D1597589

COMMUNITIES, POLITICS
AND REFORMATION IN EARLY
MODERN EUROPE

STUDIES
IN MEDIEVAL AND
REFORMATION THOUGHT

EDITED BY

HEIKO A. OBERMAN, Tucson, Arizona

IN COOPERATION WITH

THOMAS A. BRADY, Jr., Berkeley, California
E. JANE DEMPSEY DOUGLASS, Princeton, New Jersey
JÜRGEN MIETHKE, Heidelberg
M. E. H. NICOLETTE MOUT, Leiden
ANDREW PETTEGREE, St. Andrews
MANFRED SCHULZE, Wuppertal
DAVID C. STEINMETZ, Durham, North Carolina

VOLUME LXVIII

THOMAS A. BRADY, JR.

COMMUNITIES, POLITICS
AND REFORMATION IN EARLY
MODERN EUROPE

COMMUNITIES, POLITICS AND REFORMATION IN EARLY MODERN EUROPE

BY

THOMAS A. BRADY, JR.

BRILL

LEIDEN · BOSTON · KÖLN

1998

BR
307
.B73
1998

This book is printed on acid-free paper.

Library of Congress Cataloging-in-Publication Data

Brady, Thomas A.
    Communities, politics, and Reformation in early modern Europe / by
Thomas A. Brady, Jr.
        p. cm. — (Studies in medieval and Reformation thought, ISSN
0585-6914 ; v. 68)
    Includes bibliographical references and indexes.
    ISBN 9004110011 (cloth : alk. paper)
        1. Reformation—Germany.   2. Social change—Germany.   3. Germany–
–Church history—16th century.   4. Reformation—France—Strasbourg.
5. Social change—France—Strasbourg.   6. Strasbourg (France)–
–Church history—16th century.   7. Sturm, Jakob, 1489-1553.
I. Title.   II. Series.
BR307.B73   1998
940.2'3—dc21   98–34822
                                                                            CIP

Die Deutsche Bibliothek - CIP-Einheitsaufnahme

Brady, Thomas A.:
Communities, politics, and reformation in early modern Europe / by
Thomas A. Brady, Jr. – Leiden ; Boston ; Köln : Brill, 1998
    (Studies in medieval and reformation thought ; Vol. 68)
    ISBN 90–04–11001–1

ISSN 0585-6914
ISBN 90 04 11001 1

PRINTED IN THE NETHERLANDS

To Heiko A. Oberman, in friendship

"One friend in a lifetime is much; two are many;
three are hardly possible."   Henry Adams

CONTENTS

GERMANY AND EUROPE

PLACES OF ORIGINAL PUBLICATION

The chapters of this book first appeared in journals and volumes indicated, the publishers of which, as holders of copyright, have generously allowed them to be reprinted here.

Chapter 1 in *Ruling Class, Regime and Reformation at Strasbourg, 1520–1555*, pp. 1–47. Studies in Medieval and Reformation Thought, vol. 22. Leiden: E. J. Brill, 1978.

Chapter 2 in *Church History* 32 (1973): pp. 183–202.

Chapter 3 in *Städtische Gesellschaft und Reformation*, ed. Ingrid Bátori, pp. 265–91. Stuttgart: Klett-Cotta Verlag, 1980.

Chapter 4 in *Archive for Reformation History* 74 (1983): pp. 162–81.

Chapter 5 in *Archive for Reformation History* 79 (1988): pp. 262–81.

Chapter 6 in *Politics, Religion & Diplomacy in Early Modern Europe. Essays in Honor of De Lamar Jensen*, edited by Malcolm R. Thorp and Arthur J. Slavin, pp. 33–51. Sixteenth Century Studies & Essays, vol. 27. Kirksville: Sixteenth Century Journal Publishers, 1994.

Chapter 7 in *The German People and the Reformation*, ed. R. Po-Chia Hsia, pp. 14–31. Ithaca: Cornell University Press, 1988.

Chapter 8 in *Martin Bucer and Sixteenth Century Europe. Actes du colloque de Strasbourg (28–31 août 1991)*, edited by Christian Krieger and Marc Lienhard, vol. 1: pp. 129–44. 2 vols. Studies in Medieval and Reformation Thought, vols. 52–53. Leiden: E. J. Brill, 1993.

Chapter 9 in *Anticlericalism in the Late Middle Ages and Reformation*, ed. Peter Dykema and Heiko A. Oberman, pp. 167–219. Leiden: E. J. Brill, 1993.

Chapter 10 in *Germany: A New Social and Economic History*, vol. 1: *1450–1630*, edited by Bob Scribner, pp. 259–90. London: Edward Arnold, 1996.

Chapter 11 in *Journal of Modern History* 63 (1990): pp. 298–314.

Chapter 12 in *Politics and Society in Reformation Europe: Essays for Sir Geoffrey Elton on his 65th Birthday*, edited by E. I. Kouri and Tom Scott, pp. 142–57. London: Macmillan, 1987.

Chapter 13 in *Central European History* 20 (1987): pp. 229–45.

Chapter 14 in *Handbook of European History, 1400–1600. Late Middle Ages, Renaissance, Reformation*, edited by Thomas A. Brady, Jr., Heiko A. Oberman, and James D. Tracy, vol. 2: pp. 349–83. Leiden: E. J. Brill, 1995.

Chapter 15 in *Germania Illustrata: Essays on Early Modern Germany Presented to Gerald Strauss*, eds. Andrew Fix and Susan Karant-Nunn, pp. 197–216. Sixteenth Century Studies and Essays, vol. 18. Kirksville, Mo.: Sixteenth Century Journal Publishers, 1992.

Chapter 16 in *The Political Economy of Merchant Empires, 1350–1750*, ed. James D. Tracy, pp. 117–60. Cambridge: Cambridge University Press, 1991.

LIST OF ABBREVIATIONS

AEA	=	*Archives de l'église d'Alsace*
AESC	=	*Annales. Économies, Sociétés, Civilisations*
AHR	=	*American Historical Review*
AMS	=	Archives Municipales de Strasbourg
ARG	=	*Archiv für Reformationgeschichte*
AST	=	Archives du Chapître de St.-Thomas de Strasbourg
BCGA	=	*Bulletin du cercle généalogique d'Alsace*
BCorr	=	Martin Bucer. *Correspondance.* Ed. Jean Rott. Leiden: E. J. Brill, 1979–
BDS	=	Martin Bucer. *Deutsche Schriften.* Ed. Robert Stupperich, *et al.*, Gütersloh, 1964–
BNUS	=	Bibliothèque Nationale et Universitaire de Strasbourg
BSCMHA	=	*Bulletin de la Société pour la Conservation des Monuments Historiques de l'Alsace*
CH	=	*Church History*
CR	=	*Corpus reformatorum*
EA	=	*Amtliche Sammlung der älteren eidgenössischen Abschiede.* — Vols. 3–4. Zurich, Brügg, and Lucerne, 1858–86
GG	=	*Geschichte und Gesellschaft*
HJ	=	*Historisches Jahrbuch der Görres-Gesellschaft*
HZ	=	*Historische Zeitschrift*
JGO	=	*Jahrbuch für Geschichte der Oberdeutschen Reichsstädte*
JRG	=	*Jahrbuch für Regionalgeschichte*
Lenz	=	Max Lenz, ed. *Briefwechsel Landgraf Philipp's des Großmüthigen von Hessen mit Bucer.* 3 vols. Publicationen aus den K. Preussischen Staatsarchiven, 5, 28, 47. Stuttgart, 1880–91. Reprint. Osnabrück, 1965
MPIG	=	Max-Planck-Institut für Geschichte
PaP	=	*Past and Present*
PC	=	*Politische Correspondenz der Stadt Straßburg im Zeitalter der Reformation.* 5 vols. Edited by Hans Virck, Otto Winckelmann, Harry Gerber and Walter Friedensburg. Strasbourg, 1882–99; Heidelberg, 1928–33
PCSS.		See *PC*
Pol.Cor.		See *PC*

Pollet   = J. V. Pollet, ed. *Martin Bucer. Études sur la correspondance avec de nombreux textes inédits.* 2 vols. Paris, 1958–62

PSSARE = Publications de la Société Savante d'Alsace et des Régions de l'Est

QFRG   = Quellen und Forschungen zur Reformationsgeschichte

QGT.   See *TAE*

RHMC   = *Revue d'histoire moderne et contemporaine*

SCJ   = *Sixteenth Century Journal*

SFN   = Spätmittelalter und Frühe Neuzeit. Tübinger Beiträge zur Geschichtswissenschaft

SHCT   = Studies in the History of Christian Thought

SKRG   = Schriften zur Kirchen- und Rechtsgeschichte

SMRT   = Studies in Medieval and Reformation Thought

SVRG   = Schriften des Vereins für Reformationsgeschichte

TAE   = Manfred Krebs, *et al.*, *Elsaß*, parts 1–4: *Stadt Straßburg 1522–52.* Quellen zur Geschichte der Täufer, vols. 7–8, 15–16. Edited by Manfred Krebs, Hans Georg Rott, Marc Lienhard, and Stephen F. Nelson. Gütersloh, 1959–88

TQStrassburg. See *TAE*

VIEG.   See VIEGM

VIEGM = Veröffentlichungen des Instituts für Europäische Geschichte Mainz

VKLBW = Veröffentlichungen der Kommission für geschichtliche Landeskunde in Baden-Württemberg

VSWG   = *Vierteljahrschrift für Sozial- und Wirtschaftsgeschichte*

WABr   = *Luthers Werke. Kritische Gesamtausgabe. Briefe.* 18 vols. Weimar, 1930–85

Z   = Emil Egli, *et al.*, eds. *Huldrych Zwinglis sämtliche Werke.* 24 vols. Corpus Reformatorum, 88–101. Berlin and Zurich, 1905–91

ZBLG   = *Zeitschrift für bayerische Landesgeschichte*

ZC   = *Die Chronik der Grafen von Zimmern.* 3 vols. Edited by Hansmartin Decker-Hauff and Rudolf Seigel, eds. Constance and Sigmaringen, 1964–72

ZfG   = *Zeitschrift für Geschichtswissenschaft*

ZGO   = *Zeitschrift für die Geschichte des Oberrheins*

ZHF   = *Zeitschrift für historische Forschung*

ZKiG   = *Zeitschrift für Kirchengeschichte*

ZSR, KA = *Zeitschrift der Savigny-Stiftung für Rechtsgeschichte, Kanonistische Abteilung*

ZWLG   = *Zeitschrift für württembergische Landesgeschichte*

INTRODUCTION

The studies collected in the volume represent twenty-five years of research and writing. They appear here unrevised, except that errors have been silently corrected, and their topical grouping embodies the hope that their intellectual and scholarly coherence will outweigh the changes of judgment and interpretation that are inevitable over so long a time.

The studies fall into two major groups. One group deals with the oldest theme of my work, the impact of the German Reformation on the cities and of the cities on the German Reformation, with special reference to Strasbourg. Its roots lie in the time when I shifted my attention from Renaissance Italy to Reformation Germany via urban history. It was Hans Baron (1900–1988) who suggested that I investigate the career of Jacob Sturm of Strasbourg. Chapters 2 through 6 represent various stages of my work on Sturm's career over a period of more than twenty years. They range from my early study of Sturm's attempt to deal with the split between Luther and Zwingli (Chapter 2) down to a study of the Brunswick campaign, a key event in Sturm's later career (Chapter 6). These chapters reveal a shift in the center of gravity of my work on Sturm's career from the first decade of the German Reformation, which the literature heavily emphasized, to the decade of the 1540s. My book on Sturm and his world, *Protestant Politics* (1995), shows very clearly the effects of this shift.

Before the geographical and chronological dimensions ever began to expand, however, my work on Sturm underwent an even more profound change in the form of a shift of focus from his ideas to the collective social world of Strasbourg's magistrates. Chapter 1 shows the consequences of this shift, which meshed with the massive sweep of social history through American historical scholarship during the 1960s and the early 1970s. It is the most thoroughly programmatic piece I have ever published, and, some unnecessarily rhetorical flourishes aside, I do not see much in it that I would change today. I have, to be sure, subsequently refined my thinking about how the analytically derived Marxist narrative of class formation and class relations can be combined with the source-derived conception of premodern society in terms of legally defined estates, but in the main this approach to social history still seems to me the most fruitful one. It strives to meet our demands for both understanding and authenticity, allowing us to relate the past to our own times while lending our voices to "these shades from time gone, some demanding our attention, some reluctant to have it, some long thwarted into abject silence, . . . yet all there somehow, geniuses of a certain time and a certain place, and all strangely requiring only a little of our blood to return to fleeting life, to speak to and through us."[1]

By the time my first book appeared in 1978, some social historians were beginning to turn from sociology to anthropology for insights into the workings of premodern European societies. The subject that has most benefited from this turn has been the history of religion, and in the Reformation field the turn is most clearly visible in the very influential writings of Bob Scribner. His early articles embraced a social historical approach, explaining events in terms of social structures and movements and the Reformation in German cities, while his later work turned quite radically toward the study of enduring features of religion, especially religious practice and ritual.[2] The most fruitful effect of this change was to neutralize the instrumentalizing approach to religion that was pretty typical of the social history in the 1960s and 1970s. Its influence can be seen in Chapters 7 through 9, which suggest how this current affected my work. Chapter 7 continues the strongly instrumentalized approach to religion that appeared in my earlier work. That is not so true of Chapter 8, which conveys the relatively sympathetic image of Martin Bucer that reappeared in *Protestant Politics* a few years later. Chapter 9 returns to the social history of Strasbourg but for themes, communalism and groups, priests and women, I had earlier neglected. It includes the supporting documents that Katherine G. Brady and I edited together.

All of these studies on Jacob Sturm and the Reformation in Strasbourg are related in largely obvious ways to the three books I published in 1978, 1985, and 1995. The project and its genesis are adequately

---

[1] Arthur Quinn, *A New World: An Epic of Colonial America from the Founding of Jamestown to the Fall of Quebec* (Boston: Faber and Faber, 1994), p. 2.

[2] This shift can be most easily seen in the collections of Scribner's studies, *Popular Culture and Popular Movements in Reformation Germany* (London and Ronceverte: The Hambledon Press, 1987); *idem, Religion and Culture in Germany, 1400–1800* (Leiden: E. J. Brill, 1998).

described in the preface to *Protestant Politics*. Its completion required
another change, for which my training had done little to prepare
me. My working out of the main theoretical problem, the tension between social development and historical authenticity, owed much to
the debates on the transition from feudalism and to capitalism and
little at all to contemporary writings on German history. Yet the
thread I was following, the politics of the Reformation in Germany,
led toward themes of German history and German historiography,
which supplied the subjects for the second group of studies in this
volumes, Chapters 10–16. They are products of an engagement with
German history I had not anticipated.

When I began my scholarly work, there was no such thing in
America as "early modern Germany." I worked in the context of
what was called "the Renaissance and the Reformation," and for me
the bridge from Renaissance to Reformation were the cities and their
politics. This hardly surprises, for at that time there was scarcely any
tradition of teaching or writing on the German Reformation in departments of history, and the larger subject of the European Reformation stood very much in the shadow of the Italian Renaissance.
Indeed, interest in the social history of the German Reformation
hardly awakened until the mid-1960s, when Bernd Moeller's pioneering little work on *Imperial Cities and the Reformation* began to gain
a reputation in America.[3] And then it grew as a topic more in urban
than in Germany history, which as such barely existed for any period
before the later eighteenth century.

The German emigré historians, some of whom were my teachers,
had planted in America a version of German history that went back
to the Weimar Republic or, in many cases, the eve of World War I.
This version had long ago cancelled the privileged place that the
German Reformation had occupied in older versions of the national
narrative, and it had little to offer anyone who was not principally
interested in themes of successful and failed modernization. Pre-
modern history stood totally under the sway of the ideas that were

---

[3] Bernd Moeller, *Reichsstadt und Reformation*, Schriften des Vereins für Reformationsgeschichte, no. 180 (Gütersloh: Gerd Mohn, 1962). It became even better known
through the French translation, *Villes d'Empire et Réformation*, translated by Albert
Chenou (Geneva: Librairie Droz, 1966); and it appeared almost a decade later in
English as *Imperial Cities and the Reformation. Three Studies*, translated by H. C. Erik
Midelfort and Mark U. Edwards, Jr. (Philadelphia: Fortress Press, 1975). There is
a revised German text, *Reichsstadt und Reformation*, rev. ed. (Berlin: Evangelische
Verlagsanstalt, 1987).

streaming in from France, which seemed to make the received image of German history more obsolete with each passing day. Very little of the French influence bore on the interpretation of the Reformation, but almost all of it encouraged thinking about history, at least pre-modern history, in terms of continuities. In other, quite different circles the Protestant Reformation's connections to and continuities with the preceding centuries were being explored in new and exciting ways. In this respect, Heiko A. Oberman's *Harvest of the Medieval Theology* (1963) burst like a star shell over a historiographical landscape that was dominated by neo-Burkhardtian views about the discontinuity between the Renaissance and the Middle Ages.[4] The crucial intellectual turn, he argued, occurred not among Italian humanists who opposed theology and scholasticism and but among scholastic theologians.

All this had happened, or at least I was aware of it, before I became acquainted with what was happening in the two German states. During the first half of the 1960s, interest in the German Reformation as an historical event began to revive after a hiatus of more than forty years.[5] In 1961 the dean of the East German Reformation historians, Max Steinmetz, had called his colleagues to a renewal of Friedrich Engels' classic interpretation of the Peasants' War of 1525 and the German Reformation in terms of class conflict and the beginnings of capitalism as an "early bourgeois revolution."[6] Shortly thereafter, the West German church historian Bernd Moeller voiced his complaint that Reformation history had degenerated into what he called "an antiquarian exercise."[7] Yet, as he spoke, there had already

---

[4] Heiko Augustinus Oberman, *The Harvest of Medieval Theology: Gabriel Biel and Late Medieval Nominalism* (Cambridge, Mass.: Harvard University Press, 1963). Of Oberman's many relevant papers, see especially "Headwaters of the Reformation: Initia Lutehri—Initia Reformationis," in his *The Dawn of the Reformation: Essays in late Medieval and Early Modern Thought* (Edinburgh: T. & T. Clark, 1986), pp. 39–83; and "Werden und Wertung der Reformation: Thesen und Tatsachen," in his *Die Reformation von Wittenberg nach Genf* (Göttingen: Vandenhoeck & Ruprecht, 1986), pp. 15–31.

[5] See my lecture, *The Protestant Reformation in German History* (Washington, D.C.: German Historical Institute, 1998).

[6] Originally published as Max Steinmetz, "Die frühbürgerliche Revolution Deutschland 1476 bis 1535. Thesen zur Vorbereitung der wissenschaftlichen Konferenz in Wernigerode vom 21. bis 24 Januar 1960," *Zeitschrift für Geschichtswissenschaft* 8 (1960): pp. 113–24. There is an English translation in *The German Peasant War of 1525—New Viewpoints*, edited by Bob Scribner and Gerhard Benecke (London: George Allen & Unwin, 1979), pp. 9–18.

[7] Bernd Moeller, "Problems of Reformation Research," in *Imperial Cities and the Reformation*, pp. 3–4.

begun a new social history that would eventually bring the same events, Peasants' War and Reformation, into the center of an interpretation of early modern German history in social terms. This current built on the twin notions of the premodern "society based on estates" (*ständische Gesellschaft*) and the Holy Roman Empire as "the Old Empire," a rambling structure of checks and balances that allowed an immense variety of units to flourish under the umbrella of Imperial law. Feeding from an explosion of interest in the fourteenth and fifteenth centuries—the scorned nadir of the old national narrative—this current began in the 1970s to move closer to a dialogue with the East Germans. The central event in this process was the Peasants' War jubilee in 1975–76. Thereafter, while West German historians became ever more interested in the social history of the German Reformation, East German historians began a turn toward religion that reached a peak during the Luther jubilee of 1983. By the 1980s the two traditions had converged on an approach to the Reformation that emphasized both its character as a social and religious movement and its embeddedness in a comparative approach to German and European history.

Chapters 10 through 15 mark my progress in appropriating these streams of German-speaking scholarship. Oddly enough, the West Germans were harder to understand than the East Germans. Any American of my generation who worked in social history already understood the theoretical basis of East German historiography, historical materialism. West German social history, however, posed real difficulties. For one thing, it had taken up traditions, such as agrarian history, which had developed without much international contact. For another, the collapse of the Ranke-Treitschkean national narrative had plunged social history into what was most intimidating to the foreigner, local and regional history. My initiation into this current came in the 1970s from Peter Blickle's writings on agrarian history (Chapters 12 and 13).[8] It continued a bit later at the hands

---

[8] Peter Blickle, *The Revolution of 1525: The German Peasants' War from a New Perspective*, translated by Thomas A. Brady, Jr., and H. C. Erik Midelfort (Baltimore: Johns Hopkins University Press, 1981); *idem, The Communal Reformation: the People's Quest for Salvation in Sixteenth-Century Germany*, translated by Thomas Dunlap (Atlantic Highlands, N.J.: Humanities Press, 1992); *idem, Obedient Germans? A Rebuttal: A New View of German History*, translated by Thomas A. Brady, Jr. (Charlottesville, Va.: University Press of Virginia, 1997); *idem, From the Communal Reformation to the Revolution of the Common Man*, Studies in Medieval and Reformation Thought, vol. 65 (Leiden: E. J. Brill, 1998).

of urban historians, such as Heinz Schilling (Chapters 14 and 15).[9] And it eventually led me back into the fragmented, historiographically fertile world of late medieval Germany (Chapters 10 and 11). This passage has now brought me to concentrate on the problem of a general interpretation of the Holy Roman Empire's history between the Black Death and the Thirty Years' War.

The final piece (Chapter 16) represents my response to James D. Tracy's invitation to participate in a conference on merchant empires in early modern world history. Most of the contributions were framed in terms of contrasts either between Europe and Asia or between the Americas and Eurasia, about neither of which had I anything useful to say. All in desperation I began to play with the idea of a contrast between central Europe and western Europe against a global background. The result is a paper which tries, on the one hand, to define the peculiar character of European civilization during the late medieval and early modern eras in terms of a strong church, weak states, and strong warrior-merchant elites. It also tries, on the other hand, to define a distinction within that definition between a central Europe which continued the main lines of late medieval history and a western Europe which diverged in the direction of strong states, colonialism, and national consciousness. My aim in writing this piece was not to reassemble the concept of a German "special path," which I had myself criticized (in the paper here reprinted as Chapter 15). It was, rather, to reverse the conventional reading of European history from northwest to south and east by viewing western European history as an overwhelming of Latin Christendom and its transformation into Europe based on imperial nation-states and capitalist economies. This is a way of reading European history in reverse, not an alternative a complement for the other, more usual way of reading Europe from the colonized, non-European world.

The greatest pleasure in preparing this volume has been to know that it would appear, as did my first book, in "Studies in Medieval and Reformation Thought" under the editorship of Heiko A.

---

[9] Heinz Schilling, *Religion, Political Culture and the Emergence of Early Modern Society. Essays in German and Dutch History*, Studies in Medieval and Reformation Thought, vol. 50 (Leiden: E. J. Brill, 1992); *idem, Civic Calvinism in Northwestern Germany and The Netherlands, Sixteenth to Nineteenth Centuries* (Kirksville, Mo.: Sixteenth Century Journal Publishers, 1991).

Oberman. For more than a quarter of a century, we have stood, as we say, "back-to-back," acknowledging and benefitting from one another's strengths without ever feeling obliged to mute, much less to deny, our differences. It is a genuine pleasure to be able to dedicate this volume to him, small recompense for his unstinting criticism and unflagging support.

T.A.B.
Berkeley, California
12 January 1998

CHAPTER ONE

PROLEGOMENA: SOCIAL HISTORY OF
EARLY MODERN EUROPE

Historical fields, like books, have their particular histories, besides
reflecting the general movement of historical thought and changes
in research methods. The historiography of the German Reformation
is more peculiar than most, perhaps because of its origins in clerical polemics and apologetics and its continued nourishment by modern Christian confessionalism. One of the stranger chapters in its
history is the retreat into the dimmer recesses of Luther's theology
during the inter-war years. This "flight from history"[1] has largely
exhausted itself, and the study of the German Reformation has moved
back toward historical paths.

The recent study of the German Reformation as the object of historical interest shows three main lines of development. Pride of place
belongs to the new flowering of the great tradition of socialist historiography, descending from Friedrich Engels (1820–1895) and Karl
Kautsky (1854–1938), into an entire school of historical studies centered in the German Democratic Republic.[2] Secondly, there is an

---

[1] Max Steinmetz, "Probleme der frühbürgerlichen Revolution in Deutschland in
der ersten Hälfte des 16. Jahrhunderts," in *Die frühbürgerliche Revolution in Deutschland.
Referat und Diskussion zum Thema Probleme der frühbürgerlichen Revolution in Deutschland
1476 bis 1535*, ed. Gerhard Brendler (Berlin, 1961), pp. 17–52, here at p. 32. See
also Max Steinmetz, "Reformation und Bauernkrieg," in *Kritik der bürgerlichen Geschichtsschreibung. Handbuch*, eds. Werner Berthold, *et al.*, 3rd ed. (Cologne, 1970), pp. 140–
141. Important but more cautious critiques of the Luther cult are by Bernd Moeller,
"Probleme der Reformationsgeschichtsforschung," *ZKiG*, 75 (1965): pp. 246–257,
now trans. by H. C. Erik Midelfort and Mark U. Edwards, Jr., in *Imperial Cities
and the Reformation. Three Essays* (Philadelphia, 1972), pp. 3–16; and Heiko A. Oberman,
"Headwaters of the Reformation: *initia Lutheri—initia reformationis*," in *Luther and the
Dawn of the Modern Era. Papers for the Fourth International Congress for Luther Research*, ed.
Heiko A. Oberman, SHCT, 8 (Leiden, 1974), pp. 40–88.
[2] Max Steinmetz, "Reformation und Bauernkrieg in der Historiographie der
DDR," in *Historische Forschungen in der DDR, Analysen und Berichte* (Berlin, 1960), pp.
142–162; *idem*, "Forschungen zur Geschichte der Reformation und des deutschen
Bauernkrieges," in *Historische Forschungen in der DDR 1960–1970, Analysen und Berichte*
(Berlin, 1970), pp. 338–350. These volumes were prepared for the historical con-
gresses at Stockholm (1960) and Moscow (1970) and appeared as special supplements

effort to reestablish the study of the Reformation in the broad context of cultural history and the history of ideas, drawing upon the
strands (or the "tributaries," in the language of a leading exponent)
of late medieval and Renaissance thought—especially nominalism,
Augustinianism, and humanism—as conceptual tools for the analysis of Renaissance and Reformation thought.[3] Thirdly, there have
been new efforts to resolve "the Reformation" into its various forms
and find the social and political principles which seem to have determined the proliferation of forms of Reformation thought and religion.[4]
As different as these lines are from one another in methods, inten-

---

to *ZfG*, volumes 8 and 18 respectively. There is no satisfactory general history of
socialist historiography on this theme. New material on the role of Ludwig Zimmer-
mann appears in Abraham Friesen, *Reformation and Utopia. The Marxist Interpretation of
the Reformation and Its Antecedents*, VIEGM, 71 (Wiesbaden, 1974), chapter V, a work
which is otherwise vitiated by the author's hysterical characterization of Marxism
as a modern version of Joachism. The profound impact of socialist scholarship in
this field can be seen in the two volumes edited by Rainer Wohlfeil, *Reformation oder
frühbürgerliche Revolution?* nymphenburger texte zur wissenschaft, 5 (Munich, 1972), and
Der Bauernkrieg 1524–26. Bauernkrieg und Reformation, nymphenburger texte zur wissenschaft, 21 (Munich, 1975); and in two commemorative volumes, *Deutscher Bauernkrieg
1525*, ed. Heiko A. Oberman, as *ZKiG*, 85/2 (1975), and *Bauernkrieg-Studien*, ed. Bernd
Moeller, SVRG, no. 189 (Gütersloh, 1975).
  [3] See *The Pursuit of Holiness in Late Medieval and Renaissance Religion. Papers from the
University of Michigan Conference*, eds. Charles Trinkaus and Heiko A. Oberman, SMRT,
10 (Leiden, 1974), esp. the contributions by Heiko A. Oberman (pp. 3–25), William
J. Courtenay (pp. 26–59), Steven Ozment (pp. 67–92), and Charles Trinkaus (pp.
339–366); and William J. Bouwsma, "Renaissance and Reformation: An Essay in
their Affinities and Connections," in *Luther and the Dawn of the Modern Era*, pp.
127–149. This development is largely the work of scholars who write in English
and has met significant resistance wherever the formula Reformation = Luther
reigns. See the qualified resistance of Lewis W. Spitz, "Headwaters of the Reformation:
Studia Humanitatis, Luther Senior, et Initia Reformationis," in *Luther and the Dawn
of the Modern Era*, pp. 89–116, esp. pp. 112–115; the much stronger opposition of
Bengt Hägglund, "Renaissance and Reformation," in the same volume, pp. 150–158;
and the violently polemical work of Ernst-Wilhelm Kohls, *Luther oder Erasmus. Luthers
Theologie in der Auseinandersetzung mit Erasmus*, vol. I, supplementary volume 3 of the
Theologische Zeitschrift (Basel, 1972).
  [4] The chief works are Bernd Moeller, *Reichsstadt und Reformation*, SVRG, no. 180
(Gütersloh, 1962), English trans. in *Imperial Cities and the Reformation*, pp. 39–115; and
Ernst-Wilhelm Kohls, *Die Schule bei Martin Bucer in ihrem Verhältnis zu Kirche und Obrigkeit*, Pädagogische Forschungen, 22 (Heidelberg, 1963). That the older, sociologically
oriented German school of ecclesiastical history grew out of studies on the varieties
of Protestantism is convincingly argued by Manfred Wichelhaus, *Kirchengeschichtsschreibung und Soziologie im neunzehnten Jahrhundert und bei Ernst Troeltsch*, Heidelberger
Forschungen, 9 (Heidelberg, 1965). In his zeal to give Troeltsch a scholarly genealogy, however, Wichelhaus neglects the profound impression made upon Troeltsch
by the ideas of Karl Marx, a point stressed by Leo Kofler, *Zur Geschichte der bürgerlichen
Gesellschaft. Versuch einer verstehenden Deutung der Neuzeit*, 5th ed., Soziologische Texte,
38 (Darmstadt-Neuwied, 1974), p. 13.

tions, and commitments, they share the drive to re-historicize the German Reformation after a period in which Luther and his reform were placed above and beyond mortal time.

The third tendency, the search for the principles of variation within the Reformation, has in common with socialist historiography the drive toward a social understanding of the Reformation, although it employs historical sociologies far less adequate to the task than is historical materialism's class theory. One product of this tendency is the revival of interest in the "urban reform" in South Germany and Switzerland, where the civic milieu and its mentality are seen to have transformed Luther's gospel into a kind of proto-Calvinism. The most characteristic feature of the "urban reform," that which made it different and more (say some) or less (say others) effective than Luther's, was the synthesis of the new gospel with civic and humanist thought. The result was the doctrine of the sacral corporation, the identity of city and church as the collective child of God.

I. *The "Sacral Corporation" and the Urban Reformation in Germany*

1. The chief proponent of the doctrine of sacral corporatism as the best analytical key to the history of the Reformation in the German cities is undoubtedly Bernd Moeller, whose *Reichsstadt und Reformation* (1962) remains the single most influential work in this direction.[5] In his exploration of the roots of the peculiarities of the "urban reform" in the Holy Roman Empire, Moeller lays great weight on "the unique mentality of the German townspeople before the Reformation."[6] Each citizen understood "that he was part of the whole, sharing responsibility for his part in the welfare of the great organic community, the 'collective individual,' to which he was tightly bound by laws and duties."[7] The organic community, in Moeller's view, was symbolized by the oath each citizen took, which affirmed that the town "became for him the embodiment of the empire and the center of his world. It also set the absolute limits of his experience."[8] The

---

[5] There is a French version, earlier than the English one, in *Villes d'Empire et réformation*, trans. Albert Chenou, Travaux d'histoire éthico-politique, 10 (Geneva, 1966).
[6] I quote from *Imperial Cities*, 43 (*Reichsstadt und Reformation*, p. 10).
[7] *Ibid.*, p. 44 (*Reichsstadt und Reformation*, pp. 11–12).
[8] *Ibid.*, p. 45 (*Reichsstadt und Reformation*, p. 12).

importance of this mental world to the urban reform lay in the fact
that the legal and psychological corporation thus formed rejected the
sacral-temporal dualism of medieval society and saw the civic corporation as a holy community, a sacral corporation (*Sakralgemeinschaft*),[9]
through which the citizens' welfare—religious and temporal—was
seen to be mediated.[10] Although weakened during the period before
1520 by the growth of oligarchical and authoritarian tendencies in
the towns, this sacral corporatist mentality was still very powerful on
the eve of the Reformation.[11] This unitary, corporate, semi-egalitarian
mentality formed the lens through which the urban reformers of the
South—chiefly Ulrich Zwingli and Martin Bucer—adapted Luther's
gospel into a new doctrine of collective religious responsibility which,
having taken root in the citizenry through evangelical preaching, gen-
erated the popular pressure for reform that pushed the urban regimes
into *a* Reformation. The urban reform in the South "*is finally explained*

---

[9] Bernd Moeller, "Kleriker als Bürger," in *Festschrift für Hermann Heimpel zum 70.
Geburtstag zum 19. September 1971*, ed. by members of the Max Planck-Institut für
Geschichte Göttingen, 3 vols. (Göttingen, 1971–1972), II, pp. 195–224, here at p. 222.
[10] Moeller, *Imperial Cities*, p. 46 (*Reichsstadt und Reformation*, p. 13): "Material welfare and eternal salvation were not differentiated and thus the borders between the
secular and spiritual areas of life disappeared. We can grasp an essential trait of
the late medieval urban community if we characterize it as a 'sacred society.'" It
would be more correct to say that contemporary consciousness did not distinguish
clearly "material welfare and eternal salvation" (approximately the public-private
distinction of bourgeois thought), even though this is a tautology to all but the
staunchest members of the "religion vs. politics" school of Reformation history. A
sounder view is suggested by Eric J. Hobsbawm's remark: "However, insofar as religion is the language and framework of all general action in undeveloped societies . . .
ideologies of revolt will also be religious." Hobsbawm, in "Labour Traditions,"
Labouring Men: Studies in the History of Labour (London, 1964), p. 375. See esp. Natalie
Z. Davis, "Some Tasks and Themes in the Study of Popular Religion," in *The
Pursuit of Holiness*, pp. 307–336; and her "Rites of Violence," which first appeared
in *Past & Present*, No. 59 (May 1973), and is now revised in her *Society and Culture
in Early Modern France. Eight Essays* (Stanford, 1975), pp. 152–187, here at p. 155.
[11] Moeller, *Imperial Cities*, pp. 49–53 (*Reichsstadt und Reformation*, pp. 15–18). The
strength of urban corporatist traditions is stressed by Hans Morf, "Obrigkeit und
Kirche in Zürich bis zu Beginn der Reformation," *Zwingliana*, 13 (1970): pp. 164–203;
and, in a highly romanticized version, by Gerhard Pfeiffer, "Das Verhältnis von
politischer und kirchlicher Gemeinde in den deutschen Reichsstädten," in *Staat und
Kirche im Wandel der Jahrhunderte*, ed. Walther Peter Fuchs (Stuttgart-Berlin-Köln-
Mainz, 1966), pp. 79–99. Against all idealizations of the corporative character of
urban political life at the end of the Middle Ages must be set the oligarchical transformations of the guild regimes well before the Reformation. See Eberhard Naujoks,
*Obrigkeitsgedanke, Zunftverfassung und Reformation. Studien zur Verfassungsgeschichte von Ulm,
Esslingen und Schwäb. Gmünd*, VKLBW, B 3 (Stuttgart, 1958), p. 14.

by the encounter of the peculiarly 'urban' theology of Zwingli and Bucer with the particularly vital communal spirit in Upper Germany."[12]

Stressing the corporate unity of the urban populations, Moeller can lay little weight on their internal structures. True, he does recognize at least one important social distinction in the pre-Reformation towns, that between commune and clergy, which he calls sometimes "social bodies" (*Sozialkörper*) and sometimes "estates" (*Stände*);[13] and he maps the process whereby the urban clergy in South Germany were forced to become citizens—a process to which the reform movement gave a decisive impulse, although the theology of the urban reformers was not entirely comfortable with the notion that the clergy should become citizens like any others.[14] Moeller insists, however, that the principal agent of the urban reform was the entire corporation of townsfolk living in a condition of relative legal equality, and that it was the communal element that gave the urban reform its characteristic, largely medieval shape. He therefore rejects the idea of an *independent* reforming role of the urban regimes, distinct from their succumbing to pressure from the *populus*, and therefore also the possibility of the regimes acting as instruments of certain parts of the social order.[15] The unity of *populus* and *ecclesia* was complete, the hegemony of the popular will nearly so.

So far Moeller's original position: that, by adapting, "correcting," and "deepening" the gospel of Luther, the urban reformers revived, refurbished, and revitalized the old civic ideal of the sacral corporation and thereby made the gospel effective to a degree that Luther, perhaps, never achieved.[16] This transformation naturally had its consequences for the chief doctrines of the Evangelical movement. Justification by faith alone gave way to an emphasis on sanctification through an ethically formed faith operating in a social context—in a word, through love. This, like the theocratic moment with which Zwingli and Bucer altered Luther's dualistic ecclesiology, committed

---

[12] Moeller, *Imperial Cities*, p. 103 (*Reichsstadt und Reformation*, p. 67), emphasis in the original.

[13] Moeller, "Kleriker als Bürger," pp. 203, 224.

[14] *Ibid.*, esp. p. 224.

[15] Moeller, *Imperial Cities*, pp. 60–63 (*Reichsstadt und Reformation*, pp. 25–28). His assertion (p. 60) that "the urban Protestant movement in the first half of the sixteenth century had its basis exclusively among the people," is hardly weakened by the later concession (p. 62) that "we must no doubt take social factors into account" in explaining the regimes' caution vis-à-vis the reform movements.

[16] *Ibid.*, p. 90 (*Reichsstadt und Reformation*, p. 54).

Protestant historians have always seen as a reversion to or a lapse
back into medieval modes of thought.[17] There is no doubt that this
transformation did take place—or, to put it more accurately, that
the urban reforming clergy did not regard Luther as the *norma nor-
mans* to the degree that many modern Reformation scholars do—
nor that these differences are to be seen as the consequences of the
social and political milieux in which these urban reformers worked.
Moeller, at least in his early work, saw these changes as largely progressive, correcting the individualistic thrust of Luther's doctrine of
justification and the authoritarian possibilities of his dualistic ecclesiology. In his more recent work, however, it is no longer clear that
he believes that the urban reformers represent a distinct "reformed
Reformation" (as opposed to, or at least as distinct from, the "Lutheran
Reformation") which is to be regarded as a corrective to the weaknesses of Luther's doctrines and whose centerpiece is the transformed
doctrine of the sacral corporation. In his study of the integration of
the clergy into the citizenry of the Evangelical towns, Moeller writes
of the Evangelical citizenry as the "citizen community before God,
'church community'," which is no longer a "sacral community."[18]
This shift would have to mean that Moeller now regards the urban
reformers as having been faithful to Luther in that they preserved
his conception of the church which made true theocracy, or, more
accurately, the total conflation of society and church, at least theoretically impossible. Bucer and his Strasbourg colleagues, to whom
Moeller specifically refers, would have to be seen as having maintained the chief points of the Lutheran gospel and, therefore, as the
gravediggers rather than the renovators of the (already decaying)
sacral corporatist tradition.[19] Moeller's recent work, then, seems to
return to the classic position of grading the other reformers according to their faithfulness to Luther. Consequently, where Moeller once
saw the urban reform as a salutary transformation of Luther's gospel

---

[17] See in brief Wichelhaus, *Kirchengeschichtsschreibung*, pp. 178, 184. The latter is
the so-called "problem of the corpus christianum" (Wichelhaus, p. 178), which was
the chief point of attack by Troeltsch's conservative nationalist critics on his historical sociology of Christianity.

[18] Moeller, "Kleriker als Bürger," p. 217.

[19] Steven E. Ozment, *The Reformation in the Cities: The Appeal of Protestantism to
Sixteenth-Century Germany and Switzerland* (New Haven-London, 1975), p. 170 n. 26,
James M. Kittelson, *Wolfgang Capito from Humanist to Reformer*, SMRT, 17 (Leiden,
1975), however, concludes that although theologically a reasonably faithful follower
of Luther (pp. 222–237), Capito was politically a Zwinglian corporatist (pp. 200–206).

by the proto-democratic mentality and traditions of the free towns, he now tends to see the Lutheran gospel itself as more an agent for change, as the ethos which gave the coup de grâce to the spiritual world of the medieval town.

2. The change in Moeller's perspective brings him somewhat closer to the position of Ernst-Wilhelm Kohls—although not so close that the two agree on anything except the fundamental irreducibility of Luther's gospel. Kohls, too, believes that the cities of the Southwest developed a peculiar "urban theology," whose chief characteristics were its replacement of Luther's doctrine of justification by a strongly ethical and rationalistic doctrine of sanctification, and of his ecclesiology by a doctrine of collective sanctification rooted in the concept of "gemein Nutz."[20] Where, for Kohls, the first alteration of Luther's gospel was rooted in the rationalizing tendencies of urban, Erasmian humanism,[21] the concept of "gemein Nutz" derived chiefly from communal ("bürgerlich") sources and was theologized by the urban reformers of the first generation.[22]

Although Moeller and Kohls differ radically in their evaluations of these alterations of Luther's gospel by the urban reformers, regarding them as progressive and retrogressive respectively, they are very close together in their judgments of *what* the alterations were. As to sources, Kohls lays great weight on humanism—which he understands as a kind of ethical rationalism, not so different, one suspects, from Liberal Protestant theology—and correspondingly less on the political

---

[20] This is the basic argument of Kohl's *Die Schule bei Martin Bucer*, and, indeed, of nearly all of his many writings on Reformation thought. Kohls believes, against nearly the entire world of Erasmus scholarship, that Erasmus's thought formed a systematic, theological whole, a rationalistic (i.e., "humanistic") and therefore false alternative to the true theology of Luther, which it tended to corrupt wherever the two came into contact—as they did in the Upper German and Swiss towns. The groundwork for this extraordinary view Kohls laid in *Die Theologie des Erasmus*, 2 vols. (Basel, 1966), and he brings it to a climax in his *Luther oder Erasmus*, one of the most revealing documents of the entire "Luther Renaissance." The work of Luther, Kohls writes (*Luther oder Erasmus*, I, p. xiv), "ist jene Zeitenwende, in der Gott durch die Bibel und die Sakramente selbst in die Geschichte eingreift, um alle Menschen wieder unmittelbar durch die hl. Schrift auf jenen rettenden Weg der Busse und Neubesinnung zu rufen, den Gott von uns begangen wissen will und den wir in unseren philosophischen, soziologischen theologischen Landkarten gar nicht verzeichnet finden."

[21] Ernst-Wilhelm Kohls, *Die theologische Lebensaufgabe des Erasmus und die oberrheinischen Reformatoren. Zur Durchdringung von Humanismus und Reformation*, Arbeiten zur Theologie, 1st series, 39 (Stuttgart, 1969), esp. pp. 36–40.

[22] Kohls, *Die Schule bei Martin Bucer*, p. 155.

traditions of the free cities.[23] The two scholars also agree in seeing
the original bearers of the reform in the (socially undifferentiated) citizenry, although Kohls, in keeping with the religion-politics dichotomy
peculiar to his tradition, maintains that the Reformation became
"political" only when urban regimes intervened to employ the new
religion for strengthening and rounding out the institutional structure of the corporate civic order.[24] The tendencies in this direction,
Moeller and Kohls agree, were much older than the Reformation;
but neither scholar moves much beyond the analysis of a single main
feature of urban history—church-state relations for Moeller, humanism for Kohls—supposed to be chiefly responsible for the special
character of urban reformed religion.[25]

3. The concept of a "naturalization" of the Reformation in the
South German towns through the transforming power of the ideal
of the city as a holy *respublica* is quite old. Its grandfather was surely
Otto von Gierke (1841–1921), the magisterial jurist-historian, who
developed the doctrine of organic, corporate consciousness of the
medieval German urban commune, and to whom all recent employers of the doctrine pay tribute.[26] Gierke's *Genossenschaftslehre* was one
form of a continuing effort in German public thought during the
nineteenth century to find historical justification for the protection
and reconstitution of communitarian institutions in a world hostile
to all social forms except that of the self-aggrandizing individual.
And while his romantic idealization of the medieval urban commune
bears, on the one hand, similarities to the romantic, radical-liberal,
communitarian sociology of his contemporary, Ferdinand Tönnies
(1855–1936), it also has some kinship with the mainstream of conservative *Ständelehre*. Which tendency becomes dominant rather depends
on whether emphasis is laid on the organic unity of the corporation
or on the basic equality of its members. This ambiguous doctrine
was then adapted to the pre-history and history of the Reformation

---

[23] Ernst-Wilhelm Kohls, "Evangelische Bewegung und Kirchenordnung in oberdeutschen Reichsstädten," *ZSSR, KA*, 84 (1967): pp. 110–134, here at p. 116.
[24] *Ibid.*, pp. 124–130.
[25] *Ibid.*, pp. 131–133; Bernd Moeller, "Die Kirche in den evangelischen freien
Städten Oberdeutschlands im Zeitalter der Reformation," *ZGO*, 112 (1964): pp.
147–162, here at pp. 161–162.
[26] Esp. volume III of Gierke's *Das deutsche Genossenschaftsrecht*, of which see the
citations by Moeller, *Imperial Cities*, pp. 42–43 (*Reichsstadt und Reformation*, p. 10), and
Kohls, "Evangelische Bewegung," pp. 124–125.

in the German cities by another jurist, Alfred Schultze (1864–1946).[27] The completed doctrine of the shaping of the urban reform by the civic, communal traditions of the medieval German town—whether or not mixed with humanism—has gained wide currency in certain tendencies of Reformation scholarship,[28] although it has not gone unchallenged.[29]

Moeller's most recent critic is the American and self-confessed "recent convert" to the study of the urban reform, Steven Ozment.[30] Despite his *apparent* interest in social history (Ozment spares only one line for socialist historiography, the longest continuous tradition of social study of the Reformation),[31] he wants to turn the study of the urban reform back to the old paths and lead it back under the sovereignty of Luther. Thus he attacks Moeller's attempt to explain historically the variations in early Protestant thought and practice, for Ozment believes that Moeller's interpretation of Zwingli's and Bucer's theologies as welcome, progressive reinforcements of communal values against the rising tide of oligarchy reduces the value and stature of these Protestant theologies by making them too "medieval."[32] Ozment complains that Moeller's interpretation would make "the Reformation most successful where it changed religious thought and practice least,"[33] which he can do only by ignoring the entire line running from the German urban reform into Calvinism. Ozment's own interpretation, that Protestant theology gained widespread assent because of the "swelling popular desire to be rid of the psychological and

---

[27] Alfred Schultze, *Stadtgemeinde und Reformation*, Recht und Staat in Geschichte und Gegenwart, 11 (Tübingen, 1918); adapted to the Swiss towns by Leonhard von Muralt, "Stadtgemeinde und Reformation in der Schweiz," *Zeitschrift für Schweizerische Geschichte*, 10 (1930): pp. 349–384.

[28] Especially in the English-speaking world. See, for some examples, Robert C. Walton, *Zwingli's Theocracy* (Toronto, 1967), pp. xxi–xxii, and pp. 16, 29, 55n; Miriam U. Chrisman, *Strasbourg and the Reform: A Study in the Process of Change* (New Haven-London, 1967), p. 27; Harold J. Grimm, "The Reformation and the Urban Social Classes in Germany," in *Luther, Erasmus and the Reformation. A Catholic-Protestant Reappraisal*, eds. John C. Olin, *et al.* (New York, 1969), pp. 75–86, here at pp. 76–81; Basil Hall, "The Reformation City," *Bulletin of the John Rylands Library*, 54 (1971): pp. 103–148.

[29] R. W. Scribner, "Civic Unity and the Reformation in Erfurt," *Past & Present*, No. 66 (February 1975): pp. 28–60, here at pp. 28–29; Heide Stratenwerth, *Die Reformation in der Stadt Osnabrück*, VIEGM, 61 (Wiesbaden, 1971), p. 123 n. 81.

[30] Ozment, *Reformation in the Cities*, p. 1.

[31] *Ibid.*, p. 208 n. 3.

[32] *Ibid.*, p. 6.

[33] *Ibid.*, pp. 7–8.

social burdens of late medieval religion itself,"[34] is far more psychological than social and is, in fact, little more than a universalization of Luther's account of his own conversion. As for the variations in Protestantism, the departures of the urban reformers from Luther in response to different social milieux, Ozment is forced to state his belief that they never existed,[35] although the contrary was maintained longly and loudly by most parties to the doctrinal controversies of the sixteenth century.

The strength of Moeller's view of the urban reform—a strength which none of his non-socialist critics has engaged—is his return to an historical interpretation of the theology of the Reformation era[36] according to social principles of determination. He thereby picks up once more a thread of interpretation which has been lying dormant in nonsocialist scholarship since the death of Ernst Troeltsch (1865–1923).[37] Troeltsch's life-work closely paralleled what the South German urban reformers (by Moeller's account) were trying to achieve. "The victory of the 'Reformed' Reformation in the Upper German imperial cities," writes Moeller, "is finally explained by the encounter of the peculiarly 'urban' theology of Zwingli and Bucer with the particularly vital communal spirit in Upper Germany."[38] As for Troeltsch, his work on the sociology of religion "must be understood as a 'political ethic' of Protestant Christianity in the post-Bismarck era," striving to correct and shape the unavoidable democratization of modern life "through the Protestant forces of the West, recommending at the same time as a necessary corrective to this the German organic-corporative social ideal."[39]

---

[34] *Ibid.*, p. 9.

[35] *Ibid.*, p. 215 n. 71.

[36] See Steinmetz, in *Kritik der bürgerlichen Geschichtsschreibung*, 3rd ed., p. 141.

[37] Moeller, "Problems of Reformation Research," in *Imperial Cities*, pp. 4–5. "Dormant" is perhaps too strong a word, for Troeltsch's sociology of Christianity has been further developed and refined by Herbert Schöffler (see Wichelhaus, *Kirchengeschichtsschreibung*, pp. 189–192), who, however, has had little impact on the study of the German Reformation.

[38] Moeller, *Imperial Cities*, p. 103 (*Reichsstadt und Reformation*, p. 67).

[39] Eckehard Kühne, *Historisches Bewusstsein in der deutschen Soziologie. Untersuchungen zur Geschichte der Soziologie von der Zeit der Reichsgründung bis zum Ersten Weltkrieg auf wissenssoziologischer Grundlage*, dissertation, Marburg (Marburg/Lahn, 1970), pp. 166–167. Manfred Wichelhaus (see note 4 above) describes the emergence of the sociology of Christianity from the comparative study of Christian confessions, and its heyday coincides, naturally enough, with the decades before 1914–1918, when permanent world hegemony seemed to belong to the North European powers and their predominantly Protestant ruling classes. A special American variant, is the Protestantism-

In a passionate intellectual response to the Marxian critique of society and the advance of the German labor movement, Troeltsch framed the first comprehensive sociology of Christianity, his *Soziallehren der christlichen Kirchen und Gruppen*, one of the great synthetic attempts to understand the history of European Christianity in terms of its fate in the modern world. In the Protestant theological faculties in Germany, however, the future belonged not to men of the breadth and insight of Troeltsch but to Karl Holl (1866–1926) and his disciples, the creators of what came to be called "the Luther Renaissance."[40] What they could not forgive in Troeltsch was that he had

---

and-Democracy theme with its common affinity for English-speaking Calvinism. This theme, reversed into a Democracy-and-Protestantism form, has inspired an entire sociology of the Reformation era in Guy E. Swanson, *Religion and Regime: A Sociological Account of the Reformation* (Ann Arbor, 1968). Unlike the clerical scholars who would see in democracy the finest child of Protestantism (usually in its Calvinist form), Swanson reverses the causal relationship and sees in the major forms of Reformation and post-Reformation religion (ranked in the order: Catholicism, Lutheranism, Anglicanism, and Calvinism) the products of political regimes having progressively more widely distributed legislative powers. Just as the clerical version needs a primal event to serve as the source of the new, which it finds in the conversion of Luther, Swanson identifies a (purely mythical) primal event in a general political transformation which is supposed to have occurred in most of Europe during the century before the Reformation. This invention, and not the manifold errors of detail which are catalogued in the gleefully negative reviews by historians, makes the Swanson model next to useless as a theoretical construct for the guiding of historical research. Swanson's book is a particularly bald example of the myth-making power of idealist-functionalist sociology. The best recent research suggests, on the other hand, that it is difficult to correlate any significant social change in sixteenth-century Europe with the introduction of Protestant religion. See Davis, *Society and Culture in Early Modern France*, pp. 60–61, 94–95, 186.

[40] That there has not yet appeared a history of the "Luther Renaissance" is probably due to the movement's ambiguous political connections. The basic facts and the theological context, but no more, can be had from Horst Stephan, *Geschichte der evangelischen Theologie in Deutschland seit dem Idealismus*, 3rd ed. by Martin Schmidt (Berlin-New York, 1973), pp. 407–412, 427–431. For the men of the first generation, such as Karl Holl and Heinrich Boehmer, the chief inspiration was almost certainly the need to rescue Luther from the relativizing tendencies of both Roman Catholic and Liberal scholarship—the same motive which led to the founding of the Verein für Reformationsgeschichte (1901). For the next generation, the "Luther Renaissance" was a movement of struggle against Liberal Protestant theology, political Liberalism, and all forms of socialism. Its excision of Luther's thought from the historical context and elevation of his teachings into religious, political, and social norms (see, e.g., Werner Elert, *Morphologie des Luthertums*, rev. ed., 2 vols. [Munich, 1953; 1st ed., 1932]) was basically a special form of ideological warfare against the Weimar Republic, in the government of which the two chief enemies, Catholicism and Social Democracy, were allied. The hallmark of the movement was ever the doctrine of Luther as the spiritual father of the "modern world," by which was meant a rejection of nearly all foreign ideas and much of German culture (the non-Prussian, non-Protestant parts), plus the entire legacy of the French Revolution and British

been "the first to recognize dependence from economic and social-historical factors as the object of sociology of religion."[41] The new wave of the post-World War I years, however, built a many-celled structure of glosses on and textual (one is tempted to write "exegetical") studies of Luther's writings. The historicization of Luther and his works, which had been advancing all through the nineteenth century, now gave way before the effort to keep Luther's ideas free from the social and other historical elements which relativize the thought of lesser men. What passed for "Reformation history" belonged to this tradition until well into the post-World War II period, since when the guardians of this meta-historical Luther and his highly theologized reformation have been increasingly hard pressed—by the three tendencies named at the beginning of this chapter—to explain how Luther escaped the historical contingentness which is the fate of other men. Few now would dare Emanuel Hirsch's (1888–1972) fantastic identification of Luther as the sole fountainhead of all true modernity; few, indeed, would go beyond Gerhard Ebeling's plea that Luther was "uniquely responsive to events."[42]

The work of Bernd Moeller on the urban reform, which in some important respects resumes that of Troeltsch and thus represents an advance over the remnants of the "Luther Renaissance" tradition, points the way—if quite cautiously—toward the reintegration of Luther and Reformation thought into the history of the German Reformation. If his work is open to a fundamental criticism, it is so on the point that, although it tries to interpret Reformation thought historically, it does so on the basis of a highly idealized, romantic

---

Liberalism. All of this, plus what came after, belongs to the history of the "Luther Renaissance."

[41] Kühne, *Historisches Bewusstsein*, p. 163, the force of which is somewhat weakened, but not destroyed, by Wichelhaus's demonstration of a long pedigree for certain aspects of Troeltsch's sociology (*Kirchengeschichtsschreibung*, chapter 1).

[42] Quoted by Moeller, "Problems of Reformation Research," in *Imperial Cities*, p. 13, from "Luther: II," *Die Religion in Geschichte und Gegenwart*, 3rd ed., IV (Tübingen, 1960), col. 496. Ebeling is perhaps even more cautious in "Luther and the Beginning of the Modern Age," in *Luther and the Dawn of the Modern Era*, pp. 11–37, esp. pp. 33–34, 36–37. To Ebeling's characterization of Troeltsch's view of Luther's relation to medieval culture should be added the notice by Bouwsma, "Renaissance and Reformation," p. 127 n. 1. Ebeling's essay has also appeared as "Luther und der Anbruch der Neuzeit," *Zeitschrift für Theologie und Kirche*, 69 (1972): pp. 185–213. Emanuel Hirsch's position may be studied in his *Der Reich-Gottes-Begriff des neueren europäischen Denkens* (Göttingen, 1921). That besides Ebeling's cautious meta-historicization of Luther an aggressive total meta-historicization still exists, may be seen in the quotation from Kohl's *Luther oder Erasmus*, I, p. xiv, in note 20 above.

conception of urban society, the ideal of the sacral corporation. This conception, as the following paragraphs argue, is inadequate to an analysis of the urban societies of the Reformation era.

4. Whether the German towns are believed to have exerted a transforming influence on early Protestantism (Moeller and Kohls) or not (Ozment), whether that influence is believed to have been positive (Moeller) or negative (Kohls), these writers on the urban reform share a belief in the special nature of the towns. Ozment expresses this notion when he asks whether Wittenberg was so different from Zürich, implying that all Protestant theology—Luther's included—was city-born and therefore in some sense "urban," or perhaps in some sense "bourgeois."[43] At this point we can identify what is surely the most damaging weakness of the whole literature, namely, the assumption of the political, social, and cultural uniqueness of the cities.

The unique historical character of the medieval European town as a forward-looking enclave in a sea of primitive feudal society is one of the finest creations of Liberal historiography, developed and nourished in various forms by Sismondi, Villari, Gierke, and Pirenne. Whether as a vision of the urban community as an island of freedom in an ocean of servitude,[44] or as a glorification of the enterprising spirit of medieval merchants as the forerunners of modern capitalism (Pirenne, Fritz Rörig), this belief—hallowed in the textbook cliché of "the rise of the middle classes"—has never entirely lost its luster. The recent literature, strongly revisionist on this point, sees the towns as creations of, and recognizable if transformed versions of the social forms of, feudal Europe. Nowhere is this tendency clearer than in recent views of Europe's earliest urban upheaval, the Italian communal movement. As Marvin Becker has put it:

> It would be well to recall that the city did not subvert the feudal order, but instead sought to insert itself into it. Further, it would be a gross error to believe that the commune scotched feudalism. Many of the feudal institutions were included as a part of the commune, with the norms of feudal law encompassed in the communal statutes.[45]

---

[43] Ozment, *Reformation in the Cities*, pp. 7–8.
[44] A moderate version of this position is taken by Edith Ennen, "Die Stadt zwischen Mittelalter und Gegenwart," *Rheinische Vierteljahrsblätter*, 30 (1965): pp. 118–131, reprinted in *Die Stadt des Mittelalters*, ed. Carl Haase, I (Darmstadt, 1969), pp. 416–435, here at p. 422.
[45] Marvin B. Becker, "Some common Features of Italian Urban Experience (c. 1200–1500)," *Medievalia et Humanistica*, n.s. 1 (1970): p. 197 n. 8.

An extreme form of the same view is expressed by Otto Brunner:

> The constitution of the European city can be understood only in the
> total context of the "feudal" world, with which it was connected through
> its lord, the lord of the city. . . . Lordship and association are the basic
> forms of the older constitution. Although struggle occurred over the
> delimitation of their spheres of competence, yet all associative forms
> came to the fore within tile bounds of lordship and even created ele-
> ments of domination within their own area. The two structural principles
> are conceivable only together. Just those typical characteristics which
> differentiate the European city from the city-states of older civilizations
> are explicable only from the construction of the "feudal" world.[46]

Brunner, in his zeal to seal off pre-industrial Europe as a social
whole and to preserve its memory from any contamination by modern concepts of the state and modern class relations, certainly goes
much too far in seeing a harmonious relationship between towns
and the larger feudal order.

Whether called "feudal" or "aristocratic," the remarkable tenacity
and even revival of traditional, land-based social and political power
in Europe is nowadays thoroughly recognized in the literature. Henry
Kamen writes of the century after 1550, "The peculiar importance
of the aristocracy and the gentry . . . lay at this time in their almost
complete monopoly of political power and social position."[47] This is

---

[46] Otto Brunner, "Europäisches Bauerntum," in his *Neue Wege der Verfassungs- und
Sozialgeschichte*, 2nd ed. (Göttingen, 1968), pp. 199–212, here at p. 208.

[47] Henry Kamen, *The Iron Century. Social Change in Europe 1550–1650* (London-
New York, 1972), p. 129. Despite efforts to exercise the concept of feudalism from
the historical vocabulary altogether (see Elizabeth A. R. Brown, "The Tyranny of
a Concept: Feudalism and Historians of Medieval Europe," *AHR*, 79 [1974]: pp.
1063–1088), the tendency in the newer literature is to affirm the survival of feudal
institutions through the Renaissance era. For France, see J. Russell Major, "The
Crown and the Aristocracy in Renaissance France, in *Lordship and Community in
Medieval Europe*, ed. Frederic Cheyette (New York, 1968), pp. 242–251, reprinted
from *AHR*, 69 (1964); and for England, see R. B. Smith, *Land and Politics in the
Reign of Henry VIII* (Oxford, 1970), pp. 43–61, 254–258. These works concern, however, the continuation of "feudal" institutions in the juridical sense of the term
rather than feudal social formations; and the latter concept, despite the work of
Marc Bloch, has met with indifferent acceptance among non-socialist historians.
This is the main reason why there is no systematic historical sociology of what is
sometimes called "Late Medieval and Renaissance" Europe. The only serious, coherent discussion of the class structure of late feudal society and the place of the urban
bourgeoisie therein has taken place in the *ZfG*, 20 (1972), 21 (1973), and 22 (1974),
a running discussion in which a large number of younger scholars of the German
Democratic Republic took part. The discussion is an enviable achievement and one
that should be continued.

not to deny the existence, from the beginning, of an urban social moment potentially hostile to the feudal order. The cities were never—at least not since the inception of the communal movement—totally feudal in their institutions, their class systems, and their culture. In the German towns, a triple wave of revolt against established patterns of domination attests to the creation, by the freer economic conditions within the towns, of social forces contradictory to the simple division of society into rulers and ruled. After the communal movement and the movement of the guild revolts (fourteenth–fifteenth centuries), the third and final such upheaval comprised the urban plebeian participation in the anti-feudal outbursts of the late fifteenth and the sixteenth centuries—the beginnings of the urban reformation.[48] Down to the early sixteenth century at least, this ever renewed rebellion against the built-in structures of domination in the German cities is firm evidence of the continuing existence of an antagonism between urban society and the surrounding feudal order.

Much has been written about the easy flow of urban commercial wealth into the land and the movement of urban aristocrats into the nobility—what, looking at its social and political side, Fernand Braudel labelled "la trahison de la bourgeoisie."[49] The guilds, too, once seen as associations of equals embodying the principles of urban freedom, are now usually regarded as privileged corporations of promoters of monopoly.[50] We have come a long distance from the naive equations of feudalism with the land and capitalism with the cities. It is thus well to be reminded of the social and economic roots of an enduring urban "foreignness" in the late feudal world. This strangeness is most apparent at the uppermost and nethermost ends of the urban class

---

[48] Karl Czok, "Zur Stellung der Stadt in der deutschen Geschichte," *JRG*, 3 (1968): pp. 9–33, here at pp. 16–18, by far the best overview.

[49] Fernand Braudel, *La méditerranée et le monde méditerranéen à l'époque de Philippe II*, 2nd ed., 2 vols. (Paris, 1966), II, p. 68. On the entire complex of issues that lurks behind this phrase, see now Immanuel Wallerstein, *The Modern World System. Capitalist Agriculture and the Origins of the European World-Economy in the Sixteenth Century* (New York-London, 1974), pp. 273–297. So far has revision moved on the feudal origins of capitalist society, that Barrington Moore, Jr., has argued that all post-feudal social formations (capitalism, socialism, fascism) are determined by different systems of relations between lords and peasants. See his *Social Origins of Dictatorship and Democracy: Lord and Peasant in the Modern World* (London-New York, 1974; 1st ed., 1966), esp. chapter 1.

[50] Reinald Ennen, *Zünfte und Wettbewerb. Möglichkeiten und Grenzen zünftlerischer Wettbewerbsbeschränkungen im städtischen Handel und Gewerbe des Spätmittelalters*, Neue Wirtschaftsgeschichte, 3 (Cologne-Vienna, 1971).

system: at the top, where the merchants strove for "freie Kaufmann-schaft" and for new investment opportunities in the interstices and protected monopolies which appeared in the feudal order, and at the bottom, where the urban plebs, unprotected by—even exploited by—the guild system, was driven with increasing frequency into free wage labor. In France, already in the early sixteenth century, there began to emerge in literature an image of the *bourgeois* with modern features, the bourgeois as the grasping money-maker, unheedful of established social lines, rather than the bourgeois simply as town-dweller.[51]

Here is no space for an extended analysis of the place of urban communities in the late feudal society. It suffices to indicate here that the state of research—beyond all disputed questions, many of them fundamentally important—will not support the notion of the late medieval town (in Germany or elsewhere, self-governing or not) as a distinct society, politically, socially, and culturally (not to speak of economically) separate from the greater, essentially aristocratic (or neo-feudal), land-based society around it. The idea of urban self-sufficiency (temporal and sacral), therefore, requires a quite different type of analysis than what it has received at the hands of recent writers on the German urban reform. As descriptions of ideas held and promoted by urban lay and clerical leaders, the works discussed above—especially those of Moeller—have given good value. But as to the social roots and functions of the corporate ideal in urban history, these writers are silent. Silent, perhaps, because they believe the ideal to have been an adequate portrait of the basic structures of urban life. But the ideal of the sacral corporation not only ignored many aspects of urban life, it actually obscured and even denied the manifold dependency of the urban societies on the world outside the town. Nowhere is this more graphic than in Caspar Hedio's ideal-ization of the city as a great ascetic community of love—a morally self-sufficient cosmic monastery.[52] It can hardly be doubted that this and other versions of the sacral corporate ideal devised by the German

---

[51] Jean V. Alter, *Les origines de la satire anti-bourgeoise en France. Moyen âge–XVIe siècle*, Travaux d'Humanisme et Renaissance, 83 (Geneva, 1966), pp. 20–23, 109–112, 214–217.

[52] See Hedio's preface to his German version (dedicated to the regime and com-mune of Strasbourg) of Juan Luis Vives's "De subventione pauperum" (Strasbourg, 1533), reproduced by Otto Winckelmann, *Das Fürsorgewesen der Stadt Strassburg vor und nach der Reformation. Ein Beitrag zur deutschen Kultur- und Wirtschaftsgeschichte*, 2 vols., QFRG, V (Leipzig, 1922), II, pp. 170–171, no. 118. Entirely in the same vein is his *Schwörtag* sermon of 14 January 1534 (Strasbourg, Johann Albrecht, 1534), of

urban reformers drew, as Moeller has insisted, upon political and religious conceptions reaching well back into the pre-Reformation era. But that they represented the fundamental social ideal of "the people" may well be doubted.

The corporate ideal, whether in its urban or in its national form, was a typical expression of aristocratic political consciousness in Europe at the end of the Middle Ages and all through the early modern era. The ideal of society as a *communitas perfecta*, "while it may have reached down, in some form, to the lower levels of society, . . . was essentially the preserve of the dominant social and vocational groups in the state—nobles and gentry, urban patriciates, the lawyers, the clergy, the educated."[53] The urban corporate ideal thus belongs to the age of the rise and flourishing of self-governing towns, just as the national corporate ideal belongs to a succeeding age. In northern and central Italy, where the humanists early on constructed a neo-classical *paideia* for the urban aristocracies, the corporate ideal came to be expressed in a classical, rather than a Christian, idiom.[54] At Florence, however, the original home of this "civic humanism," the refashioned ideal of classical republicanism co-existed with a popular, Guelfic form of corporate patriotism, whose millennialism grew out of Christian rather than classical sources.[55]

The cities of the Holy Roman Empire were less independent, politically weaker, and smaller in size than their Italian counterparts, and neoclassicism made few permanent inroads into German urban culture before the Reformation. The corporate ideology of the German cities understandably maintained a more traditional, Christian flavor. The ideal of civic Christianity, however, is nearly an exact analogue to

which an extract is reprinted in *TQ Strassburg*, II, pp. 262–263, no. 492. See also Ozment, *Reformation in the Cities*, pp. 153–154.

[53] J. H. Elliott, "Revolution and Continuity in Early Modern Europe," *Past & Present*, no. 42 (February 1969), pp. 35–56, here at pp. 48–49.

[54] *Ibid.*, p. 50. See now J. G. A. Pocock, *The Machiavellian Moment: Florentine Political Thought and the Atlantic Republican Tradition* (Princeton, 1975), pp. 83–103, developing the line of study of "civic humanism" begun by Hans Baron in preliminary studies to and in his major work, *The Crisis of the Early Italian Renaissance* (1st ed., Princeton, 1955; 2nd ed., 1966).

[55] Donald Weinstein, *Savonarola and Florence: Prophecy and Patriotism in the Renaissance* (Princeton, 1970), pp. 35–66. It is easy to forget, given the elegant secular gleam of civic humanism, that an intensely patriotic civic Christianity flourished in the Italian city-states at the same time. See David Herlihy, *Medieval and Renaissance Pistoia. The Social History of an Italian Town, 1200–1430* (New Haven-London, 1967), pp. 257–258; Marvin B. Becker, "Aspects of Lay Piety in Early Renaissance Florence," in *The Pursuit of Holiness*, pp. 177–199, here at pp. 185–197.

the Italian ideal of civic humanism, although the concepts of virtues to be emulated, appropriated, and practiced are quite different.[56] The sacral corporatism of the Reformation era, like Italian civic humanism, was a solution to the dualism of purpose (spiritual-temporal) and power (clerical-lay) which had so troubled the lay aristocracies of medieval Europe. Two solutions to this tension, each with its peculiar concept of freedom, permitted the urban society to be viewed as a morally independent actor in history: the Italian solution of secularizing public life (civic humanism); and the German one of sacralizing it (sacral corporatism). The former solution projects the unified urban society into a history ruled by *fortuna*, the latter into a history ruled by the Christian God; but both solutions make of the urban society a new kind of historical entity, an internally integrated, externally independent collective actor. The city becomes, in a word, a nation.

It is true enough that the "myth of civic spirituality"[57] served well the immediate political needs of Zwingli, Bucer, and the other urban reformers; but the ideal of the sacral commune also represents the theological counterpart of the alliance they made with the urban regimes during the great crisis of 1524–1525.[58] It is quite true that the integration of Evangelical religion into urban corporate ideology was not total, both for theological reasons (Luther's doctrine of justification was incompatible with the notion of collective salvation) and political ones (the reformers' drive to reconstruct ecclesiastical authority). The integration was nonetheless complete enough in the early, crucial stages to leave the urban reformers helpless before a rising tide of practical Erastianism, a tide they themselves had done much to foster.[59]

---

[56] The entire literature on Florentine civic humanism has been subjected to a searching critique from the standpoint of historical-political realism by Peter Herde, "Politische Verhaltensweisen der Florentiner Oligarchie 1382–1402," in *Geschichte und Verfassungsgefüge. Frankfurter Festschrift für Walter Schlesinger*, Frankfurter Historische Abhandlungen, 5 (Wiesbaden, 1973), pp. 156–249, here at pp. 156–161, where Herde charges the (overwhelmingly American) literature with ignoring foreign (especially German) criticism and with mythologizing the Florentine republic in an idealist sense.

[57] The apt phrase is from James M. Kittelson, "Wolfgang Capito, the Council and Reform Strasbourg," *ARG*, 63 (1972): pp. 126–140, here at pp. 136–137.

[58] Sigrid Loosz, "Butzer und Capito in ihrem Verhältnis zu Bauernkrieg und Täufertum," in *Weltwirkung der Reformation*, eds. Max Steinmetz and Gerhard Brendler, 2 vols. (Berlin, 1969), I, pp. 226–232; and Kittelson, *Wolfgang Capito*, pp. 120–122, who attacks (p. 122 n. 20) but does not refute Loosz's argument. In point of fact, Mathis Zell would have made a better case study than either Bucer or Capito.

[59] A point recognized by Moeller, "Die Kirche in den evangelischen freien Städten Oberdeutschlands," pp. 159–161.

This discussion has tried to show the discontinuity between the sacral corporate ideal and the situation of the pre-Reformation town, especially in South Germany, and to suggest the political and social conditions which made such an idealized compound of real social vision and political propaganda both useful and popular. The subject leads to two, much larger questions. In the first place, the study of the literary/theological sources and the analysis of the various forms of the corporate ideal are fundamental to any explanation of the urban reform in Germany—but they also lead far beyond the history of the German towns, into the beginnings of national consciousness in Europe.[60] Secondly, there arises the question of social structures, those social formations which were partly revealed, partly disguised by the sacral corporate ideal. The historical meaning of a social ideal cannot be judged if its relation to real social structures is unknown. In other words, the significance of the corporate ideal can be gauged only by an understanding of what the objective, unidealized city was, a question not of social theology but of historical sociology.

II. *Estates and Classes: Historical Sociology and the Age of the Reformation*

1. Understanding late medieval urban society in both its structural and its dynamic aspects requires, above all, adequate conceptual tools, of which the categories of social stratification are doubtless the most important. On this ground has been renewed in the historical literature one of the deadliest struggles of the nineteenth century. When, in the post-Napoleonic era, the Liberal social theorists advanced a holistic social theory based on the doctrine of classes, the Conservatives (De Maistre, Stahl, Adam Müller) counterattacked with the romantic concept of the *Ständestaat*, the society of patriarchal, hierarchial order, in which each social stratum had its place ordained by God or by Nature.[61] While in our own century the doctrine of

---

[60] The sacral corporate ideal was translatable from the urban context to that of the territorial monarchy, just as the Italian ideal of civic activism was (see Pocock, *Machiavellian Moment*, pp. 335ff.). Martin Bucer, one of the creators of the Reformation version of the ideal of the urban sacral corporation, had surprisingly little difficulty in translating it (during his English exile, 1549–1551) into the context of the English kingdom, the result being his *De regno Christi*. On this subject, see Helmut Kressner, *Schweizer Ursprünge des anglikanischen Staatskirchentums*, SVRG, no. 170 (Gütersloh, 1953).

[61] Robert M. Berdahl, "The *Stände* and the Origins of Conservatism in Prussia," *Eighteenth Century Studies*, 6 (1972–1973): pp. 298–321, here at pp. 311–315.

classes has step-by-step invaded ever more regions of historical thought,
including thought about the structure and meaning of pre-modern
European history, there has arisen to meet this new challenge a
renewed version of the doctrine of the *Ständestaat*, the *société des ordres*.
The main battery in this counterattack is Roland Mousnier, who has
advanced in a most aggressive form his historical sociology of pre-
modern Europe in categories of estates (*ordres*).

> In the stratification into orders or into "estates," the social groups form
> hierarchies not according to the wealth of their members and their
> capacity to consume, not according to their roles in the production of
> material goods, but according to the prestige, honor, and dignity
> attached by society to social functions which have no necessary con-
> nection with the production of goods, such as the profession of arms
> or the vocation of the educated man to the magistracies.[62]

Precisely the same conception flourishes on the other side of the
Atlantic, as witness this passage from a monograph on the Knights'
Revolt of 1522:

> In fact, the very word "class" is suspect when used in this period, for
> it is a term peculiar to an "acquisitive society." The word "estate," . . .
> which was familiar to Luther's contemporaries, included more than
> the amassing of wealth. The "estate" was a "way of life," a complex
> of cultural factors emphasizing tradition and custom and hence far
> richer in content than the concept of "class." The way of life of an
> estate, including its privileges and duties and its social prestige, was
> not bound entirely to its fortune. The former was not gained solely
> through the latter nor entirely lost by its absence. It might be inter-
> esting to compare, in this respect, the flexibility of the older "estates"
> with the newer "classes."[63]

---

[62] Roland Mousnier, "Présentation," in *Problèmes de stratification sociale. Actes du colloque international (1966)*, ed. Roland Mousnier, Publications de la Faculté des Lettres
et Sciences Humaines de Paris-Sorbonne, série "Recherches," 43 (Paris, 1968),
p. 8. In the discussion, Karl Bosl (Munich) objected (p. 27) that "la seule histoire
des notions ne nous conduirait pas à une interprétation entièrement satisfaisante de
la réalité historique." Bosl's own writings are, indeed, far less romantic and more
realistic than those of the Mousnier school. See, for example, Bosl's "Kasten, Stände,
Klassen im mittelalterlichen Deutschland," in his *Die Gesellschaft in der Geschichte des
Mittelalters*, 2nd ed. rev., Kleine Vandenhoeck-Reihe, 231/231a (Göttingen, 1966;
also in *ZBLG*, 52 [1969]). This is the German version of his contribution to Mousnier's
colloquium and may be read in French in *Problèmes de stratification sociale*, pp. 13–29.

[63] William R. Hitchcock, *The Background of the Knights' Revolt, 1522–1523*, University
of California Publications in History, 61 (Berkeley-Los Angeles, 1958), p. 82. Now
common in American scholarship, this dubious estates-classes contrast seems to be

The principal theoretical defects of this conception are not direct consequences of its political intent; for, as Robert Mandrou has pointed out, the widespread notion that this position is politically neutral, while the class-oriented historical sociology of Marxist and other historians is politically committed, is patently false. The pseudo-positivism, writes Mandrou, of those who try to banish the concepts of class and class conflict from all periods before the nineteenth century, "reflects a solid political conservatism." It idealizes the image of the Old Regime

> as a refuge and a consolation in face of the ills of the contemporary world; it claims to define social relations within a double framework of entirely adequate juridical definitions—those of orders, and that of a paternalism which is pronounced perfectly legitimate in a hierarchical society: the lord protects his peasants, the king protects his fair cities and his good citizens, the master artisan his journeymen. . . .[64]

The chief defects of this historical sociology lie, rather, in two fundamental assumptions, both demonstrably false: in the first place the assumption that "classes" and "estates" are two mutually exclusive types of social formation, the one purely economic and the other rooted in privilege, esteem, and honor—in a word, in juridical and largely subjective categories; and, secondly, that because the concept of social class—the division of society into two, at least potentially hostile, social groups—was unknown before the recent era, there were no social classes before the nineteenth century.

2. There are two major objections to the position of estates *rather than* classes, one theoretical and one empirical. The theoretical objection is based on the inadequacy of estate theory as a complete historical sociology. Its great defect is that, like every form of true structuralism, it has a fatal propensity for synchronism and a corresponding inability to explain major social (i.e., structural) change. This can be easily seen if a model of society of estates is made to function as a tool of historical analysis. Such a society, as C. B. Macpherson has pointed out in his picture of "customary or status

---

gaining strength. Harold J. Grimm, for example, who wrote about urban "classes" in 1962, by 1969 denied that classes had existed in the sixteenth century. See his "Social Forces in the German Reformation," *CH*, 31 (1962): pp. 3–12, here at p. 12; and "The Reformation and the Urban Social Classes in Germany," pp. 76ff.

[64] Robert Mandrou, *Introduction à la France moderne. Essai de psychologie historique 1500–1640*, L'évolution de l'humanité, 52 (Paris, 1961), pp. 138–139.

society," allots (by custom or compulsion) the productive and regulative work within the society to discrete social groups (crudely, laborers and masters), neither of which can invade the province of the other in a regular way. This is another way of saying that there is a free market neither in land nor in labor, no arena of competition in which individuals and groups could win the material basis for wholesale changes in their social statuses. Politics, competition, in such a society can embrace only struggles among the masters for a greater share of the total social product extracted from the laborers, but the sum total (or at least the proportion) of the social product extracted cannot be significantly expanded without running the risk of massive resistance in the form of insurrections to protect and restore customary social relations.[65]

It is true enough that this model of a "status society" reproduces some features of medieval European social relations, but it is just as true that nothing like the stasis required by this model was ever achieved. From about the twelfth century onward, the development of market agriculture in Europe fuelled basic alterations in feudal obligations and thus in social relations. One result was the flourishing of the towns and all they represented. Here, where the lines of subordination and domination were more abstract (at least since the rise of the communes) than on the land, typical class relations appear in clearer, bolder relief, stripped of much of the disguising overlay of old-fashioned juridical categories. It is thus tempting to identify the towns with classes and the countryside with estates,[66] a temptation that ought to be resisted. For town and land formed a single society that was not fundamentally threatened by the growth of trade. As Wallerstein has written, "Feudalism as a system should not be thought of as something antithetical to trade. On the contrary, up to a certain point, feudalism and the expansion of trade go hand in

[65] C. B. Macpherson, *The Political Theory of Possessive Individualism; from Hobbes to Locke* (Oxford, 1962), pp. 49–50. See Wilhelm Schwer, *Stand und Ständeordnung im Weltbild des Mittelalters. Die geistes- und gesellschaftsgeschichtlichen Grundlagen der berufsständischen Idee*, Görres-Gesellschaft, Sektion für Wirtschafts- und Sozialwissenschaft, 7, 2nd ed. (Paderborn, 1952), p. 6, who contrasts the static character of estate structures with the dynamic character of class structures in an unusually clear manner.

[66] As Oliver C. Cox does in his otherwise admirable *Class, Caste and Race; a Study in Social Dynamics* (New York, 1959), here at p. 146. See the unusual schematic diagram of class and estate structures in feudal society by Johanna Maria van Winter, *Rittertum. Ideal und Wirklichkeit*, trans. from the Dutch by Axel Plantiko and Paul Schritt (Munich, 1969), pp. 80–88.

hand."[67] By far the most impressive proof, however, of the inadequacy of an historical sociology constructed of estate categories to the history of late medieval Europe is the development—beginning around 1350 and lasting for nearly two hundred years—of a state of endemic social warfare between lords and their labor force, between seigneurs and peasants—but also, it should be noted, between dominators and dominated in the towns.[68] This social warfare was rooted in a general crisis of the feudal order,[69] in which the social relations typical of the second age of feudalism (eleventh–thirteenth centuries) underwent systemic disintegration. When, as during the fourteenth and most of the fifteenth century, change and not stability is the dominant condition of social relations, such an age is relatively impervious to the static historical sociology of estates. For, except for natural causes (climate, disease) and disruption from without (invasion, cross-cultural influence), estate theory has no tools to explain large-scale historical change.

Estates did exist as social groupings in feudal Europe, they developed especially from the twelfth century onward, and they were typical phenomena of the late feudal age. The clue to the meaning of estate schemes as they appear in the late medieval sources is that estates, properly taken, embraced only those groups that participated in the structures of domination. The estates which appeared all over Europe and which found their typical and unparalleled institutional expression in the assemblies of estates which form one of the hallmarks of late medieval history,[70] these estates were in the first instance groupings of lords, of those who shared in power over others. This

---

[67] Wallerstein, *Modern World System*, p. 20.

[68] See esp. Michel Mollat and Philippe Wolff, *Ongles bleus, Jacques et Ciompi. Les révolutions populaires en Europe aux XIVe et XVe siècles* (Paris, 1970), now in English as *The popular revolutions of the late Middle Ages* (London, 1973). See also the analysis of the Ciompi revolt by Achatz Freiherr von Müller, "Ständekampf oder Revolution? Die Ciompi Bewegung in Florenz," in *Ansichten einer künftigen Geschichtswissenschaft, 2: Revolution—ein historischer Langschnitt*, eds. Immanuel Geiss and Rainer Tamchina (Munich, 1974), pp. 34–75, which is relevant to the entire question of class conflict in pre-modern Europe.

[69] František Graus, *Das Spätmittelalter als Krisenzeit*, Medievalia Bohemica, I, Supplementum I (Prague, 1969); and Ernst Werner, "Spätmittelalterlicher Strukturwandel im Spiegel neuer Forschungen: Das italienische Beispiel," *Jahrbuch für Wirtschaftsgeschichte*, (1969): pp. 223–240.

[70] Although in some regions—France, Spain, Sicily, and Flanders—the assemblies themselves antedate the division into estates, which tends to support the view that the estates represented not different parts of the population but different sectors of the "notables."

fact has been sometimes obscured by modern writers who conceive estates in terms of contemporary functionalist social theory, a task made much easier by calling upon those late medieval writers who employed anatomical metaphors to explain the relationships of the various estates to one another and to the society as a whole.[71] In the German territories, the development of estates goes hand-in-hand with the construction and expansion of the power of the territorial princes. It was then, for example, and not during the High Middle Ages or even earlier, that the lesser nobility (the *Ritter und Edelknechte*) was forged from the most various elements into the readily identifiable estate it was to form all through the early modern era.[72] In the same period, that is to say, after 1250, the typical urban social formations also appear, the commune and its division into the estates of patricians (*Honoratioren, Ehrbarkeiten*) and guildsmen (*Handwerker*). Among the aristocrats the principle of birth as the chief gateway into an estate undoubtedly always played some part—hence the development of the pseudo-biological theory of nobility of the blood in Castile and the mania for genealogy almost everywhere—but the normative principle in estate formation and maintenance of privilege was and remained the degree and form of participation in the system of lordship, of domination over other men. This was seen already by Thomas Aquinas, whose trifold scheme divides men into those who have power (the nobles), those who do not (the commons), and those in between (the *populus honorabilis*).[73] Medieval estates were not occupational status groups (*Berufsstände*),[74] a misconception which rests not least upon the tendency to view medieval societies in functionalist terms.

3. The citation of Thomas Aquinas leads from the topic of social structures to its complement, social consciousness. By "social consciousness" is meant here the variety of forms (more or less schematized) of awareness of social stratification. The importance of the topic here

---

[71] Joachim Bumke, *Studien zum Ritterbegriff im 12. and 13. Jahrhundert,* "Euphorion," Beiheft 1 (Heidelberg, 1964), pp. 138–144.

[72] For which Otto von Gierke, with his stress on the organic theory of medieval society, may be largely responsible. *Das deutsche Genossenschaftsrecht,* III, pp. 546–557.

[73] *Summa Theologiae,* I, qu. 108, art. 2. See Schwer, *Stand und Ständeordnung,* p. 35: "Völlig unbefangen erkennen Thomas von Aquin und mit ihm die anderen mittelalterlichen Theologen die Zweiteilung der Menschheit in Herrschende und Dienende auf Grund natürlicher Vorausbestimmung an. . . ."

[74] See Bumke, *Studien zum Ritterbegriff,* p. 138, but long ago (1st ed., 1934) anticipated by Schwer. On the literature of medieval estate theory, see also Ruth Mohls, *The Three Estates in Medieval and Renaissance Literature* (New York, 1933).

lies in the oft-repeated assertion that the concept of class formation—that is, the division of society into two (simple or complex),
naturally antagonistic and at least potentially hostile social groups,
based *ultimately* on the social division of labor—was quite unknown to
Europeans before its fateful discovery by certain thinkers of the nineteenth century. Furthermore, class consciousness is sometimes said
to be incompatible with the enduring characteristics—custom, privilege, the gradations of honor—of pre-modern social institutions. Theoretically, as Stanislas Ossowski has argued, there is no compelling
reason why radically different forms of social consciousness cannot
co-exist in one and the same society.[75] More specifically, two-, three-
or multi-level estate schemes, arranged in a graduated hierarchy of
privilege (and perhaps even cemented with the comforting functionalist notion of harmony), could and did co-exist in pre-modern Europe
with dichotomous schemes; built on a principle of antagonism and
(at least potential) social warfare. The subdivisions of one scheme
may very well overlap those of the other, so that the first term in
the class-oriented pairs—rich and poor, rulers and ruled, honorable
and dishonorable—might embrace groups on both sides of the estate
line that divided nobles from commoners. In such a society, Ossowski
believes, class consciousness will predominate at the top and at the
bottom of the social order, while those in between will tend to think
of themselves and others in terms of the estate hierarchy and will
therefore also accept the harmonious, "everything in its proper place"
mentality which goes with it.[76]

The schemes of estates themselves can be rather deceptive. The
classic forms, such as the three-fold division of society into *oratores*,
bellatores, and *laboratores*, probably never had much practical significance
and certainly had little or none by the sixteenth century.[77] The literary tradition of social classification contains, in fact, a bewildering
variety of *principles* of social distinction, such as divisions of society
into the estates of men and women, clergy and laity, not only among
different authors but in one and the same author.[78] When the sixteenth

---

[75] Stanisław Ossowski, *Class Structure in the Social Consciousness*, trans. Sheila Patterson
(London-New York, 1963), pp. 65–66, by far the best theoretical work on the subject.
[76] *Ibid.*, p. 67, already perceived by Botero and Bodin in the late sixteenth century (see below, notes 96–97).
[77] Mandrou, *Introduction à la France moderne*, p. 139.
[78] See Mohls, *The Three Estates*, pp. 8–9, who maintains nonetheless that estate
theory appears only in a feudal context.

century is reached, estate schemes often become either extremely
florid or very crude, without in either case attaining a consistency
in norms of classification. François de Corlieu, for example, in his
Briefe instruction pour tous estats (Paris, 1558, pp. 66ff.), discerns no less
than twenty-one "ordres," ranging from "les rois et princes," "les pas-
teurs et ministres," and "les médicins," through "le mari," "la femme"
and "les enfants," down to "les malades" and "les laboreurs."[79] This
scheme betrays not so much a complex social consciousness as a
lack of any conceptual integrity. On the other side, there is the very
simple but also inconsistent scheme advocated by Thomas Lindner
(Tilianus), author of a catechism composed (1546) for use in the
South German town of Ravensburg: "Nemlich das Predig-Amt, die
weltliche Obrigkeit und der Ehestand. Dann dise Staende haben
Gottes Wort vor sich und alle andere Staende darein gefasset."[80] If,
to Corlieu's scheme we may add Robert Mandrou's remark that
"the orders, from this time onward, no longer had the social importance attributed to them by the strictest of the jurists,"[81] then to
Lindner's text we can only add Otto Brunner's comment that "the
theoretical literature of the Middle Ages needs first to be related to
the historical reality from which it derived."[82]

On the other side, there is the ancient and rich tradition of class
consciousness, the literary expressions of which lie, since the High
Middle Ages at least, at every hand. The dichotomous scheme of
society—lords and subjects, rich and poor, gentlemen and commons—
was by the fourteenth century as common as the better-known tri-
chotomous harmonic conception of three (or more), functionally
related, divinely ordained estates. The dichotomous model came in
two versions, an aristocratic and an anti-aristocratic, popular one,
each recognizing the same social fact but giving different explanations for the fact and different (and opposed) moral interpretations
of it. The social fact is the fundamental division of society into two
kinds of persons. In the popular view, subjects and lords are at the
same time producers and parasites. An English preacher of the four-

---

[79] Arlette Jouanna, "Recherches sur la notion d'honneur au XVIème siècle," *RHMC*,
15 (1968): p. 600.
[80] Ernst-Wilhelm Kohls, ed., *Die Evangelischen Katechismen von Ravensburg 1546/1733
und Reichemweier 1547/1559*, VKLBW, A 10 (Stuttgart, 1963), p. 53.
[81] Mandrou, *Introduction à la France moderne*, p. 139.
[82] Otto Brunner, *Land und Herrschaft. Grundfragen der territorialen Verfassungsgeschichte
Österreichs im Mittelalter*, 4th ed. rev. (Vienna-Wiesbaden, 1959), p. 399.

teenth century, for example, spoke on behalf of the poor, charging the rich before God's throne:

> Our labors and goods . . . they took away, to satiate their greed. They afflicted us with hunger and labors, that they might live delicately upon our labors and our goods. We have labored and lived so hard a life that scarce for half a year had we a good sufficiency, scarce nothing save bread and bran and water. Nay, rather, what is worse, we died of hunger. And they were served with three or four courses out of our goods, which they took from us. . . .[83]

How this situation came about is explained by the ploughman in his polemic against the knight in the sixteenth-century English dialogue, "Of Gentleness and nobility," probably written by the London lawyer, John Rastell (d. 1536).[84] The ploughman, in the sacred verse of the great tradition of social warfare against the lords, sings of the golden age of equality:

> For when Adam delved and Eve span,
> Who was then a gentleman?
> But then came the churl and gathered good,
> And there began first the gentle blood;
> And I think verily ye do believe
> That we came all of Adam and Eve.[85]

Then came the fall, as the parasites began to steal from their brethren, the producers:

> For when people first began to increase,
> Some gave themselves all to idleness,
> And would not labour, but take by violence
> That other men gat by labour and diligence.
> Then they that laboured were fain to give
> Them part of their gettings in peace to live,
> Or else for their lands, money a portion;
> So possession begun by extortion.[86]

Lordship is founded in property, property began by extortion and theft.

---

[83] Norman Cohn, *The Pursuit of the Millenium*, 2nd ed. (New York, 1961), pp. 213–214.

[84] The text is printed with *The Spider and the Fly*, ed. John S. Farmer (London, 1908). I quote from Mohls, *The Three Estates*, who discusses the problem of attribution on p. 17. Rastell married Elizabeth More, Thomas's sister.

[85] Mohls, *The Three Estates*, p. 290.

[86] *Ibid.*

The lord's reply to Rastell's ploughman affirms the same social distinction—between lords and people—but explains the origin and purpose of the distinction in the manner typical of all aristocratic political theory. The development of lords out of the original equality was a measure taken by the people for their own good, establishing over themselves a group of peacemakers whose virtue they recognized and rewarded with lands and incomes:

> The people, perceiving then their goodness,
> Their great wit, discretion, and gentleness,
> Were content to give them part of the profit
> Coming of their lands, which they did get,
> As corn, cattle and such things as they won.
> But after, when that coin of money began,
> They changed those revenues, and were content
> To give them in money an annual rent.
> So for their good and virtuous conditions
> They came first to lands and possessions;
> So possessions began, and were first found
> Upon a good and reasonable ground.[87]

Lordship is rooted in the common good; the rich have their wealth by common consent and for the good of the entire society; the dignity and honor of gentlemen has been well earned and not unjustly seized. Here, in one simple poem, far from the artful archaisms and subtly constructed social pyramids of the lawyers, the entire inner meaning of the late feudal order is laid bare.

It is important to remember that the aristocratic form of class consciousness was just as strong and just as well cultivated as the popular form. The debate between the two revolved about the most ancient of social questions, the origin and meaning of social inequality.[88] A particularly vicious poetic form of the aristocratic explanation circulated in Germany before and during the Reformation. Its literary source is the sixth eclogue of the bestselling Italian poet, Baptista Mantuanus (1448–1516), cast and recast by German poets and writers, notably Hans Sachs (1494–1576) and Erasmus Alber (ca. 1500–1553). This is the story of the children of Adam and Eve, the beautiful and the ugly ones. The basic story is that Eve showed her beautiful children to God, who blessed them and ordained them to estates of high degree—kings, princes, knights, rich townsmen, merchants,

---

[87] *Ibid.*, p. 291.
[88] *Ibid.*, pp. 91–95.

and learned doctors. When Eve finally brought forward her dirty, ragged, ugly children, of whom she was ashamed (the dishonor and shame of poverty and subjection are therefore fixed in the *natural* social order), God laughed at them; but, out of pity, He also blessed them and ordained for them all the servile crafts, trades, and estates.[89] Here, in a story laced with the ugliest form of humor, derision, all who could read were taught—to their satisfaction or disappointment—that lordship and subjection, wealth and poverty, honor and dishonor, were part God's law for human society. Especially satisfied must have been the German big bourgeoisie, for whom Hans Sachs cast into verse no less than four versions of this story.[90] In his *Meisterlied* of 1546, Sachs has God's reply to Eve's query as to why children of the same parents—brothers and sisters in every sense—should be treated so differently:

> Got sprach: "es stet in meiner hant,
> das ich im lant
> mit leuten muss besetzen ein ieglichen stant,
> dazu ich den leut auserwel
> und iedem stant seines geleichen leut zu stel,
> auf das niemant
> gebrech, was man sol han."
> Also durch dise fabel wirt bedeute,
> das man zu iedem stant noch findet leute;
> dabei man spuret heute,
> wie got so wunderbar regieret,
> mit weisheit ziert, er ordiniert
> zu iedem werk sein man.[91]

But, and here was the crucial point for Sachs' audience, the rich and powerful, the lords of every kind, were the descendants of the beautiful children, the merchant as well as the king or the knight or the prince—a fundamental unity far beyond any such quarrels over status such as the knights might bring against the urban rich.

---

[89] *Ibid.*, discussing and quoting texts of Hans Sachs, who worked this theme three times in 1553 and once in 1558. This fable, which came to Germany in Baptista Mantuanus's "Eclogues" (ca. 1470), was especially popular in Philipp Melanchthon's version (1539) and especially beloved of Protestant poets and dramatists. Besides Sachs, at least seven other Protestant writers produced pieces based on this fable between 1539 and 1559. Helmut De Boor and Richard Newald, eds., *Geschichte der deutschen Literatur von den Anfängen bis zur Gegenwart*, IV, p. 2: *Das Zeitalter der Reformation 1520–1570*, by Hans Rupprich (Munich, 1973), pp. 350–351.

[90] Mohls, *The Three Estates*, pp. 92–93.

[91] *Ibid.* On the social content of Sach's poetry, see J. Münch, *Die sozialen Anschauungen des Hans Sachs in seinen Fastnachtspielen* (Erlangen, 1936).

Here is an estate scheme resting lightly on top of a basic class consciousness—a class system within an estate system. That such complex social schemes were fairly common among German writers of
this period could be easily shown.[92]

Gradually this sort of social realism penetrated all levels of social
and political theory. In France, as late as 1484, Philippe de Poitiers
could repeat the traditional wisdom about the social order:

> Everyone knows how the commonwealth is divided into members and
> estates: the clergy to pray for the others, to counsel, to exhort; the
> nobility to protect the others by arms; and the people to nourish and
> sustain the nobles and clergy with payments and produce.[93]

And another French writer, Georges Chastellain (1405–1475), maintained that the composition of such estates was fixed by divine decree.
Some years later, however, Claude de Seyssel (d. 1520) thoughtfully
allowed that the clergy were not a separate social group but were common to all levels of society, and that the possibility of social mobility—the ascent of individuals from the lower into the higher ranks of
society—was the surest specific against rebellion and social warfare.[94]

The discarding of traditional categories began earliest and proceeded most rapidly in Italy, where the recovery of classical literature combined with indigenous culture to provide the north Italians
with a rich and varied material for political thought; and the tur-
bulent history of the peninsula gave them plenty of stimulus to think
about social and political forms in new and critical ways. Most sophis-
ticated is the political sociology of Niccolò Machiavelli (1469–1527),
who not only used the dichotomous, conflict-immanent scheme exclusively but was able as well to differentiate the class systems of heavily feudal regions (where there were many "gentlemen," a "gentleman"
being one who enjoys direct power over others) and the looser, more
egalitarian social systems of the cities.[95] It was left to writers of the

---

[92] See the complicated catalogue of "estates" in *Des Teufels Netz* (ca. 1415–1418),
discussed by Mohls, *The Three Estates*, pp. 88–89.

[93] This and the following French texts are quoted and discussed by P. S. Lewis,
Later Medieval France: The Polity (London-New York, 1968), pp. 167–170, whose discussion of social consciousness is unusually good.

[94] Claude de Seyssel, *La monarchie le France*, ed. J. Poujol (Paris, 1961), p. 127.

[95] *Discorsi*, I, 55. See Alfredo Bonadeo, "The Role of the 'Grandi' in the Political
World of Machiavelli," *Studies in the Renaissance*, 16 (1969): pp. 9–30; *idem*, "The
Role of the People in the Works and Times of Machiavelli," *Bibliothèque d'Humanisme
et Renaissance*, 32 (1970): pp. 351–378.

later sixteenth century, however, to discover the importance for political stability of those persons who belonged neither clearly to the
rich and powerful nor clearly to the poor and weak—the middling
element. Jean Bodin (d. 1596), a French apostle of order, launched a
vigorous defense of class society, for, he argued against Plato and Sir
Thomas More, "equality of possessions is subversive of the commonwealth," for the preservation of which it is necessary that "the poor,
the weak, and the unprotected defer to and obey their betters, the
rich and the powerful, most willingly, with a view to their assistance,
and the advantages they hope will accrue."[96] The problem is that
such a sharp division engenders social hatred and therefore insta-
bility, so that it is dangerous not to have an "intermediate position
between the rich and the poor, the good and the bad, the wise and
the foolish." Giovanni Botero, rather less of an apologist for order,
argued a little later (1589) that society is divided among the rich, the
poor, and those who lie between the extremes; the latter are "usually the quietest and easiest to govern."[97] The middling folk are thus
seen to be the key to social peace and civil order, as they tend to
check the greater propensities to violence of the rich and the poor.

It is clear, therefore, that, well before Thomas Hobbes thought
out the first general social theory based on the principle of the free
market that every person may freely compete with and challenge the
power of every other, without the restraints of chartered privilege,
customary law, or even of religion, the ability to conceive the social
order in terms of classes and social tension and antagonism had
already become a well-established feature even of formal political
theory. Among the common people, it was probably as old as the
feudal order itself. Certainly, conceptions of society in terms of hierarchies of estates continued to flourish, just as estates themselves continued to exist right down to the opening of the modern era and,
in some places, well beyond. But the existence of such schemes does
not prove that the society of the Old Regime was a "société des
ordres" alone. Against the subtle classifications of the lawyer Loyseau,

---

[96] Jean Bodin, *Six Books of the Commonwealth*, Book 5, chapter 2 (trans. M. J. Tooley
[Oxford, n.d.], pp. 158–159).
[97] Giovanni Botero, *The Reason of State*, Book IV, chapter 2 (trans. P. J. Waley
and D. P. Waley [New Haven-London, 1956], pp. 82–83), a text pointed out by
William J. Bowsky, "The Anatomy of Rebellion in Fourteenth Century Siena: from
Commune to Signory?" in *Violence and Civil Disorder in Italian Cities, 1200–1500*, ed.
Lauro Martines (Berkeley-Los Angeles, 1972), p. 270.

the darling of the "société des ordres" literature, one may place the
clean, razor-edged rage of the parish priest of Estrepigny, Jean Méslier
(ca. 1711):

> une si étrange et si odieuse disproportion entre les différen etats et
> conditions des hommes, qui met, comme on le voit manifestement,
> toute l'autorité, tous les biens, tous les plaisirs, tous les contentements,
> toutes les richesses et même l'oisivité du côté des grands, des riches
> et des nobles, et met du côté des pauvres peuples tout ce qu'il ya de
> pénible et de facheux, savoir la dépendance, les soins, la misère, les
> inquiétudes, toutes les peines et toutes les fatigues du travail; laquelle
> disproportion est d'autant plus injuste et odieuse, qu'elle les met dans
> une entière dépendance des nobles et des riches, et qu'elle les rend
> pour ainsi dire leur esclaves, jusques-là qu'ils sont obligé de souffrir
> non seulement toutes leurs rebufades, leurs mépris et leurs injures, mais
> aussi leurs véxations, leurs injustices et leurs mauvais traitement.[98]

4. Thus far, the tendency of the argument is that class analysis is
the form of historical sociology best suited—both from the standpoint of social structure and from that of social consciousness—to
the serious study of social formations and social relations in late
medieval and Renaissance Europe, including the urban ones. Several
traditional objections to the employment of class analysis in studies
of the pre-modern era may well require some replies. First, there is
the objection that classes are "economic classes," and they reduce
the rich multiplicity of social relationships to economic relationships
only. To this it may be replied that social class is not a thing or
even a characteristic but a relationship between two or more groups
of persons which form a complete social formation; its parts, though
analytically distinguishable and susceptible to separate study, exist in
a state of tension which is part of the definition of each class. Thus,
to speak of "economic classes" is highly misleading, for the class system, whose *ultimate ground* is the structure of the economy, will, except
in times of full structural crisis, embrace every aspect of life, including politics and culture. Political power and cultural domination are
not just "mirrors" of some more fundamental relationship but are
constituent parts of the relations among social classes. The political
structure forms the primary societal controls, the culture the primary
context of self-understanding and self-definition. In "normal" times,
despite the existence of standing antagonisms which point to poten-

---

[98] *Le testament de Jean Méslier* (Amsterdam, 1864), II, p. 178, as quoted by Ossowski,
Class Structure, p. 24 n. 1.

tial conflict, the political system maintains its control and elicits patriotism, and the cultural system maintains its hegemonical effectiveness and elicits conventional piety.

A second objection, and one that has an apparent legitimacy, is to the tendency of "Marxising" historians to identify the classes of pre-industrial society with those of the age of industrial capitalism, finding the first bourgeois in every merchant and the first proletariat in every group of the urban poor.[99] Against this tendency must be said, once more it seems, that the class systems of feudal, or "late feudal" or "pre-capitalist" Europe were not those of the age of industrial capitalism, and that the confrontation and definition of classes was neither so conscious nor so precise as in the modern era. Here the structural approach, with its bias for the synchronic, the enduring, has much to contribute. The estate model of society, with its total innocence of the forces of change, is *one type* of such structural analysis that is particularly appropriate to pre-capitalist European societies, because the organization into estates was one of the features of those societies. On the negative side, feudal societies lacked the distinction between state and society—although the beginnings of such a theoretical distinction go back far beyond Machiavelli and the Italians to the medieval civilians[100]—and between the public order (of equality) and the private order (of competition and classes). The political language of the late medieval and Renaissance era was overwhelmingly that of the world of estates, the language of divinely ordained social tasks, the common good, the lack of any distinction between private and public duties.

5. Several conclusions supplied by the foregoing analysis are important to this study. In the first place, in the study of social structures of late medieval and Renaissance societies, the historian must work with estate and class categories simultaneously, realizing that the predominance of class over estate solidarities (in, for example, the study of politics) will vary according to the issue and to the social strata involved, as well as to the solidity of the social order. In the well-integrated society, whose ruling class is not rent by internal rivalries and factions, even great turbulence may not seriously shake

---

[99] I here use "Marxising" as an English rendering of the French "marxisant." Mandrou (*Introduction à la France moderne*, p. 139) employs the term "paramarxiste."

[100] Gaines Post, *Studies in Medieval Legal Thought: Public Law and the State, 1100–1322* (Princeton, 1964), pp. 333–367.

the effect of traditional political language as the carrier of traditional
values and loyalties. Secondly, the study of social consciousness—
which is not the direct subject of what follows—needs to be oriented
to an accurate understanding of social structures. Finally, the basic
lines of structure and consciousness in later medieval and Renaissance
Europe were common to the urban and the seigneurial sectors of
society; and, for the High Middle Ages onward, neither type of social
formation may be regarded as a self-sufficient whole. For the ruling
classes, this means that beyond the categories of "nobles," "seigneurs,"
and "gentlemen" for the lords in the land, and beyond the categories of "patricians," "popolo grasso," and "big bourgeoisie" for the
urban rich, we may employ the term "aristocracy" as a comprehensive term for the lords of society in the towns and in the land.[101]
This is how the term is used in the following study of the lords of
Reformation Strasbourg.

III. *Historical Method and the Study of Aristocratic Societies*

1. There are few better solvents of romantic idealization than the
assembly of as much and as precise information as possible about
individuals and groups of individuals. Much of what flies under the
modish banner of "social history" is no more than this more or less
precise study of human groups.[102] A good example of what this type
of research can achieve may be seen in the revision of scholarly
opinion about the "guild revolts," those guild-based movements
against political oligarchy in the European towns of the thirteenth
to fifteenth centuries. Once the darling of liberal medievalists, the
proto-democratic character of these movements has vanished, after
three decades of research, into thin air. What was broken in suc-

---

[101] See Kamen, *The Iron Century*, p. 129. Machiavelli (*Discorsi*, I, p. 55) actually
uses the term "gentlemen" to refer to aristocrats in the land or in town, defining
them as those who live idly on the proceeds of their possessions and who shun
agriculture or any other useful pursuit; they are most dangerous, he says, when
they also own castles and command subjects in the countryside. On the Italian term
"popolo grasso" and its counterpart, "popolo minuto," see Bowsky, "Anatomy of
Rebellion in Fourteenth-Century Siena," p. 233; and, on the London equivalents,
Sylvia L. Thrupp, *The Merchant Class of Medieval London* (Ann Arbor, 1948), pp. 14–15.
[102] Which has led Eric J. Hobsbawm to draw the distinction between social history and the history of society. "From Social History to the History of Society,"
Daedalus, 100, no. 1 (1971): pp. 20–45.

cessful revolts, it turns out, was the protected political monopoly of the old patriciates, not the domination of urban regimes by rich aristocrats. As Erich Maschke has written, the guild revolts produced "eine Erweiterung des Kreises . . . der bisher die patrizische Ratsverfassung getragen hatte. . . . Auch die Stadt der Zunftverfassung war in ihrer Führung eine Stadt der Kaufleute."[103] The guild regime, conceived as a political supremacy of artisans and other small producers, simply never existed.[104] Karl Czok, one of the closest students of the guild revolts, sees them as having brought some of the middling citizens into the inner circles of power, although he warns against seeing the struggles chiefly in class terms and recommends calling them "civic struggles" (*Bürgerkämpfe*).[105] The meaning of this revision for our understanding of the later histories of the towns has been summed up by Philippe Dollinger: "Car après comme avant le régime des villes allemandes demeure oligarchique, aux mains des plus riches."[106] Despite radical differences between their constitutions, therefore, the social complexion of the ruling class was much the same in the guild towns (Strasbourg, Ulm, Constance) as it was in Nuremberg, where there were no guilds at all.[107]

The demythologization of the German guild revolts has its forerunners and counterparts in the literature on the towns of other regions of Europe;[108] and it is gradually revising the entire approach to the social and political dynamics of the late medieval town.[109]

---

[103] Erich Maschke, "Verfassung und soziale Kräfte in der deutschen Stadt des späten Mittelalters, vornehmlich in Oberdeutschland," *VSWG*, 41 (1959): pp. 289–349, 433–476, here at pp. 475–476.

[104] Czok, "Zur Stellung der Stadt," pp. 16–17.

[105] Karl Czok, "Zunftkämpfe, Zunftrevolution oder Bürgerkämpfe?" *Wissenschaftliche Zeitschrift der Karl-Marx-Universität Leipzig*, 8 (1958–1959): pp. 129–113; *idem*, "Die Burgerkämpfe in Süd- und Westdeutschland im 14. Jahrhundert," *JGO*, 12/13 (1966–1967): pp. 40–72, here at p. 48.

[106] Philippe Dollinger, "Les villes allemandes au moyen âge: les groupements sociaux," in *La ville*, vol. 2 (Recueils de la société Jean Bodin, VII; Brussels, 1955), pp. 371–372.

[107] Wolfgang von Stromer, *Oberdeutsche Hochfinanz 1350–1450*, 3 vols., Beihefte der Vierteljahrschrift für Sozial- und Wirtschaftsgeschichte, nos. 55–57 (Wiesbaden, 1970), p. 341.

[108] Examples in Philippe Wolff, "Les luttes sociales dans les villes du Midi français, XIIIe–XIVe siècles," *AESC*, 2 (1947): pp. 452–453; Hermann Van Werveke, "Les villes belges: histoire des institutions économiques et sociales," *La ville*, vol. 2, pp. 557–558.

[109] See the critique by Gerd Wunder, "Die Sozialstruktur der Reichsstadt Hall im späten Mittelalter," *Untersuchungen zur gesellschaftlichen Struktur der mittelalterlichen Städte in Europa. Reichenau-Vorträge 1963–1964*, Vorträge und Forschungen, 11 (Constance-Stuttgart, 1966), p. 34.

Years ago, before this current was very strong, Leo Kofler asserted
the ambiguous social nature of European urban guilds:

> Despite the frequent victories of the guilds, what remained ultimately
> decisive—and not only in Germany—was that the victorious guilds-
> men sought to displace the patriciate politically but not economically.
> The social structure of the society of estates was untouched, so that
> the domination of the big bourgeoisie naturally reconstructed itself.[110]

Time has proved Kofler right.

2. The new history of the guild revolts is an example of what
may be achieved by bringing social-structural questions and empirical methods of research to traditional subject matter. For German (as
for other) towns of the late Middle Ages and the Reformation eras,
relatively new techniques have enabled historians to study urban social
structures with a precision formerly unknown. The quantification of
levels of wealth, derived from urban tax registers, has given access
to important sectors of the urban population.[111] Stratification by tax
categories works very well for social groups which, though wealthy
enough to have been regular payers of property levies, are too large
to be manageable by biographical reconstruction. The middling elements—small merchants, shopkeepers, artisans—lend themselves very
well to such treatment, by the use of which some impressive results
have been obtained.[112]

---

[110] Kofler, *Zur Geschichte der bürgerlichen Gesellschaft*, p. 119, and see pp. 123–124.

[111] See esp. Friedrich Blendinger's remarkable "Versuch einer Bestimmung der
Mittelschicht in der Reichsstadt Augsburg vom Ende des 14. bis zum Anfang des
18. Jahrhunderts," in *Städtische Mittelschichten in den südwestdeutschen Städten. Protokoll
über die VIII. Arbeitstagung des Arbeitskreises für südwestdeutsche Stadtgeschichtsforschung*, eds.
Erich Maschke and Jürgen Sydow, VKLBW, B 69 (Stuttgart, 1972), pp. 32–78. Both
the state of the literature and that of research techniques may be studied in Erdmann
Weyrauch's "Zur Auswertung von Steuerbüchern mit quantifizierenden Methoden,"
his contribution to the recent *Festgabe für Ernst-Walter Zeeden*. To the literature cited
there should be added Ingrid Bátori's contribution to the same volume, "Besitzstruk-
turen in der Stadt Kitzingen zur Zeit der Reformation," and C. R. Friedrichs,
"Capitalism, Mobility and Class Formation in the Early Modern German City,"
Past & Present, 69 (November 1975), pp. 24–29, a study of Nördlingen. My thanks
to Dr. Weyrauch and Dr. Bátori for letting me read their studies in typescript, both
of which are concrete results of their participation in the research group Sonderforschungsbereich Spätmittelalter und Reformation (Tübingen), Unterprojekt Z 2.2:
"Sozialschichtung in Städten Süddeutschlands in Spätmittelalter und Reformation,"
under the auspices of Prof. Zeeden and the direct leadership of Hans-Christoph
Rublack.

[112] Hence the efforts at quantification in *Städtische Mittelschichten* are on the whole
more successful than those in the earlier *Gesellschaftliche Unterschichten in den südwestdeutschen
Städten*, eds. Erich Maschke and Jürgen Sydow, VKLBW, B 41 (Stuttgart, 1967).

At the bottom and at the top of the urban class system, stratification by tax category is less, or not at all, satisfactory. At the bottom, because the poorest townsmen—servants, day-laborers, beggars, criminals—paid no taxes at all and, indeed, stood outside the effective system of class relations, as Friedrich Engels noted when he baptized them the "plebs."[113] The usual tax category of *habenits* reached, in fact, well up into the strata of non-paupers, and it therefore conceals persons of widely differing social positions.[114]

The top of the urban social hierarchy poses different problems. The structure of a society perpetuates itself in the documentary remains of the society—both qualitatively and quantitatively—and, for the societies of pre-industrial Europe, only among the upper classes can we reconstruct the biographies of relatively large numbers of persons. The centuries-long traditions of genealogy and heraldry, studies born of the waxing caste-like tendencies among the aristocracies of the late Middle Ages, contribute mightily to this ability. The lower classes, on the other hand, with occasional exceptions, remain faceless generalizations, interesting individual cases, or just statistics. Thus, in its reconstruct-ability, as in so many other ways, a society may be said to have belonged to, to have been the property of, its ruling class.

It has long been recognized that prosopography, or collective biography, is a useful and profitable method of studying aristocracies. Nor is it any accident that the method's greatest successes have come in the study of ancient, chiefly classical, societies; although since the work of Lewis Namier it has been employed increasingly in the study of pre-modern European aristocracies as well.[115] Some major successes have been scored in the Renaissance towns. Lauro Martines, for example has conducted two major prosopographically based studies at Florence, one of humanists and the other of notaries and lawyers.[116]

---

[113] *Der deutsche Bauernkrieg*, in *Marx-Engels Werke*, VII (Berlin, 1960), p. 346. The term "plebs" tends to be avoided by non-socialist historians, including many who find nothing objectionable about the complementary term, "patriciate."

[114] Bernhard Kirchgässner, "Probleme quantitativer Erfassung städtischer Unterschichten im Spätmittelalter, besonders in Reichsstädten Konstanz und Esslingen," in *Gesellschaftliche Unterschichten*, pp. 75–81.

[115] W. Den Boer, "Die prosopographische Methode in der modernen Geschichtsschreibung der Hohen Römischen Kaiserzeit," *Mnemosyne*, 22 (1969): pp. 268–280. On the method in general, see Lawrence Stone, "Prosopography," *Daedalus*, 100, no. 1 (Winter 1971), pp. 46–79.

[116] *The Social World of the Florentine Humanists, 1390–1460* (Princeton, 1963); *Lawyers and Statecraft in Renaissance Florence* (Princeton, 1968).

The German towns of the Reformation era have also yielded some
secrets to this method. Walter Jacob's analysis of the careers of sixty-
five politicians of Zürich during the decade 1519–1528, although the
time span is somewhat brief and his stratification categories merit
revision, is receiving deserved recognition, imitation, and adaptation.[117] Just as suggestive in another way is Hans-Christoph Rublack's
treatment of the regime of Constance and the introduction of the
Reformation there (1499–1531), part of which is based on prosopog-
raphies of the leading politicians and the clergy.[118] Rublack employs
his data not just to answer specific questions about the persons whose
biographies are reconstructed, but as an instrument to illuminate an
entire historical process in which the biographical subjects were principal actors. Thus, although his prosopographical data are not so
extensive as those of Jacob, Rublack successfully makes the transition from the study of structures (prosopography is, after all, a structural method) to the study of historical events. In this respect, his
book has few parallels in the current literature on the Reformation
in the cities of the Holy Roman Empire.[119] The most massive and
most impressive work of this kind deals not with a single city but
with an entire diocese; and, although much of the book is clearly
based on exhaustive social research at least partly of a prospographi-
cal sort, the data themselves do not, with one exception, appear in
the work itself—probably for sound material reasons. The reference

---

[117] Walter Jacob, *Politische Führungsschicht und Reformation. Untersuchungen zur Reformation in Zürich 1519–1528*, Zürcher Beiträge zur Reformationsgeschichte, 1 (Zürich, 1970). Worth consulting is René Hauswirth's review in *Zwingliana*, 13, no. 4 (1970): pp. 255–260. The principal weakness of this work is the near absence of an historical sociology and the consequent inadequacy of the stratification scheme used. Building upon this important work but with a much more developed theoretical sense is Erdmann Weyrauch's "Paper on Social Stratification. Zur Konzeptualisierung der Forschung im Unterprojekt Z 2.2" (mimeographed working paper, Tübingen, 1974), working paper no. 17 of the research group described in note 111 above.

[118] Hans-Christoph Rublack, *Die Einführung der Reformation in Konstanz von den Anfängen bis zum Abschluss 1531*, QFRG, 40 (= Veröffentlichungen des Vereins für Kirchenge-schichte in der evang. Landeskirche in Baden, 27) (Gütersloh-Karlsruhe, 1971).

[119] Territorial history in Southwest Germany is much better served, although the materials run heavily to pastors and territorial officials. Volker Press promises a vol-ume of data, including a prosopography of the Palatine officials, to accompany his *Calvinismus und Territorialstaat. Regierung und Zentralbehörden der Kurpfalz 1559–1619*, Kieler Historische Studien, 7 (Stuttgart, 1970). We may hope for a study based on Walter Bernhardt's *Die Zentralbehörden des Herzogtums Württemberg und ihre Beamten 1520–1629*, 2 vols., VKLBW, B 70–71 (Stuttgart, 1973), which is modelled on Friedrich Gund-lach's treatment of the Hessian regime. Similar repertories of the officials of Baden, Vorderösterreich, and the chief bishoprics would be extremely helpful.

is to Francis Rapp's huge *Réformes et Réformation à Strasbourg. Église et Société dans le diocèse de Strasbourg (1450–1525).*[120] As a social study of the late medieval church on a diocesan level the book is absolutely without parallel or rival, though one hopes it will not remain so. Its most remarkable feature is its deliberate linking of structural and temporal analyses, employing his researches on the social complexion of various sectors of the clergy and religious orders to explain the failures of successive reform efforts in the diocese of Strasbourg.

3. No one can long study the histories of European aristocracies without being impressed by the importance of family ties. The family as a subject of historical study is, at last, receiving the kind of attention it deserves, although there is no agreement on even the most elementary trends in family structure.[121] It is likely that, in their zeal to dispel the traditional view of the progressive nuclearization of the primitive complex stem or joint family through the disintegrating effects of urban life, Peter Laslett and his British colleagues have gone much too far in denying the importance of the complex family at any stage of Western history.[122] There is recent evidence that the complex family flourished until very late in at least certain sectors of the Central European peasantry,[123] and, for the other end of the social hierarchy, students of aristocratic social life during the Middle Ages and Renaissance have affirmed the importance of extra-nuclear family bonds.[124]

It is now clear that the thesis of unilinear, progressive nuclearization of family structure in the towns is incorrect on several counts. First, certain historical developments, especially political ones, tended to strengthen or weaken aristocratic family structure both on the land and in the towns. It is likely, for example, that the political

---

[120] Collection de l'Institut des Hautes Etudes Alsaciennes, 23 (Paris, 1974). See also René Pierre Levresse, "Prosopographie du chapitre de l'église cathédrale de Strasbourg de 1092 à 1593," *AEA*, 18 (1970): pp. 1–39.

[121] There is an excellent survey of the question by Diane Owen Hughes, "Urban Growth and Family Structure in Medieval Genoa," *Past & Present*, no. 66 (February 1975), pp. 3–7.

[122] See Peter Laslett and Richard Wall, eds., *Households and Family in Past Time* (Cambridge, 1972), pp. 1–81, an extended polemic against the historical concept of the extended family.

[123] Lutz K. Berkner, "The Stem Family and the Developmental Cycle of the Peasant Household: An Eighteenth Century Austrian Example," *AHR*, 77 (1972): pp. 398–418.

[124] Georges Duby, "Lignage, noblesse et chevalerie au la région maconnaise," *AESC*, 27 (1972): pp. 803–823, for example.

decentralization of post-Carolingian France and Italy promoted the growth of large households on the land.[125] In the Italian towns, on the other hand, the political victory of the *popolo* over the old aristocratic clans tended to have a disintegrating effect on the latter.[126] Secondly, the effect of town life on aristocratic family structure varied enormously from city to city. Whereas in Tuscany the traditional picture of progressive nuclearization is probably true, in Genoa quite the opposite happened, as the rise of the commercial aristocracy during the earlier twelfth century produced a situation in which "lineage ties became more clearly defined, more firmly patrilineal, and more frequently invoked; and the bonds of the domestic group, the joint patriarchal family, were tightened."[127] In either case extended family ties among the aristocracy, whether organized into a single or into multiple households, formed a fundamental part of aristocratic self-consciousness and a constant element of urban aristocratic politics. Lauro Martines has summarized this importance:

> The rich urban families, the oligarchical families, tended to monopolize the public forums of the cities of late medieval and Renaissance Italy. Generally speaking, they controlled the institutions of government, and their spokesmen best expressed the politico-social values that we have come to associate with those cities. Whether at Florence or Venice, Padua or Genoa, the affairs and direction of government were bound up with the practical interests of the political families. Indeed, it is not wholly metaphorical to say that government and the principal families were indivisible; and when they were not, then political violence was profound, men overturned governments and the streets were delivered to lawlessness.[128]

The strength of extended family structures may not have varied only between town and land, between town and town, and from one epoch to another, but also between class and class. Certainly the question has not been studied systematically with regard to the single most

---

[125] Hughes, "Urban Growth and Family Structure," p. 4, with references.

[126] David Herlihy, "Mapping Households in Medieval Italy," *The Catholic Historical Review*, 58 (1972): pp. 1–22. Any study of aristocratic propertyholding during this era will reveal the importance of the extended family as a social entity. The matter of actual household size is likely to have been of lesser importance to aristocrats because of their great ability to maintain family ties over considerable distances and time.

[127] Hughes, "Urban Growth and Family Structure," pp. 6–7.

[128] Lauro Martines, "The Historical Approach to Violence," in *Violence and Disorder in Italian Cities, 1200–1500*, pp. 3–18, here at p. 14.

important determinant of class, property in its various forms. It is not difficult to understand, however, that some features of aristocratic life tended to promote the maintenance of family ties beyond the individual aristocratic household. One such feature was the practice of co-enfiefment, by which a single male in each generation was the fiefholder (*Lehenträger, porteur à fief*) for a group of adult males related in the first or second degrees. Fief-holding in the Upper Rhine Valley, whether by urban or by rural aristocrats, was overwhelmingly of this kind.[129] Secondly, most aristocratic families of this region possessed a *Stammsitz*, an ancestral residence which, if a fief, was inalienable and in which each family member had some stake.[130] The practice of partible inheritance, the general rule in the German-speaking world, probably helped to weaken family ties in some cases and some periods (especially after the development of a general market in land made the liquidation and division of inheritances easy), but it may also have served to strengthen the family by keeping all siblings on the same social level. The spread of genealogy meant that aristocrats, its chief practitioners, knew better than other folks did (supposing the genealogies to be unfalsified), not only who their ancestors were, but also how closely they were related to contemporaries of the same social status. Among aristocrats, property, marriages, and status might all be considered and conserved as the goods of the complex family. This is perfectly clear from the story (ca. 1507) of Johann Werner of Zimmern and his romance with Sophia Bock (d. 1510), a rich, homely widow of Strasbourg.[131] The match was promoted by Margrave Christoph I of Baden (1453–1527), who

---

[129] Ruling Class, Regime and Reformation, pp. 86ff.

[130] *Ibid.*, pp. 129–130.

[131] The story is told in *ZC*, II, pp. 148–151, where the woman is called "Sophia Böcklin." The Bock and the Böcklin were quite distinct from each other, although tradition and heraldic evidence give them a common origin; and there is no Sophia in the Böcklin genealogy for this period, although the Böcklin descent is fairly well known. In the necrology of the commandery of the Knights of St. John at Strasbourg, however, there is a notice that Sophia Böckin (i.e., Bock) died on 8 January 1510, and she was the wife of the count of Löwenstein and the daughter of Johann Conrad Bock and Hartliebe von Andlau. BNUS, MS. 752, at 8.I. This woman can only be the rich widow of the story in the *Zimmerische Chronik*, who there marries Count Ludwig von Löwenstein. Hans Conrad Bock was a patrician senator at Strasbourg in 1466/67, 69/70, and 75/76. Hatt, p. 405. The Hans Conrad Bock who was senator in 1435, 37, 41, 43, 45, and 47, and Stettmeister in 1433, 49, 51, 53, 55, 57/58, 60/61, and 63/64 (Hatt, pp. 405, 597) is likely to have been a

wanted to help Johann Werner recoup his family's depleted resources. When Johann Werner consulted his brothers and sisters, they advised him to marry Sophia, whose lower status was somewhat enhanced by her wealth and her first marriage to a count, "then, too, he has two brothers, who—even if he damages his own descendants by this marriage—can make good, honorable marriages, fitting and in accord with their ancestry, and maintain the family in such a way that heirs will be eligible for tournaments and for the better ecclesiastical benefices."[132] Although Johann Werner did not feel compelled to follow this advice and did not marry Sophia, still the advice itself is evidence of a policy of collective maintenance and survival in one generation of an aristocratic family.

In the study of aristocracies, then, the concept of "family" must necessarily remain a complex one and not be restricted to the organization of individual households. "Family" was at once a category of familial relationship, of blood and marriage, and of property in the broadest sense of the term. "Family" was not just a household but a community maintained for the preservation and enhancement of all the forms of property that gave the family its social position: real property; capital; and cultural capital in the form of education.[133] This led to the possibility that the aristocratic family could be also a political unit, which did not necessarily mean that related office-holders always pursued together the aggrandizement of the family. It did provide, however, both informal systems of communication and possibilities of cooperation prior to and more intimate than official relationships and paths of political education, by which young aristocrats could be initiated into family political traditions and groomed to take their places in the regime.

---

different, older man. As for the *Zimmern Chronicle*, I have used the older edition by K. A. von Barack, which will be superseded when the indices are complete to Hans Martin Decker-Hauff's fine new edition.

[132] *ZC*, II, p. 149, ll. 5–11.

[133] Education as cultural capital is meant here in the sense developed by Pierre Bourdieu, "Reproduction culturelle et reproduction sociale," *Informations en sciences sociales*, 10, no. 2 (1972): pp. 45–79; now available in German in Pierre Bourdieu and Jean-Claude Passeron, *Grundlagen einer Theorie der symbolischen Gewalt*, trans. Eva Moldenhauer (Frankfurt/M., 1973), pp. 88–139.

IV. *Problems, Plan, and Purpose of this Study*

1. A prosopographical apparatus lies at the basis of this study of Strasbourg's ruling class and political elite during the Reformation era (ca. 1520–1555).[134] The "universe" of the apparatus includes every discoverable person who sat in the town's privy councils (the XV and XIII) during this time span. The lists of names had themselves to be reconstructed, as the privy councils were true *arcanae regiminis*, lists of whose members rarely appear among the registers of office-holders.[135] For a study of the social foundations of Strasbourg's politics, the composition of the "universe" was not difficult, because it has been known for a long time—at least since the work of Gustav Schmoller[136]—that the two privy councils formed, since the middle of the fifteenth century, the inner circle of power at Strasbourg. The reconstructed lists of privy councillors must then contain, as they do, all or nearly all of the principal political figures of the age, though they naturally include a good many smaller fry as well.

Given the importance of the lists as a starting point and as a basis of collection of political and social data for this study, the accuracy and completeness of the lists bear closely upon the integrity of the analysis. As to accuracy, no person has been included in the lists unless a contemporary source designates him as a XV[er] or a XIII[er], and the dates of service in the privy councils are inclusive rather than exclusive. The problems of name collection have been discussed elsewhere.[137] Suffice here to say that, in most cases, new appointments and notices of resignations and deaths are recorded in the protocols of the Senate & XXI from 1539 onward (the year at which the extant series "XXI" begins). For the preceding years, the names were gathered from a very wide variety of sources, and any lacunae in the lists fall in the 1520s rather than in any later period.

The prosopographical appendix contains biographies of 105 men who were privy councillors between 1520 and 1555, many of whom

---

[134] This appendix has not been reprinted.

[135] Thomas A. Brady, Jr., "The Privy Councils of Strasbourg (XV and XIII): A Supplement to Jacques Hatt, *Listes des membres du grand sénat de Strasbourg*," BCGA, no. 27 (1974): pp. 73–79.

[136] Gustav Schmoller, *Strassburg zur Zeit der Zunftkämpfe und die Reform seiner Verfassung und Verhaltung*, Quellen und Forschungen zur Sprach- und Culturgeschichte der germanischen Völker, XI (Strasbourg, 1875).

[137] Brady, "Privy Councils," pp. 73–74.

served also for one or more years before or after these dates. The
councillors were co-opted for life tenures, the XV from senators and
ex-senators, the XIII normally from the XV. Of the 105 known
members, the complete terms of service of 85 are known; and these
85 served for an average of just under fifteen years (14.8 yrs.). Of
the twenty-eight who were in office at any one time, nine were supposed to be patricians (*Constofler*) and nineteen to be members of the
guilds; the actual division of the 105 is 32 (30.5%) patricians and
73 (69.5%) guildsmen—or within several percentage points of the
legal ratio. The difference is to be explained by the somewhat longer
average length of tenure of the patricians vis-à-vis the guildsmen
(16.3 yrs. vs. 14.1 yrs.). Because the total period spanned by the lists
reaches 20–25 years backward and forward from the period 1520–
1555, it is impossible to say theoretically, on the basis of an average service of 15 yrs., how many names the lists *should* contain.

2. The state of the sources at Strasbourg is not particularly favorable. Some of the great staple sources of social history, such as tax
registers, court records, and treasury records, are lost nearly without a trace. Others, such as guild archives, are mere fragments.[138]
Some riches do remain, especially the under-exploited registers of
the Strasbourg notaries (series "KS"),[139] and a wealth of material
in both major Strasbourg archives on transfers of feudal and other
sorts of real property. The maxim, nevertheless, that the lower down
the class structure the more obscure the person, is doubly true in
Strasbourg. Just those records which might have allowed a reconstruction of the occupational, income, and even behavioral patterns
of the middling folk, and perhaps even some of the lower classes,
have disappeared at Strasbourg. The structure of income, for example, and the social complexion of criminality, are topics which cannot be pursued there.

These losses mean not just a loss of information but something
far more serious: except for the upper class and a few of the well-

---

[138] Jean Rott, "Artisanat et mouvements sociaux à Strasbourg autour de 1525,"
in *Artisans et ouvriers d'Alsace*, PSSARE, 9 (Strasbourg, 1965), pp. 137–170, here at
p. 160 n. 7.
[139] The Archives Municipales de Strasbourg (= AMS), Chambres des Contrats
(= KS). There is no inventory of this enormous series, although some volumes do
have contemporary indices (indexed by purchaser or lender). All the more valuable,
then, is the superb chart of the first 150 volumes, prepared by Mr. Steven Nelson,
which breaks down these volumes by *étude* and puts them into chronological sequence.
A copy of this chart is on deposit in AMS.

to-do middling folk, no social class of medieval and Reformation Strasbourg can be studied systematically by one or another of the tools of modern social history. We are thus left with chance notices of individuals and small groups, which by heroic effort can sometimes be forced to yield a coherent story.[140] What is not possible is to extend the method of the present study to such social classes. The aristocracy thus takes in the following study such a central place that it sometimes may seem that aristocracy was an essential characteristic of a social group rather than a relation of the rich and powerful to those they ruled. At the present time these other urban classes—not to speak of the rural producers—cannot be identified, comprehended, and described with anything like the precision that the aristocracy can. They remain, nonetheless, part of the definition of the aristocracy as an urban *ruling* class.

3. The plan of this work is complex. It begins with the political category of the Strasbourg privy councillors, whose 105 biographies form the initial group of data for the study. From this group, accepted on the basis of earlier institutional studies as a political elite, the study moves to the aristocracy itself as a complex social class composed of two fractions, one rentier and the other mercantile, and divided into two estates, one patrician the other of the guilds. An analysis of the elements of their integration into a single class is followed by an examination of the paths and means of aristocratic political control. This completes the first, structural part of the study, which moves from the political elite to the ruling class and back to political life.

The second, historical part of this study attempts to employ the structural analyses of the first part to reinterpret the policies and political behavior of the regime of Strasbourg, not during the entire Reformation era, but only in what—at least from the local point of view—may fairly be regarded as the two chief political crises of the age (1524–1525 and 1547–1548). Thereby is employed the unproven assumption that regimes are most likely to reveal their true social character at times of greatest stress. The bridge material (Chapter VII) between the analyses of the two crises is directed at the chief line of argument and is not meant to fill a narrative gap.

4. Several assumptions which guided the preparation of this study deserve to be stated, although no apology for them is intended. The

---

[140] A notable example is the article cited in n. 138 above.

first and most important is that historical societies were organized
into social formations which we call classes and the internal structures
of which depended *ultimately* upon the ways in which those societies
got their livings. These formations differ in structure and complex-
ity from society to society and age to age, although they have in
common the extraction of a portion of the social product from those
who produce it by those who rule. The means of extraction vary
tremendously, and so do the accompanying justifications. Taken as
a whole, Europe at the end of the Middle Ages was characterized
by social formations whose enduring characteristics were what may
be called "late feudal," although there already appear tell-tale signs
of more modern social formations.

A second assumption has to do with the role of political power
in the preservation of social structures. The aristocrats of aristocratic
societies are by definition those who rule, and the first law of aristocratic politics is collective survival, just as its mortal sin is the disruption of the state for factional, familial, or individual gain. The
much greater importance of political control to the economic domination in pre-modern societies than in the early phases of industrial
capitalism finds theoretical expression in the absence of the distinction between state and society in contemporary political theory.

Thirdly, there is the principle of social fractions,[141] those fragments
of a class which, at some time in their development, have the potential either for incorporation into the class from which they sprang
or for breaking away to form the nucleus of a new class formation.
Which alternative realizes itself depends to a great extent on specific
conditions. Hence the possibility for integration of commercial aristocracies into a larger feudal structure, despite their exhibition of
apparently anti-feudal characteristics.

A fourth assumption has to do with the significance of culture, both
high and low. The very minor role played by cultural phenomena—
chiefly theology—in this study does *not* flow from an assumption of

---

[141] The term "fraction" is here used in the sense defined by Nicos Poulantzas,
Pouvoir politique et classes sociales de l'état capitaliste (Paris, 1968), p. 88: "On désigne
par *fractions autonomes* de classe celles qui constituent le substrat de forces sociales
éventuelles, par *fractions* des ensembles sociaux susceptibles de devenir des fractions
autonomes. . . ." This work now exists in a German version, *Politische Macht und
gesellschaftliche Klassen*, trans. Günter Seib and Erika Hültenschmidt (Frankfurt a. M.,
1974). For the historical use of the term, see Czok, "Die Bürgerkämpfe in Süd-
und Westdeutschland," pp. 47–48.

the *total* dependence of culture on non-cultural phenomena, either of the substructure-superstructure or of some other type. Although popular culture is a difficult enough subject in itself, whose importance is not to be gauged by the relative paucity of literature devoted to it,[142] its relation to high culture is even more problematical. Certainly there are times when the influence of popular ideas upon high culture can be direct and measurable, as, for example, in the connection between the pronounced reevaluation of the social image of the German peasant around 1500 and the quasi-egalitarian doctrines of the early Reformation years.[143] The high culture, on the other hand, is vitally important to a grasp of the self-understanding of an entire society, together with the more specific self-consciousness of its ruling class. This covers a great deal more than direct cultural expressions of domination, although these are basically important to it. More useful here is perhaps the broader concept of cultural "hegemony," which allows a certain play to cultural traditions themselves as well as the possibility of a reciprocal force of the culture's leading ideas upon social relations and political events. The leading ideas of Reformation Germany were chiefly theological ideas, without a firm grasp of which the culture and self-consciousness of the age simply cannot be understood. That they play a relatively minor role in this study is due rather to the specific aims of the work than to an ignorance of their significance.

5. This study has a number of purposes, not all of them of the same type. There is, first of all, the desire to contribute to the illumination of the history of one of the Holy Roman Empire's most interesting cities and one of the chief centers of the German Reformation. Secondly, there is the purpose of contributing to the setting of urban history back firmly in its territorial, late feudal context. A third purpose of this work is to add to the growing basis for a general historical sociology of the late feudal era. Fourthly, the following study is designed to demonstrate the utility of the study of social groups to an explanation of the political aspects of the German

---

[142] See the wise words of Natalie Z. Davis, "Some Tasks and Themes in the Study of Popular Religion," in *The Pursuit of Holiness*, pp. 313–314.

[143] Helmut Brackert, *Bauernkrieg und Literatur* (Frankfurt/M., 1975), pp. 25–35. See the excellent analysis of the peasantry's political self-image by Horst Buszello, *Der deutsche Bauernkrieg von 1525 als politische Bewegung mit besonderer Berücksicktigung der anonymen Flugschrift An die Versamlung Gemayner Pawerschafft*, Studien zur europäischen Geschichte, 8 (Berlin, 1969), pp. 16–91.

Reformation. Finally, this book is meant as a contribution to the collective effort to liberate the field of Reformation studies from the dead hand of romantic idealism.

Nothing in this introduction is intended as a disclaimer of the internal logic of the following chapters and the conclusions to which they lead. If this book convinces some of its readers that historical investigations at the microsocial level can stand in the service of dispelling the mystery surrounding historical change, then it will have achieved its chief aim. It is a window on the workings of an extremely complex, whole society, whose historical wholeness is the analogue and determinant of the holistic understanding we seek. For the whole is ever the truth.

STRASBOURG AND THE REFORMATION

CHAPTER TWO

JACOB STURM OF STRASBOURG AND THE LUTHERANS AT THE DIET OF AUGSBURG, 1530

All through the second half of the year 1529, John the Constant, the Elector of Saxony, played a double game with the Evangelical towns of southwestern Germany. In April of that year at the Diet of Speyer, John had led a united Evangelical party in a protest against the recess of the Diet and in an agreement to form a military alliance of all the Evangelical governments in the empire. A few weeks later, John began to regret that he had allied with cities suspected of Zwinglian heresies, a step which could only aggravate his relations with the emperor. John and his advisers searched for the proper instrument by which to win favor from Charles V by abandoning their Zwinglian associates. That instrument was the Schwabach Articles, an uncompromisingly Lutheran statement of doctrine which flatly excluded the disputed Zwinglian interpretation of the sacrament of the Eucharist. John kept the southwestern towns dangling in expectation until the meeting at Schmalkalden in December, 1529. There he informed Jacob Sturm of Strasbourg and Bernhard Besserer of Ulm that his conscience forbade him to ally with the southerners so long as they supported the errors of Zwingli. Sturm and Besserer, who now began to understand John's duplicity, announced that their governments would not sign the Schwabach Articles. At the year's end, nothing remained of the solidarity the Evangelical estates had displayed at Speyer.[1]

I wish to thank the Director and Trustees of The Newberry Library and the Graduate Research Council of the University of Oregon for support in the preparation of this article. For their critical comments, I am indebted to my colleagues, Professors Gustave Alef and Val R. Lorwin of the University of Oregon, and Professor James M. Kittelson of The Ohio State University.

[1] On the origins of the Schmalkaldic League, see the pioneering study of Hans Baron, "Religion and Politics in the German Imperial Cities during the Reformation," *The English Historical Review*, 52 (1937): pp. 405–427, 614–633; and Ekkehart Fabian, *Die Entstehung des Schmalkaldischen Bundes und seiner Verfassung 1524/29–1531/35. Brück, Philipp von Hessen und Jakob Sturm*, 2nd ed. *SKRG*, no. 1 (Tübingen, 1962). The Saxon reaction which began in early June, 1529, is analyzed in detail by Wolfgang Steglich, "Die Stellung der evangelischen Reichsstände und Reichsstädte zu Karl V. zwischen

A year to the month later, Strasbourg and Ulm entered into a military alliance with John and his Lutheran clients and friends. That federation, known as the Schmalkaldic League, lasted seventeen years until 1547, when it was destroyed by military disaster. Certain changes in the political situation within the empire during 1530 made the league possible, just as political and military defeat made it collapse in 1547. This study examines, from the point of view of Strasbourg's leading diplomat, Jacob Sturm, the events which transformed the cause of a pan-Evangelical alliance from the hopeless situation of the early months of 1530 into the military union achieved by the end of the year. In particular this article will analyze the diplomatic strategy of Jacob Sturm toward the Elector of Saxony and his allies during the Diet of Augsburg (1530) in the light of Strasbourg's quest for security and of Charles V's failure to control the German schism.

I

Jacob Sturm was a member of Strasbourg's noble patriciate, a man of property.[2] When he converted to the Evangelical religion in 1523, Sturm abandoned a clerical career and entered the senate of his native city. Well born, well educated and well spoken, he moved rapidly upward through the various levels of Strasbourg's government. In 1526 Sturm became a life member of the powerful commission of the Thirteen for War. There he helped shape his city's foreign policy until his death in 1553. He also served as Strasbourg's chief diplomat for more than 25 years. His epitaph records that he served Strasbourg on 91 diplomatic missions.

Protestation und Konfession 1529/30. Ein Beitrag zur Vorgeschichte des Augsburgischen Glaubensbekenntnisses," *ARG*, 62 (1971): pp. 170–172, 181–191. Steglich's account is based on his editorship of the *Deutsche Reichstagsakten, jüngere Reihe*, 8 (2 parts; Göttingen, 1970, 1971), which covers the period between the Diet of Speier (1529) and that of Augsburg (1530). The doctrinal quarrel which provided the grounds for the clerical support of the Saxon abandonment of the southwestern towns is recounted in great detail by Walter Köhler, *Zwingli und Luther, ihr Streit um das Abendmahl nach seinen politischen und religiösen Beziehungen*. 2 vols. QFRG, 6, 7, (Leipzig, 1924; Gütersloh, 1953).

[2] The best biographical sketches are by Hermann Baumgarten, *Jakob Sturm* (Strassburg, 1876); and Otto Winckelmann, "Jakob Sturm," *Allgemeine Deutsche Biographie*, 37 (1894): pp. 5–20. A partial biography (to 1532) is the present writer's unpublished dissertation "Jacob Sturm of Strasbourg (1489–1553) and the Political Security of German Protestantism, 1526–1532" (University of Chicago, 1968).

Sturm's first diplomatic success came at the Diet of Speyer (1526), where he championed the traditional foreign policy of the Free Cities of south Germany: solidarity of the cities against the princes and firm loyalty to the emperor.[3] Sturm succeeded in holding the towns together and rejected overtures tendered by the Evangelical princes for a new, religiously-motivated, political alignment. But the urban front even then was beginning to crack under pressures produced by the religious conflict. By 1528 Sturm became doubtful about pursuing the traditional urban foreign policy. He became the first south German urban politician to argue for a new diplomacy.[4] Salvation, he believed, lay with an Evangelical alliance against the Catholic emperor and princes. For the next eighteen years (until the Schmalkaldic War of 1546/47), Sturm never wavered in his devotion to the cause of an Evangelical military and political alliance.

Since the end of the Diet of Speyer in May, 1529, Sturm had cooperated with the Landgrave of Hesse in an effort to remove the only apparent barrier to an Evangelical military alliance by bringing the Lutheran and Zwinglian preachers together. Not until the meeting at Schmalkalden in December did Sturm learn the full extent of the double game being played by John the Constant who apparently was willing to build a bridge to the emperor by abandoning his commitments to the southern towns. Sturm's grim report to the Thirteen after the Schmalkalden fiasco summarized the alternatives open to the isolated city: "In short, we have three alternatives: to await God's pleasure; to placate the Emperor; or to prepare for the Emperor's wrath."[5] The rulers of Strasbourg, who had defied Charles when they abolished the Mass less than a year ago, placed no faith in embassies to conciliate him. Three days after Sturm's report the Thirteen approved a fifteen-year military alliance with Zurich, Basel and Bern.

Strasbourg's alliance with the three principal towns of German-speaking Switzerland afforded the city some immediate military

---

[3] See Hans Baron, "Religion and Politics in the German Imperial Cities," pp. 406–411.

[4] The crucial text is in *PCSS*, 1, p. 296, no. 525 (undated, but before June 11, 1528).

[5] "Annales de Sébastien Brant," ed. Léon Dacheux, in *BSCMHA*, 19 (1901): p. 179, no. 4828. Sturm's statement of the alternatives is based on a letter to him from Landgrave Philip of Hesse, Immenhausen, October 30, 1529 (*PCSS*, 1, pp. 408–409, no. 675). On the Smalkalden meeting and on the policies of John the Constant which led him to force the doctrinal issue, see W. Steglich, "Die Stellung der evangelischen Reichsstände und Reichsstädte zu Karl V....," pp. 181–185.

protection against "the Emperor's wrath."[6] It could not bring lasting political security because the Swiss allies had no political value to Strasbourg. The Swiss towns refused to attend imperial Diets, and they rejected the jurisdictional claims of the Imperial High Court (*Reichskammergericht*). Yet these two institutions were the main arenas of imperial politics. The military threat to Strasbourg was not acute enough to drive the city out of the imperial political system and into the Swiss Confederation—the step taken by Basel in 1501. What Strasbourg required was the protection of the major Evangelical princes *within* the imperial system. Such was Sturm's conviction, which he championed in Strasbourg in spite of the centuries-long tradition of political animosity between the Free Cities and the princes.

II

In February 1530, Strasbourg learned that Charles V intended to settle the German schism at an Imperial Diet at Augsburg. Jacob Sturm proposed to his colleagues that, among other strategems, they try again to conciliate John the Constant and his friends, probably because he recognized the possibility that the effort to bring John and the emperor together might fail. Strasbourg had to be ready to exploit such a failure. Sturm's colleagues approved his proposal, though some of them distrusted all princes and favored the Swiss. They named Sturm and Mathis Pfarrer envoys to the Diet and instructed them to ask John the Constant "to ignore the dispute about the Eucharist, since we agree on the chief matter of our salvation."[7] Sturm began to prepare both the defense of Strasbourg's reform and a rapprochement with the Lutherans.

---

[6] The negotiations leading up to this alliance are described in great detail by René Hauswirth, *Landgraf Philipp von Hessen und Zwingli. Voraussetzungen und Geschichte der politischen Beziehungen zwischen Hessen, Strassburg, Konstanz, Ulrich von Württemberg und reformierten Eidgenossen 1526–1531 (SKRG*, no. 35; Tübingen, 1968), pp. 139–160.

[7] *PCSS*, 1, p. 439, no. 718: "und harin den zwispalt des sacraments nit ansehen wolten, so man im houbtstugk unserer seligkeit eins wer. . . ." Compare Sturm's view in his report to the Senate after the Marburg Colloquy ("Annales de S. Brant," in *BSCMHA*, 19, p. 175, no. 4812) and his estimate (in 1532) of what had been achieved at Marburg (*PCSS*, 2, p. 113): "Es hett aber doctor Luther sich zu Marpurg uf dem gesprech so vil vernämen lossen: wo man hette bekennen wollen die ware gegenwurtigkeit des libs und bluts Christi im nachtmol, so wolt er dises punctens halb inen bruderschaft zu beweisen nit abschlagen."

The loss of Jacob Sturm's private papers makes it impossible to form a precise view of his personal opinions on religion. Every extant statement on the subject was made in connection with his government's policies on the religious question. Sturm's critique of the Schwabach Articles reveals his commitment to a highly spiritualized interpretation of the sacraments—the chief bone of intra-Evangelical contention—similar to that of Zwingli.[8] Sturm did not deny that his city's preachers taught Zwingli's doctrine of the exclusively spiritual presence of Christ in the Eucharist as opposed to Luther's doctrine of his corporeal presence. At the same time he defended Zwingli against the charge of separating the humanity of Christ from his divinity.[9] Some months later, in the spring of 1530, Sturm composed an outline of an apology of the reforms introduced at Strasbourg, in which he suggested that the city's official view closely resembled the teaching of Caspar Schwenckfeld.[10] On the whole Sturm's remarks on the content of doctrine confirm the impression that he recognized that official religion in Strasbourg departed on some few points from the teachings of Luther.

Sturm disagreed strongly and consistently with the Lutherans on the issue of the need for complete doctrinal uniformity and the utility of formal, doctrinal statements (confessions). He recognized that attempts to define ideological differences drove the parties farther and farther apart from one another, thus obscuring their common

---

[8] Sturm's remarks to Chancellor Georg Vogler of Brandenburg-Ansbach are printed by Hans von Schubert, ed., *Bekenntnisbildung und Religionspolitik (1524–1534). Untersuchungen und Texte* (Gotha, 1910), pp. 169–182. Concerning the sacrament of baptism, Sturm said (p. 178): "Den tauff halten sie auch nit fur ein schlecht wasser, sonder fur ein widergeburt durch das wort und heiligen gaist, aber allain credentibus per fidem, in den sei er ein krefftig lebendig ding, aber bei den andern nit, doch so soll man die kinder teuffen, die weil wir nit wissen, ob sie von got zur selikait eligirt sei.—Dapei soll man aber vleissig furkommen, das die selikait allain der wurckung des heiligen gaists und dem eusserlichen werken." Concerning the sacraments in general (p. 177): "Item das auch der glaub und gaist vor dem sacrament gegeben werd und sein musz und nit erst in empfohung der sacrament, dann solliches allain testimonium fidei und bestettigung als arrobo und sigillum sei."

[9] *Ibid.*, p. 171: "Heten sie wolgemerkt, warauff der artickel gesetzt wurd, alls ob Jmaandt ainich zertailung gottes und cristi machen wolt, wie Zwinglein beschuldigt, aber nit gestendig, sei auch ire maynung nit, dann sie glaubten, das cristus gottes son, warer got und mensch, gelitten habe und gestorben sei, doch nach der menschait."

[10] Johannes Ficker, ed., "Jakob Sturms Entwurf zur Strassburger reformatorischen Verantwortung für den Augsburger Reichstag 1530," *Elsass-Lothringisches Jahrbuch*, 19 (1941): p. 152: "und wie man nitt leer, das die christen, so in warem glauben das sacrament nyssen, schlecht brott und wine empfohen, sonder den woren lib und blut Christi, der meynong, *sicut* Schwenckfelder *non ingenue describit*."

interests. An early (1525) opinion on the Mass pleaded for concentration on the common Christian faith rather than differences between the forms of the Mass and those of Evangelical services: "Both parties are Christians. May God have mercy!"[11] In the interest of civic unity, any practice or belief should be tolerated which could be defended from the Bible.[12] Sturm took precisely the same stand in the dispute with the Lutherans when he insisted that all articles of belief should be formulated in biblical language, not in the words of warring theologians.[13] Eventually Sturm came to view the eucharistic dispute as a plague, the theologians' continuation of which poisoned all of his efforts to solidify the Evangelical political front. In later years he went so far as to abstain from receiving Communion out of bitterness over this clerical quarrel.[14] Sturm's view of the eucharistic quarrel as a private dispute, so convenient for his promotion of an Evangelical league, was essentially shared by his colleagues in the Thirteen who stretched the truth when they declared:

> We have not forced anyone in our city to believe Luther, Zwingli, or the Pope, nor have we established an official position. We allow each person his own free faith; and our preachers, so far as we know, preach the clear and simple Word of God. . . . The two opinions on the Sacrament are nothing more than a verbal dispute [*wortzank*], . . . from which each draws his own understanding and meaning.[15]

---

[11] "Rathslag gottgefelliges diensts von Jac. Sturm 1525," in Strasbourg, Archives du Chapître de St.-Thomas, no. 166, fol. 129r: "sind also zu beyden theylen christen, des gott erbarm."

[12] *Ibid.*, fol. 129r: "sind noch vill ding zu tulden, und vbersehen noch zur zeit, biss gott der herr ein bessern verstand verlihen würt, domit man nit durch geschwinde fürgenommene enderung nur den handel hinder dan fürdere, . . ." *Ibid.*, fol. 128v: "Dweyl auch alle newerung ein vnglichen verstand und der halben zweyungen und verletzung der lieb bringen, mocht man in obgenanten gesang . . . so vil mit der geschrifft sich verglichen vnd verteidiget werden mocht bliben lassen."

[13] Concerning the first of the Schwabach Articles, Sturm remarked: "person und trivoltikait sind nit in der schrift und werden zu vil tailpar gesetzt. Jedoch dieweil im prauch dopey pleiben." He made a similar comment on the Introduction to the Articles: "Nit zu articulirn. Schrifftlich warheit in artickeln des glaubens zu setzen." H. von Schubert, *Bekenntnisbildung und Religionspolitik*, pp. 169–170.

[14] This fact is recorded by John Sturm, who knew Jacob Sturm well during the latter's later years. See *Quarti Antipappi tres partes priores* (Neustadt an der Hardt, 1580), pp. 166–167.

[15] The Thirteen of Strasbourg to Jacob Sturm and Mathis Pfarrer, August 17, 1530 (*PCSS*, 1, pp. 486–487, no. 782). Precisely the same view was expressed by Memmingen's envoy to the Diet of Augsburg, Hans Ehinger: "vnd jst min rautt, das wier weder lutrisch noch zwinglisch seyen, sonder Christus bevelh nach auswaisung biblischer schrifft lert man by vns. . . ." Friedrich Dobel, ed., *Memmingen in Reformationszeitalter*. 5 vols. (Augsburg, 1877–1878), 4, pp. 41–42, dated July 14, 1530.

Sturm himself put it more briefly: concerning the Eucharist the government "lets each man form his own belief, so long as he otherwise believes in God through Christ and exhibits that belief in his love for his fellow man."[16]

In their preparations for the defense of the reforms at Strasbourg, Sturm and his colleagues employed the town's chief preachers as expert advisers. Although he had studied theology in his youth, Sturm did not consider himself a theologian.[17] He normally opposed independent attempts by the clergy to intervene in political affairs, but he had not objection to using their abilities to support government policy.[18] Both Martin Bucer and Wolfgang Capito had come under Zwingli's influence during the mid-1520s, and Bucer had supported Zwingli at the Marburg Colloquy (October, 1529). Since that time Bucer had increasingly taken on the role of mediator between the two factions of Evangelical theologians, and there is no reason to doubt that by the end of 1529 Bucer was wholly committed to the policy of conciliating the Lutherans.[19] To him fell the task of composing a

---

[16] "das man hierin niemants sin verstand neme, sonder hierin ein jeden loss bliben, so verr er sonst in gott per Christum glaube und durch solchen glauben dye liebe des nachsten bezeuge." J. Ficker, ed., "Jacob Sturm's Entwurf," p. 152.

[17] Sturm studied in the theological faculty of the University of Freiburg im Breisgau between 1504 and 1509 (see T. A. Brady, Jr., "Jacob Sturm of Strasbourg," pp. 28–32). Later in his life, when he was appointed to the committee on the Interim at the Diet of Augsburg in 1548, Sturm agreed to serve, with the following reservation (*PCSS*, 4, p. 857, no. 729): "solt es aber in puncten die religion belangen gehandelt werden, dozu bekenne ich mich nit gnugsam, sondern erfordert ein ander und stattlicher man; . . . ." Whenever Sturm took part in negotiations concerning doctrine, as at Marburg in 1529, Haguenau in 1539, Worms in 1540 and Regensburg in 1541, he was always accompanied by one or more of the Strasbourg preachers.

[18] Sturm's relations with Capito were normally good (see Wolfgang Capito, *In Habakuk prophetam V. Fabritij Capitonis enarrationes* [Strasbourg, 1526], pp. A.ii.a–A.iii.b), and his friendship with Bucer is well known. One of the few real outbursts of anger in Sturm's letters occurs in his report on the trouble Capito had caused by sending letters and a clandestinely printed book to friends in Switzerland. Sturm wrote to Peter Butz from Speier, July 15, 1526 (*PCSS*, 1, pp. 263–264, no. 464): "deshalben die prädicanten nit solten hoch uf new mer acht haben, wie es do oder dort zugieng, sich auch nit uf grosz oder vest stett verlossen; dans solichs bringt argwon, als ob si sich mer uf ein fleischlichen arme dan uf Christum allein verliessen."

[19] Bucer's policy that cooperation should rest on common faith rather than precise doctrinal formulation dates at least from the weeks after the Marburg Colloquy (late October–early November, 1529), when he composed his commentary on the Schwabach Articles (see M. Bucer, *Deutsche Schriften*, III: *Confessio Tetrapolitana und die Schriften des Jahres 1531*, ed. Robert Stupperich [Gütersloh-Paris, 1969], p. 443, ll. 1–12). The influence of Zwingli on the Strasbourg preachers during the second half of the 1520s is a commonplace of the literature on the eucharistic dispute. See W. Köhler, *Zwingli und Luther*, 1, esp. pp. 730–735, 747–752, 816–817, 829–830;

statement on the Eucharist to be submitted by Sturm to the Lutheran princes at Augsburg. Bucer's document supported his government's position that full doctrinal concord was not necessary to the formation of a common political front:

> It is enough for Christians that they be assured by the Holy Spirit and free from all doubt that God, through Our Lord Jesus Christ, wishes eternally to be a Father to them.... This faith produces children and heirs of God; and, therefore, it must be maintained. Beyond that, even those who already are holy and pious may be burdened with many grievous errors.... No one, no matter how holy he may be, lives here on earth without error, ... and one often errs just when he is most certain of something.[20]

The essential points, he wrote, are faith and love: "where these exist, one should not doubt that they exhibit the spirit of God." Therefore, "one should regard as brothers and fellows in Christ all those among whom such true faith and love are found, in spite of errors and faults that may have crept in."[21] Applying this principle to the quarrel over the Eucharist, Bucer alleged that the two camps disagreed over a single, relatively minor point and that "no one is closer to the Lutherans than are the Zwinglians."[22] Bucer was not yet prepared to argue, as he later did, that the Strasbourg position was wholly in agreement with the Lutheran one.

---

and Ernst Bizer, *Studien zur Geschichte des Abendmahlsstreits im 16. Jahrhundert* ("Beiträge zur Förderung christlicher Theologie," Series 2, Vol. 46; Gütersloh, 1940), pp. 21–24. See also Jacques V. Pollet, O.P., *Martin Bucer. Études sur la correspondance.* 2 vols. (Paris, 1958, 1962), 1, pp. 9–10. Recent literature on Bucer, however, denies that Zwingli had a fundamental influence on his views. See the survey by Friedhelm Krüger, *Bucer und Erasmus. Eine Untersuchung zum Einfluss des Erasmus auf die Theologie Martin Bucers (bis zum Evangelien-Kommentar von 1530)* ("Veröffentlichungen des Instituts für europäische Geschichte Mainz," Vol. 57; Wiesbaden, 1970), pp. 3–37, and Krüger's own conclusions on pp. 225–227. This argument over Bucer's opinions does not affect the present study. All that is being maintained here is that Bucer was *by policy* a Zwinglian at Marburg and *by policy* a mediator thereafter. The relationship between his policy and his opinions is a subject for students of his biography and his theology. As for Capito, there exists no reliable, published study of his ideas and career.

[20] Bucer, *Deutsche Schriften*, 3, p. 325, ll. 1–11. The preparation of this and the other documents appended to the Instruction for the Diet probably took place during April and early May. Sturm and Mathis Pfarrer were chosen as envoys to the Diet on April 11, 1530 ("Annales de S. Brant," in *BSCMHA*, 19, 182, no. 4862). Bucer mentions the preparations in a letter of April 18 (see *Deutsche Schriften*, 3, p. 15).

[21] *Ibid.*, p. 327, ll. 7–12.

[22] *Ibid.*, p. 337, ll. 19–20: "So ist den Lutherischen noch niemand neher dann die Zwinglischen."

The central document prepared for the Diet of Augsburg was an apology for the course of the reforms at Strasbourg. Sturm drafted an agenda for this "*entschuldigung*," which served as a guide to Wolfgang Capito who composed a lengthy apology.[23] Sturm made extensive revisions in Capito's draft, excised the more polemical sections and probably eliminated the concluding discussion of doctrine. The finished version conformed to Sturm's original idea of a *defensio* rather than a *confessio*.[24] It was simply a detailed apology for the innovations in religion and ecclesiastical practice and was therefore not a direct ancestor of the confession of faith later submitted at Augsburg. Sturm's corrections and substitutions permit no doubt that he exercised full editorial control over this document. The defense of the reform was a political matter in which the clergy were not permitted to behave independently. Finally, although Capito also drafted an opinion which insisted that a council of the church alone could settle the dispute over religion, Sturm was prepared for the possibility that the entire issue would be resolved one way or another at Augsburg. In his revision of Capito's apology he added a concluding plea to Charles:

> We most humbly and firmly hope that God Almighty will . . . grant Your Majesty this grace, that, through sufficient consultation of all parties, such Christian and God-pleasing means will be found through which . . . true and lasting peace will be granted to all of Christendom, the Holy Empire and the German Nation, and through which many deaths and much corruption . . . will be avoided. And we hope that all parties will be brought to serve God Almighty in peace and unity.[25]

---

[23] Capito's "Ratschlag D" is printed in two successive redactions in *ibid.*, pp. 342–392. A comparison of the order of topics shows a dependence both on his "Copey eins vssschribens" (see *ibid.*, pp. 15–17) and on Sturm's scheme for an *Entschuldigung* of the reforms at Strasbourg (see J. Ficker, ed., "Jakob Sturms Entwurf," pp. 149–152).

[24] The later redaction of the text ("Fassung B") shows massive alterations by Sturm (see esp. *Deutsche Schriften*, 3, pp. 369, 371, 376, 377, 385, 390–391). So far as I can see, Moeller is correct in judging (*ibid.*, p. 190 n. 13) that Sturm's changes betray "immer wieder seine Bemühung um die Milderung übergrosser Schärfen." Compare Sturm's original schema (J. Ficker, ed., "Jakob Sturms Entwurf," p. 152, ll. 58–66): "Es ist auch hoch zu bedencken, domytt man nitt ursach zu gegenschrifften gebe, das man m. hern von Strossburg, der stifftspersonen oder andere nitt zu hoch anziche, sonder so vill der handel erliden mag, ir verschone und ine ir ding nitt zu ubel usslege, ... Ut sit excusatio, non accusatio." A further change between the two *Fassungen* is that the later one lacks the doctrinal section contained in "Fassung A" (Bucer, *Deutsche Schriften*, 3, p. 356, ll. 6–361, l. 25). This change probably reflects Sturm's original conception of an apology for innovations rather than a statement of belief.

[25] *Ibid.*, p. 390, ll. 23–391, l. 8.

Armed with this collection of memoranda, carefully devised to meet a variety of situations, Sturm left Strasbourg for Augsburg on May 22, 1530.

III

Charles V arrived in Germany in early summer, 1530, fresh from his reconciliation with and coronation by Pope Clement VII. When he came to Augsburg, Charles "still refused to despair of the Protestants' return to the Church, for the simple reason that he did not fully realize the extent of the dogmatic cleavage."[26] He hoped to persuade the Evangelical estates either to submit the dispute for his own decision or to restore the old ways until the meeting of a General Council. Charles' hopes were not altogether foolish. John of Saxony, too, wanted peace. He wanted religious peace with the Catholics; and he wanted good relations with Charles, not the least because he needed Charles' confirmation of his succession to the Electorate of Saxony to protect his family against the claims of its rivals, the Dukes of Saxony.[27]

---

[26] Hubert Jedin, *A History of the Council of Trent*, tr. Ernest Graf, O.S.B., Vol. 1 (London-Edinburgh-New York, 1957), p. 250. See, in general, *ibid.*, pp. 245–252; Karl Brandi, *Kaiser Karl V. Werden und Schicksal einer Persönlichkeit und eines Weltreiches* (6th ed.; München, 1961), 1, pp. 252–254. A definitive history of the Diet of Augsburg must wait until Vol. 9 of the *Deutsche Reichstagsakten, jüngere Reihe*, appears. The following studies are worth consulting on the diet as a whole: Hans von Schubert, *Der Reichstag von Augsburg im Zusammenhang der Reformationsgeschichte* (*SVRG*, no. 150; Leipzig, 1930); and Johannes von Walter, "Der Reichstag von Augsburg 1530," *Luther-Jahrbuch*, 12 (1930): pp. 1–90. On the present state of the published sources, see H. Jedin, *History*, 1, p. 250 n. 3. to Jedin's list must now be added Vol. 8 of the *Deutsche Reichstagsakten, jüngere Reihe* (Göttingen, 1970, 1971), which stops just before the opening of the Diet.

[27] No other leading Evangelical prince has been so little studied as has John the Constant (d. 1532). For the period before the Diet of Augsburg, much light is shed on John's policies by W. Steglich, "Die Stellung der evangelischen Reichsstände und Reichsstädte zu Karl V....," *ARG*, 62 (1971): pp. 161–191. There is some material on John's foreign policy in Georg Mentz's biography of his son and successor, *Johann Friedrich der Grossmütige 1503–1554* (3 vols.; "Beiträge zur neueren Geschichte Thüringens," 1; Jena, 1903, 1908), 1, chapters 2–3. See also the sketch of the foreign policy goals of the Saxon Electors of this period by E. Fabian, *Die Entstehung des Schmalkaldischen Bundes* (2nd ed.), pp. 303–307. Karl Brandi (*Kaiser Karl V.*, 1, p. 251) correctly sums up John's policy before the Diet of Augsburg: "Sie wollte Selbstbehauptung im Frieden mit der Reichsregierung."

When John arrived in Augsburg, accompanied by a crowd of his own theologians, the Lutheran party in the Diet comprised John and seven other princes, a handful of counts and about ten Free Cities. The remaining Evangelical estates were a small group of southern Free Cities that had become, in Lutheran eyes, tainted with Zwinglianism: Strasbourg, Constance, a few Upper Swabian towns and, perhaps, Ulm.[28] Ranged against these two blocs was a large Roman Catholic majority which controlled all but the Cities' house of the Diet. This alignment threatened ill for the southern towns who could expect to be the chief sacrifice on the altar of Catholic-Lutheran concord. If the two larger parties came to terms, then the southern towns could expect that the princes would resume their campaign of legislation to curb the commercial freedoms and political power of the urban ruling classes.[29] For Strasbourg the success of Charles' plans implied unremitting persecution of Zwinglianism; for the cities as a whole a new solidarity among the princes implied a new wave of anti-urban legislation. Reconciliation with the Lutheran party, whatever the price, was the only rational course open to Jacob Sturm at Augsburg.

First impressions in Augsburg were not encouraging. Sturm found a trilateral war of words issuing from the pulpits of the city: Catholics preached against Lutherans, Lutherans thundered against Zwinglians, Zwinglians ridiculed both rivals. "Such divisive preaching," Sturm lamented, "will aid the Christian cause very little, but it will certainly encourage the [Catholic] enemy."[30] Of all the Lutheran princes only Landgrave Philip of Hesse restrained his preachers. Nominally a

[28] The spread of Zwinglianism into the Swabian towns needs to be studied. The best general account is still the old work by Karl Theodor Keim, *Schwäbische Reformationsgeschichte bis zum Augsburger Reichstag* (Tübingen, 1855). On Ulm, see Eberhard Naujoks, *Obrigkeitsgedanke, Zunftverfassung und Reformation. Studien zur Verfassungsgeschichte von Ulm, Esslingen und Schwäb. Gmünd* ("Veröffentlichungen der Kommission für geschichtliche Landeskunde in Baden-Württemberg," Series B, Vol. 3; Stuttgart, 1958), pp. 71–81.
[29] See Fritz Blaich, *Die Reichsmonopolgesetzgebung im Zeitalter Karls V. Ihre ordnungspolitische Problematik* ("Schriften zum Vergleich von Wirtschaftsordnungen," no. 8; Stuttgart, 1967), pp. 37–72. On the political aspects of this struggle, see H. Baron, "Religion and Politics in the German Imperial Cities during the Reformation," pp. 407–409.
[30] Jacob Sturm and Mathis Pfarrer to the Senate of Strasbourg, Augsburg, June 2, 1530 (*PCSS*, 1, p. 447, no. 728). All of the official reports from Augsburg are in Sturm's hand; for the sake of brevity, they will be cited under his name alone. All were written from Augsburg.

Lutheran, Philip was indifferent to doctrine and was friendly to the
southern towns because he wanted their aid for his political schemes
in South Germany.[31] The Lutheran clergy, he told Sturm, behave

> as though they would much rather see our preachers, and those who
> believe in them, suppressed than that those on the side of the Pope
> and the Roman Church should be defeated. Therefore, the whole mat-
> ter will be referred to the Emperor, and the outcome will surely be
> intolerable.[32]

Philip was correct. Sturm soon learned that Charles intended to deal
with the religious question. The submission of the entire question
to the emperor would not have been especially dangerous if the
Evangelicals had been as united in 1530 as they had been at Speyer
in 1529. But they were not. On the contrary, the anti-Zwinglianism of
the Lutheran clergy suggested that the Zwinglian towns would be
totally isolated in the Diet.

   In spite of his slight chance for success, Sturm tried to approach
the Lutherans directly. He gave Bucer's memorandum on the Eucharist
to the Lutheran princes, who passed it to their own preachers, Philip
Melanchthon and John Brenz. Their expert advice was that the
princes should not ally with the southern towns since Bucer's statement was full of doctrinal errors. John of Saxony heeded his preachers and rebuffed the efforts of the Landgrave to win Sturm a hearing.
By mid-June it was clear that the direct approach would achieve
nothing: the Lutheran preachers were preparing a formal statement
of doctrine for the emperor, and John of Saxony refused to allow
Sturm to sign it.[33]

---

[31] Philip's policies and activities at Augsburg can be followed in Herbert Grundmann, "Landgraf Philipp von Hessen auf dem Augsburger Reichstag," in *Aus Reich-
stagen des 15. und 16. Jahrhunderts. Festgabe dargebracht der Historischen Kommission zur Feier
ihres hundertjährigens Bestehens* ("Schriftenreihe der Historischen Kommission bei der Bayerischen Akademie der Wissenschaften," no. 5; Göttingen, 1958), pp. 341–423. His ineffec-
tiveness at Augsburg is to be explained by the fact that he was torn between his
desire for Charles' support in his disputes with neighboring princes and his desire
to restore Duke Ulrich in Württemberg. His relations with the southern Evangelical
towns and the Swiss Evangelicals, which aimed at the latter goal, are studied at
great length by R. Hauswirth, *Landgraf Philipp von Hessen und Zwingli*, pp. 100–229.
[32] Jacob Sturm to the Thirteen, June 7, 1530 (*PCSS*, 1, p. 450, no. 732).
[33] The failure of this approach can be followed in Sturm's reports of June 2,
1530 (*Ibid.*, p. 447, no. 728), June 16 (*Ibid.*, pp. 455–456, no. 741), June 21 (*Ibid.*,
pp. 458–459, no. 746). The responses of Melanchthon and Brenz are revealed in
a trio of letters that passed between them and the Landgrave on June 11 (*CR*, 2,
pp. 92–103, nos. 718–720). See B. Moeller, in Bucer, *Deutsche Schriften*, 3, pp. 231–322.

Meanwhile, Sturm apparently decided on a more circumspect approach. Less than a week after his arrival in Augsburg, he seems to have developed a two-pronged strategy: first, to bend Strasbourg's official position on doctrine as close as possible to the Lutheran one without incurring charges of duplicity; and secondly, to expose the Lutherans to a taste of genuine Swiss Zwinglianism, beside which Strasbourg's views would seem moderate. By these means Sturm probably hoped to overcome the breach between his own government and the powerful Lutheran princes. Sturm called for Strasbourg's theological experts, Martin Bucer and Wolfgang Capito, to compose a statement of doctrine for Strasbourg. During the first week of July the two preachers stayed discretely hidden in Sturm's quarters in Augsburg while they labored over a confession of faith.[34] This document was subsequently called the Tetrapolitan Confession (CT). When Sturm canvassed the other southern towns for co-signers, only the envoys of Lindau, Memmingen and Constance agreed to sign. Konrad Zwick of Constance, who suppressed a statement from his own preachers when he signed the CT, insisted on a shorter and less polemical version of the crucial article on the Eucharist.[35]

The CT was certainly written by Bucer and Capito, although it cannot now be determined which preacher drafted what parts of the final redaction. Sturm apparently limited himself to minor corrections of style in keeping with his consistent practice of leaving doctrinal

---

The closeness with which his government followed Sturm's relations with the Lutheran princess is suggested by a special collection that Peter Butz made of extracts from Sturm's reports on the subject (in Strasbourg, Archives Municipales, AA421, no. 22, fols. 44ʳ–47ᵛ).

[34] A critical edition by Bernd Moeller in Bucer, *Deutsche Schriften*, 3, pp. 13–185, who prints two German redactions of the text, plus Bucer's Latin version. Capito's long version of Article 18, on the Eucharist, is edited by J. V. Pollet, *Martin Bucer*, 1, pp. 45–54.

[35] Jacob Sturm to the Senate, June 25, 1530 (*PCSS*, 1 p. 461, no. 749); Bernd Moeller, *Johannes Zwick und die Reformation in Konstanz* (*QFRG*, XXVIII; Gütersloh, 1961), pp. 112–113. Sturm's canvass can be followed in the reports of Hans Ehinger to Memmingen (F. Dobel, ed., *Memmingen*, 4, pp. 32–33, 35–36, 37–38, 38–39, 40–41). The refusal of the Frankfurters to sign appears in Friedrich Wilhelm Schirrmacher, ed., *Briefe und Acten zu der Geschichte des Religionsgespräches zu Marburg 1529 und des Reichstages zu Augsburg 1530* (Gotha, 1876), pp. 407–408. Sturm and Pfarrer intended to submit the version that contained Capito's long version of Article 18 (see Bucer, *Deutsche Schriften*, 3, p. 134 note w): "Dissen begriff zuuberantworten waren her Jacob Sturm vnd her Matthiss pfarer bedacht, vff das wir nit möchten geachtet werden, als ob wir das liecht flühen, auch domit nichtige gegenrede dester heller abgewendt würden."

matters to professional theologians.[36] The CT was without lasting
historical significance except as an instrument of Strasbourg's and
Sturm's foreign policy during the years between the Diet of Augsburg
and the Wittenberg Concord (1536/37). It was a hasty product,
devoid of major intellectual or literary merit, and its utility vanished
after Strasbourg drew the signatory towns into the political orbit of
German Lutheranism. Modelled, though not slavishly so, on the
Lutheran Confession of Augsburg, the CT made a significant step,
in language and substance, toward the Lutherans.[37] Bucer and Capito
moderated their language on the Eucharist, and they wisely reserved
their polemics for the Roman Catholics and the pope.[38] But the
Strasbourg confession did not hit its intended mark among the
Lutherans. When Melanchthon and Brenz read the CT, they rec-
ognized that the Strasbourgeois had taken a giant step away from
Zwinglian heresy and toward orthodoxy. But they also suspected

---

[36] Seven changes in the earlier of the two German texts have been identified as
stemming from Sturm (*Ibid.*, pp. 36, 92, 122, 126, 128, 134). All seven fall within
the category of stylistic improvements. Since all extant manuscripts, with the exception of Capito's long version of Article 18, are in secretarial hands, the puzzle of
the authorship of the various parts of the CT cannot be solved. A later Strasbourg
tradition made Bucer the sole author of the CT (see Daniel Specklin, "Collectanea,"
in *BSCMHA*, 14 [1889]: pp. 344–345, no. 2314), but this tradition is too late
(Specklin was born in 1536) to have independent value.

[37] Bernd Moeller, in Bucer, *Deutsche Schriften*, 3, pp. 19–20; Wilhelm Gussman,
Quellen und Forschungen zur Geschichte des Augsburger Glaubensbekenntnisses (2 vols.; Leipzig,
1911, 1930), 1, part 2, p. 43; E. Bizer, *Studien zur Geschichte des Abendmahlsstreits*, pp.
29–30; Gustav Anrich, *Martin Bucer* (Strassburg, 1914), p. 52. Gussman discovered
the fact that both the CT and the Confession of Augsburg were designed partly as
replies to John Eck's "404 Articles." On the debates between Eck and the Strasbourg
theologians, see Klaus Rischar, *Johann Eck auf dem Reichstag zu Augsburg 1530*
("Reformationsgeschichtliche Studien und Texte," Heft 97; Münster/Westfalen, 1968),
pp. 109–138.

[38] The longer version of the article on the Eucharist affirms the Strasbourg-
Zwingli position on the *manducatio impiorum* issue (Bucer, *Deutsche Schriften*, 3, p. 133
ll. 5–11): "Dan so das furnembst, das der Herr in disem handel gemeint hat, ist
sein gedechtnus vnd die danckbare verkhundigung seins tods, . . . so muess auch
volgen, das er von einem solichen essen geredt hab, vss dem dise gedechtnus vnd
verkhundigung entspringe. Das wur aber nur das geystlich essen sein, welchs durch
waren glauben geschicht, ..." The shorter, final version affirms that Christ "in
disem sacrament seinen waren leyb vnnd wares plut warlich zuessen vnnd trincken
gipt, zur speyss irer seelen vnnd ewigen leben, . . ." (*Ibid.*, p. 125 ll. 1–4). In Hans
Ehinger's opinion (F. Dobel, ed., *Memmingen*, 4, p. 38), "so lendt sich disse bekantnus jns sonderhaitt des sacraments halben vast auff die Zwinglische maynung." It
is impossible to tell which version of Art. 18 Ehinger had seen, but a comparison
of the two versions shows that the final one is far less explicitly "sacramentarian"
in language than the earlier version.

Bucer and Capito of playing a semantic quadrille, and they did not allow the CT to divert them from their work for John the Constant's policy of conciliating the emperor.[39]

As a bridge between Strasbourg and Saxony the CT was promising; as a bridge to Charles V it was not. Sturm tried to submit it to Charles on July 8, but the emperor dismissed him and told him to return on the morrow. When Sturm complied, he found that Charles had gone hunting, leaving a subordinate to accept the document. Few Roman Catholics at the Diet understood what the Confession said or the intent of its authors.[40] The Catholic theologians ignored the document for some time. The Lutheran estates received a reply to their statement within four weeks; the Zwinglians waited for more than fourteen weeks. Not until October 25 did Sturm and his allies receive the reply of Charles' theologians to their Confession. The reply was brutal. It ignored the substance of the CT and charged the signatories with heresy, blasphemy, impiety and wantoness. Hans Ehinger of Memmingen despondently wrote home on October 26: "we are so much and so often called heretics, worse than the people of Capharnum, worse than the Jews, and it is said that we are more unbelieving than the Devil."[41] The Catholic reply to the CT offered one more proof of what the southern Evangelical towns could expect so long as they were forced to act on their own.

---

[39] *CR*, 2, pp. 221–225, nos. 797–798.

[40] Sturm to the Senate, July 12, 1530 (*PCSS*, 1, pp. 469–471, no. 758); Hans Ehinger to Memmingen, July 14, 1530 (F. Dobel, *Memmingen*, 4, pp. 40–41). Valentin von Tetleben named the signatories as "Strasburgh, Memmingen, Lindaw und Basel" (*Protokoll des Augsburger Reichstages*, ed. Herbert Grundmann ["Schriftenreihe der Historischen Kommission bei der Bayerischen Akademie der Wissenschaften," no. 7; Göttingen, 1958], p. 90); while the Venetian envoy's reports do not even mention the Tetrapolitan Confession (see *Die Depeschen des venezianischen Gesandten Nicolo Tiepolo über die Religionsfrage auf dem Augsburger Reichstage 1530*, ed. Johannes von Walter ["Abhandlungen der Akademie der Wissenschaften zu Göttingen, philologisch— historische Klasse," New Series, Vol. 23, Part 1]).

[41] Hans Ehinger to Memmingen, October 26, 1530 (F. Dobel, *Memmingen*, 4, pp. 88–89); Jacob Sturm to the Senate, October 31, 1530 (*PCSS*, 1, pp. 529–530, Appendix A). Sturm's verbal reply to the Confutation is in his report, but he does not mention himself as the speaker. That information comes from the Nurembergers' report to Nuremberg, October 27, 1530 (*CR*, 2, p. 423, no. 931).

IV

The second stage of Sturm's strategy led him into a new relation-ship with Ulrich Zwingli. It is well known that Zwingli composed and sent to Augsburg a statement of belief, his *Fidei ratio*, largely at the urging of Sturm. Although several historians have examined the origins of Zwingli's confession, none has been able to explain why Sturm elicited this document from the Zurich reformer.[42] The affair cannot be explained by looking at the motives of Zwingli alone. On the basis of the extant Sturm-Zwingli correspondance, read in the light of Sturm's plans for and actions at the Diet of Augsburg, the explanation adopted here appears to be the most probable one, although it cannot be proven in the absence of the missing pieces of this correspondance and of Sturm's papers. The available evi-dence suggests strongly that Sturm elicited the *Fidei ratio* for his own purposes and that those purposes were part of his strategy toward the Lutheran princes. In brief the following paragraphs will show that it is highly probable that Sturm intended to ensure that the Lutheran princes and preachers could favorably compare the mod-erate opinions of Strasbourg with the radically anti-Lutheran opin-ions of Zwingli. His ultimate goal was, then, to prepare the way for a rapprochement with the Lutheran party by erasing Strasbourg's reputation for Zwinglianism and "Sacramentarianism".[43]

---

[42] See Walter Köhler, "Zwinglis Glaubensbekenntnis," *Zwingliana*, 5, no. 4 (1930): pp. 242–261; Fritz Blanke, "Zwinglis 'Fidei ratio' (1530), Entstehung und Bedeutung," *ARG*, 57 (1966): pp. 96–101.

[43] I first reached this conclusion in my dissertation, "Jacob Sturm of Strasbourg," pp. 302–303. The same explanation is suggested by René Hauswirth, *Landgraf Philipp von Hessen und Zwingli*, pp. 215–216: "Um späteren Kompromiss mit den 'Augustanern' möglichst offenzuhalten, musste man die Unabhängigkeit von Zwingli sicherstelen und nach aussen dokumentieren, am besten durch ihn selber." In his review of Hauswirth's book, Ewald Rieser complains ("Landgraf Philipp von Hessen und Zwingli. Zum Buche von René Hauswirth," *Zwingliana*, 13, no. 2 [1969]: p. 157): "Ich vermisse an dieser Stelle Hauswirths Belege, um Sturm dieses Projekt unter-schieben zu können." It is true that the state of the evidence leaves this explana-tion partly hypothetical, but it is equally true that no other theory will account for the existing evidence, *if* that evidence is viewed from the points of view of Sturm and his government. The issue at stake is not that of Zwingli's reasons for com-posing the *Fidei ratio* but that of Sturm's reasons for asking him to do so. Given the undeniable fact that Sturm pursued Strasbourg's policy of conciliating the Lutherans, both before and after they rebuffed him at Augsburg, Sturm's request to Zwingli must be viewed as serving that policy. The only possible service that Zwingli could render is the one stated by Hauswirth.

Unlike the Strasbourg preachers, Sturm had never been close to Zwingli. He had helped to initiate Zwingli into imperial politics before the Marburg Colloquy; and during a visit to the Swiss towns after the First Kappel War, he had witnessed some of the disturbing effects of Zurich's political and ecclesiastical imperialism. During February and March, 1530, Zwingli had tried to secure Sturm's support for his latest political schemes, a comprehensive, anti-Hapsburg league and a plan to strengthen Zwinglianism in the empire through a military alliance of the Swiss and Swabian Evangelical towns. Sturm apparently ignored Zwingli's request that he champion these proposals.[44]

During the second week of March, 1530, Sturm and Mathis Pfarrer had been sent by the Thirteen of Strasbourg to Basel to discuss the admission of the Landgrave of Hesse to the Swiss-Strasbourg alliance. The allies agreed to compose a common statement of doctrine for the emperor.[45] On or before May 22, however, the banker Conrad Joham and Jacob Sturm's younger brother, Peter, arrived in Basel as envoys from the Thirteen. They asked Johannes Oecolampadius, chief of Basel's church, not to send a statement to Augsburg. He agreed and passed the request to Zwingli.[46] The Thirteen's change of mind requires explanation. Between the time of the Basel negotiations (early March) and the departure of Conrad Joham and Peter Sturm to Oecolampadius (on or before May 21), Jacob Sturm prepared the plan to conciliate the Lutherans. When Sturm left Strasbourg for Augsburg on May 22, he knew that the Thirteen was trying to silence the Swiss preachers. The mission to Oecolampadius was inspired by the fear that the Swiss preachers would spoil the negotiations with John of Saxony. Sturm feared not Oecolampadius but

---

[44] Ulrich Zwingli to Jacob Sturm, February 27/28, 1530 (Z, 10, pp. 473–478, no. 986); Werner Bygel to U. Zwingli, March 3, 1530 (*Ibid.*, p. 505, no. 995); U. Zwingli to W. Bygel, March 12, 1530 (*Ibid.*, p. 508, no. 997); U. Zwingli to Johannes Oecolampadius, March 12, 1530 (*Ibid.*, p. 511, no. 998). See R. Hauswirth, *Landgraf Philipp von Hessen und Zwingli*, pp. 184–193, on these projects. On Sturm's contacts with Zwingli before the Marburg Colloquy, see *Ibid.*, pp. 147–152.

[45] *Aktensammlung zur Geschichte der Basler Reformation in den Jahren 1519 bis Anfang 1534*, ed. Emil Dürr & Paul Roth (6 vols.; Basel, 1921–1950), 4, pp. 370, 370–371, 375–377.

[46] J. Oecolampadius to U. Zwingli, Basel, May 22 [1530] (Z, 10, p. 588, no. 1028). Conrad Joham, banker and silk merchant, was a member of the Thirteen and one of the richest men in Strasbourg. He probably belonged to the pro-Swiss faction in the government. See Johannes Ficker and Otto Winckelmann, *Handschriftproben des 16. Jahrhunderts nach Strassburger Originalen*. 2 vols. (Strassburg, 1902, 1905), 1, no. 13; T. A. Brady, Jr., "Jacob Sturm of Strasbourg," pp. 65, n. 1, 163–164, 164, n. 1.

Zwingli, who might anger the Lutherans and provoke new complaints against Strasbourg.[47]

When John of Saxony refused to hear him, despite the Landgrave's intercession, Sturm changed his mind. Five days after his arrival in Augsburg, in an artful, provocative letter Sturm suggested to Zwingli that his views should be heard by the emperor.[48] Sturm tried to heighten Zwingli's feelings against Luther by sending him a copy of the printed version of the "Schwabach Articles". This document, revealed to Zwingli for the first time, gave ample proof that Luther himself, not just a few Lutheran hotheads, had reneged on the concessions he had apparently made to Zwingli at Marburg (October, 1529). Sturm cautioned Zwingli about the mode of his reply: "I advise . . . that nothing should be done by *you and your people* without prior consultation with the governments of the Christian towns." The Lutherans were preparing a formal statement of faith for the emperor: "If *you and your people* meanwhile compose apologies to the Emperor and the princes, in which you give an account of *your faith,* . . . I do not believe that *your* effort will be fruitless." The account (*ratio*) should not be submitted "without the advice of us who are working here."[49] Sturm provoked Zwingli to send a statement of faith

---

[47] The date of Sturm's departure for Augsburg is given in M. Bucer to U. Zwingli, [Strasbourg], May 25, [1530] (*Z*, 10, p. 593, no. 1031). Since Sturm knew that his government was trying to quash the plan for a common statement devised at Basel, his suggestion to Zwingli on May 31 (see note 49 below) very probably stemmed from some plan of his own. Both W. Köhler ("Der Augsburger Reichstag von 1530 und die Schweiz," p. 179) and F. Blanke ("Zwinglis 'Fidei ratio'," p. 97) concluded that Sturm was merely following the original plan; and Blanke tried to soften that contradiction by alleging that Sturm's suggestion was "half-hearted."

[48] [Jacob Sturm] to [U. Zwingli], Augsburg, May 31, 1530 (*Z*, 10, pp. 599–604, no. 1035). This and Sturm's subsequent letters are signed "psi" and addressed to "phi". Identifications of the writer and addressee are confirmed in a letter from Zurich to Bern, June 25, 1530 (*EA*, 4, 1b, pp. 677–678). Sturm explained the reasons for using code letters in his first letter to Zwingli (*Z*, 10, p. 603): "Si literas ad me daturus es, vide, ut cautius et quam tectissime deinceps scribas; nam si has, quas misisti, aliquis intercepisset, inerant quedam de inscitia et stultitia quorundam, quae etiam non sine periculo meo, ad quam scribebatur, vulgari potuissent. Scis, quam teneras quidam aures habeant."

[49] *Ibid.*, p. 604: "Si tu et tui interim 'Apologeticos' parassetis ad caesarem et principes, in quibus quam piissime, citra cuiusquam, quantum fieri potest, suggillationem fidei vestre rationem redderetis, ita tamen, ut non ederentur, nisi consultum nobis, qui hic agimus, visum fuisset, non credo omnino operam et impensam perdituros vos." Sturm was even more explicit in his letter to Zwingli on June 19 (*Z*, 10, p. 630): "Si quid in his consilii habes, rogo communices vel michi vel Catto [sc. Landgrave Philip], quanquam si ad me miseris, facile Catto comune faciam." Zwingli was probably meant to assume that the "Schwabach Articles" represented

and asked for discretionary powers over the use of that statement. Sturm's intent becomes clear when it is remembered that, three days after he wrote the first letter to Zwingli, he asked his own government to send Bucer and Capito "to give account . . . of their doctrine and belief."[50] His plan required two statements of doctrine, one from Zwingli and the other from his own city. When these facts are added to Sturm's deliberate incitement of Zwingli against the Lutherans, his intent to exploit Zwingli becomes clear.

Three weeks later (June 19 and 20), Sturm wrote again to Zwingli. He reported the composition of a new statement of faith by the Lutherans:

> You should consider whether it would not be advisable that an account also be given of our faith and of the innovations made until the present time. Although I am quite sure that the Emperor's advisers do not intend to improve the situation, yet no one knows whether or not God, in this way, wants to inform the Emperor about how falsely the Roman Pope and his people have acted. . . . Accordingly, you might prudently consider whether you and your people want to ask the Emperor to hear your account of these events.[51]

Sturm's lack of candor is striking. He did not tell Zwingli that he was pleading with the Thirteen to send Bucer and Capito to Augsburg nor that he was still trying to get permission for Strasbourg to sign the Lutheran Confession. At one and the same time Sturm was trying to sign the Lutheran statement, preparing to submit a separate statement, and trying to get a statement from Zwingli. When Sturm's letters to Zwingli are compared with those to Strasbourg, the entire scheme is almost transparent: his letters to Zwingli are totally silent

---

Luther's rejection of the agreements made at the Marburg Colloquy. Actually, the articles were more than a year old, and Sturm knew that they dated at least to November, 1529, if not earlier.

[50] Jacob Sturm to the Senate, June 2, 1530 (*PCSS*, 1, p. 447, no. 728): "möchte villeicht nit unnutz sein, das etlich e. w. predicanten auch dabei weren, irer leer und glaubens halben rechnung und antwort zu geben."

[51] *Z*, 10, pp. 633–634, no. 1046: "Verum principes Saxonum et Cattus parant se ad reddendam fidei sue rationem. Itaque tu cogita, anne consultum videatur, ut et nostri fidei sue et de his, que hactenus novarunt, rationem reddant. Nam etsi non dubitem hos, qui a consiliis sunt caesari, non huc spectare, ut rem in melius restituant, quis tamen scit, an eas via velit deus caesarem informare de his, que hactenus perperam a pontifice Romano et suis acta sunt. Itaque pro tua prudentia cogitabis, anne et per te et tuos a caesare petendum sit, ut et eorum, que hactenus gesta sunt a vobis, ratio audiatur, si forte dominus daret, ut, quod hostes nostri in salutem suam excogitarunt, in perniciem verteretur." Sturm's letters of June 19 and June 20 are in *ibid.*, pp. 625–630, no. 1045; pp. 631–634, no. 1046.

about Strasbourg's adherence either to the Confession of Augsburg
or to a separate statement, while his letters to Strasbourg are totally
silent about his suggestions to Zwingli. Sturm also covered his tracks
with great care. Except for a trio of letters to Zwingli from Augsburg
signed "psi", not an accessible scrap of documentary evidence connected him with Zwingli's *Fidei ratio*.

A messenger from Zurich gave Zwingli's statement of faith to the
imperial Vice-Chancellor for Germany on July 8, one day before
Jacob Sturm and Hans Ehinger submitted the Terapolitan Confession.[52]
Sturm may not have engineered the nearly simultaneous appearance
of the two documents, but their juxtaposition could only help his
strategy. Zwingli's *Fidei ratio* was his most personal and most forceful *Credo*. He desired nothing less than the conversion of Charles V.
Zwingli called down the judgment of God on both Lutherans and
Roman Catholics. As of old, his criticism of Luther was most forceful in the section on the Eucharist, but the tone throughout was one
of finality: he had finished with Luther. This final breach, combined
with the predictable Lutheran reaction, belies Sturm's argument that
the quarrel was a matter of semantics.

The tone, rather than its content, explains the reception of the
Fidei ratio in Augsburg. It is not known whether Charles V ever saw
Zwingli's *Fidei ratio*. Andreas Eck, a Swiss then in Augsburg, endorsed
it heartily, while Hans Ehinger of Memmingen had similar inclina-
tions but declined to support it publicly. Martin Bucer paid the price
of his involvement in Sturm's plans. He praised Zwingli's staunch
faith but deplored the polemical character of his statement. The
Lutherans reacted with predictable harshness. John Brenz denounced
the *Fidei ratio* as unbiblical, while Melanchthon declared Zwingli
insane to have sent such a document to Augsburg. All the old errors
on the Eucharist and original sin are there, he wrote Luther, plus
demands for the abolition of all ceremonies and the episcopal office.
The whole spirit of the document was more Swiss than Christian.
Luther could not bring himself to believe that Zwingli had intervened
at Augsburg on his own initiative. Behind Zwingli, he suspected,
stood the foxy Martin Bucer of Strasbourg: "And we should ally
with such men?"[53] Luther named the right city but the wrong man.

---

[52] F. Blanke, "Zwinglis 'Fidei ratio'," pp. 98–99. The *Fidei ratio* is printed in Z, 6,
no. 163.
[53] A good survey of reactions by F. Blanke, "Zwinglis 'Fidei ratio'," pp. 100–101.

Zwingli's statement of faith secured rapid and wide distribution. The Imperial Chancery, when it so desired, could maintain excellent security. Sturm, for example, could not obtain a copy of the Catholic reply to the Tetrapolitan Confession for nearly two months. He finally obtained one through his friend, the Augsburg physician Gereon Sailer.[54] Zwingli's confession, however, was known to Melanchthon on July 14; Andreas Eck had read it by July 16. There are two possible ways in which the document may have gained such rapid currency. The Imperial Chancery may have leaked it deliberately, since it suited the emperor's purpose to divide the Evangelicals further by disseminating such information. The copy Melanchthon saw circulated among the Lutheran princes, who may have secured it from the Landgrave or Jacob Sturm. Sturm after all had asked Zwingli to give him and the Landgrave discretionary powers to reveal or suppress the document.[55] It is likely, but cannot be proven, that more than one copy of the *Fidei ratio* came to Augsburg and that Sturm passed a copy through Philip of Hesse to the Lutheran princes. He took a calculated risk in doing so. Luther, who was one object of Sturm's strategy, revived all of his suspicious against Bucer; but neither Bucer nor Strasbourg was directly incriminated by Zwingli's document, and Sturm planned to vindicate them with the Tetrapolitan Confession.

See Andreas Eck to Joachim Vadian, Augsburg, July 16, 1530 (*Vadianische Briefsammlung der Stadtbibliothek St. Gallen*, eds. Emil Arbenz & Hermann Wartmann [7 parts; "Mitteilungen zur vaterändischen Geschichte," Vols. 24–25, 27–30a; St. Gallen, 1890–1913], 4, p. 217, no. 608): "Hab Zwinglii bekantnus glesen, die er dem kaiser zuschribt. Summe placet etc." Hans Ehinger's sentiments are revealed in his reports to Memmingen (F. Dobel, ed., *Memmingen*, 4, pp. 38, 39). John Brenz' opinion, dated July 12, 1530, is in *CR*, 2, p. 187, no. 777. See also P. Melanchthon to M. Luther, July 14, 1530 (*ibid.*, p. 193, no. 781); and M. Luther to Justus Jonas, July 21, 1530 (*WABr*, 5, no. 1657).

[54] Jacob Sturm to the Thirteen, August 8, 1530 (*PCSS*, 1, p. 482, no. 778): J. Sturm to the Thirteen, October 12, 1530 (*Ibid.*, pp. 527–528, no. 828). See Bucer, *Deutsche Schriften*, 3, pp. 189, 189, n. 5.

[55] See the texts quoted in note 50 above. Both the Lutheran and the Strasbourg confessions were signed and submitted by governments, not by individual theologians. Although Zwingli's confession was submitted to the emperor, it was not signed by his government, and there were no official Swiss envoys to the Diet. It is, therefore, highly improbable that Sturm simply wanted Zwingli's views to be heard by the emperor alongside those of the Lutheran and other Evangelical estates.

V

The Diet of Augsburg was one of the longest imperial convocations of the Reformation era, and Sturm spent most of it in patient vigilance, unable to influence the course of events. Charles V and the Catholic princes paid little attention to Sturm and his allies. Whereas Charles' theologians answered the Lutheran Confession within four weeks of its submission, they dawdled over the reply to the Tetrapolitan Confession for more than fourteen weeks—an accurate indication of their relative respect for the two Evangelical parties. The real business of the Diet of Augsburg involved the negotiations between the Elector of Saxony and Charles and between the Lutheran and the Catholic theologians. While John tried to assure the Saxon electorate for his son, John Frederick, his theologians strove to reach a doctrinal settlement with the Roman Catholics. If these negotiations were successful, Sturm and his allies could expect no mercy from the Diet. During the desperate days of mid-August, Sturm still hoped "that the princes will yield nothing that concerns the chief articles of their faith and their confession."[56] Sturm saw with complete clarity that the fate of Strasbourg and of the German Reformation lay entirely in the hands of Charles and the German princes. The cities were helpless. Mathis Pfarrer reported: "the cities sit here at great expense and get nothing done; for the honorable cities . . . are rarely consulted."[57]

The nerves of Strasbourg's Thirteen were not as strong as Sturm's. By mid-August they imagined a new and more conciliatory version of the "Schwabach Articles" that did not require complete agreement in doctrine:

> Therefore, we ask you to make every effort . . . to negotiate with the honorable Elector and the princes that they once again . . . have friendly discussions for the purpose of establishing a Christian League. You must convince them . . . that they should enter into a League with us . . . and not abandon us. For we want no quarrel with His Electoral Grace in the matter of the Eucharist.[58]

---

[56] Jacob Sturm to the Thirteen, August 8, 1530 (*PCCS*, 1, p. 483, no. 778).

[57] Mathis Pfarrer to Peter Butz, September 18, 1530 (*Ibid.*, p. 498, no. 792).

[58] The Thirteen of Strasbourg to Jacob Sturm and Mathis Pfarrer, August 17, 1530 (*Ibid.*, pp. 486–487, no. 782): "das si nachmols, umb ein guetlich gesprech eins christlichen verstands halb ze haben, bewilligen wolten . . . si dahin zu bewegen, das sie mit ein verstand, wie hievor davor gehandelt worden, annemen und sich deshalb von uns nit trennen lossen . . . dan ein er. rathe mit irn churf. gnoden des sacraments halben . . . kein span haben wolten."

How little Sturm's colleagues respected formal statements of doctrine is illustrated by their command that Sturm should urge the Elector to disregard both the Lutheran Confession and the Tetrapolitan Confession. Otherwise "although we are united in the chief matter and adhere to the living Word of God, we will remain divided."[59] Sturm did nothing to allay their fears when he suggested on August 24 that they prepare the city for war. To him as to them, doctrinal statements were useful or bothersome in the quest for political security.

August was Sturm's worst month. Suddenly, on the 31st, he reported that Bucer and Melanchthon "have agreed on some articles" that they are sending to Luther.[60] As his discussion with the Catholic theologians soured, Melanchthon conveniently discovered that Bucer's opinions were "not so bad as they were made out to be and were comparable to Luther's view."[61] The initiative for these discussions between the preachers of the two parties probably came from Elector John. It certainly did not come from his preachers. One of them, Justus Jonas, wrote in late August that an agreement with Bucer would be a confession of uncertainty and weakness. It was the princes and politicians who pushed the preachers together.

When the articles of Bucer and Melanchthon were sent to Luther, Sturm wrote to Landgrave Philip, who had already left Augsburg, urging that he try to persuade the elector and Luther to come to an agreement with Strasbourg and Bucer. As September wore on, no word came from Luther, and his influence with the elector meant that the latter would go no further until Luther approved. The deterioration of John's relations with Emperor Charles was reflected in Luther's new doubts about this "pious Emperor" who refused to abandon the priests for the Gospel.[62] Finally, on the day of his departure

---

[59] *Ibid.*, p. 487: "die wir doch im haubthandel einhellig und dem lebendigen gotswort anhengig sin, also zertrennt werden. . . ."

[60] Jacob Sturm to the Thirteen, August 31, 1530 (*ibid.*, p. 492, no. 786). The articles are printed in *CR*, 2, p. 224, no. 798.

[61] This opinion is attributed to Melanchthon in a Strasbourg source, which must be evaluated accordingly. See Daniel Specklin, "Collectanea," *BSCMHA*, 14, p. 346, no. 2316. Justus Jonas' view is in an opinion labelled "De missa privata" (*CR*, 2, p. 309, no. 859). The negotiations were begun at least by August 26 (see *ibid.*, pp. 315–316, no. 864, of that date).

[62] On the Landgrave's mediation efforts, see E. Fabian, *Die Entstehung des Schmalkaldischen Bundes* (2nd ed.), pp. 106–108. On the beginnings of Luther's change in his attitude toward the emperor, see H. Baron, "Religion and Politics in the German Imperial Cities," pp. 423–425, 423, n. 2; Johannes Heckel, *Lex Charitatis. Eine juristische Untersuchung über das Recht in der Theologie Martin Luthers* ("Abhandlungen der

for Torgau in Saxony the elector took a step towards Sturm. The pious wish he expressed to Sturm reflects his estrangement from Charles: "God grant His grace that all of us Protestant princes and Imperial cities will shortly come together again in a united alliance." John now needed allies, and the heterodoxy of Strasbourg appeared less grievous in the light of his current political situation. Even the Saxon Old Chancellor, pious, conservative Gregor Brück, who obeyed the Lutheran preachers and abhorred all error, recommended that his prince settle the controversy and ally with the southern towns.[63]

Since Luther would not send his blessing, Sturm sent Bucer to secure it. He attached Bucer to the departing Nurembergers with instructions to bring back Luther's approval of the Tetrapolitan Confession and an Evangelical military alliance. By the time the elector departed for Torgau, Bucer was already in Saxony with Luther. Sturm also sent Wolfgang Capito to alert the Swiss preachers to the new prospect of concord with the Lutherans.[64] The unity the Evangelical princes and towns displayed momentarily at the Diet of Speyer in 1529 now appeared on the verge of recreation. That possibility greatly outweighed the steadily worsening situation in the Diet where Charles and his majority created consternation among the Free Cities by trying to force them to accept the majority's decisions concerning religion and taxation. Sturm's object of two year's standing appeared close to success on that day in late September when John of Saxony turned his back on the pope, the emperor and the Imperial Diet.

A few days later Bucer wrote Sturm of his encouraging conversation with Luther. According to Bucer, Luther approved the Tetrapolitan Confession—or at least Bucer's interpretation of it—but he

---

Bayerischen Akademie der Wissenschaften, philosophisch—historische Klasse," New Series, no. 36; Göttingen 1953), pp. 184–191. Sturm reported, on September 10, Luther's failure to respond to the articles sent to him from Augsburg (*PCSS*, 1, p. 496, no. 789).

[63] Jacob Sturm to the Thirteen, Augsburg, September 23, 1530 (*ibid.*, pp. 499–500, no. 794); Daniel Specklin, "Collectanea," in *BSCMHA*, 14, p. 346, no. 2318; Hans Ehinger, in F. Dobel, ed., *Memmingen*, 4, p. 64. On Brück's change-of-heart, see W. Köhler, *Zwingli und Luther*, 2, pp. 235–236.

[64] The extant evidence indicates that the Strasbourg preachers were sent on their missions during the autumn of 1530 and that they were to serve their government's policy (which may or may not have been their own). Sturm sent Capito to Switzerland at the end of August (*PCSS*, 1, p. 490, no. 785); and he sent Bucer to Coburg on September 19 (*ibid.*, p. 499, no. 794): "Wir haben den Butzer . . . bemeltem Baumgartner [of Nuremberg] angehenkt. . . ."

demanded that Bucer canvass the preachers of the Swabian and Swiss towns to secure their assent to Bucer's current position.[65] He wanted assurance that the southerners were no longer heterodox. Luther never fully trusted Bucer. The entire subsequent history of the Eucharistic dispute, from Bucer's subscription to the Confession of Augsburg (1532) to the Wittenberg Concord (1536/37), shows that Luther believed that the Zwinglians were abandoning their errors for his own pure doctrine. In the end he forced the German Zwinglians to do just that.

All the necessary pre-conditions for reconciliation with the Lutherans existed by the first week in October: the dissociation of Strasbourg from Zwingli; the elector's timely change of attitude; and Luther's grudging approval of Bucer's account of the gospel preached at Strasbourg. Having received formal permission to do so, Sturm made direct contact with the Saxon agents on October 12 and 13.[66] The chief Saxon representative was Count Albrecht of Mansfeld, an activist in politics and a pragmatist in religion.

On the first day (October 12) Sturm explained the recent agreement between Bucer and Luther, in view of which the doctrinal quarrel could be seen as a thing of the past. Since Bucer and Luther "had agreed", Mansfeld should ask his prince

> that His Electoral Grace not separate from or reject the City of Strasbourg, but rather unite with it, since in faith, so far as concerns the holy Sacrament, there is no difference between His Electoral Grace and his allies and Strasbourg. And although there had been a certain verbal dispute between their preachers, there is no real dispute about the presence of the true Body and Blood. If this union and alliance is established

---

[65] Jacob Sturm to the Thirteen, Augsburg, October 5, 1530 (*ibid.*, p. 504, no. 799); M. Pfarrer to Peter Butz, Augsburg, October 12, 1530 (*ibid.*, p. 512, no. 807).

[66] The Senate of Strasbourg to Jacob Sturm and Mathis Pfarrer, October 9, 1530 (*ibid.*, p. 507, no. 802). The three extant accounts of these talks are the reports by Jacob Sturm to the Thirteen, October 15, 1530 (*ibid.*, pp. 517–518, no. 810), by Count Albrecht of Mansfeld to the Elector of Saxony, October 13, 1530 (in Karl Eduard Förstemann, ed., *Urkundenbuch zu der Geschichte des Reichstags von Augsburg im Jahre 1530.* 2 vols. [Halle, 1833, 1835], 2, pp. 726–729, no. 250), and by Konrad Zwick to Constance (Constance, Stadtarchiv, "Reformations-Akten" 4, fols. 274ʳ–276ᵛ; summary in *EA*, 4, 1b, pp. 813–816). Zwick was not a participant, and his report is based on information from Sturm. Zwick's remark that Mansfeld proposed the talks is contradicted by Sturm (*PCSS*, 1, 517). See Max Lenz, "Zwingli und Landgraf Philipp," *ZKiG*, 3 (1879): pp. 250–252, who used Zwick's report; and Otto Winckelmann, *Der schmalkaldische Bund und der Nürnberger Religionsfriede* (Strassburg, 1892), pp. 270–271, who used those of Zwick and Sturm.

between His Electoral Grace and Strasbourg, it will be useful and
encouraging for resistance and for other purposes to both parties.[67]

Mansfeld probed Sturm's meaning by asking if he might report to
Saxony that Strasbourg approved the Confession of Augsburg. Sturm
stalled; he replied that he had no such powers, but Mansfeld could
be confident that "there would be no problem there." Bucer had
read the Confession of Augsburg three times and said "that he saw
nothing wanting in it nor anything that required change."[68]

The conversation of the second day followed the pattern the Saxon
elector had established: first doctrine, then politics. Sturm danced to
the Saxon tune. Neither he nor Mansfeld possessed powers to discuss terms for an alliance, but that is what they did. First they examined the question of canvassing the Evangelical governments. The
elector would send to the northern princes and towns and recruit
them for a league; Strasbourg, aided by Ulm, would do the same
for the southern cities. Two or three envoys "from each side" would
then meet to evaluate the results "and to accept one another and to
agree upon a common defense and mutual aid; and since the matter cannot be delayed very long, as firm a commitment as possible
should be made at that meeting."[69] The failure of John's attempt to
conciliate Charles and its consequence, the impending renewal of the
Edict of Worms, now made easy what had earlier seemed impossible.

Sturm and Mansfeld went on to make an interim military arrangement, a move prompted by the growing atmosphere of religious
hostility in the Diet. Mansfeld's lord would recruit northern cavalry
for the southern towns, while the latter would gather infantry in
the south for the princes. This formula reflected the standing division
of labor between north and south Germany in the supply or mercenary troops. In two days Jacob Sturm and Albrecht of Mansfeld

---

[67] K. E. Förstemann, ed., *Urkundenbuch*, 2, p. 727. Mansfeld's report covers only
the session of October 12, while Sturm's covers only that of October 13. How little
part Mathis Pfarrer took in these talks is shown by the fact that Mansfeld calls him
"Ehr Jacob Pfaff" (*ibid.*, p. 726).

[68] *Ibid.*, p. 728.

[69] *PCSS*, 1, pp. 517–518, no. 810. Zwick stresses Mansfeld's lack of powers to
commit his lord to another meeting (Constance, Stadtarchiv, "Reformations-Akten"
4, fols. 275ʳ–275ᵛ): "Dann durch graff Albrechten von Mansfelden, wiewol durch
sich selbs on bevelch der fursten, verschiner tagen mitt ettlicher bottschafft jetz zu
Ougspurg allerlay ist geredt werden vff mainung, ob nit nochmals vff das zehand-
len were, was zu Schmalkalden ... nit mocht ain furgang haben." Sturm, too,
exceeded his instructions.

laid the groundwork for the Schmalkaldic League. John of Saxony confirmed their agreement during the first days of November, when he wrote to Strasbourg:

> The councillors we left in Augsburg have reported the statement your envoys made to them concerning the most worthy sacrament of the body and blood of Christ. Now that there exists no disagreement between us, we received that report with especial favor and enthusiasm. You have doubtless heard the opinion of Nuremburg that we, princes and cities who adhere to the cause of the Gospel, should have our advisers and deputies assemble as soon as possible.[70]

The aftermath of the Sturm-Mansfeld talks is well known. The dissolution of the Imperial Diet found the Evangelical estates still opposing Charles and now threatened by litigation to recover secularized church properties and by military action to restore Roman Catholicism in the empire.[71] John of Saxony's *volte-face* during the autumn of 1530 created the necessary will to alliance on the part of the Lutheran princes. A December meeting at Schmalkalden drafted a treaty of alliance that was subsequently ratified. The Swiss did not join. The sweet words of Bucer and Capito did not dispel from Swiss minds the suspicion that Strasbourg had betrayed them and gone over to the Lutherans. That suspicion and the continued opposition of John of Saxony to Swiss admission kept Zurich, Basel and Bern out of the Schmalkaldic League.

What did Sturm think of the results of his successful strategy? He had no illusions about the reasons for the change in the attitudes of Elector John and his theologians. The current enthusiasm for alliance, he told the Ulmers in late November, 1530, reflects the current emergency.

> Everything depends on whether we have a proper love for one another. If we are allied and this love is not present, then the alliance will have

---

[70] Ulm, Stadtarchiv, "Reichsstadt Ulm" 1201, fol. 39; an extract in *PCSS*, 1, pp. 535–536, no. 830. The military agreement by Sturm (*ibid.*, p. 518) and by Zwick (Constance, Stadtarchiv, "Reformations-Akten" 4, fols. 276ʳ–276ᵛ).

[71] The campaign against the Evangelical governments that began after the Diet of Augsburg was a series of legal suits aimed at forcing those governments to restore confiscated ecclesiastical properties to their former owners. See Robert Schelp, *Die Reformationsprozesse der Stadt Strassburg am Reichskammergericht zur Zeit des Schmalkaldischen Bundes (1524)/1531–1541/(1555)* (Kaiserslautern, 1965), pp. 58–62; Herman Buck, *Die Anfänge der Konstanzer Reformationsprozesse. Oesterreich, Eidgenossenschaft und Schmalkaldischer Bund 1510/22–1531* (*SKRG*, nos. 29–31; Tübingen, 1964), p. 511.

been made in vain; at the first sign of trouble, members will offer trivial excuses and begin to withdraw from the league.[72]

Sturm believed that he had achieved his alliance without compromising religious principle, since he thought that the elector and Luther
had agreed to ignore the trivial differences between Strasbourg doctrine and their own. He told the Ulmers: "If we attend yet another
meeting only to learn that the Elector will ally with none but those
who share his beliefs, then all this effort will be for nothing. He cannot expect that my government and others will permit him to dic-
tate the standards of faith."[73] On this point Sturm deceived himself.
The alliance he helped to engineer drew the south German Evangelical towns into the political and doctrinal orbit of the elector of
Saxony, whose thoroughgoing domination over the Schmalkaldic
League scotched the growth of Zwinglianism in south Germany.
Strasbourg no longer had the choice of maintaining a peculiar understanding of the new religion. Jacob Sturm had negotiated that choice
away, though he was unaware of this possibility during the last
months of 1530. He might have predicted the future from the letter
in which Elector John thanked him for his work in uniting the
Lutherans and the southerners:

> We did not wish to omit writing to you, whom we now know as one
> who knows best how to further the cause and who understands, bet-
> ter than others do, the grace of the Almighty. We graciously ask that
> you exert every possible effort to see that your preachers . . . adhere
> to the articles that we agreed upon.[74]

---

[72] "Erstlich wer es alles gelegen an dem, ob man ain rechte lieve anainander
hab; dann, wann man sich schon zuainander verbunden, und diselb lieb söllt nit
vorhanden sein, so were es vergebens und möcht sich ainer zur nott wol von ainer
klainfuegen ursachen ausser der halfter ziehen; deshalb vor allen dingen gutt were,
dieselb zuerst zu erlernen; . . . ." Ekkehart Fabian, ed., *Die Beschlüsse der oberdeutschen
Schmalkaldischen Städtetage*, Part I: *1530/1531* (*SKRG*, no. 9; Tübingen, 1959), p. 57.
The document is in the hand of a secretary of Ulm. In translating, I have transposed it from the third into the first person.
[73] *Ibid.*: "soll man aber anderwaid tag besuchen, und der churfurst und ander
söllen auf irer mainung verharren und zu niemant verpunden wöllen, dan die eben
das, so si glauben, so werd es aber zu nichte; dann er kundt nicht achten, das ine
sein oder ander herren masz dess glaubens geben lassen werden; . . . ."
[74] *PCSS*, 2, p. 16, no. 19: "haben wir doch nit unterlassen wollen, euch als dem,
der uns nun fur andern bekant ist, die ding auch zu furdern weis und von den
gnaden des almechtigen vor andern verstehet, zu schreiben, ganz gnediglich begerend,
ir wollet mugelichen vleis dapei haben, domit es auch der prediger halb bei euch
zwuschen uns allen vorberurts artikels halben gleichmesig gehalten muge werden."

VI

Jacob Sturm's dilemma at the Diet of Augsburg illustrates the essential weakness of the cities in the political world of Reformation Germany. Many historians have criticized the southern Free Cities for their half-hearted, cautious foreign policies. They, like sixteenth-century observers, were impressed by the enormous private fortunes accumulated by the great mercantile dynasties of the south. Private wealth, however, was not directly related to urban power. In the essential elements of power—size of territory, exploitation of subjects' resources, military capability and the strength of fortifications—the Cities were no match for the great princes. Empty treasuries were deceptive, since the princes financed their military adventures with credit rather than revenues. The Reformation destroyed the Cities' main protection, their political solidarity, leaving each city to find new allies. Within the parameters set by princely domination of the empire, every urban diplomat had to try to enhance his city's security. Jacob Sturm's strategy was just such an attempt. He lacked the ability to force the changes which made possible his goal, the formation of the Schmalkaldic League, because those changes depended entirely on the relations between Charles V and John of Saxony and his allies.

Sturm's exploitation of Ulrich Zwingli and his strategy toward the Lutheran princes exhibited the flexible, opportunistic character of his politics. Sturm strove to detach the Strasbourg preachers from their public allegiance to Zwingli and turn them toward Luther and Melanchthon. His solicitation and employment of the *Fideo ratio* duped Zwingli and helped to build a new bridge to the Lutherans. Further, Sturm's cavalier treatment of Zwingli reflected his assessment of the minimal importance of the Swiss towns in imperial politics and the limited power and availability of Swiss pikes.

Sturm's activities at Augsburg also revealed the secular thrust of his politics. Security for his native city was his goal; the main threat arose from the Catholic political response to the Reformation. Sturm never questioned Strasbourg's allegiance to the new religion, but the vulnerability of his city made him unwilling to define the public character of that religion beyond a stalwart anti-Romanism and a vague adherence to "the Gospel". Any further interpretation of the meaning of religion would only complicate Strasbourg's search for new allies. This explains the cautious attitude of Sturm and his colleagues toward all public, formal statements of doctrine. Such documents were produced, used and discarded, according to their political utility. The pragmatic element in Strasbourg's foreign policy derived from the quest for security rather than from a positive doctrine of toleration. The same motive lay behind Sturm's effort to ban the preachers from politics except as expert advisers on theology. His view of religion as a personal affair reinforced his political conviction and supported his policies. At the heart of all of Sturm's political calculations lay his desire to assure the security and prosperity of Strasbourg. Flexibility, that euphonious cousin to opportunism, was the trademark of his dealings with the Lutherans at the Diet of Augsburg.

CHAPTER THREE

PRINCES' REFORMATION VERSUS URBAN LIBERTY: STRASBOURG AND THE RESTORATION IN WÜRTTEMBERG, 1534*

Ulrich (1487–1550), third duke of Württemberg, rode into his capital city of Stuttgart on May 15, 1534, after fifteen years in exile. Driven from his lands by the Swabian League in 1519, Ulrich spent most of the intervening years as guest of his cousin, protector, and friend, Landgrave Philip (1504–1567) of Hesse, with whose backing he recovered his duchy.[1] The restoration and subsequent reformation in Württemberg marked a turning point in the political history of Reformation Germany, the last struggle in the South before the chief theater of struggle shifted to the North. It was also a turning point

---

* This study is dedicated to the scholars of the Sonderforschungsbereich 8, Spätmittelalter und Reformation, Projektbereich O and Z, who did so much to make my year in Tübingen both profitable and enjoyable. My special thanks go to my host, Professor H. A. Oberman, and to his Institut für Spätmittelalter und Reformation. This research could not have been completed without the generous support of the Alexander von Humboldt—Stiftung. My thanks also to the directors and staffs of the following institutions: the Archives de la ville de Strasbourg, the Hessisches Staatsarchiv Marburg, and the Hauptstaatsarchiv Stuttgart as well as the Center for Reformation Research (St. Louis). Katherine Gingrich Brady helped with every stage of this study.
SIGLA: AMS = Archives Municipales de Strasbourg; HStAM = Hessisches Staatsarchiv Marburg (therein: PA = Politisches Archiv des Landgrafen Philipp von Hessen); HStASt = Hauptstaatsarchiv Stuttgart; PCSS = *Politische Correspondenz der Stadt Straßburg im Zeitalter der Reformation*, edd. Hans Virck, *et al.* (Strasbourg 1882–1890; Heidelberg 1928–1933); VKLBW = Veröffentlichungen der Kommission für geschichtliche Landeskunde in Baden-Württemberg; QBLG = Quellen der badischen Landesgeschichte, ed. Franz Joseph Mone (Karlsruhe 1845–1863).

[1] On the restoration in Württemberg the basic works are J. Wille, *Philipp der Grossmüthige von Hessen und die Restitution Ulrichs von Wirtemberg 1526–1535*. Tübingen 1882, with numerous important documents; and A. Keller, *Die Wiedereinsetzung des Herzogs Ulrich von Württemberg durch den Landgrafen Philipp von Hessen 1533/34*. Dissertation Marburg 1912. Wille published some additional correspondence in: "Briefe Jakob Sturms, Stettmeisters von Strassburg". In: ZGO 33 (1880): pp. 101–115, here at pp. 103ff., to be used with Otto Winckelmann's corrections in: PCSS II. Wille, Winckelmann and other early students of this subject exploited HStAM, PA, before the reorganization that produced its present structure. Thus, the letters between Landgrave Philip of Hesse and Jacob Sturm, cited by Winckelmann as being in "Marburg Archiv (Württemberg)" are now in: HStAM, PA 2915 (Stadt Strassburg).

within the Protestant movement. Although it was greeted with joy in
many of the Protestant free cities, and although much aid for the
restoration came from the free city of Strasbourg, the cause of urban
liberty lost through Ulrich's restoration. As Heiko A. Oberman has
written: "Ulrich's restoration . . . marks the beginning of a new era,
in which the cities would have a future only as subordinate territorial administrative centers, and as such could secure no maneuver-
ing space for their own political will".[2] While furthering the cause
of Protestantism, Ulrich's recovery of Württemberg restored to power
the worst enemy of urban liberty in South Germany. It was made
possible, however, partly through the aid he received from the most
militant Protestant free city in the South, Strasbourg. The motives,
forms, and extent of this aid form the subject of the following exploration of this apparent paradox.

I. *Ulrich's Cause and the South German Free Cities, 1519–1534*

Vater unser:
Reitling is unser.
der du pist in den himmeln:
Ehing und Eßling wölln wir auch pald gewinnen.
geheiligt werde dein nam:
Hailprunn und Weil wölln wir auch han.[3]

The list of Swabian free cities in this version of "Duke Ulrich's pater-
noster" documents his fame as a scourge of urban liberties. He began
to rule in 1503, grandson and namesake of Count Ulrich "the Well-
beloved" (ca. 1413–1480); but by 1519 his subjects might have called
him "Ulrich the Well-hated", though their emnity dimmed through
the years of exile.[4] It was his attack on Reutlingen in 1519 which
brought the Swabian League down on his head and sent him on
the bitter road into exile. The free cities of the South, who played
a stronger role in the Swabian League than they would in any subsequent alliance—including the Smalkaldic League—helped to drive

[2] H. A. Oberman, *Werden und Wertung der Reformation. Vom Wegestreit zum Glaubenskampf.*
Tübingen 1977. (Spätscholastik und Reformation 2), pp. 339–340.
[3] R. Frhr. v. Liliencron (ed.), *Historische Volkslieder der Deutschen.* Leipzig 1865–1869,
vol. III, p. 239, no. 313.
[4] The irony of this change is caught by G. R. Elton, "[Ulrich's] absence, assisted
by the Austrian occupation, had turned him from a well-hated tyrant into a romantic dream to the people of the duchy". *Reformation Europe, 1517–1559.* New York
1966, 1st ed., London 1963, p. 155.

their foe from his lands, which they handed over to the Hapsburgs.[5]
The success of the Reformation in South Germany gave Ulrich
a chance to regain his lands. He first tried for aid from the Swiss
Evangelical towns. He had converted, perhaps in early 1524, to the
Swiss version of the new religion,[6] a reasonable act in view of the
proximity of his remaining territories to the spheres of influence of
Swiss cities—the great fortress of Hohentwiel to that of Zürich and
Montbeliard to that of Basel. With Swiss troops Ulrich tried to seize
his old lands under cover of the revolution of 1525, but they deserted
him before Stuttgart.[7] From this point onward, his fate depended on
the development of a Protestant alliance in Germany.

All dreams of a Protestant alliance in the southern regions of the
German-speaking world centered on the young Landgrave of Hesse,
Philip, whose sponsorship for Ulrich's cause reflected a near perfect
marriage of his friendship for Ulrich, his expansive view of his own
religion, and his ambition to be leader of the Protestant South.[8] He
dreamed of a southern anti-Hapsburg front, anchored by Hesse in
the North and the Swiss towns in the South, with the free cities of

---

[5] That the free cities were chiefly to blame for Ulrich's expulsion was alleged in
several contemporary songs. Liliencron (as note 3), vol. III, p. 241, no. 314, ll. 1–5;
pp. 252–253, no. 318, ll. 131–166; and K. Steiff and G. Mehring (eds.), *Geschichtliche
Lieder und Sprüche Württembergs*. Stuttgart 1912, p. 111, no. 28. E. Naujoks, who best
appreciates the importance of the Swabian League to the free cities of Swabia,
writes that, "Es war richtig, wenn die Fürsten hierin nicht nur einen Erfolg der
kaiserlichen Partei, sondern vor allem der Städte sahen". In: *Obrigkeitsgedanke, Zunftverfassung und Reformation. Studien zur Verfassungsgeschichte von Ulm, Eßlingen und Schwäb.
Gmünd*. Stuttgart 1958 (VKLBW 3), p. 48, and see pp. 24–28. According to E. Bock,
it is quite understandable, "daß es vor allem die Städte waren, die immer für eine
Verlängerung des Bundes eintraten, soweit sich damit nicht Änderungen verbanden,
die gegen ihre politischen Richtlinien gingen". In: *Der Schwäbische Bund und seine
Verfassungen 1488–1534. Ein Beitrag zur Geschichte der Zeit der Reichsreform*. Aalen 1968,
1st ed., Breslau 1927. (Untersuchungen zur deutschen Staats- und Rechtsgeschichte,
Old Series 137), p. 171. Ulrich's successful seige of Reutlingen (21.–28.I.1519) is
colorfully recounted by Ludwig Friedrich Heyd, *Ulrich, Herzog zu Württemberg. Ein
Beitrag zur Geschichte Württembergs und des deutschen Reichs im Zeitalter der Reformation*,
3 vols. Tübingen 1841–1844, vol. I, pp. 524–531; and that Ulrich also planned to
subjugate Eßlingen in 1519 is confirmed by G. Kittelberger, "Herzog Ulrichs Angriffs-
pläne auf die Reichsstadt Eßlingen," Jahrbuch für Geschichte der oberdeutschen Reichsstädte 17 (1971), pp. 116–119.

[6] Oberman, *Werden und Wertung* (as note 2), p. 341 n. 34. As we have no biography of Ulrich more modern than Heyd's (note 5 above), it is difficult to contest
the "heute vorherrschende Einschätzung Ulrichs als eines reinen "homo politicus".

[7] A. Feyler, *Die Beziehungen des Hauses Württemberg zur Eidgenossenschaft in der ersten
Hälfte des 16. Jahrhunderts*. Zürich 1905, pp. 264–279; G. Franz, *Der deutsche Bauernkrieg*,
7th ed. Bad Homburg v. d. H., 1965, pp. 106–107.

[8] See the excellent discussion by R. Hauswirth, *Landgraf Philipp von Hessen und
Zwingli. Voraussetzungen und Geschichte der politischen Beziehungen zwischen Hessen, Strassburg,*

Swabia and the Upper Rhine—plus Württemberg—in the center: in
fine, a southern wing of the Smalkaldic League (established 1531) to
match, in financial power and military prowess, the swarm of Lutheran
powers around the elector of Saxony.[9] Always vital to Philip's dream,
the Evangelical cities of the South became even more significant
after the collapse of Zürich's mini-imperialism after the death of
Zwingli (d. 1531). Though Ulrich's was a princely cause, Philip had
to sell it as a Protestant cause to his urban friends and clients. By
the end of 1533, this effort bore fruit, when enough Protestant cities
supported his plan to block renewal of the Swabian League, thus
opening the high road to Stuttgart.[10]

Philip's dream pitted against each other the two leading motives
of urban policy in the South—collective defence of their own liberties against their loyalty to Protestantism. To those who lay within
striking distance of Württemberg—Reutlingen, Esslingen, Heilbronn,
Weil der Stadt, Schwäbisch Gmünd, and Ulm—the restoration of
such a wolf in Stuttgart, even clad in the sheep's clothing of his new
religion, was a highly dangerous policy decision. In late 1533, Philip's
dream was but a policy; within a few months, it became history. As
Ranke noted long ago,[11] the restoration in Württemberg became
possible in 1534 because of shifts in the fortunes of the Hapsburg
dynasty and its adversaries, lending temporary advantage to France
and the German Protestant powers. The landgrave seized his chance
and made preparations for a strike against the Hapsburg regime in
Stuttgart. He turned for aid not to the Evangelical towns of Swabia,
such as Ulm and Augsburg, whose enthusiasm for the project might
well be suspect, but to Strasbourg.

Konstanz, Ulrich von Württemberg und reformierten Eidgenossen 1526–1531. Tübingen/Basel
1968 (Schriften zur Kirchen- und Rechtsgeschichte 35), ch. 1.

[9] E. Fabian, *Die Entstehung des Schmalkaldischen Bundes und seiner Verfassung 1524/29–
1531/35. Brück, Philipp von Hessen und Jakob Sturm,* 2nd ed. rev. Tübingen 1962
(Schriften zur Kirchen- und Rechtsgeschichte 1).

[10] Wille, *Philipp der Grossmüthige* (as note 1), pp. 39–40, 120ff. The dissolution of
the Swabian League is commonly attributed to the Hessian landgrave (see Bock,
Der Schwäbische Bund [as note 5], pp. 211–218), but it is now known that the Bavarians
were just as much responsible. See H. Puchta, *Die Habsburgische Herrschaft in Württemberg
1520–1534.* Dissertation Munich 1967. The continuity between the League and the
organization of the Swabian Circle is documented in the rich study by A. Laufs,
*Der Schwäbische Kreis. Studien über Einungswesen und Reichsverfassung im deutschen Südwesten
zu Beginn der Neuzeit.* Aalen 1971 (Untersuchungen zur deutschen Staats- und Rechtsgeschichte, New Series 16), esp. pp. 133–141.

[11] L. v. Ranke, *Deutsche Geschichte im Zeitalter der Reformation.* Ed. W. Andreas, 2 vols.,
Wiesbaden, n.d., vol. II, p. 81.

II. *Strasbourg and the Cause of Duke Ulrich, 1519–1534*

Herzog Ulrich, den pund hast du verachtet
den adel auch geschmecht,
den edlen fürsten auss Baiern
gehaissen ein schneiderknecht...[12]

Ich bin jung und nit alt
gerad, hübsch und wolgestalt,
gross genug und kein zwerg,
herzog und henker zu Wirtemberg...[13]

The Strasbourgeois had no major economic interests in Swabia,[14] nor had their regime ever joined the Swabian League. Ulrich's expulsion was nonetheless noted there, for Ulrich was also an Alsatian lord, who ruled the Alsatian lordship of Reichenweier/Riquewihr (his birthplace) and the county of Horburg, plus the far more important county of Montbeliard and associated lordships, which lay astride the western approach to the Burgundian Gate and thus controlled the high road from Burgundy to the Upper Rhine.[15] These western lands were the direct concern of Ulrich's brother, Count George (1498–1558), who sought refuge at Strasbourg in 1519.[16]

Ulrich's expulsion had unexpected results for some Strasbourg merchants. In late 1519 his officials at Montbeliard seized seven wagons with goods in transit from Lyons to Strasbourg.[17] They alleged that the goods were actually in transit to Ulmers or Nurembergers (*die bundtschen*) and released them only after Strasbourg's regime vouched for its merchants and forwarded the bills of lading and the

---

[12] Liliencron (as note 3), vol. III, p. 242, no. 315, stanza 7.

[13] Steiff and Mehring (as note 5), p. 111, no. 28.

[14] I have summarized the evidence on the geographical structure of Strasbourg's commerce in: *Ruling Class, Regime, and Reformation at Strasbourg, 1520–1555*. Leiden 1978. (Studies in Medieval and Reformation Thought 22), pp. 97–102, but for a detailed discussion one must consult P. Hertner, *Stadtwirtschaft zwischen Reich und Frankreich. Wirtschaft und Gesellschaft Strassburgs 1650–1714*. Cologne/Vienna 1973. (Neue Wirtschaftsgeschichte 8), pp. 1–10 and esp. pp. 115–192, making some allowances for changes during the intervening years.

[15] J. Fritz, *Die alten Territorien des Elsass nach dem Stande vom 1. Januar 1648*. Strasbourg 1896. (Statistische Mittheilungen über Elsass-Lothringen 27), pp. 49–50.

[16] Martin Crusius, *Schwäbische Chronik. Aus dem Lateinischen erstmals übersetzt und mit einer Continuation vom Jahre 1596 biss 1733 versehen von Johann Jacob Moser*. Frankfurt/Main 1733. III. x, 8 (vol. II, p. 191).

[17] HStASt, A 149/1. Two major items in the bills of lading are metal wares (esp. knife blades) and rosaries.

merchants' signs.[18] But this was minor trouble, and Ulrich's image at Strasbourg, so Wolfgang Capito reported in 1525, was very good.[19]

Neither Ulrich nor Württemberg figured importantly in Strasbourg's foreign policy until the era of the Reformation. The political tie to Philip of Hesse brought both that prince and Ulrich to Strasbourg's money market, though neither came from a dynasty which usually borrowed there.[20] Philip began borrowing in Strasbourg only in 1530[21] and Ulrich two years later, when he got 7,500 fl. (= *gulden* = Rhenish florins) secured by revenues at Montbeliard and Blamont—about all he had left.[22] Only with Philip's backing, however, could Ulrich expect *politically-motivated* aid from Strasbourg's regime, and this only because the regime had decided to make common cause with the Lutheran princes.

In a microcosm of the struggle within German Protestantism, at Strasbourg during the late 1520s a pro-Swiss, pro-Zwinglian party struggled in the regime with a pro-princely one. Leader of the latter was Jacob Sturm (1489–1553), who since 1526 had become the regime's premier diplomat and a confidant of Philip of Hesse.[23] Sturm had shared Philip's vision since 1528, when he abandoned the historic policy of urban solidarity, and he thereafter worked against the Swiss alliance and eventually led his regime into the Smalkaldic League.[24] To crown the success, the southern urban preachers signed the confession of Augsburg in 1532, and a now solid Protestant front wrang a truce from Charles V. This peace (the *Nürnberger Anstand*) was jeopardized by Philip's plans for Württemberg in 1534.

The advance of the Reformation in the South had greatly widened the circle of anti-Hapsburg powers. Strasbourg had no traditional

---

[18] The merchants involved were Friedrich V von Gottesheim, Jacob Wissbach, Batt von Duntzenheim, Conrad Joham, Diebold Olter, and Friedrich and Jacob Ingold. Except for Olter, they can be identified by consulting the index to my *Ruling Class* (see note 14).

[19] Wolfgang Capito to Ulrich Zwingli, Strasbourg, 6.II.1525: *Favor ducis* W[irttembergensis] *hic magnus est*. Huldreich Zwinglis sämtliche Werke, eds. E. Egli, *et al.*, 14 vols. Berlin/Leipzig/Zürich 1905–1959, vol. VIII, p. 299 (no. 362), ll. 4f.

[20] Brady, *Ruling Class* (as note 14), p. 155.

[21] See below, n. 36, for references.

[22] AMS VII 11/2; AMS AA 69, fol. 99; noticed in: PCSS II, p. 158, no. 154. Interest on this loan was still being paid in 1700.

[23] Brady, *Ruling Class* (as note 14), pp. 208–215, 351.

[24] On the evolution of Sturm's policy, see my "Jacob Sturm of Strasbourg and the Lutherans at the Diet of Augsburg, 1530". In: *Church History* 42 (1973), pp. 183–202, here at pp. 184–185; and now *Ruling Class* (as note 14), p. 243.

motive for or against the Hapsburgs, but a Hapsburg Württemberg now became the center of Catholic resistance to the new religion in the Southwest,[25] as well as a wedge between Protestant Hesse and its southern urban allies. A Hapsburg Württemberg could convert the loose string of territories stretching from Tyrol and Vorarlberg across Upper Swabia, the Breisgau, and the Sundgau to the Franche Comté, into the basis of a powerful territorial state.[26] With a bit of luck, the Southwest might see a Hapsburg state to match that in the Southeast—granted, that is, the traditional high degree of cooperation between the monarchy and the free cities.[27] But the rise of Protestantism made such an alliance impossible, at least in the eyes of Strasbourg's Sturm, whose foreign policy became thoroughly confessional. Sturm clearly appreciated Hapsburg Württemberg as a wedge between Hesse and the Swabian towns, as well as the anti-Protestant potential of the Swabian League.[28] He cared less about the plight of the Bavarian dukes, sealed into an iron Hapsburg ring, whom he mistrusted for confessional reasons.[29] Just as clear to Sturm

---

[25] Oberman, *Werden und Wertung* (as note 2), pp. 304–328.

[26] In the discussion of the strategic significance of Hapsburg Württemberg to the Protestants, it is often forgotten that, already before 1519, the Hapsburg dynasty ruled more land than any other power between the Lech and the Vosges and between Lake Constance and Franconia. But see P. Blickle, *Landschaften im alten Reich. Die staatliche Funktion des gemeinen Mannes in Oberdeutschland.* München 1973, pp. 96–97, on "Swabian Austria", and F. Metz (ed.), *Vorderösterreich, eine geschichtliche Landeskunde,* 2nd ed., Freiburg im Breisgau 1967, pp. 13–136.

[27] Oberman, *Werden und Wertung* (as note 2), pp. 338–339: "Schon im ersten Drittel des 16. Jahrhunderts hat der Mythos von Kaiser und Reich auch die progressivsten Kräfte in jener entscheidenden Wachstumsphase gehemmt, als es darum ging, die Einführung der Reformation in Strassburg und Konstanz (1523), in Nürnberg, Ulm und Augsburg (1524) überlokal politisch zu gestalten. . . . Nicht nur die wirtschaftlichen Sonderinteressen der Städte erwiesen sich mächtiger als ihre gemeinsame Sendung". To this must be said that Oberman 1) vastly overestimates the cultural and political potential of the free cities, 2) ignores the fact that their ruling elites freely chose the Lutheran princes over the Swiss, and 3) creates a new myth of their "gemeinsame Sendung". The key lies in his use of the word "überlokal", for it was just the weakness of the free cities—and their strength—that they could not develop into a federation of true states "à la néerlandaise", that they remained profoundly *lokal.*

[28] As soon as he accepted the idea of a confessionally-based alliance, Sturm realized that the Swabian League would have to be destroyed. To his (self-drafted) instruction for a meeting at Geislingen, drafted before 13.XII.1528, Sturm added: *Nota: verhinderung schwebischen bunds.* PCSS I, p. 306, no. 536.

[29] This is clear from his reaction to the offer of a Bavarian alliance, tendered through none other than Count Wilhelm von Fürstenberg late in 1534. See PCSS II, nos. 251, 253, 257, and esp. 259 (Sturm to Bernhard und Georg Besserer,

was the military value of Württemberg, as he later told Duke Ulrich: "for the landgrave would supply the cavalry, you the infantry, and the southern towns the artillery".[30]

In 1534 Strasbourg's regime wanted the peace preserved, but the ascendancy of Sturm and his ties to Philip were now so strong as to assure the prince a willing hearing of his war plans at Strasbourg. Sturm, to be sure, did not want to risk the peace for Ulrich's sake,[31] but he had staked Strasbourg's security on the landgrave, and he could hardly refuse him his personal support.

III. *Strasbourg Money and the Restoration in Württemberg, 1534*

> Das stündelin ist wider komn,
> das lang im land verpoten war
> dass man herzog Uolrich den fromn
> wider kecklich nennen tar
> und sprechen, er well sein erbland hon; . . .[32]

Making war required money, especially in a Germany in which armies were raised more through military entrepreneurs than through feudal levies.[33] Although he had not begun to borrow there until 1530, the landgrave was no stranger to Strasbourg's bankers. Through Friedrich II Prechter (d. 1528) and Hans Ebel (d. 1543), he had in 1532 transmitted his levy to the Swabian League's treasury at Augsburg;[34] and he was later consulted during the pursuit of Prechter's assassins.[35]

15.XII.1534). The Bavarians, and especially the chancellor, Leonhard von Eck, have been very roughly handled by Protestant historians, particularly the clerical ones, for their role in the Württemberg affair; but the double game the Bavarians played was matched by the duplicity of Landgrave Philip. See Landgrave Philip to Johann Feige, his chancellor, 30.IX.1532, quoted by Wille, *Philipp der Grossmüthige* (as note 1), p. 91.

[30] PCSS II, pp. 262–263, no. 287.
[31] See Landgrave Philip to Jacob Sturm and Mathis Pfarrer, 3.X.1533, in PCSS II, pp. 199–200, no. 204.
[32] Liliencron (as note 3), vol. IV, p. 78, no. 448, stanza 15.
[33] See F. Redlich, *The German Military Enterpriser and his Work Force. A Study in European Economic and Social History.* Wiesbaden 1964. (Supplement to the Vierteljahrschrift für Sozial- und Wirtschaftsgeschichte 47), vol. I, pp. 30–53.
[34] HStAM, PA 131, fol. 146; PA 1429, fol. 37. On these two men, who were partners and brothers-in-law, see Brady, *Ruling Class* (as note 14), in the index of personal names; and F.-J. Fuchs, "Une famille des négociants banquiers du XVIe siècle, les Prechter de Strasbourg." *Revue d'Alsace* 95 (1956): pp. 146–194, here at pp. 147–148.
[35] HStAM, PA 2915. fols. 23–25.

In 1530 Philip tried to raise 20,000 fl. at Strasbourg, but the regime lent him only half the sum, though he did get it at the relatively low interest rate of 4%.[36] The regime warned him, however, against seeking a very large loan, pleading

> that we have had ourselves to borrow a considerable sum, due to the great costs stemming from the recent peasant rebellion and other menacing developments of recent years, and especially for our extensive public works [i.e., fortifications]. For a month or more we've been trying to raise money. And without consulting and getting permission for our assembly of the Schöffen and Ammeister, we cannot lend more than 200 fl.[37]

This was not strictly true, for later the regime did lend Philip much more than 200 fl. without consulting the 300 Schöffen of the guilds; but the legal requirement of consultation did serve as a useful excuse to friendly borrowers.

The man through whom the landgrave paid the interest on this first Strasbourg loan was to be his standing connection to Strasbourg's money market, Conrad Joham (d. 1551).[38] Joham, son of a wealthy immigrant from Saverne, was a merchant in silk and metals with agents in the leading trade centers of Europe and one of Strasbourg's richest men. Not only had he regular business ties to Frankfurt am Main, a natural resort of the Hessian princes for loans, but one of his daughters married a son of Claus Stallburger, called "the Rich", a big man in that city.[39] In February, 1534, when Philip of Hesse was assured an enormous loan-plus-subsidy from France and the

---

[36] This and all subsequent Hessian loans at Strasbourg were secured by assignments (here *Verschreibung*) of the interest to princely revenues. On this practice see H. Bitsch, *Die Verpfändungen der Landgrafen von Hessen während des späten Mittelalters.* Göttingen/Frankfurt/Zürich 1974. (Göttinger Bausteine zur Geschichtswissenschaft 47), pp. 110–115. On this loan, see HStAM, K 28, fols. 263ʳ–263ᵛ; HStAM, PA 2915, fols. 44, 50ʳ–51ᵛ; PCSS I, nos. 714, 716, 732, 735.

[37] HStAM, PA 2915. fols. 44ʳ (15.IV. 1530): *das wir durch mergklichen vnd grossen vncosten, so vns vergangner bewrischer vfrur vnd anderer geschwinden leuff halb, die sich nun ettliche jor har gehalten vfgangen ist, vnnd jnn sonderheit der mergklichen vnnd schweren vnser statt gebew, so wir hieuor gethon vnd yetzt vorhaben, dohyn verursacht vnnd gedrungen werden, ein namliche summa gelts vfzenemen. Wie wir dann nun mehr ein monat lang jn vbung gestanden vnnd noch sein. Nun haben wir aber on sonder vorwissen vnd verwilligung vnsers grossen Raths Scheffel vnd Amman vber zweyhundert gulden hynweg zulyhen nit macht.*

[38] HStAM, K 28, fols. 263ʳ–263ᵛ. On Joham, see Brady, *Ruling Class* (as note 14), pp. 322–323, and the index of personal names.

[39] A. Dietz, *Frankfurter Handelsgeschichte. 4 vols. in 5.* Frankfurt/Main 1910–1925, vol. I, p. 250.

neutrality of his fellow princes, he turned to the problem of financing the recruitment of infantry (*Laufgeld, zum Anlauf*) in the South.[40] He borrowed 21,000 fl. from Conrad Joham, who "is to pay out these 21,000 fl. to my gracious lord or to his agents at Strasbourg . . .; and these 21,000 fl. shall be used for the recruitment of troops at Strasbourg".[41] Joham was to receive "for his effort, expenses, and service, and for exchange [*uff wechsel*]" more than 800 fl. at the next autumn fair at Frankfurt.[42] Joham in fact paid out 20,000 fl. to a Hessian agent, Michael Nusspicker, in two equal payments in March, 1534, and the other 1,000 fl. to one of Philip's mercenary captains, Marx von Eberstein.[43] Nusspicker disbursed most of the 20,000 fl. to other mercenary officers during the April mobilization in Lower Alsace and transferred the unspent balance (2,008 fl.) to the Hessian treasurer (*Kammermeister*), Jost von Weiters.[44]

When the Hessian recruitment mission, led by Count Wilhelm von Fürstenberg (1491–1549), arrived at Strasbourg in early April, 1534, Joham's 21,000 fl. were not nearly enough to hire and equip the troops. With Fürstenberg came two Hessian officials, Eberhard

---

[40] See Redlich (as note 33), vol. I, pp. 44–45.

[41] HStASt, A 104/2, fol. 45^r, from the copy of the war accounts of Jost von Weiters, the Hessian *Kammermeister*, sent to Stuttgart to support the landgrave's request that Ulrich pay about half the war costs. The original accounts are in HStAM, PA 359, and others in PA 352–358, 360. Jost von Weiters (d. ca. 1562) entered the Hessian treasury service by 1527 and advanced to the office of *Kammermeister* after 14.VIII.1532; he still held this office in 1555, but Herman Ungefug succeeded to it in 1562. F. Gundlach, *Die hessischen Zentralbehörden von 1247 bis 1604*. Marburg/Lahn 1931–1932. (Veröffentlichungen der historischen Kommission für Hessen und Waldeck 16), vol. I, pp. 168–170, 182, 255–259, 264; vol. II, pp. 53, 56, 63.

[42] HStASt, A 104/2, fol. 45^r, has 840 fl.; HStAM, PA 359, fol. 54^r, has 811 fl. This is the transaction described by Winckelmann in PCSS II, p. 210 n. 2.

[43] Michael Nusspicker to Landgrave Philip, Strasbourg, 17.III.1534, in: HStAM, PA 2915, fol. 250^r; Jost von Weiters to Landgrave Philip, Frankfurt am Main, 26.III.1534, in: HStAM, PA 330, fol. 3^r; Landgrave Philip to Rudolf Schenck zu Schweinsberg, ca. 19.IV.1534, in: HStAM, PA 326, fol. 53^r. Michael Nusspicker (d. after 1572), was 1540–1549 Hessian Kanzleiregistrator, 1567 Obereinnehmer der Tranksteuer. Gundlach, *Zentralbehörden* (as note 41), I, pp. 157, 245–249; II, pp. 64, 125, 131, 147. Rudolf Schenck zu Schweinsberg (d. 15.XII.1551) studied 1505 at Erfurt; 1518 Hessian vassal; 1524 married Helene, daughter of Wilhelm von Dornberg; Protestant by 1527; 1536 Landvogt zu Eschwege; 4.IV.1537 Landvogt an der Werra; 1534ff. Statthalter zu Kassel. *Ibid.*, vol. I, pp. 188–190, 206–207; II, 61, 63, 72, 97; G. Frhr. Schenk zu Schweinsberg, *Rudolf Schenk zu Schweinsberg*. Allgemeine deutsche Biographie 31 (1890): pp. 65–66.

[44] Landgrave Philip to Count Wilhelm von Fürstenberg, *et al.*, Kassel, 11.VI.1534, in: HStAM, PA 326, fol. 34^r; Weiter's account in: HStASt, A 104/2, fol. C^v, where it is noted that Nusspicker turned over 2008 fl., 4 batzen, 10d.

von Bischofferode and Rudolf Schenck zu Schweinsberg, through whom the two princes announced their declaration of war—their first official note to Strasbourg's regime—and asked for a gift, or at least a loan of 30,000 fl.: "for that part which the Stettmeister and Senate don't wish to give to us, we will both give them sufficient security. . . ."[45] In fact, before the Hessians presented their credentials, they secured an advance of 4,000 fl. from the regime, and Philip soon wrote for at least 6,000 fl. more, bringing his total indebtedness to Strasbourg's regime to 20,000 fl.[46] Strasbourg's rulers balked, just as they had in 1530, and the privy council of the XIII told

> us that they stood willing to aid Your Grace, but that they hadn't the authority and had sent the request to the Senate and to the Schöffen, but that this would mean spreading the news about. . . .[47]

The XIII in fact informed only the Senate and not the Schöffen, which, according to what they had told Philip in 1530, was illegal.[48] Nusspicker received 10,000 fl., which were "spent on the southern troops for the first half-month and for the march".[49] On the same day, April 23, the regime also decided to remit the first year's interest, though it was noted that King Ferdinand would recognize this as a politically hostile act.[50] The regime of Strasbourg thus committed itself to support the restoration in Württemberg.

---

[45] HStAM, PA 2915, fols. 268[r]-268[v], printed in: PCSS II, p. 210, no. 221: *was sie* [Stettmeister and Senate of Strasbourg] *nun uns daran nit zu hilf kommen wolten, darvor wolten wir beide inen nach notdurft verschreibung thun, das wir inen solchs widerumb gutlich und gnediglichen wollen entrichten.* In this instruction, the words *darvor wolten wir beide jnen nach notdurft verschreibung thun* replace the original *daruor sol jnen herzog Vlrich nach notdurft verschreibung thun.* HStAM, PA 2915, fol. 268[r]. Eberhard von Bischofferode, Sr., was in 1536 Oberamtmann zu Darmstadt. Gundlach, *Zentralbehörden* (as note 41), II, p. 61. Credentials for him and the other envoys from the two princes, dated Kassel, 16.IV.1534, in: AMS VII 11/2 no. 1, and AMS VII 11/3 no. 1.

[46] AMS VII 11/3, nos. 2–3; HStAM, PA 326, fols. 46[r], 50[r], 52[r], 53[r].

[47] Rudolf Schenck zu Schweinsberg to Landgrave Philip, Strasbourg, 17.IV.1534, in HStAM, PA 326, fol. 50[r]: *haben sie vns angezeigt das e. f. g. sie zu dem vnd mehernn zudienen willen, jn jrer macht stehe es aber nit, muss an einen gemeinen rath vnd scheffen gelangen, das dan ein weitleufig dingk sei. . . .*

[48] *Ibid.,* where Schenck appears confused.

[49] HStAM, PA 359, fol. 54[v] (Weiter's account); also in HStASt, A 104/2, fol. 45[v]: the sum of 1,333 fl., 5 batzen, *tregt der vffwechsel vff die X[m] an gold vff jeden fl. ii. batzen.* See also the copy of Rudolf Schenck zu Schweinsberg's accounts for the Strasbourg mission, in: HStASt, A 104/2a.

[50] Annales de Sébastian Brant, ed. L. Dacheux. In: *Bulletin de la Société pour la Conservation des Monuments historiques d'Alsace,* IIe série 15 (1892): pp. 211–279, and 19 (1899): pp. 33–260, here at no. 5048, dated 23.IV.1534: *Ist erkannt, ihnen solches anzuzeigen etc. doch so die in jahresfrist bezahlt würden den zins nachzulassen (welches König*

Mercenary troops, even when they had to fight no harder than Philip's troops did at Lauffen on the Neckar, where they scattered the Hapsburg deputy's forces on May 13, 1534, travelled on their purses. Eight days after the victory at Lauffen, Philip sent Hermann Schütz, his *Rentmeister* at Grünberg in Hesse, to Strasbourg for more money, this time for 20,000 fl.[51] Schütz was known at Strasbourg, having confiscated about 135 sheep belonging to three Strasbourg livestock merchants in 1530, because the exporters had no "passport to export sheep."[52] Once again to Schütz, the XIII replied

> that the XIII have no power to loan any of the city's money, but they must refer the requests to their lords and colleagues, the Senate & XXI; and the latter cannot lend such a sum without the permission of the Schöffen and Ammeister, who number 300 guildsmen and who are not sworn to secrecy.[53]

To Philip's offer of a new alliance among himself, Württemberg, and the southern Protestant free cities, also transmitted through Schütz, the XIII gave a cool reply, "that without peace or at least a truce, nothing fruitful could be secured in the Senate".[54] Sturm was much franker on May 22, when he pointed out to the landgrave the dire consequences of continuing the war.[55] While King Francis of France egged Philip on to an invasion of the Hapsburg hereditary lands,[56] the last thing the Strasbourgeois wanted was to lose the hard-won general peace through an escalation of the Württemberg campaign into a South German war.

Philip did get another loan in Strasbourg after the campaign. Sturm reported to him on June 17 that "I have exerted every possible energy to raise the money Your Princely Grace desires . . ., and

---

Ferdinand, wie auch anderes, . . . übel aufgenommen und empfunden). This is an extract from the protocols of the Senate & XXI.

[51] Instruction for Hermann Schütz, 21.V.1534, in: HStAM, PA 2915, fols. 270ʳ–271ᵛ, and AMS AA 411; printed in: PCSS II, p. 212, no. 228. See Wille, *Philipp der Grossmüthige* (as note 1), p. 189 n. 5. Hermann Schütz was in 1536 a *besteler diener von haus aus* and *rent*[meister] *zu Grunbergk*. Gundlach, *Zentralbehörden* (as note 41), II, p. 59.

[52] Stettmeister and Senate of Strasbourg to Statthalter and Councillors at Kassel, 15.VI.1530, in: HStAM, PA 2915, fol. 47. The livestock merchants, here called *metzger*, were Hans von Dürningen, Hans Hildt, and Hans von Frankfurt.

[53] HStAM, PA 2915, fols. 280ʳ–281ᵛ, printed in: PCSS II, p. 213, no. 229.

[54] PCSS II, p. 213, no. 229.

[55] Wille, *Briefe Jakob Sturms*, pp. 103–105.

[56] Wille, *Philipp der Grossmüthige* (as note 1), p. 265.

I have achieved success, though under conditions which you will learn" from an agent who would arrive in camp in a few days.[57] Conrad Joham wrote by the same post that "10,000 fl. are on hand, partly raised from my lords (i.e., the Senate & XXI) and partly from other sources".[58] These letters probably refer to two loans negotiated during the following week: 10,000 fl. from the civic regime at 6%, secured by revenues at Kassel and Marburg; and 5,000 fl. from the Great Hospital at 5%, secured at Homberg and Grünberg.[59] The membership of both Sturm and Joham in the regime's most powerful body, the XIII,[60] certainly smoothed the path of the loans, though Philip was charged 6% for the larger loan, which must have been the full market price for long-term money, the more usual rate being 5%.[61] The regime certainly made no financial sacrifice in granting these loans.

The Württemberg campaign of 1534 was the second most expensive of Landgrave Philip's five wars, costing nearly half a million florins, or more than the two Brunswick raids in 1542 and 1545 together and nearly four-fifths as much as the Smalkaldic War of 1546–1547.[62] Philip asked Ulrich to pay about half the bill, or 230,563 fl.,[63] in response to which Ulrich became predictably less grateful in Stuttgart than he had been in Kassel.[64] About 137,000 fl. were received in direct

[57] HStAM, PA 2915. fol. 289ʳ, cited in: PCSS II, p. 215, no. 232. The hand in which this letter is written, discussed by *Winckelmann* PCSS II, p. 215 n. 1, is not Sturm's; but the letter is surely from him. Sturm enclosed a sheet bearing news from Speyer (fols. 288ʳ–288ᵛ, dated 13.VI.1534) and the letter from Joham (fol. 290ʳ, dated 17.VI.1534; see n. 58 below); and the newsletter and the address for the whole packet are in the same secretarial hand. So also is Sturm's letter to the landgrave, Strasbourg, 22.V.1534, on fols. 277ʳ–278ʳ.
[58] [Conrad Joham] to Landgrave Philip, [Strasbourg], 17.VI.1534, in: HStAM, PA 2915, fol. 290ʳ, noticed in: PCSS II, p. 215 n. 1, where Winckelmann speculates that the writer may be Sturm. The letter is, in fact, in Conrad Joham's hand, though it is unsigned—perhaps for reasons of security.
[59] HStAM, K 28, fols. 43ʳ, 47ʳ, 82ᵛ–87ᵛ, dated 23.–25.VI.1534.
[60] Brady, *Ruling Class* (as note 14), p. 322; and pp. 165–166, on the privy council of the XIII.
[61] See the discussion of interest rates in: *ibid.*, pp. 153–154.
[62] G. Paetel, *Die Organisation des hessischen Heeres unter Philipp dem Grossmütigen*. Berlin 1897, pp. 156–157.
[63] HStASt, A 104/2, fols. 198ᵛ–199ᵛ. This is not much smaller than the sum reported by Leonhard von Eck to his masters: *Die summa gelts so Wirthemberg Hessen schuldig plybt, wurdt 300,000 laufen, ausserhalb des gelts, so der landgraf von E. f. g. dargelichen, die 50,000 kronen, so Hessen von Frankrych allererst uf nach dem vertrag emphangen, desgleichen uber das gelt, so vil fursten und stete dargestreckt haben.* Wille, *Philipp der Grossmüthige* (as note 1), p. 308.
[64] See his exchange with Philip printed in: *ibid.*, pp. 333–342; the letters are now

loans and gifts from other powers, including France, Bavaria, and Denmark,[65] but this sum may not include the public and private loans at Strasbourg.[66] At Strasbourg Philip borrowed for this campaign:

21,000 fl. from Conrad Joham, February, 1534
10,000 fl. from the civic regime, April, 1534
10,000 fl. from the civic regime, June 24, 1534
5,000 fl. from the Great Hospital, June 23, 1534,

for a total of 46,000 fl., or just under one tenth of the total war costs, and about one quarter of the war loans secured outside Hesse.[67]

IV. *Strasbourg and the Mobilization of Infantry for the Württemberg Campaign, April, 1534*

Als fünfzehnhundert dreissig vier
gezelet ward, in dem revier
bei Strassburg an der stat hinauf
versamlet sich vil volks zu hauf,
auch der landgrav auss Hessenland
mit gschütz, knecht, pferden, proviant.
Grav Wilhelm von Fürstenberg war
meister, hauptman ganzer schar,
zu fuss ir achtzehentausent gewesen,
viertausent reisige ausserlesen.[68]

Landgrave Philip raised 16–18,000 troops in 1534, an enormous force for a second-rate prince in a brief campaign; and they were mostly

---

in: HStAM, PA 3058 (besides the acts in PA 3057–3058, there are pieces of correspondence between the landgrave and his agents in Stuttgart in: HStAM, Samtarchiv, Schublade 54, no. 14).

[65] See Paetel, *Organisation* (as note 62), p. 106; and Keller, *Wiedereinsetzung* (as note 1), p. 49 and n. 16.

[66] Weiters notes 25,575 fl. *entnommen von den stetten*, which may comprise the last three sums in this list, but he nowhere identifies loans at Strasbourg. Secondary works (note 65 above), either refer vaguely to aid from Strasbourg or mention the sum of 20,000 fl. (from Winckelmann, in: PCSS II, p. 210 n. 2).

[67] Because Professor Oberman (*Werden und Wertung* (as note 2), p. 339, note 29) thanks me for the information that "die Strassburger Beteiligung an der Wiedereroberung Württembergs auf ein Viertel der Kriegskosten anzusetzen ist", I must here apologize for misleading him through erroneous preliminary calculations. The Strasbourg loans in fact amounted to about one-quarter of all loans raised outside of Hesse for the war, not a quarter of all the war costs.

[68] Liliencron (as note 3), vol. IV, p. 70, no. 447, ll. 1–10.

mercenaries, for the Hessian feudal levies could never have supplied such a force.[69] He naturally turned to the officer-businessmen whose business was war.[70] In the German military division of labor, mercenary cavalry came from the North and infantry from the South.[71] Already in September, 1533, he instructed his commander of foot to hire captains and send them through South Germany and especially to the Upper Rhine,[72] whose dense population and fragmented political structure made it an ideal recruiting ground.

Philip's commander of foot was Count Wilhelm von Fürstenberg, whose violent temperament, unbridled sexual appetites, and genius for acquiring enemies made him a fit counterpart to Duke Ulrich.[73] Fürstenberg was no friend of the exiled Württemberger, who had robbed him of an expected inheritance of Burgundian lordships;[74] but the count always served the best-paying master. Long in French service, it was he who brought Francis I and Philip of Hesse together at Bar-le-Duc in January, 1534, and served as their interpreter.[75] The infantry was to be mobilized at Geispolsheim, a Lower Alsatian village some fifteen kilometers southwest of Strasbourg. The chateau of Geispolsheim was an episcopal fief later, and possibly already at this time, belonging to none other than Conrad Joham, Philip's banker at Strasbourg;[76] while the village itself belonged to Strasbourg's Cathedral Chapter.[77]

---

[69] Paetel, *Organisation* (as note 62), chs. 1–2; H. Preuss, *Söldnerführer unter Landgraf Philipp dem Grossmütigen von Hessen* (1518–1567). Darmstadt/Marburg 1975. (Quellen und Forschungen zur hessischen Geschichte 30), p. 1.

[70] Redlich, *German Military Enterpriser* (as note 33), I, pp. 3, 30–31.

[71] E. v. Frauenholz, *Entwicklungsgeschichte des deutschen Heerwesens*. München 1937, II, 2, p. 29; R. Wohlfeil, "Adel und neues Heerwesen." In: *Deutscher Adel 1430–1555*. Ed. H. Rössler. Darmstadt 1965. (Schriften zur Problematik der deutschen Führungsschichten in der Neuzeit 1), pp. 203–233; here at p. 225.

[72] HStAM, PA 326, fol. 7, dated to before 29.IX.1533 by J. V. Wagner, *Graf Wilhelm von Fürstenberg 1491–1549 und die politisch-geistigen Mächte seiner Zeit*. Stuttgart 1966. (Pariser Historische Studien 4), p. 59 n. 121. How Landgrave Philip used the Münster crisis to mask his preparations is shown in: HStAM, PA 332, fols. 1ff.

[73] Wagner, *Wilhelm von Fürstenberg* (as note 72), p. 37.

[74] *Ibid.*, pp. 11–19. Fürstenberg married (22.X.1505) the daughter of the last lord of Neuchâtel, and he expected to divide the family's Burgundian territories (Blamont, Héricourt, Châtelot, Bourguignon, and Granges, *inter alias*) with the husband of the other daughter, Count Felix of Werdenberg.

[75] *Ibid.*, p. 57.

[76] Brady, *Ruling Class* (as note 14), p. 323.

[77] Fritz, *Territorien* (as note 15), pp. 94, 104, 111; F. Jaenger, "Geispolsheim, une exemple de village fortifié en Alsace." *Cahiers alsaciens d'art, d'archéologie et d'Histoire*, 1947, pp. 133–136.

Fürstenberg, Bischofferode, Schenck, and Count Philip of Solms left Hesse for Strasbourg on Palm Sunday (March 29), just as the twenty-eight captains were to begin mobilization.[78] Fürstenberg was a well-known character at Strasbourg, where, in the years after the revolution of 1525, his house in the Kalbsgasse had become a watering spot for young Swabian and Rhenish noblemen, to the sounds of whose revels the streets rang at night.[79] Fürstenberg had there become a Protestant converted by Caspar Hedio (1494–1552), but Jacob Sturm still mistrusted him as an opportunist.[80] The Hessian mission arrived on March 30 and went first to the Ortenburg, a great fortress on the right bank near Offenburg, visible from the roofs of Strasbourg. Returning to the city, Bischofferode, Schenck, Michael Nusspicker, and the count of Solms lodged from April 3 to 19 in the house of Antonj Tuchscher,[81] while Fürstenberg lived either at the Ortenburg, one of whose tenants he was, or in the Kalbsgasse. He took no part in the Hessians' negotiations with the civic regime. That Strasbourg's regime tolerated the assembly of an enormous army so near its walls is more convincing evidence than its loans to Philip that Strasbourg was backing the Württemberg campaign. Solms, Bischofferode, and Schenck openly recruited in the house of an official in the Wantzenau, an episcopal district north of the city, apparently under the protection of the civic regime.[82] For the Hessian recruiting was quite illegal. Although the emperor had forbidden any recruiting against his brother,[83] Strasbourg's regime allowed the Hessians to recruit among the local artillery-men,[84] and it sold them

---

[78] Rudolf Schenck zu Schweinsberg gives the itinerary in his accounts, now in HStASt, A 104/2a. See Wagner, *Wilhelm von Fürstenberg* (as note 72), p. 60, for the names of some of the captains; and HStAM, PA 355, fols. 11–12, for a fuller list, including two Fleckensteins, an Eschau, a Schauenburg, an Andlau, a Landschad von Steinach, and a Reinach.

[79] Wagner, *Wilhelm von Fürstenberg* (as note 72), p. 37 n. 215; A. Seyboth, *Das alte Strassburg vom 13. Jahrhundert bis zum Jahre 1870, geschichtliche Topographie nach den Urkunden und Chroniken.* Strasbourg 1890, p. 236 (not p. 650, as Wagner, p. 37 n. 215).

[80] PCSS II, pp. 257–258, no. 280; also quoted by Wagner, *Wilhelm von Fürstenberg* (as note 72), pp. 79–80. And see PCSS II, pp. 526–527, no. 551.

[81] Schenck's accounts in HStASt, A 104/2a, according to which they paid 15 fl., 5 batzen, 1 kreutzer, for one week's lodging; there, too, the notice of the brief trip to Ortenburg, on which see Wagner, *Wilhelm von Fürstenberg* (as note 72), p. 37.

[82] HStASt, A 104/2a; Fritz, *Territorien* (as note 15), pp. 100–101.

[83] The printed mandate is dated Toledo, 20.II.1534, of which a copy in HStAM, PA 328, fol. 2. See Keller, *Wiedereinsetzung* (as note 1), pp. 48–49.

[84] Rudolf Schenck zu Schweinsberg to Landgrave Philip, Strasbourg, 15.IV.1534, in HStAM, PA 326, fols. 42r–43v.

about 2,000 pikes for the infantry.[85] Passes were also issued to mercenaries who hurried westward over the Rhine bridge to the muster place at Geispolsheim.[86]

Fürstenberg and his captains mustered about 9,000 troops at Geispolsheim.[87] Many were certainly Alsatians, as were some of the captains, and some were surely residents and even citizens of Strasbourg.[88] No muster lists have survived, but it is known that Strasbourgeois frequently hired out as mercenaries, for lists of citizens, sons of citizens, and servants, who signed up 1546–47 contain 148 names.[89] Nobles of the town frequently became professional soldiers, and some had earlier served under Fürstenberg.[90] Recruiting was a very closely policed activity at Strasbourg,[91] and one member of the privy council of the XV, Sifridt II von Bietenheim (d. ca. 1551), even lost his offices in 1543 for aiding illegal recruiting.[92] The regime simply looked the other way in 1534, while Fürstenberg, the captains, and the Hessians recruited and mustered this great army near the city and began, on April 27, to march it northeastward toward the Rhine and the rendezvous with the landgrave. By May 4 they met him near Pfungstadt, just south of Darmstadt, and the combined armies headed for the Neckar. On May 12–13, they routed the forces of the Hapsburg deputy near Lauffen, and on the 15th they entered Stuttgart. Fürstenberg's infantry had barely seen action, but the war was over.[92a]

---

[85] Instruction for Eberhard von Bischofferode, 5.IV.1534, in: HStAM, PA 326, fol. 40^v. Strasbourg sold the Hessian officials 2,000 *lange Spiesse* at 9 albus per pike, or 318 fl. for the lot. Paetel, *Organisation des hessischen Heeres* (as note 62), p. 157. Weiter's account in: HStASt, A 104/2, fol. d^r, give the cost as 15 fl. per 100 pikes.

[86] Annales de S. Brant no. 4048, dated 25.IV.1534.

[87] Preuss, *Söldnerführer* (as note 69), pp. 359–360; Wagner, *Wilhelm von Fürstenberg* (as note 72), p. 63 n. 149.

[88] For example, Hans Kratzer and Engelhard von Spaichingen, both residents of Strasbourg. Preuss, *Söldnerführer* (as note 69) pp. 16, 51, 57.

[89] AMS IV, 86/22.

[90] Brady, *Ruling Class* (as note 14), p. 139 n. 75; QBLG II, p. 142.

[91] See, for example, AMS XXI 1539, fols. 5^r–6^r, of 11.I.1539. The *Statutenrepertorium* in AMS, an eighteenth-century index to series R (Réglements, formerly MO = Mandate und Ordnungen), has no less than forty-three entries for prohibitions of foreign military service issued by the regime of Strasbourg in the century between 1458 and 1557. See O. Stolz, "Zum Verbot des Kriegsdienstes für fremde Mächte in Deutschland im sechzehnten Jahrhundert." *Elsass-Lothringisches Jahrbuch* 21 (1943): pp. 187–213.

[92] Brady, *Ruling Class* (as note 14), p. 301.

[92a] The other large Evangelical cities of South Germany did not share Strasburg's enthusiasm for this campaign. Augsburg, probably because it feared the political consequences of an invasion of Württemberg, refused to release Sebastian Schertlin

V. *Strasbourg Propaganda for the Württemberg Campaign*

... Nun lob got in seinem reich,
dass es dazu ist komen,
das Wirtemperg ist iez geleich
dem pfawengschrai entrunnen,
hat nun gewert fünfzehen jar; ...[93]

News of the course of the campaign in the Neckar valley came to
Strasbourg's regime both through the landgrave and through its own
agent in the princes' camp.[94] Fürstenberg's mobilization could hardly
have been kept secret from the citizens, though not everyone knew
the purpose, and the rumor ran through Strasbourg that the princes
aimed at a general rebellion, just like 1525![95] In the anxious days
before Lauffen, Count George of Württemberg considered taking
refuge in Strasbourg, just as he had in 1519.[96] Although the direct
consequences of the victory to the lands on the Upper Rhine were
not great, still the event was noticed and recorded by some of the
region's chroniclers.[97] One figure, a Strasbourg lawyer, lent direct
aid to the propaganda effort to justify the campaign.

von Burtenbach into Hessian service, although Landgrave Phillip wanted Schertlin
to raise four companies of infantry for this campaign. Redlich, *German Military
Enterpriser* (as note 33), I, pp. 80–81. At Frankfurt am Main, on the other hand, the
Evangelical regime feared not Ulrich but Philip, whose demand for the local establishment of the monastery of Haina the Frankfurters resisted. In 1534 Philip urged
Frankfurt to allow his army to use the city's Main bridge, the easiest way to bring
his troops to the staging area in Upper Katzenelnbogen. When Frankfurt's regime
refused, Philip had to move westward and cross the Main on a boat-bridge near
Griesheim, which cost him much time. Relations were so bad between Frankfurt
and Philip that there was rumor that he would seize the city and crown himself
emperor. When, after the Württemberg campaign, Philip's artillery came northward
through Frankfurt, the city bristled with weapons against a surprise attack. S. Jahns,
*Frankfurt, Reformation und Schmalkadischer Bund. Die Reformations-, Reichs- und Bündnispolitik
der Reichsstadt Frankfurt am Main 1525–1536.* Frankfurt a. M. 1976. (Studien zur
Frankfurter Geschichte 9), pp. 109–113, 280–283.
   [93] Liliencron (as note 3), vol. IV, p. 95, no. 454, stanza 25.
   [94] PCSS II, p. 211, no. 266, and p. 211 n. 3.
   [95] Annales de S. Brant. no. 5049, dated 27.IV.1534: *Martin Hug soll sagen, dass
H. Landgraf und Herzog Ulrich sich sollen haben vernehmen lassen, so ihnen die Schanz nicht
geräth, wollen sie etwas anderes im sinn haben, und soll ein fähnlein, daran ein stiefel oder bundschuh stehe: habe ihm jemand gesagt, der das fähnlein gesehen.*
   [96] *Ibid.* no. 5052, dated 6.V.1534: *H. Ulrich von Wirtemberg und Landgraf von Hessen
begehren ist dieser gefährlichen läufe halb, Graf Jörg von Wirtemberg begehren würde eine zeit
lang hie zu seyn; ihm darzu gönnen, und zoll und bürgerl. beschwerde frei zu lassen. Erk.: Lassen
ruhen, so er kommt und begehrt, soll mans hie hören.*
   [97] Badische Landesbibliothek Karlsruhe, Hs. St. Blasian 12, fol. 160ᵛ: *Anno 1534
ist hertzog vlrich von wirttenberg wider in kummen in das wirdenberger landt, so nun hyne furder
von huss osterich zu affter lehen entpfohen.* This is a continuation of the Königshoven

Franz Frosch (1490–25.IV.1540),[98] city advocate of Strasbourg from 1533 until 1540, was a native Nuremberger, educated at Ingolstadt, in Italy, and at Freiburg im Breisgau under Ulrich Zasius. He worked as a procurator (1522–1525) and later assessor (1530–1532) of the *Reichskammergericht* and as chancellor of the bishop of Würzburg (1525–1530). During the 1530s, he frequently wrote legal opinions for members of the Smalkaldic League, usually on issues connected with the *ius reformandi*.

Frosch was known to Landgrave Philip through the advocate's petition to the prince on May 22, 1534, nine days after the battle of Lauffen, in which Frosch begged Philip to protect the properties of his brother-in-law at Pfullingen in Württemberg.[99] Frosch had married Felicitas, sister to Peter Scher von Schwarzenberg (d. 29.IX.1557), a long-time official of King Ferdinand.[100] Scher had fled before the invading army, and Frosch wanted Philip to intercede for him with Ulrich.

Some weeks later, the landgrave sent Jacob Sturm a set of four questions about the legality of the reconquest, requesting that Sturm either answer them or give them to the local lawyers and secure their opinions. Since this request came nearly five weeks after the princes' entry into Stuttgart, Philip probably wanted to use the replies either for propaganda or in the peace negotiations then underway. On June 29 Sturm replied that

> because I myself understand too little about the subject, being inexperienced and uneducated in the law, and because very few of our lawyers here know anything about the affair, I referred your articles to Doctor Frosch,

who would be known to the landgrave through the recent petition. Sturm enclosed Frosch's replies and recommended him as a reliable and useful man.[101] The landgrave had asked:

---

chronicle. In the Jahresgeschichten von Ober-Achern von 1471 bis 1601, printed by Mone in: QBLG III, p. 657: *In dissem jar ist auch hertzog Ulrich von Wirtemberg von dem landgrafen uss Hessen wiederumb ingesetzt worden.* These are both Upper Rhenish sources.

[98] J. Ficker and O. Winckelmann, *Handschriftenproben des sechzehnten Jahrhunderts nach Strassburger Originalen.* 2 parts; Strasbourg 1902–1905, I, p. 13, H. Winterberg, *Die Schüler von Ulrich Zasius.* VKLBW, B 18. Stuttgart 1961, pp. 38–39.

[99] Franz Frosch to Landgrave Philip, Strasbourg, 22.V.1534, in: HStAM, PA 2915, fols. 285ʳ–286ᵛ.

[100] J. Bernays, *Zur Biographie Johann Winthers von Andernach.* In: ZGO 55 (1901): pp. 28–58, here at pp. 35–38.

[101] [Jacob Sturm] to Landgrave Philip, [Strasbourg], 29.VI.1534, in: HStAM, PA 2915, fols. 310ʳ–310ᵛ, printed in: PCSS II, p. 215, no. 233.

1. Was the Swabian League justified in expelling Ulrich from his duchy in 1519?
2. Was the League's expulsion of Ulrich a breach of the land-peace?
3. Do the common law and the landpeace justify Ulrich's recovery of his land through force?
4. Is the recovery to be regarded as occurring *in continenti*, Ulrich having retained *civilis possessio* of Württemberg in exile?

Frosch replied "no" to the first two questions, "yes" to the third and "probably not" to the fourth.[102] The crucial point was Frosch's opinion that the princes, in seizing Württemberg from its Hapsburg regime, were vindicating Ulrich's legal rights.

Frosch's opinion was destined for the archives. On the day of Sturm's letter, King Ferdinand and the elector of Saxony, who was acting for the two princes, concluded the Treaty of Kaaden, which confirmed Ulrich in Württemberg, albeit as an Austrian vassal, and conceded him the *ius reformandi*.[103] This peace, far from ending Strasbourg's involvement in the restoration in Württemberg, marked only the start of a new stage of entanglement, because, as no informed spectator doubted, reformation would follow restoration.

VI. *The Strasbourgeois and the Reformation in Württemberg*

Nach Christus wort und seiner ler,
so samlest du ein grosses heer;
den wolf treib aus dem lande,
der deine scheflein hat verfürt,
verjagt, erbissen und ermordt;
reich ihn dein gnedig hande![104]

---

[102] I give them here in Winckelmann's paraphrase from PCSS II, pp. 215–216, Beilage to no. 233. The articles (fol. 295ʳ) and Frosch's replies (fols. 297ʳ–308ʳ) are in HStAM, PA 2915; and I intend to publish an edited version of them.
[103] On the treaty, see Wille, *Philipp der Grossmüthige* (as note 1), pp. 222–224, and on the *ius reformandi*, *ibid.*, pp. 246–247. Fundamental on the treaty of Kaaden and its implications for the reformation in Württemberg is the penetrating study by W. Bofinger, *Kirche und werdender Territorialstaat*. In: Blätter für württembergische Kirchengeschichte 65 (1956): pp. 75–149, here at pp. 101–120. Oberman is correct that the treaty's importance for the Württemberg reform has been "überschatzt" in the literature. *Werden und Wertung* (as note 2), p. 340.
[104] Liliencron (as note 3), vol. IV, p. 91, no. 452, stanza 18.

Through Ulrich's recovery of Württemberg with aid of the cities, especially Strasbourg, writes H. A. Oberman, "the years 1534–1536 became years of decision, because there it became evident for the first time, that two fundamental types of reformed ecclesiastical systems had developed, which would now test each other".[105] One type, represented in Württemberg by Ambrosius Blarer of Constance, was "a political theology guided chiefly by Strasbourg, which was better suited to a liberation struggle than to the consolidation of the reconquered duchy".[106] The other was a reformation "from above", the territorial church typical of Lutheran Germany, represented in newly conquered Württemberg by the Hessian military chaplain, Erhard Schnepf. Here, in the forceful introduction of the new religion into the duchy's churches and into its university at Tübingen, the only recently quieted clerical violence between the two antagonistic forms of Evangelical religion flared up once more.[107] This struggle, coming on the heels of the unexpected victory in May, brought the Strasbourgeois more trouble than they had bargained for.

Jacob Sturm certainly did not look on Württemberg as a prize to be reformed *à la* Strasbourg for the greater glory of South German Zwinglianism. Had he not, after all, duped Zwingli in 1530 and thereafter disassociated Strasbourg from Swiss Protestantism?[108] The last thing Sturm wanted was a new breach in the intra-Evangelical concord for which he had worked so long and so hard, and it was for this reason—and not because he feared that Strasbourg would lose dominant influence on the ecclesiastical reform in Württemberg—that he so strongly objected to the Treaty of Kaaden's prohibition against "sacramentarians" in Württemberg. Sturm's complaint is lost, but we have the landgrave's soothing reply:

---

[105] Oberman, *Werden und Wertung* (as note 2), p. 352.

[106] *Ibid.* To this must be said that, whatever the residual loyalty of Bucer and other Strasbourg preachers to the political principles of the Zwinglian reform, Strasbourg's regime, guided by Sturm, had chosen to associate itself with the Lutheran princes. Sturm, as I shall show in a study of his career in progress, was no friend of the "political theology" of which Oberman writes.

[107] In general, on the Württemberg reformation, see J. Rauscher, *Württembergische Reformationsgeschichte. Württembergische Kirchengeschichte* 3. Stuttgart 1934; H. Hermelink, *Geschichte der evangelischen Kirche in Württemberg von der Reformation bis zur Gegenwart. Das Reich Gottes in Wirtemberg.* Stuttgart/Tübingen 1949. Chs. 1–3; and now Oberman, *Werden und Wertung* (as note 2), ch. 13.

[108] Brady, "Jacob Sturm and the Lutherans" (as note 24), pp. 193–196.

> We also noticed in your last letter, that you are quite dissatisfied with the word "sacramentarian" in the treaty, because of the suspicion, that it might work to Strasbourg's disadvantage.[109]

"Sacramentarian" was the old Lutheran battle cry against the Swiss heresy, and Sturm feared that its revival would be of use to the king and the Catholic princes, who might seek to divide .the Protestant powers, and, he hinted, to those Lutherans who simply waited for a new excuse to take up the anti-Zwinglian vendetta once more.

> We have, however, to be concerned that the king and the mediators mean us with this word—please God, no one else will say the same— and seize the opportunity to drag us in under this name, whether we wish it or no.[110]

Sturm was thus concerned with Strasbourg's solid relations with the Lutheran powers in the Smalkaldic League, not for the opportunity to bring Württemberg within Strasbourg's ecclesiastical influence.

Sturm wrote of these dangers from Stuttgart, where he was deeply involved in the restoration. Whether or not he was truly Ulrich's "confidant",[111] Sturm did advise Ulrich on the treaty of Kaaden, which, despite his misgivings, he urged the duke to accept.[112] He also reported to the landgrave in great detail on the clerical quarrels he had experienced in Stuttgart, in which, by Sturm's account, the Lutheran Schnepf was entirely the aggressor.[113] Sturm, who was

---

[109] Landgrave Philip to Jacob Sturm, [end of July, 1534?]: *Als wir auch aus euerm nehern schreiben vermerken, das ir des worts "sacramentirer", so im vertrag verleipt, nit wol zufrieden seit, im zweifel, das es der stadt Straspurg ... zu nachteil reichen mocht.* PCSS II, p. 218, no. 236; also by Wille, "Briefe Jacob Sturms" (as note 1), p. 106.

[110] Jacob Sturm to Landgrave Philip, Stuttgart, 31.VII.1534; *wir müssen aber sorgen, das uns der konig und die unterhandler—gott woll nit jemants mehrer—mit disem wort wollen gemeint haben, und so si iren vorteil ersehen, wir wollen oder nit, und under disem namen uber-zucken. Ibid.*, p. 219, no. 237; also by Wille, "Briefe Jacob Sturms" (as note 1), p. 108.

[111] Oberman, *Werden und Wertung* (as note 2), p. 343 n. 35.

[112] Jacob Sturm to Landgrave Philip, Stuttgart, 31.VII.1534: *so hab ich ... doch daneben nit underlassen, s.g. allerlei geferlichkeiten anzuzeigen, wo s.g. den vertrag nit ratificieren solte, ...* PCSS II, p. 219, no. 237.

[113] Jacob Sturm to Landgrave Philip, Strasbourg, 26.VIII.1534: *so bedunkt mich, das M. Erhart Schnepf lasz sich auch also vernemen, als ober er die unsern fur schwermer halte, wil sich nit begnügen lassen an den worten der Sachsischen confession, die er doch selbst stellen helfen, us welchem dan die ergernüs der zweispaltung noch meher gimirkt musz werden; und nemens die papisten also ane als ein declaracion, wer die sacramentirer seien, die im frieden usgeschlossen seind.* PCSS II, p. 221, no. 239. Compare Martin Bucer to Landgrave Philip, [Strasbourg], [ca. 24.VIII.1534], in: M. Lenz (ed.), *Briefwechsel Landgraf Philipp des Grossmüthigen von Hessen mit Bucer*, 3 vols. (Publikationen aus den K. Preussischen

easily exasperated by the *rabies theologorum*,[114] told the Hessian prince that the Lutheran attacks on southern preachers were poor thanks indeed for the cities' support for the reconquest:

> it has happened through the grace of God that peace has reigned for quite a while among in the southern cities. Now we hoped that, should My Gracious Lord, Duke Ulrich, get his land back, this would further promote peace, quiet, and unity, and things should get even better. Perhaps God wills it otherwise, so that the victories and good luck don't make us haughty.[115]

Sturm recommended to Ulrich that he enforce the Confession of Augsburg as the binding norm of preaching;[116] and he asked the landgrave

> whether Your Princely Grace might find any kind of way to prevent this business; but that in any case Your Princely Grace should deal with the matter in such a way, that no one notices that the solution stems from me or from my lords or from the city of Strasbourg—for various reasons. Your Princely Grace might announce—because Your Princely Grace and the elector and other princes have accepted us into the league as being in doctrinal agreement—that so long as preaching is according to the Saxon confession, no one should be pressed beyond the words of Scripture into other words.[117]

Sturm was again thinking not of the fate of the Württemberg Reformation, but of Strasbourg's solidarity with the Smalkaldic League.

With Schnepf and his friends growling from the pulpits, Sturm's visits to Stuttgart after the conquest cannot have been very pleasant.

Staatsarchiven 5, 28, 42). Leipzig 1880–1891, I, pp. 42–43, written on the evening of Sturm's return from Stuttgart.

[114] See my "Jacob Sturm and the Lutherans" (as note 24), p. 186.

[115] Jacob Sturm to Landgrave Philip, Strasbourg, 26.VIII.1534: *solchs hat dennochten durch die gnad gottes sovil gewirkt, das bei den oberlendischen stetten itzt ein zeitlang guter fried geweszen. nun hetten wir gehofft, so min g. herr, herzog Ulrich, wider in sein land komen were, es solt zu weiter friden, rugen und enigkeit gedient haben und forthin je besser worden sein. so will es unser hergot villeicht darumb, das wir uns der victorien und glucks nit zu vil uberheben, mins bedunkens anders fugen.* PCSS II, p. 221, no. 239.

[116] *Ibid.*, p. 221.

[117] *Ibid.*, p. 222: *deshalben hab ich gedacht, ob irgen e. f. g. wege finden mocht zü verhütung desselben; doch das in alle wege e. f. g. die sachen also handelten, damit es niemant vermerken mocht, das es von mir herkeme oder auch von mein hern oder stat Straspurg, aus allerlei ursachen. es mocht e. f. g. anzeigen, dweil e. f. g. sampt andern chur. und fursten uns in die vereinigung als mithellige im glauben angenomen und das man billich gesettigt were, wan man leret, wie [die] Sachsisch confession ustrucket, das man dan nieman uber die wort, so die schrift in sich hielt, ferner zu meher worten tringen solte.*

Landgrave Philip wanted him to stay and accept a post at court, perhaps as Ulrich's *Hofmeister*;[118] but Sturm did not respond to this suggestion, although he was distantly connected with the most powerful figure at Ulrich's court.[119] Most of Sturm's later personal contacts with Ulrich involved the duke's feuds with other Evangelical powers or some other unpleasantry.

Württemberg itself, as a land about to undergo reform, meant more to Strasbourg's preachers than it did to Sturm. The leading churchman at Strasbourg, Martin Bucer, had been one of the many whose hearts went faint at the thought of the daring, even rash, strike Landgrave Philip had planned.[120] When the news of the victory at Lauffen came across the Rhine, however, Bucer was full of plans; and he and his colleagues immediately recommended Ambrosius Blarer and Symon Grynaeus of Basel to aid in reforming the church of Württemberg and the university at Tübingen.[121] It may well be true that Ulrich's own views accorded better with the southern form of the new religion than with its Lutheran one,[122] but this does not explain why he allowed the Lutheran preachers from Hesse to swarm into Württemberg and to take up the old battle against the "sacramentarians" again. Clear it is that the duke intended to take the Lutheran path to reform. It could not have been otherwise, for Ulrich was astute enough to sense that the cause of South German Zwinglianism was dying; and thus Ambrosius Blarer's "strategy of the Reformation through parish reform"[123] had no chance in Württemberg. To whatever degree the rejection of their nominee, Blarer,

[118] Landgrave Philip to Jacob Sturm, Kassel, 13.VII.1534, in PCSS II, p. 216, no. 234, with which he forwards a text of the treaty of Kaaden.
[119] This was Hans Konrad Thumb von Neuburg, Württemberg *Marschall und Hofrat*, and son of Konrad Thumb von Neuburg und Margarethe von Adelsheim. W. Bernhardt, *Die Zentralbehörden des Herzogtums Württemberg und ihre Beamten 1520–1629*. VKLBW, B 70–71. Stuttgart 1973, II, p. 675. Jacob Sturm's maternal grandmother, Ottilia von Köllen (née Schott), (d. ca. 1519), remarried Zeisolf von Adelsheim (d. 30.XII.1503). The Adelsheim came from the Baden-Palatine border lands and came into Lower Alsace in Palatine service. Brady, *Ruling Class* (as note 14), p. 80.
[120] Lenz, *Briefwechsel* (as note 113), p. 37 n. 2.
[121] Strasbourg preachers to Landgrave Philip and Duke Ulrich, Strasbourg, 18.V.1534, in: *ibid.*, pp. 36–37, no. 10.
[122] This is Oberman's view (*Werden und Wertung* [as note 2], p. 342), who, however, keys the agreement to its anti-Hapsburg component. Once back in his lands, on the other hand, Ulrich showed no inclination to entertain pan-European delusions à la Zwingli or to take any initiative in Protestant causes in Germany.
[123] The phrase is Oberman's (*Werden und Wertung* [as note 2], p. 352).

may have injured the Strasbourg preachers' pride, they themselves had already gone so far down the path toward total submission to the Lutherans, that the victory of Lutheranism in Württemberg could not be regarded as an act hostile to the interests of Strasbourg.

The university was another story, for here "everything suggests that in South Germany an academic alternative to Wittenberg and Marburg was planned".[124] Just when the Hessian recruiting and mobilization mission came to Strasbourg, Bucer was fighting unsuccessfully for the establishment of a full university at Strasbourg.[125] Three of the four universities most favored by the Strasbourgeois before the Reformation—Heidelberg, Cologne, and Freiburg im Breisgau—were still in Catholic hands, while the fourth—Basel—was hardly suitable for Strasbourg's *theological* students.[126] Hence, for Bucer and for like-minded men, the reform of the University of Tübingen took on direct significance for training their own successors; and, to their great good luck, Ulrich allowed Blarer and Grynaeus to begin the purge of the university faculty and the reform of its curriculum.[127] This effort failed, it is true, and these urban clergymen did not reshape the university to their own purposes.

Later, when the gouty old sinner in Stuttgart was dead (d. 1550), the Strasbourgeois developed much better relations with his son and successor, Duke Christoph (1515–68). Württemberg and Strasbourg theologians cooperated in the Evangelical embassy to the second session of the Council of Trent in 1551;[128] and, as the power of

---

[124] *Ibid.*, p. 344.

[125] This is connected with the Buffler foundation, which is discussed in detail by E.-W. Kohls, *Die Schule bei Martin Bucer in ihrem Verhältnis zu Kirche und Obrigkeit.* Heidelberg 1963. (Pädagogische Forschungen 22), pp. 77–82.

[126] F. Rapp, "Les Strasbourgeois et les Universités rhénanes à la fin du Moyen Age et jusqu'à la Réforme." *Annuaire de la Société des Amis de Vieux-Strasbourg* 4 (1974): pp. 11–22. Compare these figures with post-Reformation university choices, calculated by J. Ficker, *Die Anfänge der akademischen Studien in Strassburg*. In: Das Stiftungsfest der Kaiser-Wilhelm-Universität Strassburg am 1. Mai 1912. Strasbourg 1912, pp. 25–74, here at p. 58, where the popularity of Wittenberg und Tübingen after 1530 is visible. In fact, though the Tübingen figure is given for the years 1531–1567, most of this attendance is likely to have occurred after 1550.

[127] On the reform of the university, see Oberman, *Werden und Wertung* (as note 2), pp. 342–344, 357–365, 431; important new sources bearing on the involvement of Strasbourg, by B. Moeller, "Neue Nachträge zum Blarer-Briefwechsel. Zur Reformation der Universität Tübingen 1534–1535," *Blätter für Württembergische Kirchengeschichte* 68/69 (1968/69) pp. 60–80; and the dissertation of R. L. Harrison, Jr., *The Reformation of the Theological Faculty of the University of Tübingen, 1534–1555.* Vanderbilt University 1975.

[128] See PCSS V, *passim*; and V. Ernst (ed.), *Briefwechsel des Herzogs Christoph von*

orthodox Lutheranism waxed in both states after mid-century, cultural relations became closer than ever before, and Tübingen became for the first time the university of choice for the Strasbourgeois.[129]

VII. *Conclusion*

By affording to Philip of Hesse access to money and to men, the regime of Strasbourg aided the restoration in Württemberg more than did any other southern free city. It and the other cities also restrained, as the landgrave later complained, the princes from escalating the campaign into a general anti-Hapsburg crusade. "I wish", he wrote to Ulrich on August 24, 1534,

> that Jacob Sturm and the cities had given the needed money and had argued as strongly *for* an attack on the king as they in fact argued *against* it—then would have been the right time. But they gave Your Grace nothing free.[130]

But the urban politicians, including Sturm, only wanted peace and security.

Sturm and the other southern urban politicians got no comfort from the restoration and reformation in Württemberg in the short run. There was, first of all, Ulrich's old appetite for urban liberties. No sooner was he safely seated in Stuttgart again, than he began to kindle the old quarrels with Reutlingen and Esslingen and managed to begin a new one with Ulm. Sturm frequently was called upon in ensuing years to mediate these quarrels, which cannot but have weakened the bonds within the Smalkaldic League.[131] The second feature of Ulrich's restoration which proved troubling to the urban politicians was the old man's refusal to reconcile to himself and settle the

---

Wirtemberg, 4 vols., Stuttgart 1899–1907, I, nos. 172–174, 209, 231, 253, 270, 291, 305, 326, 364, 371, 386, 394, 402.

[129] See note 126 above; Ficker's calculations are cited by Oberman, *Werden und Wertung* (as note 2), p. 359 n. 70.

[130] Landgrave Philip to Duke Ulrich, Friedewald, 24.VIII.1534: *Ich wolt aber das Jacob Sturm und die Städte hätten Geld darzu geben, und so sehr gerathen den König anzugreifen, als sie es widerrathen haben . . . ware es wohl gut gewesen zu der Zeit; sie haben Euer Lieb keinen Pfennig umsonst gegeben.* Quoted in modernized form by Wille, "Philipp der Grossmüthige" (as note 1), p. 225.

[131] PCSS II, pp. 217–218, no. 235; pp. 270–271, no. 298; and Lenz, *Briefwechsel*, II, p. 245 (as note 113), no. 190. See Naujoks, *Obrigkeitsgedanke* (as note 5), pp. 105–117, on Ulrich's later quarrels with Swabian free cities.

succession upon Christoph, which, as Sturm later pointed out, only served to drive the prince deeper into the arms of his Bavarian relatives and thereby endanger what had been won in 1534.[132]

The short-time gain from Strasbourg's support of the restoration in Württemberg lay, therefore, only in a weakening of the Hapsburg strategic position in the Southwest and in a—never to be fully realized—potential increase in the material power of the Smalkaldic League. No more than a leopard changes his spots had Ulrich changed his personality, either when he converted to the new religion or when his friends helped him to recover his lands. Years later, Johann Feige, the Hessian chancellor, wrote to his prince about Ulrich: "for among the free cities there is great grumbling about him".[133] Strasbourg and Strasbourg's Sturm had aided the cause of Protestantism in South Germany in 1534, but they had substantially damaged the cause of urban liberty. Ulrich restored was again "duke and hangman of Württemberg".

---

[132] Jacob Sturm to Landgrave Philip, Strasbourg, 1.XII.1537, in: PCSS II, p. 460, no. 484; a faulty text by Wille, "Briefe Jacob Sturms" (as note 1), p. 109.

[133] Johann Feige to Landgrave Philip, Neustadt v. d. Röhn, 7.VIII.1541: *Dan ist unter den reichstetten ein gross gemurmel uber in;* . . . Lenz, *Briefwechsel* (as note 113), III, p. 136.

CHAPTER FOUR

PHASES AND STRATEGIES OF THE SCHMALKALDIC
LEAGUE: A PERSPECTIVE AFTER 450 YEARS

In the upper valley of the Werra River in the southern foothills of
the Thuringian forest lies Schmalkalden.[1] Then, as now, an iron-
working center, in 1530 perhaps 4,500 persons may have called it
their hometown. The town lay since the fourteenth century under
the condominium of the landgraves of Hesse and the counts of
Henneberg-Schleusingen; but little worthy of the wider world's notice ever happened there until the final days of the year 1530, when
the Protestant powers gathered at Schmalkalden to discuss collective
security. Frightened and angered by the wreck of Charles V's pacification policy at the Imperial Diet of Augsburg, most of the Protestant
princes and urban regimes were ready to discuss with new candor the
long-delayed military alliance in defense of their religion. When the
Hessian prince and the Saxon elector had first offered the alliance to
the leading southern free cities in 1526, the regimes of Nuremberg,
Ulm and Strasbourg had shunned it in favor of traditional, purely
southern alliance policies; and when the matter had been revived in
the spring and summer of 1529, after the great Evangelical protest
at the Diet of Speyer, the Lutherans had brought their anti-Zwinglian
campaign to its peak and wrecked the negotiations. Now, at last, the
time was ripe. On the last day of the old year, the assembled nobles
and urban envoys approved a treaty of federation and mutual protection *in causa religionis*. The day on which it took effect, February
27, 1531, may stand as the birthday of the Schmalkaldic League.[2]

Some Evangelical powers did not join: Zurich, Basel and Bern were
excluded for their heterodoxy; and Nuremberg and Margrave George
of Brandenburg-Ansbach had composed the ancient Nuremberg-
Hohenzollern feud just long enough to boycott the League together.

---

[1] Hans Patze, *Thüringen (Handbuch der historischen Stätten*, 9; Stuttgart, 1968), p. 388.
[2] The fundamental modern work on the founding of the Schmalkaldic League
is by Ekkehart Fabian, *Die Entstehung des Schmalkaldischen Bundes und seiner Verfassung
1524/29–1531/35*, 2nd ed. (*Schriften zur Kirchen- und Rechtsgeschichte*, 1; Tübingen, 1962).

Formed for six years, the alliance was renewed for another ten in
1537, and it was defeated and dispersed by the Emperor Charles V
and his allies in 1546–1547. Of this Schmalkaldic League Bernd
Moeller has written: "To a certain extent all the political, ecclesiastical and constitutional problems of the Empire also faced this League.
Yet the allies' political will was so fixed and the general situation so
favorable, that success lay within their grasp. For the next fifteen
years the Schmalkaldic League was the strongest force in the Empire,
a center for the stabilization and expansion of Protestantism, and
the emperor's chief opponent."[3]

What Moeller does not add is that the League failed to solve any
of the political and constitutional problems of the Holy Roman
Empire. Yet the League in its day combined to an impressive degree
the political wills of important sectors of the German ruling classes,
and for a decade-and-a-half it filled the role of an opposition party
to the monarchy more successfully than any previous combination
of princes had done. The League's phases and strategies, an overview
of which is the aim of this study, are illuminated by published sources
and literature with distressing unevenness.

I

The published sources for the Schmalkaldic League's history begin
with the detritus of the pamphlet wars, which has as yet barely begun
to attract scholarly attention. In 1617–1618, Friedrich Hortleder, a
princely councillor in Saxe-Weimar, published the first edition of an
enormous source-book on the causes and course of the Schmalkaldic
War, much of it from manuscripts in Weimar.[4] Normally used in
the second edition of 1645 by Hortleder's son-in-law, it provides
masses of often silently edited, incomplete and imperfectly read texts,
most of which are available in no other form. Another seventeenth-
century work, Veit Ludwig von Seckendorff's *Commentarius historicus et
apologeticus de Lutheranismo* (Frankfurt am Main, 1692), supplies a good
many other documents. Of modern sources, laying aside editions

---

[3] Bernd Moeller, *Deutschland im Zeitalter der Reformation* (*Deutsche Geschichte*, ed. Joachim
Leuschner, 4; Göttingen, 1977), p. 132.
[4] Friedrich Hortleder, *Handlungen und Ausschreiben von den Ursachen des teutschen
Krieges* (Frankfurt am Main, 1617–1618), but normally used in the second edition
(Gotha, 1645).

of the reformers' letters, three collections stand out. First, and by far the richest, is the nearly complete edition of Strasbourg's diplomatic correspondence for the years 1521 to 1555.[5] Second, there are the (to date) three heavy volumes of the correspondence of Duke Moritz of Saxony.[6] Finally, there are the immensely valuable source-books published by Ekkehart Fabian from 1956 on. These touch various aspects of the League's activities, such as the League's diets or assemblies,[7] the assemblies of the southern free cities of the League,[8] and suits against Protestant powers in the Imperial courts;[9] but in no case do they reach beyond 1536. So far as the internal and official activities of the League in the last decade of its existence are concerned, the tiny handfuls of sources in modern editions disappear beside the mountains of manuscripts that rest in the archives.

Unpublished sources are to be found, of course, in the archives of the nearly three dozen princes and free cities who were at one time or another members of the Schmalkaldic League. The two chief masses, however, lie in the state archives of Marburg and Weimar among the papers of Landgrave Philip of Hesse and Electors John and John Frederick of Saxony respectively. Divided as they are between the two German states, these rich collections will likely remain underexploited in our time. For the Marburg collection there are serviceable published inventories,[10] but in Weimar we must use the manuscript

---

[5] *Politische Correspondenz der Stadt Strassburg im Zeitalter der Reformation*, eds. Hans Virck, *et al.*, 5 vols. (Strasbourg, 1882–1899; Heidelberg, 1923–1933).

[6] *Politische Korrespondenz des Herzogs und Kurfürsten Moritz von Sachsen*, vols. 1–2, ed. Erich Brandenburg (Leipzig, 1900–1904); vol. 3, eds. Johannes Herrmann and Günther Wartenberg (Berlin, 1978). The third volume, which reaches to May 25, 1548, and subsequent ones greatly enlarge the range of documents included in this edition. On Moritz, see now Karlheinz Blaschke, "Moritz von Sachsen," *Gestalten der Kirchengeschichte, Reformationszeit* ed. Martin Geschat (Stuttgart, 1981), pp. 295–314.

[7] Ekkehart Fabian, ed., *Die Schmalkaldischen Bundesabschiede 1530–1536 (Schriften zur Kirchen- und Rechtsgeschichte*, 7–8; Tübingen, 1958).

[8] Ekkehart Fabian, ed., *Die Beschlüsse der oberdeutschen Schmalkaldischen Städtetage 1530–1536 (Schriften zur Kirchen- und Rechtsgeschichte*, 9/10, 14/15, 21/24; Tübingen, 1959–1960).

[9] Ekkehart Fabian, ed., *Urkunden und Akten der Reformationsprozesse am Reichskammergericht, am Kaiserlichen Hofgericht zu Rottweil und an anderen Gerichten 1530–1534 (Schriften zur Kirchen- und Rechtsgeschichte*, 16/17; Tübingen, 1961); *Quellen zur Geschichte der Reformationsbündnisse und der Konstanzer Reformationsprozesse (Schriften zur Kirchen und Rechtsgeschichte*, 34; Tübingen-Basel, 1967).

[10] *Politisches Archiv des Landgrafen Philipp des Großmütigen von Hessen, Inventar der Bestände*, vols. 1–2, ed. Friedrich Küch (*Publikationen aus den K. preußischen Staatsarchiven*, 78, 85; Leipzig, 1908–1910); vols. 3–4, ed. Walter Heinemeyer (*Veröffentlichungen der Historischen Kommission für Hessen und Waldeck*, 24, pp. 1–2; Marburg, 1954–1959).

reportories from the end of the sixteenth century,[11] which omit the
dates of documents and sometimes whole acts. This vast Saxon collection has been combed thoroughly only by the beavers who toiled
for the Weimar edition of Luther's works, and by the redoubtable
Heinz Scheible for his edition of the Melanchthon correspondence.

Enormous treasures lie unworked at Weimar. The documents are
there, for example, for the League's two invasions of Braunschweig-
Wolfenbüttel in 1542 and 1545, right down to the muster lists and
quartermasters' accounts, plus the papers captured at Wolfenbüttel,[12]
which have their Marburg counterpart in the looted archive of the
Habsburg regime at Stuttgart.[13] In Weimar, too, are masses of acts
concerning the restoration and restitution suits against Protestant
powers before the Imperial courts, a gold mine for studying the
spread of Evangelical religion.[14] Weimar was the major collection
point for information on these suits. Sprinkled through the Weimar
holdings are also two kinds of documents that will have to be edited
and published, if we are to get on with the later history of the
League. The first is the recesses of the League's diets, which Fabian
has published down through 1536, and of which complete series are
to be found in both Marburg and Weimar. The second group is the
correspondence between Philip of Hesse and Electors John and John
Frederick of Saxony. This very large correspondence swelled to an
enormous scale in 1546, just before the Schmalkaldic War, when
Philip and John Frederick were exchanging two and three letters
each per week, each filled with up to fifty folio sides of enclosures—
newsletters, spies' reports and information on the mustering of troops.
The archives of Landgrave Philip of Hesse are smaller in mass,
better known, and much more accessible;[15] and as Philip's chancellery

---

[11] See Hans Eberhardt, *Übersicht über die Bestände des Thüringischen Landeshauptarchivs
Weimar* (Weimar, 1959), esp. pp. 12–14 (Registrande H, Schmalkaldischer Bund;
Registrande I, Schmalkaldischer Krieg). The archiv has been renamed the Staats-
archiv Weimar.

[12] *Ibid.*, p. 13.

[13] The archive was looted at the restoration in 1534 and hauled off to Hesse.
The remaining acts are inventoried in *Politisches Archiv* (see note 10 above), I, 239–49,
under nos. 395–407. Note that nos. 396–400 were later returned to Stuttgart and
are now in the Hauptstaatsarchiv Stuttgart, series A 2.

[14] This includes the suits against members of the League (and some non-members)
all over Germany. Investigators of those suits will probably find in Weimar copies
of acts which are no longer to be had in the archives of the powers involved in
the suits.

[15] Especially as the entire section called "Politisches Archiv des Landgrafen

served as the nexus of communications between Saxony and the entire southern wing of the League, his archive duplicates much of the Weimar material. Much, but by no means all, and it is difficult to believe that fundamental advances will be made in the history of the Schmalkaldic League, except by scholars who can spend long periods for research at both Marburg and Weimar.

II

The scholarly literature illuminates the Schmalkaldic League's history very unevenly, as the state of publication of the sources would suggest. By far the best known era of this history are the years from the first tender of alliance by the Hessian landgrave and Saxon elector to the leading southern free cities until the conclusion of the intra-Evangelical concord on doctrine, the Wittenberg Concord, that is, from 1526 to 1536. Counting its prehistory the League lasted about twenty years, the course of which falls into four phases:

1. the prehistory of the League, 1526–1530;
2. the South German phase, 1531–1535;
3. the apogee of the League, 1535–1542; and
4. the North German phase, 1542–1547.

Through comments on each of these phases in turn, I can illuminate the present state of knowledge of the League's history.

The Prehistory, 1526–1530. The politicization of German Protestantism in the years 1526–1530 attracted much interest from historians during the Second German Empire. Along with other special interests, such as the right of armed resistance and the eucharistic dispute, its prehistory is perhaps the best understood aspect of the League's history.

Philipp" is available in the United States on microfilm at the Center for Reformation Research in St. Louis and can be used through inter-library loan. A very large number of letters to and from Landgrave Philip have been published, though unfortunately few of those between him and the Saxon electors. See the list (to 1955) compiled by Günther Franz and Eckhart G. Franz, eds., *Urkundliche Quellen zur hessischen Reformationsgeschichte*, vol. 3, *1547–1567* (*Veröffentlichungen der Historischen Kommission für Hessen und Waldeck*, 11, 3; Marburg, 1955), pp. 371–403. The only coherent group of letters published from this mass is Philip's correspondence with Martin Bucer, edited by Max Lenz, *Briefwechsel Landgraf Philipps des Großmütigen von Hessen mit Bucer*, 3 vols. (*Publikationen aus den K. preußischen Staatsarchiven*, 5, 28, 47; Leipzig, 1880–1891).

The Schmalkaldic League had two direct predecessors. One was the Hessian-Saxon League of Magdeburg, formed in 1526, which formulated the principle of armed defense of Evangelical religion. The second ancestor is the federation of Strasbourg, Constance and Hesse with Basel, Bern and Zurich in 1529–31, whence the Schmalkaldic League took its anti-Habsburg stance.[16] Taken together, these two forerunners flanked on the north and the west the great complex that Emperor Maximilian (d. 1519) had built in South Germany through his policies of federation and clientship in the years 1488 to 1519.[17] Maximilian's system began through association of his Austrian lands with two federations of smaller powers, the Swabian League (est. 1488) and the Lower Union (reest. 1493). It moved from success to success: Bavarian expansion blocked, 1492; Swiss expansion impeded (if somewhat feebly), 1499; Palatine Wittelsbach expansion crushed, 1504; Württemberg seized and transferred to the Habsburgs, 1519; some of wild Franconia's worst noble thugs burnt out, 1523; and the Revolution of the Common Man put down in Upper Swabia, Württemberg and Franconia, 1525. Maximilian's system provided the southern free cities' regimes with their sole protection against both individual princely dynasties and the collective power of the princes in the Imperial Diet and the Governing Council (*Reichsregiment*). In 1524–1525, just as Charles' attention was wholly engaged in the Mediterranean, the system was gradually undermined, as popular partisanship for Evangelical religion in the free cities forced their regimes to illegal measures which alienated them from the Crown. Then the Revolution of 1525 finished the wrecking of the system. By then

---

[16] On this topic see two basic modern works, by René Hauswirth, *Landgraf Philipp von Hessen und Zwingli. Voraussetzungen und Geschichte der politischen Beziehungen zwischen Hessen, Straßburg, Konstanz, Ulrich von Württemberg und reformierten Eidgenossen 1526–1531* (*Schriften zur Kirchen- und Rechtsgeschichte*, 35; Tübingen-Basel, 1968); and Wilhelm Bender, *Zwinglis Reformationsbündnisse. Untersuchungen zur Rechts- und Sozialgeschichte der Burgrechtsverträge eidgenössischer und oberdeutscher Städte zur Ausbreitung und Sicherung der Reformation Huldrych Zwinglis* (Zürich-Stuttgart, 1970), a dissertation submitted to the Free University of Berlin. Anyone who doubts that the religious issues added a wholly new dimension to these alliances, should read the Ulm regime's explanation for the formation of the Schmalkaldic League, "das ... gottes Nam, Eer, lob vnd wortt, dergleichen auch bruederlich vnnd Christenlich Lieb dardurch geaffent, gemert vnnd gefurdert werde." Ulm to Esslingen, September 30, 1531, in Helmuth Krabbe and Hans-Christoph Rublack, eds., *Akten zur Esslinger Reformationsgeschichte* (*Esslinger Studien, Schriftenreihe*, 5; Esslingen, 1981), p. 148, no. 129.

[17] The rest of this paragraph is based on my forthcoming study, *Turning Swiss: Cities and Empire, 1450–1550* (Cambridge, 1985).

the traditional policies of the "urban front" of South German cities, urban solidarity and loyalty to the Crown, could not be maintained.

It was the city of Strasbourg, long a reluctant collaborator with Maximilian's system, who blazed a trail back to the long-abandoned political alternative of "turning Swiss." For a time it seemed that many of the southern free cities might stream into a giant anti-Habsburg coalition. It was the political dream of Huldrych Zwingli, but it had been predicted as early as 1520 by Maximilian van Bergen, lord of Zevenberghen, the Brabantish nobleman who had negotiated the transfer of Württemberg from the Swabian League to Charles V. He had warned that if Charles did not take Württemberg and build it into the structure formed by Austria and the Swabian League, the estates of Württemberg would turn to the Swiss and pull all Swabia and the Rhine Valley as far down as Cologne, "the district of the free cities, into their federation, so that the German land would become one vast commune, and all authority would come to an end."[18] This alternative was averted not only because of Zwingli's death and Zurich's defeat at Kappel in 1531, nor chiefly because of the attractiveness of Lutheran doctrine, but rather because the socially ambiguous nature of the Swiss Confederacy, which combined oligarchical city-states with free rural federations, made turning Swiss a doubtful policy. The wisdom of this decision was proven in 1525. The free cities' regimes remained within the South German sphere, as defined by Maximilian's system, when they adhered to the Evangelical cause, only now the Hessian landgrave stepped into the role of oppositional leader formerly played by Bavarian, Palatine and Württemberg princes. Not until the formation of the Schmalkaldic League did this strategic situation change, for the defense of Evangelical religion brought together powers, such as Strasbourg and the Saxon elector, who had no other interest in common.

The South German Phase, 1531–1535. The structure of the Schmalkaldic League, whose constitution did not become valid until 1535, shows few innovations on that of the Swabian League. New were the lack of a noble house, the division into northern and southern districts, and the stated goal of defending one another only on religious grounds.

---

[18] Quoted by Karl Brandi, *The Emperor Charles V: The Growth and Destiny of a Man and of a World-Empire*, tr. C. V. Wedgwood (London, 1965; 1st ed., 1939), p. 121, from a document now in Hessisches Staatsarchiv Marburg, Politisches Archiv des Landgrafen Philipp, no. 396.

The princes had the upper hand, true, and both of the League's commanders were princes; but they had dominated the Swabian League from 1522 onwards, despite the earlier strong position of the free cities.[19] Probably the initial role of the free cities in the Schmalkaldic League was greater than their military potential warranted.

The League's official history opened with a stunning success in 1532, when Charles V agreed to suspend the restitution suits against Protestant powers. It was this issue, not the supposed imminence of military action by Charles against the Protestants after the Diet of Augsburg in 1530,[20] that brought the southern free cities swarming into the new League. The chief ideological issues, armed resistance and the eucharistic question, were quickly settled, one through Luther's volte-face at the end of 1530, the other through the Zwinglians' submission to the Confession of Augsburg at Schweinfurt in 1532. This phase saw a relatively low level of Saxon activity, perhaps because of John the Constant's death in 1532, but a very high level by Philip of Hesse. It was he who in 1534 engineered, with aid from France, Bavaria and Strasbourg, the solution of the outstanding question of South German politics, the restoration of Duke Ulrich in Württemberg.[21] This strike was strongly opposed by the young Saxon elector, John Frederick,[22] and by most of the other leading free cities of the South. Philip thereby restored to power the grimmest foe of southern free cities, most of whom by now had turned Protestant. Württemberg was lost to Charles and his vicar and brother, Ferdi-

[19] This development is described in the standard work by Ernst Bock, *Der Schwäbische Bund und seine Verfassungen 1488–1534. Ein Beitrag zur Geschichte der Zeit der Reichsreform*, revised ed. (*Untersuchungen zur deutschen Staats- und Rechtsgeschichte*, old series, 137; Aalen, 1968 [1st ed., Breslau, 1927]). Of more recent studies of the structure of the Swabian League, which badly needs to be researched, see Siegfried Frey, "Des Gericht des Schwäbischen Bundes und seine Richter 1488–1534. Ein Beitrag zur Geschichte der Rechtsinstitutionen des Einungswesens und ihrer Entscheidungsträger," *Mittel und Wege früher Verfassungspolitik*, ed. Josef Engel (*Spätmittelalter und Frühe Neuzeit. Tübinger Beiträge zur Geschichtsforschung*, 9; Stuttgart, 1979), pp. 224–81.

[20] See the important revisions by Wolfgang Reinhard, "Die kirchenpolitischen Vorstellungen Karls V.," *Confessio Augustana und Confutatio. Internationales Symposium in Augsburg vom 3.–7. Sept. 1979*, ed. Erwin Iserloh (*Reformationsgeschichtliche Studien und Texte*, 118; Münster i.W., 1980), pp. 62–100.

[21] See most recently Thomas A. Brady, Jr., "Princes' Reformation vs. Urban Liberty, Strasbourg and the Restoration in Württemberg, 1534," *Städtische Gesellschaft und Reformation*, ed. Ingrid Bátori (*Spätmittelalter und Frühe Neuzeit. Tübinger Beiträge zur Geschichtsforschung*, 12; Stuttgart, 1980), pp. 265–91.

[22] Georg Mentz, *Johann Friedrich der Großmütige 1503–1554*, 3 vols. (Jena, 1903–1908), II, pp. 27–28, but there is a lot more material on this in Staatsarchiv Weimar, Ernestisches Gesamtarchiv, Reg. C, no. 1069.

nand, but a Protestant Ulrich in Stuttgart was more dangerous to the Protestant free cities than the Habsburg regime had ever been.

The deep undercurrent of mistrust for this strategy of the anti-Habsburg opposition reigned above all in Nuremberg, whose regime was in 1534 just coming to the end of its remarkable six-year honeymoon with Margrave George of Brandenburg-Ansbach.[23] It is quite wrong to see in Nuremberg's refusal to join the Schmalkaldic League a policy of pure passivity. Rather, after a brief flirtation with Evangelical militancy in 1526–1529, Nuremberg eased back towards the old policies of urban solidarity and loyalty to the Crown. Once the Swabian League expired and the restoration in Württemberg, which the Swabian League's demise made possible, was accomplished, Nuremberg moved right back towards urban leagues and a pro-Habsburg policy. What is more remarkable, for a time Ulm, Augsburg and a group of smaller Evangelical free cities toyed with the same path.[24]

While it is true that the restoration in Württemberg ended, except for the coming of Evangelical religion to the Palatinate in the 1540s, the expansive phase of Protestantism in South Germany forever, it also doomed the desire to restore the old partnership between the monarchy and the free cities. Landgrave Philip had easily wrested Württemberg from Ferdinand, thereby revealing how thoroughly the Habsburg system in South Germany had been undermined by the distraction of its leaders, Charles with France, Ferdinand with the Jagellonian inheritance, and both with the Turks. These distractions, plus the new opposition backed implicitly, though probably not in fact, by the power of the Schmalkaldic League, deprived the Habsburgs of the power to police South Germany in the interests of themselves and their clients.

The Apogee, 1535–1542. The second half of the 1530s were the glory days of German Protestantism. This phase ran from the consolidation of the League (1535), the overcoming of its ideological differences (1536) and its renewal (1537), until the end of the religious colloquies in 1542. Strengthened and emboldened by new admissions, such as Augsburg (1535), a string of northern free cities

---

[23] Remarkable, that is, when it is placed in the historical context of relations between the two powers. This unfortunately does not show clearly in the study by Harold J. Grimm, *Lazarus Spengler: A Lay Leader of the Reformation* (Columbus, 1978), who does not properly connect this interlude with Nuremberg's alliance policy.

[24] *Beschlüsse der oberdeutschen Schmalkaldischen Städtetage* (see note 8 above), III, pp. 206–23.

and Albertine Saxony (1539), the League achieved in 1539 what its
smaller powers most wanted: security from the power of the Imperial courts to scotch and roll back the advance of Protestantism.
Charles continued the conciliatory policy he had followed since 1530
and which he would abandon in 1543. His price for suspension of
the suits, however, was Protestant support for and participation in
his wars and in the series of discussions, which aimed at reaching
agreement in doctrine, held at Hagenau, Worms, Regensburg and
Speyer from 1539 onward.[25] The colloquies formed the final stage
of Charles' policy of conciliation and ended, like this policy, in utter
failure. The Schmalkaldic League was now, in 1539–1540, at its zenith, and its members—apart, perhaps, from the bigamous Hessian
prince—were little inclined to make concessions.

The North German Phase, 1542–1546. This least well known phase
began when Landgrave Philip and John Frederick of Saxony decided
to make offensive war, which they naturally called a "preventive
war," on Duke Heinrich of Braunschweig-Wolfenbüttel and to employ
the League's army to crush him.[26] This decision shifted the inter-
confessional front northward in a most dramatic way. The princes'
grab of Heinrich's lands and their ruthless introduction of Lutheranism there removed the last hostile power, one who had been loyal
to Charles V from the start, on the flank of their main target of
interest. This was the great shield of prince-bishoprics that lay between
their own lands in Central Germany and Charles' beloved Netherlands: Münster, Osnabrück, Paderborn, Cologne, and Trier. This string
was the greatest prize of the Reformation struggle, greater even than
the Franconian string of bishoprics along "priests' alley," Eichstätt,
Bamberg, Würzburg and Mainz. Here the princes miscalculated, for
although Charles did nothing to save Duke Heinrich's lands in 1542,
the threat to northwestern Germany aroused him to set in motion
the train of events that would bring down the Schmalkaldic League.

---

[25] See Peter Fraenkel, *Einigungsbestrebungen in der Reformationszeit* (Wiesbaden, 1965);
Cornelis Augustijn, *De godsdienstgesprekken tussen roomskatholieken en protestanten van 1538
tot 1541* (Haarlem, 1967).
[26] See now Franz Petri, "Herzog Heinrich der Jüngere von Braunschweig-
Wolfenbüttel. Ein niederdeutscher Territorialfürst im Zeitalter Luthers und Karls V.,"
Archiv für Reformationsgeschichte 72 (1981), pp. 122–57. Petri cites (p. 138) with approval the judgment of Karl Brandi that in this era the vehemence of the confessional struggle and the pressure towards a solution by arms came chiefly from the
German princes, not from Charles V. I wholly agree, and in this light the invasion
of Braunschweig-Wolfenbüttel has to be seen as an offensive war.

Philip and John Frederick approached the problem and the opportunity presented by the German Northwest with a two-pronged
attack.[27] First, they tried to subvert the bishoprics by encouraging
their incumbents, men such as Bishop Franz von Waldeck (d. 1553)
of Münster and Osnabrück and Archbishop Hermann von Wied
(1515–1546) of Cologne, to convert openly to Protestantism and convert their prince-bishoprics into secular principalities. Second, they
egged on Duke William of Cleves-Jülich in his claim to the duchy
of Guelders. This bleeding sore in the side of the Habsburg Netherlands at last ceased to bleed in 1543, when its duke died without
direct heirs.[28] There was no chance that Charles, whose view of the
Empire was Netherlandish rather than Austrian,[29] would surrender
Guelders as Ferdinand had surrendered Württemberg nine years ago.
In fact, the princes' threats to the Netherlands probably made war
inevitable, once Charles got his hands free for action. The plunge
towards war then developed along the east-west line running approximately through Weimar, Kassel, Düsseldorf, Cologne and Antwerp.
It was fueled by the expansionist actions of the Schmalkaldic League's
two commanders in North Germany in the years 1542–1545. The
time for Charles' attack was then determined by the Peace of Crespy
on September 18, 1544, and the truce with Sultan Suleiman on
November 10 of the following year.

The Schmalkaldic League's defeat at the hands of Charles V
and his allies in 1546–1547 can be blamed partly on the incompetence of the League's commanders, especially John Frederick, who
listened long and too well to the preachers who said he was God's
chosen instrument.[30] Partly, too, it came because the League had

---

[27] See Franz Petri, "Landschaftliche und überlandschaftliche Kräfte im habsbur-
gischklevischen Ringen um Geldern und im Frieden von Venlo (1537–1543)," *Aus
Geschichte und Landeskunde. Festschrift Franz Steinbach* (Bonn, 1960), pp. 92–113; *idem*:
"Nordwestdeutschland im Wechselspiel der Politik Karls V. und Philipps des Großmütigen von Hessen." *Zeitschrift des Vereins für hessische Geschichte* 71 (1960), pp. 37–60.

[28] The background to the Guelders problem is admirably reviewed by James D.
Tracy, *The Politics of Erasmus. A Pacifist Intellectual and His Political Milieu* (Toronto,
1978), ch. 4.

[29] Volker Press, "Die Erblande und das Reich von Albrecht II. bis Karl VI.
(1438–1740)," *Deutschland und Österreich*, eds. Robert A. Kann and Friedrich E. Prinz
(Vienna, 1980), pp. 44–88, here at p. 62.

[30] There is rich evidence for these characteristics in *Politische Korrespondenz des
Herzogs und Kurfürsten Moritz von Sachsen* (see note 6 above), III, esp. the documents
cited on p. 24. If, after the Danube campaign of 1546, further evidence for John
Frederick's incompetence as a field commander were needed, the siege of Leipzig
(January 5–27, 1547) provides plenty of corroboration.

been disintegrating for some years before the war. Negotiations had
begun in 1545 for the renewal of the Schmalkaldic League, due in
1547. So deep and bitter were the divisions between South and
North, princes and cities, in the League, that it is by no means certain that the treaty would have been renewed, even had Charles not
attacked the League in 1546.[31] At the bottom of this division was precisely the same issue that had crippled the Imperial Diet in Charles'
first years, 1521–1524, the princes' attempts to exploit the financial
power of the cities for princely aggrandizement. In this case the long,
expensive occupation of Braunschweig-Wolfenbüttel proved the canker
at the League's very heart.

Constitutionally, it is true, the princes could outvote the cities by
nine votes to eight. The North German cities, however, rarely sent
full delegations to the League's diets, and splits strictly between princes
and cities were not common. Financial complaints arose from the
heavy costs borne by the cities—chiefly the southern ones, as the
northern cities rarely paid their levies—for the two invasions and
the occupation of Braunschweig-Wolfenbüttel. The southern urban
members wanted to hand the duchy over to Charles V in trust for
Heinrich's heirs, while the princes wanted to hold and milk it as
long as possible. The entire operation and the northward shift of
the chief center of confessional struggle committed these southern
urban regimes to efforts and expenses in regions largely unknown
and of little interest to either their politicians or their merchants.
The southern merchants, in fact, had a much greater stake in the
maintenance of law and order in the Netherlands, with whose cities
they traded. So it was that the abandonment of the old pro-Habsburg
policy brought these regimes a new conflict of interest, and this at
a time when the situation in the South was, by contrast, extremely
stable. Even the Schmalkaldic War brought no territorial changes in
the South. The curious contrast between the Schmalkaldic League's
initial, highly successful and vigorous phase and its disturbed later
history and defeat are to be sought not least in the fact that the rise
of the League occurred at a time when the final spread of the
Reformation in the South coincided with its first expansive phase in
the North. This not only made the northern front much more volatile, it was also responsible both for the unprecedentedly "national"
scope of the League and for its erosion in the 1540s.

---

[31] These debates can at present best be followed in vols. III–IV of the *Politische
Correspondenz der Stadt Straßburg* (see note 5 above).

III

The passage by Bernd Moeller quoted above merely hints at the Schmalkaldic League's failure to solve any of the major political problems it faced. While true, this fact should not disguise or obscure the League's political characteristics. First of all, the Schmalkaldic League covered a much larger area than any of its predecessors had done, reaching from Lake Constance to the Baltic Sea. The federations of Maximilian's day had all been restricted to South Germany, and the novel if elusive power of the religious issue is displayed in the remarkable geographical extent of an alliance which included among its members the duke of Pomerania and the city of Kempten. The Reformation therefore widened the terms of politics and created more extensive political connections between German powers than had ever existed in Maximilian's day.

A second characteristic of the Schmalkaldic League, one it shared with the old Swabian League, was its development of true state-like qualities. One sign of this was the tempo of its activities.[32] Between 1531 and 1540 the League met seventeen times for an average of twenty-four days, while the imperial Diet met only once. During its whole span of sixteen years, the League's diet averaged 1.5 meetings for 39 days per year. It also met over a much larger area and in different areas than the Imperial Diet did. While the latter continued under Charles to move back and forth across South Germany—Worms, Nuremberg, Speyer, Augsburg, Regensburg—the diet of the Schmalkaldic League met seven times at Schmalkalden, six at Frankfurt am Main, three at Worms, twice each at Schweinfurt, Braunschweig and Nuremberg, and once each at Ulm, Naumburg, Arnstadt and Eisenach. The core areas of the League were thus Franconia and Thuringia, a perceptible northward shift from the Imperial Diet's sites in the Rhine and Danube valleys.

The frequency of League diets and the League's direct negotiations with Charles clearly made the Imperial Diet unnecessary for many years, and the latter did not meet between 1532 and 1540. Its resumption in the early 1540s clearly strained the diplomatic corps of some cities, who were already burdened by the League's

---

[32] The following is based on data taken from Fabian, *Die Entstehung des Schmalkaldischen Bundes*, 2nd ed. (see note 2 above); *Politische Correspondenz der Stadt Straßburg* (see note 5 above); and sources in the Staatsarchiv Weimar.

activities.[33] Such burdens may have been responsible in part for the confused cross-currents and tensions in the League just before the war.

The statelike tendencies of the Schmalkaldic League appear also in a number of important projects, such as a common ecclesiastical constitution, a common liturgy, a common policy on ecclesiastical property[34] and the dream of a Protestant on the Imperial throne.[35] None of them came to much. A major success, on the other hand, was the development of a common legal representation before the *Reichskammergericht*, a service which functioned well for many years. Another area of success was the mediation of disputes between members, such as between the city of Ulm and Duke Ulrich of Württemberg. More importantly, perhaps, for about one decade the League blocked the authority of Imperial government over much of the Empire, including prevention of executions of the Imperial ban against such Protestant powers as the cities of Minden and Goslar.[36]

Much the most impressive achievement of the Schmalkaldic League was its role in wrecking Maximilian's system in South Germany. The collapse began, it is true, with Charles' failure to continue his grandfather's South German policy of federation and clientship, with Ferdinand's preoccupation elsewhere from 1526 on, and above all with the pressure from below on southern urban regimes for changes in religion. The League completed this dissolution and prevented the organization of a militarily effective successor to the Swabian League, despite the fact that some southern Protestant powers, including some Schmalkaldeners, wanted to restore the political ties to Charles if

---

[33] See my discussion in Thomas A. Brady, Jr., *Ruling Class, Regime and Reformation at Strasbourg, 1520–1555* (Studies in Medieval and Reformation Thought, 22; Leiden, 1978), pp. 250–56.

[34] A subject which badly needs to be studied. The oft-cited work by Hans Lehnert, *Kirchengut und Reformation (Erlanger Abhandlungen zur mittleren und neueren Geschichte*, 20; Erlangen, 1935), is not of much use. Somewhat more useful is Kurt Körber, *Kirchengüterfrage und Schmalkaldischer Bund. Ein Beitrag zur deutschen Reformationsgeschichte* (*Schriften des Vereins für Reformationsgeschichte*, 111/112; Halle 1912); and see also Friedrich Roth, "Zur Kirchengüterfrage in der Zeit von 1538 bis 1540. Die Gutachten Martin Bucers und der Augsburger Prädicanten Wolfgang Musculus und Bonifacius Wolfart über die Verwendung der Kirchengüter," *Archiv für Reformationsgeschichte* 1 (1903/04): pp. 299–336.

[35] Heinz Duchhardt, *Protestantisches Kaisertum und Altes Reich. Die Diskussion über die Konfession des Kaisers in Politik, Publizistik und Staatsrecht (Veröffentlichungen des Instituts für Europäische Geschichte Mainz*, 87; Wiesbaden, 1977).

[36] Petri, "Herzog Heinrich der Jüngere von Braunschweig-Wolfenbüttel" (see note 26 above), pp. 143–45; U. Hölscher, "Die Geschichte der Mindener Reichsacht 1538–1541," *Zeitschrift der Gesellschaft für niedersächsische Kirchengeschichte* 9 (1914), pp. 192–202.

the religious issue could be excluded. When Charles and Ferdinand reversed this neglect in the 1540s, beginning with the free knights,[37] it hardly altered the outcome. It should nevertheless be noted that Charles' great alliance scheme broached after the Schmalkaldic War, which provided for a southern and a northern league, each headed by the emperor, was anticipated by—and indeed may have originated in—a very similar plan drafted by Protestant Nurembergers in 1539!

The Schmalkaldic League also alleviated, at least temporarily, the collective pressure of the princes through the Imperial Diet on the urban oligarchies and the big commercial firms.[38] The anti-monopoly movement and proposals for new Imperial taxes reached a climax just before the Peasants' War, and the gradual crippling of the Imperial organs of rule, such as the Diet, the Governing Council and the *Reichskammergericht*, relieved this pressure for about fifteen years. The deadlock over the Reformation may help, indeed, to explain why the Reformation brought few changes in the procedures and institutions of the Diet, whose forms were largely fixed in Maximilian's reign.[39] The confessionalization of German politics made it much more difficult to maintain princely solidarity, and this was the temporary compensation for the cities' loss of their own solidarity and Imperial loyalism. By 1542, however, the old polarization reappeared in the Imperial Diet, as strong as ever, which made some southern urban politicians wonder why they had ever made common cause with some of these "ravening wolves."[40]

IV

When Ernst Troeltsch compared Lutheranism with Calvinism, he found the difference "in the active character of Calvinism, in its power for forming Churches, in its international contacts, and its

---

[37] Volker Press, *Kaiser Karl V., König Ferdinand und die Entstehung der Reichsritterschaft* (*Institut für Europäische Geschichte Mainz, Vorträge*, no. 60; Wiesbaden, 1976); *idem*, "Die Erblande und das Reich" (see note 29 above), pp. 47–48; Horst Rabe, *Reichsbund und Interim. Die Verfassungs- und Religionspolitik Karls V. und der Reichstag von Augsburg 1547/48* (Cologne-Vienna, 1971).

[38] This is based on my forthcoming work, *Turning Swiss* (see note 17 above).

[39] Rosemarie Aulinger, *Das Bild des Reichstages im 16. Jahrhundert* (*Schriftenreihe der Historischen Kommission bei der Bayerischen Akademie der Wissenschaften*, no. 18; Göttingen, 1980).

[40] The words are from Claus Kniebis (d. 1552), Ammeister of Strasbourg. Brady, *Ruling Class* (see note 33 above), *passim*, collects most of what is known about him.

conscious impulse towards expansion, and, most of all, in its capacity
to penetrate the political and economic movements of Western nations with its religious ideal, a capacity which Lutheranism lacked
from the very beginning."[41]

In principle, of course, the question of penetrating "the political
and economic movements . . . with its religious ideal" was solved for
Lutheranism in 1525, when Luther set himself against the Revolution
of 1525 and its ideal of the "godly law."[42] And while the history of
the Schmalkaldic League in general confirms Troeltsch's opinion of
the political sterility of German Lutheranism, yet it will not do to
place too great an emphasis on the League's inability to solve the
political and constitutional problems of the Holy Roman Empire.

On the question of legitimism, in particular, the Schmalkaldic
League exhibits important nuances. A test case arose in 1543–1544,
when the Protestant minority at Metz petitioned for admission to
the League, and over this request opinion divided.[43] Martin Bucer,
citing the doctrine of the *sanior pars*, argued for the admission of the
Evangelical Messins as the true, because truly Christian, representatives of their city. He was overruled, however, by the Wittenberg
theologians and John Frederick of Saxony, who opposed admission
to the League of dissident subjects of a legitimate government. In
the case of Braunschweig, on the other hand, the League threw legitimism to the winds.[44] It not only admitted the city of Braunschweig

---

[41] Ernst Troeltsch, *The Social Teaching of the Christian Churches*, tr. Olive Wyon (London-New York, 1931), p. 577.

[42] See Peter Blickle, *Die Revolution von 1525*, 2nd ed. (Munich, 1981), pp. 237–44; and the English version in Peter Blickle, *The Revolution of 1525: The German Peasants' War from a New Perspective*, tr. Thomas A. Brady, Jr., and H. C. Erik Midelfort (Baltimore, 1981), pp. 155–61.

[43] Eike Wolgast, *Die Wittenberger Theologie und die Politik der evangelischen Stände. Studien zu Luthers Gutachten in politischen Fragen* (Quellen und Forschungen zur Reformationsgeschichte, 47; Gütersloh, 1977), pp. 269–72. Wolgast (p. 269) correctly judges that with this request "ergab sich die Möglichkeit, den Bund aus einem Zusammenschluß von Reichsständen zu einer politischen Organisation aller Protestanten im Reich auszuweiten, aber auch die Gefahr, in die bestehenden Herrschaftsverhältnisse und -zuständigkeiten nachhaltig einzugreifen." The Senate of Strasbourg supported the request, pointing out that the *Schöffenmeister* of Metz, Gaspard de Heu, was a Protestant. Bucer's very interesting opinion, written to Landgrave Philip from Strasbourg, September 1, 1542, is printed by Lenz, *Briefwechsel Landgraf Philipps . . . mit Bucer* (see note 15 above), II, 83–87, no. 142.

[44] My thanks to James D. Tracy for pointing out the questionable legality of the admission of the city of Braunschweig to the Schmalkaldic League. See Olaf Mörke, Rat und Bürger in der Reformation. Soziale Gruppen und kirchlicher Wandel in

to the League, although the city was patently subject to Duke Heinrich, but the next diet of the League was staged in Braunschweig, the only time the League ever met so far north. The grab of Duke Heinrich's duchy in 1542 displays the ability of Philip and John Frederick to seize opportunities for spreading the gospel and aggrandizing themselves at the same time, a policy more in accord with the politics of Huldrych Zwingli than with those of Martin Luther. They used Luther, of course, and used him shamelessly, to provide propaganda and respectability for their plans; but then, Luther was willing to be used.[45]

The openness of these Lutheran princes to opportunity casts some doubt on the thesis of Lutheran political passivity. So does the remarkable resistance of Lutheran clergy to the Interim at the end of the 1540s.[46] Most striking, however is the revelation that Lutheranism could function to reinforce communitarian institutions and political goals in an urban setting and to stiffen communal resistance to the absolutist goals of a Calvinist prince.[47]

More than one historian has recently pronounced the German Reformation a failure. Gerald Strauss portrays the goal of German Lutheranism as the abolition of the old popular religion, plus much other popular culture, through a stern new pedagogy; and he argues that in this task Lutheranism proved a failure.[48] Steven Ozment ends his account of the Reformation in the light of late medieval thought and culture with a gloomy reflection on the unrealistically high standard Luther set for human spiritual liberation.[49] If we set our sights somewhat lower, however, than the expectation of the permanent

---

den welfischen Hansestädten Lüneburg, Braunschweig und Göttingen (Marburg, 1981), a very important Marburg dissertation, soon to be published.

[45] See the very interesting conclusion to Wolgast, *Die Wittenberger Theologie* (see note 43 above), pp. 285–99, who recognizes that the old thesis of the apolitical Luther was clearly wrong.

[46] Irmgard Höss, "Zur Genesis der Widerstandslehre Bezas," *Archiv für Reformationsgeschichte* 54 (1963), pp. 198–214: Oliver K. Olson, "Theology of Revolution: Magdeburg, 1550–1551," *Sixteenth Century Journal* 3 (1972): pp. 56–79.

[47] I refer to the pioneering Habilitationsschrift of Heinz Schilling, *Konfessionskonflikt und Staatsbildung. Eine Fallstudie über das Verhältnis von religiösem und sozialem Wandel in der Frühneuzeit am Beispiel der Grafschaft Lippe (Quellen und Forschungen zur Reformationsgeschichte, 48; Gütersloh, 1981).*

[48] Gerald Strauss, *Luther's House of Learning: Indoctrination of the Young in the German Reformation* (Baltimore-London, 1978), following his earlier study, "Success and Failure in the German Reformation," *Past and Present*, no. 67 (May, 1975), pp. 30–63.

[49] Steven E. Ozment, *The Age of Reform, 1250–1550: An Intellectual and Religious History of Late Medieval and Reformation Europe* (New Haven, 1980), p. 437.

spiritual liberation of the individual and view the achievement of German Lutheranism in the sphere of Imperial politics, then our judgment must be a tempered one. The Schmalkaldic League's achievement was an extremely limited one. It brought none of the three great problems of Imperial government—law and order, an efficient judicial system and an adequate financial basis—closer to solution. Indeed, it severely disrupted the Imperial court system for a long time.[50] What the League did accomplish was to block for a time the expansion of the Habsburg power base in South Germany and thereby prevent, for a time, the further development of the old combination of hereditary lands and client federations towards a genuine monarchy, that is, in the absolutist direction that European monarchy was taking in the sixteenth century.[51] For the failure, however, of the German monarchy to be transformed into a genuinely national government, the Schmalkaldic League alone was not to blame. Just as important was the distraction of the Habsburg brothers during this crucial generation, Charles by the Mediterranean and Netherlandish fronts against France and the Turks, and Ferdinand by the defense of the Jagellonian inheritance. They were not unaware of the importance of their grandfather's South German power base to the future of the House of Austria in Germany; but something else always proved more important.

The life of the Schmalkaldic League was linked not to national, Imperial or regional problems and solutions but to the territorial

---

[50] On this very large, inadequately researched subject, see Heinrich Bröhmer, *Die Einwirkung der Reformation auf die Organisation und Besetzung des Reichskammergerichts* (Speyer, 1931); Gerd Dommasch, *Die Religionsprozesse der rekurrierenden Fürsten und Städte und die Erneuerung des Schmalkaldischen Bundes 1534–1536 (Schriften zur Kirchen- und Rechtsgeschichte*, 28; Tübingen, 1961); Robert Schelp, *Die Reformationsprozesse der Stadt Straßburg am Reichskammergericht zur Zeit des Schmalkaldischen Bundes (1524)/1531–1541/(1555)*, 2nd (only) ed. (Kaiserslautern, 1965); Adolf Laufs, ed., *Die Reichskammer-Gerichtsordnung von 1555 (Quellen und Forschung zur höchsten Gerichtsbarkeit im Alten Reich*, 3; Cologne-Vienna, 1976), Introduction.

[51] Here I agree with R. J. W. Evans, *The Making of the Habsburg Monarchy, 1550–1700: An Interpretation* (Oxford, 1979); and with Perry Anderson, *Lineages of the Absolutist State* (London, 1974), pp. 299–309, both of whom date the rise of Austrian absolutism to the seventeenth century. It is known that at the Austrian *Generallandtag* at Innsbruck in the opening months of 1518, Maximilian broached a plan for a centralized regime for the Austrian lands, into which the imperial administration (surely a monarchical one, freed from the princes) would be integrated. His death dashed the scheme; but I have found another version of it, drafted in 1520 under Charles V, which I analyze in *Turning Swiss* (see note 17 above).

state.[52] Once the Lutheran reformation had failed to become a national reformation, from 1525 onward its fate was tied to the single form of the territorial principality: the small-to-middling state whose prince and nobles joined hands in the kind of patriarchal semi-absolutism for which Lutheran Germany became famous. In this setting Lutheranism became an important historical force. Heinz Schilling has demonstrated that Lutheranism could, under the proper conditions, prove a vital force in a communal setting, but Luther's twin political principles of referring all political questions to the New Testament and of insisting that the New Testament teaches submission to authority, cut the theoretical ground from under the doctrine of popular sovereignty.[53] Only when it was coupled with the failure of Lutheranism to develop a national program of reformation, did this doctrine of authority wed the Lutheran reformation to the territorial state. It was not so much that Lutheranism was wedded to medieval ideas and forms—Ernst Troeltsch overestimated the medieval character of German Lutheranism—but that it lacked creative force in public life. The Schmalkaldic League mirrored this impotence. It could serve well enough as a support group for the type of smash-and-grab operation the princes conducted against Braunschweig-Wolfenbüttel, but it could not integrate its members into a political union of all Protestant Christians. Between the poles of legitimism and opportunism this notion scarcely had a chance to survive. Nowhere is this crippled character of the Schmalkaldic League more visible than in its use of foreign support for its role as a German opposition party.[54] The League could use this support to hinder the Habsburg cause in Germany, but not to build itself into a political formation of genuinely national significance.

All this does not mean that the Lutheran reformation changed nothing in the political world of sixteenth-century Germany, nor that the Schmalkaldic League did not provide crucial protection for the

[52] The very best exposition of this theme known to me is by Karlheinz Blaschke: "Wechselwirkungen zwischen der Reformation und dem Aufbau des Territorialstaates," *Der Stuat. Zeitschrift für Staatslehre, öffentliches Recht und Verfassungsgeschichte* 9 (1970): pp. 347–64.

[53] Quentin Skinner, *The Foundations of Modern Political Thought*, 2 vols. (Cambridge, 1978), II, p. 19.

[54] On relations between the Schmalkaldeners and France, see now Jean-Daniel Pariset, *Humanisme, Réforme et Diplomatie. Les relations entre la France et l'Allemagne au milieu du XVIe siècle (Sociéte Savante d'Alsace et des Regions de l'Est*, série *"Grandes Publications,"* 19; Strasbourg, 1982).

young Protestant movement. It does mean, however, that the Schmalkaldic League's role in the great complex of political problems that
Germany had inherited from the fifteenth century must be characterized in negative terms: the immediate political effect of the
Lutheran reformation on this level was to help prevent the erection
of a centralized dynastic monarchy based on the centers of Habsburg
power in the German South. There is another view, of course, based
on the contention that the Schmalkaldic League performed a task
of national defense and preserved liberty against the militant and
aggressive tyranny of Charles V, who under the cover of his Austrian
and Imperial titles tried to strap Germany into Hispano-Roman
bondage. This view has little to do, however, with the historical
Schmalkaldic League. It belongs rather to the legends of 1871.

CHAPTER FIVE

ARCHITECT OF PERSECUTION: JACOB STURM AND THE FALL OF THE SECTS AT STRASBOURG*

"Government," wrote Johann Hug, a priest at St. Stephan's in Strasbourg around 1500, is preserved by religion, ". . . more than by offices or physical efforts."[1] He thereby acknowledged what Peter Munz has called "the normal pressure in all societies . . . to use religion as a means to promote social cohesion."[2] When a plurality of religions promotes division rather than cohesion, one possible response is to create a super-religion which overarches but does not threaten the practical polytheism of the subjects, such as the cult of the emperor in imperial Rome or the "civil religion" of the United States today. The small societies of the German-speaking world at the end of the Middle Ages had no chance to adopt such a grand, comfortable solution of the problem of religious diversity that arose from the Reformation movement. At most their rulers might adopt religious toleration: "a government practices toleration, when it allows to live in peace the minorities who differ from the general norm in their political or religious beliefs but do not threaten the State's existence."[3] The Protestant Reformation, which created a situation of religious plurality in many societies, did not directly promote religious toleration, but it did weaken rulers' will to persecute dissenters with the law's full rigor and to kill them.[4]

Protestant persecution of the Reformation sects is sometimes attributed to the reformers' abandonment of their own gospel. This was the view of Harold S. Bender, who asked: "May it not be said that

---

* This study is dedicated to William J. Bouwsma on the occasion of his sixty-fifth birthday.

[1] Johann Hug, *Quadrivium ecclesie Quatuor prelatorum officium quibus omnis status tum Secularis tum vero Ecclesiasticus subiicitur* (Strasbourg, Johann Grüninger, 1504), fol. 49ʳ.

[2] Peter Munz, "From Max Weber to Joachim of Floris: The Philosophy of Religious History," *The Journal of Religious History* 11 (1980): pp. 167–200, here at p. 182.

[3] Hans R. Guggisberg, ed.: *Religiöse Toleranz. Dokumente zur Geschichte einer Forderung*, Neuzeit im Aufbau. Darstellung und Dokumentation, 4 (Stuttgart-Bad Canstatt, 1984), p. 11.

[4] Claus-Peter Clasen, *Anabaptism: A Social History, 1525–1618. Switzerland, Austria, Moravia, South and Central Germany* (Ithaca and London, 1972), pp. 420–21.

the decision of Luther and Zwingli to surrender their original vision was the tragic turning point of the Reformation?"[5] This fall from the state of grace into the grace of the state formed, in Bender's eyes, the root of the animosity between what his successors would call the "magisterial" and the "radical" reformers.[6] One of them has alleged that "persecution becomes a theological necessity," once Zwingli placed "the unity of Zurich above the faithfulness of the church."[7] Persecution, however, was never a "theological necessity" but a matter of policy, for toleration is not a statement about religious or political truth but a decision not to persecute dissent. Protestant governments commonly made distinctions about dissent, and they rarely persecuted Catholic, Lutheran, or Calvinist dissent as zealously as they hounded the Anabaptists. At Strasbourg, for example, Catholics and Calvinists were tolerated, so long as they made no effort to publicize their dissent.[8] At Augsburg, to take another example, where the Protestants were split by the Luther-Zwingli controversy, opponents may sometimes have been regarded as heretics, but they were rarely so treated.[9] There was no theological reason why Protestants should have persecuted Anabaptists so much more vigorously than they did Catholics or other Protestants. There were, however, reasons why they did so from policy, that is, from their sense of duty to protect law and order and the common good. When this duty collided with the public aggressiveness of the sects, it could make a persecutor out of any magistrate, even one who was personally inclined to be tolerant.[10] Such a tolerant

---

[5] Harold S. Bender, "The Anabaptist Vision," *Church History* 13 (1944): pp. 3–24, excerpted by James M. Stayer and Werner O. Packull, eds./trans.: *The Anabaptists and Thomas Müntzer* (Dubuque, IA, and Toronto, 1980), pp. 13–22, here at p. 16.

[6] The book most responsible for spreading the magisterial-radical dichotomy is George Hunston Williams, *The Radical Reformation* (Philadelphia, 1962). See A. G. Dickens and John Tonkin, *The Reformation in Historical Thought* (Cambridge, MA, 1985), pp. 225–26.

[7] John Howard Yoder, "The Turning Point in the Zwinglian Reformation," *Mennonite Quarterly Review* 32 (1958): pp. 128–40, here from Stayer and Packull, *Anabaptists*, pp. 61–65, here at p. 65.

[8] Lorna Jane Abray, *The People's Reformation: Magistrates, Clergy, and Commons in Strasbourg, 1500–1598* (Ithaca and London, 1985), pp. 116–39.

[9] Olaf Mörke and Katarina Sieh, "Gesellschaftliche Führungsgruppen," in: Gunther Gottlieb, *et al.*, eds.: *Geschichte der Stadt Augsburg, 2000 Jahre von der Römerzeit bis zur Gegenwart*, 2nd ed. rev. (Stuttgart, 1985), pp. 301–11, here at pp. 305–07.

[10] Toleration, it must be stressed, is a matter of policy, not of conviction, and the problem of toleration was never faced by those writers, such as Erasmus, who never assumed a public position. See Marijn de Kroon, *Studien zu Martin Bucers Obrigkeitsverständnis. Evangelisches Ethos und politisches Engagement* (Gütersloh, 1984), pp. 1–7.

persecutor was Jacob Sturm (1489–1553) of Strasbourg, who during the first half of the 1530s designed the destruction of Strasbourg's sects. His is the story of a man who had every religious reason to tolerate and every political one to persecute.

I

Jacob Sturm was born in 1489 into a wealthy noble family of Strasbourg.[11] He was tutored by the humanist Jacob Wimpheling (1450–1528) and sent to study arts at Heidelberg and theology at Freiburg. Back at Strasbourg, Sturm attracted the great Erasmus's attention as a budding man of letters and was named in the *Letters of Obscure Men* as a friend of the *bonae litterae*, a point confirmed by his 1522 opinion on university reform. Like so many other well-educated young clergymen of his day, Sturm came through letters to religion and Protestantism. "If I am a heretic," he flung in Wimpheling's face in a much-cited passage, "you made me one."

Sturm's views on religion fit precisely his background. In August 1525, in the midst of his mediation work between revolutionaries and their rulers, he drafted an opinion on public worship, in which he responded to the preachers' demand that the government abolish the Mass. Sturm disagreed, "because to alter or abolish it would awaken a great deal of ill will both inside and outside the city, and because the whole matter requires further thought and deliberation by the senate."[12] The essential thing for Sturm was not the form of worship but that the preachers "should teach the people what Christ's purpose was in instituting the sacrament, namely, that we should be reminded that He saves us and that through Him we have a common Father in heaven, if only we will believe in and trust Him.... Concentration on externals plunges us into spite, quarreling, envy, and hatred against one another.... Some Christians call themselves 'Evangelicals' and the others 'papists' and 'hypocrites', while the

---

[11] Much of what follows is drawn from a study in progress of Jacob Sturm's career.

[12] Edited by Thomas A. Brady, Jr., "'Sind also zu beiden theilen Christen.' Le mémoire de Jacques Sturm sur le culte public à Strasbourg (août 1525)," in: Marijn de Kroon and Marc Lienhard, eds.: *Horizons européens de la Réforme en Alsace. Mélanges offerts à Jean Rott pour son 65e anniversaire*, Publications de la Société Savante d'Alsace et des Régions de l'Est, 17 (Strasbourg, 1980), pp. 69–75, here at p. 75, ll. 68–73.

others consider themselves the true, old Christians and the others
'Hussites' and the like. Both sides, however, are Christians, may God
have mercy!"[13]

Sturm was as good as his word. When in 1526 his government
narrowly decided "that the Mass should be preserved until the envoys
to His Majesty return," some said that Jacob Sturm "had cast the
deciding vote for the Mass."[14] Jacob Sturm's position resembled what
has been called the policy of the "masters and magistracy," the
alliance of humanistically inclined urban clergymen and scholars,
who saw in the laity's enlightenment the chief goal of reform, with
the urban oligarchs, who would close their ears to any gospel that
did not promote peace, harmony, and the *bonum commune*.[15]

In his official activities, Sturm broadly supported the South German-
Swiss theology. His comments on the Lutheran "Schwabach Articles"
in the autumn of 1529 conform in the main to that position: an
Erasmian unwillingness to go beyond the biblical language; a very
strong animus against the papacy and the old religion; a conservative defense of infant baptism; and above all an emphasis on the
individual's inner disposition—itself a product of God's election—as
a condition of divine presence in the sacraments. In an apologia he
prepared for the Diet of Augsburg in 1530, Sturm wrote, "Item, a
defense of the points concerning the Lord's Supper: that in place of
the papal Mass we have established an Evangelical Mass, that is,
the Lord's Supper; that this service is held every Sunday in specified
churches; and that we do not teach that the Christians who with
true faith receive the sacrament, receive mere bread and wine, but
they receive the true body and blood of Christ—a position deline-
ated, though not very openly, by [Caspar] Schwenckfeld."[16] This is

---

[13] *Ibid.*, pp. 75–6, ll. 76–99.

[14] *Annales de Sébastien Brant*, ed. Léon Dacheux, in *Bulletin de la Société pour la
Conservation des Monuments Historiques d'Alsace*, series 2, vol. 19 (1897–1898): no. 4701
(Sept. 24, 1526).

[15] See Heiko A. Oberman, *Masters of the Reformation: The Emergence of a New Intellectual
Climate in Europe*, trans. Denis Martin (Cambridge, 1981), pp. 187–9, 293.

[16] Johannes Ficker, "Jakob Sturms Entwurf zur Strassburger reformatorischen
Verantwortung für den Augsburger Reichstag 1530," *Elsass-Lothringisches Jahrbuch* 19
(1941): pp. 152–7, here at p. 152. On Schwenckfeld's view, see R. Emmet McLaughlin,
"The Genesis of Schwenckfeld's Eucharistic Doctrine," *Archive for Reformation History*
74 (1983): pp. 94–121; and on his teachings during his early days at Strasbourg,
see now *idem: Caspar Schwenckfeld, Reluctant Radical: His Life to 1540* (New Haven,
1986), pp. 123–46. On his relationship to Jacob Sturm (*ibid.*, pp. 152–7), McLaughlin
is properly cautious.

approximately the position incorporated in 1530 into the statement drafted at Augsburg under Sturm's eye, the Tetrapolitan Confession.[17]

Two statements reveal how Sturm viewed the Christian's prospects in the world. The first comes from 1526, when Wolfgang Capito created a serious diplomatic incident by meddling in Swiss religious politics. Sturm deplored Capito's rashness and carelessness. "It seems to me that one who undertakes to preach the gospel of Christ should freely cast body, life, honor, and property to the winds. For it is certain that the world, which never tolerated Christ while He was here on earth, will also not tolerate Him to the very end of time and will consider all, who sincerely and openly confess Him, to be knaves and rascals and will persecute them. Yet the same world will set up its own Christ, who will approve the world's show and tolerate its lusts and desires. The men of this world will make peace with their invented Christ and agree upon it, for the world always wants to be thought Christian. Therefore, whoever unmasks this counterfeit Christ and preaches the true, genuine Christ, should be resigned to never pleasing the world and to being rejected by the world, except for a little band [ein kleins hüfle] of the elect [usserwelten]. These, in whose hearts the true Christ rules and is confessed, will accept the message and will withstand and overcome the persecution."[18]

The second text comes from a letter by Sturm to Landgrave Philip of Hesse, written in 1546 on the eve of the Schmalkaldic War. "Just as religion in the time of Jesus, the apostles, and the martyrs spread against the will and consent of the Jewish and pagan authorities, so today a household, tomorrow another, then a village, and finally a whole land receives the faith, which gradually comes to prevail despite all persecution. So the restoration of the true religion—or, as we say, the reformation of the Christian faith—also gains strength. . . ."[19]

These two statements open a window into Jacob Sturm's conception of the Reformation movement, which he compared with

---

[17] James M. Kittelson, "Confessio Tetrapolitana," *Theologische Realencyklopädie*, 8: pp. 173–7, here at p. 176.
[18] Jacob Sturm to Peter Butz, Speyer, July 15, 1526, in Hans Virck, *et al.*, eds.: *Politische Correspondenz der Stadt Strassburg im Zeitalter der Reformation*, 5 vols. in 6 (Strasbourg, 1882–1899; Heidelberg, 1928–1933), 1: pp. 263–4, no. 464; and there, too, the following quote. This collection is hereafter cited *PC*.
[19] Max Lenz, ed.: *Briefwechsel des Landgrafen Philipp des Grossmüthigen mit Bucer*, 3 vols., Publikationen aus den königlichen preussischen Staatsarchiven, 5, 28, 42 (Leipzig, 1880–1897), 2: p. 450 n. 2. The passage is omitted from *PC*, 4: p. 103, no. 76.

Christianity at the beginning, when the apostles and martyrs went out to preach the gospel without protection or fear. True to his Erasmian background, he believed that truth would triumph not through an alliance with power but through the hearts of believers. There was no contradiction, at least not until one developed in the early 1530s, between his veering toward spiritualism in his own opinions and his official defense of the South German-Swiss Evangelical position.[20] What can be determined about his personal religious views, however, does not suggest support for the exclusive establishment of a church through the power of the magistrates. Based on his religious views alone, he would sooner be counted on the side of those who believed, as Jean Crespin would later put it, that "among the marks of the true Church of God one of the chief has always been that through all time she has sustained the attacks of persecution."[21]

II

During the first half of the 1530s, Jacob Sturm became the architect of persecution at Strasbourg.[22] He was thinking about the danger of free preaching during the months after the Revolution of 1525, in the course of which he had ridden into rebel camps and seen first-hand what came of allowing free preaching of the gospel. "Variety in preaching," he concluded, "will lead astray the popular mind, which is not used to such matters, and through some preachers' loud cries the people might be divided into unwholesome factions."[23] The Revolution of 1525, not the Luther-Zwingli controversy, first brought Sturm to the train of thought that led to governmental determination of Christian doctrine, to the church settlement of 1534, and to persecution.

Sturm's worries about the gospel and the common people can only have been strengthened by his experience in Switzerland in

---

[20] They do not seem, however, to fit the South German-Swiss reformation's "anticipation of both personal emancipation and of social progress." Oberman, *Masters*, p. 292.

[21] Quoted by Dickens and Tonkin, *Reformation*, p. 42.

[22] On the Anabaptists in general and at Strasbourg, I rely on Williams, *The Radical Reformation*; Klaus Deppermann, *Melchior Hoffman, Soziale Unruhen und apokalyptische Visionen im Zeitalter der Reformation* (Göttingen, 1979); McLaughlin, *Caspar Schwenckfeld*; and James M. Stayer, *Anabaptists and the Sword*, new ed. (Lawrence, KS, 1976).

[23] Wolfgang Capito to Jacob Sturm, Strasbourg, March 4, 1526, in Wolfgang Capito: *In Habakuk prophetam V. Capitonis enarrationes* (Strasbourg, 1526), p. A.ii^r.

1528. In the spring of that year, subjects in the Bernese Oberland declared their will "not to be driven from the old faith and their liberties."[24] The Bernese government struck quickly and in force, and the rebels had to surrender "unconditionally [uf gnad und ungnad]." Jacob Sturm was one of the mediators who tried to stay the harsh hand of the Bernese state from these subjects. The government warned one group of subjects to "uproot the Mass, burn and destroy the images, break up and destroy the altars, and drive out the priests immediately, [or we will] do it with might and main and acts of force, and by no means will we tolerate such disobedience."[25] These events in the Bernese Oberland reinforced the lesson Sturm had learned in 1525: the Holy Spirit's secret workings among humble people did not necessarily teach what the reformers considered to be true religion.

At Strasbourg, as at Bern—though more slowly and less ruthlessly—the new church was imposed from above through a series of acts—police of morals, a new marriage court, appointments of church-wardens—which culminated in the church ordinance of 1534.[26] Jacob Sturm's hand is visible at every stage of the settlement of 1533–1534. He served on the planning committee for the synod of 1533, over which he presided as senior president; he drafted and delivered the reports on all phases of the synod; and he presided over the drafting of the new church ordinance adopted in December 1534. The records of this entire process, through which Strasbourg's regime established their church and suppressed its rivals, everywhere bear the trace of Jacob Sturm's pen.[27]

---

[24] Quoted by Rudolf Dellsperger, "Zehn Jahre bernischer Reformationsgeschichte (1522–1532): Eine Einführung," in: *450 Jahre Berner Reformation. Beiträge zur Geschichte der Berner Reformation und zu Niklaus Manuel = Archiv des Historischen Vereins des Kantons Bern* 64/65 (Bern, 1980), pp. 25–59, here at p. 47.

[25] Quoted in *ibid.*, p. 45.

[26] On this entire process, I rely on François Wendel, *L'église de Strasbourg, sa constitution et son organisation, 1532–1535*, Etudes d'histoire et de philosophie religieuses, 38 (Paris, 1942); Miriam U. Chrisman, *Strasbourg and the Reform: A Study in the Process of Change* (New Haven and London, 1967); Marc Lienhard, "La Réforme à Strasbourg, I: Les événements et les hommes," in: Georges Livet and Francis Rapp, eds.: *Histoire de Strasbourg des origines à nos jours*, vol. 2: *Strasbourg des grandes invasions au XVIᵉ siècle* (Strasbourg, 1981), pp. 365–432; Abray, *People's Reformation*.

[27] Manfred Krebs and Hans-Georg Rott, eds.: *Quellen zur Geschichte der Täufer*, vols. VII–VIII, *Elsass. Stadt Strassburg 1522–1535*, 2 vols., Quellen und Forschungen zur Reformationsgeschichte, 26–27 (Gütersloh, 1959–1960), 2: p. 3, no. 357; pp. 15–16, nos. 365, 367; p. 35, no. 373; pp. 63, 91–2, 204–6, 271–3, 279–80, 294, 355–61, 398–9. This work is hereafter cited *TAE.*

The church settlement of the mid-1530s arose not from "theological necessity" but from policy, the desire for law and order, and it aimed to destroy not dissent in general—the Catholics were not much disturbed[28]—but the sects in particular. No sooner had the preachers persuaded the government to dismantle Catholicism, than they themselves began to be attacked by people who thought the reform had halted halfway. United in informal groups that were sealed by the common experience of adult rebaptism, they were called "Anabaptists (wieddertouffer)" or "baptists (touffer)." Though never numbering more than some hundreds at Strasbourg, they came to be perceived as a threat to established religion and public order.

Swiss Anabaptists began coming to Strasbourg in March 1526, and by early 1528 arrived the first sectarian refugees from Augsburg, who, unlike the more pacific Swiss, kept alive the tradition of Hans Hut (d. 1527), "the major executor of the apocalyptic heritage of Thomas Müntzer."[29] The newcomers soon challenged the established clergy for citizens' hearts, much as the latter had challenged the Catholic clergy earlier in the decade. Hans Denck (c. 1500–1529), a Franconian teacher who arrived in 1528, attracted to his gospel of good works, free will, and universal grace some important citizens, including the rich merchant Friedrich Ingold (d. by 1540).[30]

How Denck's gospel fulfilled the spiritual quests of respectable, educated men is illustrated by the story of Fridolin Meyger (d. 1533/1536). A native of Säckingen, an Austrian town on the Rhine above Basel, Meyger studied at Basel and became a notary in the episcopal administration at Strasbourg.[31] Around 1527 he began to listen to the Anabaptist missionaries, and by the following spring Meyger's house in the Rosenbadgasse was hosting a group who "called themselves 'the Spirit of God,' and others, who don't belong to their sect, they call 'the stinking flesh.'"[32] Caught in the general roundup of

[28] François-Joseph Fuchs, "Les catholiques strasbourgeois de 1529 à 1681," *Archives de l'église d'Alsace* n.s. 22 (1975): pp. 142–69; Abray, *People's Reformation*, pp. 118–19.
[29] Stayer, *Anabaptists*, p. 150.
[30] *TAE*, 1: p. 60, ll. 16–19, no. 64; Thomas A. Brady, Jr., *Ruling Class, Regime and Reformation at Strasbourg, 1520–1555*, Studies in Medieval and Reformation Thought, 22 (Leiden, 1978), pp. 133, 214n, 321; François-Joseph Fuchs, "Les foires et le rayonnement économique de la ville en Europe (XVIᵉ siècle)," in: Livet and Rapp, *Histoire*, 2: pp. 315–17.
[31] On Fridolin Meyger, see *TAE*, 1: p. 132 n. 8.
[32] *Ibid.*, p. 155, no. 130; and see p. 71, no. 74; p. 131 n. 2; p. 132, no. 109; p. 132 n. 8; p. 162, no. 134.

sectarians in October 1528 and again in March 1529, Meyger was twice forgiven and twice relapsed into dissent.[33]

Fridolin Meyger's odyssey offers a precious insight into the mentality of educated Strasbourgeois caught between the preachers' Reformation and the thirst for a second, more radical, one. Deeply religious since adolescence, he explained, he had first been a Catholic and then, persuaded by Erasmus and Luther, a good Evangelical. The quarrels among the reformers confused and deeply troubled him. "Then came these brethren, called 'baptists,' who were sent to me by God (I cannot describe it otherwise), uninvited to my house, and they showed me a middle way between the papacy and Luther. They relieved me of all conflict and showed me the way to a good, honorable, Christian life."[34] He denied under torture "that they want to have all things in common," or that his inner liberation meant outward rebellion against law and order: "For in this realm, gracious lords, I have given my loyalty and taken my oath to the venerable city of Strasbourg, to which I have always been true."

Like so many other devout Christians of his generation, Meyger had greeted the Revolution of 1525 as the dawn of a new era, in which the renewed Christian gospel would end the exploitation of man by man. "Please, do not be angry with me," he once pleaded to the Strasbourg preacher Martin Bucer (1490–1551), "when I confess that when the Peasants' War first began, I found no evil in it, though I did not approve the terrible things they later did. For in my heart I thought that God would work a miracle and once and for all relieve His world, so loaded down with usury that it can bear no more, and make an end to this tyranny. God forgive me, please, don't convict me of sin! God will do that, but not, I reckon, before His great day."[35]

Meyger belonged to a thin stratum of educated Strasbourgeois, mostly clergymen and ex-clergymen who thought the reform had not gone far enough, and who opposed any police of religion and morals, what they called a "new papacy." Some of them tended to the Anabaptists, others to those whom foes called "epicureans." They agreed in holding that the government had no right to compel in matters of belief. The epicureans have been called "less 'believing

---

[33] *Ibid.*, p. 235, no. 181; p. 246, no. 193a; *TAE*, 2: p. 12, no. 361; p. 110, no. 400.
[34] *TAE*, 1: pp. 235–6, no. 182, and there, too, the remaining quotes in this paragraph.
[35] *Ibid.*, p. 222, no. 172.

Christians' than liberal, tolerant humanists," who demanded "tolerance and freedom in the church in order to create space for the
Holy Spirit to operate in the individual and the individual congregation."[36] Some had enjoyed educations not dissimilar to Jacob Sturm's,
and their attitudes appealed to well-to-do folk, especially big merchants, who mistrusted all forms of moral rigorism—sooner or later
rigorists got around to usury.[37]

All of these ingredients—Swiss biblicism and pacifism, Augsburg
apocalypticism, Denckian universalism, and epicureanism—flowed
together at Strasbourg to form a heady stew, which now found
two new cooks, the elegant Silesian nobleman and prophet, Caspar
Schwenckfeld (1489–1561), and the Swabian furrier and chiliast,
Melchior Hoffman (d. 1543). Schwenckfeld came to Strasbourg in May
1529. He defended the Anabaptists, denied governmental authority
over religion, and mocked the notion of "Christian government [christ-
liche Obrigkeit]."[38] He was nonetheless careful not to form a sect,
and intercession by his powerful friends got him off with nothing
more than banishment from Strasbourg.[39] Jacob Sturm must have
been glad to see him go, especially after Schwenckfeld condemned
Sturm's alliance policy with the charge that "the preachers are trying to reach an agreement with Luther on the Sacrament... only
because carnal aid is being sought."[40]

Melchior Hoffman, who came to Strasbourg in June 1529, had
been by turns a Catholic, a Lutheran, and a Zwinglian, and at
Strasbourg he underwent a third and final conversion to the apocalyptic
tradition that reached back through the Augsburg exiles and Hans

[36] Werner Bellardi: "Anton Engelbrecht (1485–1558), Helfer, Mitarbeiter und
Gegner Bucers," *Archiv für Reformationsgeschichte* 64 (1973): pp. 183–206, here at p. 191.
See Marc Lienhard, "Les épicuriens à Strasbourg entre 1530 et 1550 et le prob-
lème de l'incroyance au XVIe siècle," in: Marc Lienhard, ed.: *Croyants et sceptiques
au XVIe siècle*, Publications de la Société Savante d'Alsace et des Régions de l'Est,
collection "Recherches et documents," 30 (Strasbourg, 1981), pp. 17–45; de Kroon,
Studien, pp. 8–23.
[37] François-Joseph Fuchs, "Les marchands strasbourgeois etaient-ils des épicuriens?" in: Lienhard, ed., *Croyants et sceptiques*, pp. 93–100.
[38] McLaughlin, *Caspar Schwenckfeld*, pp. 146–59, is by far the best account. See
also Daniel Husser, "Caspar Schwenckfeld et ses adeptes entre l'église et les sectes
à Strasbourg," in: Georges Livet, Francis Rapp, and Jean Rott, eds.: *Strasbourg au
coeur religieux du XVIe siècle*, Société Savante d'Alsace et des Régions de l'Est, collection
"Grandes publications," vol. 12 (Strasbourg, 1977), pp. 511–35, here at pp. 516–22.
[39] *TAE*, 2: p. 363, no. 581; pp. 367–8, no. 588.
[40] *Ibid.*, p. 367, ll. 11–13, no. 588.

Hut to Müntzer.[41] Hoffman taught from his cell in the Hangman's Tower, that from Strasbourg 144,000 saints would pour forth to preach the true gospel and to establish a theocracy that would endure from the extermination of the ungodly to the Second Coming of Jesus Christ. What he saw in his soul's eye, Melchiorites at Münster in far Westphalia tried to live, making Hoffman a key link between Müntzer and Münster.

The shadow of the Anabaptist kingdom at Münster lay over the entire last phase of the church settlement at Strasbourg. Communism and polygamy shocked the German ruling classes as nothing had done since 1525. Strasbourg's practical policy of toleration during the years between the Revolution of 1525 and the rise of the Anabaptists at Münster in early 1533 made the city vulnerable to being tarred with the Müntzerite-Münsterite brush, which the Lutherans wielded so vigorously against all "sacramentarians."

III

The first edict against the sects appeared over Sturm's signature—he was then ruling stettmeister—on July 27, 1527,[42] and the main campaign against the Anabaptists got underway in 1531. It was famine time. Between 1529 and 1531, thousands of poor country folk streamed into the city in search of aid. During 1530–1531, more than twenty-three thousand poor, citizens and strangers, were fed at the Almshouse, where the administrator, Lux Hackfurt, was deeply involved in Anabaptists circles.[43] In these times the Anabaptists, whom the Augsburgers reported to hold that "whoever owns property may not take the Lord's Supper,"[44] had to be seen in a new light. While the

---

[41] See Klaus Deppermann, "Melchior Hoffman à Strasbourg," in: Livet, Rapp, and Rott, eds., Strasbourg au coeur religieux, pp. 501–10.

[42] Text in TAE, 1: pp. 122–3, no. 92, republished in 1535, 1598, 1601, and 1670.

[43] Daniel Specklin, Les Collectanées, ed. Rodolphe Reuss, in: Bulletin de la Société pour la Conservation des Monuments Historiques d'Alsace, series 2, vol. 14 (1889): nos. 2298, 2306, 2322, 2330, 2332.

[44] TAE, 1: pp. 138–42, no. 116, related to the Nikolsburg Articles. The latter were held to be a forgery by Robert Friedmann, who is followed by Williams, Radical Reformation, p. 226 n. 4, and apparently by Stayer, Anabaptists, p. 164. The editors of TAE (see vol. 1: p. 143, l. 40, to p. 144, l. 10), however, and Clasen, Anabaptism, p. 461 n. 19, hold that in the absence of conclusive evidence, one cannot say that neither Hut nor his followers taught any of these doctrines.

preachers begged for permission to hold public disputations wit their rivals, the Senate and XXI preferred to rely on arrests, hearings, and banishments to break up the meetings, get rid of the leaders, and cow the followers.[45]

The most dangerous activity of the Anabaptists was their attempt to establish independent congregations, and in 1531 appeared a man who put most forcefully the case for freedom of religious organization. He was a Tyrolean mechanic named Pilgram Marpeck, whose religious odyssey duplicated that of Fridolin Meyger. Marpeck argued that the church must be independent from the government, which he held to be legitimate but nonchristian, and demanded for the Anabaptists at least one of the city's churches. In reply he got what no other sectarian had ever achieved, a fullscale disputation before the Senate and XXI, which was held behind closed doors on December 9, 1531.[46] Marpeck attacked first, allowing that "between the papists and the Lutherans the dispute is largely a temporal quarrel, born more of envy than of zeal for things divine."[47] Martin Bucer, the city's leading preacher, answered Marpeck's charges at length, but on December 11 the Senate and XXI decided to hear both sides again.[48]

Strasbourg's preachers now knew of their peril. They warned the Senate and XXI that "on account of the Common Man they should consider the matter and also restore order and punish sins, and as the citizenry alleges that there is a division within the senate, they must do away with dissension and foster unity."[49] "Everyday," they petitioned the Senate and XXI, "pious burghers here tell us how so many people in this city, in the inns and shops, in the squares, on the boats, and in the streets, blaspheme and dishonor most terribly the same Christian doctrine that our lords have confessed before His Christian Majesty and we have taught most faithfully."[50] In the streets of Strasbourg, they complained, "it is said . . . that we are murderers of the Bible and of souls; . . . that anyone, be he Jew, Turk, Catholic, or Evangelical, even if he knows nothing of Our Lord Jesus Christ, can be saved if he leads a good life and does good to his neighbor."[51]

---

[45] *TAE*, 1: pp. 188–9, no. 155; p. 200, no. 170; pp. 233–4, no. 178; p. 278, no. 225; p. 326, no. 243.
[46] *Ibid.*, p. 354, no. 277.
[47] *Ibid.*, p. 351, ll. 12–14.
[48] *Ibid.*, p. 355, no. 281; p. 356, no. 283.
[49] *Ibid.*, p. 356, ll. 33–6, no. 283.
[50] *Ibid.*, p. 357, ll. 17–21, no. 285.
[51] *Ibid.*, p. 358, ll. 6–13.

Sturm and his colleagues were now warned that they were about to undermine their standing abroad and lose control of their own Reformation. They had not intended, as Sturm noted, "when they decided to hear the two sides, to render a judgment in this matter." When it condemned Marpeck on December 18, 1531, the Senate and XXI nonetheless made its first formal doctrinal decision, and it did so on its own assumed authority.[52]

Pilgram Marpeck's expulsion inaugurated the persecution whereby Sturm and his colleagues tried to set their house in order. On the same day, they ordered the arrest of Melchior Hoffman and sent a warning to "the Spaniard [Michael Servetus], who wrote the book about the Trinity," and to Sebastian Franck "to stay out of Strasbourg."[53] By this time Strasbourg's role as the center of religious radicalism in South Germany was becoming a topic of discussion, for example, at the Schmalkaldic League's meeting at Schmalkalden in December of that year,[54] and in 1532 at Schweinfurt, Sturm had to swallow an official condemnation of Sacramentarians and Anabaptists as the price of Strasbourg's inclusion in the Peace of Nuremberg.

All through 1532, the preachers nagged the government about the sects, warning that if it did not act, God "will cast the rulers down entirely and hand the entire people over to the Devil."[55] By late November the preachers and churchwardens had ready an agenda for the synod, based on seven points: religious education of children; attendance at preaching services; discipline of former priests, monks, and nuns; treatment of the Anabaptists; church life in the villages; care of the sick and the needy; and excess in dress and other things. Their aim was "not at all, as some allege, to compel anyone to belief, but to suppress public offenses, which is the obligation of every ruler according to divine and Imperial law."[56]

Jacob Sturm agreed that it was time, "in order to combat the sects, to hold a disputation, and to hold to one [i.e., infant] baptism,"[57] but he drew the line at forcing adults to go to church. "How can they be ordered to do it?" he asked himself, "who should and would determine this? . . . It is good that they be gathered in to listen, but I don't know how. And how should transgressors be found out and

---

[52] *Ibid.*, p. 360, ll. 17–25.
[53] *Ibid.*, p. 355, no. 280; p. 395, no. 294.
[54] *PC*, 1: p. 560, no. 856, noticed in *TAE*, 1: p. 283, no. 231.
[55] *TAE*, 1: p. 549, ll. 3–9.
[56] *Ibid.*, pp. 575–8, no. 348, here at p. 575, ll. 20–3.
[57] *Ibid.*, p. 577 n. 1, l. 40.

punished? Yet, if they are not punished and warned, gradually the order will be regarded with contempt."[58] How to persecute those who were dangerous, without compelling and angering those who were not?

The Senate and XXI appointed Jacob Sturm the synod's senior president.[59] He was in the chair when the preliminary session opened behind closed doors on June 3, 1533. Sturm announced the assembly's purpose: "As much disagreement over the faith and doctrine has arisen, the senate's commissioners are to deliberate with the church-wardens, preachers, pastors, and curates about how we can achieve unity in doctrine."[60]

He might as well have tried to hold down the wind. When the first doctrinal discussions aroused a gale of grumbling, recriminations, accusations, and objections, Sturm admonished the clergy again that "this assembly was arranged solely to further the honor of God and the welfare of this city. He therefore warns and asks them to have regard for this end and stick to it and lay aside whatever one may have against another. For such actions may do great harm to this city and also to them [the clergy] as well, for they have opponents on all sides among the Catholics and the sects, who might say that their disunity is proof of their false teachings."[61] As Sturm then reported to the Senate and XXI on June 4, "the matter is more serious and bigger than my lords had realized," and "the matter will stretch out to some length."[62]

During the synod's summer session, Sturm presided over the hearings of most of the sectarian teachers, including that on July 22 of Claus Frey, a Franconian furrier, who had the poor judgment to marry a baron's sister without divorcing his own wife.[63] The furrier found no such understanding for his bigamy as Landgrave Philip of Hesse would find a few years later, and he was drowned as a bigamist on May 22, 1534.[64]

Sturm also presided over the synod's final session, which he opened on October 23, 1533, with the announcement that "the senate does

[58] *Ibid.*, ll. 30–4.
[59] Brady, *Ruling Class*, pp. 312, 317–18, 332.
[60] *TAE*, 2: p. 36, ll. 7–10.
[61] *Ibid.*, p. 43, l. 34, to p. 44, l. 10.
[62] *Ibid.*, p. 63, ll. 17–18, 32–3.
[63] *Ibid.*, p. 121, no. 410.
[64] *Ibid.*, p. 345, no. 573 n. 1.

not intend to force anyone in matters of faith, but only to suppress conspiracies [rottungen] that might lead to division of the common weal. The senate also commands the preachers to moderate their preaching, so as not to give the commune evidence of a split, and they should also examine the books of Hoffman and Schwenckfeld."[65] The synod over, Sturm and the other presidents reported in February 1534 on doctrine and in June on discipline and the sects. In their first report, Sturm noted "that the entire matter must rest on . . . whether God's Holy Word is accepted here," and the government must now decide "which of the doctrines we have heard is to be held as God's Word, for it would be fruitless to take up the other points before we have decided which one we hold to be God's Word."[66] Eight days later, on March 4, 1534, despite much reluctance, the Senate and XXI decided "unanimously [einhelliglich] . . . to remain with the oft-mentioned [Tetrapolitan] confession and the [Sixteen] articles read to the synod, and to have them preached here as the correct Christian doctrine and enforced as such. Then the presidents are commanded to deliberate and propose how we should handle the sects, which opposed this confession and these articles, suppress them in this city, and prevent their continuation."[67] Against their better judgment, the oligarchs awarded themselves the right to determine correct Christian doctrine and to persecute those who deviated from it. They did so with some reluctance, but they were by no means pushed into this act by the clergy. Indeed, what Bucer and his colleagues wanted most was not the police of doctrine but the enforcement of churchgoing and relief from the dissenters' attacks.

In June Sturm reported for the commission with a ringing declaration of support for Martin Bucer and the other Evangelical clergy, affirming that the government would neither dismiss them nor any longer tolerate the insults against them, "as though they were scoundrels, asskissers, and the like, who had never preached God's Word."[68]

Sturm could now not avoid his earlier question about compulsion in religion. "It would be good," he wrote, "if we could find a way to get the people to come to church and hear the Word of God. We think, however, that it cannot be achieved through ordinances . . . ,

---

[65] *Ibid.*, p. 178, ll. 26–31.
[66] *Ibid.*, p. 272, ll. 14–15, 23–6.
[67] *Ibid.*, p. 286, ll. 18–24.
[68] *Ibid.*, pp. 353–61, no. 557, here at p. 354, ll. 2–3, and see p. 361, ll. 6–29.

for in matters of faith, which is a voluntary act and gift of God, little can be gained through laws. Then, too, as the hearing of sermons is an external thing,[69] and not an act of faith itself, we must be concerned that such laws could not be enforced . . . in such a large community with so many parishes and sermons. . . . But if the law were not obeyed and the violators were not punished, it would only diminish the government's authority . . . and cause comment that a new papacy has been established, for, seeing that no one attends the sermons, they want to force it with laws. . . . This is the preachers' doing, so that they will have people to listen to them.'"[70] "Laws," declared Sturm, driving the point home, "make hypocrites."[71]

His reluctance to compel participation in the official church's life did not mean that Sturm wanted to tolerate its rivals: "Since we have already decided to hold to the [Tetrapolitan] confession submitted at Augsburg and the synod's [Sixteen] articles, it follows that all other sects, who oppose this doctrine, are not to be tolerated, and their supporters should be dealt with."[72] The Anabaptists were given two alternatives: either renounce their errors and conform to the civic church or leave the city within two weeks.[73]

The new church ordinance, which was read and approved on December 28, 1534, established an order that would last for half a century.[74] In the address he drafted to announce the ordinance to the 300 officials (Schöffen) of the guilds, Sturm reminded them how it had all begun. "Years ago," he wrote, "it was asserted and decided by the stettmeister and Senate and XXI and also by the Schöffen and ammeister, that in this city of Strasbourg the holy gospel was to be preached purely and clearly, and also that all sorts of anti-biblical abuses should be abolished."[75] In order to defend this decision the regime "with the knowledge and approval of Schöffen and ammeister, entered into a Christian alliance with some electors, princes, counts, and cities who agree with us on faith. This happened so that we might more peacefully hold to the confessed truth and the

---

[69] The senators deleted from Sturm's draft the words, "which might have either good or bad results."
[70] Ibid., p. 354, ll. 10–23.
[71] Ibid., p. 354 n. 2, l. 41.
[72] Ibid., p. 355, ll. 19–24.
[73] Ibid., pp. 356–7.
[74] Ibid., pp. 368–9, nos. 620–1; pp. 421–31, no. 637.
[75] Ibid., p. 422, ll. 2–6.

biblical doctrine."[76] The government had expected that this confession of the truth would lead to "the expansion of God's honor, obedience to authority, increase of brotherly love, and civic unity," but instead there arose "all sorts of heretical sects, unnecessary argument, and contentious opinions about the faith in this city, which caused many to fall away from the confessed truth and to have contempt for the doctrine and preaching of the holy gospel and its preachers alike, leading in turn through many harmful splits and divisions to considerable scandal and provocation of many Christians and to the destruction of civic peace and unity."[77] This unfortunate outcome of the Evangelical movement made the new law necessary, so as "to avert the ruin, physical and spiritual, of the whole city and its citizens."[78] How this had all happened, Sturm could not say, except to blame it on disrupters from "foreign parts."

In order to combat the sects without introducing a strict police of belief, Sturm and his colleagues seized on the sectarians' antipathy for infant baptism, "which they hold to be unchristian and an abomination before God," and decreed that all babies must be baptized within six weeks of birth.[79] The children of Strasbourg thus became spiritual hostages against future attempts at a second reformation at Strasbourg.

The irony of the situation, that a regime which had acted for the freedom of the gospel should persecute those who exercised that freedom, was driven home by Leupold Scharnschlager (d. 1563), a soap-maker, who in his broad Tyrolean accent told the Senate and XXI that "in the role of the temporal sword, you know that you have no power over faith."[80] "My dear lords," he said, "you assert and press us to abandon our faith and accept yours. That is just the same as when the emperor said to you, you should abandon your faith and accept his. Now I speak to your consciences: Do you think it right to obey the emperor in such things? Ah, well, then you might also say that we ought to obey you in such things. Then you would be obliged to reinstate all the idolatry and papal convents, also the Mass and other things."[81] Against the obdurate belief that each person

---

[76] *Ibid.*, p. 422, l. 13, to p. 423, l. 2.
[77] *Ibid.*, p. 423, ll. 5–7, 10–16.
[78] *Ibid.*, p. 425, ll. 11–15.
[79] *Ibid.*, p. 426, l. 31, to p. 427, l. 2, and p. 427, ll. 5–17.
[80] *Ibid.*, pp. 346–53, no. 476, here at p. 347, ll. 4–5.
[81] *Ibid.*, p. 348, l. 2, to p. 349, l. 11.

must judge his or her own faith, whatever the consequences for the bonum commune, Jacob Sturm and his fellow oligarchs of Strasbourg could pit only their own duty to guard the commune and its social order with the instruments of temporal power.

IV

Jacob Sturm's government decided in 1534 to institute religious persecution not from an evident desire to compel in matters of religion, but from a wish to guard the established church and the public peace and to protect their foreign policy by promoting their city's reputation for orthodoxy. The latter was endangered by the movement connected with their unwelcome prisoner, Hoffman. On November 11, 1533, Sturm relayed to his colleagues a rumor from North Germany that "Melchior Hoffman has won out here, and the whole city [of Strasbourg] holds his opinion."[82] The two cities were indeed linked in the visions of Münster's Melchiorite leaders, who "told the common folk in the city of Münster that they had a vision of three cities in the night. . . . One was the city of Münster, the second Strasbourg, and the third was Deventer. These same cities . . . God has chosen as the places where he will raise up a holy people."[83] Strasbourg's regime got its news of events in the North through Landgrave Philip of Hesse, whose two letters to Sturm about Münster bracketed the final deliberation on the church ordinance.[84]

At Strasbourg, the formation of the new church and the coming of persecution were responses to the movement from Müntzer to Münster. Sturm and his colleagues tried thereby to safeguard their two major gains of the Reformation era: the domestication of civic religious life and the pan-Protestant front with the Lutherans. These two welcome fruits of the Evangelical movement were endangered both by current Anabaptist agitation and by memories of the Revolution of 1525, the legacy of which Anabaptists were held to cherish. In Lutheran, as in Catholic eyes, radical religion meant radical poli-

---

[82] *Ibid.*, p. 204, ll. 8–9.
[83] Heinrich Gresbeck, "Bericht von der Wiedertaufe in Münster," in *Berichte der Augenzeugen über das münsterische Wiedertäuferreich*, ed. C. A. Cornelius, Die Geschichtsquellen des Bisthums Münster, 2 (Münster, 1853; reprinted, Münster, 1965), pp. 1–214, here at pp. 22–3.
[84] *PC*, 2: p. 228, no. 247; pp. 240, 247, nos. 262, 267.

tics, and the policy of persecution at Strasbourg came as a submission to this belief, despite an engrained distaste for compulsion in matters of religion.

It took ten years for the Strasbourgeois to accept willy-nilly the lesson Luther had tried for years to teach them, the one he had learned when he slipped back into Wittenberg in the winter of 1521–1522 and saw the radical changes taking place there. He had grasped immediately that once the path to individual salvation was freed from ecclesiastical authority, the Church's other functions—mainly the censorship of morals and culture—must either migrate to the state or disappear, depriving the social order of religion's support. Luther had summed up the situation in one question: "But where is the order?"[85]

Jacob Sturm, who professed to believe that doctrinal dispute was simply a "quarrel about words (wortzanck)," nonetheless trod the path of persecution in the pursuit of order. An eyewitness to the frightening scenes of 1525, he threw heart and soul into the war against the sects, though his own beliefs may not have differed much from those of the men and women he persecuted. Nothing in his vaguely Erasmian background prepared him for the hard lesson the Lutherans taught: if Christians had no community of ritual, they must form community through doctrine, or they could have no community at all. And since community could not be formed through the Common Man—that alternative was blocked in 1525—it must be formed either through the government or, what was broadly rejected as a "new papacy,"[86] the clergy. The church settlement of 1533–1534 institutionalized religious practice and persecution at Strasbourg. It created "an organization not too far removed from the model of the imperial church of the fourth and fifth centuries, and . . . provided discipline only for the group which needed it least—the clergy."[87] This limited but substantial accomplishment closed an entire phase of the Reformation at Strasbourg, a phase in which Evangelical clergy and Evangelical laity united on the need for change. On this

---

[85] See my discussion in "Luther's Social Teaching and the Social Order of His Age," in *Martin Luther Quincentennial*, ed. Gerhard Dünnhaupt (Detroit, 1984), pp. 270–90, here at pp. 280–3.

[86] See Steven Ozment, *The Reformation in the Cities: The Appeal of Protestantism to Sixteenth-Century Germany and Switzerland* (New Haven and London, 1975), pp. 151–64, for a cogent discussion of this theme.

[87] Chrisman, *Strasbourg and the Reform*, p. 224.

unity depended the startling pace of religious change in many South German cities during the 1520s. Strasbourg was not the pacesetter—that was Zurich's role—but it always ran with the best. Then, during the early 1530s, there arose the need, spurred by external political considerations and internal dissent, to reconstruct ecclesiastical authority. At this point Evangelical paths diverged, leaving Schwenckfeld, Denck, Marpeck, and many other friends of toleration on one side, and Jacob Sturm, the tolerant persecutor, on the other.

Jacob Sturm became the architect of the persecution of dissent at Strasbourg out of a twofold policy: the need to protect the settlement with the Lutheran powers, and the need to protect the loyal Evangelical clergy. Nothing in the, admittedly fragmentary, evidence about his own religious views makes such a policy necessary or even desirable. This does not mean that he was afflicted with some mysterious desire to persecute, that he was prejudiced against Anabaptists, or that he was a hypocrite. He persecuted dissent, because the dissenters threatened the alliance with the Lutherans, of which he was also the architect, and the peace of the civic church, which he had striven to free from the old order. The threats drew palpability from the situation of the times, especially in the year of Münster, and the behavior of the dissenters, and in his judgment of the threat Jacob Sturm was surely correct. He trod the path of persecution reluctantly, but he trod it nonetheless.

CHAPTER SIX

JACOB STURM AND THE SEIZURE OF
BRUNSWICK-WOLFENBÜTTEL BY THE SCHMALKALDIC
LEAGUE, 1542–1545

Summary

The war of 1546–1547 between the Emperor Charles V and the German
Protestant alliance, called the "Schmalkaldic League," grew out of a
long series of political conflicts and military enterprises, the most important of which is the subject of this study. After a long, bitter exchange
of insults and provocations, war erupted in 1542 between the Protestant
chiefs of the Schmalkaldic League—Elector John Frederick of Saxony,
Landgrave Philip of Hesse, and Duke Moritz of Saxony—and Duke
Henry of Brunswick-Wolfenbüttel, the last important Catholic prince
in North Germany. Although the invasion violated the League's constitution, they expected their southern allies to help pay for the duchy's
occupation and conversion to Protestantism. As spokesman for the
southern Protestant cities, Jacob Sturm of Strasbourg, contested the
legality of either holding the duchy or forcibly converting it to Protestantism. The bitter quarrel over this issue substantially weakened the
German Protestants on the eve of their confrontation with the emperor.
This study rests chiefly on published and manuscript correspondence
among the leaders of the Protestant alliance: Landgrave Philip of Hesse,
Elector John Frederick of Saxony, Jacob Sturm, and Martin Bucer,
the chief reformer of Strasbourg.

Between the Truce of Frankfurt in 1539 and the outbreak of war
between the Emperor Charles V and the Protestant Schmalkaldic
League in 1546, the political life of the Holy Roman Empire recovered to a great degree the rhythms to which it had moved before
1530. The Imperial Diet met regularly after a hiatus of nearly a
decade; traditional tensions between princes and imperial free cities
revived; and many princes, even Protestants, enthusiastically supported the emperor's new war with France. Only one major conflict
disturbed this restoration: in 1542 the Schmalkaldic chiefs, Elector
John Frederick (1503–1554) of Saxony and Landgrave Philip (1504–
1567) of Hesse, invaded, occupied, and introduced their religious
reformation into the lands of Duke Henry (1489–1568) of Brunswick-
Wolfenbüttel. This so-called Brunswick affair not only disrupted

imperial political life, but also disturbed relations within the Schmal-
kaldic League. One of the first to foresee this outcome was Jacob
Sturm (1489–1553), *stettmeister* and leading politician of the city of
Strasbourg and one of the League's architects. His views on the
Brunswick affair throw an especially clear light on the tensions within
the League during these years.[1]

By 1540, Duke Henry (1489–1562), called "the Younger," of
Brunswick-Wolfenbüttel stood as the last reliably Catholic ruling lay
prince on the North German plain.[2] Vigorous, able, ambitious, vain,
loyally Catholic though not especially pious, Henry, a capable ruler
and founder of the modern Guelph state, became in 1538 a commander of the League of Nuremberg, the Schmalkaldeners' Catholic
rival.[3] Duke Henry, the last, best hope of Catholicism in the north,
was a dangerous foe for the neighboring Protestant cities, Goslar and
Brunswick, whom he repeatedly menaced, and he was a maddening
rival for the Schmalkaldic chiefs, with whom he lay locked in a savage personal quarrel. His conflicts with the cities were of purely secular
origin, though the League—the southerners reluctantly—in July 1541
recognized them as "religious" and therefore within the Schmalkaldic
League's purview.[4] Meanwhile, Henry's smoldering personal quarrel

---

[1] The context for this study is provided by Thomas A. Brady, Jr., *Protestant Politics:
Jacob Sturm (1489–1553) of Strasbourg and the German Reformation* (Atlantic Highlands,
N.J.: Humanities Press, 1995). For the history of the Schmalkaldic League in general, see *idem.*, "Phases and Strategies of the Schmalkaldic League: A Perspective
after 450 Years," *Archiv für Reformationsgeschichte* 74 (1983): pp. 162–81. On the restoration of imperial politics, see Georg Schmidt, "Die Freien und Reichsstädte im
Schmalkaldischen Bund," in Volker Press and Dieter Stievermann, eds. *Martin Luther:
Probleme seiner Zeit* (Stuttgart: Klett-Cotta, 1986), pp. 177–218, here at pp. 179–80,
though I do not agree with his opinion of what I have called the "state-like" tendencies of the Schmalkaldic League.

[2] Franz Petri, "Herzog Heinrich der Jüngere von Braunschweig-Wolfenbüttel: Ein
niederdeutscher Territorialfürst im Zeitalter Luthers und Karls V.," *Archiv für Reformationsgeschichte* 72 (1981): pp. 122–58, with references.

[3] Günter Scheel, "Kurbraunschweig und die übrigen welfischen Lande," in *Deutsche
Verwaltungsgeschichte*, ed. Kurt G. A. Jeserich, Hans Pohl, and Georg-Christoph von
Unruh, vol. 1: *Vom Spätmittelalter bis zum Ende des Reiches* (Stuttgart: Deutsche Verlags-
Anstalt, 1983), pp. 741–63, here at pp. 746, 752, 755–56, 760. Heinrich's militancy
comes out in his comments on the Truce of Frankfurt (1539), Georg Pfeilschifter, ed.,
*Acta reformationis catholicae ecclesiae Germaniae concernantia saeculi XVI: Die Reformverhandlungen
des deutschen Episkopats von 1520 bis 1570*, 6 vols. (Regensburg: F. Pustet, 1959–1974), 3:
pp. 89–90, no. 55, esp. p. 89, ll. 20–30.

[4] An imperial edict against Goslar on October 25, 1540, condemned the city for
breaches of the public peace. Gundomar Blume, *Goslar und der Schmalkaldische Bund
1527/31–1547*, Beiträge zur Geschichte der Stadt Goslar, 26 (Goslar: Selbstverlag

with Landgrave Philip of Hesse flared in 1538, when the Hessians caught a Brunswick secretary with compromising documents intended for Dr. Matthias Held, the architect of the League of Nuremberg.[5] Jacob Sturm, whom the landgrave consulted, responded that

> the duke's intrigues [*Practicken*] aim to provoke the imperial estates against one another and to create the suspicion that each is in danger of attack from the other and must therefore join an alliance and begin to mobilize, so as not to allow the other side the first strike. Once both sides are convinced and are mobilized, the war will already have begun.[6]

The secretary's revelations, plus mutual acts of belligerence—Castle Wolfenbüttel fired on Landgrave Philip in April 1538, and the Saxons later returned the honor—persuaded the Schmalkaldic chiefs in late 1539 to commit their case to public opinion via the printing press, provoking a flood of pamphlets—more than sixty titles in 1542—the tone of which may be gathered from Martin Luther's contribution. "You should not write a book," Martin Luther mocked Duke Henry in the most celebrated of these pamphlets, called *Wider Hanswurst*, "until you have heard an old sow fart. Then you should gape in wonder and say, 'Thank you, beautiful nightingale, there I hear a text for me!'"[7] This war of words, in which lords of humankind

---

des Geschichts- und Heimatschutzvereins, 1969), p. 75. On the local background to the Brunswick affair, see Horst Reller, *Vorreformatorische und reformatorische Kirchenverfassung im Fürstentum Braunschweig-Wolfenbüttel*, Studien zur Kirchengeschichte Niedersachsens, 10 (Göttingen: Vandenhoeck & Ruprecht, 1959), pp. 95–98; and Blume, *Goslar*, pp. 51–52, 81–82, 91–92.

[5] Petri, "Herzog Heinrich," p. 140.

[6] Jacob Sturm to Landgrave Philip of Hesse, Strasbourg, January 17, 1539, in Staatsarchiv (hereafter StA.), Weimar, Reg. H., 2: p. 225, no. 102, fol. 208ʳ [a copy that is not in *Politische Correspondenz der Stadt Strassburg im Zeitalter der Reformation*, eds. Hans Virck, Otto Winckelmann, and Harry Gerber, 5 vols. (Strasbourg: Trübner, 1882–1898; Heidelberg: Winter, 1928–1933), hereafter *PC*]. The Recess of the Schmalkaldic League's Diet at Frankfurt, February 21, 1539, in StA Weimar, Reg. H., 2: p. 225, no. 102, fols. 2ʳ–28ʳ, here at fol. 3ʳ, notes that he revealed his name (Stephan Schmidt) and "sonst vilfeltiger kuntschafft." This happened during the crisis over the city of Minden in 1538–1539, on which see Thomas A. Brady, Jr., "A Crisis Averted: Jacob Sturm and the Truce of Frankfurt, 1539," in Monika Hagenmaier and Sabine Holtz, eds., *Krisenbewußtsein und Krisenbewältigung in der Frühen Neuzeit: Festschrift Hans-Christoph Rublack* (Frankfurt: Peter Lang, 1992), 47–60.

[7] Quoted by Mark U. Edwards, *Luther's Last Battles: Politics and Polemics, 1531–1546* (Ithaca: Cornell University Press, 1983), p. 158. On this struggle, see *ibid.*, pp. 143–62; Eike Wolgast, *Die Wittenberger Theologie und die Politik der evangelischen Stände: Studien zu Luthers Gutachten in politischen Fragen*, Quellen und Forschungen zur Reformationsgeschichte, 47 (Gütersloh: Gerd Mohn, 1977), pp. 277–78.

behaved like fishwives in the marketplace, entertained the empire for years. It became truly dangerous only because of the principals' roles in the confessional alliances.

In October 1541, the Schmalkaldic chiefs decided to act, and they met at Naumburg with Duke Moritz of Saxony to plan the strike against Henry of Brunswick-Wolfenbüttel.[8] Giving their cause the color of a religious war, so as to make their allies share the costs,[9] they declared war on July 13, 1542, and at the head of twenty thousand men took Henry's lands in a few weeks——as easily as the landgrave had seized Württemberg in 1534.[10] A jubilant Luther trumpeted "This is a truly divine victory, for God has done it all. He is the *fac totum*, and we may now hope that the last days are at hand!"[11] The conquerors installed a governor, Bernhard von Mila, who under their instructions began a reform of the duchy's church in a Lutheran sense, much as Duke Ulrich had done in Württemberg, except that in Brunswick-Wolfenbüttel there could be no legitimate claim to the *jus reformandi* except by title of conquest. Because the Schmalkaldic chiefs were determined at the very least to recover their costs, they rejected the most widely supported solution, placing the duchy in receivership ("sequestration") with its feudal lord, the emperor. The struggle of greed, zeal, and indecision drew the situation out from 1545, when they mobilized once more to defeat Henry's attempt to retake the duchy, through 1547, when Charles' victory over the Schmalkaldic League opened the way to Henry's restoration.

The Brunswick affair, more than any other, prevented the partial restoration of traditional imperial political patterns from stabilizing and containing the reformation movement in North Germany. The League's strike compromised deeply the Schmalkaldeners' standard

---

[8] The campaign plan of October 26, 1541, is printed by Erich Brandenburg, ed., *Politische Korrespondenz des Herzogs Moritz von sachsen*, 2 vols. (Leipzig: Teubner, 1900–1904; rpt., Berlin: Akademie-Verlag, 1982), 1: pp. 225–31, no. 228; and it is discussed by Max Lenz, ed., *Briefwechsel Landgraf Philipps des Grossmüthigen von Hessen mit Bucer*, 3 vols., Publikationen aus den K. Preussischen Staatsarchiven, 5, 28, and 47 (Stuttgart: S. Hirzel, 1880–1891; rpt., Osnabruck: Zeller, 1965), hereafter *Briefwechsel*, 1: pp. 155–60, and Blume, *Goslar*, p. 96.
[9] The secret plan provides "dass beide kur- und fursten als hauptleut die krigsreth [i.e., of the Schmalkaldic League] nicht anderst oder nicht ehr fordern sollen oder werden, dann so sie schon das volk im werk versammlet haben, oder im werk sein, dasselb zu versammlen; alsdann sollen sie solche krigsrethe auch erfordern." Brandenburg, *Politische Korrespondenz*, 1: p. 227, ll. 1–5.
[10] Petri, "Herzog Heinrich," p. 146.
[11] Quoted by Edwards, *Battles*, p. 154.

defense, that they were loyal both to the empire and emperor and to the true religion; it gravely weakened the League, increasing friction between South and North, and between cities and princes, when the alliance's construction came up for renewal in 1545–1546. These weaknesses heightened the emperor's temptation to meet the German situation with force, which he decided to do in 1546.

Sturm and his colleagues backed the princes' Brunswick stroke from the first. They supported the argument made by the duke's foes, the cities of Goslar and Brunswick, that however they had begun, the quarrels with Duke Henry were "religious matters" in the League's understanding, because the Duke's hatred for them as Protestants transformed the cases into "religious matters."[12] The Strasbourgeois were nonetheless touchy about respect for the League's constitutional procedures, which is probably why Landgrave Philip wanted to initiate Jacob Sturm into the secret plan against Brunswick-Wolfenbüttel even before the princes signed the highly confidential pact at Naumburg, "because, as is well known, the southerners all follow Jacob Sturm." Sturm learned of the plot at Speyer in early February 1542, when the Hessian agent Rudolf Schenck, "on special orders and under his sworn oath of loyalty" to the landgrave, revealed the three princes' plan of campaign. Sturm, the Hessian report ran, "judged the matter very positively and answered in the enclosed document [lost], which is composed in hidden words [i.e., in cipher] by Schenck."[13] The landgrave proposed to tell other southern politicians of the plan, "though not Augsburg," on Jacob Sturm's advice, "so that they will be prepared ahead of time to support the mobilization of seven thousand foot and three thousand horse for Goslar." Jacob Sturm thus knew since sometime in February 1542 that the three princes planned to invade Brunswick and assemble the League's war council post facto to approve the war. Sturm's assent to this plan is confirmed by the Strasbourg preacher Martin Bucer (1491–1550), who wrote to the landgrave in mid-March that "Sir Jacob recognizes that Your Grace's proposal is and will remain the best and swiftest way, and he doesn't doubt that the estates will be glad to take part in it."[14] At home, however, Sturm recommended

---

[12] *PC*, 3: pp. 135–38, nos. 148, 156, nos. 165, 164–65, no. 172.
[13] Lenz, *Briefwechsel*, 2: p. 56 n. 2, and there, too, the following quote.
[14] Lenz, *Briefwechsel*, 2: p. 64, no. 134. The subject is a bit obscure, but the following passage is about Duke Henry.

that this regime advise negotiations rather than war, perhaps so as
to conceal how deeply in the princes' confidence he lay.

At any event, once the invasion began, Sturm backed the princes.
On July 3 he and Ammeister Mathis Pfarrer put to their colleagues
the question: Should they back this war, which the princes had begun
in an unconstitutional manner? If they supported the war and paid
the city's share, a victory would relieve pressure on Strasbourg,
though a defeat would bring blame on "us as a cause of this evil."[15]
The Senate and Twenty-One[16] decided "we should not abandon the
princes," and instructed their Schmalkaldic war councilor, Ulman
Böcklin, that

> he should voice our complaint [against unconstitutionality], but even
> if this or that ally withdraws, the aid must be given to the commanders.
> And although the princes ignored the majority and exceeded the terms
> of the alliance, the aid should be paid according to the League's rules.

In July 1542, therefore, when the Schmalkaldic chiefs were on the
march, the Strasbourgeois threw their city's whole weight behind
the invasion of Brunswick-Wolfenbüttel. They sent Michel Han to the
Schmalkaldic cities' meeting at Ulm in July to rouse the southern
towns, whose envoys, however, bitterly criticized the princes for acting without consultation and voted only half the sum—a doubled
"month"—that the Hessian envoy had asked for. Duke Ulrich opposed
the strike against his kinsman even more strongly than the cities did.[17]

By mid-August the troubles over money began in earnest, and
when the League's diet met during the Imperial Diet of November,
the southerners began to request that southern League funds remain
in the South.[18] Soon the landgrave was complaining that the southerners still owed him 130,000 florins from the second of the two
doubled "months"—the northern cities had all paid both "months"—
and reminded the Strasbourgeois "that we borrowed money for this
campaign, which must be repaid."[19] Second thoughts were emerg-

---

[15] *PC*, 3: p. 275, no. 265, from Archives Municipales de Strasbourg (hereafter AMS), XXI 1542, fol. 245; for there, too, the remaining quotes in this paragraph. Unfortunately, the opinion by Sturm and Pfarrer is lost.

[16] The Senate and Twenty-One (XXI) were the city's permanent magistracy, including the Thirteen (XIII), a privy council for foreign affairs.

[17] Michel Han's report to the Senate and Twenty-One of Strasbourg is printed in *PC*, 3: pp. 277–78, no. 267; and the southern cities' reactions, see *ibid.*, pp. 278, 283–84, no. 271; p. 287, no. 277; pp. 289–90, no. 281.

[18] *Ibid.*, pp. 296–97, no. 288.

[19] Lenz, *Briefwechsel*, 2: p. 97, no. 146.

ing in Strasbourg's city hall, and in August the regime proposed
that the second doubled "month" be retained in the South, at Ulm,
in case it was needed there.[20] This feeling was general among the
southern allies, who did not simply refuse, as Duke Ulrich did, to
pay the second "month." According to the Hessian treasurer, the
League's southern district should have contributed for the two doubled "months"—the first levied by the commanders, the second by
the war council—a total of 207,600 florins, of which by autumn less
than half had been paid.[21] Strasbourg's regime did ask the landgrave
to fetch its share of the second doubled "month," but by this time—
October 1542—the commanders were asking for a third doubled
"month," and by this time Duke Ulrich was openly questioning the
constitutionality of the whole affair.[22] Landgrave Philip, for his part,
told the Strasbourgeois that the southerners' refusal to pay insulted
and injured him, that the cities themselves were to blame that the
third "month"—which he agreed was "too much"—had been voted
by the League's diet at Brunswick in August, and that "if this is the
way we are to operate, that the money doesn't come in until after
the war, and then only begrudgingly, we'll soon tire of this alliance."[23]

Martin Bucer greeted the Brunswick campaign as he had greeted
the Württemberg campaign eight years before, with triumphant ela-
tion, followed by anxious second thoughts. In early September, when
the duchy was won, he was filled with advice about reforming its
church and with "eternal praise and thanks to God, our Father
Almighty, who through His Son, Jesus Christ, has granted this gracious victory to His people. He will also assure that this victory will
serve to greatly expand His kingdom."[24] A month later, Bucer was
taking the discontent seriously enough to lecture the landgrave about
equity. "Our alliance is a Protestant alliance," he wrote

> in which no one should make money or seek to become richer than
> he is, but in which everyone should maintain the highest standards of
> loyalty and equality [*gleichmessigkeit*]. Equality is the basis of all com-
> munities, inequality is like the very quicksilver, which destroys every-
> thing, especially religious community.[25]

---

[20] *Ibid.*
[21] *Ibid.*, where the treasurer's statement is quoted.
[22] *Ibid.* The landgrave's receipt for Strasbourg's share of the second doubled
"month" is dated November 12, 1542, and he also bought 1,500 pikes at Strasbourg.
[23] *Ibid.*, 2: pp. 101–3, no. 148.
[24] *Ibid.*, 2: p. 83, no. 142 (from which comes the quote), and pp. 90–91, no. 143.
[25] *Ibid.*, 2: p. 96, no. 149.

And six weeks later, Bucer was warning the landgrave against those who "wanted to slip quicksilver among our princes and estates, just as Your Grace was able to do in the Swabian League."[26]

It all happened so quickly, and though the object of strife was money, of which the duchy's continued occupation sucked up enormous sums, the root of the League's discontent lay in the southern allies' resentment of their chiefs' unconstitutional invasion of Brunswick, their indignation at reports of Hessian-Saxon plundering of the duchy's ecclesiastical lands, and their fear of being branded "church robbers" and simple enemies of the public peace. At Strasbourg, the regime's support for the Schmalkaldic chiefs' line remained firm all through the autumn.[27] Yet by year's end even the loyal Strasbourgeois began to grumble about the landgrave's finances, how he had pocketed Duke Moritz's gift of 50,000 thalers, how the booty had not been assigned to cover the war's expenses, and how the princes "remain in the field with large forces and at great expense."[28]

In truth, the Schmalkaldic chiefs plundered the conquered duchy thoroughly and well, so much so "that the [duchy's] people could gain no firm hold on the gospel."[29] Their depredations against ecclesiastical and other properties, their cavalier handling of the introduction of Lutheranism, and their savage reprisals against the natives who supported Duke Henry's attempt to recover the duchy in 1545, all contributed to the memory of the Schmalkaldic League's occupation as "the old government by force."[30]

The Schmalkaldic chiefs nonetheless found themselves in the position of a dog that chases cars and then catches one. What to do with the duchy? The situation forced Jacob Sturm to face in March 1543 the consequences of the policy he had supported a year before.[31]

---

[26] *Ibid.*, 2: p. 106, no. 149.

[27] See *PC*, 3: pp. 329–30, no. 315, where the regime approves payment of both the second and third doubled "months," the razing of Castle Wolfenbüttel, appointment of a southern representative in the occupation council, and allowing Saxon-Hessian occupation for at least one year until a decision on the duchy's disposal.

[28] *PC*, 3: p. 340, no. 327, drafted by Jacob Sturm.

[29] Reller, *Kirchenverfassung*, p. 101.

[30] *Ibid.*, p. 102. On the Hessian-Saxon plundering of the ecclesiastical lands and properties, see Kurt Köber, *Kirchengüterfrage und schmalkaldischer Bund*, Schriften des Vereins für Reformationsgeschichte, nos. 111–112 (Leipzig: Rudolph Haupt, 1913), pp. 183–87.

[31] *PC*, 3: pp. 346–47, no. 330, set on March 10 and read to Senate and Twenty-One on March 17, 1543; the quotations in this paragraph are from this document. With it Sturm sent a Saxon-Hessian opinion which opposed restoration under any circumstances.

It is true, he wrote, "that it would be much better, and do more for our reputation, to sign a treaty with Duke Henry's children, to restore the land to them, and with the duke himself. That is our first choice, and so we have advised." There being no way to keep Duke Henry out of the matter, if his sons were installed, the League should negotiate with him if necessary, "so that the affair may be put to rest." The Schmalkaldic chiefs refused to put any trust in Henry or his word, but it might be possible to raze his fortresses, require his estates to go surety for his conduct, and get imperial approval of a treaty with him. Under these conditions, "we can trim his claws, so that he cannot start anything, or if he does, he must lose." It has been argued, Sturm continued, that if he gets back his lands, Henry will restore Catholicism. "We believe," however,

> that this is not sufficient reason to deprive him of his lands. This is not the reason they were taken, and when he has made an equitable treaty with Goslar and Brunswick, and when we have recovered our costs and have assurances that he will not act against us in the future, we will have no claims on the land or his subjects, which are his hereditary fief and property of His Majesty and the empire. It is none of our affair, what religion is established in such a land.

Sturm, though he agreed that Duke Henry would undo the occupying powers' ecclesiastical reforms, refused to consider this sufficient reason to reject restoration, "for otherwise we could take other papist princes' lands from them, bring the people over to our religion, and then refuse to restore the lands."[32] Nor were Henry's crimes sufficient reason to keep the lands from him, "for we are not his lord or judge, but only His Imperial Majesty has such jurisdiction. If he will not punish the duke, we may not."

Sturm doubtless appreciated the ironic aspects of comparing the Brunswick situation with that of Württemberg in 1534. Then, he and his government had backed the restoration of a prince, Duke Ulrich, who was at least as violent and lawless as Duke Henry was ever accused of being, but whose expulsion, so Sturm's legal counsel argued, had been unjust.[33] Now, he took much the same position

---

[32] When the landgrave, some months later, used this as an argument for keeping the lands, Sturm agreed that this would be the certain consequence of restoration. *PC*, 3: p. 394, no. 415, and Sturm's marginal comment at 439 n. 3.

[33] Thomas A. Brady, Jr., "Princes' Reformation vs. Urban Liberty: Strasbourg and the Restoration of Duke Ulrich in Württemberg, 1534," in Ingrid Bátori, ed., *Städtische Gesellschaft und Reformation. Kleine Schriften*, vol. 2, Spätmittelalter und Frühe

with respect to Brunswick-Wolfenbüttel—the conquerors had no right
to hold it—against the Schmalkaldic chiefs. That Ulrich turned a
Catholic land to Lutheranism and Henry would restore a Lutheranized
land to Catholicism, if he could, did not affect the law, at least not
in Sturm's eyes.

At Schmalkalden in July 1543, the allies faced the question of
Brunswick-Wolfenbüttel's disposition. They agreed to cover the campaign's deficit by allowing the land's territorial estates to sell off ecclesiastical lands, but there were bitter words against that commanders'
domination of the occupation government, especially their refusal to
have the governor swear his oath to the League, rather than to
themselves, and their objection to razing the duchy's fortresses. These
seemed clear indications that the elector and the landgrave intended
to retain the conquered lands for themselves. For Strasbourg, Sturm
admitted, the fate of the fortifications was "not very important,
because the land is far away . . . [but] the costs of the occupation
are unbearable."[34]

After the next diet of the League at Frankfurt in the autumn of
1543, the quarrel broke into the open. The League's memorial to
the emperor, which this diet had approved, hinted that under certain conditions Brunswick could be restored, but after the southern
delegates departed, the northerners excised this passage. The Strasbourgeois met this act with resignation—"since it happened, we must
put up with it"[35]—but the argument raged on into the winter, as the
landgrave strove to use Bucer to turn Sturm and his colleagues and
the Strasbourgeois collectively to turn the southern Schmalkaldic
powers.[36] He complained to Bucer that "from all this you can see
and judge, how ramshackle [baufellig] our alliance's affairs have become, and what reliance may be put on the League or on those who,
though not adhering to the Confession of Augsburg, are partly of
our faith."[37] It especially galled the landgrave that Sturm, his early
confidant in this enterprise, was becoming so "timid [cleinmutig]" and
was spreading this timidity at the league's assemblies.[38] This charge

Neuzeit. Tübinger Beiträge zur Geschichtsforschung, 12 (Stuttgart: Klett-Cotta, 1980),
pp. 265–91, esp. pp. 282–83.
    [34] Sturm's notes on the League's diet at Schmalkalden, July 1543, in *PC*, 3: pp.
418–21, no. 394, the quote at 420.
    [35] *PC*, 3: p. 434 n. 4.
    [36] *PC*, 3: p. 445, no. 420, and p. 452 n. 2; Lenz, *Briefwechsel*, 2: pp. 191–97, no. 178.
    [37] Lenz, *Briefwechsel*, 2: p. 195.
    [38] *Ibid.*, 2: p. 200, no. 179.

was true, for by the autumn of 1543, Sturm had come to believe that the invasion of Brunswick-Wolfenbüttel had violated the empire's public peace.[39]

Although Bucer tried to excuse Sturm's "timidity," he fundamentally agreed with the landgrave's view that Sturm's legalism made him timid.[40] He blamed the courts and

> the doctors [of law], who through the neglect and selfishness of other intelligent people—lords, nobles, and burghers—have become truly mighty tyrants over the laws of the German nation; they regard only their written, Roman, tyrannical law, which they employ to inflate their reputation among all estates. They can do this, because such law is so complicated and is so buried in enormous tomes, that they alone can use it.

This is the law, he complained, which the supreme court's judges used to collect all matters into the emperor's hands, and "while these doctors sit on the highest court, all princes and estates must beg them for justice." Bucer's remarks reflect his consistent belief that godly law must break human law and his acceptance of illegality for the gospel's sake, positions Sturm never shared. Bucer also shared the day's common prejudice against the learned lawyers and their jurisprudence.[41] His zeal for the gospel and Landgrave Philip's zeal for "German liberty," that is, the rights of princes, joined hands against the "timidity" of Jacob Sturm and his like, who, Bucer complained, "don't just look at the matters as they are, but they listen to the lawyers about what will and won't be approved by the supreme court, which makes them either happy or timid." Bucer could not understand Sturm's respect for learned Roman jurisprudence, which contradicted the right of free Germans to depose tyrants.

> Sir Jacob knows as well as anyone does, that by means of the Franks, God broke the Roman law of tyranny in the German lands, and He gave us the free, Frankish law, which should now be the German law, according to which, the free princes and estates may drive out such an unbearable tyrant [i.e., Duke Henry], even without the sovereign's permission. They, however, so long neglected to perform this duty . . .

---

[39] He evidently wrote this in a lost letter of October 28, 1543, to Landgrave Philip, who replied indignantly around November 20. *PC*, 2: p. 445, no. 420.

[40] Lenz, *Briefwechsel*, 2: p. 208, nos. 181, and pp. 213–15, no. 183, from which the quotations in this paragraph are taken.

[41] Gerald Strauss, *Law, Resistance, and the State: Opposition to Roman Law in Reformation Germany* (Princeton: Princeton University Press, 1986), pp. 3–30.

and from the founding of the supreme court, the doctors checked and suppressed the free, Frankish law and replaced it with the alien, tyrannical Roman law. And now that this powerful emperor grows ever stronger, and this learned court remains so obdurate, well, now Sir Jacob will see what coin has value, and what sort of law will be enforced. There is a proverb: A willing audience is more important than a good singer. The point is this: what counts is not how many rights you have, but how much you give the judge.

Jacob Sturm and Landgrave Philip finally stood face-to-face on the Brunswick affair at Speyer in February 1544. Sturm led the opposition to the princes' demand that the League throw its whole weight behind their campaign to have Duke Henry condemned for his crimes. Three times the landgrave sent for Sturm and lectured him about Brunswick. The first time, he berated the Strasbourgeois for caring only for the security of their merchants' money, and he insulted Sturm with the remark that he would rather the business were in the hands of the Council of Thirteen of the senate than in Sturm's.[42] Sturm took the diplomat's defense: he was following his instructions; if he received different ones, he would follow those. At a subsequent interview the landgrave grew calmer.[43] "We are truly astonished," he told Sturm,

> that [Duke] Henry's violent acts against Goslar and his intentions against Saxony and us don't persuade you, but you recommend that we make a treaty with him and let him come back into his lands. We know, however, that you were ever of such a mind, since the day when Rudolph Schenck told you in confidence, what the elector, Duke Moritz, and I were planning to do. Even then you concluded that we wanted to make war and were using defense merely as an excuse. If you now search your own conscience, you will surely see that we had this revealed to you because we trusted you; for you know that we have never kept anything from you, about war or about other things. We expect, therefore, since we have so trusted you, that you should not criticize but praise us.

Then, at great length, the landgrave recounted his own motives in this affair, the decisions to support the cities of Brunswick and Goslar, his and the elector's rejection of offensive war, and the League's apparent authorization of action by its commanders. "These were

---

[42] *PC*, 3: p. 462, no. 437, in Sturm's hand.

[43] I rely here on the account taken down by Simon Bing, the Hessian secretary, which is in Lenz, *Briefwechsel*, 2: p. 252 n. 4, and on Sturm's in *PC*, 3: pp. 454–55, no. 432.

the origins of the entire affair," he said, "and this is its true history." The prince pointed out that Sturm had told Schenck that he would prefer that the princes attack Duke Henry alone, "without expense to the other estates, and that it not be done for the sake of religion or reasons connected without religion," so that the Catholics would not be moved to help Henry. God, however, wishing things to happen otherwise, so ordained and 'Sir Jacob must reasonably conclude "that this affair is an act of God. And he must then not regard the affair with the eyes of this world alone."

Sturm concluded from the prince's "vehement [*heftig*]" words, as he told his colleagues at home, "that the two, elector and landgrave, have decided to retain the duchy and want therefore to prevent a peaceful settlement of this affair, no matter what we think of it."[44] He thought that if the Brunswick affair came before the emperor as judge, "there are many reasons why Duke Henry would find in this matter a more favorable judge than we would. If the judgment goes against us, we will have to pay all the costs and restore the lands."[45]

The League's majority, however, backed the princes' stand against arbitration, despite Sturm's protest. "The princes," he wrote home, "lead us ever deeper into this game. . . . It would be grievous to handle the affair in such a way that no treaty is possible; it would also be grievous to part company over this affair."[46] Sturm pleaded that to defer a settlement would only favor Duke Henry and endanger the League, since the emperor was more likely to have a free hand later than he did at the moment, "but this argument has no effect on our princes, because they are too hot and emotional against Duke Henry."[47] At this point at the latest, Sturm realized how deeply irrational the Schmalkaldic chiefs' engagement against Duke Henry had become, and how recklessly they were dragging the League after them into a position in which the entire weight of the imperial legal and military apparatus could come down on their heads. The Schmalkaldeners' collective security had always depended partly on others, princes who—whether because of personal or dynastic ties, neutralist or reformist policies, or anti-Habsburg tradition—were unwilling to see force used against the League. If Charles and Ferdinand could

---

44 *PC*, 3: p. 455, no. 432.
45 *Ibid.*, 3: p. 462, no. 437.
46 *Ibid.*, 3: pp. 463–64, no. 439.
47 *Ibid.*, 3: pp. 468–69, no. 443.

find them isolated from such benevolent non-members, that is, if they could isolate the Schmalkaldeners' from the broader German opposition, they would quickly enough settle the German schism. The Schmalkaldeners could defend the gospel against the militant Catholics alone, Sturm thought, but they could not defend princely violence against all the empire's defenders of law and order. His opinion rested on the decision which had fallen with all finality in the Peasants' War of 1525: the Reformation's fate depended on the fusion of the Protestant cause with the aims of the German princely opposition, of the gospel with German liberty.

It was the possible consequences of splitting these two causes which drove Sturm in 1544 to favor the proposal, which had come from the imperial court, to "sequester" Brunswick-Wolfenbüttel, that is, place the lands in the hands of Charles V as receiver.[48] The southern allies, weary of the expenses and dangers incurred through the occupation, tended to agree.[49] The Schmalkaldic chiefs, however, had drafted a secret proposal, according to which Duke Ulrich and Duke Ernest of Brunswick-Lüneburg would become regents until Henry's sons, at age twenty-four, took over one by one their allotted portions of the partitioned duchy, while "the choicest parts would be given to the elector and the landgrave."[50] Bucer favored this alternative, but Jacob Sturm did not, for, as Bucer told the Hessian prince,

> he is hindered by the provision of the public peace that the lands taken from a violator of the peace must revert to the feudal lord, and that the protectors of the peace may recover only their costs. From this he concludes that according to the law, we may not retain possession of the land except by force.[51]

As for the Christian duty of reformation, Sturm held that

> if we have no right to retain possession, then we are obliged to keep hands off the religion of the land as we found it, as we have done in other regions in which we've had considerable claims and connections,

[48] This legal term meant "to deposit a controversial thing with a third person as sequester." Adolf Berger, *Encyclopedic Dictionary of Roman Law*, Transactions of the American Philosophical Society, 43/2 (Philadelphia: American Philosophical Society, 1953), p. 701. The solution was first proposed by Charles' councillors in the autumn of 1543 to Duke Moritz, who forwarded it to Landgrave Philip.

[49] Lenz, *Briefwechsel*, 2: p. 260 n. 3.

[50] Roth, Friedrich, ed. "Aus dem Briefwechsel Gereon Sailers," *Archiv für Reformationsgeschichte* 1 (1903–1904): p. 144.

[51] Lenz, *Briefwechsel*, 2: pp. 259–60, no. 194, with the quoted material at 258–59; this was a crucial document for the breach between Sturm and the landgrave.

such as the prince-bishoprics, which according to all the laws of their church belong not to their possessors but to the people of God. That was the case in Metz and with others, whom we turned away, as you well know.

Had the princes had proper regard for God and religion, then the cities, Sturm thought, would not favor imperial sequestration as a solution.

The cruel irony of his position came home to Jacob Sturm during the Diet of Speyer in 1544. Not only did the Protestant chiefs rush to support the new French War—so dreaded at Strasbourg—in the hope of softening Charles on the Brunswick question, but Sturm became the target of the prowling Duke Henry, who told the emperor that in November 1543 Sturm had declared that "the French king is a good lord and chief to me."[52] His alienation from the Schmalkaldic chiefs left Sturm all the more vulnerable to such attacks.

In truth, the breach between Sturm and the landgrave had become so deep that it would never heal. "Please don't be angry at Sir Jacob's timidity," Bucer begged the landgrave

for he is loyal, but he is more afraid of illegality than of violence. . . .
He looks deeply into the matters and fears God's wrath, if things are not kept properly and in correct order. Then, too, he always goes further than he can promise to go, and our masters will truly stand by Your Princely Grace to the last.[53]

This last, at least, was true, and in the war of 1546–1547 it would cost Strasbourg dearly.

---

[52] Friedrich Hortleder, ed., *Der Röm. key.—u. königlichen Maiesten . . . Handlungen und Ausschriben, Ratschlag, Bedenken . . . von den Vrsachen dess Teutschen Kriegs Kaiser Carls des Fürsten, Sachsen vnd Hessen vnd Ihrer Chur- vnd F. G. g. Mitverwandte: Anno 1545 vnd 47* (Gotha, 1645), 1: p. 1813 (bk. 4, chap. 47): "welcher Sturm sich such unlangst in des H. Reichs Versamblung mit trutzinger, pochenden, dräwlichen Worten gegen etlicher Ständ Gesandten, . . . offentlichen hören und vernehmen lassen hat: Dass ihme der Frantzoss ein guter Herr oder Haupt sey: Dass kan er nicht verneinen. . . ." This refers to a session of 23 April 1544, in the presence of Charles V and King Ferdinand. Gereon Sailer described it to Georg Herwart, Speyer, April 25, 1544: "Den frommen her jacob Sturmen hat er [i.e., Duke Henry] gar hitzig und das her jm radt solt gesagt haben, der frantzhose sey jme ain guter herr." Roth, "Briefwechsel Gereon Sailers," 123. Sturm reported this incident to his masters (in April 1544, in *PC*, 3: pp. 488–89, no. 463), who insisted that the charges be answered, though they considered them absurd (*ibid.*, p. 495, no. 468, 500–2, nos. 470–72). In a letter of May 1, 1544, Sailer identifies the object of the charge as "der Sturm, so ain leser zw Straspurg ist." (Roth, "Briefwechsel Gereon Sailers," 135), that is, Jean (or: Johannes) Sturm, the rector of Strasbourg's Latin School.
[53] Lenz, *Briefwechsel*, 2: p. 263, no. 194.

When the allies assembled in February 1545 at Worms, where the
Imperial Diet was sitting, relations between the two Schmalkaldic
chiefs and their southern urban allies came to their nadir. The costs
and opprobrium caused by the Brunswick affair so deeply depressed
Jacob Sturm that, according to Bucer, he considered renouncing his
citizenship and leaving Strasbourg.[54] The allies' wrangling over money
at Worms depressed him ever further, and he wrote home sarcasti-
cally that, "in fine, this is enterprise from which the cities certainly will
not become rich."[55]

The Brunswick affair also cracked the solidarity between Sturm
and his colleagues in Strasbourg's regime. While he favored "a negotiated settlement," with guarantees for Lutheranism in Brunswick and
provision for repayment of the war's costs, they backed the Hessian-
Saxon policy of holding the duchy if acceptable terms for sequestration could not be gotten.[56] The landgrave, hearing of this disagreement,
tried to exploit it to undermine Sturm's role as leader of the League's
opposition party, a tactic which led Sturm to write home with great
bitterness: "I can only commend the matter to God. I could well
tolerate that someone else were sent here, who could do better than
I can." If they yielded to the princes, he insisted, "we would have . . .
given out fifty or sixty thousand florins more, all in vain."[57] Sturm
stood alone, for Bucer, weighing Sturm's "timidity" against the princes'
vigor, sided with the landgrave and even tried to influence Strasbourg's
regime for the prince and against Sturm.[58]

The Schmalkaldeners nonetheless decided with surprising speed to
deliver Brunswick-Wolfenbüttel into imperial sequestration within one

[54] *Ibid.*, 2: p. 307, no. 204.
[55] *PC*, 3: pp. 559–60, no. 526.
[56] The difference is in *ibid.*, 3: pp. 576–77, no. 546. It is worth noting that during the allies' deliberations on April 10, Sturm recommended his own rather than
his government's policy. See *ibid.*, 3: p. 580, no. 550; 590–91, no. 563; pp. 593–95,
no. 566; p. 596, no. 568.
[57] *Ibid.*, 3: p. 588, no. 560. The landgrave knew of the differences by April 24.
See Lenz, *Briefwechsel*, 2: p. 340 n. 1 (the date is corrected in *PC*, 3: p. 588 n. 2).
That the landgrave's informant was Bucer can hardly be doubted, especially in the
light of Bucer's letter in Lenz, *Briefwechsel*, 2: p. 307, no. 204.
[58] See Lenz, *Briefwechsel*, 2: pp. 346–47, no. 213; pp. 350–51, no. 214; pp. 352–53,
no. 215; *PC*, 3: pp. 598–99, no. 570. In his letter to Sturm of May 29 (*PC*, no. 3:
pp. 598–99), Bucer wrote: "Horrendum quidem est cogitatu, tradere religione fratres
talis tyranno. et quia societas germanici imperii est christiani imperii, equidem no
dubito, victoria contra tyrannum eius culpa a nostris extorta hoc officii nostris esse
impositum, ut, si valere eos id [?] dominus fert, in religione Christi hanc provin-
ciam conservent." He was precisely right. See Reller, *Kirchenverfassung*, p. 107.

month, providing that Duke Henry was not allowed into the land, and that for the time being no changes were made in the occupying regime.[59] This settlement gave Duke Henry time to act, and in mid-September he invaded his lands with eight thousand foot and fifteen hundred horse.[60] His lack of heavy guns, however, proved his undoing, for he could take neither the city of Brunswick nor Castle Wolfenbüttel. Breaking off his sieges to move against the Schmalkaldic chiefs' oncoming forces before Duke Moritz arrived, Henry met them near Kalefeld on October 14, 1545. When the superior artillery had blasted the Brunswick troops, Philip spoke to the captured duke,

> If I fell into your power, as you have into mine, you would not let me live. I, however, will treat you better than you deserve from me. You have been very foolish to disobey His Imperial Majesty by rejecting the sequestration, for had you not done that, you would not have come to this bad end.[61]

During the days when Duke Henry rode toward this second great misfortune, Jacob Sturm sat down to justify himself to the landgrave, then on campaign. All summer he had been bombarded by reproaches from the landgrave, ardent entreaties from Bucer, and hardening dissents from his colleagues in the Thirteen. "Your councillors and envoys have often heard my reasons," he wrote to Landgrave Philip on September 27, 1545,

> for I believe that even after the first blow was struck, it would have been best to negotiate, even if both sides were already mobilized, in order to prevent terrible damage to the German nation.

If the Schmalkaldeners win and keep the land,

> we must either place it in His Majesty's receivership or hold it, which will involve such expense and trouble, that our allies cannot bear it in the long run: then, I fear, the allies will be further divided. Therefore, even if we win, we will gain greater expenses and nothing more, which we cannot recover from Duke Henry or from his land or officials.

Henry had been ruined, Sturm thought, and would never again be dangerous, whereas the occupation of Brunswick formed a continuing burden to the League, not only because of the debts, but even

---

[59] Blume, *Goslar*, p. 128. The text of the Capitulation of Worms, dated July 10, 1545, is printed by Hortleder, *Von den Ursachen* (1645): bk. 4, ch. 49.

[60] Blume, *Goslar*, pp. 129–34, gives a good overview of this campaign.

[61] Quoted by *ibid.*, p. 133.

more because its example would deter other Protestant powers from joining.[62] Every time the call came for action, some would refuse support and say that this matter grew out of the Brunswick affair. "Thus the burden and expense rests on a few of us alone, and we become day-by-day fewer."

Meeting the landgrave's charges of last summer, Sturm denied that

> I look only to the advantage of my masters or of other cities, but to the common cause. As far as I can judge, if this affair continues, my masters here will perform whatever burdens the alliance places on them, if they are able—just as they have always done. It is hard, however, and in the long run will be impossible, for those of good will to bear the load alone, as others slip the harness. I am afraid it will ruin them all. May it please Your Grace to accept these words of mine and consider them. May God Almighty give Your Grace and us all grace and understanding, so that we may find the right path through this burdensome and difficult affair and the way that will praise His holy name, expand His kingdom, and advance His honor and His holy Word. May He also give Your Grace a long, happy reign.

The emotion and especially the uncharacteristic effusion in the letter's closing betray how low the relations between the two men— Hessian and Strasbourgeois, prince and noble, lord and burgher—had sunk. They would never recover.

In for a penny, in for a pound, and the costs of the second Brunswick campaign had to be piled on earlier debts and, the allies hoped, spread as widely as possible. On the day of the Battle of Kalefeld, Sturm, who, in Bucer's words, "will always do more than he promises to do," set aside his "timidity" and scruples and joined his colleague in a call to rally support for the Schmalkaldic chiefs. Since this action

> is too expensive for those powers who are engaged in the defense of Brunswick, the landgrave should circularize the other allies and tell them that the affair concerns not only those now involved but all the allies and the whole cause of true religion. They should, therefore, give aid and support and are obliged to do it. He should also send to all Protestant powers and others of the Augsburg Confession, just as to the allies, and draw them into deliberations about this common religious matter, so that the affair does not entail trouble and damages for us, and thus for our religion as a whole.[63]

---

[62] Sturm wrote this two days before Henry invaded the duchy on September 29, 1545. Petri, "Herzog Heinrich," pp. 149–50.
[63] *PC*, 3: pp. 658–59, no. 620.

Sturm thus capitulated to the landgrave's position, that the security and welfare of the Protestant powers was itself a "religious matter," and the distinction between "religious" and "worldly" was therefore largely a tactical one. Necessity rather than conviction dictated this policy to Strasbourg's regime, a committee of which—again headed by Sturm—spoke its true mind in 1546 to envoys from the northern Schmalkaldic allies. They should be told, the committee recommended, "how loyally we helped them against Brunswick, which was basically [*im grund*] not a religious matter."[64]

The Brunswick affair—the original invasion, the occupation, and the second campaign of 1545—gravely weakened the Schmalkaldic League. Not only did it lead to wrangling and petty bickering over costs—the allies accepted only a third of the landgrave's reported costs of nearly 75,000 guilders[65]—but it also created permanent mistrust in Protestant ranks and formed an important step toward the German War of 1546–1547. The quarrel exposed the hidden conflicts in the fusion of restored gospel with princes' liberty, on which the fate of German Protestantism depended. The Schmalkaldic League had based itself on the fiction that it was possible, both in politics and in law, to distinguish religious matters from secular ones. Political illusions have a way of exacting their prices, and this one was no exception.

---

[64] *Ibid.*, 4: p. 446, no. 422 (October 26, 1546).

[65] StA Weimar, Reg. H., 1: p. 670, no. 209, fols. 41ʳ–45ᵛ, dated Kassel, January 7, 1546. The first audit of accounts occurred at the League's diet at Frankfurt from February 2 to 8, 1546. The two princes were voted the remainder of the third doubled "month" plus 10,000 florins. See Jacob Sturm's diary and report in *PC*, 4: p. 32, no. 29.

CHAPTER SEVEN

IN SEARCH OF THE GODLY CITY:
THE DOMESTICATION OF RELIGION IN THE
GERMAN URBAN REFORMATION

A people's religious life, it has long been recognized, centers on the rituals that connect the people to extrahuman or suprahuman forces that can, and do, influence its collective fate.[1] A defect in ritual can lead to a people's doom, as Achilles reminded the Achaeans in the face of Apollo's wrath.[2] Explanations of such forces—myth, belief, and doctrine—arise from efforts to understand, interpret, and justify the community's situation vis-à-vis its gods and, by derivation, vis-à-vis the distribution of wealth, prestige, and power that a correct relationship demands. In complex societies, where tensions arise from the distribution of the social product, the shared symbols may be seen somewhat differently by different social groups, which in extreme cases may lead to a disruption of the ritual community and therefore to social revolt—an outcome that the ruling part of the society must naturally try to prevent. As Peter Munz has noted, there arises as a result "the normal pressure in all societies . . . to use religion as a means to promote social cohesion."[3] From this point of view, every disruption of the sacral order of ritual and myth must threaten social harmony.

Complex religious cultures, including those that offer forgiveness of sins and eternal life, do not neglect the "normal pressure"

Parts of the following essay are based on my recent book *Turning Swiss: Cities and Empire, 1450–1550*, Cambridge Studies in Early Modern History (Cambridge, 1985). I cite only quoted texts here, and I refer the interested reader to that work for additional source material.

[1] An understanding of this principle animates Bob [Robert W.] Scribner, "Cosmic Order and Daily Life: Sacred and Secular in Pre-Industrial German Society," in Kaspar von Greyerz, ed., *Religion and Society in Early Modern Europe, 1500–1800* (London, 1984), pp. 17–32.

[2] Homer, *Iliad*, Bk. I, ll. 59–67.

[3] Peter Munz, "From Max Weber to Joachim of Floris: The Philosophy of Religious History," *Journal of Religious History* 11 (1980): pp. 167–200, here at p. 182. He calls the response to this pressure mundanization, by which he means approximately what I mean by "domestication."

to promote social cohesion. The fourteenth-century Muslim philosopher Ibn Khaldūn (1332–1406) expressed this point perfectly. "Only
by God's help in establishing His religion," he wrote, "do individual desires come together in agreement to press their claims, and
hearts become united."[4] Many Latin Christian writers agreed, at least
in principle. Johann Hug, for example, a priest at St. Stephen's in
Strasbourg in about 1500, wrote that "government is preserved by
religion, more . . . than by offices or physical labors."[5]

   In medieval Latin Christendom the preservation of government
through religion was complicated by the bifurcation of authority
into *sacerdotium* and *imperium*, corresponding to a division of its elites
into lay rulers and clergy, which gave rise to a bewildering variety
of—mostly unstable—situations of governance. Right down to the
Reformation era, many writers nonetheless accepted and in principle approved this bifurcation of authority as a normal and necessary situation. One such writer was a Basel law professor, Peter von
Andlau (1415/25–1480), who in about 1470 wrote, "The world is
chiefly ruled by two forces, that is, the papal authority and the royal
power, and they are the two chief powers through which God reg-
ulates and moves the world."[6] Well and good, but many other men
strove to unite religious and temporal authority as rulers of men
sought to become masters of souls and as rulers of souls sought to
become masters of men. Symbolically it was a struggle between two
Romes. On one side, Emperor Charles V's grandchancellor, Mecurino
Arborio di Gattinara (d. 1530), announced in 1519 that the work
begun by Charles the Great would be completed by Charles the
Greatest, giving the world "one pastor and one flock."[7] At the papal
court, however, Giles of Viterbo (1469–1532) contrasted Julius Caesar,

---

   [4] Ibn Khaldūn (= ʿAbd-ar-Rahmān Abū Zayd ibn Muhammad ibn Muhammad
ibn Khaldūn), *The Muqaddimah: An Introduction to History*, trans. Franz Rosenthal,
abridged ed. by N. J. Dawood (Princeton, 1957), p. 125.
   [5] "Conseruatur autem imperium per religionem. Vnde dicit imperator rem pub-
licam magis religionibus quisquam officijs et laboribus corporis contineri" (Johannes
Hug, *Quadrivium ecclesie Quatuor prelatorum officium Quibus omnis status tum Secularis tum
vero Ecclesiasticus subiicitur* [Strasbourg, 1504], fol. 49^r). See also fol. 49^v: "Non solum
autem conservatur imperium per religionem sed etiam per pacem." On Hug, see
Charles Schmidt, *Histoire littéraire d'Alsace à la fin du XVe et au commencement du XVIe
siècle*, 2 vols. (Paris, 1879; reprinted, Nieuwkoop, 1966), 2: pp. 51–53.
   [6] Josef Hürbin, *Peter von Andlau, der Verfasser des ersten deutschen Reichstaatsrechts* (Strasbourg, 1897), pp. 130–31, from his *Libellus de caesarea monarchia*.
   [7] John M. Headley, "The Habsburg World Empire and the Revival of Ghibellinism," *Medieval and Renaissance Studies* 7 (1978): pp. 93–127, here at pp. 97–102.

who had merely believed he ruled the world, with Pope Julius II, who in fact did so.[8]

Latin Christendom's failure to resolve its peculiar structural bifurcation into either autocracy or theocracy had at least two extremely important consequences. First, it doomed every dream of uniting, under Roman imperial symbols, both military power and Christian religious authority into an empire of a classic type.[9] Second, it created the moral space in which much smaller units could become practically sovereign without the need for extreme religious and cultural localism. This process occurred most richly in Italy, where no great power emerged to usurp the weakened or shattered imperium, but another great zone of urban communal formation arose in South Germany, the lands that stretched from the foot of the High Alps northward to Germany's Central Highlands. Here the massive disturbances that accompanied the early Reformation movement during the 1520s forced the urban magistrates to trim civic religion more closely to their duty to preserve law and order under the symbol of the common good (in German the *gemeiner Nutz*, in Latin the *bonum commune*). They commonly did so by bringing religious personnel and practice more closely under their own control, pursuing what may be called a "domestication" of urban religion.

I

In the great debate over the Protestant Reformation and the origins of modernity that erupted in the middle decades of the nineteenth century, some identified in the Reformation, especially in the cities, the breakthrough to "religious freedom" or, in Engels's words, the "revolution no. 1 of the bourgeoisie." Others—notably the jurist Otto von Gierke—saw in the urban reformation the achievement by the medieval urban corporation of political, legal, and moral autonomy. Recent writing on the South German urban reform movement has highlighted its traditional, corporate thrust. Bernd Moeller, for

---

[8] John W. O'Malley, "Giles of Viterbo: A Reformer's Thought on Renaissance Rome," *Renaissance Quarterly* 20 (1967): pp. 1–11, here at p. 10 (reprinted in John W. O'Malley, *Rome and the Renaissance: Studies in Culture and Religion* [London, 1981].

[9] I mean "empire" in approximately the sense discussed by Immanuel Wallerstein in *The Modern World-System*, vol. 1: *Capitalist Agriculture and the Origins of the European World-Economy in the Sixteenth Century* (New York, 1974), p. 15.

example, wrote in 1962 that Martin Luther's southern urban colleagues—chiefly Zurich's Huldrych Zwingli (1484–1531) and Strasbourg's Martin Bucer (1490–1551)—through their emphasis on the
collectivity rather than on the individual, corrected Luther and deepened his concepts of church and state. Heiko Oberman agrees with
this estimate: "The south German Reformation expanded [Luther's]
limited purpose to include a reordering of the community; seeking
to realize the horizontal implications of the gospel within the framework of the *bonum commune*." Peter Blickle, in an even more pointed
judgment, ascribes to the urban reform "the tendency toward an
exclusive civic jurisdiction, toward communalization of the church,
and toward the rationalization of religion and piety."[10]

II

The decades before the beginning of the German Reformation heightened the perceived need for social integration in the self-governing
cities. "There was a time," wrote the Strasbourg lawyer Sebastian
Brant (1457–1521) in 1504,

> when we could rightly claim of our empire that it was lord and master
> over the world. Now, however, our society has become a haven for
> every kind of folly and vice.... Do you doubt that our end will be
> the same as the end of all the kingdoms and empires that went before
> us and all those that are still to come: dust, ashes, a scattering of rub-
> ble, a mere name? Nothing lasts in human affairs except the immor-
> tal soul.[11]

The brilliant half century between 1470 and Luther's initial blast,
indeed, brought trouble to magistrates' hearts in every South German
city hall. New threats to traditional civic order loomed both within
and beyond the walls.

---

[10] Bernd Moeller, *Imperial Cities and the Reformation: Three Essays*, trans. H. C. Erik
Midelfort and Mark U. Edwards (Philadelphia, 1975), pp. 89–90 (slightly revised);
Heiko A. Oberman, *Masters of the Reformation: The Emergence of a New Intellectual Climate
in Europe*, trans. Denis Martin (Cambridge, 1981), p. 294; Peter Blickle, *Die Reformation
im Reich*, Uni-Taschenbücher, 1181 (Stuttgart, 1982), p. 92.
[11] Sebastian Brant to Conrad Peutinger, July 1504, in *Konrad Peutingers Briefwechsel*,
ed. Erich König (Münich, 1923), pp. 32–36, here at p. 34, trans. Gerald Strauss,
in Gerald Strauss, ed., *Manifestations of Discontent in Germany on the Eve of the Reformation*
(Bloomington, Ind., 1971), p. 225.

Within the walls, the very wealth accumulated through the economic recovery further polarized society as the rich got richer and the poor poorer. Poverty's claws were, indeed, very much longer and far sharper than the cities' tax registers indicate. Europe's cities held no fixed class of "the poor," for the condition of potential poverty gripped a large part of the population and threatened a still larger part, depending on the variable economic conditions, such as harvests, prices, wages, and unemployment. As a result, in a broad sense the term "the poor" was frequently and correctly used to designate the majority of the working population,[12] for the ranks of the potential poor extended far into the fat bulge on the onion-shaped representations with which social historians describe social stratification in the premodern city.[13] The fat bulge formed a political cushion for the oligarchies that was more apparent than real, both because the ranks of the potential poor were so very much larger than those of the obviously destitute and because large sectors of the work force had no regular, legitimate channels of communication with the oligarchies. The ranks of the apprentices and wage workers, a fertile ground for discontent, composed between a quarter and a third of those gainfully occupied in the larger cities.[14] In German cities the polarization lent new substance to grievances against monopolists and usurers, which struck directly at the urban oligarchs and the sources of their wealth.[15]

Outside the walls lurked the great predators, the princes who had smashed the last South German urban league in the period 1449–1453 and who now strove to bring the free cities' assets—money

[12] On growing impoverishment in the sixteenth century, see Catharina Lis and Hugo Soly, *Poverty and Capitalism in Pre-Industrial Europe*, trans. James Coonan (New York, 1979), pp. 71–82. For German cities in particular, see Thomas Fischer, *Städtische Armut und Armenfürsorge im 15. und 16. Jahrhundert*, Göttinger Beiträge zur Wirtschafts- und Sozialgeschichte, 4 (Göttingen, 1976), pp. 17–139; Robert Jütte, *Obrigkeitliche Armenfürsorge in deutschen Reichsstädten der frühen Neuzeit: Städtische Armenfürsorge in Frankfurt am Main und Köln*, Kölner historische Abhandlungen, 31 (Cologne and Vienna, 1984), pp. 8–19.

[13] See Erdmann Weyrauch, "Über sociale Schichtung," in Ingrid Batori, ed., *Städtische Gesellschaft und Reformation*, Spätmittelalter und Frühe Neuzeit, Tübinger Beiträge zur Geschichtsforschung, 12 (Stuttgart, 1980), pp. 5–57.

[14] Knut Schulz, *Handwerksgesellen und Lohnarbeiter: Untersuchungen zur oberrheinischen und oberdeutschen Stadtgeschichte des 14. bis 17. Jahrhunderts* (Sigmaringen, 1985), pp. 37–46.

[15] See Erich Maschke, "Deutsche Städte am Ausgang des Mittelalters," here from the reprint in his *Städte und Menschen: Beiträge zur Geschichte der Stadt, der Wirtschaft und Gesellschaft, 1959–1977*, Beiheft 68 der Vierteljahrschrift für Sozial- und Wirtschaftsgeschichte (Wiesbaden, 1980), pp. 56–99, here at p. 71.

and credit, guns, and men—under their direct control. Against such dangerous lords the urban oligarchs' natural refuge was the imperial monarchy—hence the urban humanists' strident monarchism—but the Habsburgs could not guarantee law and order. Emperor Maximilian I (r. 1493–1519), a veritable "royal locust,"[16] papered his progresses with bad debts and poured the cities' money into his Italian projects. Aided by the cities, he did humble the chief South German dynasties, but he could not provide what the oligarchies most wanted—good government.

The need for guarantees of law and order grew all the more desperate with the dream of the common man as far north as Franconia of "turning Swiss"—that is, of joining or imitating the Swiss and living without lords. As the Augsburg politician Ulrich Arzt (1460–1527) wrote in 1519, "I fear that we will be pushed from behind toward the Swiss. Then the old proverb will come true: when a cow stands and moos on the bridge at Ulm, she'll be heard in the middle of Switzerland."[17] Strange prophecies circulated through South Germany, among them that the Archangel Michael "proposes to set out to reestablish a firm Christian faith on earth, so that the words of our Savior may be fulfilled: 'There shall be one flock, one shepherd [John 10:16].'"[18]

Religion, which ought to have promoted peace, justice, and unity in the service of God's honor and the common good, sometimes did just the opposite.[19] Clerical rights, privileges, and practices, however much they had been honored by earlier generations, were making laymen and laywomen in about 1500 angry and confused, providing endless provocations to disputes, quarrels, and ill will. Clerical

---

[16] Gerhard Benecke, *Emperor Maximilian I, 1459–1519: An Analytical Biography* (London, 1982), p. 128.

[17] Ulrich Arzt to Conrad Peutinger, Augsburg, 9 February 1519, quoted in Heinrich Lutz, *Conrad Peutinger: Beiträge zu einer politischen Biographie*, Abhandlungen zur Geschichte der Stadt Augsburg, 9 (Augsburg, [1955]), p. 147.

[18] Annelore Franke and Gerhard Zschäbitz, eds., *Das Buch der hundert Kapitel und der vierzig Statuten des sogenannten oberrheinischen Revolutionärs*, Leipziger Übersetzungen und Abhandlungen zum Mittelalter, A 4 (Berlin, 1967), p. 181, quoted here from Strauss, *Manifestations*, p. 235.

[19] The one adequate study of a pre-Reformation diocese reveals with great clarity how the structural deadlock between lay and ecclesiastical authority blocked all paths to reform from above. See Francis Rapp, *Réformes et Réformation à Strasbourg: Église et société dans le diocèse de Strasbourg (1450–1525)*, Collection de l'Institut des Hautes Etudes Alsaciennes, 23 (Paris, 1975).

exemptions from market laws and civic duties, clerical collection of tithes and usury, clerical quarrels between monk and priest and monk and monk, and seemingly irremediable abuses in clerical life—all these breached the commune's sense of moral security and reduced the sustenance that religion was obliged to lend to good government. No matter that the magistrates themselves helped to block episcopal efforts to improve clerical discipline nor that the clergy themselves paraded the problems before the literate laity. Episcopal reform efforts amounted to little, not least because—here the contrast with Italy is illuminating—South German bishops were not civic patriarchs but great feudal magnates and often the cities' former lords. What mattered most was not whether clerical discipline had in fact worsened or improved since earlier times[20] but that lay tolerance of clerical privileges and life-styles was declining. The seemingly natural solution—full civic control over the church and the commune's religious life—could not be attained within the bounds of the law.

The communalization of the church during the South German urban reform therefore aimed to transform the civic religious establishment from an agent of disruption into one of order. How very desperate the situation had become is evident in the plaintive cry of Strasbourg's great cathedral preacher, Johann Geiler von Kaysersberg (1445–1510), a man of impeccable life and unshakable will: "You laymen hate us priests, and it is an old hatred that separates us. Whence comes your hatred against us? I believe that it comes from our insane way of life, that we live so evilly and create such scandal."[21]

III

To this increasingly desperate situation the early Protestant reformers brought a welcome message: the identity of church and people. "The Kingdom of Christ is also external," Zwingli wrote against the Lutherans, and "a Christian city is nothing more than a Christian

---

[20] See Lawrence G. Duggan, "The Unresponsiveness of the Late Medieval Church: A Reconsideration," *Sixteenth Century Journal* 9 (1978): pp. 3–26.
[21] Johann Geiler von Kaysersberg, *Die Emeis: Dis ist das buch von der Omeissen, und auch Herr der könig ich diente gern* (Strasbourg, 1516), fol. 28ᵛ (my thanks to R. Emmet McLaughlin for sending me this text).

commune."²² Erasmus had said much the same thing in 1518 when he asked a friend, "What else is the city but a great monastery?"²³

The urban reformation's guiding principle was, in Heiko Oberman's words, "the slippery but irreplaceable concept of biblicism,"²⁴ the idea that the Bible contains binding norms of Christian social conduct. "That realm is best and most secure," wrote Zwingli, "which rules according to God alone; and that is worst and least secure which rules according to its own lights."²⁵ At Strasbourg the cathedral preacher Caspar Hedio (1494–1552) reminded the magistrates that they, together with the preachers and schoolmasters, were the pillars of civic welfare, who should find in the Bible "a vital, certain unerring guide against false doctrine, divisions and sects, and how one can survive dangerous times."²⁶ It is difficult to imagine a closer coupling of the gospel to the common good than these urban reformers preached.

The urban regimes gradually responded to the preachers' and their own citizens' urgings with a new civic religious praxis. They drafted dozens of new laws and passed them around to one another: preaching ordinances, liturgical ordinances, laws on marriage courts, laws against sectarianism, laws governing parish life, and new articles of doctrine. This praxis moved beyond mere usurpation of the episcopal functions to reshape civic religious life in an autonomous and Evangelical sense. The process briefly reawakened a sense of solidarity among the Swiss, Swabian, and Upper Rhenish cities—what a Strasbourg politician called "the good old neighborliness."²⁷ This exchange of ideas and institutions, far more than any distinctive doc-

---

²² *Huldrych Zwinglis sämtliche Werke*, eds. Emil Egli, *et al.*, 14 vols. to date (Berlin, Leipzig, and Zurich, 1905–), 14: p. 424, ll. 19–22.
²³ Desiderius Erasmus to Paul Volz, Basel, 14 August 1518, in P. S. Allen and H. S. Allen, eds., *Opus epistolarum Des. Erasmi Roterodami*, 12 vols. (Oxford, 1906–1958), 3: pp. 361–77; quoted here from *Christian Humanism and the Reformation: Selected Writings of Erasmus*, trans. John C. Olin (New York, 1965), pp. 107–33, here at p. 130.
²⁴ Oberman, *Masters*, p. 277.
²⁵ *Zwinglis sämtliche Werke*, 2: p. 346, ll. 15–18.
²⁶ Manfred Krebs and Hans Georg Rott, eds., *Quellen zur Geschichte der Taüfer*, vols. 7–8, *Elsass, Stadt Strassburg, 1522–1535*, Quellen und Forschungen zur Reformationgeschichte, 26–27 (Gütersloh, 1959–1960), 2: p. 262, ll. 19–21, no. 492. Oberman in *Masters* writes of the "political theology" that "declared the Gospel to be no more and no less than a function of the *bonum commune*" (p. 280).
²⁷ Klaus Kniebis to Bernhard Meyer, Strasbourg, 30 August 1542, in Staatsarchiv Basel, Kirchen-Akten A 8, fol. 15ᵛ.

trine, formed the practical heart of South German Zwinglianism, which radiated from the three linked centers of Zurich, Constance, and Strasbourg.

Four aspects of this civic religious praxis contained especially great integrative potential. First, the urban clergy were fully domesticated through marriage, compulsory citizenship and guild membership, and reduction in numbers, and many formerly clerical functions and resources were transferred to the communal regime. Second, the regime's assumption of episcopal authority, especially in marriage law, touched every constituent household of the commune and made possible the full coordination of patriarchal authority with governmental.[28] Third, the full domestication of worship, made possible by the total uncoupling of salvation from social life, gave birth to liturgies that were frankly designed to indoctrinate. The Catholic formula, "The norm of prayer is the norm of faith" (lex orandi, lex credendi) gave way to an Evangelical "the norm of doctrine is the norm of prayer" (lex docendi, lex orandi).[29] Fourth and finally, the formation of an autonomous civic church subordinated parish life and its pastor to the government, and all subsequent efforts to restore the integrity of the parish, chiefly through the right of excommunication, shattered in the face of governmental intransigence. In time, the Zwinglian ideal of a partnership between regime and clergy produced a thoroughgoing official control of the urban church.

The first decade of the urban reformation thus fashioned a clean, comprehensive solution to the problem of religion and civic order. The governments, emboldened by the preachers' offer of biblicist legitimacy and pressed forward by their own citizens' agitation, took control of parishes and clergy, convents and schools, and poor relief and the custody of Christian marriage. To all appearances, the Protestant free city of South Germany became the first of those godly peoples of Reformation Europe who placed themselves under the gospel understood as the *lex Christi*, or the law of Christ.

---

[28] See Thomas Max Safley, *Let No Man Put Asunder: The Control of Marriage in the German Southwest, 1560–1600*, Sixteenth Century Texts and Studies, 2 (Kirksville, Mo., 1984), pp. 121–65.

[29] Thus it is elegantly put by René Bornert in *La réforme protestante du culte à Strasbourg au XVIᵉ siècle (1523–1598)*. Studies in Medieval and Reformation Thought, 28 (Leiden, 1981), p. 596.

IV

Much is known about how the reformers' message was preached and far less about how it was received. Most arguments for a uniform reception rest on samplings of the vast flood of pamphlets aimed at the literate 10–30 percent of the urban population, though it is not yet possible to say how representative the findings are.[30] A study of the illustrations intended for the illiterate majority suggests little real doctrinal content beyond biblicism and anticlericalism. As for specific urban groups, even the ruling elites, the best documented of all the urban classes, have been studied in only a few cities.

Despite these limitations, Bernd Moeller has confidently argued that urban folk received Luther's message as he preached it and that the ruling elites displayed "a general antipathy to the Reformation" that stood in opposition to the enthusiasm of "the people." Moeller's argument rests on polls of guildsmen and guild officials (*Schöffen* and so on), which "almost always resulted in an overpowering victory for the Protestant party."[31] In contrast, the current state of knowledge about the urban reform suggests, in Günther Vogler's words, that "the movement embraced various forces and interests. They included oligarchs and humanists, artisans and journeymen, clergymen and artists, peasants and plebeians, who differed from one another in their views on both the theoretical and practical aspects of the Reformation, and who reacted variously to different situations."[32] United for a time against one target, the clergy—liberation from whose authority was seen as self-liberation with regard to both salvation and the common good—the various classes and interests soon began to split apart. Still, the fruit of their brief cooperation, the communalization of religion, was achieved without a social revolu-

---

[30] This statement is true of Bernd Moeller's programmatic "Stadt und Buch: Bemerkungen zur Struktur der reformatorischen Bewegung in Deutschland," in Wolfgang J. Mommsen, ed., *The Urban Classes, the Nobility, and the Reformation: Studies on the Social History of the Reformation in Germany and England*, Publications of the German Historical Institute, London, 5 (Stuttgart, 1979), pp. 25–39; and of most of the contributions to Hans-Joachim Köhler, ed., *Flugschriften als Massenmedium der Reformationszeit.* Spätmittelalter und Frühe Neuzeit. Tübinger Beiträge zur Geschichtsforschung, 13 (Tübingen, 1981). On illustrations, see Robert W. Scribner, *For the Sake of Simple Folk: Popular Propaganda for the German Reformation*, Cambridge Studies in Oral and Literate Culture, 2 (Cambridge, 1981).

[31] Moeller, *Imperial Cities*, pp. 62, 64.

[32] Günther Vogler, *Nürnberg 1524–1525: Studien zur Geschichte der reformatorischen Bewegung in der Reichsstadt* (Berlin, 1982), p. 323.

tion, which suggests that the urban elites favored not the old religion but the new.

A close analysis of some of the polls of guildsmen and guild officials yields not a clear but a murky picture of the allegiances of the urban elites. Nearly a dozen such polls are known from the years 1525 to 1531 in which entire citizenries or guild officials alone were polled on some reformation-related policy. Four polls were taken at Constance, two of them constitutionally mandated and two at the regime's choice. Each produced a hefty majority for the government's policy, though none was taken on the acts directly related to the change in religion, most notably the abolition of the Mass.[33] Elsewhere such polls also produced strong to overwhelming support for official policy. At Strasbourg in early 1529, for example, 184 of the 300 Schöffen voted to abolish the Mass, 94 to delay its abolition until the end of the imperial Diet, and only 1 to retain it under all circumstances. Ninety-three percent of the Schöffen thus approved the government's proposal to abolish their ancestors' central act of worship.[34]

In most cases the polls did not directly measure the strengths of Catholic and Evangelical parties. One reason is that much depended on the way in which an issue was presented. At Ulm in November 1530, minorities in the two richest guilds voted quite differently—in the *Kramerzunft* (shopkeepers' guild) for the Diet's recess and in the *Kaufleutezunft* (merchants' guild) to reject it if no General Council met within a year—though probably both minorities supported the position that opposed outright rejection of the Diet of Augsburg's recess.[35] In this poll—and in most of the others as well—a vote on one side is probably evidence of Evangelical convictions or sympathies, but a vote on the other side is not reliable evidence of Catholic ones. There was never a single line of policy, particularly foreign policy,

---

[33] Moeller, *Imperial Cities*, p. 64 n. 48. On the polls at Constance, see Hans-Christoph Rublack, *Die Einführung der Reformation in Konstanz bis zum Abschluss 1531*, Quellen und Forschungen zur Reformationsgeschichte, 40 (Gütersloh, 1971), pp. 114, 123.

[34] Miriam U. Chrisman, *Strasbourg and the Reform: A Study in the Process of Change* (New Haven, 1967), p. 172.

[35] Hans Eugen Specker, "Zwischen Gewissen und Gehorsam: Zur Reformationsabstimmung der Ulmer Bürgerschaft vor 450 Jahren," in *Die Einführung der Reformation in Ulm: Geschichte eines Bürgerentscheids*, ed. Hans Eugen Specker and Gebhard Weig, Forschungen zur Geschichte der Stadt Ulm, "Dokumentation" series, 2 (Ulm, 1981), pp. 39–46, with the voting lists reprinted on pp. 343–85. Though Specker reiterates the notion that the vote was a decision for one religion or the other (p. 39), his account of the vote of Matthäus Laupin the Elder (p. 45) makes my point perfectly.

associated with the new religion.[36] At Augsburg (a large, wealthy, and well-connected city), since about 1525 the government's inner circle had consisted of Evangelicals—mostly Zwinglians—but they did not change the civic religion and foreign policy until 1533.[37] The political cohesion and financial interests of the oligarchies, plus the binding power of traditional ties to the emperor, varied considerably from city to city,[38] and the coming of the Reformation did not obliterate their influence on civic policy.

Although the polls do not show, as Moeller maintains, that "the opposition votes came mostly from the patricians," they do reveal that urban nobles and wealthier guilds commonly backed conservative policies.[39] Only seven of the eleven officials (*Eilfer*), for example, of Memmingen's patrician *Grosszunft* appeared for a vote on 9 December 1528, and they refused to vote, because, they said, "we fear that Memmingen will not get away with this. The Mass has not yet been abolished in quite a few of the larger and smaller free cities."[40] This is the voice of prudence, not the fire of Catholic conviction. In the Memmingen poll of 1530, the wealthy Grosszunft furnished about a quarter of the fifty-one votes against rejecting the Diet of Augsburg's recess; at Ulm the heaviest opposition came from the patricians and the two wealthiest guilds, those of the Kramer and Kaufleute.[41] The rich clearly favored more cautious policies, but their ranks were not necessarily filled with Catholic recusants. This essentially social interpretation of the polls is supported by a poll of 1547 in which the Strasbourg patricians and Schöffen of the merchant guilds voted overwhelmingly for "peace with honor."[42]

---

[36] See the tortuous policy of Nördlingen as portrayed by Hans-Christoph Rublack, *Eine bürgerliche Reformation: Nördlingen*, Quellen und Forschungen zur Reformationsgeschichte, 51 (Gütersloh, 1982), p. 257, and see pp. 147–50.

[37] I am grateful to James E. Mininger for this information. The findings of Wolfgang Reinhard's team will demonstrate the dominance of Zwinglians at Augsburg. For now, see Olaf Mörke and Katarina Sieh, "Gesellschaftliche Führungsgruppen," in Gunther Gottlieb, *et al.*, eds., *Geschichte der Stadt Augsburg: 2000 Jahre von der Römerzeit bis zur Gegenwart* (Stuttgart, 1985), pp. 301–11, here at pp. 306–307.

[38] This point, which was made fifty years ago by Hans Baron in "Religion and Politics in the German Imperial Cities during the Reformation," *English Historical Review* 52 (1937): pp. 405–27, 614–33, seems to require frequent repetition.

[39] Moeller, *Imperial Cities*, p. 64 n. 48.

[40] Friedrich Dobel, *Memmingen in Reformationszeitalter*, 5 vols. (Augsburg, 1877–1878), 2: p. 70.

[41] *Ibid.*, 4: p. 22; Specker, "Zwischen Gewissen und Gehorsam," p. 45 and the lists on pp. 369–74.

[42] Thomas A. Brady, Jr., *Ruling Class, Regime, and Reformation at Strasbourg, 1520–1555* (Leiden, 1978), pp. 259–75, esp. pp. 265–68.

The reasons why the urban nobles, big merchants, bankers, and rentiers tended to favor relatively conservative policies are not far to seek. First, they had close sentimental and symbolic ties to the sacred buildings of the old faith, which had become, through their altars, glass windows, and heraldic devices, virtual showcases of aristocratic family prestige. Anyone who has strolled through Nuremberg's churches of St. Lorenz and St. Sebald can imagine how the cathedrals of Ulm, Constance, and Strasbourg once looked. Second, because of their education, books, travels, and business and diplomatic activities, the urban rich knew much about the world outside their cities' walls. Wealthy citizens were far better informed about external political forces than their social inferiors and were far more likely as well to appreciate the need for caution in the framing of policy. Unlike some modern historians, they were not likely to believe that their cities were, in fact, autonomous organisms. Third, these classes had great material interests outside their cities, such as estates, fiefs, loans to all classes of people, patronage rights, and goods in transit. Fourth, the religious schism within families probably affected the rich, whose familial ties tended to be strong and deep, more profoundly than other classes, whose families were less protected by property, politics, and genealogical memory.[43] For all of these reasons, the urban elites kept a political eye watching over their cities' walls.

The oligarchies did include recalcitrant Catholics, of course, who in a few towns, such as Rottweil and Schwäbisch-Gmünd, defended both the old faith and patrician power against popular challenges. Occasionally, for example at Basel, a resolute oligarchy could split the alliance between Evangelical religion and demands for the devolution of power.[44]

In general, therefore, it may be said that no solidly Catholic upper class in the South German free cities resisted the changes in religion. On the contrary, as Oberman notes, "members of the patriciate and the upper *bourgeoisie* of the south German cities, in the wake of longstanding efforts at communalization, tended to reject the medieval privileged church that confronted them on every hand."[45]

---

[43] Here I am following Erich Maschke, "Die Familie ist so gross, wie sie vom Familien-bewusstsein erfasst wird"; *Die Familie in der deutschen Stadt des späten Mittelalters*, Sitzungsberichte der Heidelberger Akademie der Wissenschaften, philosophisch-historische Klasse, Jahrgang 1980, no. 4 (Heidelberg, 1980), p. 14.

[44] Hans R. Guggisberg, *Basel in the Sixteenth Century: Aspects of the City Republic before, during, and after the Reformation* (St. Louis, 1982), pp. 27–31.

[45] Oberman, *Masters*, p. 293.

The urban reform enjoyed the patronage of powerful upper-class figures from the very start. The club at Nuremberg that gathered reform-minded individuals under the influence of Johann von Staupitz, for example, included such important men as Anton Tucher, Hieronymus Ebner, Kaspar Nützel, Hieronymus Holzschuher, and Sigmund and Christoph Fürer—the cream of the city's political elite. At Augsburg three of the four mayors were early Evangelicals— Georg Vetter, Ulrich Rehlinger, and Hieronymus Imhof—as was the influential Conrad Herwart. Early Evangelicals at Strasbourg included the Ammeisters Claus Kniebis and Daniel Mieg, the future Ammeister Mathis Pfarrer, the banker Conrad Joham, and Egenolf Röder von Diersburg, a noble with important connections in Baden. Many of Constance's patrician politicians became early converts, among them Bartholomäus and Thomas Blarer, Hans Schulthaiss, and Konrad Zwick, whereas at Zurich some very important people, such as the millionaire Hans Edlibach, backed Zwingli from an early point. At Frankfurt am Main, finally, two of the leading patrician figures, Hamman von Holzhausen and Philipp Fürstenberger, protected Evangelical clergymen. It is difficult to imagine what might have become of the urban reform if its agents and their ideas had not enjoyed such protection from the very first.

Applied to these cities, the commonly identified antithesis—the "official" or "magisterial" Reformation, or the "popular" Reformation— is badly conceived. The South German urban reformation was both "official" and "popular": without initial protection and support from urban aristocrats, the movement would never have survived long enough to move into the churches and the streets; without broad support from the common man, the pressure for religious change would not have developed as rapidly or as radically as it did; without the preachers' theological and personal leadership, the movement could not have been sustained; and without the oligarchies' actions, the movement could not have been turned to a domestication of urban religion. The urban reformation thus became viable when individual oligarchs supported and protected it and it became secure when the oligarchy collectively established it. In between, the movement awakened sympathy among large numbers of artisans, shopkeepers, petty officials, employees, apprentices, and servants. This class of common man, a German *popolo minuto* (Ital: "little people"), comprised those who would not normally take an active part in government but who were in touch with those who did, some of whom could expect to be consulted, personally or through their officials, in times of great crisis.

The free cities' governments protested long and loudly during the 1520s that such common folk had forced the governments to make changes in religion and would not tolerate a restoration of the old ways. This apology gains credence from the very broadness of the typical body politic. At Strasbourg, for example, a city of at most 20,000 inhabitants, some 3,500 persons were enrolled in the guilds; the comparable figure for Ulm, a somewhat smaller city, was 2,270 in 1530. If an oligarchy was backed by a large majority of a body politic of this size, it was invulnerable to internal foes, but it could not coerce or punish through ordinary means a large body of guildsmen who decided to break the law in the name of a higher law. Although Augsburg's rulers appeared at city hall in full armor during the Schilling riots in 1524, displays of force were relatively rare in the urban reformation—at least at this stage—because governments could not coerce large groups of respectable citizens who acted together in, for example, iconoclastic riots. Organized violence on behalf of Catholicism was even rarer, and most significant Catholic resistance involved religious communities, usually of women.[46] In the guilds, however, there were people who possessed the political skills to organize a movement and to orchestrate agitation and pressure on the regime, and it is almost certainly correct—though it cannot yet be demonstrated—to discern in the broad middling group of respectable citizens the social motor of the urban reformation. The decisive point came when very considerable numbers of them (there is as yet no reason to conclude that they were a majority) supported the Evangelical preachers' freedom to preach and attacked the Catholic clergy and ceremonies with militancy and perseverance. No comparable parties formed to defend the old religion with sufficient militancy or in sufficient numbers. After 1525 or so the major struggles in the

---

[46] This subject badly needs comprehensive study. For two well-known cases, see Greta Krabbe, *Caritas Pirckheimer: Ein Lebensbild aus der Zeit der Reformation*, Katholisches Leben und Kirchenreform in Zeitalter der Glaubensspaltung, 7, 5th ed. (Münster/Westfalen, 1982); Francis Rapp, "La vie religieuse du couvent de St. Nicolas-aux-ondes à Strasbourg de 1525 à 1592," *Histoire et sociologie religieuses*, Cahiers de l'Association interuniversitaires de l'Est (1962): pp. 15–30; and Lorna Jane Abray, *The People's Reformation: Magistrates, Clergy, and Commons in Strasbourg, 1500–1598* (Ithaca, 1985), p. 118.

larger cities occurred *between* Evangelicals,[47] persons committed in
some sense to the supremacy of the unadulterated Word of God.

The structure of the South German urban reformation can now
be described. A magisterial or official reform, the only kind possible short of revolution, occurred during the mid-1520s and was prolonged in some places until the early 1530s. It was carried out under
the oligarchies' custody of fundamental civic values and through their
exclusive police power; it was legitimized by the Reformation movement's biblicism and by the oligarchies' undeniable peacekeeping
authority (*jus pacificandi*). The pace of reform reflected both the jolt-
ing pressures from below, created by respectable folk who insisted
on religious change, and the cautioning influence of external forces
and events. In an age of uncertainty, the urban Reformation promised to convert civic religion from an unsettling, disruptive force into
a supportive, legitimizing force for oligarchical rule and basic civic
values. The urban elites willy-nilly seized this promise, because,
although the Reformation movement brought a solution to the problem of the clergy within the oligarchies' grasp, it created a fearsome
new situation by dividing the city in both belief and ritual. The rise
of the sects during the late 1520s gave the crucial impetus to the
formation of urban state-churches. At Strasbourg, the best-studied
case, the magistrates' actions reveal the slenderness of the connection between the proclamation of an official system of belief—a
confession of faith—and the achievement of the most rudimentary
ritual unity. Unwilling to institute either a positive policy of belief
or compulsory worship, in the end the magistrates settled for a negative ritual unity: citizens were forbidden to withhold their children
from the baptismal font.[48] The Catholic church's official ceremonies
had never, even before the Reformation, completely captured people's
full ritual life,[49] and any existing communal ritual had been grievously damaged by the Reformation movement. The long, slow path
to confessionalism began with unity not of worship but of doctrine—
"lex docendi, lex orandi."

The whole task of fashioning the people—enthusiastic, indifferent,
recalcitrant—into civic state-churches lay ahead. The enforcement of

---

[47] It is well to heed Oberman's words, in *Masters*, p. 198, about the term
"Evangelical."
[48] Abray, *People's Reformation*, pp. 104–16, with full references.
[49] This fundamental point is made by Scribner in "Cosmic Order and Daily Life."

a clerically fashioned discipline moved slowly and against much resistance.[50] The urban laity had its own ideas as to what was and was not compatible with the Christian faith.[51] Half a century after the glory days of the urban reform, a Strasbourg Jesuit named Jacob Rabus surveyed its fruits in his native city: "In poor Strasbourg you now have five or six sects among the common people. One fellow is an out-and-out Lutheran, the second a half-Lutheran, the third a Zwinglian, the fourth a Calvinist, the fifth a Schwenckfelder, the sixth an Anabaptist, and the seventh lot is purely epicurean."[52] An eighth, he might have added, was of his own faith. So much for the successful domestication of religion; so much for the identity of church and people, of gospel and common good.

V

Why did the urban reform of the 1520s fail to transform the South German towns into godly cities? The historian of religion might answer, as Peter Munz did, that very often "the momentum of religious experience has made it very difficult to contain religion within the social parameter."[53] Instead, historians of the Reformation point to the elevation of the gospel as a critical principle above the community and the common good, noting that the "properly interpreted gospel" became attached not only to the city as an oligarchically ruled commune but, more important, to what Oberman calls "the consensus of the community of true believers."[54] Although this statement precisely describes the preachers' standpoint, it is nonetheless true that the oligarchies resisted every attempt to make the Gospel

---

[50] Gerald Strauss, *Luther's House of Learning: Indoctrination of the Young in the German Reformation* (Baltimore, 1978). James M. Kittelson's study of visitation records from Strasbourg's territory has caused him to dissent from Strauss's findings; see "Success and Failure in the German Reformation: The Report from Strasbourg," *Archiv für Reformationsgeschichte* 73 (1982): pp. 153–75. His conclusions, however, at most slightly modify Strauss's work, which receives additional support from Abray's *People's Reformation*.

[51] Miriam U. Chrisman, *Lay Culture, Learned Culture: Books and Social Change in Strasbourg, 1480–1599* (New Haven, 1982).

[52] Jacob Rabus, *Christliche bescheidne und wolgegründts ablähnung/ der vermeindten Bischoffs Predigt . . . im Münster zu Strassburg* (Cologne, 1570), fol. 30ʳ. I am grateful to Lorna Jane Abray for this text.

[53] Munz, "From Max Weber to Joachim of Floris," p. 182.

[54] Oberman, *Masters*, pp. 294–95. Moeller's view is similar; see *Imperial Cities*, p. 90.

a binding norm of belief for the citizens (although they did use it as a weapon to crush the sects) or to organize true believers as "ecclesiolae in ecclesia," that is, conventicles inside the church. Only in a very limited sense did the urban laity want their hometowns to become godly cities.[55]

One powerful reason why the oligarchies did not favor too close an identification of the Gospel with the common good was that they lacked full hegemony over these concepts, just as—a point demonstrated by the wave of urban revolts[56]—they lacked full political control over their own citizens. A different conception of gospel and common good, embodied in the idea of the "godly law," had burst onto the political stage in 1525.[57] The *Twelve Articles'* rejection of serfdom, for example, on the ground that Christ had died for all men, was no less inherently "Evangelical" than was Luther's hammering on St. Paul's admonition to obedience (Romans 13). The gospel and the common good could be, and were, seen as commands to justice as well as order, both in the countryside and on the land. This view was expressed perfectly in 1524 by an Augsburg ropemaker named Ott, who was overheard to condemn the "dishonorable priests and the rich . . ., who pile up goods and money and keep the truth from us" and who were to blame for the fact that men treat one another as devils rather than as brothers. "We have always been Evangelicals," Ott concluded, "and we still are today. But truly, we have been fed many lies. If we were to follow truly the Gospel, we would all have to be like brothers."[58] A few years later another Augsburger was reported to have said that "there is only one lord, and He is in heaven, so there are none here below. If he had the money, he would be a lord, too. . . . There is no lord but God, the only true Lord."[59] This is the religious sense of wanting to "turn Swiss," to live without human lords. Ott and his kind needed "no lord but God," nor did they need the preacher's gospel, for they had "always been Evangelicals."

---

[55] Compare Bruce Lenman, "The Limits of Godly Discipline in the Early Modern Period with Particular Reference to England and Scotland," in Greyerz, *Religion and Society*, pp. 124–45.

[56] Maschke, "Deutsche Städte," p. 95 n. 206.

[57] Peter Blickle, *The Revolution of 1525: The German Peasants' War from a New Perspective*, trans. Thomas A. Brady, Jr., and H. C. Erik Midelfort (Baltimore, 1981), p. 91.

[58] Stadtarchiv Augsburg, Urgichten 1524, Produkt 3, at 27 September 1524. I am grateful to Hans-Christoph Rublack for this reference and for the following one.

[59] *Ibid.*, Urgichten 1525–1526, at 30 December 1526.

There was never only one way to couple the Gospel to the common good. If the establishment coupled it to the image of patriarchal authority in the family and hierarchy in the commune, why could the opposition not link it to the fraternal principle of cooperation? The reason was that this understanding of what it meant to be Evangelical could bring revolution to the home, the shop, the guild, the marketplace, and the city hall; no civic regime could tolerate the godly law of justice and equality. Conversely, no free city could have satisfied this understanding within the economic and social conditions then obtaining. The thirst for Christian community, which the sacramental system of the medieval church and the entire monastic tradition had sought to accommodate "without damage to the society in which it flourishes,"[60] was reinvigorated by the urban reformation, which gave it, however, no permanent home in the city. Rather, the city expelled its seekers after community to wander about until the day when a great Christian commune, built according to South German specifications, would arise at Münster on the rain-swept Westphalian plain.[61]

The urban rich and the middling folk liked this outcome well enough. They fought and rejected—as a "new papacy"—every clerical attempt to build stricter religious discipline, because an established church that demanded a fixed minimum of compliance, preached the godly nature of patriarchal and magisterial authority, and provided a religious life unburdened through the uncoupling of salvation from social life suited them perfectly.

In the end, South Germany saw no godly cities, the ruling classes' interests and ambitions had become incommensurable with the political worlds of their own hometowns.[62] Outside these classes had their business operations and investments, their fiefs and country estates; outside, too, their children sought education and often careers as well; and from outside came books and travelers, new ideas and curious tales, new inventions, and rumors and threats of war. Small and economically dependent, the South German city no longer formed

---

[60] Munz, "From Max Weber to Joachim of Floris," p. 182.

[61] On the role of communal ideas and sentiments in Münster and the continuity between the Anabaptist and post-Anabaptist eras, see R. Po-chia Hsia, *Society and Religion in Münster, 1535–1618* (New Haven, 1984).

[62] An extreme example of this incommensurabilily is presented in Olaf Mörke, "Die Fugger im 16. Jahrhundert: Städtische Elite oder Sonderstruktur?—Ein Diskussionsbeitrag," *Archiv für Reformationsgeschichte* 74 (1983): pp. 141–61.

a realm of power and imagination,[63] at least not one adequate to the talents, wealth, and ambitions of its elites' offspring. The rising world of absolutist states, whose chief business was war, had uses and rewards for urban talent and urban capital but little place for proud, self-governing little cities. The German princely states, in themselves mostly petty things, formed through confessional alliances larger systems of opportunity into which the townsmen streamed. They hardly shared, as far as we can tell, the sentiment of Machiavelli, who wrote. "I love my native city more than my own soul."[64]

---

[63] That is, society and culture, for which I borrow this phrase from Lauro Martines, *Power and Imagination: City-States in Renaissance Italy* (New York, 1979), preface.
[64] Niccolò Machiavelli to Francesco Vettori, Forlì, 16 April 1527, in *The Letters of Machiavelli: A Selection of His Letters*, trans. Allan Gilbert (New York, 1961), p. 249 (no. 225 in Alvisi's edition [Florence, 1883]). This letter was written nine weeks before Machiavelli's death.

CHAPTER EIGHT

"THE EARTH IS THE LORD'S AND OUR HOMELAND AS WELL": MARTIN BUCER AND THE POLITICS OF STRASBOURG*

"Few figures of the reformation era," writes Martin Greschat, "are so thoroughly forgotten as is this sixteenth century theologian, churchman, politician, and Christian."[1] The dimming of Bucer's reputation, which began as soon as he was dead, may best be explained by the fact that no living religious tradition claims his as founder. There are "Lutherans" and "Calvinists," but no "Bucerians." Bucer the political thinker shares the uncertainty and dimness of Bucer the churchman, not least, perhaps, because his primary frame of reference was a political form, the self-governing city-state, which had no counterparts in the Protestant world outside of southern Germany and Switzerland. Finally, Bucer the practical politician shares the same qualities, because his political efforts ended in defeat and exile. Yet, Martin Bucer was important to the first generation of German Protestant politics in general and to the politics of adopted city, Strasbourg, in particular.[2]

The story of Martin Bucer's role in the politics of Strasbourg divides rather clearly into three phases. The first phases covers Bucer's rise to political influence at Strasbourg from his arrival in the city in 1523 to the mid-1530s. In the second phase, from about 1536 to 1544, Bucer moved beyond the orbit of Strasbourg's politics to become a Protestant churchman of Imperial rank. Finally, in the third phase Bucer moved into opposition at Strasbourg and ended his career in exile in 1549. After every point since he emerged into

---

* This study is dedicated to Miriam Usher Chrisman, my mentor and my friend.
[1] Martin Greschat, *Martin Bucer. Ein Reformator und seine Zeit 1491–1551* (Munich, 1990), p. 9.
[2] Much of what follows rests on a nearly completed study of the career of Jacob Sturm. The Bucer edition has made obsolete nearly all of the older literature on Bucer as a politician. See, for example, Gerhart Schmidt, *Martin Butzer als protestantischer Politiker*, Ph.D. dissertation, Königsberg, 1936. On his political ideas, see Marijn de Kroon, *Studien zu Martin Bucers Obrigkeitsverständnis. Evangelisches Ethos und politisches Engagement* (Gütersloh, 1984).

the wider public view in 1529, Bucer's position as a Protestant church-man depended very much on his stature as a churchman of Strasbourg.

I. *Bucer's Rise to Eminence*

Bucer's story at Strasbourg during the 1520s centers on his rise from obscurity and social marginality, when he arrived in May 1523 a penniless refugee, until his emergence onto the stage of politics in 1529. He began as, in Martin Greschat's words, "a social climber," who lacked the credentials and connections possessed by Strasbourg's other reformers.[3] Whereas Bucer lacked a completed theological edu-cation, for example, Wolfgang Capito (1472–1541) had earned a doc-torate in theology from Freiburg, been a professor of Old Testament at Basel, and become "a Hebrew scholar of European eminence."[4] Again, whereas Bucer had connected himself to the notoriously ob-streperous nobleman Franz von Sickingen (1481–1523), Capito and Mathis Zell (1477–1548) had studied theology at Freiburg with Jacob Sturm (1489–1553), prominent young patrician and soon to be Strasbourg's leading politician, and Capito had been a councillor to the Elector Albert of Mainz (1490–1545).[5]

The initial structure of clerical leadership in Strasbourg's refor-mation movement took shape from late 1523 until mid-1524. Zell demonstrated his determined commitment by means of a demon-stratively public marriage to a local woman on 13 December 1523, Capito followed suit on 1 August 1524.[6] What is more, both men had secure possession of local posts before identifying themselves with religious dissent, Zell as pastor of Saint Lawrence and Capito as dean of the chapter of Saint Thomas. Bucer, by contrast, came to Strasbourg unbeneficed and without immediate prospects, and

---

[3] Greschat, *Martin Bucer*, 13: "ein sozialer Aufsteiger."

[4] James M. Kittelson, *Wolfgang Capito from Humanist to Reformer*, Studies in Medieval and Reformation Thought, 17 (Leiden, 1975), pp. 24–25.

[5] Hermann Mayer, ed., *Die Matrikel der Universität Freiburg im Breisgau von 1460–1656*, 2 vols. (Freiburg i. Br., 1907–1910), vol. 1: p. 146, pp. 161–62; Johannes Joseph Bauer, *Zur Frühgeschichte der Theologischen Fakultät der Universität Freiburg i. Br. (1460–1620)*, Beiträge zur Freiburg Wissenschafts- und Universitätsgeschichte, 15 (Freiburg i. Br., 1957), pp. 187–88. For Bucer's relations with Sickingen, see Greschat, *Martin Bucer*, pp. 48–53.

[6] William S. Stafford, *Domesticating the Clergy: the Inception of the Reformation in Strasbourg, 1522–1524* (Missoula, Montana, 1976), p. 153; Kittelson, *Wolfgang Capito*, p. 108.

although his father had once been a citizen, the magistrates initially treated him with "a good deal of reserve."[7]

Bucer's initial impetus came from the common people, the gardeners at Saint Aurelia, who elected him pastor 29 March 1524.[8] Once his post was secure, after the magistrates appropriated control over the civic parishes (24 August 1524), Bucer began to press forward. It was he who communicated between the citizens' committee and Capito in August 1524; his energy lay behind the great reform petitions to the magistrates in August and September 1524, the submission of which marked a new phase in the public presence of Evangelical religion at Strasbourg; and he drafted the memorial of October 1524, in which the Strasbourg preachers declared to the magistrates their approval of Luther's teachings.[9] Very likely, Bucer's de facto leadership dates from these days, though he freely acknowledged the primacy of Capito, whose patronage he had sought out in earlier, more difficult days.[10]

This situation—Bucer's de facto leadership under Capito's primacy—lasted through the 1520s. Bucer's stock was rising, while Capito's was not. For one thing, in 1526 Capito incurred the wrath of Jacob Sturm, whose anger at Capito's stupid provocation of the Swiss Catholic powers promoted an outburst against political clergy "who trust more to the power of this world [*uf ein fleischlichen arme*] than to Christ alone."[11] Sturm was a dangerous antagonist, for not only did his performance at the Imperial Diet of Speyer bring him great prestige just at this time, but his conservative position on religious changes made him an opponent of the preachers' campaign against the Mass. It may be doubted the Capito ever overcame Sturm's doubts about his political responsibility.

Far more seriously damaging to Capito's primacy were his flirtations with the Anabaptists, who streamed into Strasbourg during the latter 1520s. It took Bucer, who sensed what dangers these seeming

---

[7] BDS, vol. 1: pp. 346–47. See Stafford, *Domesticating the Clergy*, pp. 149–50.

[8] Greschat, *Martin Bucer*, p. 72.

[9] BCor, vol. 1: pp. 266–67, no. 73. The petitions (31 August and 3 September) are noticed in *ibid.*, pp. 267–69, nos. 74–75, and printed in BDS, vol. 1: pp. 373–76, pp. 399–404. The memorial is in BDS, vol. 1: pp. 304–44; and see BCor, vol. 1: pp. 276–77, no. 78.

[10] BCor, vol. 1: pp. 133–40, nos. 23–26; pp. 142–44, nos. 28–29; pp. 169–73, no. 37. See Kittelson, *Wolfgang Capito*, pp. 56–57. Bucer's praise for Capito's leadership is expressed in BCor, vol. 1: pp. 251–52, no. 66.

[11] Pol. Cor., vol. 1: pp. 263–64, no. 464.

innocents represented, nearly four years to convince Capito that prudence dictated that they oppose the dissenters rather than cultivate them.[12]

The first turning point in Bucer's political career came through Jacob Sturm. Since 1528 Sturm was nudging Strasbourg toward an alliance with the Lutheran princes of central Germany, chiefly Elector John Frederick of Saxony (1504–1554) and Landgrave Philip of Hesse (1504–1567). By 1529, when the Protestant party was born, Sturm's tie to Landgrave Philip became vital to this policy's future, and the two men schemed to open the path to a grand Protestant alliance by reconciling Luther to the southern Zwinglians, among whom Capito and Bucer were numbered. It was the landgrave, not Sturm, who brought Bucer into this plan, when he asked Sturm to come to the Marburg Colloquy and to bring "two judicious, unquarrelsome [preachers], who are inclined to peace and unity," one of them Martin Bucer.[13] At Marburg in the first days of October 1529, Bucer and Sturm first worked in the same harness. Their collaboration, which rested at least partly on their common adherence to the South German-Swiss understanding of the disputed doctrines, quickly bore further fruit. When, at Smalkalden in December 1529, Sturm delivered Strasbourg's objections to the "Schwabach Articles," the Lutheran princes' doctrinal price of alliance, he based them on Bucer's opinions.[14] From this point onward—through the Diet of Augsburg and the Tetrapolitan Confession (1530), the formation of the Smalkaldic League (1531), the subscription to the Confession of Augsburg at Schweinfurt (1532), the restoration in Württemberg (1534), and the Wittenberg Concord—Martin Bucer and Jacob Sturm, a cooper's son and a nobleman, worked as a political-theological team without peer in the confessional politics of the Empire.

The crowning achievement of this remarkable team came, however, not abroad but at home. Working together in perfect harmony, Sturm and Bucer smashed the Strasbourg sects and reconstructed Strasbourg's ecclesiastical order.[15] Bucer's role was so dominant, that

---

[12] Kittelson, *Wolfgang Capito*, pp. 172–88.

[13] Pol. Cor. 1: p. 382, no. 632; *Lenz* 1: p. 8. This explains why Sturm took Hedio and not Capito to Marburg.

[14] Hans von Schubert, *Bekenntnisbildungund Religionspolitik 1529/30 (1524 bis 1534). Untersuchungen und Texte* (Gotha, 1910), pp. 167–82.

[15] I have told this story in detail in "Architect of Persecution: Jacob Sturm and the Fall of the Sects at Strasbourg," ARG 79 (1988): pp. 262–81. For Bucer's perspective, see Greschat, *Martin Bucer*, pp. 127–38; and on the larger theme of toleration

Capito is described by his biographer as "Bucer's loyal ally" in this campaign.[16] When the civic synod met under Sturm's presidency in June 1533, Capito delivered the inaugural sermon and an opening prayer and then "for the most part fell silent," as Bucer debated the dissidents and pursued them one-by-one into silence or banishment. The synod ended in Capito's humiliation, as he humbly agreed to give up his "special weakness for foreign guests" and his (costly) investments in a printing firm. His defeat was total, for "nothing could have been more opposed to Capito's policy from 1526 through 1531" than the new ecclesiastical constitution (*Kirchenordnung*), which Sturm drafted, which the 300 Schöffen of the guilds accepted on 7 February 1535, and which governed official religious life at Strasbourg for the next half-century.[17] This outcome fixed the pre-eminence of Martin Bucer in Strasbourg's reformed church. As Capito acknowledged, "Bucer is our bishop."[18]

II. *Bucer at the Apogee of His Career*

The years from the mid-1530s to 1544 formed the apogee of Bucer's career in the politics of Strasbourg. They are characterized by his growing role in the reformation outside Strasbourg, indeed, far beyond the familiar world of South Germany and Switzerland and, in a few cases, beyond even the boundaries of the Holy Roman Empire.[19] His port of entry to these new fields of activity was the Smalkaldic League, formed in 1531 for the defense of the Protestant faith and extending over a vaster area—Strasbourg to Pomerania, Constance to Hamburg—than any earlier federation in German history.[20] During

and tolerance, see Marc Lienhard, *Religiöse Toleranz in Straßburg im 16. Jahrhundert*, Abhandlungen der Akademie der Wissenschaften und der Literatur Mainz, geistes- und sozialwissenschaftliche Klasse, 1991, no. 1 (Stuttgart, 1991).

[16] Kittelson, *Wolfgang Capito*, p. 193.

[17] The quoted judgment is Kittelson's in *ibid.*, p. 197. The ordinance is in QGT I: pp. 421–31, no. 637.

[18] Wolfgang Capito to Simon Grynaeus, Strasbourg, 13 September 1534, in BNUS, Th. B., 8: p. 219.

[19] His activities and reputation abroad are massively documented by *Pollet* 1, 2, 3 et 4.

[20] Ekkehart Fabian, *Die Entstehung des Schmalkaldischen Bundes und seiner Verfassung 1524/29–1531/35. Brück, Philipp von Hessen und Jakob Sturm*, 2nd ed., Schriften zur Kirchen- und Rechtsgeschichte, 1 (Tübingen, 1962); Thomas A. Brady, Jr., "Phases and Strategies of the Schmalkaldic League: A Perspective after 450 Years," ARG 74 (1983): pp. 162–81.

the first half of the 1530s, Bucer gained prominence in South Germany as a shepherd of other cities—Ulm, Augsburg, Frankfurt—away from Zwinglianism and toward conformity to Lutheranism, the price of their admission to the League.[21] The Wittenberg Concord of 1536, in which the intra-Evangelical strife was finally laid to rest, represented the triumph of this policy. It was the greatest accomplishment of the Sturm-Bucer team in foreign policy, as the crushing of the sects was their greatest domestic victory.

By 1536 Bucer had become the leading Protestant churchman in southern Germany. The subsequent growth of his reputation depended less on his service to Strasbourg than on his relationship with Landgrave Philip of Hesse. The close relationship between Bucer and the landgrave developed during the years 1538–1540 in four stages: first, in the autumn of 1539 through Bucer's consultation with the Hessian Anabaptists and his involvement in the Ziegenhain church ordinance (25 November 1539); secondly, Bucer's consultation on the treatment of the Hessian Jews (December 1538); thirdly, Bucer's strong support for the landgrave's bigamous second marriage (5 March 1540); and fourthly, Bucer's service as chief Hessian theologian at the Colloquy of Worms in 1540.[22]

Bucer's movement into the enterprise of reformation in Hesse and, beyond that, into the reformation's progress in northwestern and northern Germany, represented the beginnings of his estrangement from Jacob Sturm and from the reformation they had fashioned together at Strasbourg. At first, Bucer was elated, and shortly after the new ecclesiastical ordinance took effect, he began work on two treatises in which he justified the magistrates' authority over religion in most uncompromising language.[23] The shorter version appeared in March 1535, the longer one in the following May. In the following year, then, Bucer anchored this position in classic biblical proof text for obedience to the state, Romans 13.[24] In his 1536 commentary on this book, Bucer blasted every possible argument for an ecclesiastical authority distinct from that of the magistrates and reinforced his point with a scathing diatribe against the papacy and the Catholic

---

[21] An overview by Greschat, *Martin Bucer*, pp. 117–26.
[22] Greschat, *Martin Bucer*, pp. 164–71.
[23] "Vom Ampt der Oberkait in sachen der religion und Gotsdiensts" (10 March 1535) and "Dialogi oder Gesprechen von der gemainsame vnnd den Kirchen übungen der Christen" (17 May 1535), in BDS, vol. 6, 2: pp. 17–38, pp. 39–188.
[24] De Kroon, *Studien*, pp. 70–107.

clergy. Bucer denies any possible basis for an ecclesiastical authority separate from that of the ruler.[25] This teaching of 1535–1536 may be regarded as an act gratitude to Jacob Sturm and his fellow magistrates for ridding the preachers of the dissenters' noisy and bewilderingly confident competition.

By the early months of 1538, Bucer's mind turned from what had been gained to what had been lost: the chance for establishing a strict system of religious discipline in the reformed church of Strasbourg. The theological basis for this is the central point of his major ecclesiological treatise, "Von der wahren Seelsorge," which he wrote hastily and, as he confessed, in direct response to the religious conditions at Strasbourg.[26] Here, for the first time, Bucer laid out his belief in the special authority which committed, zealous Christians hold in the church by virtue of the Holy Spirit's authority. The idea of the church as the "kingdom of Christ" would never leave him again, and during the 1540s, when he went into opposition and then into exile, it came to dominate his theology.[27] To a very great degree, this position, and the theology of the Holy Spirit on which it rests, were a product of the victory over the sects, which liberated the entire subject for Bucer.[28]

It is possible, therefore, to see Bucer's movement into reformations outside Strasbourg at the end of the 1530s as simply an extension of his work in the city. This is no doubt partly the case, but his movement also represented a search for fields of reform activity which were free of the forces which blocked at home the formation of a disciplined Christian community. The magistrates' cold reception of "Von der waren Seelsorge" suggests that they saw quite clearly where Bucer was headed, and they blocked his plan to convert the old jurisdiction of the cathedral chapter (*Chorgericht*) into a new disciplinary court.[29] They opposed every form of compulsory religious discipline, for, having rid Strasbourg of one pope, they were not

---

[25] *Ibid.*, pp. 91–107.

[26] BDS, vol. 7: pp. 67–41, esp. 69 on the circumstances of its composition.

[27] Which is why he later gave this treatise a special place among his works. *Ibid.*, p. 70. For Bucer's ecclesiology, see Gottfried Hammann, *Entre la secte et la cité. Le projet d'église du réformateur Martin Bucer*, Histoire et société, 3 (Geneva, 1984), who, however, overestimates Bucer's consistency.

[28] See W. P. Stephens, *The Holy Spirit in the Theology of Martin Bucer* (Cambridge, 1979), p. 162.

[29] Greschat, *Martin Bucer*, p. 160.

about to establish others. As Jacob Sturm put it, "laws make hypocrites."[30] Bucer valiantly pushed the program through a new synod
in 1539, which recommended the establishment of, among other
reforms, a procedure for excommunication. The magistrates took
two-and-a-half years (May 1540–November 1542) to review these
proposals, and on 16 November 1542, which they finally rejected
the project for excommunication, "the core of an effective religious
discipline," Bucer's reform agenda sank for the last time.[31]

Bucer's domestic defeats coincided with his rise to eminence as a
Protestant churchman, a role in which he was surpassed, perhaps,
only by Philip Melanchthon (1497–1560). From the Leipzig Colloquy
of 1539 until the Regensburg Colloquy of 1542, when the restoration
of religious unity seemed to rest in the hands of a few men, of whom
Bucer was one, he moved among the great and mighty of the whole
Empire.[32] On interpretations of these events rest most of what has
been written—some of it hyperbole or even nonsense—about Bucer's
motives and stature as an ecumenical churchman.[33] Bucer truly hated
and despised the papacy and its followers and all that had to do
with Catholicism, and he truly believed in the use of compulsion in
matters of religion.[34] From the colloquies he initially hoped only for
total victory, for the thought that if the issues could be debated in
public, "the power of the Lord through His holy Word will certainly
effect and do such things, for which we shall have to thank Him."[35]
The meaning of this veiled remark is clarified by Bucer's comment
to Landgrave Philip that "without ever striking a blow, we will gradually pry the Antichrist from all his nests one-by-one."[36]

[30] QGT I: pp. 354 l. 41.
[31] See BDS, vol. 6, 2: pp. 195–99; and there, on 199, the following quote. On
this whole subject, see Thomas A. Brady, Jr., "In Search of the Godly City: The
Domestication of Religion in the German Urban Reformation," in R. Po-chia Hsia,
ed., *The German People and the Reformation* (Ithaca, 1988), pp. 14–31.
[32] Greschat, *Martin Bucer*, pp. 177–92. See, in general, Pierre Fraenkel, *Einigungsbestrebungen in der Reformationszeit*, Vorträge des Instituts für europäische Geschichte
Mainz, no. 41 (Wiesbaden, 1965).
[33] The extreme in this direction is probably represented by Heinrich Bornkamm,
Martin Bucers Bedeutung für die europäische Reformationsgeschichte, Schriften des Vereins für
Reformationsgeschichte, 169 (Gütersloh, 1952), pp. 25–31. Still the most interesting
work in the ecumenical vein is Robert Stupperich, *Der Humanismus und die Wieder-
vereinigung der Konfessionen* (Leipzig, 1936).
[34] Nikolaus Paulus, *Protestantismus und Toleranz im 16. Jahrhundert* (Freiburg i. Br.,
1911), pp. 142–75; De Kroon, *Studien*, pp. 8–23, 162; Lienhard, *Religiöse Toleranz*.
[35] *Lenz* 1: p. 94, no. 28.
[36] *Lenz* 1: p. 93, no. 27.

In the course of the colloquys, however, events drew Bucer in a different direction. One such moment came at Worms on 18 January 1540, when Bucer, Melanchthon, Johann Eck (1486–1543), and Bishop Mensing of Halberstadt signed the union formula on justification and then hugged and kissed one another like reunited brothers.[37] At Worms, briefly, Bucer became not just a Protestant but an Imperial churchman, playing for once a weightier role than Jacob Sturm did. Not only did he serve as chief theologian for Hesse, but the land-grave instructed his envoys that although "you should also hear what the other allies' envoys say, especially those of the Saxon elector, you should always listen more to Sturm's and Bucer's opinions than to anyone else's."[38] Bucer's apogee came in mid-December 1540, when the Imperial chancellor, Nicolas Perrenot de Granvelle, (1486–1550), invited Bucer and Capito to help the stalled negotiations by meet-ing secretly with two Catholic theologians. Jacob Sturm, though he thought this might help, didn't dare to authorize them to accept, so the two theologians, plagued with doubt, "whether that we might not be serving the Devil, even while intending to serve Christ," took part in the talks between 15 and 31 December.[39] They acted not for Strasbourg but for the landgrave of Hesse, who sent a back-dated instruction to cover them.[40] Bucer was neither the first nor the last Protestant to come under the influence of Granvelle, a Franche-Cômtois of great ability and compelling charm.

Bucer's prominence at Worms made a Protestant churchman of independent stature. In February 1542, Elector Hermann von Wied of Cologne (1477–1552) called him to oversee a religious reforma-tion in the prince-archbishopric.[41] This work, perhaps the most impor-tant independent commission in Bucer's career, eventually came to naught, because the Smalkaldic League failed to intervene in 1543 for the Duke William V of Cleves-Jülich (r. 1539–1592) and against

---

[37] Fraenkel, *Einigungsbestrebungen*, pp. 63–64.

[38] Günther Franz, ed., *Urkundliche Quellen zur hessischen Reformationgeschichte*, vol. 2 (Marburg, 1954), p. 341. For the larger context of Bucer, the landgrave, and the colloquies, see Gerhard Müller, "Landgraf Philipp von Hessen und das Regensburger Buch," in Marijn de Kroon and Friedhelm Krüger, eds., *Bucer und seine Zeit. For-schungsbeiträge und Bibliographie*, Veröffentlichungen des Instituts für europäische Geschichte Mainz, 80 (Wiesbaden, 1976), pp. 101–16.

[39] *Lenz* 1: p. 278, no. 101. Much later, Sturm confessed that "Buceri halb, was er privatim mit ime [Granvelle] et Gerardo [Veltwyck] gehandelt, wuste ich nit." Pol. Cor., vol. 3: p. 605 (1545), quoted by *Pollet* 1: p. 39 n. 2.

[40] *Lenz* 1: pp. 278–79, nos. 101, 517; pp. 281–82, no. 103.

[41] *Pollet* 1: pp. 96–234; 2: pp. 33–162. See Greschat, *Martin Bucer*, pp. 192–203.

the Emperor Charles V (r. 1519–1556). Indeed, this phase brought no clear victories to match Bucer's triumph over Zwinglianism in the South German free cities. Bucer's personal prestige, however, never stood higher than it did during the early 1540s.

III. *The Fall of Bucer*

The roots of Bucer's political decline lie in his worsening relations with Jacob Sturm, which, because of Sturm's dominance over the politics of Bucer's home base, external successes, such the landgrave's favor and Elector Hermann's commission, could not neutralize. Between 1539 and 1544, the apogee of Bucer's career outside Strasbourg, he and Sturm came to loggerheads over a series of important issues. First, there was the problem of the landgrave's bigamy, which Sturm believed a terrible and dangerous mistake, while Bucer, who knew about the bigamy before Sturm did, eventually sided with the landgrave.[42] Secondly, they disagreed about the beleaguered Protestant minority at Metz, whose leaders applied in 1543 for admission to the Smalkaldic League. Bucer wanted to admit them, while Sturm, who worried about the legal and political consequences, successfully opposed their admission.[43] Thirdly, the two men quarrelled bitterly over the disposal of the duchy of Brunswick-Wolfenbüttel, which the Smalkaldic commanders conquered in 1542. Sturm wanted to transfer it to Charles V's custody, while Bucer favored retaining Protestant control of the duchy.[44] On each of these issues, Bucer sided with Landgrave Philip of Hesse against Sturm.

The deterioration of his partnership with Sturm in foreign policy coincided with Bucer's involvement in a movement to subvert the regime's intransigence about ecclesiastical discipline. The story of Strasbourg's "Christian communities," conventicles of zealous believers gathered within several of the city's parishes (*eccesiolae in ecclesia*), has been told often and well.[45] In the mid-1540s, when Bucer enjoyed

---

[42] *Lenz* 1: pp. 327–91; Greschat, *Martin Bucer*, pp. 168–70.

[43] Otto Winckelmann, "Der Anteil der deutschen Protestanten an den kirchlichen Reformbestrebungen in Metz bis 1543," *Jahrbuch der Gesellschaft für lothringische Geschichte und Altertumskunde* 9 (1897): pp. 202–36.

[44] See Thomas A. Brady, Jr., "Jacob Sturm and the Seizure of Brunswick-Wolfenbüttel by the Schmalkaldic League, 1542–1545," in *Festschrift for DeLamar Jensen*, ed. Paul B. Pixton and Malcolm R. Thorp (forthcoming).

[45] Werner Bellardi, *Die Geschichte der "christlichen Gemeinschaften" in Straßburg (1546/1550)*.

all the marks of success—the deanship of Saint Thomas, a big house, a handsome salary, and a new wife—the yearning for a purer, more disciplined church left him no peace. He had come to believe that the cause of the Gospel was faltering because of the Protestants' unwillingness to submit to the discipline of the Word. "We must revive and most zealously uphold moral discipline [*zuchtordnung*] and conduct our common prayers most faithfully," he wrote to the landgrave, "for otherwise the Lord will not be with us. Our contributions of money, men, and whatever else is needed must have no other purpose or goal than to secure a proper peace and general, true reformation for the whole German nation."[46] The feeling left him no peace, and at Strasbourg he left the magistrates none. Truly, [he wrote in his catechism of 1543] if we do not acknowledge, accept, hold to, and enforce God's holy covenant better than we do now, God will break it and will no longer be our God and Savior. He will deliver us most terribly into the hands of our enemies, to our ruin, both temporal and eternal, just as he did His people of old.[47]

In the following year, 1544, the preachers formed a new type of purely clerical commission (*Convent*) to deliberate on church business under Bucer's presidency.[48] Then, at the end of 1545, the longing for a "second reformation" at Strasbourg began to assume palpable form, as conventicles took shape in two of the city's parishes.[49] Whatever Bucer's part in the conventicles' management, which he seems to have left mainly to younger clergymen, his leadership is clear from the manifesto of Strasbourg's second reformation, "Von der kirchen mengel und fahl," which the preachers submitted to the

Der Versuch einer "zweiter Reformation", Quellen und Forschungen zur Reformationsgeschichte, 18 (Leipzig, 1934; reprint, New York, 1971); Marc Lienhard, "La Réforme à Strasbourg, I: les événements et les hommes," in Georges Livet and Francis Rapp, eds., *Histoire de Strasbourg*, vol. 2 (Strasbourg, 1981), pp. 412–15.

[46] *Lenz* 2: p. 373, no. 220.

[47] BDS, vols. 6, 3: pp. 263, ll. 24–29, quoted by Greschat, *Martin Bucer*, p. 211, who links Bucer's mood at this time with his failing health and "the decline of his physical powers."

[48] Bellardi, *Geschichte der "christlichen Gemeinschaften"*, p. 22; Lienhard, "La Réforme à Strasbourg, I," p. 412. Perhaps they were spurred on by the collapse, around this time, of their hopes for reforming the diocese of Strasbourg through its new bishop, Erasmus of Limburg. See Miriam U. Chrisman, *Strasbourg and the Reform. A Study in the Process of Change* (New Haven, 1967), pp. 256–59; Lienhard, "La Réforme à Strasbourg, I," p. 404.

[49] Bellardi, in BDS, vol. 17: p. 157, though his monograph (*Geschichte*, 39) puts the beginnings during the Smalkaldic War.

Senate & XXI on Epiphany (6 January) 1546.[50] The opening sentence sets its tone:

> One of the leading causes of the current ignorance of the difference between ecclesiastical and civil government is the people's feelings of great disdain and outrage, whenever the church's power of the keys is mentioned. They have insufficient knowledge of how the two governments differ from one another and the limits of each, imagining that they are subject to the authority of the temporal ruler alone.[51]

In early 1546, therefore, only one step—divine authority for ecclesiastical offices—stood between Bucer and a solution à la Calvin to the situation at Strasbourg. The outbreak of the Smalkaldic War in June 1546 dashed this moment from his grasp, never to return.

The war worsened Bucer's relations with Jacob Sturm. Bucer, who had a weakness for crusading enthusiasm, greeted the opening of the war in 1546 as he had the campaigns of 1534 in Württemberg and 1542 in Brunswick-Wolfenbüttel.[52] The people of Strasbourg seem not to have shared his mood, as he complained to the landgrave: "Alas, we convince few people that something great is happening; they grumble about the costs, . . . If everyone had to bear the burdens every day, and eat and drink less, they would pray better and learn better. . . . We have, alas, too long and too much presumed on the immeasurable grace of Christ."[53]

To Jacob Sturm, by contrast, the outbreak of the Smalkaldic War signalled the failure of his long effort to avoid a civil war through a combination of firmness and willingness to negotiate.[54] Until late in the Danube campaign, Sturm resisted the League commanders' efforts to bring him to the front, and when he did go, he confessed to them (10 November) that he regarded the situation "with deep

[50] Edited by Bellardi, in BDS, vol. 17: pp. 151–95.

[51] BDS, vol. 17: 159, ll. 3–160, l. 3.

[52] See Thomas A. Brady, Jr., "Princes' Reformation vs. Urban Liberty. Strasbourg and the Restoration of Duke Ulrich in Württemberg, 1534," in Ingrid Bátori, ed., *Städtische Gesellschaft und Reformation*, Spätmittelalter und Frühe Neuzeit. Tübinger Beiträge zur Geschichtsforschung, 12 (Stuttgart, 1980), pp. 265–91, here at 287; *idem*, "Jacob Sturm and the Seizure of Brunswick-Wolfenbüttel."

[53] *Lenz* 2: p. 460, no. 240 (19 September 1546).

[54] See Thomas A. Brady, Jr., "A Crisis Averted: Jacob Sturm and the Truce of Frankfurt, 1539". In Monika Hagenmaier and Sabine Holtz, eds., *Krisenbewußtsein und Krisenbewältigung in der Frühen Neuzeit. Festschrift für Hans-Christoph Rublack* (Frankfurt a. M.: Peter Lang, 1992).

dejection, for I would much rather that, God willing, affairs had never brought on such a grievous war."[55] When, in January 1547, Sturm and Bucer split over whether to surrender or to resist the emperor, their partnership began to crumble away. Bucer presided over two campaigns of resistance, to the peace in 1547 and to the Interim (the emperor's provisional religious settlement) in 1548, and he lost both. He lost them mainly because Sturm and his party held the loyalty of the Schöffen against the preachers. On 27 August 1548, in a brilliant speech drafted by Jacob Sturm, the Schöffen were warned that "so long as the emperor commands obedience in the Empire of the German Nation," therefore, "as he now does, it is unthinkable that the city can hold out against him, for at last we must surrender and obey him, as others have done, or seek a lord outside the Empire."[56] When the Schöffen stood with the regime for negotiation, not resistance, magistrates were speedily sent to Bucer and the other preachers to admonish them not "to stir up the people against the pope, the king, and the emperor, for the honorable Senate will no longer tolerate that."[57] Indeed, it would not, and the second reformation at Strasbourg was over.

Why did Martin Bucer risk the work of lifetime on the card of resistance to the Interim? Had the failures and disappointments since the mid-1530s wiped away the memory of the reformation's glory days, when Bucer had truly put his fingers on the pulse of the common people, when he had faced Luther at the Marburg Colloquy, and when he climbed to eminence as the organizer of Protestant unity? Did he see resistance as the last chance for a second reformation after the cumulative disappointments of his failed campaign for ecclesiastical discipline, his rebuffs by the intransigent magistrates, his quarrels with Jacob Sturm, and the lost war? We shall never know, for not even the skilled historian can fix the motives of historical subjects. One incident, however, sheds light on the moment when Bucer set his face squarely toward the path of resistance, which led him to bitter exile amidst England's eternal fogs. It happened during the great "armored" Diet of Augsburg in 1548. After a long wait at Ulm, in case Sturm should need him, Bucer came to Augsburg

---

[55] Pol. Cor., vol. 4: p. 480, no. 451.
[56] Pol. Cor., vol. 4: pp. 1059–63, no. 816.
[57] Pol. Cor., vol. 4: p. 1065, no. 818 n. 1 (29 August).

on 30 March, "probably on his own initiative," and lodged clandestinely with Elector Joachim II (r. 1535–1571) of Brandenburg.[58]
When he first saw the text of the Interim on 2 April, the Nurembergers
reported, "said Bucer was quite pleased [*durchaus gevallen lesst*] by the
Interim, although he has some reservations about some articles, albeit
not very important ones."[59] True enough, but while Bucer professed
his lack of fundamental objections to the text, he began to realize
that if the other Protestants did not fall into line, his entire position
and influence would collapse.[60] On the 13th Bucer was arrested, first
by his electoral host, then by the emperor's men, and after some
humiliating treatment at their hands he signed the Interim on 20
April. On the same day he left Augsburg, he reached Strasbourg on
the 25th, and he began immediately to agitate against the document
he had just signed and against which, by his own admission, he had
no major objections.[61]

    In these days of late April 1548, therefore, we may set the begin-
nings of the final breach between Martin Bucer and Jacob Sturm,
because then Bucer committed himself to a course which, if successful, would undermine Sturm's authority and subvert his policy. Rallying younger clergymen to his cause, Bucer initiated them into the
tactics of the 1520s: agitation from the pulpits, formation of committed conventicles, and bombardment of the magistrates with demands
and warnings. The second reformation, therefore, aimed at victory
via the tactics of the first reformation. This was a serious mistake,
for the church at Strasbourg lay under not the divided powers of
city and bishop but the single power of the magistrates. Twenty years
had accustomed them to Jacob Sturm's firm hand at the tiller, and
though many abandoned ship during the crisis of August 1548, others,
plus the all-important Schöffen, stayed on board.

    That the negotiations with the bishop over the Interim deeply

---

[58] Greschat, *Martin Bucer*, p. 227.
[59] Pol. Cor., vol. 4: pp. 903–4, no. 747; and with greater detail in QGT IV:
p. 248, no. 1599.
[60] See his eloquent letter to the electors of Brandenburg and the Palatinate, 10
April 1548, in BDS, vol. 17: pp. 416–21. For the situation, see Greschat, *Martin
Bucer*, pp. 227–28, though I do not agree that Bucer was still swayed by memories
of the colloquys.
[61] Pol. Cor., vol. 4: pp. 918–19, no. 751 n. 7; BDS, vol. 17: p. 347, pp. 422–38.
Bucer's mind was surely made up by the time he arrived in Strasbourg, for which
see Paul Fagius to Matthias Erb, Strasbourg, 27 April 1548, in BNUS, Th. B., 19:
pp. 56–57.

shamed Jacob Sturm, did Bucer no good in the end. The indomitable Katharine Schütz, Mathis Zell's widow, reports that Sturm came to see her early in 1549, and "when he tried to speak to me, he wept so that he could hardly speak. So he knows how things stand."[62] No matter, for Bucer's banishment could now be had for the bishop's asking. Ask he did, and on 6 April 1549—twenty-seven years after he had arrived—Bucer quietly slipped out of Strasbourg.

Three weeks after his arrival in England, Bucer wrote his first and only letter to Sturm from exile, in which he confessed that "I think of you, both because of that which was introduced [i.e., the Interim], because of you personally, and mostly because of what I heard you say."[63] Reviewing their differences, he lectured Sturm that "the earth is the Lord's and our homeland as well," and that God alone is the source of law and liberty. God alone, and not the people, for rulers must build up the kingdom of Christ despite the people's weaknesses and the interests of "the rich [*accumulandi mammonae*]," until the whole world becomes one godly order, a *regnum Christi* founded on those "in whom Christ is most alive." Here, in Bucer's faith that the world could become Christ's kingdom, is the nub of the breach between Martin Bucer and Jacob Sturm, whose teamwork had raised Strasbourg to the role of capital of the South German reformation, herded the southern free cities into the Smalkaldic League, and crowned the League with the laurels of Protestant unity. Bucer believed, as he wrote to Sturm, that "the earth is the Lord's, and our homeland as well," while Sturm believed, as he had written in his great address for Strasbourg's Schöffen, that "most probably, we are not such as God will save through a miracle."[64] A lifetime in politics had taught Jacob Sturm, who was not much younger than Niccolò Machiavelli, that the earth is not the Lord's, but the lords'.

---

[62] Katharine Schütz (Zell) to Conrad Pellikan, Strasbourg, 4 January 1549, in BNUS, Th. B., 20: pp. 4–5, here quoted from Roland H. Bainton, "Katherine Zell," *Medievalia et Humanistica*, new ser. 1 (1970): pp. 25–26 n. 40.

[63] Martin Bucer to Jacob Sturm, Croydon, 13 May 1549, in Jean Rott, "Un recueil de correspondances strasbourgeoises du XVIe siècle à la Bibliothèque de Copenhague (Ms. Thott 497, 2)," *Bulletin philologique et historique (jusqu'en 1610) du Comité des travaux historiques et scientifiques 1968* (1971), 2: pp. 809–18, no. 10, here at 810; also *Rott*, Investigationes, 1: p. 303. See Heiko A. Oberman, *Masters of the Reformation. The Emergence of a New Intellectual Climate in Europe*, trans. Dennis Martin (Cambridge, 1981), p. 238 n. 137, who quotes and comments on this letter.

[64] Pol. Cor., vol. 4: p. 1061, no. 816 (27 August 1548): "das höchlich zu besorgen [ist], wir seien nit die, umb deren rettung willen der allmechtig sonder wunder zeichen tun werd."

It began in bitter reflection, this last contact between Bucer and Sturm, but then Bucer's letter took a remarkably tender turn, as the light of former days flooded in to soften his heart. "I beg you to accept my admonition as I intend it," he wrote, "for I truly love you, . . . and I am terribly concerned for your welfare [*pro tua salute*]."[65]

Conclusion

Martin Bucer came to Strasbourg in 1522 as a refugee; he left the city in 1549 as an exile, his dream of a second reformation shattered on the hard rocks of Jacob Sturm's political will and influence. Although the split between these two members of the German reformation's most remarkable team involved issues of policy, it also realized a difference which had been present since the reformation's early days. Whereas Bucer had come out of the monastery to become a clergyman, Sturm had left the clergy to become a politician. Their paths converged in the late 1520s, when the struggle to abolish the Mass was over, when Capito's admiration of the sects was undermining his leadership, and when Sturm needed a reliable churchman to serve his alliance policy. A remarkable series of successes, culminating in the crushing of Strasbourg's sects (1534) and the forging of Evangelical unity (1536), crowned their partnership. There followed the period of Bucer's growing dissatisfaction with Strasbourg's reformation and his mounting eminence as a Protestant churchman of Imperial rank. Finally, around 1544 the two partners' paths began to diverge, as Bucer tested the possibilities for a second reformation, while Sturm struggled to defend the reformation they had achieved. When Bucer needed to recreate the winning combination of the 1520s, he failed, and his second reformation was sacrificed to preserve their first reformation. The price of failure, despite Jacob Sturm's shame at what he had done, was Bucer's exile. In the last analysis, Bucer was a man of the church, while Sturm was a man of the city.

It has become fashionable, in recent years, to pronounce the German reformation a failure.[66] The judgment is plausible only if one measures the reformation's defeats against some absolute stan-

---

[65] Rott, "Un receuil," p. 814, also in *Rott*, Investigationes, vol. 1: p. 308.
[66] See, e.g., Steven Ozment, *The Age of Reform, 1250–1550. An Intellectual and Religious History of Late Medieval Europe* (New Haven, 1980), p. 438.

dard of success. Otherwise, ignorance of context disqualifies it. For the context, the conditions which alone allowed the German reformation to establish itself at all, was the decentralized and localized structure of governance in the Holy Roman Empire. This context permitted the movement to establish itself in some localities and to defend that establishment. Conversely, because the Empire had no center to conquer, as in England, the movement faltered once its initial energy was spent. What makes the German reformation's history so puzzling is that this whole process took only about twenty-five years, so that the veterans of the movement's glory days, the 1520s, had to witness the onset of its sclerosis in the 1540s. The same political context which permitted the reformation's success, prevented its further development. Jacob Sturm, who was deeply rooted in that context, the traditional structure of governance, saw and accepted this outcome, and his career began and ended in Strasbourg, the city of his ancestors. Martin Bucer, who was not deeply rooted, either as a Catholic friar or as a Protestant clergyman, could not accept this outcome, and his career began in a central Alsatian town and ended in England. Most of his last days were devoted to giving shape to his dream of the world as the kingdom of Christ. This dream went far beyond the context of Strasbourg's reformation, far beyond that of the German reformation. But it did not die, and for generations to come some Protestants would dream marshalling the world into the kingdom of Christ. They would not be German-speakers, however, and they would not be called "Bucerians" but "Calvinists."

CHAPTER NINE

"YOU HATE US PRIESTS": ANTICLERICALISM,
COMMUNALISM, AND THE CONTROL OF WOMEN AT
STRASBOURG IN THE AGE OF THE REFORMATION[1]

"You laymen hate us priests, and it is an old hatred between you and us."[2] This anguished cry comes from a work called "The Ants", a cycle of sermons preached by Johann Geiler von Kaysersberg (1445–1510) at Strasbourg and published posthumously by his Franciscan disciple, Johannes Pauli.[3] It has become well known to the current generation of reformation scholars through Francis Rapp's study of conditions in the diocese of Strasbourg between 1450 and 1525.[4] Rapp's book provides a sturdy backdrop to this study of anticlericalism at Strasbourg, which aims to examine some aspects of the problem of anticlericalism and the social integration of the clergy at Strasbourg before and during the reformation era.

Recent literature on the Holy Roman Empire in the sixteenth century offers a rich variety of reformations: "people's", "princes'", "urban", "magisterial", "radical", and "communal". Against this proliferation works a tendency to reunify the movement, most recently attempted by Hans-Jürgen Goertz, who unites the various streams of reform during the 1520s under the rubric of anticlericalism.[5] What all these

---

[1] Abbreviations specific to this paper:
AEKG = *Archiv für elsässische Kirchengeschichte/Archives de l'Eglise d'Alsace*
AMS = Archives Municipales de Strasbourg
AST = Archives du Chapître de St.-Thomas de Strasbourg
BSCMHA = *Bulletin de la Société pour la Conservation des Monuments Historiques d'Alsace*
[2] Johann Geiler von Kaysersberg, *Die Emeis: Dis ist das buch von der Omeissen, und auch Herr der könnig ich diente gern* (Strasbourg: Johann Grüninger, 1516), p. 28b: "Ir leyen hassen uns pfaffen/und ist auch ein alter hass zwischen euch und uns."
[3] On these sermons, see Eugen Breitenstein, "Die Autorschaft der Geiler von Kaysersberg zugeschriebenen Emeis", *AEKG* 13 (1938): pp. 149–98; id., "Die Quellen der Geiler zugeschriebenen Emeis", *AEKG* 15 (1941/42): pp. 141–202. On the problematical texts of Geiler's sermons in general, see Luzian Pfleger, "Zur handschriftlichen Überlieferung Geilerscher Predigttexte", *AEKG* 6 (1931): pp. 195–205.
[4] Francis Rapp, *Réformes er reformation à Strasbourg. Eglise et société dans le diocèse de Strasbourg (1450–1525)*, Collection de l'Institut des Hautes Etudes Alsaciennes 23 (Paris, 1974), p. 419.
[5] Hans-Jürgen Goertz, *Pfaffenhaß und groß Geschrei. Die reformatorischen Bewegungen in*

streams had in common, Goertz writes, was the aim "to break off
the top of the medieval pyramid of estates."[6] Inspired by his work
in Anabaptist studies, Goertz argues that the aim to integrate the
clergy into the lay community halted part-way in the Protestant cities
and lands and found its full realization only among the radical sects,
supremely among the Hutterite communities in Moravia, which at
last abolished the distinction between clergy and laity. Although he
does not claim that anticlericalism was the sole cause of the reformation,[7] Goertz does regard it as the common, radical font from
which the various streams of reformation poured forth to differentiate
themselves and to moderate their respective forces as they spread.[8]
The radical reformation was not Protestantism radicalized; Protestantism was the reformation de-radicalized.

Goertz's interesting thesis is open to several qualifications. Not
only is it unclear why all other social groups should have united in
the desire to "break off the top of the medieval pyramid of estates",
but there is no real evidence that the actors thought of their actions
in this way, nor for the existence of such a unified idea of society.[9]
The notion of society as a social pyramid with the clergy at the top
was but one of many competing conceptions in late medieval thought.
Just as common was the notion of dual, coordinated hierarchies, lay
and clerical, which were sometimes integrated into a single pyramid.
A good example is the "tree of society" (*Ständebaum*) in the famous
woodcut of 1519/20 by the Petrarch Master, which shows pope with
emperor and kings and cardinals and bishops with princes and nobles;
priests and monks, who are not shown, would presumably rank with

---

Deutschland 1517–1529 (Munich, 1987). Heiko A. Oberman has also identified anticlericalism as the initial rallying cause of the reformation movement, in "The Gospel
of Social Unrest: 450 Years after the so-called Peasants' War of 1525", now in his
The Dawn of the Reformation: Essays in Late Medieval and Reformation Thought (Edinburgh,
1986), pp. 155–78, originally published in 1976.

[6] Goertz, *Pfaffenhaß*, p. 260: "die Spitze der mittelalterlichen Ständepyramide
abzubrechen."

[7] This is noted by Tom Scott, "Historiographical Review: The Common People
in the German Reformation", *Historical Journal* 34 (1991): pp. 183–92, here at p. 192.

[8] Goertz, *Pfaffenhaß*, pp. 245, 250.

[9] Goertz takes the classic scheme of three estates seriously, though he does not
repeat the error of Robert H. Lutz, who tried to identify the "Common Man" with
the third estate in the classic, triadic scheme. See Thomas A. Brady, Jr., *Turning
Swiss: Cities and Empire, 1450–1550*, Cambridge Studies in Early Modern History
(Cambridge, 1985), p. 32 n. 86, for references.

the merchants and artisans.[10] This and other contemporary concepts cast doubt on the thesis of a single pyramid capped by the clergy.

These qualifications aside, the Goertz thesis holds far more promise than does the proposition that the virulent anticlericalism of the 1510s and 1520s erupted in direct response to clerical degeneracy. The burden of proof for this hoary favorite now lies with those who believe that the later Middle Ages witnessed a pronounced decline in clerical standards of personal behavior and learning. A younger version of this view holds that reformation anticlericalism reflects the grave psychological burdens that late medieval religion placed on the average Christian. There is no sign that the thesis of "burdensome religion" is likely to succeed where that of "corrupt clergy" has faltered.[11]

Such theses lack power to explain the fearfully explosive power of anticlericalism in the early reformation movement, because they all assume that the new anticlericalism arose as a reaction to the clergy alone, not as a critique of society as a whole. Far more persuasive is the view of Günter Vogler, that the new anticlericalism served as a powerful but transitory unifier of a wide variety of groups and their interests, and that its historical function was to facilitate both this union for action and the transitions from particular to general grievance and from religious to social criticism. "The movement's heterogeneity", he writes, "began to be more clearly discernible when it was recognized that adherents intended to apply the reform teachings

---

[10] The woodcut is often reproduced, notably in Adolf Laube, Max Steinmetz, and Günter Vogler, eds., *Illustrierte Geschichte der deutschen frühbürgerlichen Revolution* (Berlin, 1974), p. 219.

[11] The basis for such views has been eroding for some time. See, in general, Francis Oakley, "Religious and Ecclesiastical Life on the Eve of the Reformation", in *Reformation Europe: a Guide to Research*, ed. S. Ozment (St. Louis, 1982), pp. 5–32. See also Lawrence G. Duggan, "The Unresponsiveness of the Late Medieval Church: A Reconsideration", *SCJ* 9 (1978): pp. 2–26; id., "Fear and Confession on the Eve of the Reformation", *ARG* 75 (1984): pp. 153–75, who questions the corruption thesis and the burden thesis respectively. The latter was cast in its current form by Steven E. Ozment, *The Reformation in the Cities* (New Haven, 1975), pp. 22–32. James M. Stayer has recently written: "If we accept that the abuses of the clergy caused the Reformation, then we are returning to the nineteenth-century interpretation of the field. . . . I am loathe to do that because there are too many evidences of institutional, intellectual and spiritual vitality in the pre-Reformation clergy to accept that it simply collapsed by itself." James M. Stayer, "Anticlericalism: A Model for a Coherent Interpretation of the Reformation", unpublished (my thanks to him for a copy of this paper).

to secular life and the social realm."[12] Vogler cites a telling remark by Karl Marx about the need for a revolutionary moment to take on the guise of a general emancipation and to find a general enemy:

> If the revolution of a people and the emancipation of a particular class [*Klasse*] of bourgeois society are to coincide, so that one group [*Stand*] stands for all social groups, then the contrary is also true: a particular group must be despised by all others, it must embody that which blocks the desires of the others. In this case, one particular social sphere [*Sphäre*] must be the locus for the notorious crimes of the entire society, so that the liberation of this sphere may appear to be a general self-emancipation.[13]

This notion, the revolutionary transformation of one social group from objects of criticism into a general scapegoat, has the great virtue of capturing the psychological difference between revolutionary and ordinary times. It helps us to understand, for example, why the reformation movement in Germany often demonized the clergy in images and language which also seemed appropriate to Jews and Turks.[14] Based on these insights, we might see reformation anticlericalism as part of the mentality of a revolutionary situation, not as a reasoned response to escalating clerical corruption.[15] The explanation focuses less on inherent, religious characteristics of the clergy as a social group than on their relationships to the broader distinctions between wealth and poverty, power and impotence, and respectability and despicability. The dying years of our own century offer an especially good vantage point from which to understand how a specific, easily identifiable, clearly privileged group might, given the right conditions, come to be identified as the overriding source of all social ills particularly if the group had long been the object of widespread criticism and suspicions of unwarranted power and privileges.

---

[12] Günter Vogler, "Imperial City Nuremberg, 1524–1525: The Reform Movement in Transition", in *The German People and the Reformation*, ed. R. Po-chia Hsia (Ithaca, 1988), pp. 33–51, here at p. 37.

[13] Karl Marx, "Kritik der Hegelschen Rechtsphilosophie. Einleitung", in Karl Marx, *Werke*, ed. Hans-Joachim Lieber, 6 vols., 2nd ed. (Darmstadt, 1962), 1: p. 501. Vogler ("Imperial City Nuremberg, 1524–1525", p. 48) cites Karl Marx and Friedrich Engels, *Werke*, vol. 1 (Berlin, 1981), p. 388.

[14] A phenomenon noted by Heiko A. Oberman, *Wurzeln des Antisemitismus: Christenangst und Judenplage im Zeitalter von Humanismus und Reformation* (Berlin, 1981), p. 148.

[15] The same analysis could be applied to the furious, public outburst of antipapalism in Germany during the 1510s, one cause of which was surely Emperor Maximilian's violently antipapal propaganda during the Italian Wars. See Hermann Wiesflecker, *Kaiser Maximilian I. Das Reich, Österreich und Europa an der Wende zur Neuzeit*, 5 vols. (Munich, 1971–1986), 5: pp. 172–78, 462–65.

If this view has merit, it is fair to ask how the Empire's clergy got itself into this vulnerable position. Here we are helped by R. W. Scribner's recent proposal that the pre-reformation decades witnessed a "disintegration" of the clergy's power, which he classifies as economic, social, political, legal, sexual, and sacral, from the greater web of social and spiritual power.[16] This idea of "disintegration" ought to supply a starting point for detailed, comparative studies of how the clergy's position and influence was changing in relation to other groups who wielded power in one form or another. The virtue of this line of thought is that it recognizes the weakening of clerical power before the reformation, whereas both Goertz's view of anticlericalism as laicization and the older response-to-corruption thesis require just the opposite assumption—which contradicts most of what we know. It also fits much better with the known intensification of popular religious devotion in Central Europe during these decades.[17] The evidence for this upswing is abundant. Recently, for example, there has been uncovered a movement to supply the villages of southwestern Germany with something like a people's *Eigenkirche*, well before the Protestant reformers came on the scene.[18] This movement illustrates the popular appropriation of religious life, especially in the regions gripped by what Peter Blickle has called the "communal reformation". Even where perfectly orthodox, as it normally was, the move tended to push the clergy out of some long-held positions, powers, and privileges.[19] This happened earliest where popular political forces were free to act, as in Central Switzerland, where the reduction of clerical power long before the reformation removed the reasons

---

[16] R. W. Scribner, "Anticlericalism and the Reformation in Germany", in R. W. Scribner, *Popular Culture and Popular Movements in Reformation Germany* (London, 1987), pp. 243–56; id., "Antiklerikalismus in Deutschland um 1500", in *Europa 1500. Integrationsprozesse im Widerstreit: Staaten, Regionen, Personenverbände, Christenheit*, ed. F. Seibt, W. Eberhard (Stuttgart, 1987), pp. 368–82.

[17] The older views are examined by Francis Oakley, *The Western Church in the Later Middle Ages* (Ithaca, 1979), pp. 127–30, but the entire subject has been transformed by Scribner's studies on religion and ritual, which are collected in his *Popular Culture and Popular Movements in Reformation Germany*.

[18] See Rosi Fuhrmann, "Die Kirche im Dorf. Kommunale Initiativen zur Organisation von Seelsorge vor der Reformation", in *Zugänge zur bäuerlichen Reformation*, ed. P. Blickle, Bauer und Reformation 1 (Zurich, 1987), pp. 147–86; id., "Dorfgemeinde und Pfründstiftung vor der Reformation. Kommunale Selbstbestimmungschancen zwischen Religion und Recht", in *Kommunalisierung und Christianisierung. Voraussetzungen und Folgen der Reformation 1400–1600*, Beiheft 9 der Zeitschrift für Historische Forschung (Berlin, 1989), pp. 77–112. Her studies put the subject on an entirely new footing.

[19] Peter Blickle, *Gemeindereformation. Die Menschen des 16. Jahrhunderts auf dem Weg zum Heil* (Munich, 1985).

for religious communalism to demonize or marginalize the clergy.[20]
Does this mean that communalism could coexist with the other forms
of clerical power identified by Scribner, such as their sacral and
sexual powers? If so, then the role of the Protestant reformation as
the culmination of the communal reformation becomes all the more
episodic.

The problem of clerical integration and disintegration, therefore,
is central to the study of anticlericalism before and during the reformation. The following pages explore texts which help to document,
first of all, how one clergyman struggled with the problem of clerical integration, and what he anticipated and did not anticipate about
its solution. Then come texts from the heart of the early reformation at Strasbourg, which show that the consequences of the movements' drive for clerical integration differed for clergy of the two
genders, men and women. These documents appear in proper context, if we set them against the backdrop of Rapp's conclusions about
reforms and reformation in the diocese of Strasbourg.

                                    I

The works of the Strasbourg historian Francis Rapp make us better informed about clerical life and reputation in the diocese of Strasbourg, 1450–1530, than in any other of the some fifty-five dioceses
of the Holy Roman Empire.[21] Rapp's most important conclusion is
that the clergy of the diocese of Strasbourg between 1450 and 1525
were not more ignorant, avaricious, or loose-living than their predecessors of the fourteenth century had been.[22] Although there was no
general decline, Rapp nonetheless discovers at least two important
changes in clerical life during this long era, neither of which could

    [20] See Peter Blickle, "Antiklerikalismus um den Vierwaldstädtersee 1300–1500", in
this volume.
    [21] Rapp, *Réformes*; id., "Préréformes et humanisme. Strasbourg et l'Empire (1482–
1520)", in *Histoire de Strasbourg des origines à nos jours*, vol. 2, ed. G. Livet, F. Rapp
(Strasbourg, 1981), pp. 177–254; id., "Les strasbourgeois et les universités rhénanes
à la fin du Moyen Age et jusqu'à la Réforme", *Annuaire des Amis de Vieux-Strasbourg*
4 (1974): pp. 11–22; id., "Les clercs souabes dan le diocèse de Strasbourg à la veille
de la Réforme", in *Landesgeschichte und Geistesgeschichte. Festschrift für Otto Herding zum
65. Geburtstag*, ed. K. Elm, E Gönner, E. Hildenbrand, Veröffentlichungen der
Kommission für geschichtliche Landeskunde in Baden-Württemberg, series B, p. 92
(Stuttgart, 1977), pp. 265–79.
    [22] Rapp, *Réformes*, pp. 430–34,

have been accurately predicted from the literature. First, his study of clerical personnel shows a major loss of familiarity and increasing estrangement between the people of the diocese and their clergy. The clergy as a whole was recruited increasingly from outside the diocese—roughly Lower Alsace and Middle Baden—especially from Swabia, Bavaria, and the lands west of the Vosges, which means that the axis of clerical recruitment ran not along the Rhine Valley but perpendicular to it. Of 529 parish priests in the era 1450–1520 whose place of origin is known, 400 came from other dioceses.[23] The same pattern is observable among the upper clergy, especially in the cathedral chapter, which, despite the heavy representation from Alsace and the Ortenau (Middle Baden) in the fourteenth century, admitted no canon from these lands after 1455. In the other collegial chapters at Strasbourg, the proportion of natives also declined, at St. Thomas, for example, from nearly 30% to 7%. In the urban religious houses, too, the local elites, once the dominant force in the religious houses and especially in the mendicant orders, lost this position to outsiders. The sole exception to this trend involved the mendicant women's houses of the Observance, which the native elite continued to control.[24] Not surprisingly, these houses offered the stoutest resistance to the Protestant reformation, a consequence, no doubt, of the fact that the nuns' resistance "dramatized and focused the divisions within the elite."[25] The overall pattern for the years from 1450 to 1520 is neatly summed up by Rapp: "almost nothing remained of these familiar relations between the local notables and the clergy."[26] The colonization of the clergy, especially from Swabia and Bavaria, accelerated the process of estrangement of clergy from laity. Against this process the canon law was helpless, for the legal separation of the clergy from the laity had been devised for a society in which the familiar bonds between the two groups were very close, too close, for the church's comfort.

---

[23] Rapp, *Réformes*, p. 313. It is worth noting that analysis of the registers of new citizens shows a similar pattern for this period (*ibid.*, p. 314). The pattern of heavy Swabian and Bavarian immigration continued into the later sixteenth century. See Jean-Pierre Kintz, *La société strasbourgeoise du milieu du XVe siècle à la fin de la Guerre de Trente Ans 1560–1650. Essai d'histoire démographique, économique et sociale* (Paris, 1984), p. 112.

[24] Rapp, *Réformes*, pp. 284–87.

[25] Lyndal Roper, *The Holy Household: Women and Morals in Reformation Augsburg* (Oxford, 1989), p. 210.

[26] Rapp, *Réformes*, pp. 451–52.

Rapp's second major discovery is that after the agrarian depression of the fourteenth century nearly ruined the convents, foundations, and much of the benefice system, the clergy recovered through investment in agriculture and its products. By the mid-fifteenth century, clergymen and clerical corporations were playing a massive role in the financing, collection, storage, marketing, and export of foodstuffs, especially grain, from Lower Alsace and the Ortenau to poorer, neighboring regions.[27] This process accelerated a weakening of the benefice system, chiefly through commercialization and pluralism, which left large numbers of poorly paid, insecure vicars ("arme dorfpfäfflin") in the rural parishes and reduced, in general, the social status and prestige of the clergy.[28]

From Rapp's book emerges a portrait of a clergy increasingly colonized by place-seekers from other regions, the fortunate of whom shared in the profits from the burgeoning trade in foodstuffs, while the less lucky slipped into the proletariat of rural vicars. The clergy of the pre-reformation era, therefore, were socially more alien and less prestigious, but economically better off—and thus more competitive with the laity—than their predecessors had been. This situation might have been helped, had the governance of the church in this diocese not broken down. During the first half of the fifteenth century, however, the mercantile elite of Strasbourg had tried, and failed, to take over the finances of the diocese and prince-bishopric of Strasbourg.[29] Their failure left a spirit of rivalry between Strasbourg's civic elite and the whole apparatus of episcopal governance, and all subsequent efforts at clerical reform smashed against the connivance between the native lay elites and the middling and upper clergy, who formed an unloving partnership to skim the rich agriculture of Lower Alsace and the Ortenau.

---

[27] Rapp *Réformes*, pp. 435–41.

[28] Rapp, *Réformes*, pp. 265–79, 298–99, 306–18.

[29] Martin Alioth, *Gruppen an der Macht: Zünfte und Patriziat in Straßburg im 14. und 15. Jahrhundert. Untersuchungen zu Verfaßung, Wirtschaftsgefüge und Sozialstruktur*, 2 vols., Basler Beiträge zur Geschichtswissenschaft 156 (Basel, 1988), esp. pp. 502–4. Alioth has completely undermined the conventional view of Strasbourg's political history in the later Middle Ages, a classic statement of which is in Philippe Dollinger, "La ville libre à la fin du Moyen Age (1350–1482)", in *Histoire de Strasbourg* (n. 21 above), pp. 99–175. The rivalry between magistrates and bishops is dramatized in Thomas A. Brady, Jr., "Rites of Autonomy, Rites of Dependence: South German Civic Culture in the Age of Renaissance and Reformation", in *Religion and Culture in the Renaissance City*, ed. S. Ozment, Sixteenth Century Essays & Studies 11 (Kirksville, Mo., 1989), pp. 9–24.

Rapp's findings allow us to hazard an explanation of the clergy's fate at Strasbourg during the reformation. The clergy had rescued itself from financial disaster during the depression by enhancing its activities in moneylending and trading in foodstuffs; these operations made the clergy more exposed to criticism and resentment from the common people, especially the peasants; the native elites, who protected from reform a clergy with whom they shared strong economic interests but ever weaker social solidarity, sacrificed their clergy to the popular movements of the 1520s. Whether this picture can be applied as a model to other regions and dioceses, remains to be seen, but for the moment it may underpin an investigation of some aspects of clerical integration at Strasbourg before and during the reformation.

II

Johann Geiler von Kaysersberg (1445–1510), who was cathedral preacher at Strasbourg from 1478 until his death, is widely recognized as an acute diagnostician of the problems of Christian life in general, and of clerical life in particular, during the generation before the onset of the Protestant reformation.[30] This reputation is very old, for the historical consciousness of Protestant Strasbourg long revered Geiler as chief forerunner to the city's reformation. Caspar Hedio, for example, a Protestant who was Geiler's successor but one as cathedral preacher of Strasbourg, remarked in 1526 that

> the more I read Dr. Kaysersberger, the more he pleases me, for when I read his writings, I find that he identified and understood the problem quite well. The time, however, was not yet ripe.[31]

---

[30] The best introduction to Geiler's career is by Francis Rapp, "Jean Geiler de Kaysersberg (1445–1510), le prédicateur de la cathédrale de Strasbourg", in *Grandes figures de l'humanisme alsacien. Courants, milieux, destins*, ed. F. Rapp, G. Livet, Publications de la Société Savante d'Alsace et des Régions de l'Est, Collection "Grandes Publications" 14 (Strasbourg, 1978), pp. 25–32, plus many sections of Rapp, *Réformes*. Still worth consulting is Charles Guillaume Adolphe Schmidt, *Histoire littéraire de l'Alsace à la fin du XVᵉ et au commencement du XVIᵉ siècle*, 2 vols. (Paris, 1879; repr., Nieuwkoop, 1966), 1: pp. 337–461.

[31] Jacob von Gottesheim, "Les éphemerides de Jacques de Gottesheim, docteur en droit, prébendier du Grand-Choeur de la Cathédrale (1524–1543)", ed. Rodolphe Reuss, *BSCMHA*, 2nd ser., 19 (1898): p. 271. See also *ibid.*, "1527. Dominica post

A generation later, the Protestant town architect Daniel Specklin (ca. 1536–1589) fixed Geiler's reputation by including in his *Collectanea* a notice about Geiler's sermon before the Emperor Maximilian I at Strasbourg during the Bavarian War of 1504.

> At the end of his sermon, Dr. Kaysersberger referred once again to the problem of reform. If, he said, pope, bishop, emperor and king will not reform our unspiritual, insane, godless way of life, God will raise up one who will do it and will reestablish our ruined religion. I hope to see the day and to become his disciple, but I am too old. Many of you, however, will live to see it, and please remember me then and what I said.[32]

Emperor Maximilian, Specklin notes at another place, "also experienced Dr. Luther's reformation and surely must have thought often about Dr. Kaysersberger."[33] Protestant Strasbourg acknowledged its indebtedness to Geiler for his attacks on the problem of reform before, in their view, the time was ripe. Their respect for him as a diagnostician of reform corroborates the Strasbourg laity's affection for him in his own day, and if this stature possessed a theological basis, it lay in his adaptation of mystical theology to lay piety, not in the degree to which he did or did not anticipate Luther's teaching on justification.[34]

Valentini, 17. Februarii, D. Caspar hedio fecit concionem merdianam, praedicavit de cadaveribus sepeliendis etra urbem, extulit Dominum Joannem Keyserpergium, . . ." See, too, the testimony of Otmar Nachtigall, in the preface to his *Dye gantz Euangelisch Hystorie wie sie durch die vier Euangelisten, yeden sonderlich, in kriechischer sprach beschrieben, in ain gleychhellige unzertaylte red ordenlich verfasst* (Augsburg, 1525): "Ich hab in meiner kinthayt von Doctor kaysersberger in seinen predigten zu Strasburg gethon, vnd sonst in seynem hauss ayns tayls, also vil haylsamer lere empfangen, die mir darzu geholffen, das man mich zeycht, ich sey kain weltmensch."

[32] Daniel Specklin, "Les Collectanées", ed. Rodolphe Reuss, *BSCMHA*, 2nd ser., 14 (1889): no. 2190. Specklin, Strasbourg's first municipal architect, wrote a two-volume chronicle, of which only fragments survive. Johannes Ficker and Otto Winckelmann, *Handschriftenproben des 16. Jahrhunderts nach Straßburger Originalen*, 2 vols. (Strasbourg, 1902–1905), 2: p. 99.

[33] Specklin, "Les Collectanées", no. 2167.

[34] This last is the question pursued by E. Jane Dempsey Douglass, *Justification in Late Medieval Preaching. A Study of John Geiler of Keisersberg*, SMRT 1 (Leiden, 1966; 2nd ed., 1989), who judges—correctly, I believe—that Geiler was no proto-Lutheran. A new and fruitful approach to this subject, Geiler's relationship to the reformation, is opened up by Herbert Kraume, *Die Gerson Übersetzungen Geilers von Kaysersberg: Studien zur deutschsprachigen Gerson-Rezeption* (Munich, 1980). It has been expanded to Geiler's whole mystical theology in an unpublished dissertation by Georges Herzog, "Mystical Theology in Late Medieval Preaching: Johann Geiler von Kaysersberg (1445–1510)", (Boston University, 1985).

Geiler's opinions and programs are contained in the huge corpus of his sermons, which is now once again attracting the kind of
scholarly attention it deserves.[35] His social ideas, including his ecclesiology, have attracted only scattered attention.[36] This neglect is all
the more remarkable, because not only does Geiler pronounce on
many particular issues of the day, such as anticlericalism and clerical social integration, but his general social outlook diverged radically from those of the Alsatian humanists among whom he is often
numbered.[37] For Geiler stood close to the movement that Peter Blickle
has called "the communal reformation".[38]

Geiler's relationship to religious communalism, which frames his
other social views, including his program for the clergy, is suggested
by three aspects of his thought. First, he believed that human laws
must be judged by divine laws, which sounds much like the fundamental principle of religious communalism, the supremacy of the
"godly law".[39] Geiler broaches the question in the preface to his
"21 Articles" of 1500:

> These articles state the customs, statutes, and usages of the city of
> Strasbourg. One must approach them cautiously and consult godfear-
> ing, honorable, wise, and learned experts in Imperial, canon, and divine
> law, to see whether these customs, usages, and statutes are not opposed
> to Christian principles and God's laws. Otherwise the city's rulers
> and inhabitants might, through their observance of such statutes, cus-
> toms, and usages, fall from God's grace and into eternal damnation
> of their souls.[40]

Geiler's godly law is not yet the godly law of the Peasants' War,
which would tie the concept to the "pure gospel" and localized it

---

[35] The fullest discussion of the literature on Geiler is by Herzog, "Mystical Theology, pp. 19–31.

[36] See, for example, Jakob Strieder, *Studien zur Geschichte kapitalistischer Organisationsformen. Monopole, Kartelle und Aktiengesellschaften im Mittelalter und zu Beginn der Neuzeit*,
2nd ed. (Munich, 1935), pp. 189–92.

[37] Rapp, *Réformes*, pp. 150–70, develops very clearly the contrast between Geiler's
reform program, based on preaching, and the "programme médiocre" of Jakob
Wimpheling and the other local humanists.

[38] Peter Blickle, *Gemeindereformation. Die Menschen des 16. Jahrhunderts auf dem Weg
zum Heil* (Munich, 1985).

[39] Blickle, *Gemeindereformation*, pp. 59–67. An investigation of this theme should
begin with Geiler's views on natural law. See Peter Bierbrauer, "Das Göttliche Recht
und die naturrechtliche Tradition", in *Bauer, Reich und Reformation. Festschrift für Günther
Franz zum 80. Geburtstag*, ed. P. Blickle (Stuttgart, 1982), pp. 210–34.

[40] Johann Geiler von Kaysersberg, *Die ältesten Schriften*, ed. Léon Dacheux (Freiburg
i. Br., 1882; reprint, Amsterdam, 1965), p. 3.

in the Bible.[41] God's laws, for example, do not yet stand in judgment on the laws of Empire and church.[42] Geiler nonetheless teaches a recognizable form of the ideal of godly law, which monitors, corrects, and even vacates human law.

A second connection between Geiler and communalism is his republicanism. In the absence of adequate restraints, Blickle has noted, communal political organization tended to evolve into republican forms of governance well before any full-blown republican theory emerged in the German-speaking world.[43] The German cities, at least as compared with those of Italy and the Netherlands, proved poor nurseries of political theory of any kind, including republicanism.[44] There may be political ideas, however, where there is no true theory, and Geiler's political ideas took a decidedly republican turn. In his sermons on "The Ants", for example, he examines the governments of several species of animals to shed light on human society. This is a convention, of course, the best known contemporary example of which may be the remark of Ottaviano Fregoso (†1524) of Genoa in Baldesar Castiglione's *Book of the Courtier*: "deer, cranes and many other birds, when they migrate, always choose a leader whom they follow and obey; and bees, almost as if they had discourse of reason, obey their king with as much reverence as the most obedient people on earth."[45] Like Fregoso's opponent, Pietro Bembo (1470–1547), Geiler chooses the republican side of the argument, though unlike the Venetian he accepts the analogy between animal and human government. In his sermon cycle on "The Ants", Geiler compares human society to that of the ants, whom he sets in the political context of the animal kingdom as follows:

---

[41] Blickle, *Gemeindereformation*, pp. 62–64.
[42] See, *Gemeindereformation*, p. 67, where Blickle warns against seeing in the godly law too radical a negation of tradition, that is, of the "old law". I follow Vogler, "Imperial City Nuremberg, 1524–1525", pp. 38–39, in seeing biblicism as a sign of the movement's radicalization.
[43] Peter Blickle, "Communalism, Parliamentarism, Republicanism", trans. T. A. Brady, Jr., *Parliaments, Estates and Representation* 6 (1986): pp. 1–13.
[44] See Heinz Schilling, "Gab es im späten Mittelalter und zu Beginn der Neuzeit in Deutschland einen städtischen Republikanismus? Zur politischen Kultur des alteuropäischen Stadtbürgertums", in *Republiken und Republikanismus im Europa der Frühen Neuzeit*, ed. H. Koenigsberger, Schriften des Historischen Kollegs, Kolloquien 11 (Munich, 1988), pp. 101–44, here at p. 142, with whose argument I agree.
[45] Baldesar Castiglione, *The Book of the Courtier*, trans. Charles Singleton (Garden City, N.Y., 1959), p. 304.

There are two sorts of animals. Some, such as bears and lions, are solitary. Other animals live together, such as doves and chickens, which fly together in a flock. . . . Sheep, too, move about in large flocks. We humans must be together. A man can never be self-sufficient, we all need one another ("man is a political animal"). The ants, too, live together, for these small creatures live together with large numbers in one anthill with no leader, no prince, and no teacher.

Whereas some animals, such as cranes and herring, have leaders, "the ants have no king", says Geiler, overlooking the fact that ants do have queens. Over them, as over humanity, stands only God, for "we know very well that God is the common ruler of all creatures, and there can be no government on earth without the commune."[46]

His view of the Swiss Confederacy, the most important example of communally based political autonomy, forms Geiler's third connection to communalism. Geiler had been born at Schaffhausen, a free city which joined the Confederacy in 1501. At that time, after the Swabian War of 1499, the Alsatian humanists turned against the Swiss, who had long been allies of the Alsatian communes, and supported the House of Austria and the idea of imperial monarchy.[47] Geiler, by contrast, understood why the Swiss had gone to war with the emperor. They were victims of bad government and arrogant rulers, he thought, just as the poor, especially poor women, are the victims of arbitrary and uncaring urban magistrates.

And when a poor widow or a poor woman comes, they [the officials] say to her: "Do you think that we've nothing more to do than deal with you?" . . . Then she's referred to the ammeister or sent to [privy council of] the XV, and so forth. The judges are supposed to help them, and most of all under communal governments, such as rule Strasbourg, Mainz, and Nuremberg, the widows and orphans should be relieved of lengthy judicial procedures. Sometimes a suit goes for thirty years. What created Switzerland? It was the arbitrariness of the officials and their failure to give expeditious justice. Read the histories!

---

[46] Geiler, *Die Emeis* (1516): pp. xii^v–xiii^v.

[47] The chief example is Wimpheling. See Guy Marchal, "Bellum justum contra judicium belli. Zur Interpretation von Jakob Wimpfelings antieidgenossischer Streitschrift 'Soliloquium pro Pace Christianorum et pro Helvetiis ut respiscant . . .,' (1505)", in *Gesellschaft und Gesellschaften. Festschrift zum 65. Geburtstag von Professor Dr. Ulrich Im Hof*, ed. N. Bernard, Q. Reichen (Bern, 1982), pp. 114–37. On this movement in general, see Dieter Mertens, "Maximilian I. und das Elsaß", in *Die Humanisten in ihrer politischen und sozialen Umwelt*, ed. O. Herding, R. Stupperich, Mitteilungen der Kommission für Humanismusforschung 3 (Boppard, 1976), pp. 177–200.

The closing passage is nothing less than an adaptation to the free city—the officials named have Strasbourg titles—of the saying, "Question: What makes Switzerland grow? Answer: The lords' greed", which we find, among other places, on the title page of the great programmatic pamphlet of the Peasants' War, *An die Versamlung gemainer Pawrschafft* (1525).[48]

Once Geiler's communalist stance is recognized, it can be seen to underpin most of his ideas about society and government. Whether he speaks of nobles or peasants, the message is the same: government exists for the sake of the community, not the community for the sake of government. It is not that he merely contrasts the ideal of nobility with the reality, though he does that,[49] or that he abhors the nobility's characteristic arrogance, as in this passage from his cycle of sermons based on *The Ship of Fools* by his friend, the city attorney Sebastian Brant (1459–1521):

> The fifth bell means to take pride in one's nobility. O, you foolish black horse, you, you take pride because the peacock's feathers made your father and your ancestors noble because of their virtues; but you are ennobled by your vices. You foolish black horse, they were noble and you are not.[50]

He lashes out, too, at the rich burghers' longing to be thought noble and the obsessive inflation of titles. He cites, for example, the proverb, "Whoever is rich, wants honor (i.e., nobility)", the aptness of which is documented by the sigh of Hans Armbruster in der Brandgaße, "he whom God has made rich, also wants honor."[51]

The greatest of the nobles were the princes, and in the German cycle based on Brant's *Ship of Fools*, Geiler exposes their foolishness:

> The sixth bell means to pursue one's own interest. What prince is not guilty of this bell? They all pursue their own goals, not one of them

---

[48] "Wer mehret Schweiz? Der Herren Geiz." *"An die Versammlung gemeiner Bauernschaft." Eine revolutionäre Flugschrift aus dem deutschen Bauernkrieg (1525)*, ed. Siegfried Hoyer, Bernd Rüdiger (Leipzig, 1975). The author is unknown, though Christian Peters has made a case for Andreas Bodenstein von Karlstadt. Christian Peters, "An die Versammlung gemeiner Bauernschaft (1525)", *Zeitschrift für bayerische Kirchengeschichte* 54 (1985): pp. 16–28.

[49] See, for example, the quotes from his *Nauicula sive speculum fatuorum* (Strasbourg, 1510), by Léon Dacheux, *Un réformateur catholique à la fin du XVᵉ siècle, Jean Geiler de Kaysersberg* (Paris, 1876), p. 210 n. 1, which measure the reality against the ideal.

[50] Geiler, *Narrenschiff* (Strasbourg, 1520), p. 182ᵛ.

[51] Geiler, *Navicula penitentie* (Strasbourg, 1511), fol. VI E.

pursues God's goals. . . . Nor have they any sympathy with their neighbors. If my side of the wall is cool, they say, I'm doing all right.[52]

Such rulers, Geiler predicts, will come to a bad end:

> They will be devoured one-by-one, like the oxen who were eaten by the wolf, because they wouldn't help one another. Everyone wants to rule himself, and some even abandon the jurisdiction of the [Holy] Roman Empire. Just so, when one brand after the other is pulled out of the stove [*felix*], the fire goes out. A ruler should pursue the common good, for which purpose he was elected. Therefore, he should be content with his salary and seek no more.

Here Geiler interprets Swiss disobedience to the Holy Roman Empire—of which he does not approve—as an understandable reaction to the princes' selfish greed.

Geiler tends to believe that princes and their spiritual counterparts, bishops, form the main source of the world's ills, especially in the burghers' world. He writes:

> Now look at the prelates, how they behave in the cities in both spiritual and temporal affairs, and you see how they wear the bell. Don't you see how the prelates and princes through their bad example are the cause and source of destruction of the whole earth? They mislead the poor sheep who follow them.[53]

In keeping with this attitude, when he wishes to present images of spiritual authority, Geiler chooses familiar types. He speaks, for example, of "Christ, the community's merchant", by which he means—as we can infer from his violent views against usury and usurers—one who serves the commune in an important way.[54]

Geiler once preached an entire sermon cycle in which he interpreted in a religious sense the status and duties of a village headman (*Dorfmeier*). The headman is distinguished, Geiler says, by the fact that he is elected by, and responsible to, the commune.

> The custom is that a headman is elected by the commune and receives from it authority and power over the commune. Even though he is installed by the village's seigneur, his authority comes originally from

---

[52] Geiler, *Narrenschiff* (Strasbourg, 1520), p. 195^r; and there, too, the following quote.
[53] *Ibid.*, p. 106^v.
[54] Geiler, *Das Buoch Arbore humana* (Strasbourg, 1521), fol. 43^{r-v}; id., *Brösamlein* (Strasbourg, 1517), pp. 47^v–48^r; id., *Narrenschiff* (Strasbourg, 1520), pp. 185^{r-v}; id., *Das Evangelibuch* (Strasbourg, 1515), p. 30^v.

the commune, which elected his predecessors. And whoever is elected
by the commune, is elected for the commune's sake and not for his
own sake. Therefore, whoever is in authority ought to consider that
he belongs to the commune, not the commune to him. He therefore
should not raise himself over those who elected him, the officials who
act for the commune.[55]

Geiler's belief in the rightness of popular election ran very deep,
and, like the author of *An die Versamlung gemainer Pawrschafft*, he felt
election of rulers far superior to hereditary rule. In the sermons on
the *Ship of Fools*, for example, he says,

The fifth bell means to elect rulers for their family and their nobility.
This is a sign of great foolishness, to fill offices out of friendship and
because of nobility, and to disregard the pious and the wise. All
Germany is filled with this foolishness, for bishops are elected not for
their chastity or their holiness; magistrates are not elected for their
wisdom, but because of their nobility and their families. Thus come
fools, mischievous and stupid men, into the government.[56]

These texts illustrate the degree to which Geiler's communal ideal
consisted not just of formal characteristics, such as election, but also
of a deep antipathy for the domination of the world by inherited
power.[57] There is very little substantive difference between his social
ideal and that of the author of *An die Versamlung gemainer Pawrschafft*,
the radical pamphlet of 1525.

And what of the clergy, Geiler's own estate? Geiler's ideal could
be inferred from what I have said above, but that is not necessary.
In one place he speaks of "a common person, who serves the whole
community, such as a bishop, a priest, an ammeister", which makes
the priest and bishop officers of the civic church.[58] Further on in
the same text, he reinforces his point:

The Son of Man is not come to be ministered to but to minister. All
rulers, temporal and spiritual, should hear this and should believe not
that the commune belongs to them, but they to the commune. The
communes exist not for their sake, but they for the commune's sake.
They are the commune's servants.

---

[55] Geiler, *Das Buoch Arbore humana* (Strasbourg, 1521), fol. 135^r.

[56] Geiler, *Narrenschiff* (Strasbourg, 1520), pp. 194^v–95^r.

[57] See his portrayal of the ideal and the reality of the nobles, in Geiler, *Narrenschiff*
(Strasbourg, 1520), p. 182^v; id., *Navicula sive speculum fatuorum* (Strasbourg, 1510),
Turb. LXXVI C, F, and G.

[58] Geiler, *Postille*, part II, 5, quoted by Dacheux, *Un réformateur catholique*, p. 544
n. 2.

The most striking dramatization, however, of Geiler's ideal of the clergy's integration into communal life comes in his cycle of sermons on the ants.[59] Geiler compares Christian society to an anthill, an image not unknown to modern anticommunist polemics, though there the similarity ends. Following Aristotle, he says, one may divide people into three groups: "One part consists of the working folk, the 'artisans', as we call them, such as tailors, cobblers, etc. The second is the burghers, and the third is the nobles." The first group, the workers, he compares with those ants who carry bodies to the graves. They are the vast majority, and each has his task: "These are the artisans, of which there are many kinds on this earth. This kind makes shoes, another farms, another can't farm, and I must preach." Each employs his craft to nourish himself and his children, with something left over, "so that he can also help the poor."

The second group is like the ants who carry in the food, for it does much good by teaching.

> These are the clergy, who should live by alms, sing, read, and praise God, since they can't chop and plough or make shoes. We don't do these things that we should do, but we get our sustenance nonetheless, for the wine and corn is packed into our cellars. This is all given to us so that we might celebrate the Mass and do our other duties, not so that we can collect three or four whores apiece, as the proud college boys at the bishop's court do.

Geiler's clerical ideal contains no hint of lordship, for "thus we clergy, monks, priests, and nuns eat up your work. You nourish us, so we should repay temporal with spiritual goods. To have much property, however, such as rents and dues, wine and grain, and then fail to offer spiritual goods in return, this angers the people." The laity should not respond, "we should take half the property which the priests have. Why should they have so much property? They have too much." Truly, Geiler sighs, "many priests do have too much, but you shouldn't for that reason take it away. I don't know where it will end, if you start taking away from all who have too much. It would injure many people. If you took the priests' property, God knows, what would happen then." Rather, give "the priests and the convents their proper incomes, and otherwise watch carefully and see that they live correctly and perform the duties for which they hold and enjoy what they have."

---

[59] Geiler, *Die Emeis*, pp. 8ᵛ–9ᵛ.

Behind Geiler's plea lies less a desire to defend property rights in general than a vision of the clergy's necessary contribution to the common good. It is the prayers and sacramental functions of the clergy, he believes, which link the communities spiritually with one another. The clergy "do much good, not only for themselves but also for all others. It is so, for when they and you are in the state of grace, whatever a friend of God does, the others all share in it." The chief, but not exclusive, role in maintaining the spiritual inter-dependence of communities, falls to the clergy. "When a priest at Rome says Mass in the state of grace", Geiler says, "you benefit from his action. And when you here at Strasbourg pray the Our Father in the state of grace, the priest at Rome benefits from it. That is *participium*." Recognizing that his hearers would meet this idea with skepticism, Geiler goes on: "You ask, 'how can that happen? How can someone at Rome share in what is done here'?" He tries to meet such questions with a version of the paramount metaphor of all corporatist-communal thinking.

> It happens just as with a human being, who has many organs. The limbs and organs are weak and ill, the fingers slack, the ears pointed, and the mouth pale. Then you eat a little soup or porridge, and though the stomach receives the porridge, all the organs benefit from it. The toes on your foot become strong; the fingers become red again; the mouth and all the organs become stronger. Each limb begins once more to move as it needs to. So, in like manner, when a just person does a good deed, the others all benefit from it.

This spiritual communalism, therefore, is neither created nor main-tained exclusively by the clergy.

One final point illustrates the civic and communal character of Geiler's clerical ideal. The third group of persons is compared with the third sort of ants, who show the right way to others. Here Geiler places "the nobles, prelates, and especially bishops and doctors". The proper office of the bishop, he says, is "to preach and to teach the way to heaven. . . . For this reason St. Paul tied the two offices, pas-tors and doctors, together, for their task is to herd the sheep as pas-tors and teach and instruct them as doctors." This passage proves that Geiler's is not just a new version of the tired old feudal triad of *oratores, bellatores,* and *laboratores*.[60] His clergy are divided among all

---

[60] See Thomas A. Brady, Jr., "Luther's Social Teaching and the Social Order of His Age", in *Martin Luther Quincentennial*, ed. G. Dünnhaupt (Detroit, 1985), pp. 270–90.

three of the social groups: the preacher in the first; the priest in the second; and the bishop in the third. The legal unity of the clerical estates here yields to a division of labor which is both material and spiritual.

Geiler's benign view of the bishop as a kind of local patriarch may reflect conditions in the diocese and city of Strasbourg, where the bishop had access to his cathedral church only at the sufferance of the civic magistrates. To be sure, the Strasbourgeois were quite unaccustomed to seeing their bishop in a pastoral role, and when Bishop William of Honstein (r. 1506–1541) came to Strasbourg at Corpus Christi 1508 and said Mass in the cathedral, Sebastian Brant rushed to the archives to discover precedents. He found that no bishop had said Mass at Strasbourg for 150 years.[61] On the other hand, the bishop was no lord in the city, and the magistrates reminded him of this fact as often as they thought necessary. When Bishop William came to be enthroned in 1507, for example, and complained of the restrictions they placed on his entourage, the magistrates set him straight. "It pertains to the Senate of the city of Strasbourg", they replied, "to order, mobilize, command, and forbid in their city, just as they please. Enough said."[62] At Strasbourg, therefore, the bishop's power was far weaker than, say, at Worms, where the bishop conducted a long feud against the city, and the clergy engaged in an especially humiliating exodus in 1499.[63]

In Geiler's vision, the clergy are servants, not lords. The church, the only necessary supra-communal body, is a structure of grace rather than of lordship, and its bonds are neither exclusively sacramental nor exclusively clerical. Geiler's vision is thus a kind of Christian clerical Guelfism, an alliance of local community and universal Church, and a far cry from the caesaropapist Ghibellinism of many German humanists.[64]

---

[61] Sebastian Brant, "Bischoff Wilhelm von Hoensteins waal und einritt. Anno 1506 et 1507", in *Code historique et diplomatique de la Ville de Strasbourg*, ed. Louis Schneegans, 2 vols. (Strasbourg, 1845–47), 2: p. 296.

[62] *Ibid.*, p. 296.

[63] Scribner, "Anticlericalism", p. 251.

[64] I have treated this theme—universal church and local autonomy—in a forthcoming study, "The Rise of Merchant Empires—a European Counterpoint". On the German humanists' political loyalties, see John M. Headley, "The Habsburg World Empire and the Revival of Ghibellinism", *Medieval and Renaissance Studies* 7 (1978): pp. 92–127; id., "Germany, the Empire and *Monarchia* in the Thought and Policy of Gattinara", in *Das römisch-deutsche Reich im politischen System Karls V.*, ed. H. Lutz (Munich, 1982), pp. 15–33; Mertens, "Maximilian I. und das Elsaß" (n. 47

Finally, it is important to remind ourselves that this is a dream, a vision, an ideal, and while it reflected realities, it was not itself reality. Geiler was hardly faint-hearted about reform. In 1492, when he discussed with the bishop and the civic magistrates the prospects for reform in some of the worst religious houses, Geiler is said to have recommended as follows:

> We should take those nuns who not only are whores but who have secretly killed their own babies, stuff them in a sack, and throw them in the river. The monks and priests who are implicated or assisted in these crimes should be beheaded with a sword.[65]

Not only would the bishop not "lay a hand on consecrated persons", but "the nobles and magistrates, who had daughters, sisters, and other female relations and friends in the house, wouldn't act without papal permission", even though "Dr. Kaysersberger said he would take responsibility for the act before God, pope, emperor, and bishop." It was the same old story, clerical reform blocked by the powerful laity. By 1492 or so Geiler's belief in the possibility of reforming the secular clergy began to falter, and though he hoped longer for a reform of the regulars, by 1508, two years before his death, he had given up. He declared that "the best thing to do is to sit in one's own corner and stuff one's head into a hole, seeking only to follow God's commandments, to do good, and thereby to gain eternal salvation."[66]

Geiler was correct in believing that he would not live to see reform, but it did come within two decades of his death and at the hands of men who had known and admired him. One of them was Stettmeister Jacob Sturm (1489–1553), who had stood at Geiler's deathbed in 1510, and who in 1523 abandoned both his own clerical

---

above), pp. 177–200. We badly need a new understanding of the German humanists' political ideas and loyalties, which continue to be characterized vaguely as "patriotism" or "nationalism". See, for example, Noel L. Brann, "Humanism in Germany", in *Renaissance Humanism: Foundations, Forms, and Legacy*, ed. A. Rabil, Jr., vol. 2: *Humanism beyond Italy* (Philadelphia, 1988), pp. 123–55, here at pp. 137–41. By contrast, Quentin Skinner, *Foundations of Modern Political Thought*, 2 vols. (Cambridge, 1978), 1: pp. 235, 238, recognizes the socially conservative, politically monarchist tendencies of northern humanism in general.

[65] Specklin, "Les Collectanées" (n. 32 above), no. 2164; and there, too, the quotes in the following sentence.

[66] Geiler, *Die Emeis*, 22ʳ. See Rapp, "Jean Geiler de Kaysersberg (1445–1510)" (n. 30 above), p. 29: "Jusqu'en 1492 à peu près, Geiler crut qu'une réforme du clergé séculier était possible." Rapp (*ibid.*, pp. 29–30), offers the clearest picture of Geiler's ideal of clerical reform.

career and the old faith.[67] In very many ways, the ecclesiastical reform undertaken by Sturm and his fellow magistrates between 1527
and 1534 realized Geiler's ideal of integrating the clergy in communal life.[68] The clergy surrendered their separate legal status and
most of their property, and those who remained conformed very well
to Geiler's ideal of pastoral office. The presidency of the Strasbourg's
Church Assembly, for example, much resembled Geiler's ideal of
the bishop as one who "teaches and shows the way to heaven."[69]
The differences, however, were also great. The Protestant reformers
stripped away the entire edifice of trans-local spiritual exchange, and
they and the magistrates made war on the religious orders, both the
lax and the strict, to which Geiler had felt a special attachment.
Geiler had not foreseen that integration of the clergy might lead to
a purely pastoral clergy and thus to the disappearance of the religious
orders. Nor had he any inkling of the effect that integration might
have on the most vulnerable sector of the clergy, the women.

III

"The female religious life", Lyndal Roper has written, "was understood through a metaphor at once social and sexual: the nun was
the bride of Christ."[70] While the convents used the language of kinship—the nuns were "sisters"—they "created a series of relationships
which were at odds with civic kin structures." The most important
of such structures was the patriarchal household, the solidification of
which—one of the major facts of contemporary urban life—cast even
graver doubt on "an option which ensured that wifehood was not
the only socially valued role for women." The nuns' chief role as

---

[67] Jakob Wimpheling, *Opera selecta*, vol. 2: Jakob Wimpfeling and Beatus Rhenanus,
Das Leben des Johannes Geiler von Kaysersberg, ed. Otto Herding and Dieter Mertens
(Munich, 1970), p. 18, no. 84, ll. 837–48; also in Joseph Anton Riegger, *Amoenitates
literariae friburgenses* (Ulm, 1775–1776), pp. 124–25.
[68] François Wendel, *L'Eglise de Strasbourg, sa constitution et son organisation, 1532–1535*,
Etudes d'histoire et de philosophie religieuses 38 (Paris, 1942); Miriam Usher
Chrisman, *Strasbourg and the Reform: A Study in the Process of Change* (New Haven, 1967);
William S. Stafford, *Domesticating the Clergy: the Inception of the Reformation in Strasbourg,
1522–1524* (Missoula, Mont., 1976); Lorna Jane Abray, *The People's Reformation:
Magistrates, Clergy, and Commons in Strasbourg, 1520–1599* (New Haven, 1985).
[69] Abray, *People's Reformation*, pp. 72–76, 159–60.
[70] Roper, *Holy Household*, p. 206; and there, too, the remaining quotes in this
paragraph.

part of the clergy, of course, was the one specified by Geiler for all clergy: their prayers and, for the priests, Masses conferred spiritual benefits on all Christians. The reformation's message concentrated sacral power in spoken words, it stripped the world of holy things and actions, and radically localized the sense of church, all changes which tended to strip the cloistered orders of their spiritual utility and to expose them to charges of parasitism. For the women, whose gender entered into all their relationships, the blow fell very early and doubly hard, for not only did Protestant city governments harass, bully, and even force them to dissolve, but the new, Protestant clergy had no place for them.[71] Whether its discipline was harsh and authoritarian or mild and affectionate, the patriarchal household received reinforcement from the reformation, both as symbol through the elimination of a rival way of life for women and through the repatriation of women who had chosen that way of life.

The convent of St. Nicolaus-in-Undis had been founded in the thirteenth century in one of Strasbourg's swampy suburbs, hence the reference in its name to "waves" or water, though the locals Germanized it to mean "among the dogs" (*zu den Hunden*).[72] In the later Middle Ages, St. Nicolaus-in-Undis and the eight other mendicant women's houses remained the province of the native elites, and the spread of the practices of the Observance among the six Dominican convents had renewed their reputation for austerity and strictness.[73] In 1522 one of the young women living at St. Nicolaus-in-Undis was fourteen-year-old Margarethe Kniebis, who had entered the house at the age of nine and now wanted to begin her novitiate.[74] This, Margarethe's father decided, was not to be.

---

[71] Merry E. Wiesner, "Nuns, Wives, and Mothers: Women and the Reformation in Germany", in *Women in Reformation and Counter-Reformation Europe: Public and Private Worlds*, ed. S. Marshall (Bloomington, 1989), pp. 8–28, here at pp. 9–10.

[72] Medard Barth, *Handbuch der elsässischen Kirchen im Mittelalter* (Strasbourg, 1960–1963; reprint, Brussels, 1980), coll. 1386–88; Luzian Pfleger, *Kirchengeschichte der Stadt Straßburg im Mittelalter*, Forschungen zur Kirchengeschichte des Elsaß 6 (Colmar, 1941), p. 87; Adolph Seyboth, *Das alte Straßburg vom 13. Jahrhundert bis zum Jahre 1870* (Strasbourg, 1890), p. 222.

[73] Socially, Strasbourg's mendicant women's houses probably resembled the much better documented Augsburg convents, on which see Roper, *Holy Household*, pp. 207–9.

[74] This story comes from AMS, II 7/20, fols. 26ʳ–29bisᵛ; noticed with an excerpt in *Humanisme et Réforme à Strasbourg. Exposition organisée par les Archives, la Bibliothèque et les Musées de la Ville* (Strasbourg, 1973), pp. 51–52, no. 108; partly printed by Jean Lebeau and Jean-Marie Valentin, eds. *L'Alsace au siècle de la Réforme 1482–1621. Textes et documents* (Nancy, 1985), p. 193. The text is printed in the appendix,

Claus Kniebis was a wealthy, university-educated rentier, who had entered the Senate from the Smiths' Guild in 1512 and in 1519 gained the ammeistership, the commune's highest office.[75] In April 1522, while representing Strasbourg in the Imperial Diet at Nuremberg, Kniebis had begun to move toward the reformation movement, which may or may not have inspired him, once back home, to intervene in his daughter's plans. On 22 June he came with his mother's brother, Hug Meyer, who was a priest and a vicar in the cathedral chapter, to St. Nicolaus-in-Undis for an interview with his daughter and with the prioress, Ursula von Mörßmünster.[76] Kniebis refused the proposal that Margarethe be allowed to enter the novitiate, and before she might even think about it, two or three years hence, "his wish is that she live in his house for a time and test herself in the world."[77] Margarethe reminded her father that "I've said to you many times that I don't want to leave, that I don't want to be in the world. If you force me, God will forgive me, for my will is never again to be in the world." Kniebis grew angry and retorted, "even if you don't want to leave, you must leave. You must leave, even if you do so in the Devil's name." "In his name I won't leave," Margarethe responded, "but in God's name and in obedience to God's will. For you brought me into this house and offered me to God with your own hands." Now the prioress intervened and proposed that the novitiate be put off, with the provincial's permission, until

---

Katherine G. Brady and Thomas A. Brady, Jr., eds., "Documents on Communalism and the Control of Women at Strasbourg in the Age of the Reformations", no. 1. In subsequent references, this edition is referred to as "Documents", with document number and lines.

[75] Thomas A. Brady, Jr., *Ruling Class, Regime, and Reformation at Strasbourg, 1520–1555*, SMRT 22 (Leiden, 1978), pp. 326–27; Jean Rott, "Un recueil de correspondances strasbourgeoises du XVIe siècle à la Bibliothèque de Copenhague (Ms. Thott 497,2°)", in *Bulletin philologique et historique (jusqu'en 1610) du Comité des Travaux Historiques et Scientifiques 1968*, (1971), 2: pp. 749–818, here at pp. 756–58; Jean Rott, "La Réforme à Nuremberg et à Strasbourg. Contactes et contrases (avec des correspondances inédites)", in *Homage à Dürer. Strasbourg et Nuremberg dans la première moitié du XVIe siècle*, Publications de la Société Savante d'Alsace et des Régions de l'Est, series "Recherches et Documents" 12 (Strasbourg, 1972), pp. 91–142, here at pp. 99–100. The studies by Rott are reprinted in Jean Rott, *Investigationes Historicae. Eglises et société au XVIe siecle. Gesammelte Aufsätze*, ed. M. de Kroon and M. Lienhard, 2 vols. (Strasbourg, 1986), 1: pp. 250–52, 399–400.

[76] On Hug Meyer, see Brady, *Ruling Class*, p. 146 n. 97.

[77] "Documents", no. 1; and there, too, the remaining quotes in this paragraph. Following the prioress' account, I have transposed the conversation into direct address. "Documents", refers to the documents appended to this chapter and cited by number.

Margarethe turned seventeen, and that meanwhile she should continue to live in the community. No, Claus Kniebis replied, that would
not do, and he would come to fetch her home in two day's time.

Next day the prioress decided to write to Margarethe's mother,
Ottilia Rot, and "ask her humbly to play the loyal mediator among
the father's anger, the daughter, and us."[78] Two days later, she also
wrote to Kniebis himself and pleaded "that he should forgive us,
leave off his anger, and become our good friend." He replied that
"he will do anything else we want, but he must take his daughter
away." But he did not come, and Margarethe, as the prioress told
her mother, "waited day after day, filled with anxiety and fear, until
he should fetch her. . . . Thus the child wasted away visibly in body
and strength, because of her grief and sorrow."

Finally, on Friday after St. Martin's Day (14 November)—not two
days but nearly five months after his first threat—Kniebis and his
uncle, Hug Meyer, came once more to the convent. There ensued the
final interview among them, Margarethe, and Ursula von Mörßmünster. The prioress turned to the young woman and said with sad,
ritualized solemnity, "I would rather see you lying in a grave than
see you go out into the world. But if he demands to have you, then
I give you from my hand to his hand, from my care to his care."
She reminded Margarethe to meditate on the brevity of life and on
the last things in the hope, perhaps, that the woman could maintain something of her old spiritual life in her father's house. Then
she turned to the ammeister and said,

> this is your daughter, whom I give from my hand into your hand,
> from my care into your care. Please God, that you care for her well.
> I give you a good, devout, innocent child. Please God, that you keep
> her so, and if you do not, then we are absolved of responsibility before
> God and before you.

Nine days later, on Sunday, 23 November 1522, Kniebis and his
brother-in-law, Dr. Michael Rot, fetched Margarethe from the convent
to her parents' home in Dragon's Street.[79]

---

[78] *Ibid.*; and there, too, the remaining quotes in this paragraph and those in the
following one.

[79] Seyboth, *Das alte Straßburg*, p. 178. Dr. Michael Rot (d. after 1533), who figures
in the documents analyzed below, was active at Strasbourg by 1515, when he
drafted an opinion for the regime about the reform of the civic hospital. Later,
after the events narrated here and in the following paragraphs, he married a woman
(name unknown), who died in 1555 and left some money to the hospital. During
the early 1530s Rot served as churchwarden at New St. Peter's Church, and he

We know something about this story's aftermath. Claus Kniebis became the political leader of the Evangelical movement, served again as ammeister in the year of the Peasants' War, 1525, and remained a strongly committed Evangelical until his death in 1552. He knew how to do well by doing good, for he, Dr. Rot, and their dependents were some of the few Strasbourgeois to enrich themselves from properties of the dissolved religious houses.[80] Margarethe Kniebis never returned to her convent. She resided at her parents' home until 1525, when at the age of nearly seventeen she was married to Caspar Engelmann, a well-to-do cloth merchant.[81] She married into her father's own set, the nouveaux-riches, mostly cloth merchants, who played such a prominent role in Strasbourg's government during the reformation generation.[82] As for the nuns at St. Nicolaus-in-Undis, despite its discipline this redoubtable community lost many of its nuns just after the great Peasants' War of 1525.[83] It nonetheless endured far into the post-reformation era until the magistrates decided

---

helped to draft the church ordinance of 1534. Otto Wickelmann, *Das Fürgsorgewesen der Stadt Straßburg vor und nach der Reformation bis zum Ausgang des sechzehnten Jahrhunderts. Ein Beitrag zur deutschen Kultur- und Wirtschaftsgeschichte*, QFRG 5 (Leipzig, 1922; repr., New York, 1971), vol. 1: pp. 25–26, and vol. 2: p. 260; Manfred Krebs and Hans-Georg Rott, eds., *Elsaß. Stadt Straßburg 1522–1535*, QFRG 27–28 (Gütersloh, 1959–1960), vol. 2, pp. 95, 135, 178–79.

[80] Brady, *Ruling Class*, pp. 144–46.

[81] Their marriage agreement, dated 12 September 1525, records her dowry of 300 fl. and his *Morgengabe* of 100 fl. Caspar, son of Christoph Engelmann (1494–1541), a cloth merchant and senator, and Margarethe Surgant (1498–1540) of Thann in Upper Alsace; he was Schöffe 1535 and Zunftmeister 1541 of the Guild zum Spiegel; he and Margarethe Kniebis lived since February 1527 in a house they rented from the chapter of St. Thomas; their son, Heinrich, was a Schöffe zum Spiegel 1563–1573, and he and his two brothers formed a firm to sell cloth; Caspar renounced his citizenship on 21 July 1548 during the crisis of the Interim at Strasbourg. F.-J. Fuchs, "Engelmann", *Nouvelle dictionnaire du biographie alsacienne*, vol. 7 (Strasbourg, 1986), p. 813; Karina Kulbach, "Ascendances des enfants d'André Sandherr (1672–1737) et d'Anne Salome Oestringer, de Colmar", *Bulletin du Cercle Généalogique d'Alsace*, 31 (1975): pp. 63–70; AMS, KS 18, fol. 100^r, AMS, KS 19, fol. 115; AMS, Corporation du Miroir, 5. Much of this information comes from F.-J. Fuchs of Strasbourg, to whom my thanks.

[82] See Brady, *Ruling Class*, pp. 183–84.

[83] The convent's manager (*Schaffner*) drew up ca. 1525 a list of "Volgende Closterfraüwen sindt nach dem Bauren krieg auß dem Closter St. Claus in vndis allhie zu Strasburg kommen vnd weltlich worden", which contains the following names: Subprioress Margarethe Rötin, Susanna Pfaüren, Maria Gerhartin, Ursula Ehingeren, Magdalena Stürmin, Margareth Böcklerin, Anna Heüsin, Anne Wurme, Veronica Mehen, Juliana Bÿsin, Appolonia von Heÿdelberg, Paulina Furtherin, Ursula Spitzlerin, N. Neuischin, Margreth von Waltzhut, Agneß Dolden, Elizabeth Hüsen, Barbara Eppen, Elizabeth Beÿnen, Margen Stürmin, Maria Durbchen, Margreth Müllerin. AMS, II 7/20, fol. 42^r.

on 8 April 1592 to close it, and its nuns were taken into the Dominican community of St. Mary Magdalene.[84] Of all the women's houses at Strasbourg, those of the Dominican Observance survived the longest, despite the endless campaigns of vilification by the Evangelical preachers and intermittent harassment by the regime, a process which began in 1525 under the eye of the ruling ammeister, Claus Kniebis.[85] The nuns' resistance, as Lyndal Roper has written of Augsburg, "dramatized and focused the divisions within the elite", from whose daughters the convents recruited.[86] The repudiation of their way of life by the reformers and followers split families at Strasbourg, as it did elsewhere. No case at Strasbourg is so well documented as that of the Poor Clares at Nuremberg under the redoubtable Caritas Pirckheimer (1467–1532).[87] We do know of other cases of removals, however, mostly carried out by prominent Strasbourgeois who repatriated their female relations. This happened, for example, to Clara Sturm, who was removed from the convent of SS. Margarethe and Agnes by her two brothers, Jacob and Peter, in 1524.[88] Both their father's family, the Sturms, and their mother's kinsmen, the Schotts, long enjoyed especially strong ties to the houses of the Dominican

[84] Francis Rapp, "La vie religieuse du couvent Saint-Nicolas-aux-ondes à Strasbourg de 1525 à 1592", *Études de sociologie religieuse*, Cahiers de l'Association interuniversitaire de l'Est (1962), pp. 1–16; Pierre Levresse, "La survie du catholicisme à Strasbourg au XVIe siècle", in *Strasbourg au coeur religieux du XVIe siècle. Hommage à Lucien Febvre*, ed. G. Livet, F. Rapp, Publications de la Société Savante d'Alsace et des Régions de l'Est, Collection "Grandes publications" 12 (Strasbourg, 1977), pp. 457–69, here at p. 462. Five other communities survived the reformation era intact: the women's houses of St. Mary Magdalene and SS. Margarethe and Agnes; and the men's houses of the Carthusians, the Knights of St. John, and the Teutonic Knights. F.-J. Fuchs, "Les catholiques à Strasbourg de 1529 à 1681", *AEKG* 38 (1975): pp. 141–69, here at pp. 142–43.
[85] See AMS, II 57/7, two letters from the prioress and community of SS. Margarethe and Agnes, another Dominican house, to Ammeister Kniebis concerning the replacement of their confessor by the wardens (*Pfleger*). On the struggle of the women's houses to maintain their religious life, see Fuchs, "Les catholiques à Strasbourg", pp. 156–61.
[86] Roper, *Holy Household*, p. 210.
[87] The best study is still Gerta Krabbel, *Caritas Pirckheimer. Ein Lebensbild aus der Zeit der Reformation*, 5th ed., Katholisches Leben und Kirchenreform im Zeitalter der Glaubensspaltung 7 (Münster, 1982 [1940]), esp. pp. 86–197; and see Klaus Guth, "Caritas Pirckheimer. Kloster und Klosterleben in der Herausforderung der Zeit", in *Caritas Pirckheimer. Eine Ausstellung der Katholischen Stadtkirche Nürnberg, Kaiserburg Nürnberg, 26 June–8 August 1982* (Munich, 1982), pp. 13–29.
[88] Brady, *Ruling Class*, pp. 351–53; Rapp, *Réformes*, p. 520. The convent, which dated back to the union of two communities of Dominican women, held out until the French Revolution. Barth, *Handbuch*, coll. 1369–70, pp. 1381–84.

Observance.[89] The two younger Sturm brothers nevertheless removed Clara from her convent, where she had lived for sixteen years and was, unlike Margarethe Kniebis, almost certainly a professed nun. A number of other removals occurred, or were attempted, about the same time by men of equal rank.[90]

The story of Margarethe Kniebis captures in midstream the pressure placed on this sector of the clergy by the reformation movement and its consequences for familial relations. Although at first glance Kniebis' actions seem to be a predictable—given his commitment— rescue of his daughter from the monastic life, which Luther had decreed to be worse than useless, on closer scrutiny the document reveals Kniebis' action to have been more paternal than Protestant. He argued not that Margarethe's chosen way of life was worthless or harmful but that she was too young to take first vows, and that he wanted her to live in the world for a few years before deciding to remain in the convent for the rest of her life. Indeed, the prioress says that until he was angered, he consented to let her live in the community, though not to take vows.[91] Once angered, "he swore that he would fetch her in two days' time", and when he did fetch her, nearly five months later, she never returned. Perhaps this story catches the ammeister in religious midstream, when the new faith

---

[89] Their aunt, Magdalena Sturm (†1520), and their sister, Margarethe (†1530), were nuns at St. Nicolaus-in-Undis, and two aunts and two uncles were buried at the men's Dominican house. AMS, II 7/20, fol. 42ʳ; and see Thomas A. Brady, Jr., "La famille Sturm aux XVᵉ et XVIᵉ siècles", *Revue d'Alsace* 108 (1982): pp. 29–44, here at pp. 32–33, for further documentation. Anna Schott, a great-aunt on the Schott side, had been a nun at SS. Margarethe and Agnes, and her family was said to have a "special love" for the Dominicans. Bibliothèque Nationale et Universitaire de Strasbourg, Ms. 1058, fol. 166ᵛ; Charles Guillaume Adolphe Schmidt, *Histoire littéraire de l'Alsace* (n. 30 above), 2: p. 9 n. 20, p. 29 n. 78; Dacheux, *Un réformateur catholique*, pp. 426–27.

[90] Other actions of this kind are known. Jacobe Spender, for example, was removed by her father, Jacob Spender († ca. 1525), from St. Nicolaus-in-Undis on 25 November 1522. AMS, II 7/20, fol. 29ʳ, noticed in *Humanisme et Réforme à Strasbourg*, p. 52; and on the father, a privy councillor, see Brady, *Ruling Class*, pp. 210, 223, 379, 382, 391. Adolf von Mittelhausen, a noble senator, tried to remove his daughter from SS. Margarethe and Agnes in 1522. AST 37, fols. 48ʳ, 59ᵛ. Mathis Wurm von Geudertheim tried four times between September 1522 and February 1523 to force his sister, Anna, from the convent of St. Nicolaus-in-Undis, which she had entered in 1512. See Jean Rott and Gustave Koch, "De quelques pamphletaires nobles", in *Grandes figures de l'humanisme alsacien*, pp. 135–45, here at pp. 139–45 (reprinted in Rott, *Investigationes Historicae*, 2: pp. 575–85).

[91] Documents", no. 1; and the remaining quotes in this paragraph are from *ibid.*

could prompt his doubts about his daughter's choice but did not yet grip him so firmly as to demand immediate action.

Other male patricians likely underwent similar experiences. Local law seems to have permitted them to remove kinswomen, even adults, from their convents, perhaps based on residual right of guardianship over the women. Once their communities no longer shielded them, the nuns perhaps came under a law of 1500—protested to no avail by Johann Geiler—which provided that all widows "shall be given a guardian without their knowledge or will."[92] This law merely illustrates the progressive deterioration of women's legal rights in sixteenth-century Europe, including the Holy Roman Empire.[93] The fate of women from communities attacked or dissolved in the wake of the reformation movement, therefore, must be seen in this larger light. The attack on the women's communities represented not only a confessional act against Catholicism but also an affirmation of the patriarchal household's rights over women. This process enjoyed widespread popular support because of the widespread doubts about women's inability to manage either their properties or their sexuality.[94] By disrupting and dissolving the communal religious life of women, therefore, the reformation movement eased such doubts by promoting the consolidation of male authority over women's religious life. This improved domestication of women formed one aspect of the reformation's integration of the clergy.

IV

Authority and gender enter richly into another story about the relationships between the domestication of women and the integration of clergy. It, too, involves what Scribner calls the "sexual power" of the clergy.[95] Strasbourg certainly rivalled other major South German

---

[92] Geiler, *Die ältesten Schriften*, p. 19.

[93] Merry E. Wiesner, "Frail, Weak, and Helpless: Women's Legal Position in Theory and Reality", in *Regnum, religio et ratio. Essays Presented to Robert M. Kingdon*, ed. J. Friedman, Sixteenth Century Essays & Studies 8 (Kirksville, Mo., 1987), pp. 161–69. On the economic basis of the deterioration, see id., *Working Women in Renaissance Germany* (New Brunswick, N.J., 1986), esp. pp. 149–85, 187–98; Susan C. Karant-Nunn, "The Woman of the Saxon Silver Mines", in *Women in Reformation and Counter-Reformation Europe*, ed. S. Marshall, pp. 28–45, here at pp. 42–43.

[94] Roper, *Holy Household*, p. 229. See *ibid.*, pp. 211–28, on the closing of convents, a process much better documented at Augsburg than at Strasbourg.

[95] Scribner, "Anticlericalism", pp. 246–48.

cities in its number of high- and loose-living clergymen, and the
notorious clan of the Wolfs of Eckbolsheim contained some of the
worst. Its head, Thomas Wolf, Sr. (1445–1511), was the son of rich
peasants at Eckbolsheim, who studied at Erfurt, Basel, and Bologna.[96]
Wolf collected benefices and books, conducted an active law practice, and consorted with humanists without being one. Upon his
death, his fine house at New St. Peter's was sacked by his brother,
Caspar, whose gang of mercenaries looted the plate and drank up
the cellar. Wolf was the very type of the pre-reformation gentleman-
clergyman, a "master-pluralist" who dabbled in all that was fashionable, lived well off the church, and performed as an efficient
opponent to the efforts of Bishop William III of Strasbourg to reform
his clergy in 1509.[97] Wolf's brother, Andreas, married Katherine
Meyer and had four sons by her, all clergymen. The best of the lot
was Thomas, Jr. (1475–1509), who followed in his uncle's footstep
as a pluralist, though he made a better mark as a humanist and,
one assumes, lived more modestly, for he was a particular favorite
of Geiler's.[98] The Wolfs who interest us here are two of his brothers, Johann Andreas and Cosmas, both canons of New St. Peter's
at Strasbourg.[99] The brothers, themselves notable womanizers, became embroiled in the worst clerical scandal of the immediate pre-
reformation years. The case involved one Johann Hepp of Kirchberg,
a canon of St. Thomas at Strasbourg, who had seduced a young
country girl, brought her to Strasbourg as his mistress, and then
kidnapped her when she mysteriously fell ill; after her death he had
been arrested by Strasbourg's regime and let go, whereupon he sued

[96] On the Wolf family, see also Schmidt, *Histoire littéraire*, 2: pp. 58–60; Jean Rott,
"The Library of the Strasbourg Humanist Thomas Wolf, Senior (†1511)", in *The
Process of Change in Early Modern Europe* ed. P. Bebb and S. Marshall (Athens, Ohio,
1988), pp. 33–58, here at pp. 33–34; Rapp, *Réformes*, p. 292 n. 63, pp. 299–300,
302–4; Miriam Usher Chrisman, *Lay Culture, Learned Culture: Books and Social Change
in Strasbourg, 1480–1599* (New Haven, 1982), pp. 41, 61, 82.
[97] Rott, "The Library of the Strasbourg Humanist", pp. 33, 35.
[98] According to Matern Berler, "Chronik", p. 114. This Wolf was a minor humanist and holder of four benefices, of whose career Chrisman (*Lay Culture*, p. 82) writes
that "he spent more time collating the Latin inscriptions he had brought from student days in Italy than in pursuing questions of doctrine or theology."
[99] This is based on Jean Rott, "Clercs et laiques à Strasbourg à la veille de la
Réformation: Les tragiques amours du Chanoine Jean Hepp et ses procès (1512–
1521)", *Annuaire des Amis de Vieux-Strasbourg* 9 (1979): pp. 15–52; and id., "Pfaffenfehden und Anfänge der Reformation in Straßburg. Die Streitigkeiten des Johannes
Murner mit den Brüdern Wolff und dem Jung Sankt Peter-Stift daselbst (1519–
1522)", in *Landesgeschichte und Geistesgeschichte* (n. 21 above), pp. 279–94 (reprinted in
Rott, *Investigationes Historicae*, 1: pp. 313–50, 351–67).

Strasbourg at Rome for violation of clerical immunity. The city's
case was handled by Hans Murner, brother to the much more famous
Franciscan writer and a terror to wayward clergymen. In 1509 his
sister, Anna, had been seduced and left pregnant by Friedrich von
Beyern, a chaplain at Old St. Peter's Church and bastard son of
the late bishop of Strasbourg. Murner's involvement in the Hepp
case brought him into conflict with the Wolf brothers, who took
Hepp's part and who had, Murner believed, designs on a woman
he called his kinswoman but whom the Wolfs called "his good little whore". After several threats and broken windows, on the nights
of 21 and 22 January 1522, the matter came to blows in wild scenes
staged in the cemetery of New St. Peter's Church. On the second
night, Murner and three armored companions, who were armed with
boar spears, ambushed the Wolfs and three others. In the petition
which he submitted next day to his employers, Murner raged against
"these unworthy, alleged clergymen", who constantly offend the
citizens, "sparing no respectable man's wife or child."[100] This notorious case combined clerical concubinage, clerical crime, clerical
violence, all protected by the web of clerical immunities and ecclesiastical jurisdiction, for eventually Murner was excommunicated at
Rome, notice of which was posted at Strasbourg on Christmas Day
1519. The affair caused Nicolaus Wurmser (1473–1536), who was dean
of the chapter of St. Thomas, to which the Wolfs belonged, to ex-
claim in his diary, "Oh, it is such a wondrous thing that the clergy
are hated by everyone and have no defenders!"[101]

This tangled series of scandals, which unfolded in the last pre-
reformation years, colored the mood at Strasbourg about clerical behavior and formed, therefore, part of the psychological background
to the case of Drenss vs. Hedio. The gist of the case is related in a
fragmentary minute of the Senate & XXI of Strasbourg for 14 May
1524. It says that Augustin Drenss charges

> that Dr. Hedio has taken his sister in marriage, and this was done
> through the connivance of Sir Claus Kniebis and Dr. Michael Rot,
> who seduced the sister and her mother with smooth words, so that
> they were betrayed and humiliated.[102]

[100] Quoted by Rott, "Pfaffenfehden", p. 282.
[101] Rott, "Pfaffenfehden", p. 294 n. 71: "Or res auditu mirabilis, quod clerus
tanto odio est omnibus, ut nullum defensorem habeat!" On Wurmser, see Ficker
and Winckelmann, *Handschriftenproben*, 2: p. 53.
[102] "Annales de Sébastien Brant", ed. Léon Dacheux, *BSCMHA*, 2nd ser., 19
(1899): p. 95, no. 4521.

The object of this complaint was the wedding of Dr. Caspar Hedio and Margarethe Drenss on St. John the Baptist's Day 1524.[103] The clergyman is the historian Caspar Hedio (1494–1552), a native of Ettlingen near Karlsruhe, who had studied theology at Freiburg im Breisgau and served successively as vicar at St. Martin's Church in Basel, cathedral preacher at Mainz, and since September 1523 cathedral preacher at Strasbourg.[104] He was, therefore, Geiler's successor but one in the cathedral's pulpit.

Augustin Drenss († 3 May 1552) was a substantial citizen. He came from one of the Gardeners' guild's most prominent families, three of whom—including Augustin—served the guild in the privy councils between 1483 and 1557.[105] Augustin, though a truck gardener, was also a moneylender, and his father had been wealthy enough to serve the commune mounted.[106] Augustin's wife was Aurelia Rot, whose sister, Ottilia, was married to Claus Kniebis, and both were kinswomen of Dr. Michael Rot. Drenss vs. Hedio, therefore, is a familial matter which got out of hand, one of those many instances of the intermingling of private and public life.[107]

The case is unusually well documented. Besides Augustin Drenss' original petition, we have the responses of Claus Kniebis, Dr. Michael Rot, and Agnes Drenss, mother of Margarethe and Augustin, plus a final statement by Drenss himself.[108] August Drenss came to the Senate for justice, and he reminds the magistrates that, according to local law and ancient custom,

> no one may entice or lead away a child from its father behind his back. Whoever is found to have assisted in such an act, whether by word or deed, is to be punished. If the child is fatherless, the guardian

---

[103] Sebald Büheler, "La chronique strasbourgeoise", ed. Léon Dacheux, *BSCMHA*, 2nd ser., 13 (1888): p. 71.

[104] On Hedio, see Ficker and Winckelmann, *Handschriftenproben*, 2: p. 60; Charles Spindler, *Hédion. Essai biographie et littéraire*, theol. dissertation (Strasbourg, 1864).

[105] Brady, *Ruling Class*, pp. 113, 181, 387.

[106] *Ibid.*, p. 307. Augustin was the son of Agnes N. and Andres Drenss, who served three two-year terms as senator from the Gardeners' Guild between 1482 and 1497; Andres appears among the mounted burghers in the civic muster lists of his time. Jacques Hatt, *Liste des membres du grand sénat de Strasbourg, des stettmeistres, des ammeistres, des conseils des XXI, XIII, et des XV du XIIIe siècle à 1789* (Strasbourg, 1963), p. 557; AMS, IV p. 86.

[107] Their marriage took place before October 1526. AMS, KS 19, fol. 292^v. Aurelia Rot and her daughter are called Dr. Rot's "mumen", that is, female relations in undetermined degrees. AST, 69/3. fol. 8^v.

[108] "Documents" nos. 2–6.

named according to the statute by you, my gracious lords, is to be
regarded as standing in a father's place.[109]

Dr. Hedio, Drenss claimed, had nonetheless

decided and brazenly plotted to take as his wedded wife my sister,
Margarethe Drenss, secretly, without the knowledge, and against the
wills of the guardian and of myself, as I am told. And he did as follows. Michael Rot, doctor of medicine, invited my sister and her mother
to his house to dine. Secretly and without their knowledge, as I have
been told, he also invited Dr. Caspar Hedio. Then Sir Claus Kniebis,
the ammeister, also arrived, and the two men smoothly told daughter
and mother that vows should be exchanged, as common rumor said
they already had been. My mother and sister, however, very properly
demurred, replying that it was not right to do such a thing behind
the backs of her guardian, brother, and friends.[110]

Kniebis and Rot, however, assured mother and daughter that they
would fix the matter with him, Augustin, which they tried to do several days later. Meanwhile, Margarethe was staying in Dr. Rot's
house, "even though there is no wife in his house." Drenss, however, refused his consent and told his mother, sister, and others that

my sister must give up the priest and marry a good, honest citizen,
and I will dower her with 100 florins from my own property. For the
doctor is a clergymen, and they are forbidden to marry not only by
local law and custom, but also by the laws according to which
Christendom has lived for a thousand years and more. From this marriage, too, will come considerable disadvantage to me and mine, not
to mention the scandal. For a proper, conscientious Christian ruler
cannot allow such an act, but must forbid and disallow it, for it is
unthinkable that such a mischievous undertaking be permitted to can-
cel and cast aside both papal and imperial law. Otherwise, my sister
would rightly be regarded as called a public sinner and a whore. If
she bears children by the aforementioned doctor, and her mother and
grandmother were already dead, the children could not inherit from
either woman, for they would justly be regarded as bastards.[111]

Drenss, therefore, asked the magistrates to force Hedio "to desist
from his undertaking and to have nothing to do with my sister or
my relations, except at law." If that is not possible, he asks them to
support his attempts to find redress in other courts,

---

[109] "Documents", no. 2.
[110] "Documents", no. 2.
[111] "Documents", no. 2.

for if it should happen, that it were considered proper and permissible for any priest or monk to take with impunity and by fraud and trickery a child or other relation from a respectable citizen, without his knowledge and against his will, that would be a scandalous thing. What that might lead to, my lords can well imagine.[112]

So they might have, but the subsequent responses of Claus Kniebis, Caspar Hedio, and Agnes Drenss did not corroborate Augustin's allegations.

Kniebis responded angrily that "I, one of your ammeisters, had to listen to this petition, in which I and my brother-in-law are not a little insulted." Kniebis related that Caspar Hedio had just happened by, as he was told, "to have a friendly talk [with Dr. Rot] about all sorts of things, as scholars do", and after a while Agnes and Margarethe Drenss knocked at the door. As they were his kinswomen ("mumen"), Rot let them in and explained that about a month ago he had invited them to come "and see, how I keep house."[113] The conversation turned to the secret betrothal of Margarethe Drenss and Caspar Hedio three weeks before, which gossiping tongues were now spreading about, "so they thought it perhaps better to send for a good friend of the house, before whom they could say their vows." Several were asked, and Claus Kniebis, who was sitting at dinner, agreed to come, though he wasn't told why he was wanted. That he learned only at Dr. Rot's house, and "they proposed to me that, since they were already betrothed, to unite them in marriage publicly. Which I at first refused, protesting that some one else should do that, as I was not a priest."[114] They all persisted, however, so Kniebis

> talked to the mother and her daughter (whom I hadn't known before), shook hands with them and greeted them. Then I asked the daughter and Dr. Caspar separately whether each desired to wed the other. And after each said, "yes", I united them in marriage and wished them much happiness, peace, and grace.[115]

After the wedding dinner, mother, newlyweds, "and some others" begged Kniebis and Rot "to go to Augustin Drenss, their son, brother, and brother-in-law, and asked him in a most friendly way to give

---

[112] "Documents", no. 2.
[113] "Documents", no. 3.
[114] "Documents", no. 3.
[115] "Documents", no. 3.

his consent to the marriage, which he had not approved."[116] Next day they did so, taking three others who were "our dear and good friends and kinsmen".[117] Augustin's reply was curt and simple: he would go after Dr. Hedio, find him, and strangle him. Kniebis, fearing the worst, commanded Augustin "in the name of the Senate" to keep the peace, an act which Drenss later denounced as an attempt to exploit the ammeister's office for personal advantage.

Dr. Hedio, the bridegroom, also replied to Augustin Drenss' charges, mainly, he said, "because I must be unimpeded in my office, to which God has called me, for the advancement of his honor and of the salvation of many souls."[118] The marriage occurred, he asserted, "with the knowledge, will, and approval of the honorable Agnes Drenss, her mother and my dear mother-in-law." He confirmed the betrothal and the details of the wedding three weeks later, as related by Claus Kniebis, whose intervention with Augustin Drenss he justified. As for the allegation that clergymen may not marry, Hedio thought it known to everyone now,

> that the Lord God, who stands above all laws and all kings of the earth, never forbade marriage to anyone, but on many occasions approved it. But about five hundred years this divine ordinance was abolished through the arbitrariness and violence of Pope Gregory VII, who acted tyrannically and against God's law. This led to the ruin of [clerical] behavior, which can be accepted and approved by no Christian ruler who regards Christ as Lord set above all human legislators.[119]

The Word of God, he warned in the spirit of the glory days of the reformation movement,

> which abides eternally, through which were created heaven and earth, not only shatters the canon law but also dashes to the ground the whole world, Hell, and the Devil—indeed all who undertake anything against God's will.

Hedio then tempered this outburst with another defense of his right to marry, and then he ended his response.

---

[116] "Documents", no. 3. The mention of Drenss as "brother-in-law" does not mean that Kniebis' wife, Ottilia Rot, was present, for among those who went to get Augustin's consent was Mathis Rot, who may well have been brother to Ottilia, Aurelia, and Michael Rot.

[117] They took with them Drenss' kinsman, Jacob Drenss, and Lorentz Graff († 8/9 July 1553), XV^{er} from Drenss' own Gardeners' Guild and described as Kniebis' "vetter". "Documents", no. 3. On Graff, see Brady, *Ruling Class*, p. 316.

[118] "Documents", no. 4.

[119] "Documents", no. 5.

Much the most interesting of the three responses to Augustin's charges came from his mother, for from Agnes Drenss we learn enough about the dynamics of will and interest to make sense of the story. Dr. Hedio, she affirmed, "courted my dear daughter, Margarethe, as a pious, upright gentleman ought to do."[120] He made his suit known to mother, daughter, son, and friends, to which Augustin had replied that "concerning the marriage, whatever pleased me and my daughter, would please him as well." As soon, however, as Augustin learned that the women were inclined to accept Hedio's suit, he "acted improperly through words and gestures." She attributed that to the "bad lads" whose company Augustin kept, "who oppose all that fosters God's Word and Christian uprightness, for, under-standably enough, they hate the gospel." She hoped that sound preaching would soften her son's heart and make him recognize "that holy matrimony is permitted and even recommended by God to everyone, and that just because the clergy have been forbidden to marry, scandal and vice have flourished and flourish still."[121] The duty, however, of every good Christian to help see that "the divine, holy institution of marriage should drive out the improper, shame-less way of life of some clergyman", was lost on Augustin.

Agnes was moved to her decision, she said, "by the daily, clear preaching of the gospel in this city of Strasbourg, which would not be allowed by Your Graces, or attended by so many respectable citizens, were it not truly divine and Christian."[122] The decision to accept Hedio's suit, therefore, was made by Agnes, for her daughter "while she was in my care she always obeyed my will."[123] Fortified by the advice of "quite a few of my relations, friends, and chums, all honorable and pious folk", Agnes Drenss decided "that this marriage will be pleasing to God and beneficial and useful to my dear daughter, and will in no way be shameful to my son", providing he followed good rather than evil counsellors.

Agnes' decision, we learn, lay behind her visit, Margarethe in tow, to Dr. Rot's house on St. George's Day, which she made without notifying the doctor. Upon finding Hedio there, Agnes "spoke with him about the gossip, and we two decided that, . . . with my daughter's consent, which she had already given him, to arrange the wedding

---

[120] "Documents", no. 5.
[121] "Documents", no. 5.
[122] "Documents", no. 5.
[123] "Documents", no. 5.

now in order to stop the gossip."[124] Now she asked their host to send for the ammeister to preside over the wedding. Like Hedio, Agnes Drenss was careful to say that Kniebis knew nothing of the matter until he arrived. The ammeister, "since our request was reasonable and in accordance with godly law, could not refuse", and he united them in marriage, wished them well, and stayed for the wedding dinner—having missed his own. There were no "smooth words", as Augustin alleged, nor any coercion, nor yet any pressure from Dr. Rot.

It was not the gospel alone, as we learn from Agnes Drenss, that made her and Margarethe so receptive to Hedio's suit. The daughter, she asserted, "is mine and not my son's, and we told him that after he had turned away so many previous suitors, he was rejecting this one purely because of his unbelief [*unglauben*] and the counsels of evil folk." In fact, "he cannot forbid us anything which we have not put in his power, so I think we have committed no grave sin." They did not consult Margarethe's guardian, true, but "we think we were not obliged to do so, having so many good relations and friends whose advice we followed." The long and the short of it was, "sooner or later, it had to happen."

Against this battery of responses, poor Augustin Drenss had few weapons left. Probably he recognized that as the magistrates had decided to protect other married priests, they would not make an exception of their cathedral preacher, especially if they had to injure an ammeister in order to do so. Drenss appealed to their belief that women, being weak, can easily be exploited, for anyone could see, he alleged in his final statement, that just as his mother "was used in the original affair, so is she further manipulated in this one, for if Dr. Caspar's response and those of my mother and others are compared, one can easily tell that they are all arrows from the same quiver."[125] The whole matter showed very clearly, "how the new Evangelical teaching has the aim to bring contention and division between father, mother, and children." Although he professed his willingness "to acknowledge and hold her as mother all my life, despite this new doctrine", he blamed Agnes for arranging this wedding in the absence of the guardian and the family's friends.[126] It

---

[124] "Documents", no. 5.
[125] "Documents", no. 6.
[126] "Documents". no. 6.

was simply not true, Augustin said, "that I would approve no man for my sister." He'd found several good prospects for her, "but she would take only this one [i.e., Hedio]."[127]

The game was up, and Augustin Drenss knew it. He closed his second statement with a bitter comment on the illegality of what had happened.

> That priests and monks should once more be allowed to marry, is against both papal and imperial law. Nor, according to Your Graces' ancient customs and the usage of Christendom for many centuries, may the child of a priest, legitimate or illegitimate, inherit.

With this final shot, Drenss withdrew his complaint.[128]

The story behind Drenss vs. Hedio is less a tale of the reformation movement at Strasbourg than one of the Drenss family and the impingement of the reform on their relations. The movement bitterly split families, and though many of them later patched over their differences, as the Drenss family was to do, others never did.[129] The movement's point of entry into this story is Agnes Drenss, the story's key figure, whose energy and decision brought the entire affair to a head. She wanted her daughter, Margarethe, properly settled, while her son, Augustin, turned away suitors, either because he didn't want to pay her dowry or because he simply opposed his mother's authority over Margarethe. Perhaps he changed his mind about Hedio's suit—Agnes says that he originally did not oppose it—because of his mother's enthusiasm for preaching that conveniently attacked the rule of mandatory clerical celibacy. Marriage of priests, after all, had come to Strasbourg only half a year earlier, when on 18 October 1523 Anton Firn (†1545) announced his marriage, and

---

[127] "Documents", no. 6: "dann ich gearbeit das sie den schaffner zu Sant Catharina oder Våltin des Schultheÿssen sun von Wangen zu der ee nemen."

[128] *Annales de Sébastien Brant*, no. 4521: "Hat Drens endlich revocirt."

[129] This was true, for example, of the family of Franz Frosch (1490–1540), a lawyer from Nuremberg who served as city attorney of Strasbourg from 1533 until his death. Three years later, his sister, Gertrud, came from Nuremberg to announce that in a codicil to his will her brother had stipulated that none of his property should go to his two brothers-in-law, who were members of religious houses. AMS, KS 48/I, fols. 61ᵛ–62ʳ. These will have been members of the Scher von Schwarzenburg family, from which Frosch's wife, Felicitas, came. Jacob Bernays, "Zur Biographie Johann Winthers von Andernach", *Zeitschrift für die Geschichte des Oberrheins* 60 (1901): pp. 30, 33, 35–38. On Frosch, see Ficker and Winckelmann, *Handschriftenproben*, 1: p. 23; Hans Winterberg, *Die Schüler von Ulrich Zasius*, Veröffentlichungen der Kommission für geschichtliche Landeskunde in Baden-Württemberg, series B, 18 (Stuttgart, 1961), pp. 38–39.

CHAPTER NINE

on 3 December the pastor of the cathedral parish, Mathis Zell (1477–1548) publicly married a local woman, Katharine Schütz (1497/98–1562).[130] The magistrates vacillated well into the new year, though they continued to interpose themselves between bishop and priests even after the citation on 24 January of the priests to Saverne for disciplinary action. The bishop's letter of excommunication of married priests was published at Strasbourg on 3 April, but on 18 March the magistrates had taken the decisive step to block any further prosecution. This affair, which aroused great interest and partisanship at Strasbourg, was well advanced before the end of 1523, when Caspar Hedio arrived from Mainz to assume the cathedral pulpit. And at least five weeks before his wedding day (23 April), a Strasbourgeoise could marry a priest at Strasbourg with the assurance that her husband would not lose his benefice. And Dr. Michael Rot must have invited Margarethe Drenss and her mother to visit him just after the Senate & XXI had decided to block episcopal prosecutions of married priests.

This chain of events liberated Agnes Drenss from her son's will, or whims, and emboldened her to push forward the match between Margarethe and her betrothed. Not that this action was out of character, for her statement shows her to have been the real head of the Drenss household and to have had a very firm, untroubled conscience about what she had done. So much so that her son's allegation about her manipulation by Hedio, Kniebis, and Rot—women are weak, after all—was almost certainly false.

Augustin Drenss' motives are more difficult to construe, for though he insists on enforcement of the law and makes clear his dislike for "the new doctrine", his two statements contains very little in the way of positive comments on religion. Perhaps he wished to be saved Margarethe's dowry, perhaps he simply played the tyrant, though, if so, by his mother's account he did so desultorily. What is certain is that he saw this marriage as just another case of clerical misbehavior, another priest invading the sanctity of a burgher's home to get at his women. He wanted, ironically enough, what the Protestant reformers wanted, a chaste, disciplined clergy, though he rejected their solution, clerical marriage.

---

[130] The most detailed account of these events and the bishop's magistrates' reactions is in Stafford, *Domesticating the Clergy*, pp. 151–65.

Claus Kniebis' role in Drenss vs. Hedio is more difficult to judge. Augustin Drenss' complaint cannot have put him in much danger, given the recent movement of the Senate & XXI against the bishop, though it clearly angered him, especially the charge that he had misused his ammeistership in a private matter. Kniebis' role in the wedding nonetheless entered that zone of lawlessness which lay between the local regime's repudiation of episcopal jurisdiction over the clergy and marriage and its own' assumption of jurisdiction over marriage.[131] The transition hardly affected official views on what made a valid marriage, namely, the exchange of vows (*sponsalia*) in the absence of coercion or impediments.[132] According to the ritual ordinance then formally still in effect in the diocese of Strasbourg, this was supposed to take place outside the church, usually on the steps, to be followed by a Mass and blessing of the union in the church.[133] The Protestant marriage services, drafted by Diebold Schwarz (1485–1561) in 1524 and Martin Bucer in 1525, moved the central act into the church, as vows were now to be exchanged in church, before a clergyman, and as part of a wedding service.[134] In this, as in most other things pertaining to marriage, the Protestants made few radical changes.[135] According to canon law, the only impediment to the validity of the Drenss-Hedio marriage was Hedio's

---

[131] François Wendel, *La mariage à Strasbourg à l'époque de la Réforme 1520–1692*, Collection d'études sur l'histoire du droit et des institutions de l'Alsace 4 (Strasbourg, 1928), pp. 97–118. On this question in general, see Lyndal Roper, "'Going to Church and Street': Weddings in Reformation Augsburg", *PaP* 106 (February 1985): pp. 62–101, here at pp. 64–67, with full references; and id., *Holy Household*, pp. 132–64.

[132] See Thomas M. Safley, "Civic Morality and the Domestic Economy", in *The German People and the Reformation*, ed. R. Hsia, pp. 173–90, here at p. 175, for references.

[133] Wendel, *La mariage*, pp. 214–19, prints the passages from this book and from Diebolt Schwarz's ritual. On the changes in the conception and liturgy of marriage, see René Bornert, *La réforme protestante du culte à Strasbourg au XVIe siècle (1523–1598): Approche sociologique et interprétation théologique*, SMRT 28 (Leiden, 1981), pp. 553–69. On Diebold Schwarz, a local man, see Ficker and Winckelmann, *Handschriftenproben*, 2: p. 61.

[134] Bornert, *La réforme protestante du culte*, p. 561: "Le mariage est célébré à l'église."

[135] See Thomas M. Safley, *Let No Man Put Asunder: The Control of Marriage in the German Southwest, a Comparative Study, 1550–1600* (Kirksville, Mo., 1984); id., "Civic Morality and the Domestic Economy", pp. 173–90. The researches of Safley and Lyndal Roper do not bear out the contention that the Protestant reformation transformed marriage. See, for this view, Steven Ozment, *When Fathers Ruled: Family Life in Reformation Europe* (Cambridge, Mass., 1983). Indeed, as Lyndal Roper has written, "the Protestant view of marriage approximated more closely to German townspeople's traditional notions of how a marriage was made" than the Catholic sacramental theory of marriage did. Roper, "'Going to Church and Street'", p. 65.

status as a priest. The wedding's private setting nonetheless violated deep sensibilities of German townsfolk, who held that publicity, "going to church and street", contributed in an important way to a completed marriage.[136]

The rancor aroused by this affair seems to have faded away within a few years. Augustin Drenss converted to the new religion by 1529, when he was churchwarden (*Kirchenpfleger*) at St. Aurelia's, which was Bucer's first parish and a font of Strasbourg's reformation. Drenss entered the Senate from the Gardeners' Guild in 1536 and the privy council of the XV in 1542.[137] The restoration of peace between him and Margarethe is suggested by the fact that two of her eight children were boys named "Augustin", each whom died at the age of five.[138] She lived to be very old, and in her widowhood her guardian, prescribed by Strasbourg's law, was Nicolaus Hugo Kniebis, Claus' son.[139]

V

Taken together, the sources presented above yield some insights into the disintegration and reintegration of clerical power in one local setting. They show, for one thing, that the process went much deeper than the legal and political integration of the clergy—the priests became citizens and members of guilds—which is the only aspect of clerical integration that has been well studied.[140] Johann Geiler, who sensed the disintegration on all sides, also felt that the root of anticlericalism lay in the breakdown of the grand system of material and spiritual exchange that underlay universal church's existence as a grand community of sacramental grace and prayer. His explanation for the decay was the laity's perception that "the priests have too

---

[136] Roper, "'Going to Church and Street'", pp. 66–67. The campaign against clandestine marriage characterized all marriage legislation of the time. See Safley, "Civic Morality and the Domestic Economy", pp. 175–76.

[137] AMS, KS 18, fol. 218ʳ, dated 16 April 1529, which mentions him as one of the "verordnete pfleger des wercks zu St. Aurelien". See Jean Rott, "Die 'Gartner', der Rat und das Thomaskapitel", in Jean Rott, *Investigationes Historicae*, 2: pp. 177–80.

[138] Augustin in 1537 and Augustin Chrysostomus in 1542. Six of these children died before age fifteen. Wilhelm Horning, *Beiträge zur Kirchengeschichte des Elsasses vom 16.–18. Jahrhundert*, 7 vols. (Strasbourg, 1881–1887), 7: pp. 1–3.

[139] AMS, V 14/112 (1571).

[140] Bernd Moeller, "Kleriker als Bürger", in *Festschrift für Hermann Heimpel zum 70. Geburtstag zum 19. September 1971*, edited by the Max-Planck-Institut für Geschichte, 3 vols. (Göttingen, 1971–1972), 2: pp. 195–224; id., *Pfarrer als Bürger* (Göttingen, 1972).

much", but his sole remedy, short of expropriation, was that the clergy must be urged to moderation and to more faithful devotion to service. His emphasis on communal service—bishop and priests are servants of the community—probably stood in tension with his sacramental conception of the common good, for it is clear from his anticipation of listeners' questions that stronger skepticism attached to the universal than to the local exchange of spiritual and material goods between clergy and laity. This, in turn, suggests that domestication, cutting the local church off from the greater church, might be the most effective path to integration. For this reason, it is surely correct to identify (with Scribner) the clergy's sacral power as the critical aspect of their power, and to say that the reformers' attack on the sacramental notion of the church made possible a provisional reintegration of the clergy through a whole series of measures.[141] These measures included suppression of the *privilegium fori* and spiritual jurisdiction, expropriation, abolition of mandatory celibacy, mandatory clerical citizenship, dissolution of the convents, and a great reduction in the numbers of clergy. Together they constituted perhaps the principal social change wrought by the Protestant reformation in the Holy Roman Empire, the magnitude of which is undiminished by our recognition that, after a decent interval, a new clericalism succeeded the old.[142]

The austere Geiler may well have underestimated, on the other hand, the importance of the clergy's sexual power and the burgher's longing to have it controlled. Both the facts and the obvious remedy had long been recognized, for example, by the anonymous priest who wrote in the late 1430s *The Reformation of the Emperor Sigismund:*

> It may be a good thing for a man to keep himself pure, but observe the wickedness now going on in the Church! Many priests have lost their livings because of women. Or they are secret sodomites. All the hatred existing between priests and laymen is due to this. In sum:

---

[141] Scribner, "Anticlericalism", p. 249: "Sacred power can be taken as a measure of all other clerical pretensions, and can be seen as the ultimate fountain of all kinds of anticlericalism. . . . What seems to have aroused most lay anger was three things: clerical claims to exercise a monopoly of sacred power; their demand that this be provided only in return for payment; and their readiness to deny their priestly services, often for light causes and often because of the inability of layfolk to pay." Much the same point—desacralization as the condition for radical change—is made on a grander scale by Carlos M. N. Eire, *War Against the Idols: The Reformation of Worship from Erasmus to Calvin* (Cambridge, 1986).

[142] Scribner, "Anticlericalism", pp. 254–56.

> Secular priests ought to be allowed to marry. In marriage they will
> live more piously and honorably, and the friction between them and
> the laity will disappear.[143]

Luther and the other Protestant reformers accepted this diagnosis
and its remedy, which they supplied with a theological justification.[144]
They thus canonized in word and deed one traditional diagnosis of
and remedy for anticlericalism, but it was not Geiler's diagnosis,
nor his remedy. In this respect, the Strasbourg Protestants' respect
for Johann Geiler rested on a very limited kinship between his imagined reform and their accomplished one. The Protestants shared
Geiler's ideal of the clergy devoted to communal service but not his
view of the clergy's role in the church as a community of sacramental grace and prayer. It was Luther, not Geiler, who opened the
path to integration of the clergy through desacralizing them and
their social role, and he thereby brought down the walls against
reform that Geiler had attacked in vain. Luther's attack on this sacramental view of the church may well have constituted his most
powerful contribution to the urban reformation; it was certainly his
major contribution to overcoming late medieval anticlericalism.

As Geiler had hardly anticipated the coming desacralization of the
clergy, he certainly could not have foreseen its effects on the regular clergy, men and women. The story of Margarethe Kniebis cannot be explained as a lay reaction to clerical abuses, for her father
removed her from one of the strictest religious communities at Strasbourg, into which he had brought her some years before. Only Claus
Kniebis' changed sensibilities explain this act, and the same may
well be true of other removals, such as that of Clara Sturm. Here,
again, the events must be seen in the light of the Protestant reformers' attacks on the religious orders in general and the women's
houses in particular. Their attack succeeded in part because their
theology empowered the burghers' deep views about the proper place
of women. As Luther put it in 1523, "a woman is not created to
be a virgin, but to conceive and bear children."[145] He and the other

---

[143] "The Reformation of the Emperor Sigismund", trans. Gerald Strauss in *Manifestations of Discontent in Germany on the Eve of the Reformation* (Bloomington, 1971), pp.
14–15.

[144] Ozment, *When Fathers Ruled*, pp. 3–9.

[145] Quoted in Ozment, *When Fathers Ruled*, p. 17, from Martin Luther, *Ursach und
anttwort das iungkfawen kloster gottlich verlassen mugen* (Wittenberg, 1523).

reformers did not cause men to remove their kinswomen from convents so much as they legitimized action based on the burgher's sensibilities about relations between the genders.[146] Such sensibilities were by no means universal among the burghers, and particularly not among the upper class, whose daughters had long populated the urban convents. During the struggle over the house of the Poor Clares at Nuremberg, for example, male patricians reacted in different ways to pressure to remove their kinswomen from the convent. The patrician Christoph Kress (1484–1535), for example, bluntly told his fellow magistrates what he thought: "I have told my sister that if one cowl is not enough for her, she may wear three, one on top of other. And then we'll see who will try to forbid it or to take them away from her."[147] Next day, however, male members of the Ebner, Nützel, Tetzel, and Fürer families arrived at St. Clara's to fetch their daughters home. Some women, like Margarethe Kniebis, had to be forced to leave, but others were glad to go, sometimes—as with Felicitas Peutinger, who left St. Katherine's at Augsburg—against parental wishes.[148]

It has been argued that in this "liberation of women from cloisters", the Protestant reformers "were particularly concerned . . . to free nuns from their cloisters, and allow them to rejoin society", because of the "reformers' own recent appreciation of the joys of marriage."[149] Perhaps, but our judgment ought to pay attention both to the views of the women who were subject to such "liberation" and to the fact that they were being "liberated" from one type of authority into the hands of another, the male authority of fathers, brothers, guardians, and husbands. This aspect is neatly expressed by Prioress

---

[146] The story thus confirms Roper's judgment that Protestant reformers brought the understanding of marriage, and of all matters of gender, closer to the burghers' own views. Roper, "'Going to Church and Street'", pp. 65–70.

[147] Related in *Die "Denkwürdigkeiten" der Caritas Pirckheimer (as den Jahren 1524–1528)*, ed. Josef Pfanner, Caritas Pirckheimer Quellensammlung, vol. 2 (Landshut, 1962), p. 75, ll. 38–76, l. 1. These men came from the political cream of Nuremberg's oligarchy. See Phillip N. Bebb, "Humanism and the Reformation: The Nürnberg *Sodalitas* Revisted", *The Process of Change in Early Modern Europe*, ed. P. Bebb and S. Marshall, pp. 59–79, here at 65. On Kress, see Jonathan W. Zophy, "Christoph Kress, Nürnberg's Foremost Reformation Diplomat" (Ph.D. diss., Ohio State University, 1972).

[148] Roper, *Holy Household*, p. 210.

[149] Ozment, *When Fathers Ruled*, pp. 9, 12–13; the first phrase quoted is a subhead in a chapter entitled, "In Defense of Marriage", which contains an eloquent defense of the Protestant reformers.

Ursula von Mörßmünster's formula of re-commendation—"I give her from my hand to your hand, from my care to your care"—which laicized Margarethe Kniebis and reintegrated her into communal life by passing her back from a woman's authority to that of a man. The world of the burghers, especially Protestant burghers, had no place for female authority, even when women did not altogether lack power.[150]

This picture of the mutual reinforcement of the urban reformation, clerical integration, and the control of women is contradicted, but only apparently, by the story of Drenss vs. Hedio. One has only to recognize the connection between celibacy and the sacral power of the clergy, both for men and for women, in order to appreciate how their desacralization through the reformers made possible the control of their sexuality as part of their integration. Agnes Drenss and her son, Augustin, did not disagree about the desirability of having a chaste clergy, only about how that goal was to be achieved. He called on the regime to enforce the canon, Imperial, and local laws; she referred to the new gospel as providing a remedy, marriage of the clergy, for the evil of which they both disapproved. They agreed on this, at least in principle, for in practice personal interests—the desires respectively to marry off the daughter and to save the dowry—may have weighed heavily with both mother and son. The actions of Agnes Drenss show that in the absence of a father, authority over dependent women could devolve on the mother rather than on the son, not only in practice—as we should expect—but also in the eyes of the magistrates. The case also illustrates the intertwining of private with public affairs, for though born of a familial dispute, Drenss vs. Hedio was also highly political, both because it involved the conflict over religion which then occupied the city, and because of an ammeister's involvement.[151] Agnes Drenss had her way against her son, Caspar Hedio got his bride, and only in the irregular form of the wedding does the story bear the stamp of the tran-

---

[150] I do not mean only that former monks could remain clergy and former nuns could not, though this is true (see Wiesner, "Nuns, Wives, and Mothers", p. 10). Rather, I mean the exclusively male character of civic language and political sensibility, on which see Lyndal Roper, "'The common man', 'the common good', 'common women': Gender and Meaning in the German Reformation Commune", *Social History* 12 (1987): pp. 1–21 here at pp. 2–5.
[151] The dichotomy of public and private does not adequately express the consistent differences between male and female lives, at least not in early modern Europe. See *ibid.*, p. 21; Wiesner, "Nuns, Wives, and Mothers", p. 9.

sition period when the gospel shattered laws. Otherwise, this story and its outcome fit the broad pattern of the urban reformation, in which the desacralization of the church opened the way to a settlement of the question of reform, which had so bedeviled Johann Geiler. It enabled the integration of the clergy into the commune through their conformity to the only social ideal—the patriarchal household—for which the burghers had thoroughgoing respect. With different results, naturally, for men and for women.

Do these materials and stories shed any light on the conclusions framed by Francis Rapp? Perhaps. For one thing, they suggest that the important changes of the pre-reformation had less to do with clerical behavior than with lay standards of behavior for the clergy, which were based on their standards for themselves. They were becoming intolerant not just of a clergy that misbehaved but of one that lived differently. If anything, the holiest nuns and the most austere priests threatened their own ideals more deeply than did dissolute nuns and whoring priests, for the success of a celibate way of life relativized and therefore devalued, by its very success, their own ideal of the harmonious and hierarchical household. To burghers who were ever more used to running their own affairs and having their own way, the very existence of wayward clergy eased the moral pressure placed on their own ideal way of life by the existence of another, stricter, harder way to salvation. This sensibility—relief at the clergy's imperfections—lies behind much of the anticlerical humor of the pre-reformation era. A wayward clergyman might arouse anger, but not spiritual intimidation. The reformation made such humor obsolete, at least in principle at Strasbourg and other reformed cities, as an old and extremely varied way of life was suppressed. With it went the old jokes, such as one composed by the young Peter Schott (1460–1490), Jacob Sturm's great-uncle, who as a schoolboy at Sélestat is said to have penned these lines:

> These three things you should never let into your home:
> An old ape, a young priest, or wild bears.[152]

---

[152] "Alt aff, jung pfaff, dazu wilde Bären/Soll niemand in sein Haus begehren." Geiler, *Das Buoch Arbore humana* (Strasbourg, 1521), p. 91. The couplet is also quoted in *Works of Peter Schott (1460–1490)*, ed. Murray A. Cowie and Marian L. Cowie, 2 vols., University of North Carolina Studies in the Germanic Languages and Literatures 41, 71 (Chapel Hill, 1963–1971), 1: p. 266, no. 234; and Schmidt, *Histoire littéraire*, 2: p. 4 n. 7. On Schott, see *Works of Peter Schott*, 2: pp. xxii–xxxi; Schmidt, *Histoire littéraire*, 2: pp. 2–35.

APPENDIX: DOCUMENTS ON COMMUNALISM AND THE CONTROL OF WOMEN AT STRASBOURG IN THE AGE OF THE REFORMATION

The following six documents are edited by Katherine G. Brady and Thomas A. Brady, Jr. according to the following guidelines.

- Only initial letters of sentences and proper nouns are capitalized; all other words begin in lower case.
- Punctuation follows the rules for modern German, and long sentences are often broken into shorter ones.
- All abbreviations are resolved.
- Except for verbs, words with prefix "zu" are normally put together.
- The distinctions between vowel "i" and consonant "j" and between vowel "u" and consonant "v" and "w" have been normalized.
- The letters "f" and "v" are interchangeable.

For analysis of the documents and information on the persons mentioned in them, readers are referred to the study they accompany. The editors express their gratitude to Dr. Jean-Yves Mariotte, Director of the Archives de la Ville de Strasbourg, for his kind assistance.

DOCUMENT NO. 1

Claus Kniebis removes his daughter, Margarethe, from the
Convent of St. Nicolaus-in-Undis, Strasbourg, 1522

SOURCE: Archives Municipales de Strasbourg, II 7/20, fols.
26ʳ–29bisᵛ.
HAND: Ursula von Mörßmünster, prioress of St. Nicolaus-in-Undis.[1]

[fol. 27ʳ] Anno xvᶜ xxii uff den xᵐ ritter dag[2] ist Herr Claus Kniebis[3]
bei uns an der winden gewesen und bei siner dochter, Margreden,[4]
die het in frintlich gebetten, um gotts willen ir zu gönnen, das versuch jor an zu legen, si sige im xiiii jor. Das hat er ir abgeslagen,
geseit, wann si xvi oder xvii jor alt werde, und nit e, si es echter
zu der selben zit nach sin will oder gutbeduncken. Er welle si aber
ain zit lang vor in sinen huß in der welt versächen und probieren.
Het si sich vast übel gehebt, in ernstlich do fur gebetten, zu im geseit
zu vil molen, si well slechtlich nit hinuß, well nit in der welt sin.
Werde er si aber hinuß zwingen, welle si vor got entschuldiget sin,
müß dennocht ir will, nimmer me werden in der welt zu sin, und
derglichen vil und me wort. Do ist der vater erzürnt warden uber
unß und die dochter, het geseit, well si nit hinuß, so müß si hinuß.
Si soll hinuß gon, glich in ein tufel namen. Het si geseit, in dem
namen well si nit hinuß, si well in gottes namen, und umb gotts
willen hin sin, in der meinung, er si öch harin geben hab, und mit
siner eigen hant selbs zu opfer gefürt. Und het in aber frintlich gebetten, umb gotts willen er soll si hinlossen, und wir öch. Und hab ich
im zu geseit, ich woll im die dochter lossen still ston mit dem versuch jor, bis si xiiii jar alt si. Do zwischen werden unser obren[5]
komen, will ich im sin meinung sagen, will er zu losse, si so lang
bitz xvii jar lossen gon, well ich gehorsam sin. Will er aber einan-
ders, will ich aber gehorsam sin und in das selb öch lossen wissen.
Disse red geschach vor dem, das er so erzürnt was, und [er] nam
das an. Aber zu lest, do er also erzürnt was, swür er, er wolt die

---

[1] The hand is an old-fashioned, late fifteenth-century hand, perhaps because of
the prioress' age, or perhaps because the nuns preserved an older style of writing.
[2] Ten Thousand Knights' Day, 22 June 1522.
[3] Ammeister Claus Kniebis (1479–1552).
[4] Margarethe, daughter of Claus Kniebis.
[5] I.e., the Dominican provincial.

dochter in zweien dagen holen. Es müst also sin, und slechtlich nit anders. Bei dissen ist zu gegen geweß Her Hug Meiger,[6] vicarius der hohen stift.

Uff den abend des dags der vergangnen geschicht, schreib ich der frowen[7] ein brieflin, bat si demüticlich, ein getruwe mittlerin zu sin zwischen dem zorn des vaters, der dochter, und unser.

Do noch am dritten dag[8] habe ich dem herrn selbs geschriben, und die dochter auch, in demüticlich um gotts willen gebetten um verzühung, sinen zorn abzulossen und unser guten frint zu sin. Het er unß entboten, er wolle unß dun, alles das uns lieb ist. Er well aber slechtlich die dochter hinuß haben.

Uff dise wort ist die dochter genug betrüpt und ellend, von der x^m ritter dag untz uff Martini[9] het [sie] alledag mit engsten und schrecken gewartet, wenn er si holen welle. Denn er ir noch unß do zwischen chein ander antwort geben het, den i mol, iii oder iiii mol zwischen der zit unß entboten bei unsern schafner, er si noch des willens, sin dochter hinuß zu nemen, er well si nit bei unß haben. Also ist das kint ellend gangen, sich verjomert und betrübt, das si zusehenlich an iren lib und kreften abgenomen hett, das ich es jriencie[10] halb nin hab mögen sehen noch liden. Ist er öch do zwischen nie zu unß kommen haruß, das ichs hot mögen mit im reden.

Also hab ich siner frowen der dochter mutter uff zinstag S. Martins dag einen brief geschriben, wie die dochter sich verellende und betrüpt si, an iren lib abnemen, [und] si geboten, den herrn frintlich zu bitten, das er der dochter zu friden helf, wie den die copi des briefs lutet also gezeicht.[11] Also ist Herr Claus Kniebis dem schriben noch mit dem alten herrn, Herr Hug Maiger, kommen uff Fritag noch Martini,[12] het gesait, er hab in dem. . . .[13]
[fol. 27^v blank]
[fol. 28^r] Min liebs kint, do stat din vater. Der hat dich geben in dis closter, in meinung zu sin der will, das gevallen im die ere gottes

---

[6] Hug Meyer, priest and vicar in the cathedral chapter, brother to Claus Kniebis' mother.

[7] Ottilia Rot, sister to Dr. Michael Rot.

[8] 25 June 1522.

[9] St. Martin's Day, 11 November 1522.

[10] iwwerenzi = übrig, übereinzig. Charles Schmidt. *Wörterbuch der Straßburger Mundart* (Strasbourg, 1896), p. 54.

[11] Here a flower is drawn.

[12] 14 November 1522.

[13] The remainder of this paragraph is missing.

und diner selen seliklich. In der selben guten meinung hant wir dich
um gotts willen angenommen, und dich nun im fünften jor nit mit
cleiner arbeit erzogen und gelert. Jetzt ist eß nun der will dins vaters,
das du solt bei unß [nit] sin, und will dich bei im duß haben.
Und het unß getröwen, wo wir dich [nit] im gutwilliclich geben,
well er etwas zu richt, das wir dich im müssen geben. Des tröwes
und gewalts wollent wir nit warten sin, darumb wollent und müssen
wir dich im geben. Ich wolt dich aber lieber sehen in ein grab legen,
denn das ich dich müß sehen in die welt gon. So er dich aber je
haben will, so gib ich dich uß miner hant in sin hant, uß miner
sorg in sin sorge. Wir stossent dich nit uß und wellent dich öch
unußgestossen haben, denn du hests nit verschuldet. Du waist, das
dich der convent lieb und wert gehebt het, und noch. Ich bin dir
vil inert gemess, das hab ich dir im besten gedon. Ich hab dich nit
wellen betrügen oder verfüren, das ich dir zum ersten zäigte das
süß, und so du gebunden wurdest, das bitter. Ich hab dir von erst
wollen zäigen das bitter, ob es dich rüwen wolt. Das es dich ruwete,
öb du gebunden wurdest, darumb solt du mir es nit fur übel. Und
gesegne und behüt dich got, liebs kint. Und ich bitt dich, hab got
alwegen vor ögen, gedenck die kürtze diß lebens, wie alle ding
zergont als der röuch. Das end aller ding, so uff erden sint, ist der
bitter dot. Der kant und blibt nit uß. Bedenck den spruch, daß wiß
manns, do er spricht, mensch gedenck diner lesten stend, so gesin-
destu niemer. Schrib in din hertz die vier lesten ding, der wir warten
sint, die unfelich kommen, und nit ußbliben, das ist der dot, das lest
streng urteil gottes, die ewige fröid. Die gab der Her bereit hett,
denen die in lieb haben, und die ewige verdampnuß, die denen
bereit ist, die sich von got abwenden.

Das ist uwe dochter, die gib ich uch uß miner hant in uwer hant,
uß miner sorg in uwer sorg. Nun welle got, das ir si wol versorgen.
Ich gib uch ein gut, fromm, unschuldig kint. Got woll, das ir eß
also behalten, und wo ir harnoch anders begegnen wurd, wellen wir
vor got und vor uch entschuldiget sein.

[fol. 28ᵛ blank]

[fol. 29ʳ] Uff Sonndag noch Presentacionis Marie, ist Sant Clemens
dag,[14] het der Kniebis sin dochter uß dem closter gerissen. Im geholfen
Michel Rot.[15]

---

[14] St. Clement's Day, 23 November 1523.
[15] Dr. med. Michael Rot, brother-in-law to Claus Kniebis.

Uff S. katherinen dag Anno xxii hat Jacob Spender[16] sin dochter, Jacobe, uß dem closter genommen.

[fol. 29bis^v] Diß ist wie Her Klaus Kniebis sin dochter uß unßren kloster mit gewalt genomen hatt und wie mutter Ursel von Morschminster zur selben zit priorin und öch der convent sich dorin gehalten haben.

DOCUMENT NO. 2

Drenss vs. Hedio: Petition of Augustin Drenss
[14 May 1524]

SOURCE: Archives du Chapître de St.-Thomas, Strasbourg, 69/2, fols. 5^r–6^r.

HAND: Augustin Drenss.

[fol. 5^r] Strengen, edlen, erenvesten, ersamen, frumen, fursichtigen, wisen, gnödigen herren. Wie wol durch euer, meiner gnödigen herren, ordnung, artickel und altem herkhomen bei hochen penen und strafen verboten, das do nieman khainem vater sin khind wider sinen willen und im zu ruck zu usseren zu verenderen oder zu entziechen. Und welcher do funden wurdt dar zu sollichem hilf oder rat thon hett, der soll deß gestraft werden. In welchem fall wo das khind vaterloß wer, ein vogt von euch, minen gnödigen herren, im geben nach inhalt dis artickel fur ein vater geacht soll werden. Uber sollichen artickel gar unangesechen hat kurtzer verschiner ziten Doctor Caspar Hedion, predicant im munster, understanden und im furgenomen, Margret Thrensin, meins schwoster, heimlich und on wissen und wider willen eins vogt und minen, als irs elichen bruders, im zu elichen gmahel, als mich anlangt, understanden anzumassen. Und das durch sollich mittel, es hat Michael Rott, doctor der artznei, benante miner schwoster sampt ir mutter in sin huß zu tisch geladen und darzu heimlich on wißen der mutter und der dochter, als ich wisen mag gehabt, und verhalten bestimpten Doctor Caspar Hedion. Darzu ouch beruft, hernach worden Herr Clauß Kniebis alt ammeister ouch khommen, die do mit glatten worten die dochter und mutter beredt, das do etwas zusagens und der handschlag als die red offenlich

beschehen soll sin und wie wol gemelt min mutter und schwöster
sich mit zimlichen worten ab ziechen wellen, sagende, das inen sollichs nit hinder irem vogt bruder und fruntschaft gepuren welle. Aber
gemelten personen min lieb mutter und schwester nit von handen
laßen wellen, besunder gesagt, es werde khein mangel haben, gemelter
Herr Claus Kniebis und Doctor Michel wellendt sollichs bei mir
abtragen. Als ouch an anderen tag darnach si baidt mit dem schafner
in der Ellenden Herberg zu mir khomen und mich mit glatten worten
uberreden wollen, hab ich mich gegen inen hören lassen, das kheiniß
wegs darzu gehellen welle, mit mer worten etc. Uff sollichs gemelter
Kniebis [fol. 5ᵛ] mir den friden gepoten. Ist nit euwer, meiner herren,
ordnung, gemelter Hedion were dann zu gegen gewesen. Aber in ab-
wesen einer parthi ist frömdt zuhoren on geheiße der oberkheit, ein
burger dem anderen frid zubieten.[17] Und uber sollich alles ist ge-
dachts min schwester in gemeltz Doctor Michels huß, welher doch
khein eefrow in sinem huß haben ist,[18] muß ich und mein fruntschaft
zu diser zit gott befelchen. Sollich alles ist geschehen uber das ich
bei meinem schweher, Mathis Rotten, und ander gemelten Doctor
Rott, Hedion und Kniebis dar zugepötten und bitten lassen. Ouch
ich zu meiner mutter, schwester und anderen, do mir sollichs furkhe-
men, gesagt, min swester solle der pfaffen mießig ston und sunst
einen erlichen frummen burger nemen, so wil ich mines gutzs ir hundert gulden zu irem eigenthum fursetzen. Und diewill aber der doctor geisthlich und sollich ee nit allein nit landtlöfig und bruchlich
funden, ouch wider alle recht geisthlich und weltlich, dero si die
Cristenheit dusent jar und noch lenger gebrucht hat, und ouch daruß
mir und den meinerm nit kleiner nachteil, schandt und schmach erwachsen möcht, dann wo ein ordenliche geburende oberkheit der
Cristenheit sollich handel nit nach lassen wurd sunder verbieten und
kheins wegs gestatten, als zu erachten, geschehen werd. Dann je nit
gloublich, das durch frevel furnemen ettlicher und der wenig bep-
stlich und keiserlich recht umgestossen und zuruck geworfen mag
werden. Als dan wurd billich mein swester wie ein offne sunderin
und metz geacht und gehalten. Verer, wo sie bei benantem doctor
khind uberkhomen wurdt und die mutter oder großmutter mit tod

---

[17] The practice of "geboter Friede" was an admonition to keep the peace, that
is, refrain from violence, until a matter could be settled at law or by arbitration.
[18] Dr. Michael Rot later married. His widow, whose name is unknown, died
in 1555.

abgeen solten, mochten solliche khindt verlassens gutz mit kheinem
rechten erben sin, darum dann sie billich als uneelich geacht wur-
den, Welches alles, gnödigen herren, nit zu kleinem nachteil, schmach
und schanden mir und den minen dienen möcht. Und diewill dann
sollich vermeint ee durch benanten doctor und ander als obluwt
wider euwer, meiner gnödigen herren, ordnung und alten herkhomen
gehandlet und furgenomen ist und nach allen [fol. 6ʳ] rechten sollich ee nit sin khan und mag, bitt ich undertenigklich, euch meine
genödigen herren, ir wolt mich und die minen als euer gnaden burger zu guten und gnaden bedencken, und mit oft benanten doctor
verschaffen, das er von solchem sinem furnemen abstandt miner
swester und minem, anders dann mit dem rechten mussig gan. Wo
aber sollich je sin nit möcht, der zuversicht ich doch zu euch, meinen
herren, bin, bitt ich euer gnad, ir wolt mir nit zu wider sin sunder
bewiligung thun, das ich an anderen orten vor geburenden richtern
und fur die sollich hendell gehören mit dem rechten ersuchen mög.
Dann solt es je do hin khomen, das ein jedem pfaffen und munch
zimmen und geburen wolt, on witer ungeltnuß einem frumen bider-
man und burger sine khindt oder verwanten wider wissen und willen
zu betriegen und zu bescheissen, wer sollich schimpflich zu hören.
Und was dar uß erwachsen möcht, khunnen ir, meine gnödigen herren, wol ermessen. Hierin ich dan unzweifelter hoffnung und zu ver-
sicht bin, ir, meine gnödigen herren, werden mir als einem burger
beraten und beholfen sin, damit mein beger als obluwt der billicheit
und rechten nach stathaben möge. Oder aber wo sollichs nit kheiner
parthi zu beladen, wil ich anderweg dem rechten und billicheit nach
an orten und enden, da sich sollichs geburt, zu rechtvertigen nit
underlassen, euwer gnad zum aller hochsten anrufende etc.

Euer gnödigen wißheit undertöniger burger

Augustinus Trenß, burger zu Straßburg etc.

[fols. 6ᵛ, 7ʳ⁻ᵛ blank]

DOCUMENT NO. 3

Drenss vs. Hedio:
Response of Dr. Michael Rot and Ammeister Claus Kniebis
[ca. 14 May 1524]

SOURCE: Archives du Chapître de St.-Thomas, Strasbourg, 69/3, fols. 8^r–9^v.
HAND: Claus Kniebis.

[fol. 8^r] Strengen, erenvesten, fursichtigen, ersamen und wisen gunstigen heren. Euer ersamen wißheit hat uff nest vergangen pfingst aben[19] verlesen horen, ein vermeinte supplication, so durch Augustin Trensen ingeben, darin er den wurdigen der heiligen gotlichen schriften hochgelerten lerer, Doctor Casparn Hedion, sin schwoger, schwerlich verunglimpftet und verclaget etc. Darzu den hochgelerten Doctor Micheln Rot, min schwogern, und mich, Clausen Kniebiß etc., als ob wir zu etwas gescheften, die unß nit geburten, und im zu nit kleiner schmach, nachteil und schanden reichten geholfen, und darzu mit glatten worten sin muter und schwester beredt. Und uber daß si sich mit zimlichen worten abziehen wollen, sollen wir si nit von handen lossen wollen etc, alles inhalt gemelter siner vermeinten, erdichten, unworhaftigen supplication etc. So dann ich als ein altammeister bei euch, min herrn, gesessen und sollichs verlesen horen, darin min schwoger und ich unser eren nit klein (so dem also were) geschmecht, hat mir gebürt, sollichs zu verantwurten. Und hab uff daß mol mich protestiert vor euer wißheit, die schmach schriften, wie sich gebürt zu siner zit zu rechtvertigen, als ich von wegen mins schwogers und min uff hüt aber protestiert haben will, [MARGIN: protestiert mich ouch wes hie anzeigt wurt, keiner ander meinung, dann unß zu verantwurten und die worheit als vil wir wissen, dar zu thun, do mit euwer wißheit erfar, mit was fugen der gegentheil suppliciert]. Und uff daß ich die obigen sin vermeint unworhaftig supplication mit der worheit, als vil die unß belangt, verantwurdte, hab ich die zit der selbigen abgeschriften begert, die mir von euch, min herrn, gutlich zu gelossen, die ich dann als bald minem schwoger, als dem, den si ouch zum hochsten belangt, angezeigt. Der hat si dem obigen herrn Doctor Casparn, als dem principal beclagten, ouch

---

[19] Pentecost Eve, 14 May 1524.

nit wollen verhalten, und anzeigt, sich dem nach wissen zu richten etc. Und uff daß ir, min herrn, der worheit bericht werden, so hat es die gestalt und ist ergangen, als harnach volget. Namlich, sagt Doctor Michel, min schwoger, das er uff den selben tag den obgemelten Doctor Casparn weder frow Anges Trensen noch Jungfrow Margred, ire dochter, keins geladen als von Augustin ußerthalb der worheit angezeigt. Aber si nit on, es si Doctor Caspar in sin, Doctor Michels, als in [fol. 8ᵛ] sines guten und lieben frinds und gönners, huß komen, und als gelerte lute von allerlei frintlich gesprech gehabt. Und als si ein gut wile bieinander gewesen, on aller menschen schühe oder forcht, nit heimlich [MARGIN: als Augustin sagt] verhalten, ist im on wissen genante frow Agnes Trensen und Jungfrow Margred, ir dochter, an daß thor komen anklopfende. Die er, Doctor Michel, als sin mumen²⁰ ingelossen und frintlich entpfangen, die do gesagt (als ouch wor ist), er, Doctor Michel, habe vor iiii wochen do vor ungeverlich si geladen, si sollen eins zu jme komen und sehen, wie er huß halte etc. Daruff so konnen si wie er das begert witer, als nun si in Doctor Michels huß gewesen, haben si witer gesprech gehalten und einander angezeigt, wie vil red iren halben allenthalben in der stat sei von dem, als si ungeverlichen vor iii wochen einander mit der hand verheissen die ee. Und haben doch sollichs willen gehabt zu verbergen bitz noch Pfingsten. So aber also vil red do von sei, so dunckte si gut, daß si jemants guter frind beschicken und vor den selben sollichs offentlich ouch theten und bekanten etc. Doruff si etlich beschickt und under andern, so hat in dem nacht imbiß genanter min schwoger mich, Clausen Kniebiß, ouch selb erbeten, mit im in sin huß zu gon zu etlichen guten frinden und mir nit eroffnet, was ich thun solte. Also bin ich mit im gangen in sin huß. So bald ich darin komen, hab ich Doctor Casparn, Jungfrow Margreden, ir muter und andern, so ouch darzu beschickt, do funden, die mich bericht, warumb ich also beschickt, und mich gebeten, wie woll si der sach mit einander dohin eins und die ee einander gelobt, so bitten si mich, doch si zu samen zu geben ouch offentlich. Des ich mich gewidert und vermeint, es solt das einander thun dann ich, so ich doch nit priester were etc. Und doch uff ire begere mich bereden lossen, daß ich bewilligt, und die mutter und die dochter (die ich vormals nit kandte) angesprochen, inen die handt geboten und gegrußt, und also Doctor Casparn und die dochter jeglichs

---

²⁰ That is, his kinswoman.

gefragt, ob es des andern zu der heiligen ehe begere etc. Und noch
ire antwort als si beidersit jo sagten, zusamen geben und vil glücks
friden und genod gewinscht etc. [fol. 9ʳ] Und sunst hab ich, Clauß
Kniebiß, die mutter und die dochter weder mit glatten noch mit
rüwen worten angesprochen, ouch gar nit zu thun oder zu lossen
beredt, ouch si nit behalten oder si nit von handen lossen wollen
(als er erdichtlich on worheit schriftlich anzeigt), sunder nit anders
dann wie hie vor angezeigt mit ire geredt. Was ouch gar nit not,
dann die sach vorhin beschlossen gewesen (als si sagen). Nach disem
sind wir gesessen zu tisch und bei einander das nachtmol frölich
genomen, und noch dem nachtmol haben genanter Doctor Caspar,
frow Agnes Trensin und ire dochter Doctor Micheln, min schwogern,
und mich mit sundern fliß und ernst gebeten, daß wir und etlich
andere mit unß sollen gon zu Augustin Trensen, iren sun, bruder
und schwoger, und in uff das frintlichst ansuchen und bitten, das er
sin willen (dann er des nit wol zu friden sei) darzu gebe und inen
thu das inen liebe sei, daß wollen sei in alle weg ouch thun. Daß
hab ich uff ir flissig bitt bewilligt und mich vor mols nit erboten,
ouch nit do von geredt oder sei etwas vertrost, als er, Augustin,
unworhaftiglich anzeigt. Uff den andern tag²¹ bin ich mit Doctor
Michel und den schafner in der herberg²² hinuß gangen und uff der
gartner stuben under wagner²³ funden die ersamen unser lieben und
guten frind und vettern Lorentzen Grofen,²⁴ Mathis Roten²⁵ und
Jacob Trensen.²⁶ Die haben wir bericht, wes wir willens, und si
gebeten, unß ouch helfen, frintschaft zu behalten und machen etc.
In dem haben wir Augustin obigen ouch beruft und mit im wie
obstat vilfaltig geredt und umb gottes willen sin selbs, sins weibs,
kinder, und fruntschaft willen, sin willen abzustellen. Darin er mit
vil andern worten anzeigt, er were bedocht, des mochten wir Doctor

---

²¹ 24 April 1524.
²² Lux Hackfurt († 6 April 1554), since 15 August 1523 manager (*Schaffner*) of the
municipal poor house. Johannes Ficker and Otto Winckelmann, *Handschriftenproben
des 16. Jahrhunderts nach Straßburger Originalen*, 2 vols. (Strasbourg, 1902–1905), 2: p. 78.
²³ The guildhall of the Gartner unter Wagnern, one of three halls of the Gardeners'
Guild.
²⁴ Lorentz Graff († 8/9 July 1553), gardener; married 1534 Katharina Apt; XVᵉʳ
from the Gardeners' Guild 1524–1542; Evangelical by January 1524. Thomas A.
Brady, Jr., *Ruling Class, Regime, and Reformation at Strasbourg, 1520–1555*, SMRT 22
(Leiden, 1978), p. 316.
²⁵ Obviously the physician's kinsman.
²⁶ This may be the Jacob Drenss who as a clergyman studied at Heidelberg in
1512–1514. Brady, *Ruling Class*, p. 308.

Caspar sagen, er wolt im noch gon, so lang biß er Doctorn Casparn betrete, so wolte er in erwürgen, oder er muste es im thun. Mit vil anderen, trotzigen, unfrindtlichen trow worten uber unser aller vil faltige bitt und ermanen, so wir theten, mit dem das wir im anzeigten, was im schand daruß [fol. 9ᵛ] erwachsen mochte etc. Als er aber daruff behart, gedocht ich, wo ein burger dem andern vor schaden sein mocht und in sunderheit vor todschlegen, das er sollichs zuthun schuldig, und zeigt im an. Die wil er also uff sinen furnemen verhart und dann ich sollichs horte, so were ich schuldig, daß (so vil mir moglich) zu furkomen und gebote im do mit in gegenwertig obgenanter siner und unser guten frind, nitzt in ungutem gegen Doctor Casparn, siner muter, und schwester ouch gegen den, so darin verwant weren, furzunemen mit der thät. Sunder hette er ansprach an jeman, solte er mit recht thun, friden halten, das gebiete ich im als euer, des Radts, als hoch in den friden zu gebieten hette etc. Uff sollichs er wider antwort gab, gebiete ich zum friden, so wolte er die nit halten etc. Uber sollich alles haben wir alle in mer gebeten, von sinem fursatz abzuston. Er verharret aber, wie er gesagt, dem nach zu komen, und haben also mussen ungethan abscheiden. Also ist es und nit anders ergangen. So nun ir min herrn hören, daß diser handel gar nit ist, als er in anzeigt, und die so die obigen vermeint unworhaftig supplication erdicht. So ist uff diß mol Doctor Michels, mines schwagers, und min underthenig bitt und beger, Augustin Trensen als dem, der unß unbillich, schmechelich antast in siner vermeinten erdichten supplication und clag, absolvieren mit körung costens und in ein ewig stil schweigen uff legen, vor behalten Doctor Michel und mir zu gelegener zit dise injurii, wie recht und sich geburt zu rechtvertigen. Hie mit euer er, wißheit flissig anrufen, hoff ouch, euer wißheit werd Doctor Michel und mir glouben geben, als den die sich bitzhar (als wir hoffen) unverwißlich gehalten. Beger ouch zu meren bericht, wo not, alle, die ee do bei gewesen, deßhalb zu verhoren.

Euer strengen, fursichtigen, wisen gehorsamen burger

Doctor Michel Rot und

Clauß Kniebiß

DOCUMENT NO. 4

Drenss vs. Hedio: Response of Dr. Caspar Hedio
[ca. 14 May 1524]

SOURCE: Archives du Chapître de St.-Thomas, Strasbourg, 69/4,
fols. 10ʳ–11ᵛ.
HAND: Caspar Hedio.

[fol. 10ʳ] Strengen, ernvesten, fursichtigen, ersamen und wisen gendi-
gen herrn. Nach dem in kurtzverruckten tagen Augustinus Trenß,
mein lieber schwager, mir zu ruck und on alle verkündung ein supplication euer gnaden uberantwort,²⁷ und verlösen hat lassen, darin
er mich und andere treffeliche personen unbillich beclagt, und der
massen euer gnaden anbracht, das weder mir noch in zu schweigen
geburen wil. Dan wie wol ein jeden christen schmach oder lesterung
umb der gerechtigkeit willen zu leiden befollen, sollen wir doch der
onwarheit und boßheit mit unserm schweigen kein kraft oder zunemen nit gestatten. Namlich, so sollichs auch unsern nesten belangen
ist, als in dieser handlung der ersame, fursichtige, und weise Her
Claus Kniepse, altammeister, und der hochgelert Her Doctor Michael
Rott unverdienet, wie dan euer gnaden vernemen werden, gezogen
sindt. Und weiter, dieweil ich in meinem bevelch, zu dem ich durch
gots berufung verordnet bin, gern onstroflich sein wolte, zu mherem
furgang der ehr gots und vieler menschen seelen heil, hab ich
angezeigte meins schwagers anclag, und mein und gemelter miner
herrn veronglimpfen nach minem besten vermogen zu entschuldigen,
und zu verantworten nit mogen underlassen, so vil mich von noten
sin beduncken wil. Sag hiruff zum ersten, das mein wil oder gmüt
nie gewesen, und noch nit sei, wider die gebot gots, uß denen ich
wol weiß, das man vater und mutter gehorsam sin soll, noch euer,
miner herren, als weltlicher oberkeit satzung, die wider gots gebot
nit streben, zereissen oder zeubertreten. Darumb mir unbillichen
zugelegt wurt, das ich wider inhalt euer gnaden artickel Junckfrow
Margret zu den ehe erworben habe, dan es ist mit wissen, wollen,
und gutem wolgefallen der ersamen frowen Agnesen Trensin, irer
mutter, miner lieben schwiger beschehen, wolche darumb wol mag
verhort werden. Ich wolte mich auch in mein hertz schemen, das

---

²⁷ Document No. 2.

man mit warheit von mir sagen mochte, wie ich jemans sein dochter oder kind mit list betrug oder alfantz[28] hette understanden zu entweren. Bin auch ungezweifelt, euer gnaden artickel möge in diesem fal der strenge nach nit verstanden werden, das von noten sei, ein bruder, schwester oder vogt in einicher vermehelung zebegrussen, und si darumb zu ersuchen, vorab wo die mutter zu gegen [fol. 10ᵛ] und die dochter zu iren verstendigen jaren kommen ist, auch in ander werbungen von inen etwas hindernuß befunden were etc. Als aber Augustin, mein schwager, mit der lenge erzelet, mit was mittel die dochter wider iren willen mit glatten worten dahin berot sol sin durch Her Claus Kniepsen, Doctor Michaeln und mich, sag ich bei hohem glauben, das beden itzgenanten, min herrn und mir, sollichs ungillich zugemessen wurt. Dan vor und ehe ungeverlich fur iii wochen hat min schwiger vnd ir dochter mir zulößlich antwort und zur heiligen ehe bewilligung geben, mit diesem anhangk, das wir zu gelegner zeit unß des handels, als der gotlich und gerecht vor nimans nit zu bergen, offentlich vernemen lassen wolten. Wie dann uff Georgii[29] in bisein Her Claus Kniepsen und Doctor Michael, beider miner herrn, beschehen ist, on allen widerwillen der mutter und der tochter, des ich mich abermals uff ir verhor gezogen haben wil. Nach dem allen, als der handtschlag beschehen ist, hab ich fruntlicher mei-nung Her Claus Kniepsen und Doctor Michaeln gepeten, sich zu meinem schwager, Augustin, zu verfugen und dieser geschehener handlung gutig zu berichten, da mit zwischen unß frid und einigkeit, deren ich mich alles vermogen bevlissen, erhalten wurde. Was aber ungeschickter, unfruntlicher und heftiger trowwort er, min schwager, ußgestossen, ist nit von noten zuerzelen. Doch ist Her Niclaus Kniepß, als burger und des regiments vertrawter, in den friden zegepieten verursacht worden. Uber daß mein schwager schimpflicher weiß furbringt, wie Doctor Michael, unangesehen, das er kein eheweib hab, sin schwester und mein gemahel bei im uffenthalte, als ob Doctor Michael, so eins unredlichen gemüts were, das er schmach oder laster gedachte zuzufugen einer frommen dochter; und je nimans ist, der uff Doctor Michael mit der warheit etwas so arges gedencken oder in sin nemen mochte. Das aber Augustin, mein schwager, wei-ter meldet, mir als ein geistlicher, ein [fol. 11ʳ] eheweib zunemen nit gepuren wölle, angesehen das sollichs nit landleufig und geprauch-

---

[28] Deceit, trick (from MHG: *alevanz*).
[29] St. George's Day, 23 April 1524.

lich, auch in geistlichen und wöltlichen rechten verboten ist etc. Das selbig der lenge nach zu entschüldigen, ist nit von nöten. Dan menglichen zu wissen, das got der Her, der uber alle recht und uber alle künig der erden ist, die ehe nie verboten, sunder jedes gelegenheit nach gepoten hat. Aber in derthalb v^c ongeverlich durch gewalt und mutwil Gregorii des Bapsts des sibenden[30] dise gotlich ordnung tyrannisch und wider gots recht und gbot gewert worden ist, zu grossem abbruch aller erbarkeit, wolchem on zweifel kein christliche oberkeit, die Christum fur ein haupt, und uber alle gesatzgeber haltet, anhangen und bestetigen mage. So sind wir nit frevele menschen in geringer zall, die das geistlich recht zuruck werfen etc., wie dan Augustin, mein schwager, anregt, oder andere die si supplication mir zu dienst begriffen haben, sonder das wort gots, das in ewigkeit wert und bleiben wurt, dadurch himel und erden beschaffen sin, das verwurft nit allein geistlich recht sonder stosset zu boden auch die gantz welt, hell und teufel, gewaltiglichen, namlich, so sich wider den rat gots uffzubouwen onderstön. Dorumb mich hochverwundert, so got der Her die ehe, die dan an kein person uff erden in sunderheit gepunden ist, durch die gantz heilig geschrift, so hoch bevor hat und rümbt, das in min schwagers namen so schimpflich furgeben wurt, als ob sin schwester bei mir wie ein offne sunderin oder metz wonen solle. Darzu wer auch on not, das er so grosse sort trüge, wie das gut solte geteilt werden, dan so sich der fal, das got lang wenden wölle, begebe, weiß man wol vermög gemeiner recht und einer loblichen stat ordenung etc. Darumb, gnediger herrn, angesehen das got der Her frei gelassen und jederman erlaubt, ja gepoten hat, wer sich nit enthalten mag, das er in die ehe komme, und ich als ein frummen man geburt, umb ein frummen tochter geworben, auch si mit [fol. 11^v] willen, wissen und gehel ir beder, der mutter und tochter, zum ehegemahel erlangt, und darin dem gebot und bevelch gotts nach gehandlet. Dan der Her sagt, was got zusamen verfügt, sol der mensch nit scheiden oder trennen.[31] Item, verlasse der mensch vater und mutter und hang an seinem weib.[32] Und ich auch kein gepot euer, miner herrn, darin ubergangen, weiß ich minen gemahel min leben lang nit zu verlassen. Bin auch ungezweifelt, ir, min gnedigen herrn, als liebhaber gotlicher gepot und

---

[30] Pope Gregory VII (r. 1073–1085). He means, of course, about 500 years ago.
[31] Matt. 19:6.
[32] Gen. 2:24.

christlicher freiheit, werden mich bei dem, so got zugehört, als euern gehorsamen burger gnediglich handhaben und beschirmen. Und wo Augustin, mein schwager, je vermeinte, das ich unbillich und wider euer gnaden artickel gehandelt haben solte, das sich doch mit der warheit nimmer erfunden wurt, wil ich im vor euer gnaden zurecht sin, und erkante straf darumb erwarten und gehorsamlich leiden. Dan ich niemans sein kind beschissen hab oder noch zethon in willens bin, als dan mich meins schwagers supplication gern veronglimpfete. Wil hiemit euer gnaden undertheniglich gepeten haben, mit Augustin, meinem schwager, gutlich zuverschaffen, als er mich und andere der sachen halb ongeschmecht, ongeirt und bekummert lasse. Dan ich in fruntschaft, liebs und guts zubeweisen geneigt bin, wo ich das umb euer gnaden sampt und sunder beschulden oder verdienen konndte, wolt ich allerzeit onverdrossene fleiß erfunden werden.

 Euer strengen, fursichtigen, wißheit undertheniger
  burger und diener,
   Doctor Caspar Hedio, predicant im Münster zu
   Straßburg

DOCUMENT NO. 5

Drenss vs. Hedio: Response of Agnes Drenss
[ca. 14 May 1524]

SOURCE: Archives du Chapître de St.-Thomas, Strasbourg, 69/5, fols. 12^r–13^v.
HAND: Secretarial hand.

[fol. 12^r] Strengen, ernvesten, ersamen, weisen, gnedigen, gunstigen herren. Mit besunder beschwerdt und hertzen leidt, als woll zuvermuten, hab ich vernomen, wie mein son Augustin Trenß uß unwissend villeicht oder mher, als ich woll acht, uß anreitzung und verhetzung etlicher ungotsferchtigen unruwigen leudt, denen woll ein anderns were angestanden, wo si gott und iren statt bedencken wolten, habe etliche theure und dapfere menner gegen euer gnaden schwerlich zuverunglimpfen, sich undernomen und das gesparter worheit, nemlich den ersamen weisen und die hochgelerten und erbarn Her Niclaus Kniebis, alt Ammeister, und Doctor Michael Rodt, beide

mein lieben vettern, und Doctor Caspar Hedio, predicanten im
Munster, nun meinen lieben vertrauwten dochterman, do mit den
nun euer gnaden eigentlichen bericht,[33] wie die sach ergangen habe.
Und dester fuglicher alle uneinigkeit und zweitracht hinlegen moge,
so sag ich unverholen vor euer gnaden mit der warheit, das der
hochgelert, christlich Doctor Caspar Hedio, predicant im Munster,
umb mein liebe dochter, Margaredt, gewarben hat, wie das einem
fromen, zuchtigen herren und man geburen mag, hat [MARGIN:
an mein son] mich und mein dochter geschickt, gemelten meinen
lieben vettern und herren, den hochgelerten Doctor Michael Rodt,
der on zweifel mein und meiner dochter wolfart nit weniger begert
zu furdern, dan eben mein son, und freilich vil mher dan alle sin
rath geber. Dem auch mein son zuantwort geben hat, was der ehe
halb mir und meiner dochter gefelligk und gelegen sei, sol im auch
gefelligk und gelegen sein. Daruff ich und mein dochter unß ein zeitlang zubedencken genomen haben. So bald aber mein son gemergkt,
das wir, ich und mein dochter, die in meinem gewalt sich alweg
nach meinem willen gehalten hat, ob angebotener ehe nit groß
scheueten, hat er sich ungepurlich genug ertzeigt mit worten und
geperden. Das hab ich do zu mol zu geben bösen jungen, die on
das allem dem entgegen sind, daß das gottlich wort und christlich
erberkeit vermag die auch der mossen leben, das sie nit on vrsach
das licht des evangelii hassen.[34] Und hab also die sach lossen anston,
verhoffet durch die teglichen predigen des gotlichen worts wurt er,
wie ich das genugsam erkent hab, ouch erkennen, das die heilig ehe
jederman von got zugelossen [fol. 12ᵛ] und vergunt ist. Und freilich,
die weil daher, das den geistlichen die ehe verpoten gewesen ist, so
groß schand und laster furgangen ist, und noch furget, ein jeder
frommer christ nit allein sinem vermogen dartzu helfen solt, das
durch die gottlich und gebenedeite ehe das ungeschickt, unverschampt
leben etlicher geistlichen abtreiben wurd. Diese erkantnuß hat aber
villeicht durch teglich der gotlosen hinderhalten bei meinem son nit
wollen komen. Do ich im dan genug hab vorgeben, vill meher dan
ich als ein mutter schuldigk gewesen, und gesehen, das er uß keinem
guten christlichen grundt wieder unß an getragene ehe gewesen ist,
hab ich bewegt uß teglichen hellen predigen des evangelii, so in

---

[33] Document No. 3.
[34] This passage attests to the existence in mid-1524 of popular opposition to the
Evangelical preachers.

dieser loblichen Stat Straßburhgk geschehen, und aber euer gnaden frilich nit geschehen liessen, nach auch so ein merckliche erbare burgerschaft die horten, wo sie nit christlich und gotlich weren, mein dochter obgemeltem Doctor Caspar zu einem ehegemahel mit irem willen zugesagt, do zu mir auch nit wenig meiner verwanten frundt und sunst gute gunner—erbar, frumm, redlich leudt, die mein son noch jeman anders in kein weg schmehen mag mit der warheitt, geraten haben. Und bin auch ungetzwifelt, wie solche ehe gott gefelligk, also soll si auch fuglich und gantz nutzlich sein meiner lieben dochter, dero sich auch mein son gar nit dorft beschemen, so er gott vor augen wolt haben und mer folgen denen, die im guts gonnen in der warheit, dan denen die durch in villeicht etwas ungluck wolten anrichten. Und ist diß geschehen achtag nach Ostern.[35] Nach diesem, als ich kein besserung an meinem son sahe, dem ich doch gerne hette gehofirt, wo er nur nit so gar heßlich geton hette, ob dem, das doch gotlich und billich ist, sein wir, ich und mein dochter, uff Sant Jorgen tagen[36] gemelts Doctor Michaels unsers lieben vetterns hauß komen. Dan zumal on sein Doctor Michels wissen, der uns dan wol ein monat zu vor geladen hat, etwan ein mol zu im zu komen in sein hauß, do wir dan Doctor Caspar offentlich und nit heimlich gehalten in befunden. Und nach dem ich mit im fruntlich red gehapt [MARGIN: und wir vermerckt], das wir allenhalb im geschrei gewesen,[37] haben wir unß entschlossen, on Doctor Michels zu thon, die weil wir doch einer verwilligung noch der zeit hoffen mechten bei meinem son und ich im [fol. 13ʳ] doch mit willen meiner dochter, si im schon zuvor zugeseit hatte, den handt streich zu thun und den leiten uß dem geschrei zuhelfen. Und die weil wir besorgten, das dan nun beschicht, hab ich Doctor Michael gepeten, das er Her Niclaus Kniepsen wolt vermogen, das er si oftgedochtem Doctor Caspar und mein dochter zusamen geb. Hab auch sust noch andern meinen lieben frunden etlichen geschickt, als aber die gescheft halben nit mochten komen. Und Her Nicolaus Knieps kam, den Doctor Michael von seinem essen beruft hat, und des handels auch nit bericht, biß das er in zu unß in sein hauß brocht hat, hab ich und Doctor Caspar in gepeten, er wolte sie zusamen geben und also ein zeug sein, der versprochenen und redlich uffgerichten ehe. Das

---

[35] 4 April 1524.
[36] 23 April 1524.
[37] That is, there was gossip about their secret betrothal.

er, die weil unser beger billich und gottlichem [MARGIN: rechten
gemeß] nit kindte abschlagen, und hat sie also uff unser bitt zusamen
geben, glucks gewunscht, und druff bei unß im nachtmol blieben,
und mit einigem wort wider dartzu noch von geroten, ich schweig,
das er mit glatten worten mich oder mein dochter solte hinder gangen sein, vil weniger getzwongen. Wie dan auch Doctor Michael der
uber sein erste werbung, als wol gegen meinem son als gegen mir
gethon, auch weder zu noch von geroten hat, dann allein das er
alweg gestanden ist, wie er schuldig und ein jeder christ, das solche
ehe gottlich und billich sei. Des ich selb ouch solchen grundt hab
und weiß sampt meiner dochter, so haben wir auch bed solchen
geneigten willen zu oftgemeltem Doctor Caspar, also einem getruwen
lerer der gantzen stadt, das so es nit geschehen were, muste es noch
heute bei tag geschehen. Dan die dochter mein und nit meins sons
ist. Wir haben in lang genug vor augen gehabt, etwa manchen
erlichen werbern haben wir umb seindt willen abgeschlagen, so hat
im dieser[38] allein uß ein unglauben und böser leut reitzung nit gefallen.
Die weil dan er unß nit zuverbieten hat, ob wir dan schon uff sein
verbot nit geben haben, acht ich wir haben nit hoch gesundet. Den
vogt haben wir uß vrsach nit gefragt, acht wir seins auch nit schuldigk
gewesen. Vill guter verwanter frundt haben wir gehabt, und irem
roth gefolgt, hat unß auch in kein weg geruwen. Und sag frei und
onverholen, wie vor, so es noch nit geschehen were, must es nach
geschehen. Darumb, gnödige herren, ist am euer gnaden mein under-
[fol. 13ᵛ] thenigk, demutige bitt, ir wollent dem unworhaftigen fur-
tragen meins sons kein glauben geben, sonder wie ich die sach in
der warheit ertzelt hab, also kein zweifel haben, es sei alles der
massen ergangen. Und wollent verschaffen mit meinem son, das er
mich mein liebe dochter und vertrauweten dochterman unbemuhet
und on geschmecht lasse, sampt mein andern gnödigen hern und
frunden, die er mit der unworheit unbillich euer gnaden furtra-
gen hat. Doch im uff diß mol, wo er anders von seinem ungeschickten furnemen wolte abston seiner unwissenthalb, und des argen
anreitzens des sich etlich böß leut, als ich gontzlich in glauben gut
vrsach hab, gegen im iben, vertzeihen, das er also mit der unworheit
meine lieben herren und frundt Her Niclaus Knieps, Doctor Michael
und Doctor Caspar gegen euer gnaden zu unglimpfen understanden
hat. Dan so er je in seinem ungeschickten unchristlichen furnemen

---

[38] I.e., Dr. Caspar Hedio.

wolte furfare und also frevenlich gotlichen gepot entgegen hande-
len, mich als sein mutter, deren er in billichen sachen als diese ehe
ist gehorsamen soll, uß gotlichem rechten nit erkennen, so betzeug
ich mich des offentlich hie vor euer gnaden, meinen gnödigen herren, das ich in auch nit hinfurt fur ein son erkennen wurde, das
dan im und seinen kinden keinen frummen bringen wurdt. Diß hab
ich die worheit zubetzeugen und zuentschuldigen, meine lieben herren
und frundt, so mein son oder die, so im die supplication begriffen
mit der unworheit haben wellen ver unglimpfen, do mit auch unei-
nichkeit und zweitracht mochte hingelegt und recht christliche einigkeit uffgericht werden, im besten nit wollen bergen, mit anhangenden
bitt, euer gnaden wolle mich als ein witfrauwe sampt meiner dochter
und verwanten dochterman, euer gnaden burger altzeit in gnedigem
befelch haben.

    Euer strengen, fursichtigen wißheit alltzeit gehorsame
      burgerin,
        Agnes Trensin,
        Andres Trensen seligen verloßne witfrauwe.

DOCUMENT NO. 6

Drenss vs. Hedio: Second Petition of Augustin Drenss
4 June 1524

SOURCE: Archives du Chapître de St.-Thomas, Strasbourg, 69/6,
    fol. 14^{r-v}.
HAND: Augustin Drenss.

[fol. 14^r] Strengen, erenvesten, fursichtigen, ersamen, wisen, gnödigen herren, demnach uff min warhaftig supliciern und ingeprachte
supplication[39] Herr Claus Kniebiß und Doctor Michel Rott, ouch
mein lieb mutter und Doctor Caspar, predicant, gegen supplicatio-
nes,[40] ire handlung, so ich euch, min gnödigen herren, angepracht,
zu beglimpfen angezeugt, laß ich alles zu diser zit in sinem werd
beston. In ansehung, das der gegenteil muntlich und schriftlich furtreg
nit rechtlichen wiß, als ich ouch nit in recht ingebracht haben werd

---

[39] Document No. 2, Petition of Augustin Drenss.
[40] Documents 3, 4, and 5.

und will, und alles, so ich in miner supplication ingepracht, doch mit protestation do zemal noch ietz nimandt damit zuinjurieren besunder allein zu behilf miner noturft, ist selbs von miner lieben mutter wie gehandlet ist, als mir angezeigt, gehort worden. Und als gemelt min muter selbs durch ein geschrift verantwurt,[41] ist lichtlich abzunemen, wie sie hindergangen ist. Sie im ersten handel da me angelegen uberredt, vill mer in disem fall. Dan so Doctor Caspar verantwurtung und stilus ouch dargegen miner muter und der andren fur ougen gnomen wirdet, sindt pfill uß einem kocher. Diewill Her Claus Kniebiß ouch Doctor Michell alle handlung gestandt, doch nit mit uff satz besunder mit einer hupschen beschonung, pringt der handel selbs deßhalb ein claren verstandt. Und wie wol jetz die neu evangelisch leer so vill wircken will, das vater und mutter und ire khinder ouch eegemächt[42] und andre fruntschaft zu widerwertigkeit und zertrennung khomendt, als jetz leider, gott erbarmß, zwischen miner lieben einigen sweseter gewesen und miner lieben muter, alß sie sich vor eueren gnaden schriftlich hören lassen, sie wolle mich nit fur einen sun mer haben, befunden wirdet, wil doch ich sie unangesehen dise neue leer fur ein muter mein leben lang erkhennen und haben. Hoff, eß sie gotz gepot und will. Dann wo sollichs nit were, wolte ich euere gnaden wol witer wissen anzuzeigen. Ich hette ouch geachtet, wo sach also schlecht ergangen, als [der] gegenteil angezeigt hette, billich einigen frundt oder vogt von minem vater oder mutter darzu beruft. Were wol alß erlich und billich, dann [der] gegenteil niemandt dar bei gehept, dann die personen obbestimpt. Und das euer gnaden mag erwegen, das [der] gegenteil gern etwaß wider mich inprechte, zeit er an, wie ich miner swester kheinen man zunemen vergunstigen. So doch das widerspill offenbar ist, dann ich gearbeit, das sie den schafner zu Sant Catharina[43] oder Vältin des Schultheissen sun [fol. 14ᵛ] von Wangen[44] zu der ee nemen. Diser[45] hat aber ir allein gefallen. Diewill dann, gnödige herren, luwt miner vor ingeprachter supplication verstanden nach der lenge gehort, das pfaffen und munch ee wider haben sollendt, weder bäpstlich und keiserlich satzung und recht ist, ouch euer, miner gnödigen herren,

---

[41] Document No. 4, the petition of Agnes Drenss.
[42] Spouses (from MHG: *egemechide*).
[43] Unidentified.
[44] Unidentified.
[45] I.e., Dr. Caspar Hedio.

alten herkhomen, ouch in aller cristenheit vill hundert jar nie inge-
pruch gewesen, und namlich uff disentag khein erbfall den khinden,
so von pfaffen, eß sei in oder vsserthalb der ee, zu gelassen wurdet.
Mag euer gnaden wol erwegen, waß sollichs min geschlecht erlich
frundtschaft, so lieb und leid vill jar mit diser statt erlitten, ein inse-
hen haben, damit die neuerung niit mir und miner frundtschaft nit
angefangen werde. Will also lut miner vorigen supplication als ein
armer burger den handel zu erwegen und zu bedencken, und also
eueren gnaden ergeben, mit namlich geding, waß sich mit der zit
zu tragen möchte, das mir euere gnaden solliches mines ernstlichen
anhaltes nit in vergeß stellen wellendt.

   Euer wißheit undertäniger burger
      Augustin Trenß

GERMANY AND EUROPE

CHAPTER TEN

ECONOMIC AND SOCIAL INSTITUTIONS IN LATE MEDIEVAL GERMANY

One morning in the year 1338, as the Emperor Charles IV lay sleeping, a young knight woke him with the cry, "Sire, get up, the Last Day has arrived, for the whole world is covered with locusts!" Charles arose, dressed, and went out to see how large the swarm was; he rode nearly 30 miles without coming to the end of it.[1] Ten years later, a tremendous earthquake rocked the Carinthian town of Villach and threw down its castle, monastery, churches, and walls, while the earth opened up in the middle of the city and poured out water and sulphur, killing at least 5,000 persons. The plague—it was the dreadful new Black Death—that followed closely on this catastrophe raged so fiercely in Vienna, "that in a single day 1,200 bodies were buried in St. Colman's cemetery. . . . The great mortality was blamed on the Jews, and . . . the common people rose up in the towns of Stein and Krems, . . . seized the Jews, and killed them all."[2] Famine, earthquake, plague, pogrom—signs of the fourteenth century, signs of the waning middle ages, signs of crisis so many and massive that historians call it an "age of crisis".[3]

The economic crisis began in the 1310s—at least three decades before the Black Death raged across Latin Christendom in 1347–1350—and it lasted more or less until the 1470s and 1480s, when all the principal economic indicators—population, settlement, prices—began to indicate recovery.[4] This secular rhythm, a 150-year trough between

---

[1] *Vita Caroli quarti. Die Autobiographie Karls IV.*, ed. E. Hillenbrand, ch. 10, quoted by Hartmut Boockmann, *Stauferzeit und spätes Mittelalter. Deutschland 1125–1517* (Berlin, 1987), p. 228.

[2] Quoted by Karl Brunner and Gerhard Jaritz, *Landherr, Bauer, Ackerknecht. Der Bauer im Mittelalter. Klischee und Wirklichkeit* (Vienna/Cologne/Graz, 1985), p. 121.

[3] Frantisek Graus, *Pest-Geissler-Judenmorde. Das 14. Jahrhundert als Krisenzeit*, Veröffentlichungen der MPIG LXXXVI (Göttingen, 1987), p. 555.

[4] On the agrarian cycle, the current state of knowledge is described by Thomas W. Robisheaux, "The World of the Village", Thomas A. Brady, Jr., Heiko A. Oberman, and James D. Tracey, eds., *Handbook of European History, 1400–1600. Late Middle Ages, Renaissance, and Reformation* I (Leiden, 1994), pp. 79–112.

the economic boom of the high middle ages and the more laboured expansion of Fernand Braudel's "long sixteenth century", frames the late medieval era in the Holy Roman Empire from the Swiss Jura to Pomerania and from Flanders to the Hungarian border. In this space lived perhaps 14 million persons on the eve of the Black Death, a figure which dropped to c. 10 million by 1450 and did not recover pre-plague levels until the mid-sixteenth century.[5] Human densities, which were always highest in the Empire's western and southern sectors, reached a peak of 45 persons/km² in Brabant (1435) and the Lower Rhenish region, dropping to perhaps 23 persons/km² (c. 1300) in Saxony and half that in Silesia. Most of the people lived in one of the approximately 170,000 settlements, including 4,000 towns and cities, within the boundaries of the Empire (in 1300 almost exactly the size of Germany in 1937). In the fourteenth century only Cologne—and perhaps Prague—reached 40,000, the size of Roman Trier in the fourth century, and no city in the Empire rivalled contemporary Venice, Milan, Florence, or Paris, though at least four others—Brussels, Metz, Lübeck, and Danzig—surpassed 20,000. Seven other cities had around 20,000, and over a dozen more exceeded 10,000, but, outside of the Empire's densely settled north-west, its towns typically housed fewer than 2,000 souls.

From the end of the medieval boom through the long depression and into the age of recovery, the Empire's peoples adapted inherited customs and practices in response to the great new forces, and created or developed the characteristic social and economic institutions of pre-industrial Central Europe. The new forces produced the long agrarian depression: the fall or stagnation of populations and grain prices, the recession of cultivation and settlement, the expansion of market relations, and the appreciation of the value of human labour relative to land. The general economic movement favoured the town over the land and the peasants over their lords, so that the depression's global effect was to devolve, in the absence of strong centralised government, more and more self-management and even self-governance into the hands of the common people. The late medieval era thus advantaged the Central European common people relative to their social betters in both town and countryside, though to call this harsh era their "golden age" is perhaps going too far. Yet the peoples of

---

[5] These figures are taken from Wilhelm Abel. Substantially lower ones (10 million and 7.5 million respectively) are given by Peter Moraw.

this harsh, freer era proved extremely creative. If the medieval expansion had created the Empire's basic social topography—the patterns of forest and clearing, the roads, and the villages and towns—the later middle ages fixed the economic and social institutions that would structure social life until the Empire's demise: the household, the guild, the commune, and the firm.[6] Only one institutional system— the church—retained a much older structure, for its shapes reached back to the post-Carolingian centuries and beyond.

I. *Household*

Theoretical and taxonomic considerations aside, the predominant small community in which late medieval German-speakers lived was the household (*Haus*), the basic unit of co-residence, production, and reproduction in the towns as on the land.[7] Nearly all we know about the structure and size of late medieval households comes from the cities, and there from the middle and upper classes; but we may accept in general that the late medieval German household conformed to the northern European type based on a nuclear couple who had first married rather late—perhaps the mid-20s—and at roughly the same age, and who, together with their children and servants—perhaps seven to nine persons in all—formed the important unit of co-residence and production.[8] The urban regimes recognized these fact by requiring that all citizens "keep fire and smoke", that is, maintain a household in the city.[9] In principle, in the city

---

[6] And, of course, the territorial state, which falls outside this chapter's scope.

[7] Michael Mitterauer and Reinhard Sieder, *The European Family. Patriarchy to Partnership from the Middle Ages to the Present*, trans. Karla Oosterveen and Manfred Hörzinger (Chicago, 1982), p. 8; Erich Maschke, *Die Familie in der deutschen Stadt des späten Mittelalters*, Sitzungsberichte der Heidelberger Akademie der Wissenschaften, Phil.-hist. Klasse, Jahrgang 1980, no. 4 (Heidelberg, 1980), pp. 11–15. I agree with the reservations expressed by Mitterauer and Sieder (p. 9) about using the term "the whole house" (*das ganze Haus*), for which see Otto Brunner, "Das 'ganze Haus' und die alteuropäische 'Ökonomik'", in Brunner, *Neue Wege der Verfassungs- und Sozialgeschichte*, 2nd ed. (Göttingen, 1968), pp. 103–27 (originally published in 1958). A survey of the entire subject of household and family in a European context is Merry E. Wiesner, "Family, Household, and Community", in Brady *et al.*, *Handbook of European History, 1400–1600* I, pp. 51–78.

[8] Jan de Vries, "Population", in Brady *et al.*, *Handbook of European History, 1400–1600* I, pp. 1–50.

[9] I give the form used at Strasbourg, "feuer und rauch halten", but there are many others.

as on the land, only those who owned their own houses were allowed
to have families—the nobility, the burghers, the peasants, but not
the servants, the journeymen, or the farmhands. Yet, our scanty evidence suggests the towns' resident poor (*Hausarmen*) also formed and
lived in households, which were typically composed, like those of
solid burghers, of a man, his wife (*uxor, husfrauw, wieff*), their children and possibly grandparents, the remnants of a "deracinated and
fluid" multi-generational family.[10]

Many households were headed by women, whose discriminatory
exclusion from many trades made them disproportionately poor.
Among 2,400 taxpayers surveyed at Trier in 1364, for example, a
quarter—but two-thirds of the female heads of households—belonged
to the poorest class. Women could and did head urban households,
however, despite the customary law which still placed each woman
in the custody (*mundium, Munt*) of a man, usually a father or a husband, a norm which in practice often bent to the economic reality
of the household.[11]

Kinship, an older and in some respects alternative principle of
social organization, continued to flourish without threatening the
household's predominance. The kin community, based on real or
fictive descent from a common ancestor, bore in German the name
Geschlecht (pl. *Geschlechter*) but in Latin a variety of names—*familia,
gens, progenies, genus, stirps*, and *genealogia*—which suggests its fluidity as
contrasted to the solid monotony of the term *Haus*.[12] The feeling for
kin or family in this sense remained as strong among the German-
speakers as among the other peoples of Christendom, for whom it
formed the primary metaphor for their religious sense of community
as the great body of the kinsmen and kinswomen of Jesus Christ.[13]
This powerful religious metaphor kept kinship on people's minds,
and so did the confusingly contradictory rules that delimited poten-

---

[10] Maschke, *Die deutsche Familie*, p. 11, based on the members of the "Elenden-
Bruderschaft", in Trier, 1437–1465.

[11] *Ibid.*, p. 33; Martha C. Howell, *Women, Production, and Patriarchy in Late Medieval
Cities* (Chicago, 1986), pp. 9–46. For evidence of practice, see Erika Uitz, "Zur
gesellschaftlichen Stellung der Frau in der mittelalterlichen Stadt", *Magdeburger Beiträge
zur Stadtgeschichte* I (1977): pp. 20–34, esp. the table after p. 34.

[12] Maschke, *Die deutsche Familie*, p. 13; Brunner, "Das 'ganze Hause' und die alteuropäische 'Ökonomik'", pp. 42–3.

[13] For the religious importance of spiritual kinship in late medieval religion, see
John Bossy, *Christianity in the West, 1400–1700* (Oxford, 1985); and on the family as
a social metaphor in general, see Mitterauer and Sieder, *The European Family*, pp. 2–3.

tial marriage partners on the basis of consanguinity, even though the church did not really succeed in imposing its authority over "the forms and patterns of marriage at all levels" until the sixteenth and seventeenth centuries.[14]

In practice the shape of family had become very fluid and its size as large, Erich Maschke wrote resignedly, "as family sense made it".[15] The point can be illustrated from wills at Lübeck: the widow Alheyd Wessel named in her second will of June 1354 thirteen relatives from three generations as her heirs; Elisabeth, the childless widow of Conrad Cruse, named in 1351 as heirs her sister's four children, four grand-nieces, and her brother-in-law's three children; and Gerhard Warendorp, a substantial merchant, named in two wills of 1356 and 1359 twenty persons, including eight maternal uncles and a paternal uncle and aunt.[16] The Lübeck wills show a family sense which extended over great distances but embraced, at most, the four generations of living memory. Different limits can be seen in the household books kept by wealthy southern merchants. When, for example, Lucas Rem (1481–1541) of Augsburg brought his great-grandfather's list (*verzeichnus*) up to date, he included only his own line of descent and excluded collaterals, which means that his sense of family was long but narrow.[17]

The Rems belonged to the very top of the smaller, more favoured of the two classes recognized by late medieval urban social discourse, rich (*dives, reich*) and poor (*pauper, arm*). The civic tax registers give us a more nuanced insight into the shapes of wealth and poverty among urban households, and allow us to see them *ensemble* as a social structure. Around 1500 the possession of property worth 25–30 fl. or an income of 15 fl. per annum—the absolute minimum for a single person—meant true poverty. The possession of property worth 100 fl. meant modest prosperity, those who possessed 500 fl. were

[14] Jack Goody, *The Development of the Family and Marriage in Europe* (Cambridge, 1983), p. 148. I do not mean to slight the importance of these restrictions, and Goody (p. 145) cites the example of the Imperial Recess of Mainz in 1439, which asked the church to reduce the prohibitions to the second degree.

[15] Maschke, *Die deutsche Familie*, p. 15.

[16] Ahasver von Brant, ed., *Regesten der Lübecker Bürgertestamente des Mittelalters*, Veröffentlichungen zur Geschichte der Hansestadt Lübeck, 18, 24 (2 vols. Lübeck, 1964–1973) II, p. 76, no. 535; pp. 26–7, no. 444; pp. 102–3, no. 587, here cited from Maschke, *Die deutsche Familie*, p. 18.

[17] This document is evaluated in *Ibid.*, pp. 19–22. Maschke's treatment of this genre (pp. 19–30) suggests that the strong familial sense it documents does not yield much to the famous Florentine *ricordi*.

rich, and more than 5,000 fl. made one the late medieval equivalent of a millionaire. A nest-egg of 200 fl. was considered "quite a lot of money".[18]

The relationship between urban social stratification and economic structure may be illustrated by comparing tax-payers at Lübeck in 1460 with those of Augsburg in 1475: the rich and upper middle classes made up 18 per cent and 4.9 per cent, the middling ones 68 per cent and 27 per cent, and the poor 14 per cent and 66 per cent respectively.[19] Deficiencies of data aside, these figures reveal dramatically different social structures: Lübeck, a classic late medieval shape of an onion or turban—small point, large middling bulge, and modest base; and Augsburg, a pyramid shaped by the rapid development of large-scale production for export—tiny super-rich point, modest middling sector, and very large base. The key to social and political stability, of course, lay in the social and political behaviour of the bulge of middling folk.[20]

Most late medieval households, of course, formed and lived not in the cities but in the thousands of villages, hamlets (*Weiler*), and dispersed rural settlements, where the interplay of household and kinship responded to customary laws of inheritance of status and property, the presence of economic opportunity, and "the gradual, long-drawn-out process" of "the transfer of authority from parents to children".[21] This process was regulated by inheritance regimes, and modern research teaches us great caution about assuming fixed correspondences between family structures and inheritance customs, the more so because rural families cannot be traced until the coming of parish registers in the middle years of the sixteenth century. No one, however, doubts that customary law powerfully influenced the inheritance of status and property during the later middle ages. In this era the line between servility and freedom, for example, was still quite visible, and its enforcement devolved, along with other legal functions, on the rural communes. At Ettenheimmünster in Baden,

---

[18] Walter Jacob, *Politische Führungsschicht und Reformation. Untersuchungen zur Reformation in Zürich 1519–1528*, Zürcher Beiträge zur Reformationsgeschichte I (Zurich, 1970), pp. 102–3.

[19] Isenmann, *Die deutsche Stadt*, pp. 266–7.

[20] Erich Maschke, "Mittelschichten in deutschen Städten des Mittelalters", in Maschke, *Städte und Menschen. Beiträge zur Geschichte der Stadt, der Wirtschaft und Gesellschaft 1959–1977* (Wiesbaden, 1980), pp. 275–305.

[21] David Warren Sabean, *Property, Production, and Family in Neckarhausen, 1700–1870* (Cambridge, 1990), p. 16.

a manorial court (*Dinghof*) composed of leading male householders (*von mengem erberen Manne*) dealt with the offspring of a servile father and a free mother. If both parents were servile, they judged, the child would follow its mother, but if the father is servile and the mother free, the child should be servile and not follow its mother.[22]

The agrarian depression none the less eroded servility, along with the old patterns of management and governance of the manor, and created opportunities by loosening the rules of inheritance. Although the German-speaking lands are famous for their division into zones of partible and impartible inheritance, we cannot establish a clear correlation between impartible inheritance, size of holding, and the formation of a stem or multi-generation family, which was in any case predominant only in the eastern Alpine lands.[23] We may suppose that rules of impartibility encouraged larger, more complex households, and that partibility made the formation of stem families unlikely, but the evidence all comes from a later era.[24] Indeed, the typically fixed and regular patterns of rural inheritance in the German-speaking lands is a product less of the medieval than of the early modern era, when rising population pressure and the state's fiscal interest encouraged strict and uniform regulation of the generational transfer of real property. Even then, the state's preference for impartibility on fiscal grounds did not extinguish the great zones of partibility in the Rhineland, Württemberg, Baden, Lower Franconia, Hesse, south-western Westphalia, and parts of central Germany (Thuringia, south-west Saxony, southern Hanover).[25] This is so because different forces

---

[22] Günther Franz, ed., *Quellen zur Geschichte des deutschen Bauernstandes im Mittelalter* (Darmstadt, 1974), p. 418, no. 186 (24 Feb. 1363).

[23] John W. Cole and Eric R. Wolf, *The Hidden Frontier. Ecology and Ethnicity in an Alpine Valley* (New York, 1974), pp. 181–2, show that adjacent regions with similar ecologies but different inheritance systems could in fact emerge with farms of similar size, though they do not study typical farming landscapes.

[24] The literature on the stem family in the eastern alpine lands centres on the early modern era, not the late medieval period. See Michael Mitterauer, "Familiengröße—Familientypen—Familienzuklus", *GG* I (1975): pp. 235–55; Lutz Berkner, "The Stem Family and the Developmental Cycle of the Peasant Household. An Eighteenth Century Example", *AHR* LXXVII (1972): pp. 398–418; *idem*, "Inheritance, Land Tenure and Peasant Family Structure. A German Regional Comparison", in Jack Goody, Joan Thirsk, and E. P. Thompson, eds., *Family and Inheritance. Rural Society in Western Europe, 1200–1800* (Cambridge, 1976), pp. 71–95.

[25] On the geography of inheritance, see Barthel Huppertz, *Räume und Schichten bäuerlicher Kulturformen in Deutschland. Ein Beitrag zur deutschen Bauerngeschichte* (Bonn, 1939), pp. 25–7, and map 1, who also describes (pp. 27–9) the debate about why some regions (especially the south-west) practised partibility and others impartibility and concludes that there are no environmental reasons for it.

acted for different rules of inheritance—the state for impartibility
and population pressure for partibility—so that the two systems might
come to pre-dominate in neighbouring regions, as, for example,
Upper Swabia (impartibility) and Württemberg (partibility).[26]

It is difficult now, so powerful is the image of a static middle ages,
to imagine the opportunities that opened up for young people to
form new households during the late medieval agrarian crisis. Many
fields were abandoned and whole settlements disappeared—perhaps
23 per cent of the total—ranging from low levels (10 per cent) in
the Netherlands, to higher ones (17 per cent) in Alsace, and highest levels (40 per cent) in Brandenburg, Mecklenburg, and Hesse's
uplands. A survey of the Mark Brandenburg in 1375 found "an
empty, deserted land" (öde, wust land), of which only a third to a half
was occupied.[27] The shift of the land-labour ratio favoured the farmers by giving opportunities to find land and found households. How
peasants seized such opportunities is suggested by an undated late
medieval customary (Weistum) from western Germany, which says
that if a stranger should ask for land, the village mayor (Schultheiß)
should take the stranger up behind him on his horse and ride out
into the land. When the stranger saw land which pleased him, he
should dismount and mark the place, whereupon the mayor should
mark off 15 Morgen (5.4 ha) for him to farm.[28]

Such evidence conveys the impression of an age, from about 1350
to about 1450, when very favourable conditions reigned for the formation and preservation of farming households and constitution of
villages as groups of households. Villages averaged perhaps 12 households and 70 persons, who were related to one another in complex
ways: consanguinity, affinity, godparenthood, co-ownership, employment, indebtedness, and faction. Although the village was a bastion
of equality, compared with the society as a whole, every village
formed a hierarchy of households. At the top were the rich, influential
families, who in regions such as Westphalia (where they were called

---

[26] Sabean, *Property, Production, and Family*, p. 15, who also suggests the impossi-
bility of correlating family patterns with inheritance customs before the introduction of parish registers in the sixteenth century.
[27] Wilhelm Abel, "Landwirtschaft 1350–1500", in Hermann Aubin and Wolfgang
Zorn, eds., *Handbuch der deutschen Wirtschafts- und Sozialgeschichte* I (Stuttgart, 1971),
p. 303.
[28] Wilhelm Abel, *Agrarian Fluctuations in Europe. From the Thirteenth to the Twentieth
Centuries*, trans. Olive Ordish (New York, 1980), p. 79.

Schulten) and Franconia might pay as much tax as a well-to-do burgher in a nearby town. Such households formed the backbone of many small territories, such as the abbey of Göß in Styria, the boundaries of whose 25 large farms (*Meierhöfe*) survive to this day.[29]

The middling farmers, called *Vollbauern* or *Huber*, possessed one or more *Hufen* of ploughland and formed the stable element in every village. Below them stood the cotters (*Häusler*), who rented house and garden but, having little or no right to ploughland, worked in others' fields or as artisans or loggers. Below all these farmers stood those who lacked full rights in the village, called by different names in the different regions, who were often younger, non-inheriting brothers of full and middling peasants. A 1486 tax register from the county of Mark, a smallish territory on the Lower Rhine, offers a glimpse into rural stratification: a ninth of the 3,766 households had property worth less than 12.5 fl., of whom 38 per cent were too poor to pay any tax (*nil habet*); of the fifth worth more than 125 fl. each, only 2 per cent could pay nothing; and two-thirds of the tax-paying farmers were middling men with holdings worth between 20 and 125 fl.[30]

Most noble households also formed and lived in the countryside, where they shared the peasants' vulnerability to the price scissors created by falling revenues and rising costs of labour and manufactured goods. As the Bavarian Estates complained in 1510, "all the grain and other things, which the peasant must sell to pay his taxes, are in little demand now; but the things he must buy in the town do not fall in price and are not regulated by law, but they cost ever more."[31] Such conditions indeed favoured the burghers, who began in the later middle ages to invade the countryside as moneylenders and even as landlords, providing the nobles with competition they could rarely withstand.[32] The depression threatened the noble household more than it did the peasants, who at least benefited from cheaper and more accessible land; and it did so earliest and most strongly where agriculture was already market-oriented and demesne

---

[29] Peter Moraw, *Von offener Verfassung zu gestalteter Verdichtung. Das Reich im späten Mittelalter 1250 bis 1490* (Berlin, 1985), p. 89.

[30] Wilhelm Abel, *Geschichte der deutschen Landwirtschaft vom frühen Mittelalter bis zum 19. Jahrhundert*, Deutsche Agrargeschichte II (Stuttgart, 1962), p. 132.

[31] Quoted in *Ibid.*, p. 131 n. 1.

[32] Rolf Kießling, *Die Stadt und ihr Land. Umlandpolitik, Bürgerbesitz und Wirtschaftsgefüge in Ostschwaben vom 14. bis ins 16. Jahrhundert*, Städteforschungen, series A, XXIX (Cologne/Vienna, 1989); Tom Scott, *Freiburg and the Breisgau. Town-Country Relations in the Age of Reformation and Peasants' War* (Oxford, 1986).

farming had declined, as in the Upper Rhine Valley. A study of sixteen families of lesser (*ritteradlige*) nobles in the fourteenth-century
Ortenau, a district of Middle Baden, reveals that a community of
noble households—they endowed masses and even built a chapel
together to serve their dead—suffered grievously from the fall of
grain prices and the debasement of coinage, which depressed their
incomes faster than those of their tenants.[33] The plunge in their fortunes stabilized around 1400, but other evidence indicates that southwestern rural nobles' incomes remained depressed right to the end
of the later middle ages.[34]

This picture of the noble household standing helpless before the
agrarian depression can none the less be misleading. One of the
defining characteristics of nobles, lineage or descent, helped them to
defend themselves against the ravages of the economic depression.
They used it, for example, to guard their monopoly of many clerical
corporations, such as the cathedral chapter, by enforcing requirements
for noble ancestry—the "four-ancestor rule" as used at Freising and
Regensburg, the "sixteen-ancestor rule" at Bamberg, Würzburg, and
Mainz—for admission. Strasbourg, most aristocratic of all, admitted
only men whose families held seats in the Imperial Diet, which meant
that, as Desiderius Erasmus once quipped, Jesus Christ lacked sufficient
noble ancestors to become a canon of Strasbourg.[35]

Then, too, in complicated noble lineages fortunate households
could make up the losses suffered by less fortunate ones. This process can be seen in the history of the lords (since 1467, barons) of
Fleckenstein, the most successful noble lineage of Lower Alsace during
the later middle ages.[36] They recouped some of their late fourteenth-

---

[33] Hans-Peter Sattler, "Die Ritterschaft der Ortenau in der spätmittelalterlichen Wirtschaftskrise", *Die Ortenau* XLII (1962): pp. 220–58; XLIV (1964): pp. 22–39; XLV (1965): pp. 32–57; XLVI (1966): pp. 32–58. The chapel, built at Neuweier in 1329, is noted in pt. II, vol. 44, p. 31.
[34] K. O. Müller, "Zur wirtschaftlichen Lage des schwäbischen Adels am Ausgang des Mittelalters", *ZWLG* III (1939): pp. 285–328, who found that two-thirds of the Swabian lesser nobility had annual incomes less than 200 fl., while only 2 per cent enjoyed incomes over 800 fl.
[35] *Die Chronik der Grafen von Zimmern*, eds. Hansmartin Decker-Hauff and Rudolf Seigel (3 vols., Darmstadt, 1964–1972), III, p. 72, II, pp. 37–38: "Christus het [in] das collegium, da sie nit dispensirt, nit angenomen werden megen."
[36] Peter Müller, *Die Herren von Fleckenstein im späten Mittelalter. Untersuchungen zur Geschichte eines Adelsgeschlechts im pfälzisch-elsässischen Grenzgebiet*, Geschichtliche Landeskunde XXXIV (Stuttgart, 1990). The Fleckensteins were the only Alsatian family that was able to found a miniature territorial state.

century losses by entering Palatine service in the next century, but the failure of one line, the Dagstuhls, to produce sufficient and timely heirs depressed its fortunes in comparison with its kinsmen. The family as a whole, however, survived the depression in good shape, thanks as much to political environment as to improved economic conditions.[37] This story reminds us that bonds between lines and between households provided types of support—for example, in the mortgage, sale, and purchase of lands and rents, and providing surety for loans—lacked by the burghers generally and the peasants almost universally.

While evidence from the south-west reveals hard times for the lesser nobles, the picture further east, in Saxony, shows more light and shadow, perhaps because the greater degree of economic autarchy in the more sparsely populated east helped noble households better to withstand the depression's effects. Hans von Honsperg of Klöden, for example, reported to the electoral Saxon treasury in 1474 that his incomes barely met household expenses. For cloth alone he allotted annually the equivalent of 41,700 kg of rye, half for himself, a third for his wife, and the rest for his daughters. This was less than half the limit (100,000 kg of rye) that Regensburg's sumptuary law placed on the price of a single dress for a burgher's wife or daughter. Burghers often lived far better than country gentlemen did, and not only in the east. In 1519 Lucas Rem of Augsburg, for example, spent half again as much (991 fl.) on a single wedding as the Swabian knight Werner von Zimmern had paid (650 fl.) in 1453 for an entire village.[38]

There are none the less signs of modest if rough prosperity in the (self-assessed) tax returns of the Saxon nobles in 1474. Seiffard von Lüttichau, lord of Kmehlen on the Bohemian-Lusatian border, for example, described his considerable household: wife, daughter, four sons, two squires, secretary, bailiff, watchman, carpenter, lady's maid, cook, children's nanny, and others—a total of twenty-four persons.[39]

---

[37] *Ibid.*, pp. 292–5.

[38] Abel, *Agricultural Fluctuations*, p. 76; *idem, Geschichte der deutschen Landwirtschaft*, p. 129.

[39] Franz, *Quellen*, pp. 570–5, no. 228, used by F. R. H. Du Boulay, *Germany in the Later Middle Ages* (London, 1983), pp. 73–4, 87, 174–6. This household, it may be noted, was larger than that of a dowager duchess in Hannoversch-Münden in 1397–1398, which contained 20–30 persons; Wilhelm Abel, "Neue Wege der handwerksgeschichtlichen Forschung", in Abel, ed., *Handwerksgeschichte in neuer Sicht*, Göttinger Beiträge zur Wirtschafts- und Sozialgeschichte I (Göttingen, 1978), pp. 1–25, here p. 11.

This junker was also lord of five villages, perhaps 1,000 souls, from whose rents he and his folk lived roughly but well—his inventory includes spices, figs, almonds, and raisins—though he complained that his barns and fish-ponds lay in ruins.

II. *Guild*

Just as the lineage cushioned the noble household, the guild shielded the burgher household against the shocks of the late medieval age of crisis. Trade and manufacturing, the late medieval German city's most important economic functions, were managed, trade partly and manufacturing almost entirely, through corporations called "guilds".[40] It is customary to distinguish between two types of guild, the older merchants' guild (*Gilde*), which went back to eleventh-century antecedents and was chiefly a north German form, and the newer artisans' and shopkeepers' guild (*Zunft*), which emerged in south Germany around 1200 and slowly spread northward. The many names—*Gilde* and *Amt* in north Germany, *Innung* in central Germany, *Zeche* in Austria, Bavaria, Bohemia, Moravia, and Silesia, and *Zunft* in south Germany—all refer to an institution which, in Otto von Gierke's words, "combined religious, social, moral, private, and political goals".[41] A community of fortune of persons having common economic and social interests, the guild regulated their work, represented and defended their liberties, managed their spiritual lives and social welfare, and, in many cities, shared in the governance of the city.[42] The guild consisted of three overlapping communities. First, it was an economic association which possessed an exclusive right to conduct a trade or trades and jurisdiction over all aspects of the trades, which was exercised by a guildmaster (*Zunftmeister*) and guild court (*Schöffen, Sechser, Zwölfer*). Secondly, the guild was a religious confraternity (*Seelzunft*), which assumed religious obligations, managed burials, and marked the anniversaries of deaths (*Jahrzeiten*), and to which a good

---

[40] Fundamental is Eberhard Isenmann, *Die deutsche Stadt im Spätmittelalter 1250–1500. Stadtgestalt, Recht, Stadtregiment, Kirche, Gesellschaft, Wirtschaft* (Stuttgart, 1988), here pp. 299–319. See also Erich Maschke, "Deutsche Städte am Ausgang des Mittelalters", in Maschke, *Städte und Menschen*, pp. 56–99.

[41] Otto von Gierke, *Das deutsche Genossenschaftsrecht* (4 vols., Berlin; 1868–1913; repr. Graz, 1954), I, p. 228.

[42] Isenmann, *Die deutsche Stadt*, pp. 315–19.

many outsiders, including clergy, might belong. Thirdly, the guild maintained a social club (*Stube, Gesellschaft*), often separate from its headquarters as a trade association (*Laube*). Guilds also varied greatly in size, from a dozen or so masters in the small towns of south-western Germany to 300 weavers at Frankfurt in 1387 and 700 gardeners at Strasbourg around 1500.

Like the household, the guild was thus both an economic and a social institution. Just as the household was a unit of co-residence and production supplemented by literal kinship relations, the guild was an association of producers and sellers supplemented by religious and social relations of fictive or spiritual kinship. The economic core of the guild was monopoly (*Zunftzwang*), which bound to guild membership the right to exercise a trade and access to the civic market, the control of production processes and the quality of products, and limitation of production to specific places—notably not the countryside.

Only master artisans, traders, merchants, and shopkeepers could be full members of an urban guild, though journeymen and apprentices enjoyed a kind of passive membership and shared the guild's protection. Admission to a guild depended on ability to demonstrate free, legitimate, and honourable birth, performance of an apprenticeship and journeymanship (2–8 years, though 2–4 years was normal), a probation period (1–3 years), and, since the early fourteenth century, execution of a masterwork. New guildsmen had normally to become citizens (*Bürgerrecht*), to pay a fee (*Zunftkauf*), and either to furnish arms for militia service or to pay a fee (*Harnischgeld*). Such was the model guild in its classic, south German form between the fourteenth and the sixteenth centuries. While in the south the guilds tended to become subsidiary corporations of the urban communes, giving the masters political voice and weight, over most of northern Germany and in a few southern towns, notably Nuremberg, the older mercantile elites maintained their political monopolies.

The number of a city's guilds was determined not by the number of its trades but through political negotiation: 15 at Basel, 13 at Zurich, 28 (later 20) at Strasbourg, 7 at Überlingen, 17 at Ulm, 12 at Magdeburg, 16 at Danzig, and 50 at Lübeck. The number of crafts, on the other hand, underwent an explosive increase during the later middle ages. There were 148 trades in 1378 and 191 in 1440 at Frankfurt am Main, and 206 at Erfurt around 1500. Frankfurt had 32 metalworking trades alone, while Nuremberg had more than 40 trades, and by 1420 more than 500 masters worked in the iron branch there. Hamburg had 457 brewers in 1376; Cologne 200 weavers around 1400.[43] Specialization and strict control of quality brought some German products to high reputation by the fifteenth century, such as Constance's linens, Nuremberg's metalwares, Augsburg's and Ulm's fustians, and Solingen's knives. This soaring reputation of German craftsmen tends to hide the parallel growth of the humbler service and victualling trades, whose numbers reached astonishing levels for such small populations: 71 butchers at Nuremberg (1363), 116 at Lübeck (c. 1370), 109 at Basel (1451), and 75 at Frankfurt am Main (1481); 187 brewers at Lübeck (1407), 182 at Wismar (1464), 378 at Danzig (1416), and 457 at Hamburg (1378).[44]

These figures suggest the degree to which the urban common good (*gemeiner Nutz*) depended on the prosperity and discipline of its artisanate which bore the main brunt of civic taxation. The inculcation and enforcement of this discipline fell to the guilds, for

> with the objective norms of craft and status (*Stand*) went a strict moral code, which demanded exemplary moral conduct from the entire households—master, wife, journeymen, and apprentices—both at work and in social intercourse. The code forbade them to associate at home or in public with persons of evil reputation and provided the norms for their way of life in all matters, including how they dressed and ate. The guild encased (*überformte*) family and household.[45]

The guild, from this point of view, was the middle instance in the hierarchy of household, guilds, and commune.

From another point of view the guild looked like a federation of households formed to serve common economic, social and religious needs. It did so, in part, by closing off access to work and markets to non-members. This is clearest in its economic functions the cartel-like character of which has been subject to a very long debate.[46] Guilds restricted the sizes of shops (one or two journeymen was usual), the rights to practise a craft or sell manufactured goods, and access to raw materials, and they engaged in many kinds of price-fixing. During the fifteenth century, too, guilds and regulated crafts began

---

[43] Rolf Sprandel, "Gewerbe und Handel 1350–1500", in Aubin and Zorn, *Handbuch der deutschen Wirtschafts- und Sozialgeschichte*, I, pp. 335–6.

[44] Isenmann, *Die deutsche Stadt*, pp. 342–3.

[45] *Ibid.*, p. 312.

[46] See Reinhard Ennen, *Zünfte und Wettbewerb. Möglichkeiten und Grenzen zünftlicherischer Wettbewerbsbeschränkungen im städtischen Handel und Gewerbe des Spätmittelalters*, Neue Wirtschaftgeschichte III (Cologne/Vienna, 1971).

to restrict the numbers of masters: Nuremberg set a limit of 12 master bronzesmiths, while Hamburg reduced the master coopers from 200 in 1437 to 150 in 1458 and 120 in 1501. These acts were exclusions, but even more exclusionary were the restrictions on males who had no households and on women, whether heads of households or not.

Domestic servants, apprentices, and journeymen made up the bulk of the urban working poor, who lacked the independence to form households and economically belonged to the have-nots (*habenitse*).[47] These servants (*Knechte*), who worked for wages and keep, made up about quarter (22–28 per cent) of the populations of fifteenth century cities. Many of them were domestic servants, who served in every urban household of substance and belonged to its inner core. They might well be persons of respect—in 1441 and again in 1459, "our maid, Grete", stood godmother to sons of Augsburg's Jakob Fugger[48]—but their disability lay in that, while in service, they could not form households of their own.

One type of servant, the journeyman, had no household of his own, though he could hope to form one as a master. Journeymen—apprenticeship became a distinct status only in the fourteenth century—worked under masters for a fixed term, most commonly six months, of service (*Dienst*), and despite their English name (the German *Geselle* has no such connotation), the requirement to travel began to appear only in the mid-fifteenth century and did not become general until around 1600. During the fifteenth century, the guilds began to regulate wages (*Lidlon*), work hours—8–16 hours for an average of 11–12 hours per day, about 256 days per year minus free ("blue") Mondays—and other conditions. The journeyman's nominal wage—a third to a half in cash—often remained fixed for very long periods, even in the face of great price fluctuations, as at Frankfurt am Main, for example, where construction workers were paid at the same weekly rate from about 1350 until 1553.

The guilds supervised journeymen in part to reduce competition for their labour and in part to counter their own corporate activity, for the journeymen called themselves "comrades" (*Geselle*, from

---

[47] Erich Maschke, "Die Unterschichten in der mittelalterlichen Städte Deutschlands", in Maschke, *Städte und Menschen*, pp. 306–79.

[48] Maschke, *Die deutsche Familie*, p. 48. This was Jakob the Elder (d. 1468), not his far more famous son, Jakob the Rich (1459–1525).

Saalgenosse) and organized in imitation of the masters with whom they worked very closely—rarely more than two journeymen per shop in the Rhenish cities. Such journeymen's guilds (*Knechtzünfte*) began to appear in the Upper Rhenish cities, especially among the weavers, and flourished from about 1350 until about 1410—the period of rising real wages. The journeymen also formed regional and sometimes transregional brotherhoods with rules, treasuries, assemblies, courts, and religious activities. The journeyman bakers of Strasbourg and Freiburg even built and maintained their own chapels in the civic hospitals. They also staged strikes, the first by journeyman belt-makers at Breslau in 1329 and the most spectacular in 1470 by Strasbourg's journeyman furriers, who decamped to Haguenau and called out their comrades all through the region. Gradually, however, the masters, allied to the communes, harnessed the journeymen to the allied structures of commune, guild, and household and undermined their ability to organize and bargain, and by the mid-fifteenth century they worked under a single set of regulations from northern Switzerland to Cologne.

The journeyman was at least potentially a full-fledged master; the working woman was usually not. The role of gender in the interplay of household and guild was complicated. The city depended on women's work and working women, both within the household and outside it.[49] Women worked in retail trades in all cities. At Nuremberg, for example, women worked as tailors, shopkeepers, money-changers, and innkeepers; Speyer recognized "women merchants" (*koufmennine, koufvrouwe, institutrices*); Lübeck allowed a female shopkeeper (*cremersche*) to continue her work after marrying a guildsman; women belonged to the confraternity of the ironmongers at Trier in 1285; and women made up more than half (27 of 52) of the retail grocers (*Gremper*) in a Strasbourg list of the fifteenth century.[50]

Women also worked in shops as artisans, sometimes as masters. At Lübeck female masters (*sulvesvrouwen*) were active in many crafts; at Strasbourg around 1430, 25 women were members of the cloth

[49] The following paragraphs are based on *ibid.*, pp. 35–45; Isenmann, *Die deutsche Stadt*, pp. 314–15; Margarete Wensky, *Die Stellung der Frau in der stadtkölnischen Wirtschaft im Spätmittlalter* (Cologne, 1981); Martha C. Howell, *Women, Production, and Patriarchy in Late Medieval Cities* (Chicago, 1986); Merry E. Wiesner, *Working Women in Renaissance Germany* (New Brunswick, NJ, 1986). For the European context, see *idem, Women and Gender in Early Modern Europe* (Cambridge, 1993), pp. 102–6.

[50] Maschke, *Die deutsche Familie*, pp. 36–7.

guild (*Tucherzunft*), and in 1484 the guild ordered that the guild's women (*frowenspersone*) should perform all duties of a guild member with the exception of the city watch; and at Basel in the late thirteenth century, women were active in several trades, including the plasterers and the coopers.[51] Many guilds recognized the "widow's right" to continue her husband's shop, though sometimes only to complete current work. The role of women in a given branch varied enormously, even in neighbouring regions. It was very important in the draperies of Douai in Flanders, far less so in those of Lier in Brabant.[52]

A special case is presented by late medieval Cologne, where the role of women in guilds assumed an unprecedented and unmatched proportion. A few of Cologne's guilds—tailors, harness-makers, cloth-cutters—discriminated against women, but many others did not, including the needle-makers, purse-makers, furriers, sash-makers, and weavers of linen, fustians, and woollens, as well as the butchers. And in Cologne, alone in the German-speaking world, women artisans formed their own guilds of yarn-makers, gold-spinners, and silk-weavers. The last-named counted between 1437 and 1504 a total of 116 masters and 765 apprentices.[53]

The entire development of women's participation in retail sales, crafts, and the corresponding guilds reflected the economic realities of rising wages and rising prices for manufactured goods.[54] Against it stood the feelings represented by the ideal of the burgher's household, a closed and secure unit represented to the outside world of guild and commune by its male head. In effect, in the burgher's world all social roles were, in the last analysis, gendered roles, and when the economic trends changed after 1450 with the recovery of populations and prices, such views began to make themselves felt in a new way.[55] Gradually, as work became scarcer and cheaper, and access to the guilds' privileges correspondingly more valuable, women were pushed out of many trades and lost their rights in many guilds.

---

[51] *Ibid.*, p. 37.

[52] Howell, *Women, Production, and Patriarchy*, pp. 161–73.

[53] Wensky, *Die Stellung der Frau*.

[54] But probably not a permanent surplus of women in the cities. This widespread notion goes back to Karl Bücher; it is demolished by Kurt Wessoly, "Die weibliche Bevölkerungsanteil in spätmittelalterlichen und frühneuzeitlichen Städten und die Betätigung von Frauen im zünftigen Handwerk (insbesondere am Mittel- und Oberrhein)", *ZGO* LXXXIX (1980): pp. 69–117.

[55] See esp. Lyndal Roper, *The Holy Household. Women and Morals in Reformation Augsburg* (Oxford, 1989).

292   CHAPTER TEN

The beginnings of this process, most of which belongs to the succeeding, early modern era, can be detected in the fifteenth century.[56] At Frankfurt, for example, where nine of the twenty guilds and brotherhoods had had provisions for women in the fourteenth century, only three of them did so after 1500. Women continued to perform "women's work", such as the needle trades, midwifery, and certain kinds of baking, but their day as active participants in the corporate economic and social institutions of the German-speaking cities was past.[57] The location of the limits to which late medieval economic reality stretched attitudes about work and gender is illustrated by the near-total absence of women from the institutions that drove large-scale and long-distance economic operations, firms, and mining syndicates.

III. *Firm*

Many kinds of economic operations in the late medieval Empire—long-distance trade and banking, mining operations, and certain other branches, such as printing—were conducted not by corporate associations of producers or sellers but by entrepreneurs operating by means of what is here called a "firm".[58] Varieties of firms in the late medieval Empire did all long-distance trade and most banking. Along the roads—the great constrictor of trade—and rivers and across the northern seas, the German merchants transported goods produced and consumed by the Empire's peoples. Their two most important networks connected the Hanseatic merchants to the trade of the North and Baltic seas and the southern cities' merchants to the trade of the Mediterranean basin.[59]

The two chief zones of German trade evolved quite different institutions. Hanseatic firms were small—two to four partners—and formed for a short term—usually a single venture. The Lübecker Hermann Mornewech, for example, formed or renewed eighteen different firms

---

[56] On this trend, see Heide Wunder, *"Er ist die Sonn, sie ist der Mond". Frauen in der frühen Neuzeit* (Munich, 1992), pp. 120–5.

[57] Wiesner, *Working Women in Renaissance Germany*.

[58] John H. Munro, "Patterns of Trade, Money, and Credit", in Brady *et al.*, *Handbook of European History, 1400–1600* I, pp. 147–96.

[59] Based on Sprandel, "Gewerbe und Handel 1350–1500", pp. 347–52; Isenmann, *Die deutsche Stadt*, pp. 358–80.

between 1323 and 1335. This practice, plus the assembly of capital from wide circles, including rural nobles, clergymen, and even harbour workers, spread the northern trade's high risks. So did the Hanseatic merchants' custom of avoiding specialization in trade. Their operations were protected by a vast economic and military federation of cities, the Hansa itself, which from its centre at Lübeck stretched out its two wings in the Baltic and North Seas to protect its merchants' trade along the axis Novgorod-Reval-Visby-Lübeck-Hamburg-Bruges-London. Westward flowed the wax, timber, rye, fish, copper, and furs; eastward went salt, cloth, and other manufactures; and along both wings flowed German beer. Although by the fifteenth century the Germans began to feel the challenge to which they would later succumb, from the Hollanders, until the end of the later middle ages the Hanseatic League remained cock of the north, so powerful that it made war on Denmark (1426–1435), the Netherlands (1438–1441), and England (1470–1474).

The contrast between Hanseatic and southern merchants' practices has been characterized thus: "the Hanseatic merchant had businesses, the South German merchant had a business."[60] The southerners founded powerful, long-lasting firms, often around a single family, in which the principal partners supplied both capital and management skills, for an average of four to six years, often renewed. The evolution of the southern firms is illustrated by the Great Ravensburg Company, established by three Swabian merchant families in 1380, which from its headquarters around Lake Constance strove to monopolize the linen trade through thirteen offices scattered from Ravensburg to Barcelona. At its height the company had partners from 121 families, all burghers of free cities, and 117,000 fl. in working capital. Whereas the Ravensburg company was run by a troika of partners and avoided banking, Jakob Fugger (1459–1525) ran his family-based firm, pursued both trade and finance, and over the years 1484 to 1524 made 15–20 per cent per year to the Ravensburgers' 7.5 per cent. By 1510, when his firm was worth about 245,000 fl., he had surpassed the Ravensburgers for good.

Although the south German merchants never dominated the trade of any land outside the Empire, they operated all through the area

---

[60] Jacob Strieder, *Studien zur Geschichte kapitalistischer Organisationsformen. Monopole, Kartelle und Aktiengesellschaften im Mittelalter und zu Beginn der Neuzeit*, 2nd ed. (Munich/Leipzig, 1935), p. 97.

bounded by the line Rome-Seville-Lisbon-Toulouse-Paris-Antwerp-London-Lübeck-Cracow-Lvov/Lemberg-Constantinople. The Nuremberg firms, which since 1350 operated in all sectors, formed true economic conglomerates, combining long-distance trade in goods, large manufacturing enterprises, and mining operations with banking and the trade in offices and regalian rights. Nurembergers pioneered in all areas and all branches from the early fourteenth century, only to be overhauled after 1470 in certain sectors by Augsburg firms. Like the Nurembergers under the Luxemburg dynasty in the fourteenth century, the Fuggers and lesser Augsburg firms bound their destinies to the Habsburg dynasty at the end of the fifteenth. A deposit of 300,000 fl.—two-and-a-half times the Ravensburg Company's entire capitalization—by Bishop Melchior von Meckau of Brixen (Bressanone) suggests the scale on which they operated. The firms spread the techniques they learned from others, chiefly the Italians, such as double-entry book-keeping (introduced by Praun and Tucher of Nuremberg in 1476–1484) and the bill of exchange. From the early 1400s onwards the Nurembergers, and later the Fuggers, codified their knowledge in books modelled on Francesco Balducci Pegolotti's *La Practica della mercatura* (1337–1340).

Despite the spread of guilds, there were always some branches in which production could be and was organized by merchant-investors. The handiest instrument for such situations was the *Verlag*, a term which comes from the verb *vorlegen* in the sense of "to extend credit".[61] The investor, usually a large merchant or a firm, extended credit in cash (*Geldverlag*) or materials and tools (*Gezeugverlag*) to the producers in return for an exclusive right to buy the products at a fixed price. This system was suited to branches, such as mining, in which the producers themselves could no longer raise the amounts of capital they required. It was also a powerful instrument for the extension of urban economic power over the hinterland and for co-ordinating whole regions' economies with those of large cities.[62] Versions of it achieved great prominence in the new, or newly re-organized, industries of the later fifteenth century, notably mining and printing.

---

[61] Isenmann, *Die deutsche Stadt*, pp. 353–6; Bernhard Kirchgäßner, "Der Verlag im Spanngsfeld von Stadt und Umland", in Erich Maschke and Jürgen Sydow, eds., *Stadt und Umland* (Stuttgart, 1974), pp. 72–128.

[62] Hektor Ammann, *Die wirtschaftliche Stellung der Reichsstadt Nürnberg im Spätmittelalter*, Nürnberger Forschungen XIII (Nuremberg, 1970), pp. 194–224; Kießling, *Die Stadt und ihr Land*.

During the later fifteenth century, mining in the Empire expanded from a subsidiary branch conducted by small, part-time producers, such as the *Eisenbauern* of Styria and Carinthia, into what became by 1500 the greatest industrial branch in Europe.[63] The major watershed came in the second half of the fifteenth century when Central Europe witnessed an explosion of mineral production, largely because of technological improvements in drilling, drainage, and ventilation, which permitted the exploitation of previously untappable gold, silver, and copper deposits in the Saxon-Bohemian Erzgebirge, in the alpine regions of the Tyrol, Styria, and Carinthia, and in Upper Hungary. The scale of this upsurge may be suggested by what happened in Salzburg's Gastein valley, a silver region, the population of which rose from c. 1,800 in 1456 to c. 3,000 in 1497 to 5,000 (of whom 1,200 were miners) in the following century. In the Tyrol, the greatest mining region in Europe, by the early sixteenth century the industry employed perhaps a quarter of the entire population.

Three aspects of the mining boom provided special opportunities to urban firms. First, the mines and smelters required capital far in excess of what could be raised by the syndicates of miners or supplied by any other local source. Secondly, the regalian right to mine, in the Empire a prerogative of princes, suggested a partnership between mining princes and urban firms to exploit mines, smelters, and metal markets to mutual advantage. And thirdly, the mines, the chief form of rural industry, lay far beyond the reach of the urban guilds, which strove with might and main to crush every shoot of rural industry.[64] These factors, plus the tremendous demand for metals, made mining an ideal sector for the operations of firms.[65]

The Nurembergers again led the way, having gained control of the Carpathian metals trade as early as 1396–1412. Around 1450 they began to invest in the first modern smelters (*Saigerhütten*) in Thuringia, and in 1478 investors from Nuremberg, Bautzen, and Cracow (Jan

---

[63] Michael Mitterauer, "Produktionsweise, Siedlungsstruktur und Sozialformen im österreichischen Montanwesen des Mittelalters und der Frühen Neuzeit", in Mitterauer, ed., *Österreichisches Montanwesen. Produktion, Verteilung, Sozialformen* (Vienna, 1974), pp. 234–315; K. Klein, "Die Bevölkerung Österreichs vom Beginn des 16. bis zur Mitte des 18. Jahrhundert", in Heimold Helczmanovszki, ed., *Beiträge zur Bevölkerungs- und Sozialgeschichte Österreichs* (Vienna, 1973), pp. 47–112.

[64] Sprandel, "Gewerbe und Handel 1350–1500", p. 339.

[65] Isenmann, *Die deutsche Stadt*, pp. 351–2; Adolf Laube, *Studien über den erzgebirgischen Silberbergbau von 1470 bis 1546*, 2nd ed. (Berlin, 1976); Strieder, *Studien zur Geschichte kapitalistischer Organisationsformen*; Mitterauer, *Österreichisches Montanwesen*.

Thurzo) negotiated a half-interest in the Goslar mining district called
Trostenfahrt in return for the erection of a modern smelter. They were
also heavily involved in exploiting the Saxon silver bonanzas of the
Erzgebirge at Annaberg and Schneeberg. Once the capitalists gained
access to the mines through agreements with the princes, they got
control by buying up shares (*Kuxen*) in the highly fragmented mining syndicates (*Gewerke*). The operation was then tied together by
contracts (*Käufe*), paid in advance, for deliveries of metals to the
princes. In effect, the developments since 1470 enabled princes and
investors to exploit the ore deposits, and the miners, on a scale
unknown to the old, co-operative mining syndicates.

The system worked much the same way in the great mines of the
Tyrol, where silver production tripled and copper more than doubled between 1470 and 1520.[66] Starting at Villach in Carinthia in
1495, the Fuggers of Augsburg gained a dominant position in Europe's
greatest mining region. They organized the production and sale of
metals and held a monopoly of the import of foodstuffs, in return
for which they lent huge sums to Emperor Maximilian I (r. 1493–1519),
who owed them and other Augsburgers about 6,000,000 fl. at his
death in 1519.[67]

New methods or machinery sometimes favoured exploitation by
firms rather than by guilds. The rising cost of wages in the later
middle ages made labour-saving devices, such as the silk-spinning mill,
which Walter Kesinger brought from Lucca to Cologne in 1412/13,
all the more desirable.[68] One such new process that well suited the
institution of the firm was printing with movable type, which emerged
during the 1450s in the firm which Johann Gutenberg (Gensfleisch)
of Mainz had organised in 1448. The branch's profit depended on
using relatively cheap raw materials—paper cost a third of parchment—
and the relatively high literacy of the German burghers, and soon
printed books cost about a fifth as much as manuscripts. Under these
conditions, printing firms spread through the Empire during the second half of the fifteenth century, until by 1500 about 300 presses
were operating in about 65 cities. Of the 450 known printers of this
era, very few came from the older crafts, but more than 100 were

---

[66] Sprandel, "Gewerbe und Handel 1350–1500", pp. 340–2.
[67] Hermann Wiesflecker, *Kaiser Maximilian I. Das Reich, Österreich und Europa an der Wende zur Neuzeit* (5 vols., Munich, 1971–86) V, pp. 576–80.
[68] Isenmann, *Die deutsche Stadt*, pp. 347–8.

university men, many of them clergymen. Almost all the printers were investors, organizers, and managers of their firms, though few became rich from the trade. The greatest of them, Anton Koberger of Nuremberg, is said to have employed 100 employees working 25 presses.

Around 1500, on the eve of the early modern era, it might have seemed as if the firms were taking over the world. This was certainly the impression conveyed by the anti-monopoly movement of the 1520s, and it was certainly fostered by theologians such as Johann Geiler von Kaysersberg (1445–1510), who defended the corporatist ethic from his pulpit in Strasbourg's cathedral:

> The Holy Sacrament should be refused those who buy as cheaply as possible and those who sell as dearly as possible . . . for this is against brotherly love. You should add a modest profit, also your trouble and effort, but to buy as cheaply and sell as dearly as you can, that is false![69]

In fact, around 1500 the corporate way of life was enjoying the last phase of its golden age. It was partly protected by the fact that it had evolved from its economic base a socio-political institution well suited to the management of small social orders through the coordination of households and, in the cities, guilds. This institution was the commune.

IV. *Commune*

The commune (*Gemeinde*), a sworn association of heads of household for the purposes of governance—the defence of homes and rights, the management of everyday life, the provision of justice, and representation to the outside world—arose from origins in the thirteenth century to become the most characteristic social institution of the common people in the late medieval Empire. The comparability of rural and urban communes is now widely accepted.[70] There were

---

[69] Quoted by Strieder, *Studien zur Geschichte kapitalistischer Organisationsformen*, p. 62. See Thomas A. Brady, Jr., *Turning Swiss. Cities and Empire, 1450–1550* (Cambridge, 1985), pp. 120–30.

[70] To the credit, above all, of Peter Blickle. See his *Deutsche Untertanen. Ein Widerspruch* (Stuttgart, 1981); *idem*, *The Communal Reformation. The Quest for Salvation in Sixteenth-Century Germany*, trans. Thomas Dunlap (Atlantic Highlands, NJ, 1992), pt. 3. The following is based on Günter Vogler, "Dorfgemeinde und Stadtgemeinde zwischen

important differences, but their basis, the contrast between agriculture
and trade and manufacturing, was not great. More than two-thirds
(67.1 per cent) of the Empire's cities were either small agricultural
towns (*Ackerbürgerstädte*) or contained at least some farmers, and in
some rich regions, notably Alsace, large numbers of urban guildsmen were actually engaged in some form of agriculture.[71] Whether
in the town or in the village, the commune was an oath-bound association, admission to which depended on the possession of a farm
or a house; its assembly possessed the power to form statutes (*Satzungen,
Weistümer*) for the purposes of securing justice and regulating the use
of common property. The commune's decisive norm was the common good, service to which was binding on all members. Neither
in the village nor in the town did the commune include, even by
inference (as it did women and children), all residents, nor was it
ever a purely associative institution.

Even where, as in the imperial free cities, the lord's authority disappeared, the commune evolved a city council as a governing institution, which soon began to consider itself a "ruler" (*Obrigkeit*) and
the citizens its "subjects" (*Untertanen*).[72] From its origins in the thirteenth
century, the German urban communal regime developed into a fully-
fledged city-state with council (Rat), town clerk (*Stadtschreiber, Ratschreiber*),
and attorney (*Consulent, Syndicus*), judicial functions, taxation, military
organization, and welfare institutions.[73] It may be argued that these
communes and their regimes were primarily political rather than
social or economic, but, in truth, in these milieux such distinctions
are not very helpful. The commune and its regime were both social
and economic institutions, because there were no boundaries between
private and public life in the towns, and the civic regime, like the
guild regime, reached its fingers into every aspect of the burghers'

Feudalismus und Kapitalismus", in Peter Blickle, ed., *Landgemeinde und Stadtgemeinde
in Mitteleuropa*, HZ, Supplement XIII (Munich, 1991), pp. 39–64, here pp. 39–51.

[71] Anne-Marie Imbs, "Tableaux des corporations alsaciennes, XIVᵉ–XVIII siècles",
and Jean Rott, "Artisanat et mouvements sociaux à Strasbourg autour de 1525",
in *Artisans et ouvriers d'Alsace*, Publications de la Société Savante d'Alsace et des
Régions de l'Est IX (Strasbourg, 1965), pp. 35–45, 158. The percentage of *Ackerbürgerstädte* is based on a survey of 1911 towns by Renate Schilling, cited by Vogler,
"Dorfgemeinde und Stadtgemeinde", p. 46.

[72] There is a classic statement of this dualistic principle by Otto Brunner, "Souver-
änitätsproblem und Sozialstruktur in den deutschen Reichsstädten der frühen Neuzeit",
in his *Neue Wege der Verfassungs- und Sozialgeschichte*, 2nd ed., pp. 294–321, here p. 303.
For the European context, see Steven Rowan, "The Urban Community. Rulers
and Ruled", in Brady *et al., Handbook of European History, 1400–1600* I, pp. 197–230.

[73] See the superb systematic description by Isenmann, *Die deutsche Stadt*, pp. 131–98.

economic and social lives. The burgher's government dealt with war and peace, assaults and insults, fashion and finance, goods and services, bread and wine, taverns and brothels, beggars and bishops, clothing and trash, and marriage, birth, and death.[74]

In some sectors, the late medieval communal regimes did not just manage, they pioneered, and in none more notably than in finance. Urban regimes managed by merchants and other burghers practically invented the entire foundations of finance and banking in the Empire. They adapted to this purpose their favourite instrument, annuities (*Renten*), for which the purchaser deposited a fixed sum in return for a guaranteed annual income. Originally "perpetual" (*ewig*), that is, non-redeemable, in the fourteenth century annuities generally became negotiable and redeemable, and perpetual ones were commonly forbidden (1240 in Lübeck, 1360 in Vienna, 1439 in Frankfurt). For small folk the annuity was the most popular form of social insurance, especially after the introduction of life annuities (*census vitalitius*, *Leibgedinge*), i.e. annuities paid only for the life of the purchaser, on which the interest gradually fell from 12–15 per cent to a standard 5 per cent at the end of the fifteenth century. The sale of annuities drew very large sums from private hands toward public purposes. Lübeck's Castorp brothers, for example, around 1490 held civic debt to the sum of 30,000 Lübeck pounds. The inability to redeem such debts led to the continuing need to service them. At Basel, for example, service on the public debt rose from around 2 per cent of total civic outlay in the 1360s to over 50 per cent by the 1430s, and remained above 30 per cent for most of the rest of the century.[75] The communal regime was indeed an organ of justice and governance, but it was also the foremost urban economic institution.

The late medieval German urban communes exhibit many variations in their histories and shapes. There were many intermediate phases between the first consular regimes around 1200 (Utrecht, 1196; Lübeck, 1201; Cologne, 1216) and the full-blown southern guild regimes of the fourteenth and fifteenth centuries, just as there were many urban communes which never gained full autonomy, for example, the many towns of the German east which were endowed by the princes with some rights of self-government.[76] The late medieval

---

[74] See the splendid overview in *Ibid.*, pp. 146–60.

[75] Josef Rosen, "Zins und Zinsaufwand", in Rosen, *Finanzgeschichte Basels im späten Mittelalter. Gesammelte Beiträge 1971–1987* (Stuttgart, 1989), pp. 170–3.

[76] Isenmann, *Die deutsche Stadt*, pp. 109–13, is clear and nuanced on these gradations.

phase of urban development none the less possessed its own characteristic signatures. The first was the conjuncture, collision, and collaboration of the communal development, on the one side, and the rise
of the guilds, on the other. This process, which drew strength from
the appreciation of the value of human labour during the depression, gave the economic and social weight of the middle—the bulge
in the onion—political weight and voice.[77]

Civic struggles—another name for guild revolts[78]—produced typical
guild-based constitutions at Strasbourg in 1334, Zurich in 1336, Augsburg in 1352/68, Braunschweig in 1374, Lübeck in 1380/84, Cologne
in 1396, Hamburg in 1484.[79] Often the guilds won and held a substantial share of civic offices—one-half at Ulm, two-thirds at Strasbourg,
and, briefly, all at Basel—but elsewhere their bid for sharing power
was beaten back by the older elites. At Lübeck, for example, a city
ruled by the merchants, the guilds (*Ämter*) lost their independent jurisdiction in 1384 and functioned only as reporting bodies (*Ruginstanz*)
for the civic regime, while from around 1400 the guilds of Danzig,
Stendal, and Hamburg were allowed to meet only in the presence of
two councillors. Over much of north Germany, indeed, though not at
Cologne, the guilds remained regulated crafts, closely supervised by
a non-guild ruling group. The most notorious example of this outcome in south Germany was at Nuremberg, where the mercantile
elite crushed the guilds with the emperor's aid in 1348; thereafter
the city knew only various types of regulated crafts (*Handwerke*).

Where the guilds did gain direct access to communal government,
it did not mean that artisans as such ruled the towns. Plain artisans
did sit in the council chambers of many (especially southern) German
towns during the later middle ages, but the ominous gap between
their economic needs and the onerous but poorly remunerated civic
offices tended to keep the main weight of civic business in the hands
of the well-to-do, who in the Upper Swabian towns were called "men
of leisure" (*Müßiggänger*).[80] This tendency, plus the growing complica-

[77] Erich Maschke, "Mittelschichten in deutschen Städten des Mittelalters", in
Maschke *Städte und Menschen*, pp. 275–305.
[78] Karl Czok, "Die Bürgerkämpfe in Süd- und Westdeutschland im 14. Jahrhundert",
Jahrbuch für Geschichte der oberdeutschen Reichsstädte XII–XIII (1966–1967): pp. 40–72.
[79] Sprandel, "Sozialgeschichte 1350–1500", p. 378.
[80] Isenmann, *Die deutsche Stadt*, p. 139; and see Erich Maschke, "Verfassung und
soziale Kräfte in der deutschen Stadt des späten Mittelalters, vornehmlich in Oberdeutschland", in Maschke, *Städte und Menschen*, pp. 170–274.

tion and tempo of civic business, stimulated a pronounced trend toward oligarchy—more offices in the hands of fewer, richer families—
and sometime around 1450 came the watershed between an age of
devolution of political voice to the guildsmen and an age of its re-
concentration in the hands of the noble and mercantile elites.[81] Gradually, the great age of popular activism in the towns came to a
close—Maschke counted 170 disturbances between 1301 and 1520—
as the economic recovery and falling real wages reinforced the oligarchical trend and made the guild towns more and more like
Nuremberg, where, as Dr. Christoph Scheurl noted in 1516, "the
common folk [*das gemain völklein*] have no authority, as they properly
should have none, for all authority comes from God, and governance is granted to only those few who are specially gifted by the
special wisdom of Him who created nature and all things."[82]

The history of rural communes in the late medieval Empire displays
great variations.[83] In general, it is recognized that the commune
(*Gemeinde*), as a sworn association of the principal male householders
of a village, took shape in the space left by the disintegration of the
primary economic and social unit of the preceding era, the manor.
Like its urban counterpart, the rural commune was older than the
economic crisis that set in after 1300, though it acquired its classic
form only gradually, in the depression's wake, as rights of local governance associated with the manor disintegrated into separable and
often separate components—landlordship (*Grundherrschaft*), mastery of
serfs (*Leibherrschaft*), and judicial authority (*Gerichtsherrschaft*).[84] The process, which occurred earlier in the other settled areas of Germany

---

[81] Isenmann, *Die deutsche Stadt*, pp. 132–3; Vogler, "Dorfgemeinde und Stadtgemeinde", pp. 49–50. See Thomas A. Brady, Jr., *Ruling Class, Regime, and Reformation
at Strasbourg, 1520–1555*, Studies in Late Medieval and Reformation Thought XXII
(Leiden, 1978), pp. 163–96, where the trend is documented from the mid-fifteenth
century.

[82] Christoph Scheurl's famous "Epistel über die Verfassung der Reichsstadt
Nürnberg", in *Die Chroniken der fränkischen Städte. Nürnberg* V vol. 5 Chroniken der deutschen Städte, XI (Leipzig, 1874); repr. Göttingen, 1961, pp. 781–804, here p. 791.
On the number of urban revolts, see Maschke "Deutsche Städte am Ausgang des
Mittelalters", p. 95 n. 206. The effect of falling real wages on popular political
activity is argued by Jean-Pierre Kintz *La Société Strasbourgeoise du milieu du XVIᵉ siècle
à la fin de la Guerre de Trente Ans 1560–1650. Essai d'histoire démographique, économique
et sociale* (Paris, 1984).

[83] Robisheaux, "The World of the Village", pp. 99–102.

[84] See Heide Wunder, *Die bäuerliche Gemeinde in Deutschland* (Göttingen, 1986); idem,
"Die ländliche Gemeinde als Strukturprinzip der spätmittelalterlich-neuzeitlichen
Geschichte Mitteleuropas", in *Landgemeinde und Stadtgemeinde in Mitteleuropa*, pp. 385–402.

than east of the Elbe, created a new space for the rural commune.

The typical rural commune was a sworn corporate association of households, each represented by its adult male householder—communal government was almost exclusively a male affair—and presided over by a mayor (*Schultheiß*) and a village court (*scabini, jurati, Schöffen, échevins*) of six, eight, or twelve men. This body co-operated with, rivalled, and sometimes superseded the nobles' local governance, especially where property rights and territorial government were greatly fragmented. At Ebersmünster in Lower Alsace, for example, the abbot as both seignieur and landlord nominated the village mayor, while at Hüningen, which belonged to the abbot of St. Alban in Basel, the village elected its administrator (*Meier*), who assessed taxes with the aid of four or six full farmers (*Huber*).[85] Here, as elsewhere in southern Germany, the general tendency during the later middle ages was for local rule to pass from seignieurial into communal hands.

No general notion of liberty, but only "specific and precise rights", underlay this intensely local development.[86] There did arise a notion, however, that somehow things were out of joint on the land, or, as the Strasbourg merchant and mystic Rulman Merswin (1307–1382) put it, "the peasants in these villages live like animals, lacking all fear of God, and they have become wicked and quite proud, and are of quite perverse mien".[87] Where feudal governance was weak, they became truly obstreperous, as rural federations combined into permanent, sworn associations to pacify and defend the countryside. In the Swiss forest cantons, the Graubünden, and the Valais, mature political federations developed on a communal basis, and unsuccessful attempts to "turn Swiss" in this sense erupted in Vorarlberg, the Tyrol, the Swabian Allgäu, and the belt of lands from Lake Constance west to Alsace during the fifteenth century.[88] If they did not succeed

---

It is now recognized that rural communes were typical of central Europe as a whole, not just their classic landscape in the Empire's southern and western lands. Wunder, *Die bäuerliche Gemeinde*, pp. 63–7; and see the contributions of Karlheinz Blaschke, Hartmut Harnisch, Evamaria Engel, and Carl-Heinz Hauptmeyer to *Landgemeinde und Stadtgemeinde in Mitteleuropa*, pp. 119–44, 289–384.

[85] Henri Dubled, "Grundherrschaft und Dorfgerichtsbarkeit in Elsaß vom 13. bis zum 15. Jahrhundert und ihr Verhältnis zueinander", *Deutsches Archiv für Erforschung des Mittelalters* LXVII (1961): pp. 518–19.

[86] Du Boulay, *Germany in the Later Middle Ages*, p. 172. For the very wide regional variations in rural communes, see Wunder, *Die bäuerliche Gemeinde*, pp. 67–77.

[87] Franz, *Quellen*, p. 479, no. 187 (c. 1370).

[88] Brady, *Turning Swiss*, pp. 34–42.

in imitating their Swiss neighbours, at least they were able to push their ways into established territorial diets (*Landschaften*).[89] This occurred chiefly in the Empire's southern belt, which was also the main theatre of the sixty or so rural revolts between 1336 and 1525.[90]

One important cause of rural revolts, which often were organized by communes, arose from their lords' efforts to recover what the agrarian crisis had taken. One way to do this was to retain labour on the land by offering very favourable terms, as the prince-bishop of Augsburg did at Pfronten in the Allgäu in 1403, or heritability of tenures, as the provost of Berchtesgaden did in 1377.[91] Another was to reinforce servile customs: some south German abbots demanded that their serfs swear, on pain of a heavy fine, never to leave the land.[92] Harsher yet, since around 1400 some south German lords began to restore full servility by revoking the rights to free mobility and to free choice of guardian or marriage partner.[93] It was partly this temporary reversion to serfdom that lay behind the Upper Swabian rebels' complaint in 1525 that serfdom "is pitiable, given that Christ has purchased and redeemed us with his precious blood, the shepherd the same as the Emperor".[94]

In the southern lands, this relapse into servility did not succeed in either quashing the rural communes or keeping them out of the territorial parliaments.[95] East of the Elbe, however, a very different story unfolded. The rural communes of the eastern lands harked back to the Netherlands and the Weser and Elbe marshes, whence their founders had migrated.[96] As in Old Germany, the communes formed, often under very favourable circumstances, during the age

---

[89] Peter Blickle, *Landschaften im Alten Reich. Die staatliche Funktion des gemeinen Mannes in Oberdeutschland* (Munich, 1973).

[90] Peter Bierbrauer, "Bäuerliche Revolten im Alten Reich. Ein Forschungsbericht", in Peter Blickle, ed., *Aufruhr oder Empörung? Studien zum bäuerlichen Widerstand im alten Reich* (Munich, 1980), pp. 62–5.

[91] Franz, *Quellen*, pp. 497–501, no. 196; 479–83, no. 188. The first document is summarized (somewhat inaccurately) by Du Boulay, *Germany in the Later Middle Ages*, p. 174.

[92] Abel, *Geschichte der deutschen Landwirtschaft*, p. 127.

[93] Claudia Ulbrich, *Leibherrschaft am Oberrhein im Spätmittelalter*, Veröffentlichungen des MPIG LVIII (Göttingen, 1979), p. 256.

[94] "Articles of the Peasants of Memmingen, 24 February–3 March, and the Reply of the Memmingen Town Council", in Tom Scott and Bob Scribner, eds., *The German Peasants' War. A History in Documents* (Atlantic Highlands, NJ, 1991), p. 78, no. 3.

[95] See Blickle, *Revolution of 1525*, pp. 171–80.

[96] Wunder, *Die bäuerliche Gemeinde*, pp. 35–7; Du Boulay, *Germany in the Later Middle Ages*, pp. 176–8.

of German-speaking colonization, which the Black Death brought to
an end. Yet in some parts of the east, notably in East Prussia, the
rural communes continued to expand their competencies until well
into the fifteenth century.[97] For a number of reasons, however, such
as ethnic diversity in the villages, expansion of urban power, and
the late and deep effects of the depression, the rural communes of
the east never gained political representation in the territorial parliaments, leaving the rural folk open to a solution to the labour problem
from above. Although the agrarian depression may not have caused
the east Elbian "second serfdom" of the early modern era, its deep
and late inroads on rural economies surely weakened the peasants'
abilities to defend their liberties.[98] Nothing shows more clearly the
importance of circumstances than the dramatically different fates of
the farming folk in the two zones of the German-speaking world.

V. *Others*

The explosive development of corporate forms among the Empire's
common people—household-guild-commune in the towns, household-
commune on the land—is one of the most remarkable aspects of
late medieval German history. It led, as Italian observers of the
German towns noted, to levels of popular politics known nowhere
else in Europe.[99] So intense was the corporate process in the towns,
indeed, that the "commonalty" (*Gemeinheit*) of all householders "sometimes emerges as a legitimate political category, distinct from the traditional patriciate on the one hand, and the 'brotherhood' of the guilds
on the other".

The cities contained, however, groups of persons whose way of
life drew them away from this corporate order, either because they
were drawn toward different social spheres, where different values
reigned, or because the corporate order itself excluded them. The

---

[97] Wunder, *Die bäuerliche Gemeinde*, p. 58.
[98] The chief force behind enserfment and the formation of the latifundia (*Gutsherr-schaft*) east of the Elbe was the export boom in grain during the sixteenth century. Peter Kriedte, *Peasants, Landlords and Merchant Capitalists. Europe and the World Economy, 1500–1800*, trans. V. R. Berghahn (Cambridge, 1983), pp. 27–30.
[99] A fact noted by Italian observers. See Antony Black, *Guilds and Civil Society in European Political Thought from the Twelfth Century to the Present* (Ithaca, NY, 1984), p. 74; the following quote on p. 71.

first possibility applies to the urban patricians.[100] Whether their origins were purely mercantile, as at Lübeck and Hamburg, largely noble and ministerial, as at Metz, or mixed noble and mercantile, as at Strasbourg, Ulm, Augsburg, and Nuremberg, their common ethos was the desire for "honour", that is, for the respect and prestige claimed by who lived nobly. The Strasbourgeois Hans Armbruster spoke for them all about 1477: "Whom God has granted riches, also wants honour."[101] "Honour" in the noble sense meant living nobly, that is, without work; it meant the expansion of a sense of family from the household to the lineage; it meant dress, manners, and recreation—such as jousting—which the common folk might enjoy but could not emulate. This honourable style of life attracted both the offspring of rural nobles, such as Nuremberg's Paumgartners, and those of merchants, such as Strasbourg's Wurmsers. At Hamburg and Freiburg im Breisgau, at Rostock and Frankfurt am Main, they bought land, rents, and castles, became seigneurs, jousted with rural nobles, and sometimes married their daughters. Such men sat beside merchants and craftsmen in the town halls, but in their clubs—Lübeck's *Zirkelgesellschaft*, Lindau's *Sünfzen*, and Strasbourg's *Hohensteg*—they decided who was socially acceptable and who was not. The Nurembergers could speak freely in 1489 what the other patricians all thought, namely, that only he was an "honourable and worthy man" (*ehrbar und bescheiden Mann*), "who lives nobly and honestly, deals in nothing dishonourable, and pursues no craft" (*wer sich ehrbar und redlich hält, nichts Unehrbars handelt oder Handwerk treibt*).[102]

Those repelled by the corporate order included the unemployed, under-employed, and seasonally unemployed; fatherless families, poor widows and spinsters, orphans, and beggars, plus the itinerants (*fahrende Leute*)—lepers, gamblers, prostitutes, quack physicians, poor students, and unemployed soldiers—and the practitioners of "dishonourable trade", such as cesspool cleaners, renderers, gravediggers, travelling players, and, universally, executioners, who plied "the most dishonourable of the dishonourable professions".[103] Their numbers are hard to grasp, though when Basel counted mouths in preparation for a

---

[100] Ingrid Bátori, "Das Patriziat der deutschen Stadt. Zu den Forschungsergebnissen über das Patriziat besonders der süddeutschen Städte", *Zeitschrift für Stadtgeschichte, Stadtsoziologie und Denkmalpflege* II (1975): pp. 1–30.
[101] Quoted by Brady, *Ruling Class*, p. 49.
[102] Quoted by Isenmann, *Die deutsche Stadt*, p. 246.
[103] Werner Danckert, *Unehrliche Leute. Die verfemten Berufe* (Berne, 1963), p. 23.

siege in 1444, they reckoned the propertyless at 20–30 per cent of
the city's population.[104] These truly poor were disproportionately
female. At Strasbourg, when civic poor relief was established in 1523,
a survey found that 69 per cent of the persons needing assistance
were women, and that 79 per cent of the needy women (versus 21
per cent of the men) lived alone.[105] These poor, native (*Hausarmen*)
and itinerant, lodged where they could in cellars, alleyways, and back
courts, where 24.6 per cent of tax-paying Lübeckers lived in 1460.[106]
They had special claim on the surplus that the church dispensed
through hospitals (*Spitäler*) and poor-houses (*Almosen*), the most important of which was Cologne's great Hospital of the Holy Spirit, where
700 poor folk ate each day.[107]

Repelled, too, were the Jews. Once eligible for citizenship on the
same basis as Christians, savage persecutions at the time of the Black
Death pushed them into countryside and the shadows, from which
they did not re-emerge for nearly four centuries. The late medieval diaspora brought Jews into about 500 places where no previous
settlement is known, leaving larger communities of 150 or more in only
two dozen towns—all south of a line from Dortmund to Goslar to
the Baltic sea coast.[108] With the destruction in 1519 of Regensburg's
Jewry, in 1500 nearly 15 per cent of the city's residents, the disaster
and the diaspora became complete.

One other group stood largely outside the new social and economic
institutions associated with the corporate structure of household, guild,
and commune. It was, oddly enough, the clergy. Oddly, because the
regular clergy supplied the oldest public models for social organization on the basis of fraternity rather than kinship. Oddly, too, because
the clergy, especially the mendicants, supplied the religious language
for that order's justification, linking the idea of the common good—
the foundation value of guilds and communes—to the Christian virtue

---

[104] Sprandel, "Gewerbe und Handel 1350–1500", p. 379.

[105] Thomas Fischer, *Städtische Armut und Armenfürsorge im 15. und 16. Jahrhundert*,
Göttinger Beiträge zur Wirtschafts- und Sozialgeschichte IV (Göttingen, 1979), pp.
128–9.

[106] *Ibid.*, p. 115 n. 1.

[107] Franz Irsigler and Arnold Lassotta, *Bettler, Gauker, Dirnen und Henker, Randgruppen
und Aussenseiter in Köln 1300–1600* (Cologne, 1984), p. 47.

[108] Alfred Haverkamp, "The Jewish Quarters in German Towns during the late
Middle Ages" (unpublished paper). My thanks to Professor Haverkamp for allowing me to read this. See also Isenmann, *Die deutsche Stadt*, pp. 100–1.

of *caritas* (altruistic love).[109] As the new guild regime at Augsburg announced in 1368, it intended "with God's help to ordain and establish all things in the best, safest and most Christian way".[110]

The parish, the most common form of community in the Empire, represented medieval Christianity's most important adaptation to European conditions.[111] The parish's congregation formed a community and was so regarded throughout the middle ages, and pastor (*rector ecclesiae*) or his vicar (*vicarius*), who was responsible for its spiritual welfare and sacramental life, could be regarded either as his flock's leader or as its lord.[112] Thus dualism of associative and hierarchical features replicated the character of all other "communal" institutions and was, therefore, in itself nothing provocative. Yet as communal institutions grew denser in the later middle ages, external patronage, which meant the right to nominate priests and sometimes to collect the tithe, tended to grow more irksome. In the cities, where the number of parishes bore little relationship to the population's size—28 at Erfurt, at least 20 at Cologne, 9 each at Strasbourg and Regensburg, 6 at Augsburg, 2 at Nuremberg, and only one at Frankfurt am Main, Bamberg, Freiburg im Breisgau, and Ulm—something could be done about patronage. The Ulmers, for example, in 1446 took pride in paying the immense sum of 25,000 fl. to the abbot of Reichenau for their church's patronage, thereby acquiring "a higher stage of control over the church" than any other power in medieval Europe.[113] In the towns, too, the parishes competed with other churches, both in the urban skyline and for the citizens' hearts, and the major ecclesiastical towns, those "German Romes", sprouted

---

[109] Antony Black, "The Individual and Society", in J. H. Burns, ed., *The Cambridge History of Medieval Political Thought*, c. 350–c. 1450 (Cambridge, 1988), p. 596.

[110] Quoted by Black, *Guilds and Civil Society*, p. 71.

[111] See, in general, Léopold Genicot, *Rural Communities in the Medieval West* (Baltimore, MD, 1990), ch. 4; Isenmann, Die deutsche Stadt, ch. 5; Dietrich Kurze, *Pfarrerwahlen im Mittelalter. Ein Beitrag zur Geschichte der Gemeinde und des Niederkirchenwesens*, Forschungen zur Kirchengeschichte VI (Cologne/Graz, 1966).

[112] See Wolfgang Reinhard, "Die Verwaltung der Kirche", in Kurt G. A. Jeserich, Hans Pohl, and Georg-Christoph von Unruh, eds., *Deutsche Verwaltungsgeschichte I: Vom Spätmittelalter bis zum Ende des Reiches* Stuttgart, 1983), pp. 156–7; Karl Siegfried Bader, "Universitas subditorum parochie-des Pfarrers Untertanen. Zur Auffassung und Bezeichnung der spätmittelalterlichen Pfarrgemeinde", in Klaus Obermayer, eds., *Festschrift Hans Liermann zum 70. Geburtstag* (Erlangen, 1964), pp. 11–25, reprinted in Karl Siegfried Bader, *Ausgewählte Schriften zur Rechts- und Landesgeschichte* (3 vols., Sigmaringen, 1984) II, pp. 240–54.

[113] Kurze, *Pfarrerwahlen im Mittelalter*, p. 388.

spires like barley fields: by 1350 Cologne had 11 collegiate chapters, 20 religious houses, 19 parishes, 24 autonomous and 20 other chapels, and 62 houses of *béguines* and *béghards*; and Erfurt, the most churched town in Central Europe, possessed 2 chapters, 22 monasteries, 23 other churches, 36 chapels, and 6 hospitals, plus 28 parishes.[114]

In the countryside things were quite different: the parish church was the only church, if the village were lucky enough to possess one, and the patronage rights of distant lords grew the more intrusive the firmer the local communal structure became. The range of patrons was immense. In Alsace they included nobles and commoners, monasteries and convents, and clerical corporations of every conceivable description.[115] The village communes tried to gain control over the patronage and the tithe of existing churches and, where none existed, to found and endow them with repatriated tithes.[116]

One aim of this "communal reformation", the roots of which lay well back in the later middle ages, was to use the tithe to support the village poor.[117] This corresponded to the immense expansion of charitable institutions in the towns, often under clerical leadership or control—hospitals, poor-houses, orphanages, and schools.[118] Their rise was nourished by the ethos of spiritual kinship and fraternal love that formed the heart of popular Christianity, for "the state of charity, meaning social integration, was the principal end of the Christian life, and any people that claimed to be Christian must embody it somehow, at some time, in this world".[119] Charity, which involved both the living and the dead and aimed both at peace in this world and at eternal salvation in the next, lay behind the donations that jammed the churches with altars, retables, windows, tombs, tablets,

---

[114] Isenmann, *Die deutsche Stadt*, p. 211.

[115] Luzian Pfleger, *Die elsässische Pfarrei. Ihre Entstehung und Entwicklung*, Forschungen zur Kirchengeschichte des Elsaß III (Strasbourg, 1936), pp. 113–46.

[116] Kurze, *Pfarrwahlen*; Rosi Fuhrmann, "Die Kirche im Dorf. Kommunale Initiativen zur Organisation von Seelsorge vor der Reformation", in Peter Blickle, ed., *Zugänge zur bäuerlichen Reformation*, Bauer und Reformation I (Zurich, 1987), pp. 147–86; *idem*, "Dorfgemeinde und Pfründstiftung vor der Reformation. Kommunale Selbstbestimmungschancen zwischen Religion und Recht", in *Kommunalisierung und Christianisierung. Voraussetzungen und Folgen der Reformation 1400–1600*, Peter Blickle und Johannes Kunisch, eds., ZHF Supplement IX (Berlin, 1989), pp. 77–112; Peter Blickle, "Antiklerikalismus um den Vierwaldstättersee 1300–1500. Aufriß eines Modells, weshalb es nicht zur Reformation kommt", in Peter Dykema and Heiko A. Oberman, eds., *Anticlericalism in the Late Middle Ages and Reformation* (Leiden, 1992), pp. 115–32.

[117] Blickle, *Communal Reformation*.

[118] Isenmann, *Die deutsche Stadt*, pp. 183–90.

[119] Bossy, *Christianity in the West*, p. 57.

and chapels, as the living endowed masses for the souls of their kin, natural and spiritual. The urban rich endowed by family, the middling folk by confraternity, a kind of "consensual parish" that boomed in such cities as Lübeck (over 70) and Cologne (80) around 1350 and Hamburg (99) around 1520—and sometimes grew to enormous size—4,000 in Ulm's Rosary Confraternity (est. 1483).[120] Their charitable activities swelled the flow of prayers and wealth to the hospitals and poor-houses. Most of them drew their resources from donations of the burghers, such as Cologne's Dr. Peter Rynck, who in 1500 left 4,300 marks to clothe and feed "the poor foundlings, who are cared for as abandoned and unwanted children".[121]

In this story of expansion, one point seems clear. The expanding institutions—confraternities, hospitals, and poor-houses—were all lay religious institutions, even when clerically led. The numbers of dioceses and deaneries (subdivisions of dioceses) remained fixed in their earlier sizes and configurations; collegiate churches did not grow in numbers or importance; and the patterns of monastic life changed very little, if at all.[122] Only one type of purely ecclesiastical institution did continue to grow during this age, rural parishes, but only in villages which for some reason—poverty, custom, or oversight—had hitherto lacked parishes of their own. Otherwise, while the later middle ages was very rich in new or newly prominent lay economic and social institutions, it was very poor in new clerical ones.[123]

Reflection on the fit between the older, clerical, or clerically led institutions and the newer or newly prominent lay corporate institutions sheds some light on this contrast. The archetypal form of clerical community, the monastery, was based on the separation of genders and communal property. The lay communities of the late medieval Empire, by contrast, were based on the co-ordination of genders and more exclusive forms of property peculiar to the household.[124] Here we seem to encounter a genuine divide, a difference not of religious

---

[120] This phrase from Gabriel Le Bras is quoted by Isenmann, *Die deutsche Stadt*, p. 223. See Robert W. Scribner, "Elements of Popular Belief", in Brady *et al.*, *Handbook of European History, 1400–1600* I, pp. 231–62, here pp. 241–2.

[121] Irsigler and Lassotta, *Bettler, Gauker, Dirnen und Henker*, p. 47.

[122] Reinhard, "Die Verwaltung der Kirche", pp. 143–76.

[123] See John Van Engen, "The Church in the Fifteenth Century", in Brady *et al.*, *Handbook of European History, 1400–1600* I, 305–30.

[124] I mean more the notion of property and its purpose than its precise legal status, for, as David Sabean points out, by the sixteenth century in regions of partible inheritance such as Württemberg, ownership was strictly individual; Sabean, *Property, Production and Family*, p. 16.

belief but of moral sensibility, for the burghers and, perhaps, the peasants were coming to see the fulfilment of God's command in terms
of a way of life based on labour structured both by age and by gender. The imperial church might in time have adjusted to this sensibility, and probably did so in many ways, but not enough and not
swiftly enough. Its immobility stemmed partly from its incorporation,
long ago, into the Empire's very structure, partly from its economic
basis in an increasingly archaic institution, the benefice, and partly
from its vulnerability to the imperial nobility's rapacious use of the
church to soften the depression's worst effects.[125] Most of the upper
nobles probably shared Emperor Frederick III's belief that "what the
priests own, belongs to our treasury" (*Pfaffengut ist unser Kammergut*).[126]
When the clerical corporations responded successfully to the agrarian crisis, as they did in the diocese of Strasbourg, their very success fomented conflict with the laity provoked by clerical usury and
clerical involvement in the trade in foodstuffs. Their wealth, in turn,
drew many foreigners—Swabians, Bavarians, and Lorrainers—into
the region, which also tended to estrange the laity from their clergy.[127]

The new anti-clericalism of the pre-Reformation decades arose
partly from this growing unconformity between clerical social institutions and those of the laity, to which they had to some degree
provided models and values. The burghers, and perhaps also the
peasants, increasingly saw the world less as a family bound by ties
of kinship and more as a household structured by the conservation
of and transmission of property and by division of labour according
to gender and age.[128] This new world valued service over mediation,
instruction over ritual, and thrift over display.

---

[125] Dietmar Willoweit, "Die Entwicklung und Verwaltung der spätmittelalterlichen
Landesherrschaft", Wolfgang Reinhard, "Die Verwaltung der Kirche", and Dietmar
Willoweit, "Das landesherrliche Kirchenregiment", in Jeserich *et al.*, *Deutsche Verwaltungsgeschichte* I, pp. 77–8, 165–7, 361–2; Gerhard Kallen, *Die oberschwäbischen Pfründen
des Bistums Konstanz und ihre Besetzung (1275–1508). Ein Beitrag zur Pfründgeschichte vor
der Reformation*, Kirchenrechtliche Abhandlungen XLV–XLVI (Stuttgart, 1965), pp.
188–95; Jörn Sieglerschmidt, *Territorialstaat und Kirchenregiment. Studien zur Rechtsdogmatik
des Kirchenpatronatsrechts im 15. und 16. Jahrhundert Forschungen zur kirchlichen Rechtsgeschichte
und zum Kirchenrecht*, XV (Cologne/Vienna, 1987).
[126] Wiesflecker, *Kaiser Maximilian I.* I, p. 79; V, pp. 156–7.
[127] Francis Rapp, *Réformes et réformation à Strasbourg. Église et société dans le diocèse de
Strasbourg (1450–1525)*, Collection de l'Institut des Hautes Études Alsaciennes XXIII
(Paris, 1974), pp. 265–79, 284–7, 298–9, 306–18, 313, 430–4, 435–41, 451–2.
[128] Among the common people, I think, this is nearer the mark than Bossy's
thesis of a direct passage from spiritual kinship to individualism; Bossy, *Christianity
in the West*. I owe much of this insight to David Sabean's writings.

One side of this nonconformity impressed Johann Geiler of Kaysersberg at Strasbourg. He sensed that the laity felt that "we should take half of what the priests own. Why should they have so much property? They have too much."[129] His answer was to try to teach the Strasbourgeois that the clergy returned spiritual goods for material ones, forming with the laity one vast division of spiritual and material labour. Geiler believed that the anti-clerical sentiments he commonly witnessed—"You laymen, you hate us priests!"—flowed from the laity's incomprehension of this truth. He was half right. For another moral sentiment had emerged from the long evolution of lay society and its institutions over the later middle ages, from the first shadows on the medieval boom around 1300 through the Black Death in the late 1340s, the agrarian depression of the following century, and the quickening recovery after 1450. This strong, new sentiment, like most others, had long been taught by the clergy. It held that God intended men and women to live and work together.

---

[129] Johann Geiler von Kaysersberg, *Die Emeis. Dis ist das buch von der Omeissen, und auch Herr der kónnig ich diente gern* (Strasburg, 1516), 28[b]. See Thomas A. Brady, Jr., "You Hate us Priests": Anticlericalism, Communalism, and the Control of Women at Strasbourg in the Age of the Reformation, in Dykema and Oberman, eds., *Anticlericalism in the Late Middle Ages and Reformation*, pp. 167–207, on which this paragraph is based.

CHAPTER ELEVEN

IMPERIAL DESTINIES: A NEW BIOGRAPHY OF THE EMPEROR MAXIMILIAN I*

There are historical works of such a rare monumentality that volume-by-volume reviews can hardly do them justice; Hermann Wiesflecker's *Kaiser Maximilian I* is one of these. Wiesflecker, whose *Maximilian* crowns his long career at the University of Graz in Styria, tells how the work's idea came to him in 1945 (1: p. 2),[1] as he stood before the tomb of the Emperor Maximilian I (r. 1493–1519) in the bombed out Church of St. George in Wiener Neustadt. He had written his Ph.D. dissertation at Vienna on Maximilian's efforts to acquire the County of Gorizia, and now Leo Santifaller's (1890–1974) reorganization of the edition of the medieval emperors' acts (*Regesta imperii*)[2] set him on his path. Wiesflecker assumed responsibility for the volume (vol. 14) on Maximilian, moved in 1948 to Graz, and became professor there in 1961. The students he sent forth brought back more than 20,000 documents, selected from a total of perhaps 100,000, out of which they wrote more than ninety dissertations and twenty other research papers (more than half of them by women). Wiesflecker's *Maximilian* forms the summit of this pyramid of scholarship.

---

* Hermann Wiesflecker, *Kaiser Maximilian I: Das Reich, Österreich und Europa an der Wende zur Neuzeit* (Munich: R. Oldenbourg Verlag, 1971–1986); vol. 1, *Jugend, burgundisches Erbe und Römisches Königtum bis zur Alleinherrschaft, 1459–1493* (1971): xvi + 608 pp., DM 68.00; vol. 2, *Reichsreform und Kaiserpolitik, 1493–1500: Entmachtung des Königs im Reich und in Europa* (1975): xvii + 576 pp., DM 76.00; vol. 3, *Auf der Höhe des Lebens, 1500–1508: Der grosse Systemwechsel: Politischer Wiederaufstieg* (1977): xxviii + 624 pp., DM 98.00; vol. 4, *Gründung des habsburgischen Weltreiches: Lebensabend und Tod: 1508–1519* (1981): xxviii + 692 pp., DM 125.00; vol. 5, *Der Kaiser und seine Umwelt: Hof, Staat, Wirtschaft, Gesellschaft und Kultur* (1986): xxxii + 904 pp., DM 180.00.

[1] References to volume and page number(s) are to Wiesflecker's *Maximilian*.

[2] See Alphons Lhotsky, *Österreichische Historiographie*, Österreich Archiv, Schiftenreihe des Arbeitskreises für österreichische Geschichte (Vienna: Verlag für Geschichte und Politik, 1962), pp. 189–90. On Santifaller, see Wolfgang Weber, *Biographisches Lexikon zur Geschichtswissenschaft in Deutschland, Österreich und der Schweiz: Die Lehrstuhlinhaber für Geschichte von den Anfängen des Faches bis 1970* (Frankfurt am Main: Peter Lang, 1984), pp. 493–94. On the Regesta imperii, see Leo Santifaller, *Das Institut für österreichische Geschichtsforschung: Festgabe zur Feier des zweihundertjährigen Bestandes des Wiener Haus-, Hof- und Staatsarchivs*, Veröffentlichungen des Instituts für österreichische Geschichte, vol. 11 (Vienna: Universum Verlag, 1950), pp. 39–40.

The *Maximilian* itself also has a pyramidal shape. The first four volumes follow the king-emperor[3] from childhood to the beginning of his reign in 1493; through the first Italian Wars to the nadir of his power (1493–1500); through his recovery and the zenith of his power (1500–1508); and through the second Italian Wars to his death. Volume 5, which is topically organized, recapitulates the material under the headings of policy and politics, religion and the church, culture, warfare, administration, and finance. The final chapter summarizes the entire work.

I

Why does the Emperor Maximilian I warrant such monumental treatment? Wiesflecker set out to rescue the emperor's historical image from the Rankean school. Leopold von Ranke (1795–1886), in his *History of the Latin and Teutonic Nations, 1494–1514* (1824), dismissed Maximilian's personality as having "little to do with history" and asserted that the emperor's career "is that presentiment of the future greatness of his dynasty which he had inherited from his father, and the restless striving to obtain all that passed to him from the House of Burgundy."[4] Maximilian's policies, he thought, "were concentrated, not upon the Empire, for the real needs of which he evinced little real care, and not directly upon the welfare of his hereditary lands, but upon the realization of that sole idea," the idea of "universal monarchy over all the Latin and Teutonic nations." God, however, "willed it that this should not happen. The development of the Latin and Teutonic nations that had just begun, would have been interrupted and hindered thereby."[5] Instead, God channeled Maximilian's energies and powers into the House of Austria's future, leaving Europe a clear ground for the infant nations and Germany a clear ground for the Reformation.[6]

---

[3] Though never crowned by the pope, Maximilian declared himself emperor at Trent in 1508.

[4] Leopold von Ranke, *History of the Latin and Teutonic Nations (1494 to 1514)*, trans. G. R. Dennis (London: George Bell, 1909), p. 98.

[5] *Ibid.*, p. 228.

[6] See Leonard Krieger, *Ranke, The Meaning of History* (Chicago: University of Chicago Press, 1977), p. 112: "Ranke invoked God, as He had been traditionally invoked by historians, when he wished to place some causal link in the gap between events and their unexpected consequences."

Whereas Maximilian, in Ranke's view, struggled for universal rule and created the House of Austria, the German princes strove for "a real unity of the nation in opposition to the imperial power" but created nothing, an outcome which emerged at the Diet of Cologne in 1505.[7] A decade later, when he returned to this crucial point in his *German History in the Age of the Reformation*, Ranke asked himself: "Was it even possible to return to measures which had already proven themselves impracticable? Had territorial sovereignty not already developed too far to permit the princes to welcome such comprehensive and innovative measures? . . . One might imagine at most that at this point a committee of princes might have taken all power into its hands; but no one could expect them to surrender their position in favor of the king."[8] Germany's national reformation was to come not through the princes but through the Protestant movement against the Roman papacy.

Ranke had come to the German Reformation from his *History of the Popes*, and he moved on to write his *Prussian History*. This journey partly recapitulated and partly anticipated what Adolf Stoecker would one day call "the hand of God in history from 1517 to 1871."[9] Well before 1871, however, Ranke's disciples had opened the battle to make the German past serve the coming German state. It began with a debate over the national versus the universal aims of the medieval Empire between two Prussian historians, the Düsseldorf Protestant Heinrich von Sybel (1817–1895) and the Paderborn Catholic Julius Ficker (1826–1902), professors, respectively, at Munich and Innsbruck.[10] Sybel, who once called himself "four-sevenths professor and three-sevenths politician," believed in the state's duty to determine the nature and limits of human freedom and held that all of Germany's history had to be judged against its need for a strong national state.[11]

---

[7] Ranke, *History of the Latin and Teutonic Nations*, p. 225.

[8] Leopold von Ranke, *Deutsche Geschichte im Zeitalter der Reformation*, ed. Willy Andreas, 2 vols. (Wiesbaden: Emil Vollmer, 1957), 1: p. 75.

[9] Quoted by Karl Kupisch, "The 'Luther Renaissance,'" *Journal of Contemporary History* 2, no. 4 (1967): p. 41.

[10] Weber, *Biographisches Lexikon*, pp. 145–46, 595–96; the literature is collected by Wiesflecker, *Kaiser Maximilian I*, 1: p. 15 n. 27; and by Hellmut Seier, "Heinrich von Sybel," in *Deutsche Historiker*, ed. Hans-Ulrich Wehler (Göttingen: Vandenhoeck & Ruprecht, 1971), 2: pp. 24–38.

[11] Seier, pp. 25, 27. On Sybel's statism, see Georg G. Iggers, *The German Conception of History: The National Tradition of Historical Thought from Herder to the Present*, rev. ed. (Middletown, Conn.: Wesleyan University Press, 1983), pp. 116–19.

The man who measured Maximilian against this norm was the Thuringian Heinrich Ulmann (1841–1931), professor of history at Greifswald from 1874 to 1912.[12] For the *Habilitation*, Ulmann turned from the Middle Ages to the early sixteenth-century struggle of Duke Ulrich of Württemberg (1487–1550) against Emperor Maximilian, which led to Ulrich's expulsion from his lands in 1519.[13] This work prepared him for his two-volume study of Maximilian's reign, which from its appearance in 1884–1891 shaped Maximilian's place in the neo-Rankean canon. Ulmann's Maximilian is an unstable, fantasy-ridden dreamer, a self-serving schemer, and an Austrian exploiter, who reigned over a Germany that needed a wise and steady hand, a far-seeing statesman, and a true German patriot.[14] The book is not a biography of Maximilian but a "history of the Empire under Maximilian."[15] It is the story of the struggle between Maximilian and Elector Berthold of Mainz (d. 1504), the leader of the electoral and princely opposition. In contrast to Ulmann's own day, "at that time the truly realistic national policy was to build the parliamentary institutions into an effective form which could restrain every particularism [*Sonderwillen*]."[16] Maximilian, Ulmann thought, had been strong enough to prevent the formation of an effective government, "which would have had to share with the estates," "but he could hardly restore to effectiveness the corroded prerogatives of the medieval monarchy." His failure led to the succession "at the decisive moment" by "a foreigner in feeling and manner of thought" and brought the Empire for a century into dependence on "the point of view and interests of Spanish rulers."

For Ulmann, as for Ranke, the Reformation brought a wondrous compensation for the lost national state: "It is . . . a living sign of the inscrutable guidance of human affairs that the failure of the Imperial reform in a parliamentary sense . . . made the establishment of the ecclesiastical reformation in our country easier. The disobedience to the Edict of Worms [1521] and even the protest at Speyer [1529]—how much more difficult would they have been, had the

---

[12] On Ulmann, see Weber, *Biographisches Lexikon*, p. 611.

[13] Heinrich Ulmann, *Fünf Jahre württembergischer Geschichte unter Herzog Ulrich, 1515–1519* (Leipzig: J. G. Cotta, 1867).

[14] See Wiesflecker, *Kaiser Maximilian I*, 1: pp. 15–19.

[15] Heinrich Ulmann, *Kaiser Maximilian I*, 2 vols. (Leipzig: J. G. Cotta, 1884–1891), 1: p. iii.

[16] *Ibid.*, p. vi; there, too, the remaining quotes in this paragraph.

laws of 1495 and 1500 been enforced?"[17] The Germans thus owed the possibility of their Reformation to the Austrian Maximilian, whose impracticality, mercurial behavior, Machiavellian diplomacy, reckless spending, imperious arrogance, utopian dreaming, and general political incompetence Ulmann displayed on page after page.

Ulmann's easily became the orthodox portrait of Maximilian and the Imperial reform, for the Rankean succession dominated the chairs of academic history in Wilhelmine Germany.[18] Inspired by history's momentous judgment on Germany in 1870–1871, their "historicism"—the "one main tradition of German historiography"[19]—discarded Maximilian as a selfish, irrelevant dreamer and left him to the Austrians, who didn't want him, at least not until Wiesflecker came along.[20]

Ulmann's work also shaped the image of Maximilian abroad, especially in England. It inspired, for example, T. F. Tout, who in his chapter on "Germany and the Empire" in the *Cambridge Modern History* (1903) wrote that since "there was no very great or essential dissimilarity between the condition of Germany under Frederick III and that of France of the Armagnac and Burgundian feuds," Germany's failure to emulate the "national monarchies" then developing in France, Spain, and England had to count as the chief result of Maximilian's reign.[21] Tout formed a grim judgment on the emperor's character: "A review of the political history of Germany brings out Maximilian's character almost at its weakest. Yet the impression derived from his calamitous European wars, his ineffective negotiations, and his pitiable shifts for raising money is even more unfavourable."[22] Berthold of Mainz, by contrast, was "the one statesman who strove with great

---

[17] *Ibid.*, p. vii.

[18] See Wolfgang Weber, *Priester der Clio: Historisch-sozialwissenschaftliche Studien zur Herkunft und Karriere deutscher Historiker und zur Geschichte der Geschichtswissenschaft, 1800–1970*, Europäische Hochschulschriften, ser. 3, vol. 216 (Frankfurt am Main, Bern, and New York: Peter Lang, 1984), pp. 208–9. Weber is able to connect an astounding 57 percent of all professors of history in the German-speaking world, 1800–1970, to Ranke's school. On its confessional character, see Weber, *Priester der Clio*, pp. 291–92, 326–33.

[19] Iggers, *German Conception of History*, p. 3.

[20] This interesting point is made by Lhotsky, *Österreichische Historiographie* (n. 2 above), p. 213, who draws a contrast to Switzerland.

[21] T. F. Tout, "Germany and the Empire," in *Cambridge Modern History*, ed. A. W. Ward, G. W. Prothero, and Stanley Leathes, vol. 1, *The Renaissance* (Cambridge: Cambridge University Press, 1903), p. 280.

[22] *Ibid.*, p. 322.

ability and consummate pertinacity to realise the ideal of a free, national, and united German State."[23] Because "monarchy, and monarchy only, could be practically efficient as the formative element in national life," and "since the German monarchy refused to do its duty, German unity was destined not to be achieved."

As for Ranke and Ulmann, for Tout the Reformation turned national defeat into victory of a kind. Reviewing the literary expressions of German patriotism under Maximilian, he concluded that "it was the national idea that gave unity of direction and aim to the German Renaissance, and inspired all that was best in German Protestantism." Then, through the long centuries "when there was no German State there remained a German nation, able to hand on the great traditions of the past which could realise . . . the ancient ideal of Berthold of Mainz, that side by side with the German nation there should also be a German National State."[24]

Ulmann's view long held sway in England. Geoffrey Barraclough's *The Origins of Modern Germany*,[25] for example, which appeared just after World War II, told that though Maximilian often claimed "that his policy was directed to assuring Germany its proper place among nations and protecting its rights against foreigners . . . it is difficult for the scrupulous historian to find in it anything but the dynastic interests of the Habsburg house."[26] Maximilian's reign thus ushered in "the conflict between Habsburg dynastic policy and German interests, which henceforward was endemic in German history."[27]

In Germany, by contrast, the fall of monarchies in 1918 had set historical thinking about states and nations in flux. In 1932, for example, Willy Andreas's popular *Deutschland vor der Reformation* presented a new, more balanced view of Maximilian and Berthold and judged that, although Maximilian had not held a "coherently national point of view," yet "to demand a German goal for his foreign policy is to miss the point, for the norms of later ages cannot be applied to statesmen of earlier ones."[28] Such a higher historicism, of course,

---

[23] *Ibid.*, p. 300; and the remaining quotations in this paragraph are on pp. 300–301.

[24] *Ibid.*, p. 328.

[25] Geoffrey Barraclough, *The Origins of Modern Germany* (Oxford: Blackwell, 1946; rev. ed., 1947).

[26] *Ibid.*, p. 363.

[27] *Ibid.*, p. 366.

[28] Willy Andreas, *Deutschland vor der Reformation: Eine Zeitenwende* (Stuttgart: Deutsche Verlags-Anstalt, 1932), p. 232. On Andreas, a Protestant from Karlsruhe, see Weber, *Biographisches Lexikon* (n. 2 above), pp. 8–9.

undercut the Ulmannian orthodoxy, though it did not rehabilitate Maximilian. The rehabilitation came first not for Maximilian but for his grandson and successor, Charles V (r. 1519–1556), and its architect was the Göttingen historian Karl Brandi (1868–1946).[29] A Westphalian Catholic, like Ficker, and a medievalist by training, Brandi published in 1937 a volume called *The Emperor Charles V: The Growth and Destiny of a Man and of a World-Empire*, as it sounds in C. V. Wedgwood's elegant English version of 1939.[30] In Brandi's view, Charles "formed out of the collection of inherited lands a new European, and in some senses trans-oceanic, imperial system, a world-empire which was based uniquely not on conquest but on the dynastic idea and a unity of faith."[31] Charles allowed large parts of the old empire—the Netherlands, Lorraine—to slip away, though by splitting the Habsburg inheritance he drove Austria and the other German Catholic states closer together. All this and more flowed from a man "whose tension filled life was nonetheless given an inner unity by the dynastic idea, which in Charles proved more vital and effective than anywhere else in world history."[32]

From his title onward, Brandi's *Charles* revised Rankeanism by returning to the master's original view. And what Brandi did for the grandson, Hermann Wiesflecker has done for the grandfather. By adopting precisely Brandi's conception—the union of the dynastic idea with the notion of a unified Christian *imperium*—Wiesflecker finesses Ulmann's concentration on the problem of a German national state by returning to a Rankean view older than Rankeanism: Maximilian's union of universalism and dynasticism. That is not all, for Wiesflecker's Maximilian also formed the Austrian lands into historic Austria. Only since 1945, when there is no longer a single German state, could this problem—the formation of Austria—come into historical focus as the centerpiece of a work on Maximilian.[33]

---

[29] Weber, *Biographisches Lexikon*, pp. 61–62.

[30] Karl Brandi, *Kaiser Karl V: Werden und Schicksal einer Persönlichkeit und eines Weltreiches* (Munich: F. Bruckmann, 1937), many times reprinted. I cite from the 6th ed. of 1961 and from *The Emperor Charles V: The Growth and Destiny of a Man and of a World-Empire*, trans. C. V. Wedgwood (London: Jonathan Cape, 1965). A second volume of *Quellen und Erörterungen* appeared in 1941. The study has also appeared in French, Spanish, Italian, and Dutch.

[31] Brandi, *Kaiser Karl V.*, 1: p. 11.

[32] *Ibid.*, p. 13.

[33] The influence of the postwar situation on the entire subject is already visible in R. G. D. Laffan, "The Empire under Maximilian I," in *The New Cambridge Modern History*, vol. 1, *The Renaissance, 1493–1520*, ed. G. R. Potter (Cambridge: Cambridge University Press, 1957), pp. 194–223.

II

The central theme of Wiesflecker's *Maximilian* is the emperor's grand policy, the set of goals which dominated political, diplomatic, and military operations through his entire reign and shaped his relations with the other great powers, his German vassals and subjects, and his own Austrian lands. Wiesflecker sees in Maximilian, as Brandi saw in Charles V, a ruler whose policies were rational, if not necessarily "modern," and whose chief problem was matching resources to goals.

Wiesflecker's most original idea may be his conception of the starting point for Maximilian's grand policy: the Burgundian Netherlands, where in the years between 1477 and 1489 the young prince from backward Austria discovered a civilization built on a union of "the French courtly tradition with the burghers' power in the southern Netherlands."[34] Maximilian returned to the Empire "a complete Burgundian (*ein völliger Burgunder*)" (1: pp. 228, 389), who "saw and judged the politics of the hereditary lands, the Holy Roman Empire, and Europe with a Burgundian eye" (1: p. 389). From this Valois Burgundian legacy came the overriding goal of Maximilian's grand policy, the restoration of "the Christian world-empire, for which all else was but means" (5: p. 410). He aimed to rebuild the Christian imperium of the Ottonians, Salians, and Hohenstaufen, to achieve coronation at Rome, to go on crusade and win Constantinople from the Ottomans, and to usher in an age of universal peace.

By the age of thirty, therefore, Maximilian resembled less his phlegmatic, parsimonious father, Emperor Frederick III (r. 1440–1493) than he did his flamboyant father-in-law, Duke Charles the Bold (r. 1467–1477), the "Latin upstart (*welscher Gesprotze*)" whom he met only once, at Trier in 1473 (1: p. 97). Though Austrian in many things, such as his tiny court and frugal way of life, in many others, such as his military innovations, his notions of administration, his love of display, and his use of propaganda, Maximilian became a Burgundian. From Burgundy came, above all, his grand policy's primary axioms: the primacy of the West and the struggle against France. Opposed by that most expansive military power of the age,

---

[34] Walter Prevenier and Wim Blockmans, *The Burgundian Netherlands*, trans. Peter King and Yvette Mead (Cambridge and New York: Cambridge University Press, 1986), p. 371.

Maximilian always lacked sufficient men and money, hence his restless search for allies—Brittany, Aragon and Castile, England, the papacy—and wealthy clients—the Netherlands and Milan—to provide what the German electors and princes would not give. He understood the situation perfectly: whereas, he joked, he was a "king of kings," whose vassals could do as they pleased, the French monarch was a "king of animals," whose subjects had to obey (5: p. 5).

In time Maximilian had to moderate his policy toward France, if not his feelings, and resign himself to the survival of a strong, independent French kingdom. The turning point came in the years 1503–1506, when he abandoned his "great plan of war" (1496) for the conquest and partition of France (2: p. 40). In the Netherlands he had inherited his father-in-law's motto, "I dared to do it! (*Je l'ay emprint*)"; the terrible defeats of 1496–1500 taught him a new motto, "Moderation! (*Halt Mass!*)" (1: p. 112; 3: p. 409).

Not even the wealth of Milan could finance Maximilian's ambition to rescue Italy from France and restore it to the Empire. Before he was dragged off in 1500 into French captivity, Duke Lodovico Sforza (1451–1508) gave Maximilian his niece's hand in marriage and subsidies to the tune of 1 million florins. In return there came only a standing French presence in or threat to Lombardy and an unhappy queen, surrounded by a flock of Milanese exiles whom the Germans called "the children of Israel" (2: p. 263; 5: p. 382). But Maximilian, who saw in Italy "the foundations of Imperial authority" (1: p. 396), would not give up. "I don't want that Italy, which is mine," he once said in his rough Latin, "should fall into other hands" (2: p. 26).

Though presaged by the Spanish double marriage of 1496/97, the winning combination came together only in the last phase of the Venetian War of 1508–1517, much too late to bring victory to Maximilian. Through Aragon, whose estates were as intractable as the German ones, Castilian military power flowed in to settle the Italian question—but not in Maximilian's time, and not in favor of Austria or Germany.

Wiesflecker places great emphasis on the divergences between the goals of Maximilian's policies and their consequences. Maximilian helped to save both the Netherlands and Italy from French domination but failed to bind them closer to the Empire: in the Netherlands he provoked a greater sense of solidarity and autonomy; in Italy he broke ground for the Spanish hegemony. Charles V's dazzling heritage and universal claims masked these consequences, but not for long.[35]

III

Maximilian's grand policy more nearly succeeded on the eastern front, where he laid the basis for Austria's beginnings as a Danubian power. Maximilian secured Habsburg claims to the Hungarian-Bohemian succession through the Treaty of Bratislava (1491) and two Hungarian wars, and he won consent to them from the Jagiellonian kings of Hungary-Bohemia and Poland-Lithuania. It meant a complete reversal of the Hungarian predominance under King Matthias Corvinus (d. 1490), and the long peace with the Turks allowed Maximilian—at the cost of two campaigns and an ocean of debts— to win out over a Magyar nobility that feared him "more than the Turks or the Devil" (1: p. 286).

Wiesflecker's portrayal of Maximilian's eastern policy and its consequences far surpasses in clarity and connectedness anything in the older literature. He defends Maximilian's eastern diplomacy against modern—mainly Polish—critics and notes how much the king contributed to widening European horizons to the east.[36] The Austrian discovery of Muscovy, he notes with pride, coincided with the Spanish discovery of America (1: p. 317).

Wiesflecker may well make too little of the larger reasons for the disparity between Maximilian's western failures and his eastern successes. From Paris to Moscow, a west-east gradient operated on every level: states became less centralized, armies less modern, diplomats less experienced, and alliances less volatile. In the field, for example, despite his skills and his creation of the *Landsknechte*, the first German infantry to rival the famous Swiss, he could rarely beat the French or the Venetians, while he rather easily dispersed the Magyars. His

---

[35] See M. J. Rodriguez-Salgado, *The Changing Face of Empire: Charles V, Philip II and Habsburg Authority, 1551–1559*, Cambridge Studies in Early Modern History (Cambridge: Cambridge University Press, 1988).

[36] But see now Krzysztof Baczkowski, "Der jagiellonische Versuch einer ostmitteleuropäischen Grossreichsbildung um 1500 und die türkische Bedrohung," in *Europa 1500: Integrationsprozesse im Widerstreit: Staaten, Regionen, Personenverbände, Christenheit*, ed. Ferdinand Seibt and Winfried Eberhard (Stuttgart: Klett-Cotta Verlag, 1987), pp. 433–44.

diplomats vastly expanded Habsburg horizons, established the first ties to Muscovy, influenced relations between the Teutonic Order and Poland, and brought the Catholic kings of the East together in 1515 in an unprecedented show of amity. He also initiated a frontier defense system that would serve the eastern Austrian lands well in the later Turkish Wars. He may therefore fairly be called the father of Austria as a Danubian state, the three-hundred-year existence of which outshines anything he accomplished in the West.

IV

In Wiesflecker's *Maximilian* there is no "German problem," only two opposed policies: Maximilian wanted the German electors and princes to grant him troops and money for his struggle to restore the Empire; they refused to back his "foreign adventures." Maximilian came to the Imperial throne with more good will and greater kingly qualities than his reclusive, secretive, almost provincially Austrian father had ever enjoyed, and he brought skills from the far more centralized and efficient Burgundian state. His reform program aimed to secure regular taxation and a standing army from the Empire's German-speaking heartlands, an agenda roughly in tune with the fifteenth-century reform tradition of such writers as Nicholas of Cusa (2: pp. 202–3; 3: p. 69).[37] Maximilian was from the first willing to share the Imperial government with the electors and princes, if they were willing to help pay for his wars.

If not, Maximilian would go his own way. When the reforms voted at Worms in 1495 stalled, Maximilian simply created his own royal organs of Imperial government; when the opposition seized the government from him at Augsburg in 1500, he did not fight them; and when the princes' government at Nuremberg failed in 1501–1502, he began to reconstruct the royal one. His one great object was to break down the obstacles to royal access to the Empire's wealth, which he desperately needed for his restoration projects in the Netherlands and Italy, for his eastern policy, and for his long proclaimed, never undertaken crusade against the Ottoman Turks.

---

[37] See Eberhard Isenmann, "Integrations- und Konsolidierungsprobleme der Reichsordnung in der zweiten Hälfte des 15. Jahrhunderts," in Seibt and Eberhard, eds., pp. 115–49.

The German princes had no taste for foreign wars or enhanced royal power, and the creation of a German "national state" was the furthest thing from their minds. They come off quite badly in Wiesflecker's account, mainly because of their lack of dedication to anything but increased particularism. Though Berthold of Mainz possessed a certain vision of stronger government in the hands of the electors and princes, he lacked the personal qualities of leadership needed to build lasting institutions. His great victory came at the Diet of Augsburg in 1500, when the estates took over the government and supreme court and moved them to Nuremberg, only to have them die within a year. Wiesflecker's Berthold was a party politician rather than a statesman, capable of scolding the princes to become "united like the Swiss" (2: p. 267) but not of inspiring obedience to the laws the diet had made. Though Maximilian railed at the princes as "German sheep (*deutsche Hammel*)" (1: p. 35), he forgave them, even the sullen old Elector Palatine, whose power he crushed in 1504; but his hatred pursued Berthold of Mainz beyond the grave. The irreconcilable differences between king and primate, as much as anything else, doomed the Imperial reform, except for a few struggling new institutions, such as the supreme court (*Reichskammergericht*) (5: pp. 2–3).

By Wiesflecker's account, there is plenty of blame to pass around for the failure of king and estates to give the Empire what most critics wanted, a more effective central government through a stronger monarchy. He does neglect, however, the absence of external threat as a factor in the growth of princely particularism. Except for the eastern Austrian lands, the German-speaking world experienced no serious external military threat between the Hussite Wars of the 1430s and the Thirty-Years' War, a fact which helps to explain the failure of royal centralism in the Empire.

Wiesflecker's *Maximilian* thus lays to rest the myth of the Imperial reform as a conflict between German national interests and Austrian dynastic ones. The chief issue lay deeper, in the clash between irreconcilably different conceptions of the Empire. For Maximilian it was the Empire of his ancestors, reaching right back to Charlemagne, the shield of Christendom and guardian of the church; for the princes, it was the realm of German-speaking nobles, shorn of the bothersome Romance- and Slavic-speaking peripheries. For the king it was still the Holy Roman Empire; for the princes it had already become the Holy Roman Empire of the German Nation. Very few princes took any part in the king's external affairs, which they considered to be mere "adventures," and after the departure of Elector Frederick (d. 1525) of Saxony from the court in 1498, no great prince held office in the Imperial regime.[38] Not even the king's victory in the Bavarian War of 1504 turned them permanently to his party.

The Bavarian War formed the great turning point of Maximilian's reign, for it gave him a chance to crush his strongest foes, the Palatine Wittelsbachs, to acquire new lands in the Inn Valley, and to cow the Imperial opposition. At this point, after the great Diet at Cologne in 1505, Maximilian might have tried to subjugate the remainder of South Germany and form it into a core state. Instead, he turned to Hungary, then back to Italy, where he became embroiled in a catastrophic nine-year war. Maximilian's failure to use his German victory in Germany confirms Wiesflecker's view of the secondary place of German affairs in Maximilian's grand policy. The Imperial estates had the power to refuse the role of milch cow; the Austrian lands did not.

V

The well-known saying that Austria should flourish through marriage rather than through war may well reflect the Austrians' sufferings for the sake of Maximilian's wars. Wiesflecker's chapters on Austria are the most splendid part of his *Maximilian*, for they are solidly researched, thoughtful, and free of the Rankean ghost that haunts his chapters on the Empire.

Maximilian once said that he would sooner allow the Empire to be ruined than his Austria (1: p. 35), but the truth is that no one ever drove the Austrian lands closer to destruction than he did. It was not out of love for them but out of zeal for war that he formed an Austria out of the five eastern duchies, the Tyrol, and Vorarlberg and the western lands. He needed money and troops for his diplomacy, wars, and upkeep, and if the other Germans would not pay,

---

[38] 5: pp. 8–10. Wiesflecker attributes to Frederick very modest abilities (5: pp. 35–42) and speculates that but for his protection of Luther, he would hardly be remembered (5: p. 42). For a very different judgment, see Ingetraut Ludolphy, *Friedrich der Weise, Kurfürst von Sachsen, 1463–1525* (Göttingen: Vandenhoeck & Ruprecht, 1984), pp. 177–93, who largely accepts the neo-Rankean view of Maximilian. Frederick was Maximilian's first cousin once removed, as his grandmother was the king's aunt.

Austria must. He squeezed the lands, especially the Tyrol, to exhaustion to feed his Italian operations, and he so undermined their liberties that centralization won, as it were, by default.

Ulmann had accused Maximilian of bleeding Germany for Austrian interests; Wiesflecker demonstrates that the opposite was true. He estimates that during the era of the later Italian Wars, roughly 1508–1517, Austrian revenues averaged 500,000–1 million florins/year, while the rest of the Empire contributed just under 50,000 florins/year. Based on Maximilian's own estimate to the Diet of Constance in 1507, Wiesflecker also sets the total Imperial costs of his reign at 25 million florins, of which something more than 70 percent was spent on war. Lack of money was the fundamental weakness of his policy, and even Austria could not produce the sums he needed in his later wars. Need drove him into the hands of the Augsburg firms, especially the Fuggers, who held an enormous share of the mountainous debts—perhaps 6 million florins in all—he left at his death. Wiesflecker sums up: "Maximilian conducted grand policy on credit, and Austria had to pay the bill" (5: p. 204).

How did he do it? Maximilian, as his father once said, was a "wastrel (*Streugütlein*)" (5: p. 564). In his semi-autobiographical *Weisskunig*, the king agreed: "I am not a king of money, but I wish to reign over the people and over those who have money; every king fights his enemies with men and money; a warlike regime and reputation count for far more than does money" (3: p. 229). It was worse than that, for though punctilious to a fault about his honor, he lacked all morals about money. Every florin was spent, mortgaged, and promised ten times over before it ever came in; he set his courtiers a model for their infamous venality; he sometimes had to leave his queen behind as pledge for his debts; and he borrowed continuously from his servitors—large sums from top officials, tiny ones from servants—and never repaid them. Those who liked him tried to make excuses, as the Augsburg merchant Lucas Rem did: "He was pious but not very intelligent, and he was always poor, ... while his councillors, who were mostly scoundrels, dominated him entirely" (3: pp. 245–46). But, in truth, the man whom the Venetians mocked as "Maximilian the Penniless (*Massimiliano pocchi danari*)" (1: p. 21) was the most venal of all. The top officials, though they imitated their master in such matters, served him relatively well. In Wiesflecker's hands they emerge from the shadows for the first time—Tyroleans and Swabians, mostly, from petty noble or burgher backgrounds, with the occasional lucky peasants' son thrown in. Among them were a few Burgundians, who seem for a while to have set the tone.

There is an old debate about Burgundian versus native origins for the Tyrolean governmental reforms, which Maximilian began in the 1490s and on which the centralization of the Austrian lands rested. The most commonly accepted view, which follows an argument made in 1922 by Theodor Mayer (1883–1972) for native origins, can now be discarded.[39] Wiesflecker demonstrates not only the Tyrolean reforms' conformity to Burgundian models in allocations of function and offices, plus the presence of Burgundians at Innsbruck, but also the use of such Burgundian terms as *Stat* and *Finanz*, all of which led the Austrians to call the central administration "the Netherlandish government" (2: pp. 175–85; 5: pp. 205–6, 209). The reforms gave each group of Austrian lands—the five eastern duchies, the Tyrol, and Vorarlberg and the western lands—its own government; they divided the governments functionally into regime, court, and treasury; and they set the Innsbruck government over the others. The reforms' overriding goal was greater revenue, and their success may be judged from the fact that while the Innsbruck treasury could hardly support the court of Duke Sigmund, who resigned the Tyrol to Maximilian in 1490, under Maximilian it financed the Italian Wars (5: p. 209).

The Tyrol, with its heart at Innsbruck, its fabled mineral wealth, its beloved hunting preserves, and its easy access to South Germany and North Italy, formed the "pivot point" of Maximilian's Austria.[40] The Tyroleans showed little of the anticentralist resistance which made governmental centralization so difficult in the eastern duchies. The Tyrol always paid more than its share of Austrian taxes, and its capital, Innsbruck, hosted the great pan-Austrian diet of 1518, when Maximilian introduced his final plan for uniting the governments of

---

[39] See Christoph Link, "Die Habsburgischen Erblande, die bömischen Länder und Salzburg," in *Deutsche Verwaltungsgeschichte*, ed. Kurt G. A. Jeserich, Hans Pohl, and Georg-Christoph von Unruh, vol. 1, *Vom Spätmittelalter bis zum Ende des Reiches* (Stuttgart: Deutsche Verlags-Anstalt, 1983), p. 476. Theodor Mayer (1883–1972), who was from upper Austria, was a disciple of Alfons Dopsch; see Weber, *Biographisches Lexikon* (n. 2 above), pp. 371–72.

[40] The term comes from Volker Press, "Die Erblande und das Reich von Albrecht II. bis Karl VI. (1438–1740)," in *Deutschland und Österreich*, ed. Robert A. Kann and Friedrich E. Prinz (Vienna: Böhlau Verlag, 1980), pp. 44–88, here at p. 54. See Thomas A. Brady, Jr., *Turning Swiss: Cities and Empire, 1450–1550*, Cambridge Studies in Early Modern History (Cambridge: Cambridge University Press, 1985), pp. 51–52.

Austria and the Empire (4: pp. 305–20; 5: p. 218).[41] When his grandson and successor, Archduke Ferdinand (1503–1564), completed the
centralization of Austria in 1526, the year of Mohacs, Austria's center was about to shift to Vienna, Wiener Neustadt, and Prague. It
was nonetheless the old emperor, Maximilian, who created Austria
out of the Habsburgs' German-, Italian-, and Slovene-speaking lands.
He centralized them at Innsbruck; his motive was revenue for the
Italian Wars, and his attention was hardly distracted by the acute
suffering which his policies caused the common people, especially
during the terrible years from 1513 to 1517.

Austria could not play this role of the core, which the German
princes had refused, and so, in his ruthless penury, Maximilian delivered his Austrians into the hands of the great South German firms.
"The rise of the House of Habsburg," Wiesflecker writes, "was possible
only in cooperation with South German capital," and "the emperor
was forced to permit the firms to exploit his lands and to lay off his
debts on their peoples" (5: p. 583). One object of his expenditures,
and one alone, redounded to the Austrian peoples' benefit: the union
with Hungary, which provided a shield in the coming Turkish Wars.
Otherwise, the creator of Austria was its relentless exploiter, a fact
which Wiesflecker recognizes but which his method prevents him
from dramatizing. For that one must turn to other books.

VI

Wiesflecker's readers have to share—as Maximilian would have—
the historian's surprise at the eruption in 1518 of the first signs of
the coming Reformation storm. It is not that he ignores the church,
for he portrays Maximilian as a typical fifteenth-century ruler, pious
and predatory, plundering the church in good Habsburg tradition.
From his father he learned that "What the priests have is ours
(*Pfaffenhab ist unser Kammergut*)" (1: p. 79; 5: p. 156); in the Netherlands
he learned his Valois father-in-law's caesaro-papist claim to be pope
and emperor in his own lands (5: p. 157). He dispensed Austrian
and Imperial benefices, appropriated monastic revenues, laid hands
on the proceeds of crusade indulgences, and tried to treat the popes

---

[41] Brady, *Turning Swiss*, pp. 89–91.

as mere Imperial patriarchs. That did not work, faced as he was by popes who were individually more than a political match for him and whose refusal to obey prompted his outburst that "throughout my whole life, no pope has ever kept his word to me" (4: p. 414).

All this is in the *Maximilian*, but it does not help to explain the coming of the Reformation, which broke in on Germany just as Maximilian was dying. Wiesflecker does recognize the place of religious conceptions and language in the Imperial reform tradition, from Nicholas of Cusa to the Upper Rhenish Revolutionary, who appeared and was ignored at the Diet of Worms in 1495 (2: pp. 201–8; 5: pp. 122–24). He sees, too, how the Imperial discourse of political reform excluded both issues of church reform and the voices for reform—peace, justice, and law and order—of the burghers, officials, and common people. Such folk had "not the slightest chance of being heard," because the upper classes "saw in the Imperial reform nothing more than a constitutional struggle for control of Imperial government" (2: p. 227). Wiesflecker is also aware of storm signs, for though he does not notice that the year of Maximilian's accession, 1493, also saw the first rural revolt (*Bundschuh*) on the Upper Rhine, he does acknowledge the powerfully unsettling effects in Germany of the long Italian Wars—so much so, that "without the Venetian War there would have been no Knights' Revolt and Peasants' War in the 1520s" (5: p. 553).

Why then the surprise when, at Augsburg in 1518, the crust of Imperial political discourse cracked open to allow dissident, even shrilly critical voices to sound in the Empire's highest forum? The answer must be that Wiesflecker has lost one of the Rankean tradition's essential insights: the link between the failure of state building and the peculiar form and success of the German Reformation. This link cuts to the heart of the Empire's character. Nowhere else in Europe did the union of temporal and spiritual power take such durable and decisive forms as it did in the Holy Roman Empire, where by 1500 the church found itself so mired in the established social order that reform from within had become impossible.[42] What was more natural than to connect the church with the deep social problems of justice and law and order? Such, in fact, was the attitude of the

---

[42] This is the essential lesson of the best study of the pre-Reformation church, Francis Rapp, *Réformes et réformation à Strasbourg: Église et société dans le diocèse de Strasbourg (1450–1525)* (Paris: Ophrys, 1974).

common man, who, however much he might appreciate Luther's biblicism, remained deaf to all talk of a separation between the notion of justice and the "true gospel" and "godly law."[43] The Reformation movement of the 1520s, therefore, including the revolts and the Peasants' War, were partly consequences of the failure of king, electors, and princes to establish an effective central government in the Empire. This failure enabled sentiments for the reform of religion to acquire revolutionary potency.

While he sees that Luther's appearance at Augsburg in 1518 gave opportunity for his reform ideas to spread through German public opinion (4: p. 416), Wiesflecker does not comprehend the connection between Luther's reformation and the seething demands and the popular hunger for reform. Neither, it must be admitted, did Luther himself. Maximilian's own blindness to what was happening—he was too busy buying electoral votes for his grandson—should not blind us to the importance of Augsburg in 1518 as a rehearsal for Worms in 1521. What the failure of reform from above had determined was that in the Empire, unlike other lands affected by the Reformation, reform would be tried from below.

VII

Wiesflecker's splendid *Maximilian* is in some ways a recognizable, though not typical, accomplishment of the dominant Austrian way of doing history. That way tends to empiricism, to the criticism of documents rather than the critique of history, and at its worst to exhaust its energies "in footnotes," as Alphons Lhotsky (1903–1968) once charged.[44] Even its strong tradition of medieval social history still carries the antitheoretical bias it received at the hands of its great master, Alfons Dopsch (1868–1953).[45] Whatever the reasons for this marked hostility to political economy and historical sociology,[46]

---

[43] See Peter Blickle, *Gemeindereformation: Die Menschen des 16. Jahrhunderts auf dem Weg zum Heil* (Munich: R. Oldenbourg, 1985).

[44] Alphons Lhotsky, *Geschichte des Instituts für Österreichische Geschichtsforschung, 1854–1954*, Mitteilungen des Instituts für Österreichische Geschichtsforschung, supp. vol. 17 (Graz and Cologne: Böhlau Verlag, 1954), p. 118.

[45] Weber, *Biographisches Lexikon*, pp. 109–10. See the very good study by Hanna Vollrath, "Alfons Dopsch," in *Deutsche Historiker*, ed. Hans-Ulrich Wehler (Göttingen: Vandenhoeck & Ruprecht, 1980), 7: pp. 39–54.

[46] See the highly interesting but confusing book by Günter Fellner, *Ludo Moritz Hartmann und die Österreichische Geschichtswissenschaft: Grundzüge eines paradigmatischen*

it means that history painted on a very broad canvas can be viewed only from the top down. This is especially true of a work cast on a Europe-wide stage, as is Wiesflecker's *Maximilian*. Not only do the common people get pushed to the margins, but in addition politics, diplomacy, and wars press economies and religion into the shadows. This is why, despite his evident sympathy for the common people and their sufferings and dreams, Wiesflecker seems surprised at the vehemence of the voices that sound as the old emperor is dying. The German Reformation disrupted a political stalemate; Wiesflecker explains why the stalemate occurred but not why it was so suddenly disrupted.

The weakness of theoretically conscious social history in Austria, it has recently been charged, arises from the Austrian historians' subservience to German historicism, which in an older generation led to support for "austrofascism" and even Nazism.[47] This is rather too simple. It is true that the Austrian historians—Wiesflecker (5: p. xxxii) is no exception—commonly bow to Ranke, but the profoundly statist and Protestant bias of classic German historicism did not easily fit Austrian conditions. In pre-1918 Austria, the concept of "nation" attached not to a language or culture but to the Austrian state, of which Maximilian could fairly be called the founder.[48] The fall of this state in 1918 might have sent Austrian historians back to study

---

Konfliktes, Veröffentlichungen des Ludwig-Boltzmann-Institutes für Geschichte der Gesellschaftswissenschaften, vol. 15 (Vienna and Salzburg: Geyer-Editionen, 1985), esp. pp. 86–99.

[47] This is Fellner's main argument in *ibid.*, see esp. pp. 80–99, 325–68. He believes that "historicism" as a philosophy and a cultural politics was tantamount to pan-Germanism, at least in Austria. Historicism, however, was a Protestant, chiefly liberal Protestant, philosophy of history, as I have argued in "From the Sacral Community to the Common Man: Reflections on German Reformation Studies," *Central European History*, vol. 20 (1988), and its colonization of a largely Catholic historical establishment must have created more strains than Fellner can see. There are clues to these strains, though Fellner does not see them, in his treatment of Hugo Hantsch (1895–1972), the Benedictine monk and historian, who appears in his book, first, as a "competitor [Konkurrent]" of the "austro-fascist" historians, then as one "loyal to the austro-fascist regime [dem austrofaschistischen System loyal gegenüberstehend]," and much later as one who was interned at Buchenwald and then banished to a rural parish. Fellner, pp. 329, 331, 357. See Weber, *Biographisches Lexikon*, pp. 204–5.

[48] As Alexander von Helfert wrote in 1853, "Nationalgeschichte ist für uns nicht die Geschichte irgendeiner Gruppe . . . sondern die Geschichte eines durch geographische und politische Notwendigkeiten vereinigten Volkes, das derselben Staatsgewalt untertan ist und denselben Gesetzen gehorcht" (quoted by Ernst Joseph Görlich, *Grundzüge der Geschichte der Habsburgermonarchie und Österreichs*, 3d ed. [Darmstadt: Wissenschaftliche Buchgesellschaft, 1988], p. 11).

its formative age, Maximilian's age, but they did not go.[49] Instead,
they shifted toward the concept of "the people [das Volk]" as the
enduring basis of history, and since there was no historic "Austrian
people" or "Austrian nation," Austrian historical writing of the interwar
era tended toward pan-Germanism, including, in some cases, the
National Socialist variety.[50] Some, such as the eminent Heinrich
Ritter von Srbik (1878–1951), a disciple of Dopsch, passed entirely
into the National Socialist movement.[51] Srbik was a true believer in
a great pan-German state, in which all religious, confessional, and
class differences would dissolve into a common historical consciousness. His projection of the pan-German heritage back to the foundations of the Austrian state in the early sixteenth century combined,
as one critic has noted, "medieval Christian universalism with blood,
mostly German blood, uniting state and soul."[52] A superficially similar path was trod by the medievalist Otto Brunner (1898–1982), who
tried to free all of premodern history from the state-centered vision
of the German historicists and found the fabric of premodern history rather in a variety of social groups, ranging from the household to the race.[53] Brunner's populism, which he later stripped of
its racialist elements, led him to a view of social history which bears
close resemblance to the "structuralist" history of more recent times,
especially in its more vehemently antistatist forms. His achievement
represents in many ways an extension to all premodern history of
the principles announced but never developed by Alfons Dopsch,
who had tried to show that the main structures of social history (like
Karl Lamprecht, he called it "cultural history [*Kulturgeschichte*]") survive the rise and fall of states.[54]

The main Austrian tradition may therefore be seen as "historicist"
in its bias against theory, but not in its rejection of the development
of the state as history's core. Once its devaluation of the state had
been detached from pan-Germanism after 1945, this tradition, chiefly

---

[49] See Lhotsky, *Österreichische Historiographie* (n. 2 above), pp. 212–13, on the atmosphere after 1918.
[50] This is portrayed, if unevenly, by Fellner, pp. 325–50.
[51] Weber, *Biographisches Lexikon* (n. 2 above), pp. 561–62. See Helmut Reinalter,
"Heinrich Ritter von Srbik," in *Deutsche Historiker*, ed. Hans-Ulrich Wehler (Göttingen:
Vandenhoeck & Ruprecht, 1982), 8: pp. 78–95.
[52] Fellner, p. 331.
[53] See Weber, *Biographisches Lexikon*, p. 72. I have learned much about Brunner
from an unpublished paper by James Van Horn Melton (to whom my thanks).
[54] Vollrath (n. 45 above), pp. 41–47.

through Brunner's influence, inspired a new view of the "Old Empire" between the later Middle Ages and the French Revolution. What the Rankeans had long regarded as the dark night of German particularism and weakness, punctuated only by Martin Luther, the Peasants' War, the Thirty Years' War, and the rise of Prussia, has blossomed as "the early modern era," different but no less interesting than what went before and came after.[55] It has been made possible by the integration of political history into social history, largely along the lines recommended by Dopsch and practiced by Brunner.

Austrian history poses powerful barriers to a similar evolution, not least because it provides no long-term continuities in the relationships between peoples and states. When Alphons Lhotsky (1903–1968) reviewed Maximilian's reign, he concluded that "this was hardly the foundation of an energetic territorial government, much less of a successful royal policy. If Germany seemed to face the alternatives, either to acquire a republican-corporate constitution represented by Berthold von Henneberg or to be united by the Habsburgs under a national monarchy, in fact there was neither the power for the former nor the will for the latter. The Habsburgs themselves, however, had to choose between universal dynastic policy or Austrian state policy, and by choosing to pursue both they caused many odd entanglements."[56] Hermann Wiesflecker's *Maximilian* shares much of Lhotsky's skepticism toward the old connections between nations and state building. If he is also cool toward social history, Brunnerian or otherwise, it may well be because in Austria, at least for his generation of historians, social history still bears the taint of its associations with pan-German racialism.

This situation helps to explain the weakness of the national element, any national element, in the *Maximilian*, for Wiesflecker never deviates from the triple-tiered stage of his story—Europe, the Empire, Austria—which he replicates in summary chapters to most of the volumes. Wiesflecker is a Tyrolean, a native of Lienz in the East Tyrol, who attended school at Bressanone/Brixen in the (already Italian) South Tyrol and Schwaz before his studies at Vienna, Innsbruck,

---

[55] See Heinz Schilling, *Aufbruch und Krise: Deutschland, 1517–1648* (Berlin: Siedler Verlag, 1988), pp. 9–12.

[56] Alphons Lhotsky, *Das Zeitalter des Hauses Österreich: Die ersten Jahre der Regierung Ferdinands I. in Österreich (1520–1527)*, Veröffentlichungen der Kommission für Geschichte Österreichs, vol. 4 (Vienna: Hermann Böhlaus Nachfolger, 1971), p. 64. On Lhotsky, see Weber, *Biographisches Lexikon*, pp. 349–50.

and Rome.[57] His road to the *Maximilian* began under the guidance
of Leo Santifaller, a South Tyrolean from Kastelruth near Bressanone/
Brixen. He is thus the son of a land divided between two relatively
young states, Austria and Italy, and a member of a generation for
whom his teachers' most obvious national identification, the German
nation, is not possible. The unity of his story, therefore, lies on none
of its three levels—European, Imperial, or Austrian—but in the unity
of temperament, education, thought, ambition, and action in the person of the king-emperor himself. In this sense, the *Maximilian* is a
true biography, which seeks its coherence in the unity of thought
and action. Here, within—not in the future of any of the peoples
who appear on its three stages—is the *Maximilian*'s heart.

[57] Weber, *Biographisches Lexikon*, pp. 659–60.

CHAPTER TWELVE

THE COMMON MAN AND THE LOST AUSTRIA
IN THE WEST: A CONTRIBUTION TO
THE GERMAN PROBLEM[1]

One of the persistent peculiarities of German history is "the idea of a *Sonderweg*, or German historical aberration."[2] The currently most prominent version of the idea holds that "the central point about Germany's passage to 'modernity' was the lack of synchronization between the economic, social, and political spheres", with the result that "Germany did not have a bourgeois revolution of the normal kind associated with England, France, or the United States".[3] There is another notion of a German *Sonderweg*, ideologically related to the first, which holds that Germany failed in the sixteenth century to imitate "the growing signs of organised strength, the growing unity of national consciousness, the growing reality underlying the pomp of dynamic monarchy",[4] which may be identified in contemporary England, France, or Castile. The deficit attributed to this second *Sonderweg* is not the bourgeois revolution of the eighteenth century but the Protestant Reformation, sometimes in its guise as the "early bourgeois revolution". What is at stake in this notion of *Sonderweg*, again, is not the class character of the new Germany created in 1871, but its confessional character. The point was perfectly made by Adolf Stoecker, the Prussian court preacher, who exulted that "the Holy German Evangelical Empire is now achieved", in which "we can see the hand of God from 1517 to 1871!"[5]

The twentieth century has made a historical curiosity of the quarrel of *großdeutsch* and *kleindeutsch* over the shape of the German state.

---

[1] This study draws on my recently published *Turning Swiss: Cities and Empire, 1450–1550* (Cambridge Studies in Early Modern History) (Cambridge/New York, 1985), where references will be found for statements otherwise unsupported here.

[2] David Blackbourn and Geoff Eley, *The Peculiarities of German History Bourgeois Society and Politics in the Nineteenth Century* (Oxford/New York, 1984), p. 10.

[3] *Ibid.*, pp. 6–7.

[4] G. R. Elton, *Reformation Europe, 1517–1559* (New York, 1963), p. 304.

[5] Quoted by Karl Kupisch, "The 'Luther Renaissance'", *Journal of Contemporary History*, II, 4 (October 1967), p. 41.

What survives is a myth of the German national *Sonderweg* in the sixteenth century. Two examples from very different corners may illustrate how widely it is held. The English historian A. J. P. Taylor has written:

> The first years of Charles V were the moment of Goethe's phrase which, once lost, eternity will never give back. The moment for making a national middle-class Germany was lost in 1521 perhaps forever, certainly for centuries. By 1525, it was evident that the period of national awakening had passed, and there began from that moment a steady advance of absolutism and authoritarianism which continued uninterruptedly for more than 250 years.[6]

From another point of view Max Steinmetz, dean of the German Democratic Republic's historians of the Reformation era, contends that "The early bourgeois revolution, which culminated in the Peasants' War, represented the first attempt of the popular masses to create a unified national state from below."[7]

Neither historian specifies the term "national", though one suspects that each means Germany in something like the configuration of 1871. Neither specifies the political meaning of a national—as distinct from a patriotically-minded—"middle-class" or the "popular masses".

There are at least two serious objections to the general view expressed by Taylor and Steinmetz. The first is that the "national" states created in sixteenth-century Europe were, with the exception of the Netherlands, centralised, dynastic monarchies, which possessed the attributes of absolutist states—civil bureaucracies, taxation, standing armies, diplomatic corps, and claims to sovereignty—and which had war as their chief business. Far from being creations of "middle-classes" or "popular masses", such states represented "the new political carapace of a threatened nobility", which now required the state's mediation for its extraction of the surplus.[8] In some parts of Europe, state-building forces also arose from the burghers and even the ranks of the peasantry. Such forces were strong in a belt of lands that

---

[6] A. J. P. Taylor, *The Course of German History* (London, 1945), p. 162.

[7] Max Steinmetz, "Theses on the Early Bourgeois Revolution in Germany, 1476–1535", in Bob (Robert W.) Scribner and Gerhard Benecke (eds.), *The German Peasant War of 1525—New Viewpoints* (London, 1979), pp. 9–18, here at p. 17.

[8] Perry Anderson, *Lineages of the Absolutist State* (London, 1974), p. 18. For an illuminating case study of how this mediation worked, see Hermann Rebel, *Peasant Classes: The Bureaucratization of Property and Family Relations under Early Habsburg Absolutism* (Princeton, NJ, 1983).

stretched across the northern foot of the Central Alps, where they tended politically not toward absolutism but toward republics based on the representation of urban and rural communes.[9] It is conceivable that in regions of Germany where the nobles were weak, such forces might have combined under royal leadership to form a state which would have been monarchical but not absolutist.

A second objection to the statements by Taylor and Steinmetz concerns the concept of the "nation". A close examination of the Holy Roman Empire's structure at end of the Middle Ages reveals a system that was centred firmly in the South. Not only did the High Court and Governing Council, created in the reform era of 1495–1521, sit in the South, but the Imperial Diet was also predominantly southern in its meeting sites, membership, and attendance. The Habsburg dynasty, which ruled the empire continuously since 1440, had its dynastic lands entirely in the south. Austria stretched from the borders of Hungary to those of Lorraine, and it was never combined administratively with the Habsburg Netherlands except for the brief years of personal union between Maximilian I's death in 1519 and Archduke Ferdinand's assumption of rule over Austria in 1522. In the opening decades of the sixteenth century this dynasty was faced not with the creation of a "national" Germany on a bourgeois, popular, or any other basis, but with the formation and consolidation of an Austrian system of lordship and clientage solid enough and rich enough to serve as a basis from which to strengthen its power over the rest of the empire. The creation of such a basis may well have lain within Habsburg grasp around 1520, but the chance was shattered by a combination of forces and events that doomed the basis that was then forming, Austria's kingdom in the west.

I

Shortly before Christmas 1519, a Brabantine nobleman named Maximilian van Bergen rode into Augsburg to negotiate with representatives of the Swabian League about the transfer of the duchy of Württemberg, which the League had conquered from its reigning duke, to King Charles of Spain, who was also King of the Romans

---

[9] See Peter Blickle, "Communalism, Parliamentarism, Republicanism", *Parliaments, Estates and Representation*, VI, 1 (1986): pp. 1–13.

and emperor-elect. "Your Majesty should be thoroughly convinced",
Bergen wrote to his master,

> that this land of Württemberg is a large and important territory, and
> that Your Royal Majesty can procure no greater advantage than to
> bring it into Your Majesty's hands. This is so because it lies in the
> middle of the Holy Empire and borders on some of Your Royal
> Majesty's hereditary Austrian lands. If Württemberg is added to them,
> then Your Royal Majesty would have, as archduke of Austria, ade-
> quate power *vis-à-vis* the disturbers of the peace in the German lands.
> Your Majesty should also consider that he could thus all the better
> maintain law and order in the Holy Empire, and that the common
> folk in Württemberg wish nothing more than to join the obedience of
> Your Royal Majesty and the House of Austria.[10]

The alternative, Bergen thought, would be the destruction of the
Swabian League by the princes, who would

> shove the cities aside and enjoy a "free government" in the Empire.
> Your Majesty can well imagine how much obedience you would then
> command! Also, once the cities see what is happening, His Majesty
> can be assured that nothing less will happen than that all these cities
> will join the Swiss, and thereafter the whole land of Swabia and the
> Rhine Valley all the way down to Cologne would join as well. God
> grant that it might go no further! We are firmly convinced that the
> princes who thus intrigue do not sufficiently consider what they do;
> for if it develops so far in this direction, they will be expelled by their
> own subjects, who would then join these others; and in the end the
> whole German land would become one vast commune, and all the
> lords would be expelled.[11]

Bergen thus laid before his sovereign the two political paths that
South Germany might reasonably take. The townsmen and other
commoners might well support a strong House of Austria, if it could
keep the peace in the South and provide good government. Otherwise, they would try to "turn Swiss", that is, either to join the Swiss
confederation or form "new Switzerlands" in imitation of the old.
Monarchism and communal federalism were thus not contrary policies but alternatives.

The wisdom of Bergen's comments in the winter of 1519–1520 can
be judged only in the context of the dead emperor's reign. Three
years before he succeeded his father, Emperor Frederick III, in 1493,

---

[10] Quoted in *Turning Swiss*, pp. 107–8.
[11] Quoted in *ibid.*, pp. 110–11.

Maximilian became lord of Tyrol and Western Austria (*Vorderöster-reich*), a belt of lands stretching from Vorarlberg across Upper Swabia and the lands west of Lake Constance—the Hegau, Klettgau, and Breisgau—to the Sundgau in southern Alsace. Tyrol now became the pivotal point of Habsburg Austria, based on its control of the strategic Brenner Pass, its mining wealth, and its position as the bridge between the western and eastern parts of Austria. What Western Austria lacked were major cities and all the good things cities provided—guns and foodstuffs, credit and men, for although the neighbouring lands were, by Central European standards, rela-tively highly urbanised, most of the cities had acquired self-rule and owed obedience to Maximilian only as King of the Romans and later as emperor. Maximilian gathered them under the Austrian eagle's wings through two strategies: he made them Habsburg clients through membership in political federations he organised; and he offered the big merchant bankers very lucrative business through chartered monopolies, loans, and purveyance to the royal court.

The cities of the neighbouring lands, Swabia and the Upper Rhine Valley, had exercised little military power since the princes had smashed the last German urban league in the Cities' War of 1449–1453. The Swabian cities drew near the House of Austria with lit-tle resistance, for Maximilian knew what they wanted. In 1488 he organised the free cities, along with the free nobles and prelates of Upper Swabia, into the Swabian League, which only had to show its teeth through a mobilisation in the Lech Valley in 1492 in order to restore Duke Albert IV of Bavaria to good behaviour. The next year Maximilian corralled the Upper Rhenish powers, some of whom had refused to join the Swabian League on the grounds that they were "too distant", into a league called the Lower Union. The reconstitu-tion of the Lower Union was a cunning act. The original Lower Union formed in 1474 of Alsatian powers, the duke of Lorraine, and the House of Austria, and it allied with the "Upper Union", the Swiss confederation, in the League of Constance against Burgundy in the same year. Together the allies caught and killed the Burgundian governor on the Upper Rhine, invaded and plundered Burgundy, and in 1475–1477 smashed the Burgundian power in three glorious battles. The reconstituted Lower Union of 1493 formed the west-ern, Rhenish wing of Maximilian's system of clientele.

Maximilian's South German system dominated the region from the earlier 1490s until well after the king's death in 1519. In 1492 it

halted Bavarian expansion in Upper Swabia; in 1499 it fought a dis-
astrous war against the confederation, from which it nevertheless
emerged relatively unscathed; in 1504 it crushed the expanding power
of the Palatine Wittelsbachs on the Upper Rhine; and in 1519, just
after the old king's death, the Swabian League invaded Württemberg
and expelled Duke Ulrich, its wild, reckless ruler. The humiliations
of the Swabian War of 1499 aside, Maximilian's system was a most
effective instrument of the free cities and Austria against the chief
princely dynasties of the South. After the Swabian League expired in
1533, a Protestant Nuremberger lamented its demise: "The Swabian
League was the proper form of the German Nation. It was feared
by many, and in many ways it protected and sustained the public
peace and law and order."[12]

Maximilian bound the urban rich to his person and his treasury
through many types of connections. His legendary penury meant
opportunity to the urban bankers, those of Augsburg in particular,
to whom he owed about 3 million florins at his death, 1.3 million
to the Fuggers alone. In return they got chartered monopolies for
the import of foodstuffs into the alpine lands and for the exploitation of Tyrol's rich silver and copper mines and smelters. Of the
1.5 million florins his Tyrolean mines annually produced, perhaps
a tenth remained unmortgaged and came to Maximilian. A very
large portion of the commissions and orders for the court, ranging
from clothes to books to paintings to gems to armour to guns to
funeral monuments, went to the city folk, who supplied the notoriously slow-paying court on speculation. So dependent did he
become on the urban merchants that in 1508, when the Italian Wars
had ruined his finances beyond all hope, the king even tried to assume
direct royal jurisdiction over the great firms of South Germany, just
like his jurisdiction over the Jews.

Maximilian also showed himself in the cities, moving from town to
town like a "royal locust" and papering his progress with bad debts.
He recruited personnel for his court in the towns—secretaries and
councillors, humanists and poets, artillerymen and physicians. He
bound many of the urban elite to his person through vassalage, hon-
orary appointments, literary commissions, and familiar ties, such as
standing godfather to the baby daughter of Claus Jörger, an upstart
cloth merchant at Strasbourg. He did not inspire much awe. As a

---

[12] Quoted in *ibid.*, p. 18.

young prince, when he and his father had been unable to pay their bills in 1474, the good burghers of Augsburg threw dung at him in the streets. Here, at Augsburg in the Lech Valley, Maximilian's favourite route northward from Italy and Tyrol, the king was most at home; here he owed the most money, and here the big folk knew him best. When he died, the Augsburg merchant Wilhelm Rem wrote the king's epitaph:

> The emperor was Austria's lord, he was pious but not especially intelligent, and he was always out of money. In his own lands he had given away so many cities, castles, rents, and dues, that very little came to him.
>   His councillors were genuine scoundrels, and they completely dominated him. Almost all of them grew rich, while he was poor. And whoever wanted a favor from the emperor, . . . he had to pay bribes to the councillors, who got it done. When, however, an adversary came to court, they also took money from him and gave him charters which contradicted the earlier ones. The emperor stood by and let it all happen.[13]

Dr. Erasmus Topler of Nuremberg, who lived for five years at court, put it more succinctly: "for the nature of this court [is] dedicated to deals (*finanzen*)."

The positive responses with which Maximilian's overtures and programmes were received among the urban ruling classes found their most lasting expression among the South German humanists, who propagated a monarchist and pro-Austrian ideology during Maximilian's era. At Nuremberg, Augsburg, and Strasbourg, the leading literary lights all did their part to spread the fame and glory of the House of Habsburg, men such as Jacob Wimpheling at Strasbourg, who lashed out with fury at those who suggested that Alsace had ever been ruled by Latins, and Conrad Peutinger of Augsburg, who spent his spare time composing Habsburg genealogies. It was for the glory of the Habsburgs that this generation of humanists stitched together the unbroken line of majesty from Maximilian right back to Augustus.

Behind this elegant hyperbole lay hard calculation. The oligarchies of this generation faced severe threats to their power and independence both without and within the city walls. Without lay the great princes, who coveted the cities' resources and laid siege to their liberties, either individually through attempts to mediatise the

---

[13] Quoted in *ibid.*, p. 87, and there, too, the following quote.

cities and incorporate them into their territories—the fate of Mainz, Boppard, and Erfurt—or collectively in the Imperial Diet, where the princes staged in the early 1520s a whole series of attacks on commerce in general and the chartered monopolies in particular. Added to these political threats were the more straightforward predations of the robber-nobles, such as Cuntz Schott, who specialised in collecting hands from Nuremberg merchants, which heightened the already acute need for law and order.

Within the city walls, the fabric of hegemonic values—justice, peace, and unity in the service of God's honour and the common good—was beginning to unravel. The mounting wave of urban revolts during the first two decades of the century differed in some respects from earlier upheavals, for they arose less from political ambition and more from need. The economic boom that began in South Germany around 1470 lasted until about the middle of the sixteenth century, but despite the signs of urban wealth—it was the age of Holbein, Grünewald, Riemenschneider, and Dürer, of Jakob Fugger the Rich and the Welser colonisation of Venezuela, of the golden age of German printing and of the *Landsknechte*—despite such signs the cities witnessed a growing polarisation of wealth. Poverty's sharp claws reached much further up the social structure than the urban tax registers reveal, for above the actual poor were the potential poor, those threatened by the falling real wage. The consequence was that the ranks of the potentially poor embraced in many cities the bulk of the work force,[14] while at the same time the apprentices and wage-workers—up to a third of those gainfully occupied in some cities[15]—had few organisations through which to express their grievances.

Faced with such forces, the urban oligarchies drew ever nearer the monarchy, especially when, early in Charles' reign, the princes mounted their campaign against the great firms under the slogan of anti-monopoly. In the summer of 1523, they sent an embassy to the emperor at Valladolid in Spain, which begged Charles to assume direct rule in Germany, deposing the Governing Council and High Court and presumably bypassing the Imperial Diet, or to direct his

---

[14] Robert Jütte, *Obrigkeitliche Armenfürsorge in den deutschen Reichsstädten der frühen Neuzeit. Städtische Armenfürsorge in Frankfurt am Main und Köln* (Kölner historische Abhandlungen, XXXI) (Cologne/Vienna, 1984), pp. 8–19.

[15] Knut Schulz, *Handwerksgesellen und Lohnarbeiter. Untersuchungen zur oberrheinischen und oberdeutschen Stadtgeschichte des 14. bis 17. Jahrhunderts* (Sigmaringen, 1985), pp. 37–46.

brother, Archduke Ferdinand, to rule Germany in his place. The further development of this proposal was blocked for the moment by the envoys' lack of powers to commit their cities to direct financial aid to the monarch, but the proposal itself represented a direct development of the political partnership of cities and crown in Maximilian's time.

What was true of the free cities' oligarchies applied, *mutatis mutandis*, to the elites of the territorial towns as well. Or so Maximilian van Bergen alleged, and his view is confirmed for Württemberg, at least, by the strongly pro-Austrian sentiments among the smalltown notables (*Ehrbarkeit*) in the duchy. Just as in the free cities, however, in Württemberg the elites had important ties to the Swiss confederation. Not only did their spendthrift duke, Ulrich, owe large sums of money to Swiss creditors, but Württemberg was one of the regions that regularly supplied the confederation with grain. Bergen expressly attributed to them the same motives he ascribed to the governments of the free cities: if Austria could not guarantee law and order, they would seek it from the confederation.

II

These were the tendencies and policies that brought Maximilian, as ruler of Tyrol and Western Austria, as head of the House of Austria, as leader of the Swabian League and Lower Union, and as King of the Romans and emperor, together with the South German burghers and especially those of the southern free cities. The tendencies were both objective—trade and security—and subjective—monarchism and Austrian feeling, and the policies groped toward an ever closer association of crown and cities. At the same time, there emerged a notion of forming Austria, particularly Tyrol and the western lands, into a more adequate basis for the system of Austrian clientage in South Germany and for the domination of the Holy Roman Empire.

The relatively advanced state of Tyrolean administrative institutions made the land a reasonable base for state-building. Although the origins of a territorial administration built up of collegial bodies having specific competencies (finance, etc.) for the entire territory reached back well before Maximilian's time, and although the king himself, driven by the need to find money for his political schemes, destroyed nearly as much as he created, by the early 1500s Tyrol

had the most advanced administrative bureaucracy in the German-
speaking world.[16] The combination of a relatively efficient bureaucracy and abundant revenues from mining ought to have made Tyrol
a powerful state, as it did the two Saxonies, had Maximilian not
drained the country for his plans in Italy and elsewhere.

There is ample evidence that Maximilian nonetheless recognised
the need for a stronger centralised government for Tyrol and the
other dynastic lands. His first project, framed in 1516, was to transform Austria into a separate kingdom, to be cut out of Charles'
fabulous heritage and given to Archduke Ferdinand as Austrian
king, a plan which foundered on Charles' objections. Two years later,
he broached to an assembly of envoys from all of the Austrian lands
a plan for a central government for Austria and the empire. In the
new State Council (*Hofrat*) would sit five councillors from Eastern
Austria (the five Austrian duchies), four from Western Austria, and
four royal nominees, plus five from the rest of the Holy Roman
Empire. His purpose, as he explained, was to promote "our own
welfare and that of our lands and subjects" by establishing "at the
proper time and place, a neighbourly union, agreement, and league
with the estates of the Holy Empire, or, if that is impossible, at least
with the principalities and lords that border on our Austrian lands".[17]

The emperor also promised to establish a central Austrian treasury and chamber of accounts at Innsbruck, plus separate provincial
regimes at Vienna, Innsbruck, and Ensisheim in Alsace. Though
approved by the wary deputies, the plan came to nothing, largely
because the emperor's new defeats at the hands of the diet of
Augsburg in 1518 were closely followed by his own death.

The consolidation plan of 1518, which foresaw a united, centralised Austria, flanked by the Swabian League, as a base from which
to strengthen royal authority in the empire, was not just a passing
fancy of Maximilian, a ruler admittedly given to fancies. A newly re-
discovered document from the archives of the short-lived (1520–1534)
Habsburg regime at Stuttgart repeats the vital parts of the Innsbruck
plan and adjusts the Austrian part of it to make room for an Austrian
Württemberg.[18] The plan may come from Bergen's pen, and it cer-

---

[16] Theodor Mayer, *Die Verwaltungsorganisationen Maximilians I. Ihr Ursprung und ihre
Bedeutung* (Forschungen, zur inneren Geschichte Österreichs, XIV) (Innsbruck, 1920;
reprinted Aalen, 1973), pp. 57–63, 75–85.
[17] Quoted in *Turning Swiss*, p. 90.
[18] It is edited in *ibid.*, pp. 235–41.

tainly fits his vision of the need for a strong, centralising hand in Austria as the basis for Habsburg domination of South Germany, lest the duchy turn Swiss, "for the land Württemberg lies near the Swiss, and should it join them and they admit it, then other lands— Tyrol and Inner and Outer Austria—would also be lost, and also all Swabia and the regions down to Cologne. Bavaria, too, would doubtless fall".[19]

One way or another, Bergen believed, South Germany would evolve into a larger, stronger state. It may perhaps be forgiven a Netherlander that he foresaw neither the blockage of both Austrian and Swiss expansion nor its result: stable, long-term, domination by the territorial princes.

The potential Austrian state in the west can now be described. It was a political structure having its administrative head at Innsbruck and its financial heart at Augsburg. The Austrian dynastic lands, with their subsidiary centres at Vienna, Ensisheim, and Stuttgart, formed the system's core, surrounded by federations of clients, among whom the free cities played the most promising and most vital role. For the urban oligarchies feared the unstable social forces within their walls, while without they sensed a threat less from the aggressions of individual princely dynasties than from the collective effort to make the cities, and their resources, truly subject to the Imperial Diet. The oligarchies needed a stronger guarantee of the monarchy, but the Swiss confederation remained a strong second best.

III

What happened to the Austrian kingdom in the west? There are several traditional explanations of the political development of Germany in the sixteenth century. The first held that the Habsburg dynasty failed, because of its foreign attachments and engagements, to devote itself to the formation of a national monarchy in Germany, while its devotion to an alien, Roman, church deprived the Germans of their one chance for a national Lutheran religion. A second view held that the Reformation and the revolt of the Protestant princes against Charles V saved Germany from an absolutist monarchy in the Spanish style. A third view argued that by splitting the German people over

---

[19] Quoted in *ibid.*, p. 111.

religion the Protestant Reformation itself was responsible for the lack of a German national state. To these three traditional arguments we may add two more recent ones. One is Max Steinmetz's opinion that the failure of the Peasants' War in 1525 doomed the chances for a German national state because the German bourgeoisie betrayed the popular cause, just as they would again in 1848. Another attitude beams with favour upon the actual political evolution of the Empire, which it fondly calls "the Old *Reich*", and it is not free of a certain nostalgia for the unsystematic, uncentralised, comfortably aristocratic politics of an age when the German burghers felt their strongest attachments to their own home towns. The events of the sixteenth century appear hardly to have disrupted the evolution toward this condition.

Each of these views suffers from a blindness toward the social basis of German politics in the age of the Reformation. The first traditional view rests on one correct perception, the preoccupation of Charles V and Ferdinand I with non-German engagements. The situation for a continuation of Maximilian's South German system looked very good in 1522, when Ferdinand arrived as Austria's new lord. The Württemberg notables rallied to the best government in the duchy's recent memory, and the Habsburg officials struggled with the territorial Estates to reduce Duke Ulrich's mountainous debts and restore solvency to the duchy. In Tyrol and the eastern Austrian duchies, which Ferdinand found in a state of revolt, he was able to satisfy some grievances and restore the lands to order. In January 1527, Ferdinand was even able to issue a decree for a unified Austrian government (*Hofordnung*), which in Maximilian's time had remained but a dream. Ferdinand was an extremely able prince, better educated, more thoughtful, and more tolerant than his elder brother, and in time he might well have become the creator of the Austrian kingdom in the west. What intervened, however, was the Turkish invasion of Hungary in 1526 and the death of his brother-in-law, King Louis, at Mohács. Thereafter his overriding political aim, the creation of a realm for his own descendants, came to centre on his two royal crowns, those of Bohemia and Hungary, for the defence of which he bled Austria white, and though he did become King of the Romans in 1531, his main achievement lay not in the government of Germany but in the creation of the eastward-looking Austria—Hungary of early modern times. Vienna, not Innsbruck, became this land's political centre.

As for Charles V, once he reluctantly surrendered the Austrian lands to Ferdinand, he regarded the Holy Roman Empire chiefly as a source of revenue and religious quarrels. The glue of his vast system was not military but fiscal, and he rarely used his moments of real advantage—Castile after the *Comuneros*, Italy after Pavia, or Germany in 1547–1548—to install genuinely absolutist political forms. This is a major objection to the second traditional view, that the Reformation saved Germany from a Latin-style tyranny. When Charles V did have the German opposition in hand, at the imperial diet of Augsburg in 1548 after his victory over the Schmalkaldic League, his plan of political reform looked nothing like an absolutist agenda. He proposed not strict centralism but a double system of federations under his own presidency, a plan which owed more to the Swabian League than to absolutist monarchy. His suppression of the guild regimes in a series of southern free cities between 1548 and 1552, which has also been cited as proof of his centralising aims, was also nothing of the sort. The direct model came not from Spain or Italy but from good, solid, loyalist, Protestant Nuremberg.[20]

The third traditional view suffered from an excess of nostalgia. Without some centralisation and bureaucratic efficiency, South Germany could hardly have been defended against the Ottoman Turks, and the centralisation occurred in Austria alone, because the Germans of the rest of the empire would not submit to it. A structure as large as the Holy Roman Empire simply could not have been governed according to the standards of western European monarchy without a genuinely imperial system of government, with its centralised bureaucracy which drew the surplus to the centre and exported force to the periphery.

The fourth view, that represented here by Steinmetz, derives, despite its Marxist dress, from the old Liberal notion that the chief historical role of the bourgeoisie was to create the centralised modern state. It appears in many forms, among them Fernand Braudel's thesis of the "treason of the bourgeoisie".[21] An Italian model would

---

[20] The persistent belief that Charles suppressed twenty-eight guild regimes for religious reasons is laid to rest by Eberhard Naujoks (ed.), *Kaiser Karl V. und die Zunftverfassung. Ausgewählte Aktenstücke zu den Verfassungsänderungen in den oberdeutschen Reichsstädten (1547–1556)* (Veröffentlichungen der Kommission für geschichtliche Landeskunde in Baden-Württemberg, Reihe A XXVI) (Stuttgart, 1985), pp. 7–26, 335–9.

[21] Fernand Braudel, *The Mediterranean and the Mediterranean World in the Age of Philip II*, trans. Siân Reynolds (2 vols. New York, 1973), vol. II, pp. 725–34. Braudel much

yield, of course, quite the opposite conclusion about the politics of the bourgeoisie. The very existence of a "national bourgeoisie" in sixteenth-century Germany is a myth derived largely from taking too seriously the historicising effusions of such humanists as Jacob Wimpheling and Ulrich von Hutten.

The fifth view, that the institutional development of Germany was little influenced by the eruptions of the 1520s, suffers from a conservative myopia about the sources and directions of German politics in the sixteenth century. There existed in sixteenth-century South Germany an important tendency toward state-building in the western European style, which was frustrated partly by the failure of Habsburg leadership and partly by the massive intervention of the common man in South German politics in the later Middle Ages.

IV

The missing element in an explanation of Austria's failure in the west is to be found in the role as neighbour and model of Austria's most ancient foe, the Swiss confederation. The confederation represents the only successful European republic built upon an alliance of city-states with federations of free rural communes. It thus presented two faces to its northern admirers: its oligarchically ruled cities, such as Berne and Zürich, closely resembled their non-Swiss counterparts, such as Constance, Reutlingen, or Ulm; its rural federations, however, had no counterpart outside the confederation, and their freedoms exerted a strongly attractive power on the common people of South Germany, both rural and urban alike. To "turn Swiss" meant to live without lords, as a songster wrote about the Battle of Leipheim in Upper Swabia in 1525:

> The peasants tried to learn
> Evil tricks from the Swiss
> And become their own lords,
> But we baptized them in a different faith,
> And whoever didn't get away,
> He was soon cut down.[22]

---

softens this judgement in his *Civilization and Capitalism, 15th–18th Century*, vol. II: *The Wheels of Commerce*, trans. Siân Reynolds (New York, 1982), p. 594.

[22] Quoted in Brady, *Turning Swiss*, p. 35.

Reports that the common people wanted to "turn Swiss" came from as far north as Franconia, and by 1500 it was proverbial that the whole of South Germany had at least the potential to join or imitate the Swiss. Ulrich Arzt, mayor of Augsburg and a president of the Swabian League, wrote to Conrad Peutinger in 1519 that he feared the old prophecy would come true, that "when a cow stands on the bridge at Ulm and moos, she'll be heard in the middle of Switzerland".[23]

Such reports do not mean that the farming populations of South Germany stood ready to pour into the confederation, or that they hated the House of Austria, but they do mean that reports had spread widely of people elsewhere who worked the land without lords and managed, and defended, their own affairs. Whether the free institutions of the Swiss upland stockmen could have survived among farmers on flatter terrain remains to be studied. The existence of such sentiments, however, corresponded to the objective peculiarity of the rural federations as one pillar of the confederation, and the extension of the Swiss model further northward, where the many cities already had their freedom, would have meant—if possible— the political and military liberation of much of the land. This, in turn, could well have threatened the economic, but not political, subordination of the land to the towns through marker relationships. Whether or not the objective interests of the land conflicted with those of the urban artisans and wage-workers,[24] therefore, the very notion of giving the land its freedom ought to have made the urban upper classes more strongly monarchist and pro-Austrian.

The history of the urban front, which reached its pro-centralist peak just before it foundered on the religious question, reveals the importance of the early Reformation—and not just the Revolution of 1525—as a massive, brief intervention of the common man into South German politics. Brief though it was, it was massive enough to force religious change far more rapidly than the oligarchs might have wished, if they wished for it at all, for it forced them to illegalities which estranged them from their monarch. The views of Charles himself, though he was no fanatic, naturally played a certain role. So did the varying political traditions of the major South

---

[23] This and the following texts are quoted in *ibid.*, pp. 38–40.
[24] A point made by Tom Scott in "The Peasants' War: A Historiographical Review", *Historical Journal*, XXII (1979): pp. 957, 966.

German free cities. The correspondence nonetheless holds good that the stronger the popular Reformation movement the more radical an anti-Austrian and even anti-monarchist external policy the city's oligarchs were willing to consider. Zürich, Constance, and Strasbourg blazed the way. What they were not willing to consider, however, was that the rural folk should have the same freedom to respond to the Gospel that the burghers themselves claimed, the friendship between Zwingli and Michael Gaismair notwithstanding. The coming of the Reformation, therefore, did not alter the terms of South German politics sufficiently to bring the "middle of Switzerland" any further north, much less to the bridge at Ulm, but it did disrupt the basis of Austrian influence in South Germany long enough to make that basis irretrievable. The Austrian paralysis, which spread like wildfire at Maximilian's death and reached a first peak in Archduke Ferdinand's helplessness during the Revolution of 1525, reached a second, fatal peak in 1534, when the Habsburg brothers allowed Landgrave Philip of Hesse to pluck Württemberg from the lifeless Austrian grasp.

The Austria in the west failed, not so much because it lacked the institutions of the early modern state, "independent of the household, bureaucratically organized in national departments, but responsible to the crown",[25] but because, when the Reformation broke in upon it, time, fiscal need, and the quest for security had not yet begun to lead the South German burghers and petty nobles over the bridge of monarchist and pro-Austrian sentiment into the administrative arms of Austria itself. To have made anything lasting of this opportunity, the Habsburgs would have to have had a much freer hand than they had ever had, or Austria would have had to rank higher in their priorities than it ever did. Their loss owed something, however, to the intervention of the common man.

An illumination of the early modern German *Sonderweg* does not explain the modern one. Neither, however, ought to be regarded, as each commonly is, in a too narrowly national context. The Reformation and its political consequences were but one force which "helped to depose Germany from the place of first importance which it had intermittently held since the ninth century".[26] The greater

---

[25] G. R. Elton, *The Tudor Revolution in Government: Administrative Changes in the Reign of Henry VIII* (Cambridge, 1953), p. 425.

[26] Elton, *Reformation Europe*, p. 324, and there, too, the following quote.

context is dominated by the fact that "above all, in this age Europe was tilting away from the landmass to the oceans—to that open side where success awaited the enterprising few to the benefit of the many". And, one might add, to the confusion, sorrow, and grief of many others.

CHAPTER THIRTEEN

FROM THE SACRAL COMMUNITY TO THE COMMON MAN: REFLECTIONS ON GERMAN REFORMATION STUDIES

Oliver St. John Gogarty tells that during a bus trip to Connemara, he engaged a fellow traveller in conversation about the unseasonable weather. "Ah," replied the stranger, "it isn't this time of year at all."[1] That Irishman's astonishment came to mind when I heard that the Conference Group for Central European History would sponsor a session on the German Reformation. It is a rebuke, surely, to those who believe, as someone recently argued, that the truly significant part of German history begins at 1871 or—my informant was not precise on this point—perhaps 1918 or even 1933. And, indeed, our papers reveal that much of what is going on in German Reformation studies bears on the broader interpretation of German history.[2]

R. Po-chia Hsia reviews the chief research topics of the social history of the Reformation during the past quarter-century, casting his account in fairly specialized terms. I will try to provide a larger context for his and Peter Blickle's findings and specify what they contribute to the larger picture of the German Reformation. These tasks require me to range deeper into the historiographical past than our panelists have done and to deal with some matters to which they could only allude.

I

The papers open with references to the writings of Bernd Moeller, and together they tell how a quarter-century's labors have both built upon, revised, and sometimes refuted Moeller's theses. Although Hsia

---

[1] Oliver St. John Gogarty, *It Isn't This Time of Year at All: An Unpremeditated Autobiography* (Garden City, N.Y., 1954), p. 17.

[2] The neophyte has easy access to the field through two recent publications: Steven Ozment, ed., *Reformation Europe: A Guide to Research* (St. Louis, 1982); and A. G. Dickens and John Tonkin, *The Reformation in Historical Thought* (Cambridge, Mass., 1986).

correctly cites Alfred Schultze as a source of Moeller's union between
the Reformation and German urban communalism, Moeller's leading
idea—the urban reformers adapted Luther's message to the burghers'
communal mentality—probably owes less to Schultze's purely legal-
institutional view than to the ideas of the Swabian theologian Ernst
Troeltsch (d. 1923).[3] Troeltsch's life work was a critique of German
Protestantism, for he aimed to warn his fellow Protestant Christians
that the tradition of German Lutheranism alone could never provide the basis of a stable, German, Christian civilization.[4] What his
own tradition lacked, a sense of fully Christian, fully modern universalism, he sought in a recovery of the full range of Protestant social
values and ideas. In his greatest work, *The Social Teaching of the Christian
Churches*, Troeltsch searched Calvin's Geneva and the world of the
sects and spiritualists for the protomodern attitudes he found wanting in the socially backward worlds of Luther's Saxony and German
Lutheranism.[5] He ignored, however, the German-speaking cities—
the *Social Teachings* contains only four passing references to Huldrych
Zwingli of Zurich and three to Martin Bucer of Strasbourg[6]—and he
continued to think of Lutheranism as peculiarly German and Calvinism as peculiarly "western."[7] The Great War mightily reinforced this
habit of thought.

[3] Almost nothing produced by the older Troeltsch reception in America can be
relied upon today. In West Germany there is a "Troeltsch Renaissance" underway,
which is producing at last detailed information on his biography. See Horst Renz
and Friedrich Wilhelm Graf, eds., *Troeltsch-Studien: Untersuchungen zur Biographie und Werk-
geschichte* (Gütersloh, 1982). In English one may begin with Robert J. Rubanowice,
Crisis in Consciousness: The Thought of Ernst Troeltsch (Tallahassee, Fla., 1982); and Robert
Morgan and Michael Pye, trans. and eds., *Ernst Troeltsch: Writings on Theology and
Religion* (Atlanta, 1977), which provides on pp. 253–55 a useful bibliography of
Troeltsch's writings in English.

[4] The main instrument of this argument was his distinction between Old and
New Protestantism, which Christoph Weber detects in his thought as early as 1900.
Christoph Weber, *Der "Fall Spahn" (1901): Ein Beitrag zur Wissenschafts- und Kulturdiskussion
im ausgehenden 19. Jahrhundert* (Rome, 1980), p. 25 n. 82.

[5] Ernst Troeltsch, *Die Soziallehren der christlichen Kirchen und Gruppen* (Tübingen, 1912,
1922), translated by Olive Wyon as *The Social Teaching of the Christian Churches* (New
York, 1931).

[6] *Soziallehren*, pp. 681–82, 752, 773–74, 812 (English: *Social Teachings*, pp. 626, 669,
677–78, 703).

[7] Developed most fully in the essays collected in *Deutscher Geist und Westeuropa:
Gesammelte kulturpolitische Aufsätze und Reden*, ed. Hans Baron (Tübingen, 1925; reprint,
Aalen, 1966); its flavor may be sampled in English in Ernst Troeltsch, "The Ideas
of Natural Law and Humanity in World Politics", in Otto Gierke, *Natural Law and
the Theory of Society, 1500–1800*, trans. Ernest Barker (Cambridge, 1934, 1950), pp.
201–22.

The next step was taken by Wilhelm Bofinger, whose 1957 Tübingen dissertation extended Troeltsch's analysis to the South German and Swiss cities and argued that the urban reformers' adaptation of Luther's message to the burghers' mentality formed a sound, progressive, decidedly "western" tradition of German Protestantism.[8] Bofinger—a Swabian, like Troeltsch—wrote at a time when the transformation of a defeated Germany into two German states stimulated thought about, on the one hand, German traditions unconnected with the Prusso-Saxon Northeast and, on the other, possible connections of German Protestant Christianity to "the West." This line of thought— western Protestant Christianity, too, is of German origin, and German Protestantism, too, is western and democratic—found its fruition in Moeller's famous essay of 1962. Moeller, who is neither a Swabian nor even a southerner, made his intention crystal clear in *Reichsstadt und Reformation*, the final sentence of which reads, "In the form of modern Anglo-Saxon democracy, however, despite many new and different ideas, a piece of medieval German urban civilization has returned to Germany."[9] He alludes, of course, to the 1949 constitution of the Federal Republic of Germany.

Moeller's work may also be located in a broader framework of German writing on the Reformation, now almost two hundred years old, which long supplied an important idiom to the debate about the meaning of German modernity and what it means to be a German. Though often attributed to Ranke, the construction and care of this tradition owes far more to his epigones. The master, it is true, was conventionally confessional—he once said of his only Catholic student, Carl Adolf Cornelius, "I was friendly to him, even though he was a Catholic."[10] There was nonetheless a deep qualification to Ranke's celebration of the Reformation in his *Germany in the Age of*

---

[8] Wilhelm Bofinger, "Oberdeutschtum und württembergische Reformation: Die Sozialgestalt der Kirche als Problem der Theologie- und Kirchengeschichte der Reformationszeit" (unpublished diss., Tübingen, 1957). Part of it has been published in Wilhelm Bofinger, "Kirche und werdender Territorialstaat: Eine Untersuchung zur Kirchenreform Herzog Ulrichs von Württemberg," *Blätter für württembergische Kirchengeschichte* 65 (1965): pp. 75–149.

[9] Bernd Moeller, *Reichsstadt und Reformation*, Schriften des Vereins für Reformationsgeschichte, 180 (Gütersloh, 1962), p. 76: "In den modernen angelsächsischen Demokratie aber ist, nach vielen Wandlungen und neben manchem anderen Gedankenelement, auch ein Stück mittelalterlichen deutschen Städtewesen nach Deutschland zurückgekehrt." This sentence is missing from the French and English translations.

[10] Quoted by Wolfgang Weber, *Priester der Clio: Historisch-sozialwissenschaftliche Studien zur Herkunft und Karriere deutscher Historiker und zur Geschichte der Geschichtswissenschaft*

the Reformation, the flagship work of Reformation historiography.[11] Ranke, as Leonard Krieger has shown, approached the Reformation less as a moment of national liberation than as a fulfillment in a particular ("national") aspect of a Latin Christianity whose other, universal, moment had already been realized in medieval Catholicism.[12] It is also true, however, that as his perspective turned "German and political" rather than "universal and theological,"[13] "the result was still to leave universal history without a demonstrable empirical embodiment in modern times."[14]

The Prussian school and the neo-Rankeans made a virtue of this lack, and German historicism grew up as an apology for the State in general and the Prusso-Germanic imperial state in particular. From their commanding domination of academic history,[15] Ranke successors poured a vision of history "From Luther to Bismarck" into the hearts and minds of Germany's Protestant *Bildungsbürgertum*.[16] This voice, which reached its formal peak during the Luther jubilee of 1883,[17] hardened the master's old-fashioned prejudice into the deep bigotry of the neo-Rankeans. For Max Lenz, Hermann Oncken, and

---

1800–1970, Europäische Hochschulschriften, ser. III, vol. 216 (Frankfurt a. M., Bern, and New York, 1984), p. 218.

[11] Dickens and Tonkin, *The Reformation in Historical Thought*, pp. 167–75.

[12] Leonard Krieger, *Ranke: The Meaning of History* (Chicago, 1977), pp. 158–77, and esp. p. 162, where he says of Ranke's *German History in the Age of the Reformation*, "But to understand both Ranke's purpose and execution aright, this national emphasis should be construed in apposition rather than opposition to his universal theme."

[13] As it had been in his earlier *History of the Popes*. See *ibid.*, p. 161. For a different view, which serves up once again the wearisome and false characterization of Ranke as positivist and nationalist, see Hayden White, *Metahistory: The Historical Imagination in Nineteenth-Century Europe* (Baltimore, 1973), p. 174.

[14] Krieger, *Ranke*, p. 178.

[15] Weber, *Priester der Clio*, pp. 208–9. Weber is able to connect an astounding 57% of all professors of history in the German-speaking world, 1800–1970, to Ranke's school. On its confessional character, see *ibid.*, pp. 291–92, 326–33.

[16] See Karl Kupisch, "'Von Luther zu Bismarck': Zur Kritik einer historischen Idee," in his *"Von Luther zu Bismarck": Zur Kritik einer historischen Idee—Heinrich von Treitschke* (Berlin and Bielefeld, 1949), pp. 1–47. Kupisch elsewhere characterizes this mentality as follows: "Die Linie von Luther zu Bismarck bezeichnete den providentiellen Geschichtsweg der Deutschen, der in Worms 1521 begonnen hatte und in Versailles 1871 zum Abschluss gekommen war." Karl Kupisch, *Durch den Zaun der Geschichte: Beobachtungen und Erkenntnisse* (Berlin, 1964), p. 261. Note, however, the judgment of Fritz Fischer, "Der deutsche Protestantismus und die Politik im 19. Jahrhundert," *Historische Zeitschrift* 171 (1951): pp. 473–518, here at p. 494, that church circles regarded the war of 1870 with caution. As for Bismarck and Luther, see the assessment by Rudolf von Thadden, "Bismarck—ein Lutheraner?" in *Luther in der Neuzeit: Wissenschaftliches Symposion des Vereins für Reformationsgeschichte*, Schriften des Vereins für Reformationsgeschichte, 192 (Gütersloh, 1983), pp. 104–20.

[17] Vintage examples of jubilee addresses are Heinrich von Treitschke's "Luther

their like, the slogan "From Luther to Bismarck" became a dogma and the struggle against Catholic spiritual servility a sacred duty.[18]

In this historicist marriage of Reformation and modernity, social and ideological motives flowed together. The defense of the Reformation against "ultramontanism" guarded the near-monopoly of Protestants, especially Prussian Protestants, in academic chairs of history, because it enabled the incumbents to set professional standards which were objectively neutral in form but thoroughly confessional in inspiration. According to Karl Kupisch, "the theological hermeneutic of German Protestantism, whose role in the development of the humane sciences can hardly be overestimated, yielded its secular fruit in the discipline of history and in the person of Ranke."[19]

Historicism, therefore, which Georg G. Iggers has called "the one main tradition of German historiography,"[20] fostered a tradition of Reformation historiography which was deeply presentist, profoundly political, and decidedly confessional. The Reformation became a vital topos of this tradition, both through its idealization of the State and through its presentation of the Reformation as the spiritual birth of the new Germany and of Martin Luther as the model of the modern German.[21]

The image of Luther as the quintessential German is relatively

---

und die deutsche Nation," accessible in English as "Luther and the German Nation," in Heinrich von Treitschke, *Germany, France, Russia, and Islam* (New York, 1915); and Albrecht Ritschl's "Festrede," trans. David W. Lotz, *Ritschl & Luther: A Fresh Perspective on Albrecht Ritschl's Theology in the Light of His Luther Study* (Nashville and New York, 1974), pp. 187–202.

[18] Weber, *Priester der Clio*, 331, quoting Hermann Oncken. For Lenz and the confessional character of academic history, see Christoph Weber, *Der "Fall Spahn,"* pp. 33–41; and on the neo-Rankeans, see Hans Schleier, "Die Ranke-Renaissance," in Joachim Streisand, ed., *Studien über die deutsche Geschichtswissenschaft*, 2 vols. (Berlin, 1965), 2: pp. 99–135, esp. p. 115.

[19] Karl Kupisch, *Die Hieroglyphe Gottes: Grosse Historiker der bürgerlichen Epoche von Ranke bis Meinecke* (Munich, 1967), p. 17. This is a second, less well developed side of the argument of Weber, *Priester der Clio*, pp. 332–33.

[20] Georg G. Iggers, *The German Conception of History: The National Tradition of Historical Thought from Herder to the Present*, rev. ed. (Middletown, Conn., 1983), p. 3.

[21] Thomas Nipperdey has recently testified to the idea's enduring power: "Wer wie ich protestantisch geboren ist und das nicht nur als Zufall, sonder bewusst aufnimmt, neigt dazu, die weltgestaltende Bedeutung Luthers und des Luthertums für die Geschichte der Modernität in Deutschland, für Persönlichkeit und Verhaltensweisen wie für die Gestaltung von Gesellschaft und Kultur hoch und positiv einzuschätzen. Das muss man heute laut sagen, weil es für lauter Selbstzweifel und Kritik unterzugehen droht." Thomas Nipperdey, "Luther und die Bildung der Deutschen," in Hartmut Löwe and Claus-Jürgen Roepke, eds., *Luther und die Folgen: Beiträge zur sozialgeschichtlichen Bedeutung der lutherischen Reformation* (Munich, 1983), pp. 13–27, here at p. 27.

new. Early on, Luther had functioned in German Protestant culture as an apocalyptic prophet, then as a thaumaturgic holy man.[22] His first important political role was not national but universal, as he appears in this prayer by the Prussian philosopher Johann Gottlieb Fichte, voiced in the year of the Jacobin ascendancy in Paris (1793): "O Jesus and Luther, holy patron saints of liberty, who in your times of humiliation seized and with titanic power smashed the chains of humanity, . . . look down now from your heights upon your descendants, and rejoice at the sprouting grains now waving in the wind."[23] Luther here served as a patron saint of the cause of universal Christian liberation. To enlightened German Protestants, indeed, Luther alone survived the Enlightenment's relegation of the Reformation to the barbarous past. As Goethe wrote to a friend in the jubilee year of 1817: "between ourselves, there is nothing of interest in the whole matter except the character of Luther. . . . Everything else is confused rubbish, with which we are still daily burdened."[24]

By the middle decades of the nineteenth century, the struggle for a new Germany transformed the images of Luther and his Reformation in accord with the Protestant middle classes' passage from liberal reformism to nationalist enthusiasm for Bismarck's "revolution from above." The transformation of Luther into the patron saint of the new German empire emerged full-blown in the Luther jubilee of 1883. Heinrich von Treitschke marked the jubilee by affirming that "the act of liberation proceeded from the struggles of an honorable German conscience," which reveals "the utter contrast between Romance and Germanic sensibilities." To Treitschke, Luther's Reformation "presented our nation with a form of Christianity that corresponded to the thirst for truth and untamable independence of the German nature, just as the Roman Church corresponds to the logic and aestheticism of the Romance peoples, and the Orthodox Church

---

[22] That the apocalyptic image of Luther was well founded in his own view of the world has recently received powerful support from Heiko A. Oberman, *Luther: Mensch zwischen Gott und dem Teufel* (Berlin, 1983), soon to appear in English. See above all the writings of R. W. Scribner especially "Luther Myth: A Popular Historiography of the Reformer," *London German Studies* 3 (1986): pp. 1–21; and "Incombustible Luther: The Image of the Reformer in Early Modern Germany," *Past and Present*, no. 110 (1986): pp. 36–68. Both studies are now accessible in Scribner's *Popular Culture and Popular Movements in Reformation Germany* (London and Ronceverte, W. Va., 1987), pp. 301–22, 323–54.

[23] Heinrich Bornkamm, *Luther im Spiegel der deutschen Geistesgeschichte*, 2d ed. (Göttingen, 1970), p. 220.

[24] *Ibid.*, p. 216, from a letter dated 22 Aug. 1817.

to the semi-oriental bondage of the Graeco-Slavic world."[25] Luther had now become both the font of a specifically German form of Christianity and the prophet of a Christian form of German nation-hood. Treitschke, a fiercely anti-Catholic husband of a Catholic wife, lived and breathed the idea of Germany as a Protestant nation. "It remains true," he wrote, "that the Protestant faith is the true faith of the German people, and only where it lives does our nature develop its full power."[26]

The final stage of Luther's political domestication speaks with the voice of the Saxon church historian Heinrich Bornkamm: "We find him in German history never behind us, but always before us. Ever and again he arises among us and bestrides with his terrifying direct-ness the path of the German people. Only when we see the unity of his form and his grim mission, do we understand Gerhard Ritter's words: 'He is us: the Eternal German.'"[27] On this November 10, 1934, Luther's 451st birthday, Bornkamm celebrated the ultimate stage of a German civic culture conceived as a kind of "Nachfolge Lutheri."[28]

II

Two voices—one Catholic, one socialist—dissented from the Rankean-Prussian-historicist view of the German Reformation. In the post-Napoleonic era, some German Catholics took a relatively positive view of Luther's Reformation. The theologian Johann Adam Möhler, for example, developed "a deep sympathy with Reformation ideas" and held that "Luther's doctrine of the Church is nevertheless not

---

[25] Heinrich von Treitschke, "Luther und die deutsche Nation," quoted by Born-kamm, *Luther im Spiegel der deutschen Geistesgeschichte*, pp. 261–63.

[26] Quoted by Hermann Haering, "Über Treitschke und seine Religion," in *Aus Politik und Geschichte: Gedächtnisschrift für Georg von Below* (Berlin, 1928), pp. 218–79, here at p. 249. For Treitschke's confessionalism, see Ludwig Freiherr von Pastor, *Tagebü-cher—Briefe—Erinnerungen*, ed. Wilhelm Wühr (Heidelberg, 1950), pp. 94–96, 100–1.

[27] Heinrich Bornkamm, *Luther und der deutsche Geist*, Sammlung gemeinverständlicher Vorträge und Schriften aus dem Gebiet der Theologie und Religionsgeschichte, 170 (Tübingen, 1934), p. 20. Compare the resigned comment of Georg Wünsch in 1921: "Luther war ein Volksmann, aber er ist keiner mehr und kann auch mit allen Anstrengungen nicht mehr dazu gemacht werden." Georg Wünsch, *Der Zusammenbruch des Luthertums als Sozialgestaltung* (Tübingen, 1921), p. 6.

[28] That the modern Luther cult served primarily the need for a sense of continuity of the German past with the events of 1871 and 1918 is the view of Kupisch, *Durch den Zaun der Geschichte*, pp. 337–41.

false, though it is one-sided."[29] The Rhenish journalist Joseph von Görres, too, found much to admire in the Reformation: "Truly, it was a great and noble movement of the German people which the Reformation produced. The Latin peoples may reject it without reservation, but we Germans can and may not do so, for it arose out of the most inward spirit of our nation."[30] And the church historian Johann Ignaz von Döllinger was captivated by the national character of Luther's ideas and movement: "Though Luther is the only founder of a religion whom the German nation has ever produced, he is also—in his entire being, his aims and his actions, his virtues and errors—the true man of the people, the most genuine type of Germanness."[31]

By this time—Döllinger spoke this judgment in the Luther jubilee year of 1883—a younger, more critical voice, goaded by Bismarck's anti-Catholic laws, had already begun to examine the Reformation in a very different light. Johannes Janssen, a priest from Xanten in the Lower Rhenish region, chose to rebut Ranke and the Rankeans with a massive work on fifteenth- and sixteenth-century Germany.[32] With unmatched prolixity and a breathtaking command of the sources, Janssen sought to demonstrate how the Protestant Reformation had wrecked German culture's most glorious age.

Against Janssen rose a mighty chorus of professors and pastors to accuse him of "religious fanaticism," "refined tendentiousness," "systematic sophistry," "historical prestidigitation," and the purveyance of "poisonous bouquets," though in after years it became more common simply to disqualify him with the term, "ultramontane."[33] Both Janssen and his critics belonged to a new, more bitterly confessional and

---

[29] Dickens and Tonkin, *The Reformation in Historical Thought*, p. 180; Bornkamm, *Luther im Spiegel der deutschen Geistesgeschichte*, p. 331.

[30] Quoted by Bornkamm, *Luther im Spiegel der deutschen Geistesgeschichte*, p. 328, from *Der Katholik* 15 (1825): p. 279, though Bornkamm's own exposition (85) characteristically emphasizes the more negative judgment in Görres's 1821 essay, "Europa und die Revolution."

[31] Quoted by Bornkamm, *Luther im Spiegel der deutschen Geistesgeschichte*, p. 339, from an address of 1883. See Georg Schwaiger, "Luther im Urteil Ignaz Döllingers," in Moeller, ed., *Luther in der Neuzeit*, pp. 70–83; and, more generally, Dickens and Tonkin, *The Reformation in Historical Thought*, pp. 181–83.

[32] Johannes Janssen, *Geschichte des deutschen Volkes seit dem Ausgang des Mittelalters*, 8 vols. (Freiburg i. Br., 1876–1894) (English: *History of the German People at the Close of the Middle Ages*, trans. M. A. Mitchell and A. M. Christie, 17 vols. [London, 1896–1910]). See Dickens and Tonkin, *The Reformation in Historical Thought*, pp. 183–84, which is too brief to be very helpful. For the literature, see C. Weber, *Der "Fall Spahn,"* p. 17 n. 47.

[33] Janssen collects these epithets in his rebuttal, *An meine Kritiker* (Freiburg i. Br.,

politically more volatile age, and in their writings one senses, in Heinrich von Srbik's words, "how mightily foamed the passions of the confessional Christian parties, struggling over issues of religion and church, and the passions of the German political groups in the years of Bismarck's *Kulturkampf* . . . in this younger generation, to which both Janssen and his critics belonged."[34]

The violence and tenacity of Janssen's critics focused on his celebrated portrait of Luther, but behind his attack on the German Reformation lay his true target, the Prusso-Germanic state. Janssen, despite his current reputation as a conservative, did not celebrate uncritically the entire medieval past but rather the golden age which, but for the Reformation, German culture should have experienced. In a sense, therefore, he accepted the "Luther-to-Bismarck" thesis that 1871 was a consequence of 1517, so that his massive erudition threatened not so much Ranke's achievement as the use to which Ranke's epigones had put it in fashioning the ideas of 1871. To Prusso-German modernity he posed not so much the Middle Ages as an alternate German modernity, as one can sense in his work's opening celebration of "Johann Gutenberg's invention of the printing-press and the use of movable type, . . . [as] the mightiest and most important [invention] in the history of civilisation. . . ."[35] The golden age it ought to have ushered in became tragically aborted by the Reformation, which strengthened the forces of particularism, commercialism, and tyranny. The central actor of Janssen's history is thus neither Luther nor the pope, but the German people and its cultural creativity, which the Protestant reformers, allied with the princes, maimed through their "reformation from above." There was a brief time, he admitted, "when Luther was the most popular man in Germany," but after the Peasants' War the Reformation became the ally of the particularist State and aided the princes rather than the people.[36] Nothing infuriated Janssen critics more than his dethronement of Luther's achievement and the Bismarckian State and their

1884), p. 2. The term "ultramontane" was used by historians who should have known better, such as G. P. Gooch, *History and Historians in the Nineteenth Century* (London, 1913; reprint, Boston, 1959), pp. 513–16.

[34] Heinrich Ritter von Srbik, *Geist und Geschichte vom deutschen Humanismus bis zur Gegenwart*, 2 vols. (Munich and Salzburg, 1951), 2: pp. 57–58.

[35] Johannes Janssen, *History*, 1: p. 1.

[36] See Janssen, *An meine Kritiker*, pp. 116–22. The two volumes of Janssen apology for his *History* are structurally very different from the work itself. His critics focused very heavily on his irreverent portrait of Luther, and it is this running battle, not

replacement center stage by the moral welfare and cultural creativity of the German people.[37] In Janssen's view, Luther's sacrifice of those values to his own ambitions and to the power of the State made the new Germany possible, and only his blindest foes failed to recognize that his guns, ostensibly aimed at Wittenberg, in fact fired on Berlin. He gave a new, intolerable meaning to the slogan, "From Luther to Bismarck."[38]

Marxian socialism raised a second voice of dissent against the canonical interpretation of the German Reformation.[39] The story of this dissent is essentially that of its principal expression, Friedrich Engels's *The Peasant War in Germany*, which is too well known to require much recounting here. Engels portrayed the German Reformation as aspect and outcome of a mighty social movement, which in 1525 failed to achieve its two objective tasks—the abolition of feudalism and the creation of a centralized national state—and thereafter became a tool of princely greed and particularism. Two things alone survived the wreck: the impossible but portentous communistic vision of Thomas Müntzer and the courage and vitality of the German common people. Engels, like Janssen, believed that the people needed for the realization of its true cultural potential the guidance of a supranational institution—for Engels the communist movement or party, for Janssen the Catholic Church—and, again like Janssen, he thought that whatever its progressive origins, the Reformation had betrayed itself and the people after 1525. The two

the *History* itself, which has fixed Janssen's historiographical place. Contemporary authors are all the more vulnerable to this distortion, because the *History* is so long and so prolix, hence there is no accessible, adequate, modern evaluation of Janssen's work and its historiographical and cultural-political significance. The treatments in English are all derivative and conventional.

[37] Along with Karl Lamprecht, Janssen is one of the fathers of *Kulturgeschichte* in Germany. Christoph Weber notes that there "lag auch schon bei Janssen ein, wenn auch unsichtbarer, Übergang zu kulturgeschichtlichen Kriterien in der Religionsgeschichte vor." *Der "Fall Spahn,"* p. 18.

[38] Thomas A. Brady, Jr., "From Prussia via Luther to Hitler: A Rejoinder," in James F. Harris, ed., *German-American Interrelations, Heritage and Challenge: Joint Conference held at the University of Maryland, April 2–April 5, 1984* (Tübingen, 1985), pp. 89–94.

[39] On Karl Marx's early assessments of Luther and the Reformation, see Günter Vogler, "Martin Luther und die Reformation im Frühwerk von Karl Marx," in Moeller, ed., *Luther und die Neuzeit*, pp. 84–103. The literature on the interpretation of the German Reformation in the light of historical materialism principles is easily accessible through Dickens and Tonkin, *The Reformation in Historical Thought*, pp. 234–63; Andreas Dorpalen, *German History in Marxist Perspective. The East German Approach* (Detroit, 1985), pp. 99–123.

visions differed radically, of course, in their evaluation of what might have come from the great Peasants' War, but they both condemned the consequences of the Reformation: narrow particularism, petty tyranny, and social and cultural backwardness. They shared, too, an ultimate faith in the fundamental humanity of the common people, which gave the German past a moral significance for the German future.[40]

<h1 style="text-align:center">III</h1>

This was the situation of Reformation studies—a historicist orthodoxy dogged by two dissents—when Ernst Troeltsch and his Heidelberg colleague Max Weber intervened just before the Great War. They shifted the center of discussion from the State and Martin Luther to the social and social-psychological impact of European social development on Christianity and of the Reformation on European civilization, and, like Engels and Janssen, they viewed the German Reformation as revolutionary in original intent but conservative in ultimate effect. Neither Weber nor Troeltsch enjoyed much immediate influence on Reformation studies.[41] Weber was studied chiefly by sociologists, while Troeltsch's work was savagely counterattacked from the Luther Renaissance, that late-blooming flower of "the German conception of history."[42] Only the end of the Third Reich, in the spiritual fortunes of which many of the leading Reformation historians were implicated—one thinks of the Lutherans Heinrich Bornkamm, Emanuel Hirsch, and Paul Althaus and the Catholic Joseph Lortz—cleared the ground for a revival, reassessment, and reexamination of the old dissenting traditions' themes. This process dominates the modern field of the social history of the Reformation.

---

[40] The similarities between Catholic and socialist interpretations of the Reformation, and especially of its connections with the Peasants' War, have been noted many times, though never studied. See Abraham Friesen, *Reformation and Utopia: The Marxist Interpretation of the Reformation and Its Antecedents*, Veröffentlichungen des Instituts für Europäische Geschichte Mainz, 71 (Wiesbaden, 1974), pp. 169–70, 249–50.

[41] See Dickens and Tonkin, *The Reformation in Historical Thought*, pp. 264–76.

[42] Karl Kupisch, "The 'Luther Renaissance,'" *Journal of Contemporary History* 2, no. 4 (Oct. 1967): pp. 39–49. For other references, see Thomas A. Brady, Jr., "Luther's Social Teaching and the Social Order of His Age," in Gerhard Dünnhaupt, ed., *Martin Luther Quincentennial* (Detroit, 1985), pp. 270–90, here at p. 285 n. 6.

Since about 1960 new forms of the old dissents have flowered in
two great streams. The elder and more powerful is that of Engels,
which has flourished most prominently and fruitfully in the German
Democratic Republic.[43] At first it seemed as if the new communist
Germany would exalt Thomas Müntzer as the Luther Renaissance
had exalted Luther, making him, perhaps, "the eternal communist."
By 1961, however, the broader historical-materialist vision had been
recovered, reordered, and reformulated by Max Steinmetz and his
disciples into the thesis of the Reformation as early bourgeois revolution.[44] Over the past quarter-century important modifications have
been made to Engels's conception. For one thing, the topics of the
bourgeoisie and its relationships to feudal society and to early capitalism have been pursued in a far subtler fashion. Second, it is considered essential to reintegrate the German Reformation into European
history and to link its revolutionary or protorevolutionary character
to the subsequent wave of European revolutions. Third, while Reformation history has been one of the chief arenas of struggle between
socialist and bourgeois historiography in the Germanies there has
emerged a general tendency in the GDR to rethink the old categories.[45] It has borne fruit not only in the reconsideration and modi-
fication of Luther's image in connection with the jubilee of 1983, in
which Gerhard Brendler's Luther biography played a major role,[46]
but also in a broader inclination to loosen the connections of the
Reformation with the current politics of the two Germanies. As
Walther Schmidt wrote in the *Zeitschrift für Geschichtswissenschaft* in
1985, "Historisiert werden muss auch das Geschichtsverständnis."[47]

[43] Dickens and Tonkin, *The Reformation in Historical Thought*, pp. 256–62; Dorpalen,
German History, pp. 99–123.
[44] Max Steinmetz, "Die frühbürgerliche Revolution in Deutschland (1476–1535)—
Thesen," in Gerhard Brendler, ed., *Die frühbürgerliche Revolution in Deutschland: Referate
und Diskussion zum Thema Probleme der frühbürgerliche Revolution in Deutschland 1476–1535*
(Berlin, 1961), pp. 7–16 (English: "Theses on the Early Bourgeois Revolution in
Germany (1476–1535)," in R. W. Scribner and Gerhard Benecke, eds., *The German
Peasant War of 1525—New Viewpoints* [London, 1979], pp. 9–19).
[45] See Brent O. Peterson, "'Workers of the world unite—for God's sake!' Recent
Luther Scholarship in the German Democratic Republic," in James D. Tracy, ed.,
Luther and the Modern State in Germany, Sixteenth Century Essays & Studies, 7 (Kirksville,
Mo., 1986), pp. 77–100.
[46] Gerhard Brendler, *Martin Luther: Theologie und Revolution* (Berlin, 1983).
[47] Walter Schmidt, "Zur Entwicklung des Erbe- und Traditionsverständnisses in
der Geschichtsschreibung der DDR," *Zeitschrift für Geschichtswissenschaft* 33 (1985): pp.
195–212, here at p. 196.

The second stream of the social history of the Reformation, the one described by Hsia, also owes something to the legacy of Friedrich Engels, but whereas the Marxist-Leninist school frames the issue in terms of capitalism vs. feudalism, this school casts it in terms of communalism vs. the authoritarian state.[48] As Hsia has put it, communalism "symbolizes the anti-feudal, populist, and anti-authoritarian legacy in German history," as it "forges a link between the democratic present and a populist past." This theme underlay Bernd Moeller's 1962 essay on the reformation in the free cities, and it underlies much of subsequent literature, both German and North American, on the urban reformation.[49] Occasionally, of course, someone with roots in both streams points out that communalism meant different things to different social classes, and that the ideal of communal solidarity could be an instrument of liberation in some hands or an instrument of hegemony in others. In the main, however, few historians of its Swiss-South German homeland have challenged the validity of the communalism-authoritarianism antithesis, though others, notably Heinz Schilling, have argued for a similar phenomenon, based on Dutch influence, in North Germany.[50] Hsia himself has even weighed in with a formidable study of conflict between communal and authoritarian forms of Catholicism at Münster.[51] On the whole, the evidence for a populist North, which Hsia suggests may be a mirror image of the South, is not very impressive. The Ditmarsh peasants were brave folk and tough fighters, but popular communalism still seems an odd growth in the northern cities, and no one has yet produced evidence to convince me that Schilling's "Turning Dutch" served

[48] See the programatic statement by Peter Blickle, "Thesen zum Thema—Der 'Bauernkrieg' als Revolution des 'Gemeinen Mannes,'" in Peter Blickle, ed., *Revolte und Revolution in Europa: Referate und Protokolle des internationalen Symposiums zur Erinnerung an den Bauernkrieg 1525 (Memmingen 24.–25. März 1975)*, Beiheft 4 der Historischen Zeitschrift (Munich, 1975), pp. 127–31 (English: "The 'Peasant War' as the Revolution of the Common Man—Theses," in Scribner and Benecke, eds., *The German Peasant War of 1525*, pp. 19–22).
[49] See Thomas A. Brady, Jr., "The Reformation's Fate in America: A Reflection," in Sherrin Marshall and Phillip N. Bebb, eds., *The Process of Change in Early Modern Europe: Essays in Honor of Miriam Usher Chrisman* (Athens, Ohio, 1988), pp. 17–31. See, in general, Kaspar von Greyerz, "Stadt und Reformation: Stand und Aufgaben der Forschung," *Archiv für Reformationsgeschichte* 76 (1985): pp. 6–63.
[50] See Heinz Schilling, *Konfessionskonflikt und Staatsbildung: Eine Fallstudie über das Verhältnis von religiösem und sozialem Wandel in der Frühneuzeit am Beispiel der Grafschaft Lippe*, Quellen und Forschungen zur Reformationsgeschichte, 48 (Gütersloh, 1981).
[51] R. Po-chia Hsia, *Society and Religion in Münster, 1535–1618* (New Haven and London, 1984).

anything like the model function in the North that "Turning Swiss" did in the South.[52]

The most important new thesis in Reformation social history since the early 1960s is Peter Blickle's argument for a distinct peasant reformation, of which his current paper offers the latest formulation, but for the full form of which one must consult his *Gemeindereformation* of 1985.[53] Moeller, as Blickle correctly notes, never considered the possibility of an active peasant role in the Reformation, but this was also true of Troeltsch and of the whole historicist tradition going back to Ranke, who, not knowing what else to do with the Peasants' War, called it "a natural event" (*ein Naturereignis*) to distinguish it, I suppose, from properly historical events.[54]

Long before he began to deal with the Reformation as such, Peter Blickle was tracking the causes, processes, and consequences of communalism among the South German peasants.[55] He mapped a great movement, which began around 1350 and culminated but did not die in the tremendous revolt of 1525. The peasants, emboldened by their experience of self-management in the villages, tried to build or reform state formations to suit their own conditions of life. In his *Habilitationsschrift* of 1973, the political side of this argument is already in place; and in his *Revolution of 1525* of 1975, he is already engaged,

---

[52] Heinz Schilling, "Die deutsche Gemeindereformation: Ein oberdeutsch—zwinglianisches Ereignis vor der 'reformatorischen Wende' des Jahres 1525?" *Zeitschrift für historische Forschung* 14 (1987): pp. 325–32. This is not to deny the international importance of Dutch republicanism though this subject is but broached by J. V. Polisensky, *The Thirty Years' War*, trans. Robert Evans (Berkeley and Los Angeles, 1971), pp. 21–23, 264–65. The criticial, rural component in the Swiss model is missing from the Dutch one, which corresponds to the weakness of communal elements in northern Netherlandish agriculture. See Jan De Vries, *The Dutch Rural Economy in the Golden Age* (New Haven and London, 1974), pp. 55–67.

[53] Peter Blickle, *Die Gemeindereformation: Die Menschen des 16. Jahrhunderts auf dem Weg zum Heil* (Munich, 1985).

[54] Hans-Christoph Rublack, "Forschungsbericht Stadt und Reformation," in Bernd Moeller, ed., *Stadt und Kirche im 16. Jahrhundert*, Schriften des Vereins für Reformationsgeschichte, no. 190 (Gütersloh, 1978), pp. 9–26.

[55] See especially Peter Blickle, *Landschaften im alten Reich: Die staatliche Funktion des gemeinen Mannes in Oberdeutschland* (Munich, 1973); *idem*, *Die Revolution von 1525*, rev. ed. (Munich, 1981) (English: *The Revolution of 1525: The German Peasants' War from a New Perspective*, trans. Thomas A. Brady, Jr., and H. C. Erik Midelfort [Baltimore, 1981]); *idem*, *Die Reformation im Reich*, Uni-Taschenbücher, no. 1181 (Stuttgart, 1982); *idem*, "Social Protest and Reformation Theology," in Peter Blickle, Hans-Christoph Rublack, and Winfried Schulze, *Religion, Politics and Social Protest: Three Studies on Early Modern Germany*, ed. Kaspar von Greyerz, Publications of the German Historical Institute London (London, 1984), pp. 1–23.

as Engels had become engaged, with the Reformation. Gradually, the logic of this connection has shaped a new thesis, the thesis of the peasants' reformation, which Blickle now holds to be both a "subordinate part of the communal reformation" and the "fruition of the communalization of rural society." It formed one wing of the greater "communal reformation" that embraced both the towns and the land.[56] Blickle's thesis is the most important new departure in the social history of the Reformation since Bernd Moeller's 1962 essay on the urban reformation. If it has not yet gained general assent, there is nonetheless growing conviction that the Reformation was not only, in A. G. Dickens's celebrated words, "an urban event."[57]

Several aspects of Blickle's achievement attract my attention. First, his larger portrait of communalism breaks the far-too-national framework of the debate on the urban reformation. Blickle has drawn the wider, European implications of the political side of his argument in a 1985 paper that sketched the potential of communalism as the basis of a grand alternative to European absolutism.[58] Here emerge his ideas about the connections between peasant communalism and modern democracy, which form an alternative to the now debatable notion that democracy is a creation of the bourgeoisie.[59] The ecclesiastical side of his argument, which he elaborates in this paper, may well turn out to possess similarly international implications, and future investigations into rural parish life—a subject barely scratched for most of Europe—may show that here, too, the Swiss and South

[56] See Franziska Conrad, *Reformation in der bäuerlichen Gesellschaft: Zur Rezeption reformatorischer Theologie im Elsass*, Veröffentlichungen des Instituts für Europäische Geschichte Mainz, 116 (Wiesbaden, 1984); Peter Blickle, ed., *Zugänge zur bäuerlichen Reformation*, Bauer und Reformation, 1 (Zurich, 1987).

[57] See, for example, Hans-Christoph Rublack, "Is There a 'New History' of the Urban Reformation?" in E. I. Kouri and Tom Scott, eds., *Politics and Society in Reformation Europe: Essays for Sir Geoffrey Elton on his Sixty-Fifth Birthday* (London, 1987), pp. 121–41, here at p. 122: "the Reformation . . . was also much more than an urban event." This is not to say that Blickle's interweaving of urban and rural movements has gained general assent, least of all from Tom Scott, *Freiburg and the Breisgau: Town-Country Relations in the Age of Reformation and Peasants' War* (Oxford, 1986), pp. 229–35. Dickens's comment—"the Reformation was an urban event"—comes from his *The German Nation and Martin Luther* (New York, 1974), p. 182.

[58] Peter Blickle, "Communalism, Parliamentarism, Republicanism," trans. Thomas A. Brady, Jr., *Parliaments, Estates and Representation* 6 (1986): pp. 1–13.

[59] And debatable not only for Germany. See David Blackbourn, "The Discreet Charm of the Bourgeoisie: Reappraising German History in the Nineteenth Century," in David Blackbourn and Geoff Eley, *The Peculiarities of German History: Bourgeois Society and Politics in Nineteenth-Century Germany* (Oxford and New York, 1984), pp. 173–74.

German developments were simply the most advanced types of much wider process of the communalization of rural religious life.

My second point is that Blickle's argument has reached the point at which a major consideration of ritual religious life is warranted.[60] In the beginning, Blickle's attention to religious life concerned religious ideas almost exclusively. Now he and his students have plunged into the study of rural religious institutions, and they have begun to uncover the formation in Switzerland and South Germany of a proprietary church (*Eigenkirche*) of the Common Man, to which the Reformation put an end. In the absence, however, of attention to everyday religious life, particularly religious ritual, the thesis of "the Christianization of rural society" must remain incomplete. Even so, it is currently the most powerful rival to the more fashionable "acculturation thesis."

A third point concerns the relationship between rural religious life and what Blickle calls "the official church." These ecclesiastical initiatives on the part of the villagers seem to me no more and no less "official" than was the *Eigenkirche* of the aristocracy.[61] It is true, however, that the German union of governmental and religious authority in the hands of the bishops gave the movement for communalization a strong anti-episcopal potential, something its Italian counterpart largely lacked; it is also true that this union, which helped to make the German church the pasture of the German aristocracy, posed the strongest possible barrier to the reform of local religious life on a communal basis. This is probably why communalization in the empire acquired a revolutionary edge it elsewhere lacked.

My fourth point returns to the story of the two dissents from the Luther- and State-centered doctrines of "the German conception of history." With the rise of the communalism thesis, especially in Blickle's formulation, and with the rethinking of the early bourgeois revolution, there is taking shape a point of view which combines Engels's anti-feudalism with Janssen's anti-statism. We may tentatively describe

---

[60] Its starting point should be R. W. Scribner, "Cosmic Order and Daily Life: Sacred and Secular in Pre-Industrial German Society," in Kaspar von Greyerz, ed., *Religion and Society in Early Modern Europe, 1500–1800* (London, 1984), pp. 17–33, now reprinted in Scribner's *Popular Culture and Popular Movements in Reformation Germany*, pp. 1–16.

[61] Jörn Sieglerschmidt, *Territorialstaat und Kirchenregiment: Studien zur Rechtsdogmatik des Kirchenpatronatsrechts im 15. und 16. Jahrhundert*, Forschungen zur kirchlichen Rechtsgeschichte und zum Kirchenrecht, 15 (Cologne and Vienna, 1987), pp. 1–36.

its vision as follows. There was an anti-feudal revolution in the southern and central parts of the German-speaking world in the first quarter of the sixteenth century; the revolution culminated a long era of
the social and local devolution of control over everyday life, including religious life, which was without parallel in the rest of Europe;
it was touched off by new pressures from above and fueled by the
early Protestant preaching, the intentions of which at most overlapped
those of the common people; its overall failure stimulated a centralization of government on the territorial level, made possible the rise
of confessionalism, and slightly improved conditions for the deploy-
ment of capital; and the whole process was made possible, as Engels
wrote, by the high degree of decentralization, that is, freedom in the
pre-modern sense. Engels was wrong to tax the movement for not
creating an absolutist monarchy; Janssen was wrong to dream that
the Church, itself deeply mired through the benefice system in the
fragmentation of property and sovereignty, might have escaped the
consequences of feudalization and particularism.

The Reformation is no longer a major battleground in the struggle
for the definition of modernity or of what it means to be a German
in the modern age. The vision of the Reformation on which we are
converging, however, bears vital relevance to the civic lives of both
German states, for, gradually, the outlines are coming into view of
the deepest and oldest tradition of self-government in all of Europe.
Its visibility, ironically enough, has become possible only through the
ignominious death of "the German conception of history."

CHAPTER FOURTEEN

THE HOLY ROMAN EMPIRE, 1555–1648

Begun in strife, concluded in slaughter—such was for long the image of German history between the Religious Peace of Augsburg in 1555 and the Peace of Westphalia in 1648. For Leopold von Ranke and his disciples, who framed it, the era's great mystery was that the awakening between 1495 and 1520 should have yielded not a national state and a national church but 300 years of religious divisions and political weakness.[1] Nowadays, when Rankean presuppositions have sloughed away, a very different picture has emerged of the Reformation's settlements in the Holy Roman Empire.

I. *Preliminary Settlements*

Some settlements fell in the reformation movement's first two decades. The Peasants' War, which engulfed the southern and central sectors in 1524–1526, was settled by the princes, and with it the possibility of a general reformation from below.[2] Its Anabaptist successor movement was settled when the city of Münster fell to Imperial troops in 1535.[3] The Swiss reformation's settlement came in 1531 with Zurich's defeat and Zwingli's death at Kappel.[4] These settlements left Lutheranism after the mid-1530s as the Empire's sole form of Protestant reformation.

The Lutheran reformation's survival depended on an adequate political representation of its interests at the Imperial level. At the end of the 1520s, its leaders gathered behind the Elector of Saxony, ably seconded by Landgrave Philip of Hesse (1504–1564). They gained

---

[1] W. Schulze (1987): pp. 46–49. See in general, Dickens and Tonkin (1986).

[2] Peter Blickle, in *Handbook of European History 1400–1600. Late Middle Ages, Renaissance, Reformation*, eds. T. A. Brady, Jr., H. A. Oberman, J. D. Tracy (Leiden, New York, Köln, Brill, 1995), vol. 2: pp. 161–92.

[3] James Stayer, *ibid.*, vol. 2: pp. 249–82.

[4] Muralt (1980); J. Wayne Baker and Miriam U. Chrisman, in Maltby (1992): pp. 47–74, 105–28.

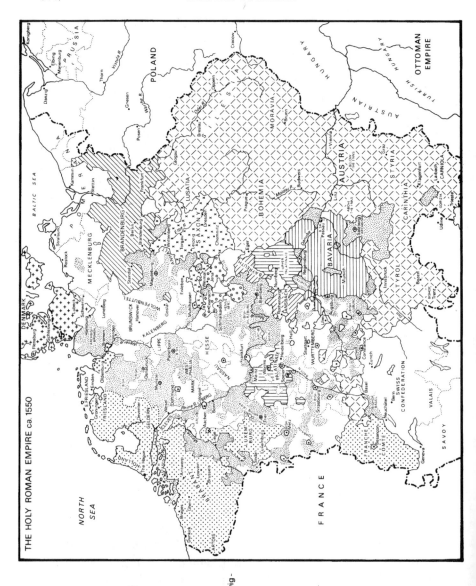

THE HOLY ROMAN EMPIRE ca. 1550

HABSBURG LANDS
  Austrian line
  Spanish line
WETTIN LANDS
  Albertine line
  Ernestine line
HOHENZOLLERN LANDS
  Brandenburg line
  Franconian line
WITTELSBACH LANDS
  Bavarian line
  Palatinate line
OLDENBURG DYNASTY
  Denmark - Schleswig-
    Holstein
  Oldenburg
  Ecclesiastical
    territories
  Imperial cities
  Boundary of the
    EMPIRE

a collective voice through their protest (whence "Protestants") against the Imperial Diet of Speyer in 1529 and their statement of faith (Confession of Augsburg) submitted at Augsburg in 1530, and through the military alliance, called the "Smalkaldic League," which they founded in 1531. Between then and the Smalkaldic War of 1546–1547, Lutheran reformations gained time and space to spread, to grow strong, and to assume their characteristic geographical contours and institutional shapes, though not yet their doctrinal consolidation.[5]

Geographically, Lutheran gains were remarkable: three of the four lay electorates; all of the lay principalities in the northern Empire except for Cleves-Jülich; most of the lay principalities in the southern parts of the Empire, except Bavaria, Austria, and part of Baden; and all but a handful of the 65 or so free cities, though many retained important Catholic minorities. By mid-century, all of these territories and cities were "Protestant" in the sense that their rulers, princes or magistrates, professed to be "Evangelical" and not "papist." In addition, nearly a dozen bishoprics, concentrated in the Empire's northeastern quadrant, were taken or threatened, along with countless monasteries and innumerable other church properties.[6] By the 1550s the Lutheran reformation had assumed most of the geographical configuration it would maintain into the modern era.[7]

Institutionally, the Lutheran advance was equally impressive. Rulers, magistrates, and clergy had acted with impressive speed to adopt and adapt Luther's dualistic ideal—the ruler to keep law and order, the clergy to proclaim God's Word and administer the sacraments.[8] In theory, the clergy's authority was grounded in the Word alone; in practice, the Lutheran ministers could not—and many would not, or not until too late—guard religious life from intervention at will by princes and magistrates. Consequently, in the Empire with few exceptions the Protestant reconstruction of church life was undertaken by clergymen under the authority, with the permission, and as employees of princes and magistrates. It was against this type of fusion of church and state that John Calvin struggled at Geneva with some success and with important consequences for the history of Calvinism.

[5] Schilling (1988a): pp. 227–39; Rabe (1991): pp. 317–461; Brady (1995): pp. 206–352.

[6] Cohn (1987); Schindling (1980).

[7] Greyerz (1980).

[8] Martin Brecht, *Handbook of European History 1400–1600. Late Middle Ages, Renaissance, Reformation*, eds. T. A. Brady, Jr., H. A. Oberman, J. D. Tracy (Leiden, New York, Köln, Brill, 1995), vol. 2: pp. 129–59.

The fusion was hardly without precedent. Since the fifteenth century the obligation to care for the churches and monasteries had come to be regarded as a normal part of princes' and magistrates' duties.[9] In 1526 a formal magisterial right to reform (*ius reformandi*) was enshrined in Imperial law by the Imperial Diet, which declared that until a general council overcame the schism, each ruler and urban regime would act "in such a way as he will be responsible for to God and the emperor."[10] This act conferred formal religious legitimacy on the Empire's late medieval structure of dispersed governance. It also scuttled forever the fifteenth-century program of a comprehensive reform of Empire and church.

It is difficult, because of the strife and stalemate that soon followed, to recapture the ebullient mood of those halcyon days of the German Reformation, when many Protestants believed they might live to see true religion capture the entire Empire. Their hearts stirred in the early 1540s at the declaration by Elector Herman of Cologne that he would convert to the new faith if he could retain his prince-archbishopric. "In time," exulted Chancellor Gregor Brück (1482–1557) of Saxony, "our party could set up its own King of the Romans, to whom the whole Empire could be made subject and obedient, . . . and there should be no more priests."[11] It was not to be. The Cologne project faltered. Aided by Duke Moritz of Saxony—the "Judas of Meissen," his fellow Protestants named him—in 1546–1547 the Emperor Charles V crushed the Smalkaldic League, and in the following year he compelled the Protestants to accept a provisional religious settlement, called the "Interim".[12] At this point, when the schism seemed almost ended, Moritz of Saxony undertook a remarkable reversal of fortunes. Backed by the French king, he rose in revolt, drove the emperor from the German lands, and signed with King Ferdinand, Charles' brother, the Treaty of Passau. This document contained the substance of the Religious Peace of Augsburg of 1555: each of the emperor's immediate subjects, the "Imperial estates," would have the right to decide which religion his subjects would practice.[13]

---

[9] Berndt Hamm, *ibid.*, vol. 2: pp. 193–227; M. Schulze (1991); Moeller (1987).
[10] Quoted by Brady (1995): p. 55.
[11] Quoted by *ibid.*, p. 258.
[12] Rabe (1971).
[13] Lutz (1964); the texts of 1552 and 1555 may be conveniently consulted in Kastner (1994): pp. 520–31, nos. 159–60.

II. *The Religious Peace of Augsburg (1555) and Its Legacy*

At the Diet of Augsburg in 1555, Ferdinand I (r. 1556–1562) made good on his promise to sponsor a purely political—though provisional—settlement to the Empire's religious schism.[14] The Religious Peace incorporated the religious status quo (as of 1552) into the Empire's public peace (*Landfriede*): "In order to prevent the permanent division and the ruin of the German nation, our beloved fatherland, we have agreed ... [that] His Imperial Majesty and we, the Imperial estates, ... shall maintain the following religious peace (*Religionsfriede*), together with all provisions of the ... the established public peace."[15] The Peace guaranteed that princes, prelates, and magistrates of the Catholic faith should peacefully co-exist with those of the Confession of Augsburg, and the parties would treat "the disputed religion in no other way than by Christian, friendly, peaceful means and paths to a unanimous, Christian understanding and conciliation."[16]

The Religious Peace made rulers responsible for the religious welfare, and ultimately the consciences, of their subjects. Some years later, a Greifswald law professor, Joachim Stephan, coined for this rule the historic tag: "whose the rule, his the religion [*cuius regio, eius religio*]."[17] The Peace made two exceptions to this rule. First, in free cities where both religions were practiced, they would share the magistracies and the churches. Second and far more important, a codicil called the "Ecclesiastical Reservation," which Ferdinand promulgated without Protestant consent, protected the ecclesiastical states by forbidding secularization if a prince-bishop should turn Protestant. In return, though secretly, Ferdinand guaranteed limited religious toleration to Lutheran subjects of Catholic prince-prelates (*Declaratio Ferdinandei*).

This settlement froze the Empire's late medieval constitution as an aristocratic association and blocked the Empire's way toward centralized rule in a western European sense. The Peace also contained several inherent flaws. One was the possible unenforceability of the Ecclesiastical Reservation. Another was the Diet's lack of a way to suspend, in matters touching religion, the principle of majority rule

---

[14] Heckel (1959).
[15] Quoted by Schilling (1988a): p. 241.
[16] *Ibid.*, p. 242.
[17] Heckel (1968): p. 80.

it had adopted in 1512. A hundred years and a long war later, these problems, too, were settled in 1648.[18]

The Decades of Coexistence, 1555–1585

The skilled pragmatism of Emperor Ferdinand I, Emperor Maximilian II (r. 1564–1576), and Elector August I of Saxony guarded the Empire's peace for nearly a generation. In South Germany's bi-confessional free cities, Lutherans and Catholics enjoyed the same religious and political rights, shared the magistracies and use of the churches, schools, and welfare institutions, and with some frequency married across religious boundaries. Similar conditions obtained in a few territorial states, notably in the prince-bishopric of Münster in Westphalia, where the official liturgy was a Mass with German hymns and the communion in both kinds.[19] Religious co-existence was long the norm in the Lower Rhenish duchies of Cleves-Jülich, where for years Duke William V (r. 1539–1592) looked the other way while Calvinist and Lutheran congregations formed within his lands alongside Catholic parishes in which communion was received in both kinds.

It is nevertheless easy to exaggerate the Empire's possibilities for religious, as distinct from political, coexistence, for the schism had already cut deeply into everyday life. In 1549, for example, young Duke Erich II (1528–1584) of Brunswick-Calenberg had written that unless his wife, Duchess Sidonia (1518–1575) of Saxony, returned to "the old, true Christian faith" and abandoned her Lutheran heresy, he could not continue to live with her as man with wife.[20] It was a time drawing boundaries, for which purpose lay to hand a rich vocabulary of division, created by the pamphlet wars of the 1520s and 1540s, which portrayed the world as a battleground between the servants of Christ and those of Antichrist.[21] A Lutheran "Song for Children to Sing," published in 1569, begged:

> Lord, preserve us in Your Word
> And send death to Pope and Turk,

---

[18] See Duchhardt (1991): pp. 147–53, on the entire development.

[19] Hsia (1984): p. 199.

[20] *Politische Korrespondez des Herzogs und Kurfürsten Moritz von Sachsen*, vol. 4, eds. Johannes Hermann and Günther Wartenberg, Abhandlungen der Sächsischen Akademie der Wissenschaften zu Leipzig, Philologisch-historische Klasse, 72 (Berlin, Akademie Verlag, 1992), p. 510, no. 438.

[21] Scribner (1981).

Who hate Jesus Christ, Your only Son,
And aim to throw Him off His throne.[22]

Meanwhile, events abroad were also working against the Empire's peace. After the Peace of Cateau-Cambrésis (3 April 1559) proclaimed an end to sixty-five years of Habsburg-Valois wars, during the following decade lengthy civil wars, fortified by religious conflict, erupted in the kingdom of France and in the Habsburg Netherlands.[23] In these lands Calvinism, a younger, more aggressive, and more internationally minded faith than German Lutheranism, squared off to fight a reviving Catholic Church.[24] Because of the international character of the confessions, every escalation of confessionalization consolidation and religious strife abroad tended to narrow the political space for the spirit of accommodation on which the Religious Peace depended.

Confessional Strife Escalates

A new, harder, and more aggressive tone took definite shape during the 1580s. Confessional strife erupted over the Pope Gregory XI's new calendar (24 February 1582), according to which the day after 4 October would be the 15th. Its adoption by Emperor Rudolph II without consultation touched off a new pamphlet war.[25] Unlike the 1520s, however, when Luther and his supporters had out-produced, out-written, and out-argued their disunited Catholic opponents, by the 1580s the Catholics were able to give as good as they got, using the printing press both to attack the Protestants and to defend their own devotions, both old and new.[26] In some places, notably at Augsburg, the calendar dispute sparked disturbances of a kind unknown since the days of the Peasants' War, as Protestants fought against being yoked by the new papal calendar:

The pope is brother to the Turk;
May Jesus Christ strike them both
Down into Hell with their calendar,
For the Devil is their bosom pal.[27]

---

[22] Ernst Walter Zeeden, in Zeeden (1985): pp. 333–36.
[23] See Wirsching (1986).
[24] Oberman (1992).
[25] Traitler (1989): pp. 141–52.
[26] Chrisman (1982): p. 81; Chaix (1981); Soergel (1993): pp. 5–6.
[27] Quoted by Vocelka (1981): p. 268. For Augsburg, see Roeck (1991): pp. 84–88; Warmbrunn (1983): pp. 360–64.

These strong words express the spirit of *confession*, that is, "intellectual and organizational hardening" of the religious communities into
"more or less stable church structures with their own doctrines, constitutions, and religious and moral styles."[28] The currently debated
"confessionalization hypothesis" holds that the three confessions—
Lutheran, Reformed, and Catholic—were moving on three parallel
but separate tracks, though at different speeds, toward the same goal:
the regulation of religion and society in a Christian sense.[29] In many
respects, such as the stricter supervision of marriage,[30] this is true,
but the hypothesis cannot do justice to the radical sense of binary
struggle that was growing stronger and stronger since the 1580s. The
Empire had entered the confessional age.

III. *The Reformed Advance*

The Coming of Calvinism

The Calvinist or "Reformed" faith formally entered the Empire
around 1560 with the conversion from Lutheranism of the Palatine
Elector Frederick III (1515–1576).[31] As the French and Netherlandish
struggles deepened, Reformed congregations were forming at Aachen,
Metz, Trier, in the united duchies of Cleves-Jülich, and on the North
Sea coast at Emden and Bremen. Gradually, whole Lutheran principalities were converted to Calvinism, beginning with the Palatinate
around 1560, and by 1620 two of the lay electors—Brandenburg
and the Palatinate—were Calvinists, along with five Silesian dukes,
the prince of Anhalt, the landgrave of Hesse-Cassel, seventeen Imperial
counts, and the city of Bremen.[32] Although not impressive in total

---

[28] Zeeden (1958): p. 251, and (1965): p. 9.
[29] The clearest formulation is by Schilling (1992): pp. 205–46, and in *Handbook
of European History 1400–1600. Late Middle Ages, Renaissance, Reformation*, eds. T. A.
Brady, Jr., H. A. Oberman, J. D. Tracy (Leiden, New York, Köln, Brill, 1995),
vol. 2: pp. 641–82. On confessionalization, see Reinhard (1983); Schilling (1988b),
and in English in (1992); Hsia (1989): pp. 1–9. On the individual confessions, see
Schilling (1986), Rublack (1992), and Reinhard and Schilling (1994); and for a geographical treatment, Schindling and Ziegler (1989–1993).
[30] Safley (1984). Even so, Zschunke (1984) finds divergent patterns of fertility
among the confessions.
[31] Press (1970); Cohn (1985): pp. 148–50. There is an important overview by
J. F. G. Goeters, in Schilling (1986): pp. 44–59; and in English see Knox (1977).
[32] See Cohn (1985): pp. 135–40, with map.

land mass or aggregate population, the Reformed advance also threatened Electoral Saxony—which twice (1571–1574 and 1586–1591) came under the influence of "crypto-Calvinist" elites—Brandenburg, where in 1613 Elector John Sigismund (1572–1619) announced his conversion to Calvinism, Baden-Durlach, and Schleswig-Holstein. Each of these threats foundered on resistance by Lutheran elites.[33]

By the early 1590s the advance of this third, illegal Imperial confession seemed irresistible. Thirty years later, Abraham Scultetus (1566–1624), a former court preacher at Heidelberg, described the Calvinist mood at this time:

> I cannot fail to recall the optimistic mood which I and many others felt when we considered the condition of the Reformed churches in 1591. In France there ruled the valiant King Henry IV, in England the mighty Queen Elizabeth, in Scotland the learned King James, in the Palatinate the bold hero John Casimir, in Saxony the courageous and powerful Elector Christian I, in Hesse the clever and prudent Landgrave William, who were all inclined to the Reformed religion. In the Netherlands everything went as Prince Maurice of Orange wished, when he took Breda, Zutphen, Hulst, and Nijmegen.... We imagined that an *aureum saeculum*, a golden age, had dawned.[34]

Then, however, "within twelve months the elector of Saxony, the count palatine, and the landgrave all died, King Henry deserted the true faith, and all our golden hopes went up in smoke."

Reformed Structures

The German-speaking Reformed reformation developed differently from its French and Dutch counterparts in that, with few exceptions, it was a reformation from above, initiated by rulers who exploited their *ius reformandi*—guaranteed by a Religious Peace that did not recognize their faith.[35] Free presbyteries and classes in the Franco-Dutch style did flourish in the duchies of Cleves-Jülich and in East Frisia, especially at Emden, where the constituting synod of the Dutch Reformed Church met in 1571.[36] The typical Reformed church in

[33] Klein (1962); Nischan (1994).
[34] Quoted by Cohn (1985): p. 135; and there, too, the remaining quotes in this paragraph.
[35] Schilling (1988a) and (1986); Münch (1978), who exaggerated the role of nobles in the consistories.
[36] See Robert M. Kingdon, *Handbook of European History 1400–1600. Late Middle*

the Empire nonetheless developed as a territorial church of a classic caesaropapist kind.

The center of the Reformed faith lay from the first at Heidelberg, to which refugees flowed from France, the Netherlands, and the German Protestant states—e.g., Strasbourg—that had opted for orthodox Lutheranism.[37] Heidelberg's university became the center of a Reformed network that included the universities of Marburg and Frankfurt an der Oder, the academies of Herborn and Bremen, and a score of secondary schools of the first rank.[38] The Heidelberg Catechism, published in 1563, became the normative Reformed statement of faith (in 129 questions and answers) until far beyond the confessional era. And the court at Heidelberg—the German Geneva—served as Reformed Germany's political headquarters, especially under the regent John Casimir (1543–1592), who campaigned alongside the French Protestants and maintained diplomatic ties to all of Calvinist Europe. Despite two brief Lutheran restorations in 1576–1583 and 1583–1610, the Rhine Palatinate continued to form a second hub—alongside the Dutch Republic—of Calvinism in Central Europe. From Heidelberg the faith spread into other principalities, such as the group of Imperial counties in the Wetterau, along the Middle Rhine's right bank, where, under the leadership of Count Johann VI of Nassau-Katzenelnbogen, there developed highly modernized and centralized institutions of ecclesiastical and civil governance.[39]

In Europe the Reformed faith fed from the intensifying sense of confrontation with Rome; in the Empire it grew as a "Second Reformation" almost exclusively at Lutheran expense.[40] The "Second Reformation," as defined in 1596 by Wilhelm Zepper (1550–1607), professor of theology at Herborn and Inspector in the (Reformed) church of Nassau-Dillenburg meant that a reformation of life had to follow the earlier reformation of doctrine. The first generation of reformers, he explained, had had "so much to do" to reform "doctrine as the principal matter against the violent intrigues, rage, and insane behavior of the pope and his crew," that they had no time to reform

---

Ages, Renaissance, Reformation, eds. T. A. Brady, Jr., H. A. Oberman, J. D. Tracy (Leiden, New York, Köln, Brill, 1995), vol. 2: pp. 229–47.

[37] Press (1970); Abray (1985): pp. 142–62.

[38] See Cohn (1985): pp. 137–38.

[39] Glawischnig (1973); Georg Schmidt, in Schilling (1986): pp. 184–213.

[40] The concept is debated by William Heinrich Neuser and Heinz Schilling, in Schilling (1986): pp. 379–86, 387–437.

the manner of living. At that time, indeed "the work of Christian discipline was not yet rightly understood" and was decried as a new form of papal servitude. Now, however, it was time "to take in hand a proper reformation in the other chief matter, the Christian way of life."[41]

Reformed Politics

To the strict Lutherans, this Reformed agenda seemed proof that the Calvinists, having perverted true doctrine, aimed to subvert true religion as well. Seemingly untouched by the old yearning for unity and emboldened by the fierce, bloody struggles against Catholicism in France, England, and the Netherlands, the Calvinists also threatened the Religious Peace. Their weakness in the Empire nevertheless forced their leaders to seek toleration under the Peace by touting their faith as consistent with the Confession of Augsburg. This assertion came to a test at the Diet of Augsburg in 1566, when Duke Christoph of Württemberg (1515–1568), the foremost Lutheran prince in South Germany, complained about the "heretical catechism" (of Heidelberg). In reply the Elector Palatine Frederick III, Christoph's cousin and exact contemporary, stated the Reformed case for continuity with the original Protestant Reformation. The Lutheran princes, though they believed not a word, sheepishly shared Duke Christoph's admission that if Frederick were condemned, "the persecutions in France, Spain, the Netherlands and other similar places would grow at once by heaps, and by that condemnation we should be guilty of shedding their blood."[42] August of Saxony's pragmatism prevailed once more, and for the next half century, the Reformed faith lived in the Empire as a legally "Lutheran" shadow confession.[43]

Even though the Lutheran powers dared not absolutely deny the Reformed claim to be Protestants, their fury against Calvinism could rage very hotly. When the second pro-Calvinist attempt on Electoral Saxony collapsed in 1601, and the chancellor who favored it was going to the block, the executioner's sword bore the inscription, "Calvinist, beware!"[44] In the same spirit, Matthias Hoe von Hoenegg

---

[41] Quoted by Paul Münch, in Schilling (1986): pp. 296–97.
[42] Hollweg (1964): p. 387.
[43] Martin Heckel, in Schilling (1986): pp. 11–43, here at p. 31.
[44] Lutz (1983): p. 349.

(1580–1645), a Saxon court preacher, posed his question, "whether, how, and why one should have more to do with and trust more the Papists than the Calvinists."[45] The Calvinists replied in kind, meting out to Lutherans treatment fully as brutal as what the Lutherans complained of in the Catholic territories. In 1604 the "Second Reformation's" full weight fell on the University of Marburg, a famous nursery of Lutheran pastors, now to be converted to the Reformed faith by Landgrave Moritz (1572–1627) of Hesse-Cassel. When some students and faculty resisted, Moritz's troops drove them into Lutheran-Hesse Darmstadt, where from Giessen (raised to a university in 1607) they launched a mighty stream of polemic against their Reformed expropriators.[46]

The anomalous position of the Reformed as the smallest but most aggressive of the three Imperial confessions around 1600 helps to explain the political weakness of German Protestantism. It was a matter of perspective. Whereas the view from Heidelberg and Amsterdam saw the main body of German Protestants as backward but promising brethren in the great struggle against the papal Antichrist and his Habsburg lieutenants, the view from Dresden and Stuttgart looked on Calvinists as dangerous fools, ready to imitate Huldrych Zwingli, Jan van Leiden, and Thomas Müntzer in grasping the sword in the gospel's name.

IV. *The Lutheran Rally*

Precisely when Calvinism began to penetrate the Empire during the 1560s, Lutheranism lay locked in the midst of a thirty-year doctrinal struggle over the legacy of Martin Luther.[47]

The Way to Concord

The doctrinal quarrels began in the aftermath of the Smalkaldic War between Philip Melanchthon's "Philippist" party and the Gnesio-

---

[45] Neveux (1967): p. 11.

[46] Gross (1975): pp. 105ff.

[47] See Martin Brecht, in this *Handbook of European History 1400–1600. Late Middle Ages, Renaissance, Reformation*, eds. T. A. Brady, Jr., H. A. Oberman, J. D. Tracy (Leiden, New York, Köln, Brill, 1995), vol. 2: pp. 148–52. There is a good overview by Rabe (1991): pp. 507–14.

Lutheran (Grk.: *gnesios* = legitimate) party headed the Dalmatian theologian Matthias Flacius (1520–1575). The issues were fundamental: 1) whether salvation rested exclusively on God's grace (a continuation of the debate with the Catholics); 2) the manner of Christ's presence in the Eucharist (a continuation of the debate with the Zwinglians); and 3) proper relationship between the church and temporal authority (an issue critical to all confessions). The Flacians' insistence on the sovereignty of the gospel resembled militant Protestantism of the west European Calvinist-Puritan type, all the more so in that it created Protestant resistance theory to justify the right of "inferior magistrates" to resist monarchs. "When the superior authority undertakes to persecute its subjects with violence and injustice," the preachers in besieged Magdeburg proclaimed in 1550, "and to subvert divine or natural law, true doctrine, and divine services, . . . the inferior authority is obliged by divine command to maintain itself and the subjects against his superior."[48]

Ten years later, Melanchthon's death opened yet wider the floodgates of theological discord. The struggle fed from the rivalry between the two Saxonys, the dominant Albertine state being a Philippist bastion and the remnant Ernestine state the fortress of Gnesio-Lutheranism.[49] The unifying efforts, by contrast, came from the west, Brunswick and Württemberg, where the Calvinist challenge seemed more palpable, and it was Jacob Andreä (1529–1590), professor of theology and chancellor of the University of Tübingen, and the Lower Saxons Martin Chemnitz (1522–1586) and Nikolaus Selnecker (1530–1592) who pushed hardest for doctrinal agreement. Meanwhile, in Electoral Saxony during the first half of the 1570s, the Philippists at Wittenberg— Luther's old university—were working secretly for an understanding with the Calvinists. When Elector August I purged these "crypto-Calvinists" in 1574, a corner was turned toward Lutheran doctrinal unification on an anti-Calvinist basis.

The main phase of reunification began in March 1577, when theologians assembled in the old Benedictine abbey of Bergen, an Ottonian foundation outside the walls of Magdeburg. Their twelve articles codified Lutheran doctrine against the "sects and conventicles" and against the Reformed and Catholic challenges. They agreed "to commit ourselves exclusively and only, in accordance with the pure,

---

[48] Quoted by Schilling (1988a): p. 292.
[49] See Ernst Koch, in Schilling (1986): pp. 60–78.

infallible, and unalterable Word of God, to that Augsburg Confession which was submitted to Emperor Charles V at the great imperial assembly in Augsburg in the year 1530."[50] The *Book of Concord*, which also contained several other doctrinal statements (called "symbols"), was published in 1580, the fiftieth anniversary of the Confession of Augsburg. It appeared over the signatures of fifty princes, 38 free cities, and no fewer than 8,000 clergymen.[51] This successful rallying of Lutheranism came just in the nick of time, before the Reformed challenge reached its peak, and before the Catholic revival was fairly underway.

Success and Failure in the Lutheran Reform

Although Lutheran churches existed in Scandinavia and scattered through the German diaspora in eastern Europe, they exerted little influence on Lutheranism in the Empire, which remained the most purely German in personnel and temperament of the three Imperial confessions. In many ways, too, it remained the confession least changeable and most bound to the past, a pastors' church in which most pastors came from pastoral families.[52] Some indeed have argued that Lutheranism represented a failed reformation. Gerald Strauss has argued that Lutheran clergy of the first and second generations certainly developed an aggressive program of religious and moral pedagogy, based on principles which have come to be recognized as the common pedagogy of the confessional era: self-discipline, obedience, self-control, and the acceptance of paternal, pastoral, and princely authority. This program, however, foundered on popular resistance to the new discipline.[53]

Strauss' argument about the Reformation's failure has been much debated. With dubious yield, for the debates have mixed indiscriminately urban successes with rural failures. Most of the Empire's people, after all, lived in villages, where old ways, including religious ones, stubbornly resisted all reformers. The Jesuits, for all of their successes, met their match in the villages of the prince-bishopric of

---

[50] Theodore G. Tappert, ed., *The Book of Concord. The Confessions of the Evangelical Lutheran Church* (Philadelphia, 1959), pp. 8–9. See Brecht and Schwarz (1980).
[51] Lohse (1980).
[52] The evidence is summarized by Hsia (1989): pp. 14–16. For the background, see Scribner (1987): pp. 123–44.
[53] Strauss (1978).

Speyer, where the Capuchins, a reformed branch of the Franciscans, had later to do the whole job again.[54] Very rarely did the rural folk have the luxury of choosing their religion, and when they did, as in parts of the Swiss Confederacy and the associated states of Valais and Graubünden, they defended their own ways with great tenacity, the Reformed communities of the Toggenburg against the Catholic abbot of St. Gallen not less stoutly than the Valtellina's Catholic Italian-speakers against their Reformed occupiers from the Graubünden.[55]

The debate about the Reformation's success or failure rarely considers what barriers to religious change from above were posed by the Empire's deeply fragmented governance and considerable local autonomies. Consider how the Lutheran faith came to Ödenwaldstetten, a very poor village lying east of the Neckar Valley in the Swabian Jura.[56] The village's lord was the Catholic abbot of Zwiefalten, whose lay protector (*Vogt*) was the Lutheran duke of Württemberg. Nothing much happened at Ödenwaldstetten until the parish priest died in 1558. When the abbot asked Duke Christoph's permission to install another "Mass priest [*Messpfaffe*]," Württemberg's ruler decided that it was time to bring the gospel to the village. Two likely candidates declined the post after inspecting the situation, because "they could not detect that the mayor, officers, and jurors have any special love for the holy gospel. Also, they found a very small, cramped, crumbling . . . rectory, in which no clergyman could possibly live with wife and children. And in the little church they found all sorts of papist trash, which the people continue to honor."[57] The village court consulted the Lutheran superintendent at Urach, Johann Otmar Mayländer, who organized occasional preaching at Ödenwaldstetten by a nearby pastor. When, however, he visited the village at Pentecost 1559, Mayländer was astounded to see the villagers in solemn procession, led by a volunteer Catholic priest from a nearby village, and he admonished the villagers to leave off their papistical ways. In the end, when the abbot would not pay to renovate the ruined rectory, the villagers accepted a Lutheran pastor, who served a heavily Catholic flock under their Catholic lord, the

---

[54] Forster (1992).
[55] Stadler (1980): p. 624; Head (1994).
[56] Fritz (1989).
[57] *Ibid.*, p. 40.

abbot. Not until around 1610 did villagers cease to demand a Catholic
priest, and far into modern times, it was told, Ödenwaldstetters nod-
ded to the spot on the church's wall where the image of the Virgin
had once stood. Finally, when the village passed from Zwiefalten to
Württemberg in 1750—200 years after Luther's death—the Lutheran
reformation was complete at Ödenwaldstetten. This story suggests
the immense difficulties under which the Lutheran reformation—and
all other reformations—labored in the countryside.[58] Against Catholicism, Lutheranism had the added burden of a preaching message
which condemned the past to a society based on the continuities of
household, farmstead, and cultivation, and which deprecated "works,"
that is, human deeds and labor, to people whose lives were composed of works alone.

All three confessions were essentially town-bred, and the formation of clear confessional identities came more easily in the cities.[59]
Naming was a particularly visible sign of identity, in the Empire as
elsewhere in transalpine Europe. In bi-confessional Augsburg, by the
early seventeenth century Lutherans were displacing the name "Maria"
for their daughters by the confessionally neutral "Regina," while
for boys, though "Hans" and "Johann" held pride of place in both
confessions, the Lutherans turned toward Old Testament names—
"Abraham," "Elias," and "Daniel"—and the Catholics to "Michael"—
a great Counterreformation favorite—and "Ignaz."[60] Gradually, too,
confessionally mixed marriages, which had been common before the
1580s, became less so, as the confessional lines hardened. Being on
one side or the other, or moving from one side to the other, could
mean the difference between survival and ruin, since in mixed communities, such as Augsburg, nearly all social welfare institutions were
administered on a confessional basis.[61]

Lutheran Politics

Although Lutheranism changed slowly, its achievements were not
unimpressive. By the 1580s the confession possessed a clear standard
of identity in the *Book of Concord* and a durable, bedrock policy of

[58] See, e.g., Robisheaux (1989).
[59] See Abray (1985), Warmbrunn (1983), and Roeck (1991) for examples.
[60] Roeck (1991): p. 295.
[61] *Ibid.*, pp. 296–97.

loyalty to the Imperial constitution in general and the Religious Peace of 1555 in particular. Indeed, it was the Lutheran jurists, not the Catholics, who developed the strongest tradition of pro-monarchical legal thought.[62] The concentration of Lutheran powers—Saxony, Brandenburg, and their dependents—in the east, where the Ottomans seemed at least as threatening as the Catholics, helped the confession's political leaders to resist being pulled by the Calvinist politicians into the maelstrom of the western European religious wars. The most purely Imperial of the three Imperial confessions, the Lutherans had most to lose if the Religious Peace were disrupted. Count Henry of Isenburg (1565–1601), a Lutheran progenitor of Calvinist heirs, stated their position best: "Peace is better than war, for it is uncertain who will win."[63]

V. *The Catholic Revival*

"My church and I are destroyed," wrote Hildesheim's prince-bishop to Rome in 1545.[64] At that time and for long after, the emperor's policy of conciliating the Protestants dampened the freedom and will of many of the Empire's Catholic prelates to undertake a vigorous defense of their faith. During these decades odd conditions obtained, mixed orders of worship were common, the state of ecclesiastical property was chaotic, and in some places the same man might serve as a Catholic priest and a Protestant pastor.[65] By the mid-1560s, however, change was in the wind. In 1566, three years after the Council of Trent rose for the last time, the Roman Curia, now convinced of the hopelessness of dealing with the emperor and the Imperial Diet, began to negotiate with individual bishops about introducing the Tridentine reforms.[66] The Catholic revival began with individual bishops' acceptance of the Tridentine profession of faith and promises to obey the council's canons and decrees, which were gradually incorporated via diocesan synods into the local laws.[67]

---

[62] Gross (1975).
[63] Quoted by Schilling (1988a): p. 291.
[64] Quoted by Bauerreiss (1965): p. 280.
[65] Zeeden (1965): pp. 74, 77; Evans (1979): p. 15.
[66] Bireley (1988): p. 13.
[67] See Molitor (1967) for a model study.

Foundations of Catholic Revival

Rome's most important contribution was to train a cadre of modern clergy at the German College (*Collegium Germanicum*), which was founded at Rome in 1552 and reorganized by Jesuits in 1573. Its graduates—in the early days mostly Netherlanders and Lower Rhinelanders—comprised an ever increasing proportion of the Catholic bishops and cathedral canons in the Empire. During the early 1580s the papacy also established permanent nuntiatures at Graz (1580) and Cologne (1584), which became important switching points for the process of Catholic reform in the Empire.[68]

Further help came from the Society of Jesus's efforts to begin the modern training of priests in the Empire.[69] Their schools, many of them founded in episcopal residential cities, became the nurseries of the Catholic reform, as the free cities had been those of the Protestant one.[70] Such schools appeared at Dillingen (for Augsburg) in the 1550s, at Mainz in 1561, at Würzburg also in the 1560s, at Eichstätt in 1584, and at Bamberg in 1586.[71] The Society, first established in the Empire at Cologne in 1544, grew even more rapidly, rising from 273 members organized into two provinces in the mid-1560s to nearly 2,500 in three provinces (Rhenish, South German, and Austrian) by the 1620s.[72] Such were its successes, so quickly did the Jesuits provide the Empire's intact Catholic communities with religious leadership and able defenders through pulpit and pamphlet, that both friend and foe tended to overestimate their powers. The Society flourished in the cities, but not in the countryside, and in Bavaria, where the Jesuits worked to great effect from pulpits, in schools, in the theater, and in the University of Ingolstadt, they took little or no part in the revitalization of the religious culture of shrines and pilgrimage that so effectively armored Bavarian Catholicism against Lutheran influence.[73] In the prince-bishopric of Speyer on the Upper Rhine, the Jesuits' efforts in the villages failed altogether, and reform had to be reestablished by the Capuchins, a far more demotic order.[74]

---

[68] P. Schmidt (1984); Reinhard (1971).
[69] O'Malley (1993).
[70] Rublack (1978).
[71] May (1983): pp. 254–55, 242–45, 366–67, 277, 574.
[72] Based on figures summarized by Hsia (1989): p. 48.
[73] Soergel (1993): pp. 89–90, 34–36, 152–54.
[74] Forster (1992).

Gradually, too, the older religious orders drew themselves together and were mobilized for the Catholic reform.[75]

The Ecclesiastical States

The key to reform was the clergy, especially the hierarchy—prince-bishops, abbots, abbesses, and cathedral canons—who, though remaining as aristocratic as ever, gradually began to change their ways of life.[76] Archbishop Wolf Dietrich von Raitenau (1559–1612) of Salzburg, a nobleman from south of Lake Constance, illustrates the transition from old to new.[77] Wolf Dietrich studied for five years at the German College in Rome before succeeding in Salzburg at the age of eighteen. There he blended the old ways with the new. He accumulated benefices with the zeal of a pre-Reformation prelate, and he even sought Rome's permission to marry Salome Alt, the lovely daughter of a Salzburg magistrate, by whom he fathered ten children. Wolf Dietrich's policies, however, fully justified Pope Sixtus V's admonition "to break the blows of the heretics and turn their deadly shots back on themselves." He introduced the Tridentine pastoral agenda at Salzburg, began to reform clerical life, harnessed the younger religious orders to the task of reform, and began—in precise imitation of Sixtus V at Rome—the Baroque transformation of Salzburg. Wolf Dietrich also had the bad judgment to clash with Duke Maximilian I (r. 1598–1651) of Bavaria, which led to his deposition and incarceration.

Archbishop Wolf Dietrich represented a Catholic version of the typically Imperial fusion between centralized authority and religious reform.[78] He and the other prince-bishops—twelve of the sees had been lost to the Lutherans—were crucial to the success of Catholic reform, because, outside of Bavaria and Austria, most of the Empire's intact Catholic communities lived under ecclesiastical lords.

---

[75] Seibrich (1991).

[76] For orientation, see Wolfgang Reinhard, in Jeserich, Pohl, and Unruh (1983): pp. 143–76; Schindling (1987); for details see Schindling and Ziegler (1989–1993); and for the later history see Peter Hersche, in G. Schmidt (1989): pp. 133–51.

[77] Ortner (1981); Schindling and Ziegler (1989–1993): vol. 1: pp. 72–85. The story of Wolf Dietrich is recounted by Schilling (1988a): pp. 284–88.

[78] Reinhard (1989); and see Bireley (1990), for Counterreformation state-craft.

Bavaria

The Bavarian dukes early assumed the leadership of the Catholic revival, because the emperors from Ferdinand I through Rudolph II were tied to the need to conciliate both the Imperial estates and the estates of the Habsburg lands.[79] In Bavaria, by contrast, already in the early 1560s Duke Albert V's (r. 1550–1579) defeat of his heavily Lutheran territorial nobility enabled the duchy to become the linchpin of the Empire's Catholic reform in a Tridentine sense. Albert called the Jesuits to Munich and to his university at Ingolstadt, and he made the Landsberg League (1556–1598) a military instrument for the protection of Catholic interests.

Duke Albert also began to push Catholic Wittelsbachs into endangered episcopal sees, a policy which yielded its first major fruit in the early 1580s at Cologne. Cologne's archbishop, Gebhard Truchsess von Waldburg (r. 1577–1583), converted to Protestantism and tried to retain his see. This act challenged the Ecclesiastical Reservation and touched off the "Cologne War" (1583–1585), which nearly became a major war. While Emperor Rudolph stood by helplessly, Duke William V (r. 1579–1593, d. 1626) secured the claim of his younger brother, Ernest, to the see and began thereby the 180-year history of the great Rhenish see as a Bavarian secundogeniture. The securing of Catholicism at Cologne, in collaboration with the Spanish regime at Brussels, made possible the stabilization of the Catholic position in the Empire's entire northwestern sector, and it did so at a time when the emperor was caught between the Ottoman threat and the need to conciliate the Protestants.

The Austrian Lands

Protestantism's initial penetration of the Austrian lands met little resistance from a deeply enervated church.[80] As in Bohemia, Bavaria, and elsewhere, the new faith quickly allied with the landed nobility's struggle to preserve its liberties against princely centralism. By the early 1580s, it has been argued, most nobles and many burghers in the Austrian lands had turned to the new faith.

---

[79] Albrecht (1977a) and (1977b); Lutz (1977); Schindling and Ziegler (1989–1993): vol. 1: pp. 56–71.
[80] Schindling and Ziegler (1989–1993), vol. 1: pp. 86–101, 102–17, 188–33, 134–52; Reingrabner (1976).

The Austrian Counterreformation, it has also been argued, represented the triumph of "a universal (imperial) ideology and a revived cosmopolitan (Catholic) Church" over "the vestiges of Renaissance and the ruins of Protestantism."[81] If true, this helps to explain the revival of a church once so deeply enervated that a survey of Lower Austrian monasteries in 1563 counted 122 houses containing 463 monks, 160 nuns, 199 concubines, 55 wives, and 443 children.[82] The rulers did supply some essential impulses to reform, notably Maximilian II's creation in 1567–1568 of a Monastic Council (*Klosterrat*) for Upper and Lower Austria.[83] Such measures alone nevertheless cannot account for the rapid decline of the Lutheran cause after 1580. Unfavorable economic conditions helped to account for the decline of the nobles, and the Habsburg rulers accelerated the change through the creation of new Catholic nobles, but so did Catholic successes in the struggle for reform at the level of the local seigniory and the rural monastery.[84] Among rural folk, surely, the Protestant advantage was not so great as has sometimes been asserted, for the Protestant nobles never possessed more than about half of the pastorates in the Austrian lands, and the majority of those were castle chaplaincies.[85]

Much depended, too, on Ferdinand I's division of the Austrian lands in 1564 among his three sons, whose capitals lay at Vienna, Graz, and Innsbruck.[86] While Lutheranism strongly penetrated the "lower lands" of Upper and Lower Austria, it was weaker in Inner Austria (Styria, Carinthia, and Carniola), and much weaker yet in the western lands of Tyrol and Vorarlberg. At Graz and at Innsbruck the Catholic reform received decisive dynastic support long before it did in the "lower lands." There, except for Vienna with its durable Catholic majority, the Catholic reform began to succeed only after the great rural insurrection of 1594/97, which the Protestant-led estates crushed. Thereafter, the Protestant clergy were driven out of the cities and into the castles for refuge.[87]

Vienna, demoted to a provincial capital by Rudolph II in favor of Prague, posed a special case. In the 1580s a strong champion of

[81] Evans (1979): p. xxiii.
[82] *Ibid.*, p. 4.
[83] Jeserich, Pohl, and Unruh (1983): here at pp. 512–13; Patrouch (1994).
[84] MacHardy (1982): pp. 82–83, based on Lower Austrian data.
[85] Patrouch (1994): pp. 75–76.
[86] The division is explained in Jeserich, Pohl, and Unruh (1983): p. 472; and by Evans (1979): pp. 158–62.
[87] Schindling and Ziegler (1989–1993): vol. 1: pp. 126–29.

Catholic reform emerged there in the person of Melchior Khlesl
(1552–1630), son of a Protestant baker in Vienna, a graduate of
Jesuits schooling, and delegate of the bishop of Passau in the Aulic
Court at Vienna. He became the heart and soul of the struggle to
beat back the Protestant challenge in Lower Austria, though the
effort faltered after 1600, when "the brothers' quarrel [*Bruderzwist*]"
between Rudolph and Matthias brought Catholic reform to a standstill.
For a time, it even seemed as if there would be an Austrian version
of Rudolph II's "Letter of Majesty" (1609), which confirmed the religious liberties of the Bohemian estates. In fact, the moment for action
by the Protestant Austrian nobles was already past, and when the
estates turned to arms against Archduke Ferdinand of Inner Austria,
who came to the Bohemian throne in 1617 and to the Imperial
throne as Emperor Ferdinand II in 1619, it was already too late.
Catholicism, in the 1550s to 1570s an apparently doomed religion
in both the Empire and the Austrian lands, had become by century's end the strongest of the three confessions.[88]

VI. *The Failure of Imperial Politics*

"There is no more friendship on this earth," the poet Theodore
Höck groaned in 1601, "and each has become Devil to the other."[89]
It was, indeed, a hard age, this late sixteenth century, and over its
reputation stands the somber image of the reclusive Emperor Rudolph
II, hiding himself away in the great Hradcany Castle at Prague, "for
long stretches mentally ill, so disordered and irrationally frightened
that he let imperial business slide for months and years, so depressed
that he thought himself bewitched and even attempted suicide."[90]
Meanwhile, all around him the leaderless Empire disintegrated into
mistrust, resignation, and mutually hostile armed parties.[91]

One may not blame the listless emperor for the times, which were
indeed hard. There is mounting evidence that during the 1590s
Europe fell into a general crisis which adversely affected all of its

---

[88] Parker (1987): p. 19, marks the turning point in the Empire at the Cologne
War (1583–1588).
[89] Evans (1973): p. 278.
[90] Midelfort (1994): p. 128.
[91] The following is based on Evans (1973) and (1979).

lands and all aspects of its peoples' lives.[92] Not only was religious strife becoming more intense, but there were new waves of revolts in the cities and on the land.[93] By far the most ominous and most revealing sign of the crisis, however, was the onset of the great witch panic.

The Witch Panic

Between 1580 and 1660 Europe shuddered to the great witch panic, to which the Empire contributed about half of the 40–50,000 persons executed for the crime of witchcraft.[94] Its main phase began in the 1580s with an unprecedented wave of denunciations, prosecutions, and executions. In the southeast, the best studied region, about 75% of the executions for witchcraft occurred between 1586 and 1630, whereas in two core regions of witch hunting, Franconia and southwestern Germany, the peaks came later and resulted in many more executions (ca. 8000 vs. ca. 1800 in Bavaria and Austria).[95] The prosecutions of witches found broad approval among the common people, though not necessarily for the same reasons as it did among the elites. The latter were split, the strongest proponents of religious renewal—Catholic and Protestant—tending to be more in favor of prosecutions, but in general the skeptics gradually gained the upper hand and dampened or stopped the prosecutions earliest in the most strongly governed states.[96]

The Search for Order

Against the chaos that threatened the Empire and the world stood forces which were, given the age's reputation, deceptively powerful. At the center formed by the Rudolfine court worked a heterogeneous aristocracy which represented "the belief in a single universal authority and the total, all-embracing conception of society."[97] In

---

[92] Clark (1985).

[93] Schilling (1985); Roeck (1991): pp. 62–66; Schilling (1988a): pp. 380–81.

[94] See Brian P. Levack, in this *Handbook of European History 1400–1600. Late Middle Ages, Renaissance, Reformation*, eds. T. A. Brady, Jr., H. A. Oberman, J. D. Tracy (Leiden, New York, Köln, Brill, 1995), vol. 2: pp. 607–40; Midelfort (1972).

[95] Behringer (1988): pp. 414–15.

[96] *Ibid.*, p. 417 and n. 39.

[97] Evans (1973): p. 284.

origin Renaissance rather than medieval, their ideal centered not on
a Church Universal but a universal monarchy, the tasks of which
were "to preserve the mental and political unity of Christendom, to
avoid religious schism, uphold peace at home, and deliver Europe
from the Ottoman menace."[98]

The Rudolfine ideology of universal monarchy tried to promote
Imperial stability by two means: protection of the Religious Peace
and struggle against the Ottomans. The former aim was served by
a remarkably successful record of political adaptation and innovation.
Since Charles V's day much of the Imperial Diet's work, such as
judicial review and financial administration, had come into the hands
of the Circles (*Reichskreise*) and a new institution, the *Reichsdeputationstag*,
a kind of executive committee of the Diet.[99] In the 1590s the latter
body assumed the task of regular review of the Imperial Chamber
Court, which continued to expand its work despite competition from
another new institution, the purely royal Imperial Aulic Court (*Reichshofrat*, est. 1559).

The Ottoman struggle tested the effectiveness of all Imperial institutions. When war came again in 1593, the Habsburg propagandists
set out to deploy anti-Ottoman sentiment against the confessional divisions. Their warnings resonated with the sentiments of many others,
among them Peter Waldner of Augsburg:

> Because the Empire's princes are so contentious
> The Turk has become so powerful.
> There is no peace in Christendom,
> So that he grazes where he will.
> He knows well how things stand,
> That there is no peace in Christendom.[100]

Such sentiments long mortgaged the tactic of tax refusal, which the
Protestant princes had employed so effectively against Charles V.
From 1576 to 1603, indeed, the Imperial estates voted generous taxes
against the Ottomans and, more astonishingly, paid them—rather,
they persuaded their own subjects and estates to pay them. The new
Imperial tax administrator (*Reichspfennigmeister*, est. 1566), collected
more than 80% of the Imperial taxes levied between 1576 and
1606—a miraculous level, considering the Empire's history. Between

---

[98] *Ibid.*, pp. 2–3.
[99] Dotzauer (1989): p. 27.
[100] Quoted by Schulze (1978): p. 61 n. 99. See Vocelka (1981): pp. 246–78.

Charles V's abdication in 1556 and the end of the Ottoman War in 1606, the Empire paid more than 30,000,000 fl. for war against the Ottomans.[101] "While it lasted," Winfried Schulze has written, "the Ottoman threat posed an important, consolidating force in the Empire and preserved its political structure from collapsing earlier than it did."[102] Indeed, by the early years of the seventeenth century, it seemed as if the Imperial system had weathered the storms of the Reformation era and was moving down the same path on which the kingdoms of Europe's western tier were treading, toward greater centralization, cohesion, and internal uniformity.

Imperial Breakdown

The Imperial politics based on the Religious Peace of 1555 withstood internal shocks which might have broken a more fragile state. The first major test of confessional co-existence came in the early 1580s, when Spanish and Bavarian forces faced off against German Calvinist and Dutch troops in the "Cologne War." The crisis passed, and the Catholics kept the see. A similar case opened in 1592 at Strasbourg, where a double episcopal election produced Catholic and Protestant claimants to the see. Again there was threat of major war, again it was averted, and again the Catholics held the contested see. A third case involved the long confessional strife in the free city of Aachen, where the Protestant congregations had organized too late, after 1555, to be protected by the Peace. There was much internal strife and threats of external intervention, but the Catholics held the day, and in 1614/16 the Protestants were expelled from the city. In all three cases, the Catholics won out because the Catholic forces— the emperor, Bavaria, and the Spanish regime at Brussels—worked together more easily than did the western Calvinist and eastern Lutheran princes.

The Catholics possessed a tremendous advantage in a Catholic emperor, even though Rudolph's religious mentality favored the mystical, the miraculous, and the dynastic, and he abhorred confessionalism and Rome.[103] When he could make up his mind, however, he generally favored the Catholic side, as he did in a fourth case,

---

[101] Schulze (1978): p. 369.
[102] *Ibid.*, p. 366.
[103] See Evans (1973): pp. 84–115.

called the "Four Monasteries Case." This was a group of suits brought
by Catholic monasteries against Protestant princes, all of which the
Imperial Chamber court decided in a Catholic sense—though in fact
the judges probably never intended to address in principle the issue
of ecclesiastical property and the *ius reformandi*.[104] No matter, for when
the case came before the *Reichsdeputationstag*'s visitation of the court
in 1600/1, the Protestant members demanded its referral to the Diet,
the Catholics refused, and both sides left the meeting in a huff. This
destroyed the effectiveness of both the *Reichsdeputationstag* and the
Chamber Court and left only the Imperial Diet to oppose the creeping paralysis of Imperial governance. Then, in 1606 the Truce of
Zsitva Torok with the Ottoman Sultan, who was pressed in the east
by a Persian attack, removed the last major external restraint on
confessional aggressiveness.[105]

This was the situation in 1608, when a dispute erupted over
Catholic religious rights in the Protestant-dominated free city of Donauwörth. When the magistrates refused to protect Catholic religious
processions, the *Reichshofrat* decided against them, and the emperor
appointed the Duke Maximilian of Bavaria—not the commander
of the Swabian Circle, the (Protestant) duke of Württemberg—to
execute the sentence. Bavarian troops occupied the town, long an
object of Bavarian policy, and Catholicism was restored. This action
had ominous consequences, because the ensuing quarrel disrupted
the Imperial Diet of Regensburg in 1608, which dissolved in acri-
mony without framing a recess. "This Diet had such an unfortunate
end and consequence," wrote a Mainz secretary at the end of his
minutes, "that it dissolved with nothing accomplished."[106] As the fear
of war swept over the Empire, Rudolph II, paralyzed by his bitter
quarrel with his brother, Archduke Matthias, failed to act.

With the Diet disrupted and the emperor quiescent, the confessional parties hardened into confessional alliances. At Auingen near
Nördlingen on 14 May 1608 came into being the Protestant Union,
in which normally traditionally loyal Lutheran cities—Nuremberg,
Strasbourg, and Ulm—joined, though Elector Christian II of Saxony
stayed aloof. In response, the Catholic League came into being at
Munich on 10 July 1609. At first it comprised chiefly South German

[104] Rabe (1976).
[105] See Press (1991): pp. 161–94, for an overview.
[106] Quoted by Vocelka (1981): p. 154.

prelates, and its finances were closely tied to the Bavarian treasury, but in 1610 it admitted the electors of Mainz, Cologne, and Trier and two Austrian archdukes. Not only had the League greater extent than the Union, but its common confession, which the emperor officially shared, gave it greater cohesion.

Now, the old system shattered, the Empire seemed to plunge toward confessional war—and then stopped once more. The last great pre-war crisis developed over the succession to the Lower Rhenish conglomerate state of Cleves-Jülich. At the death of the childless and hopelessly insane Duke John William in 1609—the year of the Twelve Years' Truce between Spain and the Dutch—the chief claimants were the wives of Count Palatine Philip Louis (a devout Lutheran) and Elector John Sigismund of Brandenburg (a convert to Calvinism). At first they collaborated against a Catholic regency council headed by the dowager duchess. Meanwhile, the Protestant Union, torn between two Protestant claimants, stood pat, the emperor sat silent at Prague, and northwestern Europe mobilized for the general war the Empire most feared. At this moment (14 May 1610) came the assassination King Henry IV of France, just as the royal army was about to move, and all powers stood down. Even when Philip Louis's son, Wolfgang Wilhelm, converted to Catholicism, the confessional alliances still did not move, and by 1614 the dispute was settled by partitioning the duchies between the two chief claimants.

The final blow to the Imperial peace came in 1618 in Bohemia. Rudolph's brother and heir, Emperor Matthias, was succeeded in Bohemia in 1618 (and in the Empire in 1619) by Archduke Ferdinand of Inner Austria (Emperor Ferdinand II). Born in 1578, Ferdinand was the first Holy Roman emperor who was wholly a child of the confessional era. His succession came at a difficult time, for Europe's rulers and politicians were waiting for the Twelve Years' Truce between Spain and the Dutch Republic to expire (in 1621), expecting it would be followed by another general European war. At Prague the Protestant nobles who led the Bohemian estates decided to forestall the uncertainty of that event by revoking their election of Ferdinand and putting a Protestant in his place. As Polyxena Lobkovic, wife of the Bohemian chancellor, remarked, "things were now swiftly coming to the pass where either the Papists would settle their score with the Protestants, or the Protestants with the Papists."[107] Bolstered

---

[107] Quoted by Parker (1987): p. 44.

by promises from Christian of Anhalt (1586–1630), the mind behind
the Protestant Union, plus the Upper and Lower Austrian estates
and the Prince of Transylvania, the Bohemian leaders chose themselves an alternative king. Their foolhardy choice fell on the young
Elector Palatine, Frederick V (1596–1632), "a man who had never
seen either a battle or corpse, . . . a prince who knew more about
gardening than fighting."[108]

VII. *War and Settlement*

The long, terrible war of 1618–1648 deserves study in its own right,
for the guise in which it appears here, as the culmination of the
Empire's Reformation settlement,[109] pushes to the margin some of
the most interesting questions, such as the war's economic and social
effects,[110] in favor of its political dimensions. Two questions need to
be raised: Why did the war go on so long? Why did the war end
in a restoration of the Religious Peace of 1555?

The Long War

The war lasted for thirty years because of the overwhelming quality
of Emperor Ferdinand II's victories in the war's first ("Bohemian")
phase in 1618–1623 and second ("Danish") phase in 1624–1629. His
success tempted Ferdinand to declare measures that frightened his
opponents, both in the Empire and abroad. His Bohemian settlement, though radical, lay within the bounds of the Imperial constitution—assuming that Bohemia lay in the Empire—and within the
rights stipulated to rulers by the Religious Peace. *Cuius regio, eius
religio.* The Austrian Protestants fell under the same rule, and they
fell alone. The transfer of the Upper Palatinate to Bavaria also lay
within royal prerogative, and one could argue that awarding the Palatine electorate to Bavaria kept it with the same dynasty and did
not, therefore, violate the Golden Bull of 1356. It was difficult, however, to justify constitutionally the Edict of Restitution of 1629,

---

[108] Quoted in *ibid.*, from a Czech source.
[109] *Ibid.*; Schormann (1985); a good, brief overview by Bonney (1991): pp. 188–203.
[110] The long debate is summarized by Christopher R. Friedrichs in Parker (1987):
pp. 208–15; and by Schormann (1985): pp. 112–20.

which ordered restoration of all church lands and bishoprics secularized since the Treaty of Passau in 1552, not because of its strict
interpretation of the Religious Peace, but because it was unilaterally
issued by the emperor. Still, at this time, around 1630, "the political leaders of Germany were free to determine their own destiny,"
for although the war between Spain and the Dutch Republic had
resumed, and although both branches of the House of Austria had
become embroiled once again in a major war with France in Italy,
"as long as the German princes remained neutral and unattached,
there was still a chance for peace."[111] Then, in late June 1630, King
Gustavus Adolphus of Sweden landed in the Empire, beginning the
war's third, "Swedish" phase of 1630–1634. He came, as he said, to
restore the status quo of 1618, for "while an elector can sit safe as
elector in his land, and a duke is a duke and has his liberties, then
we are safe."[112] After he fell (Lützen, 1632), and after his army was
defeated (Nördlingen, 1534), France intervened to begin the war's final
"French" phase (1635–1648).

Settlement and Restoration

The Thirty Years' War ended in an Imperial restoration, because
leading Imperial princes of both major confessions were moved by
the desire to restore the Imperial constitution, so that the Empire
would escape both foreign domination and a "Latin servitude" to
the House of Austria. This program underlay both the Catholic
League's pressure for the dismissal of Albrecht of Wallenstein (1583–
1634), Ferdinand's most successful general, and the Saxon elector's
perennial refusal to throw his resources whole-heartedly against the
emperor. The moment for restoration seemed to strike after the
Swedish defeat at Nördlingen in September 1634, when the impending French intervention pressed Emperor Ferdinand to make peace
with the leading Protestant princes, Saxony and Brandenburg. The
Peace of Prague (30 May 1635) ended the Imperial civil war, made
the Swedish army's position in Germany hopeless, combined the
hitherto hostile forces into an Imperial army, and restored the voice
of pragmatism and compromise to Imperial counsels. Had it not

---

[111] Parker (1987): p. 111.
[112] Quoted by Michael Roberts, "The Swedish Dilemma, 1633–1641," in Parker
(1987): p. 157; and there, too, the following quote.

been for the French "war of diversion," which aimed to fight Spanish power in Germany rather than "in the bowels of France," the end of the Empire's war would have ended the war in the Empire as well.[113] As it was, since the mid-1630s the old Imperial political order had begun to reconstitute itself beneath the surface of ceaseless struggle. The electors were meeting periodically, and in September 1640 the Imperial Diet convened at Regensburg for the first time since 1613. The greatest internal barrier to restoration was removed in 1641, when, over the papal nuncio's protest, Emperor Ferdinand III withdrew the Edict of Restitution. During the next six years, each French victory stiffened his resolve, and that of the leading Catholic and Lutheran princes, to make peace.

The Peace of Westphalia of 1648 completed this restoration.[114] The treaties in the main confirmed the Religious Peace of 1555, with three important changes: the Calvinist faith was recognized; the fixing of 1624 as the status quo settled the dispute about the Ecclesiastical Reservation; and the formation of two religious caucuses, the *corpus evangelicorum* and *corpus catholicorum*, which cut across the Diet's historic structure, enabled this parliament to incorporate the Empire's confessional division into its structure of governance. In addition, the Empire lost important groups of lands, the Swiss Confederacy and the Dutch Republic, from its southwestern and northwestern corners respectively.

With the Peace of Westphalia the Imperial constitution triumphed over the religious forces unleashed by the Protestant and Catholic reformations. The long war spelled defeat for two alternative visions. One was the renewed Reformed vision fashioned at Heidelberg, which held that German-speaking Protestantism's rulers should fuse their policies and resources with those of foreign Protestant rulers into a gigantic, Europe-wide league against the Habsburgs and Rome. The second was Ferdinand II's Catholic dream of extending to the Empire his style of rule, which, though it has been called "confessional absolutism," substituted religious orthodoxy for structural centralization.[115] Each of these visions looked beyond the traditional politics of compromise and accommodation to a new kind of universalism, which was neither medieval nor did it lie on the "mod-

---

[113] The quoted passages come from Parker (1987): p. 144.
[114] Dickmann (1959).
[115] R. J. W. Evans, "The Imperial Vision," in Parker (1987): pp. 83–88.

ern path" toward absolutist centralism and the national state. The twin Imperial settlements of 1555 and 1648 defeated these projects for renewal in favor of the Imperial structure that had emerged from the fifteenth century: a monarchy caged by constituted aristocratic liberties. It would endure for another 150 years.

Bibliography

Abray, Lorna Jane. *The People's Reformation: Magistrates, Clergy, and Commons in Strasbourg, 1520–1599.* New Haven, 1985.

Albrecht, Dieter. "Die kirchlich-religiöse Entwicklung. Zweiter Teil: 1500–1745." In *Handbuch der bayerischen Geschichte*, ed. Max Spindler, vol. 2: pp. 626–56. 2d ed. Munich, 1977a [1966].

———. "Das konfessionelle Zeitalter. Zweiter Teil: Die Herzöge Wilhelm V. und Maximilian I." In *Handbuch der bayerischen Geschichte*, ed. Max Spindler, vol. 2: pp. 351–410. 2d ed. Munich, 1977b [1966].

Bauerreiss, Romuald, O.S.B. *Kirchengeschichte Bayerns.* Vol. 6, *Das sechzehnte Jahrhundert.* Munich, 1965.

Behringer, Wolfgang. *Hexenverfolgung in Bayern. Volksmagie, Glaubenseifer und Staatsräson in der Frühen Neuzeit.* Munich, 1988.

Bireley, Robert. *The Counter-Reformation Prince: Anti-Machiavellianism or Catholic Statecraft in Early Modern Europe.* Chapel Hill, 1990.

Bireley, Robert, S.J. "Early Modern Germany." In *Catholicism in Early Modern History. A Guide to Research*, ed. John W. O'Malley, S.J., 11–30. St. Louis, 1988.

Blaschke, Karlheinz. *Sachsen im Zeitalter der Reformation.* SVRG, vol. 185. Gütersloh, 1970.

Bonney, Richard. *The European Dynastic States, 1494–1660.* Oxford, 1991.

Brady, Thomas A., Jr. *Protestant Politics: Jacob Sturm of Strasbourg and the German Reformation.* Studies in German Histories. Atlantic Highlands, N.J., 1995.

Brecht, Martin, and Reinhard Schwarz, eds. *Bekenntnis und Einheit der Kirche. Studien zum Konkordienbuch.* Stuttgart, 1980.

Chaix, Gérard. *Réforme et Contre-Réforme catholiques. Recherches sur la Chartreuse de Cologne au 16ᵉ siècle.* 3 vols. Analecta Cartusiana, vol. 80. Salzburg, 1981.

Chrisman, Miriam U. *Lay Culture, Learned Culture: Books and Social Change in Strasbourg, 1480–1599.* New Haven, 1982.

Clark, Peter, ed. *The European Crisis of the 1590s.* London, 1985.

Cohn, Henry J. "Church Property in the German Protestant Principalities." In *Politics and Society in Reformation Europe: Essays for Sir Geoffrey Elton on his Sixty-Fifth Birthday*, eds. E. I. Kouri and Tom Scott, pp. 158–87. London: Macmillan Press, 1987.

———. "The Territorial Princes in Germany's Second Reformation." In *International Calvinism, 1541–1715*, ed. Minna Prestwich, pp. 139–65. Oxford, 1985.

Dickens, Arthur Geoffrey, and John Tonkin. *The Reformation in Historical Thought.* Cambridge, Mass., 1986.

Dickmann, Fritz. *Der Westfälische Frieden.* Münster, 1959.

Dotzauer, Winfried. *Die deutschen Reichskreise in der Verfassung des alten Reiches und ihr Eigenleben (1500–1806).* Darmstadt, 1989.

Duchhardt, Heinz. *Deutsche Verfassungsgeschichte 1495–1806.* Urban-Taschenbücher, vol. 417. Stuttgart, 1991.

———. *Protestantisches Kaisertum und altes Reich. Die Diskussion über die Konfession des Kaisers in Politik, Publizistik und Staatsrecht.* Wiesbaden, 1977.

Evans, R. J. W. *The Making of the Habsburg Monarchy, 1550–1700. An Interpretation.* Oxford, 1979.
——. *Rudolph II and His World.* Oxford, 1973.
Forster, Marc R. *The Counter-Reformation in the Villages: Religion and Reform in the Bishopric of Speyer, 1560–1720.* Ithaca, 1992.
Fritz, Eberhard. *dieweil sie so arme Leuth: Fünf Albdörfer zwischen Religion und Politik 1530–1750. Studien zur Kirchengeschichte der Dörfer Bernloch, Eglingen, Meidelstetten, Oberstetten und Ödenwaldstetten.* Quellen und Forschungen zur Württembergischen Geschichte, vol. 9. Stuttgart, 1989.
Glawischnig, Rolf. *Niederlande, Kalvinismus und Reichsgrafenstand (1559–1584). Nassau-Dillenburg unter Graf Johann VI.* Schriften des hessischen Landesamtes für geschichtliche Landeskunde, vol. 36. Marburg, 1973.
Greyerz, Kaspar von. *The Late City Reformation in German: the Case of Colmar, 1522–1618.* VIEG, vol. 98. Wiesbaden, 1980.
Gross, Hanns. *Empire and Sovereignty: A History of the Public Law Literature in the Holy Roman Empire, 1599–1804.* 2d ed. Chicago, 1975.
Head, Randolph C. *Early Modern Democracy in the Grisons: Society and Politics in a Swiss Mountain Canton.* Cambridge, 1994.
Heckel, Martin. "*Autonomia* und *Pacis Compositio.* Der Augsburger Religionsfriede in der Deutung der Gegenreformation." *ZSR, KA* 45 (1959): pp. 141–248.
——. *Deutschland im konfessionellen Zeitalter.* Deutsche Geschichte, vol. 5. Göttingen, 1983.
——. *Staat und Kirche.* Munich, 1968.
Hollweg, W. *Der Augsburger Reichstag von 1566 und seine Bedeutung für die Entstehung der Reformierten Kirche und ihres Bekenntnisses.* Neukirchen, 1964.
Hsia, R. Po-chia. *Social Discipline in the Reformation: Central Europe, 1550–1750.* London and New York, 1989.
——. *Society and Religion in Münster, 1535–1618.* New Haven, 1984.
Jeserich, Kurt G. A., Hans Pohl, and Georg-Christoph von Unruh, eds. *Deutsche Verwaltungsgeschichte.* Vol. 1, *Vom Spätmittelalter bis zum Ende des Reiches.* Stuttgart, 1983.
Kastner, Ruth, ed. *Quellen zur Reformation 1517–1555.* Darmstadt, 1994.
Klein, Thomas. *Der Kampf um die zweite Reformation in Kursachsen 1586–1591.* Mitteldeutsche Forschungen, vol. 27. Cologne and Graz, 1962.
Klueting, Harm. *Das konfessionelle Zeitalter 1525–1648.* Stuttgart, 1989.
Knox, R. Buick. "The Making of a Reforming Prince: Frederick III Elector Palatine." In *Reformation, Conformity and Dissent. Essays in Honour of Dr. Geoffrey Nuttall,* ed. R. Buick Knox, pp. 44–69. London, 1977.
Lohse, Bernhard. "Das Konkordienwerk von 1580." In *Kirche und Bekenntnis,* ed. Peter Meinhold, pp. 94–122. Wiesbaden, 1980.
Lutz, Heinrich. *Christianitas afflicta: Europa, das Reich und die päpstliche Politik im Niedergang der Hegemonie Kaiser Karls V. (1552–1556).* Göttingen, 1964.
——. "Das konfessionelle Zeitalter. Erster Teil: Die Herzöge Wilhelm IV. und Albrecht V." In *Handbuch der bayerischen Geschichte,* ed. Max Spindler, vol. 2: pp. 297–350. 2d ed. Munich, 1977 [1966].
——. *Das Ringen um deutsche Einheit und kirchliche Erneuerung. Von Maximilian I. bis zum Westfälischen Frieden 1490 bis 1648.* Propyläen Geschichte Deutschlands, vol. 4. Berlin, 1983.
MacHardy, Karin J. "Der Einfluß von Status, Konfession und Besitz auf das politische Verhalten des niederösterreichischen Ritterstandes 1580–1620." In *Spezialforschung und "Gesamtgeschichte,"* ed. Grete Klingenstein and Heinrich Lutz, pp. 56–83. Wiener Beiträge zur Geschichte der Neuzeit, vol. 8. Munich, 1982.
Maltby, William S., ed. *Reformation Europe: A Guide to Research, II.* St. Louis, 1992.
May, Georg. *Die deutschen Bischöfe angesichts der Glaubensspaltung im 16. Jahrhundert.* Vienna, 1983.

Midelfort, H. C. Erik. *Mad Princes of Renaissance Germany*. Charlottesville, 1994.

——. *Witch Hunting in Southwestern Germany, 1562–1648: the Social and Intellectual Foundations*. Stanford, 1972.

Moeller, Bernd. *Reichsstadt und Reformation*. 2d ed. Berlin, 1987 [1962].

Molitor, Hansgeorg. *Kirchliche Reformversuche der Kurfürsten und Erzbischöfe von Trier im Zeitalter der Gegenreformation*. VIEG, vol. 43. Wiesbaden, 1967.

Münch, Paul. *Zucht und Ordnung. Reformierte Kirchenverfassungen im 16. und 17. Jahrhundert (Nassau-Dillenburg, Kurpfalz, Hessen-Kassel)*. SFN, vol. 3. Stuttgart, 1978.

Muralt, Leonhard von. "Renaissance und Reformation." In *Handbuch der Schweizer Geschichte*, vol. 1: pp. 389–570. 2d ed. Zurich, 1980 [1970].

Neveux, J. B. *Vie spirituelle et vie sociale entre Rhin et Baltique au XVIIᵉ siècle de J. Arndt à P. J. Spener*. Publications de la Faculté des Lettres et Sciences Humaines de Paris-Nanterre. Paris, 1967.

Nischan, Bodo. *Prince, People, and Confession: The Second Reformation in Brandenburg*. Philadelphia, 1994.

Oberman, Heiko A. "*Europa afflicta*. The Reformation of the Refugees." *ARG* 83 (1992): pp. 91–111.

O'Malley, John W., S.J. *The Early Jesuits*. Cambridge, Mass., 1993.

Ortner, Franz. *Reformation, katholische Reform und Gegenreformation im Erzstift Salzburg*. Salzburg, 1981.

Parker, Geoffrey. *The Thirty Years' War*. London, 1987 [1984].

Patrouch, Joseph F. "The Investiture Controversy Revisited: Religious Reform, Emperor Maximilian II, and the Klosterrat." *Austrian History Yearbook* 25 (1994): pp. 59–78.

Press, Volker. *Calvinismus und Territorialstaat. Regierung und Zentralbehörden der Kurpfalz 1559–1619*. Kieler Historische Studien, vol. 7. Stuttgart, 1970.

——. *Kriege und Krisen. Deutschland 1600–1715*. Die Neue Deutsche Geschichte, vol. 5. Munich, 1991.

Rabe, Horst. "Der Augsburger Religionsfriede und das Reichskammergericht 1555–1600." In *Festschrift für Ernst Walter Zeeden*, ed. Hansgeorg Molitor, Horst Rabe, and Hans-Christoph Rublack, pp. 260–80. Reformationsgeschichte Studien und Texte, suppl. vol. 2. Münster in Westfalen, 1976.

——. *Deutsche Geschichte 1500–1600. Das Jahrhundert der Glaubensspaltung*. Munich, 1991.

——. *Reichsbund und Interim: Die Verfassungs- und Religionspolitik Karls V. und der Reichstag von Augsburg 1547/48*. Cologne and Vienna, 1971.

Reingrabner, Gustav. *Adel und Reformation. Beiträge zur Geschichte des protestantischen Adels im Lande unter der Enns während des 16. und 17. Jahrhunderts*. Forschungen zur Landeskunde von Niederösterreich, vol. 21. Vienna, 1976.

Reinhard, Wolfgang. "Katholische Reform und Gegenreformation in der Kölner Nuntiatur 1584–1641." *Römische Quartalschrift* 66 (1971): pp. 8–65.

——. "Reformation, Counter-Reformation and the Early Modern State: A Reassessment." *CHR* 75 (1989): pp. 383–404.

——. "Zwang zur Konfessionalisierung? Prolegomena zu either Theorie des konfessionellen Zeitalters." *ZHF* 10 (1983): pp. 257–77.

Reinhard, Wolfgang and Heinz Schilling, eds. *Die katholische Konfessionalisierung. Akten eines vom Corpus Catholicorum und Verein für Reformationsgeschichte veranstalteten Symposions, Augsburg, 1993*. Gütersloh, 1994.

Robisheaux, Thomas. *Rural Society and the Search for Order in Early Modern Germany*. Cambridge, 1989.

Roeck, Bernd. *Als wollt die Welt schier brechen. Eine Stadt im Zeitalter des Dreißigjährigen Krieges*. Munich, 1991.

Roper, Lyndal. *The Holy Household: Women and Morals in Reformation Augsburg*. Oxford, 1989.

Rublack, Hans-Christoph, ed. *Die lutherische Konfessionalisierung in Deutschland. Wissenschaftliches Symposium des Vereins für Reformationsgeschichte*. SVRG, no. 197. Gütersloh, 1992.

———. *Gescheiterte Reformation. Frühreformatorische und protestantische Bewegungen in süd- und westdeutschen geistlichen Residenzen.* Spätmittelalter und Frühe Neuzeit. Tübinger Beiträge zur Geschichtsforschung, vol. 4. Stuttgart, 1978.

Safley, Thomas Max. *Let No Man Put Asunder: the Control of Marriage in the German Southwest. A Comparative Study, 1550–1600.* Kirksville, Mo., 1984.

Schilling, Heinz. *Aufbruch und Krise. Deutschland 1517–1648.* Berlin, 1988a.

———. "The European Crisis of the 1590s: the Situation in German Towns." In *The European Crisis of the 1590s*, ed. Peter Clark, pp. 135–56. London, 1985.

———. "Die Konfessionalisierung im Reich. Religiöser und gesellschaftlicher Wandel in Deutschland zwischen 1555 und 1620." *HZ* 146 (1988b): pp. 1–45.

———, ed. *Die reformierte Konfessionalisierung in Deutschland—Das Problem der "Zweiten Reformation." Wissenschaftliches Symposion des Vereins für Reformationsgeschichte 1985.* SVRG, vol. 195. Gütersloh, 1986.

———. *Religion, Political Culture and the Emergence of Early Modern Society. Essays in German and Dutch History.* SMRT, vol. 50. Leiden, 1992.

Schindling, Anton. "Die Reformation in den Reichsstädten und die Kirchengüter. Straßburg, Nürnberg und Frankfurt im Vergleich." In *Bürgerschaft und Kirche*, ed. Jürgen Sydow, pp. 67–88. Stadt in der Geschichte, vol. 7. Sigmaringen, 1980.

———. "Reichskirche und Reformation. Zu Glaubensspaltung und Konfessionalisierung in den geistlichen Fürstentümern des Reiches." In *Neue Studien zur frühneuzeitlichen Reichsgeschichte*, ed. Johannes Kunisch, pp. 81–112. Zeitschrift für Historische Forschungen, suppl. vol. 3. Berlin, 1987.

Schindling, Anton, and Walter Ziegler, eds. *Die Territorien des Reichs im Zeitalter der Reformation und Konfessionalisierung. Land und Konfession 1500–1650.* 4 vols. Katholisches Leben und Kirchenreform im Zeitalter der Glaubensspaltung, vols. 49–52. Münster i.W., 1989–93.

Schmidt, Georg, ed. *Stände und Gesellschaft im Alten Reich.* VIEG, Abteilung Universalgeschichte, Beiheft 29. Stuttgart, 1989.

Schmidt, Peter. *Das Collegium Germanicum in Rom und die Germaniker.* Tübingen, 1984.

Schormann, Gerhard. *Der Dreißigjährige Krieg.* Göttingen, 1985.

Schulze, Manfred. *Fürsten und Reformation. Geistliche Reformpolitik weltlicher Fürsten vor der Reformation.* Spätmittelalter und Reformation, n.s., vol. 2. Tübingen, 1991.

Schulze, Winfried. "Concordia, Discordia, Tolerantia. Deutsche Politik im konfessionellen Zeitalter." In *Neue Studien zur frühneuzeitlichen Reichsgeschichte*, ed. Johannes Kunisch, pp. 43–79. Zeitschrift für Historische Forschungen, suppl. vol. 3. Berlin, 1987.

———. *Reich und Türkengefahr im späten 16. Jahrhundert. Studien zu den politischen und gesellschaftlichen Auswirkungen einer äußeren Bedrohung.* Munich, 1978.

Scribner, Robert W. *For the Sake of Simple Folk: Popular Propaganda for the German Reformation.* Cambridge, 1981.

———. *Popular Culture and Popular Movements in Reformation Germany.* London, 1987.

Seibrich, Wolfgang. *Gegenreformation als Restauration. Die restaurativen Bemühungen der alten Orden im Deutschen Reich von 1580 bis 1648.* Münster, 1991.

Soergel, Philip M. *Wondrous in His Saints: Counter-Reformation Propaganda in Bavaria.* Berkeley and Los Angeles, 1993.

Stadler, Peter. "Das Zeitalter der Gegenreformation." In *Handbuch der Schweizer Geschichte*, 2d ed., vol. 1: pp. 571–672. Zurich, 1980.

Strauss, Gerald. *Luther's House of Learning: Indoctrination of the Young in the German Reformation.* Baltimore, 1978.

Theibault, John. "The Rhetoric of Death and Destruction in the Thirty Years War." *Journal of Social History* 27 (1994): pp. 271–90.

Traitler, Hildegard. *Konfession und Politik. Interkonfessionalle Flugschriftenpolemik aus Süddeutschland und Österreich (1564–1612).* European University Studies, series 3, vol. 400. Frankfurt am Main, Bern, New York, and Paris, 1989.

Vocelka, Karl. *Die politische Propaganda Kaiser Rudolfs II. (1576–1612)*. Veröffentlichungen der Kommission für die Geschichte Österreichs, 9. Vienna, 1981.

Warmbrunn, Paul. *Zwei Konfessionen in einer Stadt. Das Zusammenleben von Katholiken und Protestanten in den paritätischen Reichsstädten Augsburg, Biberach, Ravensburg und Dinkelsbühl 1548–1648*. Wiesbaden, 1983.

Wirsching, Andreas. "Konfessionalisierung und Außenpolitik. Die Kurpfalz und der Beginn der französischen Religionskriege (1559–1562)." *HJ* 106 (1986): pp. 333–60.

Zeeden, Ernst Walter. *Die Entstehung der Konfessionen. Grundlagen und Formen der Konfessionsbildung im Zeitalter der Glaubenskämpfe*. Munich, 1965.

———. "Grundlagen und Wege der Konfessionsbildung in Deutschland im Zeitalter der Glaubenskämpfe." *HZ* 185 (1958): pp. 249–99.

———. *Konfessionsbildung. Studien zur Reformation, Gegenreformation und katholischen Reform*. Stuttgart, 1985.

Zschunke, Paul. *Konfession und Alltag im Oppenheim. Beiträge zur Geschichte von Bevölkerung und Gesellschaft einer gemischtkonfessionellen Kleinstadt in der frühen Neuzeit*. Wiesbaden, 1984.

CHAPTER FIFTEEN

SOME PECULIARITIES OF GERMAN HISTORIES IN THE EARLY MODERN ERA

Summary

Professor Brady, an expert on the historiography as well as the history of the Holy Roman Empire, looks again at the idea of Germany's *Sonderweg*, both its positive versions among the followers of Leopold von Ranke and some negative ones after World War Two. Noting that the Holy Roman Empire, in view of its long survival, cannot have been as weak as is alleged, he examines "three dominant characteristics of the Holy Roman Empire during the early modern era: first, the traditional, non-national character of the imperial monarchy; second, the prominence of small states; and third the active participation in public life by the church in the guise of the three confessions. . . ." Brady shows how these features already set Germany apart from the nations to its west, as, one after another, they diverged from the late medieval European pattern into "centralized governance, commercialized warfare, and seaborne empire." With frequent reference to the work of Peter Blickle, Brady points to the rural communes of the Rhine and Danube basins. Here ideas of liberty and quality persisted among peasants and villagers and provided a model that was feared by some and emulated by others, even beyond the region. Such popular communalism included control of religion. The people adhered tenaciously to their own variety of Christianity and resisted confessionalization. Thus, Brady concludes, only after 1800 did Germany really begin its *Sonderweg*—toward, not away from, the West.

And without the vehemence of passion history was only chronicle.

Gerald Strauss[1]

I

The bewildering political map of central Europe before 1800 displays "the contrast between posture and power" in the old Holy Roman

---

[1] Gerald Strauss, *Historian in an Age of Crisis: The Life and Work of Johannes Aventinus, 1477–1534* (Cambridge: Harvard University Press, 1963), p. 247.

Empire.[2] Strewn across it are purple blotches for ecclesiastical territories and bright red pimples for the free cities; and the explorer
who digs behind the big, showy pieces—Prussia, Austria, Bavaria,
and Saxony—finds curious things: Imperial free abbesses and prince-
provosts, heads of military-religious orders and free knights, and free
peasants, notably the thirty-nine free villages and hamlets on the
Leutkirch Heath in Upper Swabia, whose folk until 1806 appointed
their sheriffs and judges and owned no lord but the emperor. No wonder later writers wrote the empire's epitaph with a sense of wonder-
ing incomprehension.[3] Lord Bryce spoke in 1866 for the majority:

> So, too, is the Holy Empire above all description or explanation; not
> that it is impossible to discover the beliefs which created and sustained
> it, but that the power of those beliefs cannot be adequately appre-
> hended by men whose minds have been differently trained, and whose
> imaginations are fired by different ideals.... Something more suc-
> ceeding generations will know, who will judge the Middle Ages more
> fairly than we, still living in the midst of a reaction against all that is
> mediaeval, can hope to do, and to whom it will be given to see and
> understand new forms of political life, whose nature we cannot so
> much as conjecture.[4]

Long reflection on our incomprehension still whets one's sympathy
for the perennial attempts to plot a straight line from some point in
the Germanys' pasts to Germany's present in 1871, 1914, 1933,
1945, or even 1990. Every line so drawn pays tribute to the idea of
a German special path or *Sonderweg*, a course on which the Germans
diverged from the patterns of the European "West," whether the
latter be understood as "Western civilization," "modern Europe,"
"modernity," "the modern world," "democracy," "freedom," "the
free market," "civilization," or even—more candidly—England, perhaps flanked by France and the Low Countries.[5]

Though the negative form of the idea of *Sonderweg* took shape during the Great War as an inversion of one of the "ideas of 1914,"[6]

---

[2] *Idem*, "The Holy Roman Empire Revisited," *Central European History* 11 (1978):
pp. 290–301, here at p. 291.
[3] *Ibid.*, pp. 290–91.
[4] James Bryce, *The Holy Roman Empire*, rev. ed. (New York: Clarke, Given and
Hooper, n.d.), p. 388.
[5] I comment on this point in "The Rise of Merchant Empires, 1400–1700: A
European Counterpoint," in *The Economics of Merchant Empires*, ed. James D. Tracy
(Cambridge and New York: Cambridge University Press, 1991).
[6] See Klaus Schwabe, "Zur politischen Haltung der deutschen Professoren im

SOME PECULIARITIES OF GERMAN HISTORIES

an older, positive form "had been developed, with widely varying meanings, since the early nineteenth century as a by-product of the development of modern German national consciousness."[7] It was largely the work of the academic historians, those self-appointed guardians of the New Germany's political culture, who "rationalized German history of the eighteenth and nineteenth centuries as a meaningful historical process which culminated in 1871."[8] They helped to create "the ideology of the German way," a vision of "the special problematic of German history, which arose from the Germans' political life in a European context and included the specific political and cultural accomplishments of the Germans."[9]

The classic point of origin for "the German way" lay in Martin Luther and his reformation. "Within German historical scholarship," writes Jaroslav Pelikan, "the Reformation occupies a position analogous in some ways to that of the Civil War in American historiography, as the crucial and (in a quite literal sense of the term) epoch-making event by which the nature of an entire national community and of its history has been defined."[10] This idea reflects the character of academic history in the Second Empire as a Protestant discipline, scarcely disturbed by the marginalized dissents of Catholics, Social Democrats, and others.[11] Ranke's disciples, who gave the

Ersten Weltkrieg," *Historische Zeitschrift* 193 (1961): pp. 60–34; *idem, Wissenschaft und Kriegsmoral. Die deutschen Hochschullehrer und die politischen Grundfagen des Ersten Weltkrieges* (Göttingen: Vandenhoeck and Ruprecht, 1969).

[7] Bernd Faulenbach, *Ideologie des deutschen Weges. Die deutsche Geschichte in der Historiographie zwischen Kaiserreich und Nationalsozialismus* (Munich: C. H. Beck, 1980), p. 6.

[8] *Ibid.*, p. 7. This sense of the historians as political tutors to the nation is forcefully expressed by Gerhard Ritter's *Geschichte als Bildungsmacht. Ein Beitrag zur historisch-politischen Neubesinnung* (Stuttgart: Deutsche Verlags-Anstalt, 1947). See, for comparison, William H. McNeill, "Mythistory, or Truth, Myth, History, and Historians," and "The Care and Repair of Public Myth," in his *Mythistory and Other Essays* (Chicago: University of Chicago Press, 1986), pp. 3–22, 23–42.

[9] Faulenbach, *Ideologie des deutschen Weges*, p. 6.

[10] Jaroslav Pelikan, Leopold von Ranke as Historian of the Reformation: What Ranke Did for the Reformation—What the Reformation Did for Ranke," in *Leopold von Ranke and the Shaping of the Historical Discipline*, ed. Georg G. Iggers and James M. Powell (Syracuse: Syracuse University Press, 1990), pp. 89–98, here at p. 90. On the role of the Reformation in the idea of "the German way," see Faulenbach, *Ideologie*, pp. 125–31.

[11] For the social basis, see Wolfgang Weber, *Priester der Klio. Historisch-sozialwissenschaftliche Studien zur Herkunft und Karriere deutscher Historiker und zur Geschichte der Geschichtswissenschaft 1810–1970*, Europäische Hochschulschriften, ser. 3, no. 216 (Frankfurt, Bern, and New York: Peter Lang, 1984), pp. 208–9. See my comments in "From the Sacral Community to the Common Man: Reflections on German Reformation Studies," *Central European History* 20 (1987): pp. 229–45, here at pp. 235–39.

tone, echoed "the Master's" dictum, that "[in the Reformation era]
for the first time the German spirit assumed a general form without regard to a foreign model."[12] They treasured and guarded
his identification of "the German nation, or at least its 'productive,'
future-oriented sections, with Protestantism," and they tended "to
summarize the whole of German history under the heading 'From
Luther to Bismarck.'"[13]

The positive form of this idea of *Sonderweg* was a casualty of the
era from 1918 to 1945, though in the opinions of some, notably
Gerhard Ritter, it lived far into the postwar age.[14] Its negative form
proved more durable. Geoffrey Barraclough's influential *Origins of
Modern Germany* pronounced that "generations of strife" and "the religious changes" of the Reformation era "brought about . . . a further
rise in the power of the princes, which ushered in the period of
princely absolutism."[15] A. J. P. Taylor added with customary certainty
that "the moment for making a national middle-class Germany was
lost in 1521 perhaps forever, certainly for centuries."[16] And the Leipzig
historian Max Steinmetz wrote that the Reformation era witnessed
the failure of "the first attempt of the popular masses to create a
unified national state from below."[17] These quotes testify to the power
of the old idea of the *Sonderweg* as sixteenth-century Germany's path
away from "the West."

Nowadays, after a long generation of several Germanys, boundaries are once again coming into flux. It is a time for reflection on

---

[12] Quoted by Faulenbach, *Ideologie*, p. 125.
[13] Wolfgang J. Mommsen, "Ranke and the Neo-Rankean School," in *Leopold von
Ranke and the Shaping of the Historical Discipline*, pp. 136–37. See Karl Kupisch, *Durch
den Zaun der Geschichte. Beobachtungen und Erkenntnisse* (Berlin: Lettner-Verlag, 1964),
pp. 337–41.
[14] See Gerhard Ritter, *Europa und die deutsche Frage. Betrachtungen über die geschichtliche
Eigenart des deutschen Staatsdenkens* (Munich: Münchner Verlag, 1948), esp. pp. 7–150;
in English: *The German Problem: Basic Questions of German Political Life, Past and Present*,
trans. Sigurd Burckhardt (Columbus: Ohio State University Press, 1965), pp. 9–150.
On Ritter's place in this tradition, see Faulenbach, *Ideologie*, *passim*; and on the role
of Luther and the Reformation in Ritter's thought, see Klaus Schwabe, "Zur
Einführung: Gerhard Ritter Werk und Person," in *Gerhard Ritter. Ein politischer Historiker
in seinen Briefen*, ed. K. Schwabe and Rolf Reichardt, Schriften des Bundesarchivs,
33 (Boppard am Rhein: Harald Boldt, 1984), pp. 22–31.
[15] Geoffrey Barraclough, *The Origins of Modern Germany*, 2nd rev. ed. (Oxford: Basil
Blackwell, 1947), p. 373.
[16] Quoted by Thomas A. Brady, Jr., "The Common Man and the Lost Austria
in the West: A Contribution to the German Problem," in *Politics and Society in
Reformation Europe: Essays for Sir Geoffrey Elton on his 65th Birthday*, ed. E. I. Kouri and
Tom Scott (London: Macmillan, 1987), pp. 142–43.
[17] Quoted by Brady, *ibid.*, p. 143.

inherited truths, even apparently discarded ones. Recent literature on the Reformation and early modern eras sheds much light on the old thesis of the German *Sonderweg* since the sixteenth century. It undermines in particular the residual credibility of the belief that in the Reformation era the German-speaking world embarked on a path of authoritarian political development, which led it away from the path taken by the peoples of western Europe and thus from the common European heritage.

II

Two recent developments cast bold new light on the histories of German-speaking peoples in the early modern era: a new picture of their world as a whole, and the discovery of the movement for popularly based, decentralized governance at the end of the Middle Ages. The traditional picture of the Holy Roman Empire during the early modern era offered merely a series of stepping stones from the politically supine late medieval empire to the wars of liberation against Napoleon. The stones, Heinz Schilling recently noted, were named "Peasants' War," "Luther and the Reformation," "Thirty Years' War," and "Frederick II and Prussia."[18] Thirty years of research in the presence of multiple German states have changed this picture entirely by thrusting into the foreground three dominant characteristics of the Holy Roman Empire during the early modern era: first, the traditional, non-national character of the imperial monarchy; second, the prominence of small states; and third, the active participation in public life by the church in the guise of the three confessions, Catholic, Lutheran, and Reformed or Calvinist.[19]

Though not free of occasional whiffs of conservative nostalgia, the effort to rehabilitate the empire as a successful political structure has gone a long way toward forcing us to a new appreciation of its durability and relative workability. If we begin with its revitalization during the reigns of the emperors Maximilian I (r. 1493–1519) and

---

[18] Heinz Schilling, *Aufbruch und Krise: Deutschland 1517–1648, Das Reich und die Deutschen* (Berlin: Siedler, 1988), p. 9.

[19] H. Schilling, "Vom Aschenbrödel zum Märchenprinzen—Geschichtswissenschaft und historisch-politische Kultur in Deutschland," in *Wes Geistes Wissenschaften? Zur Stellung der Geisteswissenschaften in Universität und Gesellschaft, Vortragsreihe der Justus-Liebig-Universität Gießen im Wintersemester 1988/89*, ed. H. Schilling and Conrad Wiedemann (Gießen: Verlag der Ferber'schen Universitätsbuchhandlung, 1989), pp. 35–49, here at p. 42.

Charles V (r. 1519–1556), the empire's three-hundred-year life does not rank it among the most ephemeral of European states and state-like formations. Much evidence has accumulated, too, to show that its judicial, law-keeping, fiscal, and military structures were tolerably effective, provided one accepts their differences from comparable organs of the centralized national monarchies of western Europe. In Gerald Strauss's memorable words, "Though clearly an awkward colossus with a baroque façade and a labyrinthine structure, the Holy Roman Empire no longer strikes us as quite the sideshow monstrosity depicted in the older historiography."[20] Assiduous scholars have documented the workings of imperial institutions, such as the High Court (*Reichskammergericht*) and the regional bodies (*Kreise*), which "performed concretely and effectively what the empire as a whole stood for but could not do: the preservation of fragmented sovereignty, of the privileges of the weak as well as the strong, and of the complex and shifting political relationships on which the feudal order in Germany rested."[21]

The durability of the Holy Roman Empire is closely linked to the second characteristic, the prominence of small states. We may begin with the conventional comparison, which holds, with justice, that the state building process occurred in the German-speaking world on a "territorial" level rather than a "national" one. What does this mean? Once upon a time, it meant that, unlike the Portuguese, Spanish, French, and English, the German nation evolved no centralized state adequate to its needs. This meaning, however, loses all force in the face of our recognition that nations as we know them are more or

---

[20] Strauss, "The Holy Roman Empire Revisited," p. 301. For orientation to the literature, see Volker Press, "The Holy Roman Empire in German History," in *Politics and Society in Reformation Europe*, pp. 51–77; Georg Christoph von Unruh, "Die Wirksamkeit von Kaiser und Reich," in *Deutsche Verwaltungsgeschichte*, ed. K. G. A. Jeserich, H. Pohl, and Georg Christoph von Unruh, vol. 1: Vom Spätmittelalter bis zum Ende des Reiches (Stuttgart: Deutsche Verlags-Anstalt, 1983), pp. 270–78.

[21] Strauss, "Holy Roman Empire Revisited," pp. 296–97. On the *Reichskammergericht*, see V. Press, *Das Reichskammergericht in der deutschen Geschichte*, Schriftenreihe der Gesellschaft für Reichskammergerichtsforschung, no. 3 (Wetzlar: Gesellschaft für Reichskammergerichtsforschung, 1987). On the *Kreise*, see James Allen Vann, *The Swabian Kreis: Institutional Growth in the Holy Roman Empire, 1648–1715*, Studies Presented to the International Commission for the History of Representative and Parliamentary Institutions, vol. 53 (Brussels: Éditions de la librairie encyclopédique, 1974); Helmut Neuhaus, *Reichsständische Repräsentationsformen im 16. Jahrhundert. Reichstag—Reichskreistag—Reichsdeputationstag*, Schriften zur Verfassungsgeschichte 33 (Berlin: Duncker and Humbolt, 1982).

less creations of the states, rather than vice versa. "Nations," writes Ernest Gellner, "can be defined only in terms of the age of nationalism," which is "essentially, the general imposition of a high culture on society [and the] generalized diffusion of a school-mediated, academy-supervised idiom, codified for the requirements of reasonably precise bureaucratic and technological requirements."[22]

Sixteenth-century Europe did witness the emergence of a new type of state, but it had less to do with national community than with three interlinked characteristics: centralization, militarization, and empire.[23] The "national" kingdoms of Europe's western tier were all conquest states, built and rebuilt through the subjugation of some peoples by others. "The new monarchy," V. G. Kiernan writes, "bore an essentially warlike character that it was never to lose. War for it was not an optional policy, but an organic need, . . . [and] the whole state apparatus that rulers were putting together piecemeal was largely a by-product of war."[24] Political consolidation began with conquest and ended with "an exchange of resources, including plunder, to merchants in return for goods and credit."[25] War and trade were complementary ways of gaining control of what had belonged to others, and their marriage was consummated in the military revolution, in which innovations in management, organization, and weaponry spread like wildfire across sixteenth-century Europe.[26]

---

[22] Ernest Gellner, *Nations and Nationalism* (Ithaca, London: Cornell University Press, 1983), pp. 55, 57. See Bernard Guénée, *States and Rulers in Later Medieval Europe*, trans. Juliet Vale (Oxford: Basil Blackwell, 1985), pp. 49–65. See also John A. Hall, *Powers and Liberties: The Causes and Consequences of the Rise of the West* (Berkeley: University of California Press, 1985), pp. 217–23, who argues that nations in the modern sense are the agendas of nation building, which result from the state's drive for development.

[23] This paragraph recapitulates my argument in "The Rise of Merchant Empires, 1400–1700," in which the notes provide access to the literature.

[24] V. G. Kiernan, "State and Nation in Western Europe," *Past and Present* 31 (July 1965): pp. 20–38, here at p. 31.

[25] Eric R. Wolf, *Europe and the People without History* (Berkeley: University of California Press, 1982), p. 105. As Charles Tilly so pungently puts it, "War making and state making—quintessential protection rackets with the advantage of legitimacy—qualify as our largest examples of organized came." Charles Tilly, "War Making and State Making as Organized Crime," in *Bringing the State Back In*, eds. Peter B. Evans, Dietrich Rueschemeyer, and Theda Skocpol (Cambridge: Cambridge University Press, 1985), pp. 169–91, here at p. 169.

[26] See the masterful synthesis by Geoffrey Parker, *The Military Revolution: Military Innovation and the Rise of the West, 1500–1800* (Cambridge: Cambridge University Press, 1988); also William H. McNeill, *The Pursuit of Power: Technology, Armed Force, and Society since A.D., 1000* (Chicago: University of Chicago Press, 1982), pp. 79–81.

Charles Tilly has characterized this process with the pungent comment that "war making and state making—quintessential protection rackets with the advantage of legitimacy—qualify as our largest examples of organized crime."[27] Although some of the military innovations behind it sprang to life in the German-speaking world—one thinks of Swiss infantry and of the German *lansquenets* and *Reiter*—their political consequences made very slow headway in the empire. This was so partly, perhaps, because during the two centuries between the Hussite Wars (1420–1433) and the Thirty Years' War (1618–1648), the empire's German-speaking heartlands enjoyed relative respite from major wars, and partly because the major German-speaking military power, Austria, was for long engaged in wars of a quite un-European type.[28] By the eighteenth century, of course, one German-speaking power, Prussia, had managed to become large enough, ambitious enough, and predatory enough to imitate the western monarchies, but its poverty, unnourished by seaborne empire, forced Prussia to super-militarize itself into a social caricature of them.[29] Eighteenth-century Prussia thus became the first part of the German-speaking world to try to remake itself in the image of the West.

The other, smaller German states hardly tried to keep pace. T. C. W. Blanning's study of eighteenth-century Mainz reveals how the hopelessly "backward" ecclesiastical principalities, of which the empire contained dozens, illustrate "the astonishing ability of the political and social establishment in Germany to absorb, adapt and even utilize progressive and potentially disruptive forces."[30] All in all, it is at least likely that, with the exception of Prussia and perhaps the Austrian borderlands, the inhabitants of the empire, especially in its southern regions, retained far more local control of their institutions and bore less crushing burdens of taxation for military and imperial purposes than did the subjects of the western European monarchs. For this order, which in most respects preserved what had been built during the later Middle Ages, they paid a double price.

---

[27] Tilly, "War Making and State Making," p. 169.

[28] I have made this point in "Imperial Destinies: A New Study of the Emperor Maximilian I," *Journal of Modern History* 63 (1991): forthcoming; and see Parker, *Military Revolution*, pp. 35–38.

[29] This argument about imitation owes not a little to Perry Anderson, *Lineages of the Absolutist State* (London: NLB, 1974), pp. 195–278.

[30] T. C. W. Blanning, *Reform and Revolution in Mainz, 1743–1803*, Cambridge Studies in Early Modern History (Cambridge: Cambridge University Press, 1974), p. 3, quoted by Strauss, "Holy Roman Empire Revisited," p. 299.

First, the decentralized polity left the empire susceptible to civil war (in the seventeenth century) and invasion (in the eighteenth). Secondly, from one of medieval Christendom's heartlands the German-speaking world became a part of the less developed semiperiphery as the centralized monarchies of the West promoted development through their competitions for empire.

The third major characteristic of early modern Germany flowed from the Reformation. Across the length and breadth of the empire there arose after 1555 "more or less stable church structures with their own doctrine, constitutions, and religious and moral styles," the formation of which proceeded in close cooperation with the territorial states.[31] They are called "confessions," and their uncovering and mapping have become a major theme of the historiography of post-Reformation Germany.[32] Beginning with Ernst Walter Zeeden, historians have laid bare the development of a firm sense of collective religious identity in the two generations between the Peace of Augsburg (1555) and the onset of the Thirty Years' War (1618) and in the two generations between the war's end and the early eighteenth century.[33] These four generations, not the Reformation generation, created the confessional map of the German-speaking world and linked the structure, welfare, and work of the churches more closely to the power of the states than had ever before been the case. Confessionalization is thus to be seen as the specially German form of Christian reform in the Reformation and Counter-Reformation, and as a modernizing force, as in concert with the state the churches promoted rationalization bureaucracy, social discipline, individualism, and a sense of supraethnic community.[34]

A traditional monarchy, small states, and widespread confessional networks—these three characteristics reveal how organically the Holy

---

[31] Robert Bireley, S.J., "Early Modern Germany," in *Catholicism in Early Modern History. A Guide to Research*, ed. John W. O'Malley, S.J., Reformation Guides to Research 2 (St. Louis: Center for Reformation Research, 1988), pp. 11–30, here at pp. 11–12, quoting Ernst Walter Zeeden.

[32] For orientation to the literature, see Bireley, "Early Modern Germany," pp. 25–29.

[33] Ernst Walter Zeeden, *et al.*, eds., *Repertorium der Kirchenvisitationsakten aus dem 16. und 17. Jahrhundert in Archiven der Bundesrepublik Deutschland*, vol. 1: *Hessen* (Stuttgart: Klett-Cotta, 1982), p. 16 (introduction).

[34] Bireley, "Early Modern Germany," p. 12, citing the work of Jean Delumeau. See in general Wolfgang Reinhard, "Gegenreformation als Modernisierung? Prolegomena zu einer Theorie des konfessionellen Zeitalters," *Archiv für Reformationsgeschichte* 68 (1977): pp. 226–51; idem, "Zwang zur Konfessionalisierung?" *Zeitschrift für historische Forschung* 10 (1983): pp. 257–77.

Roman Empire of the early modern era prolonged and filled out the
structures of late medieval Germany, namely, the weak royal power,
the emergence of territorial states, and the interpenetrating of lay and
clerical institutions and forms of authority. In the light of these features, and measured against the characteristics of Europe around, say,
1350, in the eighteenth century the Germanys were the most European lands in transalpine Europe. They had adhered more or less
to a common pattern from which the countries of Europe's western
tiers, one after the other, had diverged into the enterprise of centralized governance, commercialized warfare, and seaborne empire.

III

Nowhere in the German-speaking world did the old ways and old
patterns endure longer or with greater tenacity than in the old imperial heartlands in the Rhine and Danube basins. Nowhere did
people counter more stoutly the "western" political strategy—concentration and state building—with their own strategy of dispersion
and parliament and commune formation.[35] The development of
communes, which allowed the ideals of liberty and equality to take
root in the structures of local life, preceded by several centuries the
struggle for succession to feudal governance between the partisans of
concentration and those of dispersion. The German-speaking South,
especially between the central highlands and the Alps, fostered and
fixed decentralized forms of governance with special effectiveness
and longevity.

Peter Blickle has usefully defined communalism as the movement
which, between about 1250 and about 1500, transferred local governance from feudal magnates to corporations of townsmen and villagers.[36] Urban communes are a well-understood force in European

---

[35] Gerald Strauss, *Law, Resistance, and the State: The Opposition to Roman Law in
Reformation Germany* (Princeton: Princeton University Press, 1986), p. 96.
[36] Peter Blickle, *Deutsche Untertanen. Ein Widerspruch* (Munich: C. H. Beck, 1981),
pp. 51–54; *idem*, "Der Kommunalismus als Gestaltungsprinzip zwischen Mittelalter
und Moderne," in *Gesellschaft und Gesellschaften. Fetschrift zum 65. Geburtstag von Ulrich
Imhof*, eds. Nicolai Bernard and Quirinus Reichen (Bern: Wyss, 1982), pp. 95–113;
idem, "Communal Reformation and Peasant Piety: The Peasant Reformation and
Its Late Medieval Origins," *Central European History* 20 (1987): pp. 216–28, here at
pp. 221–23. For an overview of Blickle's ideas, see Brady, "From the Sacral Community," pp. 242–44. See also Heide Wunder, *Die bäuerliche Gemeinde in Deutschland*
(Göttingen: Vandenhoeck and Ruprecht, 1986).

history, but rural communes, though they also appeared in many parts of Europe—including France and England[37]—came to play a lasting role in local, sometimes even in regional, governance only in certain parts of the Holy Roman Empire, namely, the German South, or roughly the upper basins of the Rhine, the Rhone, and the Danube, which also formed a zone of intense and lasting communal formation in the towns.[38] Here, by contrast with Italy, the communal ethos did not give way to signorial experiments or atrophy into a deadened oligarchical order.[39] What is far more startling, however, than the vitality of urban communes is the rise of rural ones. Though not unknown in other European lands, rural communes developed most lavishly and freely in the Alpine uplands, where the weak fabrics of royal and feudal authority allowed the countryside to awaken from the long sleep of history without motion.[40] The communes acquired political aspirations, they sometimes gained voice in territorial parliaments, and in a few favored places they formed independent rural republics. Where else did rural folk ever claim, as the people of the Valais did in 1619, "to be a free people, as in a free republic"?[41]

---

[37] This subject needs to be disentangled from the notorious statism and individualism of the French and English literatures respectively. I have commented on the literature's treatment of French rural communes in "The Rise of Merchant Empires, 1400–1700," at n. 86. On English rural communes, see Clifford S. L. Davies, "Die bäuerliche Gemeinde in England (1400–1800)," trans. Helmut Gabel, in *Aufstände, Revolten, Prozesse. Beiträge zu Bäuerlichen Widerstandsbewegungen im frühneuzeitlichen Europa,* ed. Winfried Schulze, Geschichte und Gesellschaft. Bochumer Historische Studien 27 (Stuttgart: Klett-Cotta, 1983), pp. 41–59, here at pp. 52–55; Margaret Spufford, *Contrasting Communities: English Villages in the Sixteenth and Seventeenth Centuries* (Cambridge: Cambridge University Press, 1974).

[38] On communalism in general, see Antony Black, *Guilds and Civil Society in European Political Thought from the Twelfth Century to the Present* (Ithaca: Cornell University Press, 1984). On the geography of German-speaking communalism, see Brady, *Turning Swiss: Cities and Empire, 1450–1550,* Cambridge Studies in Early Modern History (Cambridge, New York: Cambridge University Press, 1985), pp. 5–6, 9–11, 28–30; Peter Blickle, "Kommunalismus und Republikanismus in Oberdeutschland," in *Republiken und Republikanismus im Europa der frühen Neuzeit,* ed. Helmut G. Koenigsberger and Elisabeth Müller-Luckner, Schriften des Historischen Kollegs. Kolloquien 11 (Munich: R. Oldenbourg, 1988), pp. 57–75, here at p. 74.

[39] H. Schilling, "Gab es im späten Mittelalter und zu Beginn der Neuzeit in Deutschland einen städtischen 'Republikanismus'? Zur politischen Kultur des alteuropäischen Stadtbürgertums," in *Republiken und Republikanismus,* pp. 101–43, here at pp. 115–16.

[40] I allude to Emmanuel Le Roy Ladurie, "History that Stands Still," in E. Le Roy Ladurie, *The Territory of the Historian,* trans. Ben Reynolds and Sian Reynolds (Chicago: University of Chicago Press, 1979), pp. 1–27.

[41] Quoted by Blickle, "Kommunalismus und Republikanismus in Oberdeutschland," pp. 57–75, here at p. 57. Schilling, "Gab es ... einen städtischen 'Republikanismus'?"

Although the formation of communes in the German-speaking world dates back to the thirteenth century, it took on political significance in the fourteenth century and maintained it until the sixteenth.[42] The movement's most spectacular creation, the Swiss Confederacy, arose from the union in 1291 of what a later pamphleteer called "the poor little bunch of peasants, . . . the Swiss."[43] During the next two hundred years, the confederacy underwent a political and military expansion that made it the only rural-urban federation in European history. It exerted considerable political influence on its neighbors, and it acquired the image of a nemesis of the South German feudality. Briefly, the confederates "gained world-historical significance" for "the Swiss way of war."[44]

The Swiss Confederacy also exerted a powerful demonstration effect on the rest of South German communalism.[45] Not only did the Swiss actively support the formation of "little Switzerlands" in neighboring lands, such as the Swabian Allgäu, Vorarlberg, the Graubünden, and the Valais, but they also provided the entire zone with a model of state construction from the bottom up. When the communal movement rose to its last peak in the first quarter of the sixteenth century, this model of governance worked powerfully in all the regions in which local communal authority was already well established.[46] One such region was the Tyrol, the subject in 1525 of a most imaginative popular constitution, the basis for which is illustrated by this report of 1421 from the Stubai Valley: "When a judge is to be appointed in the Stubai, the neighbors have the right to elect three of the neighbors and present them to the prince's sheriff; he then chooses a judge from among the three, whichever seems best."[47] So

---

p. 143, believes that Blickle's unification of urban and rural communes under the term "communalism" is too specially German, but that is also true of the phenomenon itself.

[42] Blickle, "Kommunalismus and Republikanismus in Oberdeutschland," p. 72.

[43] "An die Versammlung gemeiner Bauernschaft," in *Flugschriften der Bauernkriegszeit*, eds. Adolf Laube and Hans Werner Seiffert (Berlin: Akademie-Verlag, 1975), p. 133, l. 33.

[44] Hans Delbrück, *Geschichte der Kriegskunst im Rahmen der politischen Geschichte*, vol. 4: *Neuzeit* (Berlin, 1920; reprinted, 1962), p. 1.

[45] For details, see my *Turning Swiss*.

[46] Blickle, *The Revolution of 1525: The German Peasants' War from a New Perspective*, trans. Thomas A. Brady, Jr., and H. C. Erik Midelfort (Baltimore: Johns Hopkins University Press, 1981), pp. 171–80.

[47] Blickle, *Gemeindereformation. Die Menschen des 16. Jahrhunderts auf dem Weg zum Heil* (Munich: R. Oldenbourg, 1985), p. 175.

powerful did this demonstration effect become by 1520, that a Netherlandish councillor warned the Emperor Charles V that without a strong royal hand, "the whole German land would become one vast commune."[48]

The confederacy also symbolized communalism's menace to aristocratic power. By 1500 the identification of "Swiss" with "peasant" and "rebel" had become a cliché of South German political discourse, the content of which is revealed by a late fifteenth-century verse which warns the nobles that:

> The common man can't be beaten
> For the Swiss take no prisoners.
> Therefore, let's get out of here,
> For they are wild with anger
> And will murder and despoil
> The nobles on the spot.[49]

This same image inspired Emperor Maximilian in 1499 to call the Swiss "wicked, crude, contemptible peasants, who despise virtue, nobility, and moderation in favor of arrogance, treachery, and hate for the German nation."[50] When he discovered how deeply such vices had penetrated his own army, the emperor flung his glove to the ground and cried, "You can't fight Swiss with Swiss!"[51]

The word "Swiss" thus came to stand for "the common man," another contemporary term, which Blickle has defined as "the peasant, the miner, the resident of a territorial town; in the imperial cities he was the townsman ineligible for public office."[52] The name distinguished all such folk from those who by birth, wealth, prestige, power, or simple self-regard were wont to say to themselves, as Owen Glendower does in I Henry IV (III.1), "I am not in the roll of common men." The phrase, "the common man," included women and children only by vague association, though the Swiss tended to relative liberality in these matters. After the Battle of Marignano, for example, widows of the fallen were permitted to speak in the Landesgemeinde,

---

[48] Quoted in my *Turning Swiss*, p. 111.

[49] Rochus Freiherr von Liliencron, ed., *Die historischen Volkslieder der Deutschen*, 5 vols. (Leipzig, 1865–1896; reprint, Hildesheim: Georg Olms, 1966), 1: p. 433, no. 93, ll. 184–88. I take the translation from my *Turning Swiss*, p. 36.

[50] Hermann Wiesflecker, *Kaiser Maximilian I. Das Reich, Österreich und Europa an der Wende zur Neuzeit*, 5 vols. (Munich: R. Oldenbourg, 1971–1986), 2: p. 337, 5: p. 76.

[51] *Ibid.*, 2: p. 347.

[52] Blickle, *Revolution of 1525*, p. 124.

or assembly, of Schwyz; and in Uri, Unterwalden, and Zug the age of political majority was set at fourteen, instead of twenty-five or thirty, the usual age in urban communes.[53]

Lest we be tempted to place a political "Golden Age of the Common Man" in our textbooks alongside the ever-rising middle class, we should remember that the zone of real liberation from feudal lordship remained relatively small, mainly those uplands which, though poor, were also relatively open both to the outside world and to internal change.[54] What became reality in such regions remained merely an agenda among the lowland farmers, who lacked not the political will but the armed force. Machiavelli put the point with his usual terseness: "The Swiss are heavily armed and wholly free." ("Svizzeri sono armatissimi e liberissimi.")[55]

The time for political action proved rather brief, for the long late-medieval depression, which fed popular aspirations by raising the value of human labor, gave way to the sixteenth-century increase of people, prices, and state authority, which undermined the security, and hence the potential or actual political voice of working people in the South German towns, as well among the artisans and journeymen as among the working women;[56] it had the same effect on the land, as well in the nucleated villages of Franconia as in the dispersed settlements of Upper Austria.[57] All in all, during the sixteenth cen-

---

[53] Louis Carlen, *Die Landsgemeinde in der Schweiz. Schule der Demokratie* (Sigmaringen: Jan Thorbecke, 1976), pp. 12–13. In general, however, Lyndal Roper is correct in arguing that communal institutions remained closed to women's participation. See her study, "'The Common Man,' 'the Common Good,' 'Common Women': Gender and Meaning in the German Reformation Commune," *Social History* 12 (1987): pp. 1–22.

[54] Pier Paolo Viazzo, *Upland Communities: Environment, Population and Social Structure in the Alps since the Sixteenth Century*, Cambridge Studies in Population, Economy and Society in Past Time (Cambridge: Cambridge University Press, 1989), esp. pp. 154–73.

[55] *The Prince*, ch. 12, in Niccolò Machiavelli, *The Chief Works and Others*, trans. Allan Gilbert, 3 vols. (Durham: Duke University Press, 1958), 1: p. 48; Italian: *Il Principe e Discorsi sopra la prima deca di Tito Livio*, ed. Sergio Bertelli, 2nd ed. (Milan: Feltrinelli, 1968), p. 55. See Leonhard von Muralt, *Machiavellis Staatsgedanke* (Basel: Benno Schwabe and Co., 1945), p. 127, who cogently connects this sentence with the title of *Discorsi*, 1: p. 55: "Where there is equality a princedom cannot be established; where there is none, a republic cannot be established." *The Chief Works and Others*, 1: p. 306; Italian: *Il Principe et Discorsi*, p. 254.

[56] Jean-Pierre Kintz, *La société strasbourgeoise du milieu du XVIᵉ siècle á la fin de la Guerre de Trente Ans 1560–1650. Essai d'histoire démographique, économique et sociale* (Paris: Editions Ophrys, 1984); Knut Schulz, *Handwerksgesellen und Lohnarbeiter. Untersuchungen zur oberrheinischen und oberdeutschen Stadtgeschichte des 14. bis 17. Jahrhunderts* (Sigmaringen: Jan Thorbecke, 1985); Merry Wiesner, *Working Women in Renaissance Germany* (New Brunswick, N.J.: Rutgers University Press, 1986).

[57] Thomas Robisheaux, *Rural Society and the Search for Order in Early Modern Germany*

tury the common people became more vulnerable, more divided, more subject to manipulation and pacification, and more concentrated on survival than they earlier had been.[58] This new, harder time took the political steam from South German communalism.

Some historians, it is true, hold that objective economic conflicts of interest made impossible any cooperation between popular political aspirations in town and land.[59] The record nonetheless documents instances of such cooperation, especially in the great Peasants' War, when heavy action often found burghers standing by the peasant rebels. Here, for example, is an eyewitness account by Jacob Sturm of Strasbourg from the free city of Heilbronn in April 1525:

> The rebels moved to Heilbronn, where, after threats to cut down the vines and pressure from the common man, especially from the women, the honorable senate had to open the city to them on Easter Tuesday [April 18]. Today [April 22] their commander, Jörg Metzler of Ballenberg, came with many other captains into the city and moved into a special chamber in the city hall. They hold their deliberations there, having posted their own men at the gates, and do what they please.... The Heilbronners have to put up with all this.

Perhaps, but Sturm also reported how many Heilbronners joined the rebels:

> A placard has been posted ordering all citizens and journeymen who want to join the army to assemble at one of the gates. The senate had to let depart anyone who will.

Heilbronn's mayor stood weeping at the gate as his people streamed out to join the rebels.[60] The behavior of these and many other burghers in 1525 recalls to mind an old Saxon legal adage: "Only a wall separates burgher from peasant."

(Cambridge: Cambridge University Press, 1989); Hermann Rebel, *Peasant Classes: The Bureaucratization of Property and Family Relations under Early Habsburg Absolutism, 1511–1636* (Princeton: Princeton University Press, 1983).

[58] The general trend, of course, affected most of Europe. See Peter Kriedte, *Peasants, Landlords and Merchant Capitalists: Europe and the World Economy 1500–1800*, trans. V. R. Berghahn (Cambridge: Cambridge University Press, 1983), pp. 18–60.

[59] This is the position of Tom Scott, *Freiburg and the Breisgau: Town-Country Relations in the Age of Reformation and Peasants' War* (Oxford: Clarendon Press, 1986). His skepticism is shared by Schilling, "Gab es ... einen Republikanismus?" p. 143; *idem*, "Die deutsche Gemeindereformation. Ein oberdeutsch-zwinglianisches Ereignis vor der 'reformatorischen Wende' des Jahres 1525?" *Zeitschrift für historische Forschung* 14 (1987): pp. 325–32.

[60] Jacob Sturm to Strasbourg, Heilbronn, April 22, 1525, in *Politische Correspondenz der Stadt Straßburg im Zeitalter der Reformation*, eds. Hans Virck, *et al.*, 5 vols. (Strasbourg: J. H. Ed. Heitz; Heidelberg: Carl Winter, 1882–1933), 1: p. 196, no. 344.

Political cooperation between burghers and peasants reflected the many correspondences between urban and rural communal life.[61] The town had its wall, the village its fence; the town its council and mayor, the village its jurors and headmen; the town its law book, the village its regulations (*Weistümer*). Town and land also shared a political discourse based on "traditional guild and communal ideals of corporate friendship, brotherhood and love" and the unifying values of peace and the common good.[62] In the town halls and the village courts, men spoke of "law and order," "justice," "neighbors," "the common good," "the honor of God," "Christian brotherly love," and,' by the eve of the Reformation, the "godly law." This vocabulary served, on the one hand, the magistrates of Nuremberg, who introduced a law book of 1478 with the statement,

> As peace, concord, and due obedience of the whole community is protected, defended and promoted by an appropriate and fair administration of justice—therefore, to the praise of God and to the salutary and blessed increase of the common weal of this honorable city, as well as of the entire community, these statutes have been codified.[63]

It also served, on the other hand, rural communes such as that of Pfalzen in the Tyrol, which in 1417 opened a statute with these words:

> To all who may see, hear, or read this open document, we, the body of neighbors who reside in the village of Pfalzen, have established, constructed, and made with enthusiasm, unanimity, and sound judgment a union (*ain ainung*), in order to promote the honor, piety, and welfare of our descendents. We therefore establish, decree, and order that. . . .[64]

By the fifteenth century, the South German and Swiss rural commune had become a tiny but structurally and morally complete counterpart to its urban sister.

The South German-Swiss communal experience is striking, not because of communal formation itself, which occurred in many parts

---

[61] See Blickle, "Kommunalismus und Republikanismus in Oberdeutschland," p. 72; *idem, Gemeindereformation*, pp. 167–79.

[62] Black, *Guilds and Civil Society*, pp. 69–70. See Blickle, *Gemeindereformation*, pp. 196–204.

[63] Quoted by Hans-Christoph Rublack, "Political and Social Norms in Urban Communities in the Holy Roman Empire," in Peter Blickle, Winfried Schulze and Hans-Christoph Rublack, *Religion, Politics and Social Protest. Three Studies on Early Modern Germany*, ed. Kaspar von Greyerz (London: George Allen and Unwin, 1984), p. 26, the translation of which I have slightly revised.

[64] Blickle, *Gemeindereformation*, p. 173.

of Europe, but because in this zone communalism entered the realm of governance and, however briefly and incompletely, devolved political voice upon ordinary people. Not on all persons, of course, nor on the most ordinary, for the big folk—patricians and merchants in the towns, inheriting heads of prosperous households in the village— almost always set the tone of communal life. Yet, by European standards communalism created political voice for remarkably broad strata of the population.

Equally striking is peasant participation in the parliamentary governance of many small South German states, mainly in an arc across the Swiss Confederacy's northern boundaries, reaching from the Tyrol and Vorarlberg in the east to Baden and the prince-bishopric of Basel in the west.[65] Through their representation in these parliaments, and often through the courts as well, the rural communes defended their collective rights, sometimes with great success.[66] In the absence of centralized territorial states, individuals, too, could pursue justice very high into the empire's judicial hierarchy. There was, for example, the case of Linsers Hans, a peasant from around Wolfisheim near Strasbourg. Hans's trouble began in a Wolfisheim tavern one winter afternoon in 1524, when a dispute over a sale led to drawn knives and a stabbing. After convictions by a civil proceeding before the village court and by a criminal hearing before the seigneur, Linsers Hans appealed to the senate of Strasbourg and, failing to get his way there, to the High Court of the Holy Roman Empire (*Reichskammergericht*). What is more astonishing, when the High Court sent for the record of the trial of first instance, the village court of Wolfisheim produced the indictment, the testimonies, and the verdict—all in writing.[67]

The documentation of such institutions, movements, representation, and rights has become the stuff of historical literature on early modern Germany. They formed one sector of the much despised

---

[65] F. L. Carsten, *Princes and Parliaments in Germany from the Fifteenth to the Eighteenth Century* (Oxford: Clarendon Press, 1959), p. 424. The point has been developed thoroughly by Peter Blickle, *Landschaften im alten Reich. Die staatliche Funktion des gemeinen Mannes in Oberdeutschland* (Munich: R. Oldenbourg, 1973).

[66] See Winfried Schulze, *Bäuerlicher Widerstand und feudale Herrschaft in der frühen Neuzeit*, Neuzeit im Aufbau, vol. 6 (Stuttgart-Bad Cannstatt: Frommann-Holzboog, 1980).

[67] Strasbourg, Archives Départementales du Bas-Rhin, 3B 707: Linsers Hans vs. Arbogasts Hans. The stabbing took place on January 7, 1524. The dossier is incomplete, and the appeal's outcome is unknown. My thanks go to Leah C. Kirker for her transcription and analysis of the dossier's central document.

German particularism, that bewildering, confusing, decentralized, and unnational structure, which protected, on the one hand, the growth of Bavaria and Prussia as important states and, on the other hand, the liberties of Tyrolean valleys, the burghers of Strasbourg, Memmingen, and Isny, the upland communities in the southern Black Forest, and the villages of the "Free Folk on the Leutkirch Heath." If this picture clashes radically with the fashionable view of European rural society as "stable, stabilized, and balanced,"[68] locked in the nearly timeless sleep of the *longue durée*, the puzzle must be unraveled elsewhere and by others.

IV

Communalism sought, as much as did centralized states, to bond to itself the power of religion, through which "individual desires come together in agreement to press their claims, and hearts become united."[69] Zurich's reformer, Ulrich Zwingli (1485–1531), acclaimed the importance of religious bonds to the urban community: "a Christian city is nothing more than a Christian commune."[70] Religious communalism, however, was by no means restricted to the cities, and we are gradually learning that parallel to religious communalism in the German-speaking cities, which culminated in the urban reform, ran religious communalism on the land, which culminated in the "rural reformation."

The reigning orthodoxy about popular religion in late medieval and early modern Europe is informed by the Anglo-French acculturation thesis, which holds that Christianity hardly influenced the rural people until the seventeenth century, when "seeking to eliminate the worship of saints and to put an end to the cult of the dead, . . . Catholicism finally found itself digging its own grave."[71] Undeterred

---

[68] Emmanuel Le Roy Ladurie, "Rum Civilization," in *The Territory of the Historian*, pp. 79–110, here at p. 103.

[69] Ibn Khaldûn, *The Muqaddimah: An Introduction to History*, trans. Franz Rosenthal, abridged ed. N. J. Dawood (Princeton: Princeton University Press, 1957), p. 125.

[70] *Huldreich Zwinglis sämtliche Werke*, eds. Emil Egli, *et al.*, 14 vols. to date (Berlin, Leipzig, Zürich, 1905–), translated by Thomas A. Brady, Jr., "In Search of the Godly City: The Domestication of Religion in the German Urban Reformation," in *The German People and the Reformation*, ed. R. Po-chia Hsia (Ithaca: Cornell University Press, 1988), p. 20.

[71] Le Roy Ladurie "Rural Civilization," pp. 99–101. See the trenchant critique

by such solemnities, Peter Blickle and his team at Bern have begun to uncover a deep, broad movement of religious communalization in the pre-Reformation era.[72] Through their headmen and courts, villages requested the establishment of parishes and the provision of parish priests, and they often demanded both a voice in the nomination of pastors and the repatriation of alienated tithes to support their priests.[73] Where such rights were secure, they were defended, as in the village of Ehringen near Nördlingen, where the village statutes proclaimed "that the commune of Ehringen has the power to elect its pastor . . ., and if the commune is not satisfied with him, it may give him notice within three months."[74] In central Switzerland the communes installed and deposed their priests, some of whom had to submit to annual reviews and confirmations. Such rights were extremely rare outside the Swabian-Alemannic and Alpine lands, and they were by no means the rule within this region.

The fundamental problem of pre-Reformation religion, it seems, was the localization of control of the religious personnel, institutions, and resources so as to provide more faithful, more regular, and cheaper religious service by the clergy to the laity. By 1500, perhaps only one hundred of the three thousand or so towns in the empire had acquired the right to appoint their own parish priests, though there was mounting pressure to transfer patronage rights and tithes to the towns and villages. The Reformation gave this movement a powerful legitimating idea: the godly law, God's plan for the world as contained in the Bible. Based on the godly law, the Reformation movement's twin goals around 1520 became the preaching of the Word of God and local control of religious life. The

---

of this thesis by Richard C. Trexler, "Reverence and Profanity in the Study of Early Modern Religion," in *Religion and Society in Early Modern Europe, 1500–1800*, ed. Kaspar von Greyerz (London: George Allen and Unwin, 1984), pp. 245–69.

[72] Blickle summarizes the findings in "Communal Reformation and Peasant Piety: The Peasant Reformation and Its Late Medieval Origins," trans. David Luebke, *Central European History* 20 (87): pp. 216–28. For the historiographical context, see his introduction to *Zugänge zur bäuerlichen Reformation*, ed. Peter Blickle, Bauer und Reformation 1 (Zürich: Chronos, 1987), pp. 11–18. What follows is based on this collection, on Blickle's own *Gemeindereformation*, and on Franziska Conrad, *Reformation in der bäuerlichen Gesellschaft. Zur Rezeption reformatorischer Theologie im Elsass*, Veröffentlichungen des Instituts für europäische Geschichte Mainz 116 (Wiesbaden: Franz Steiner, 1984).

[73] See Rosi Fuhrmann, "Die Kirche im Dorf. Kommunale Initiativen zur Organisation von Seelsorge vor der Reformation," in *Zugänge zur bäuerlichen Reformation*, pp. 147–86.

[74] Quoted by Blickle, *Gemeindereformation*, p. 181.

connection between biblicism and local control is visible everywhere, even where the local communes had no political aspirations.
Such was the case in the margraviate of Brandenburg-Ansbach in
Franconia, where Margrave Casimir installed a new pastor at Wen-
delstein in 1524. Immediately, the headman and court of the village
instructed the pastor that "we hold you to be no lord but only a
servant (*ein Knecht und Diener*) of the community, so that we have to
command you, and not you us. And we order you to proclaim faithfully the Gospel and the Word of God purely and clearly, according to the truth and without human additions."[75] In 1525 the rebel
armies of Upper Swabia formed their "Christian Association" "to
the honor and praise of God Almighty, to the exaltation of the holy
Gospel and God's Word, and to the furtherance of justice and the
godly law"; and they proclaimed that "we want henceforth to have
the power and right for the entire commune to appoint and depose
its pastor."[76] Finally, the Ilanz Articles of April 1524 bound the
Graubündners as follows: "So that the Word and Christ's doctrine is
proclaimed more faithfully to the common man, who should not be
led into error, from henceforth no one, whether pastor, chaplain,
monk, Roman appointee, or of whatever status he may be, shall be
appointed to any post, if he does not reside among our Leagues."[77]
Behind this provision lay the desire for regular, inexpensive, and
faithful service by the clergy to the laity, which, it was believed,
could be secured only through local control.[78]

Religious communalization aimed to secure the benefits of a rich
and varied ritual life, the popularity of the symbols and actions of
which by no means disappeared with the coming of the Reformation.[79]
The Christianity of ordinary, German-speaking folk, indeed, impresses

---

[75] Quoted by Blickle, *Gemeindereformation*, pp. 27–28.
[76] *Ibid.*, p. 34.
[77] *Ibid.*, pp. 52–53.
[78] Our one satisfactory study of a pre-Reformation diocese confirms this belief.
Francis Rapp, *Réformes et reformation à Strasbourg. Église et société dans le diocèse de Strasbourg (1450–1525)*, Collection de l'Institut des Hautes Études Alsaciennes 23 (Paris;
Editions Ophrys, 1974).
[79] This is the main message of Robert W. Scribner's pioneering studies of religious
ritual, which are now easily accessible in Robert W. Scribner, *Popular Culture and
Popular Movements in Reformation Germany* (London, Ronceverte: Hambledon Press,
1987), especially "Cosmic Order and Daily Life: Sacred and Secular in Pre-Industrial
German Society," p. 116; "Ritual and Popular Belief in Catholic Germany at the
Time of the Reformation," 1748; and (previously unpublished) "Ritual and Reformation," pp. 103–22.

through "the extraordinary tenacity of popular resistance to imposed doctrines and observances," as exemplified by its startling power to clothe a new figure, such as Luther, in old garments, the attributes of a Catholic saint.[80] After reflection on this power, Gerald Strauss suggests that following the Reformation's "early hyperactive and emotionally charged heroic phase," the common people tenaciously resisted the Reformation's attempt "to replace the permissive climate of medieval Catholicism with an authoritarian creed."[81]

This stubborn quality of popular Christianity often resisted confessionalization quite successfully. Cases are known, for example, from the mid-sixteenth century of men who served simultaneously as Catholic priests and Protestant pastors.[82] Where no strong state developed to impose and guard confessional boundaries, popular Christianity never lost this quality. This was the case in the Graubünden, a land— now in Switzerland—which possessed three languages, two confessions, one small city (Chur), and hardly any state. Once past the (extremely disruptive and savage) Wars of Religion, its people settled into a way of life in which the two confessions functioned in a common culture.[83] At least this is the conclusion suggested by stories of how it fell to the Capuchin priests to protect both Catholic and Protestant Bündner communities from demons and other evil spirits.[84] Of the most famous such priest, Eberhard Walser, Capuchin superior ("*dr Supeeri*") at Mastrils, it was said that "he drove many devils over the Mastrils hill and out of the Prättigau."[85] Father Walser died in 1905.

A story from the town of Ilanz (Romansh: Glion), the ancient market town of the Surselva, also illustrates the transconfessional role

---

[80] Gerald Strauss, *Luther's House of Learning: Indoctrination of the Young in the German Reformation* (Baltimore: Johns Hopkins University Press, 1978), p. 302. See R. W. Scribner, "Luther Myth: Popular Historiography of the Reformer," and "Incombustible Luther: the Image of the Reformer in Early Modern Germany," in his *Popular Culture and Popular Movements*, pp. 301–22, 323–54.

[81] Strauss, *Luther's House of Learning*, pp. 30–33.

[82] Bireley, "Early Modern Germany," p. 13, citing Ernst Walter Zeeden, *Die Entstehung der Konfessionen. Grundlagen und Formen der Konfessionsbildung im Zeitalter der Glaubenskämpfe* (Munich: R. Oldenbourg, 1965), pp. 74, 77.

[83] For orientation, see Friedrich Pieth, *Bündner Geschichte*, 2nd ed. (Chur: F. Schuler, 1982), pp. 119–250.

[84] See Scribner, "Ritual and Popular Belief in Catholic Germany at the Time of the Reformation," pp. 44–47, for an explanation of why this remained a Catholic task.

[85] Arnold Büchli, *Mythologische Landeskunde von Graubünden. Ein Bergvolk erzählt*, 4 vols. (Disentis: Desertina, 1989), 1: pp. 574–75.

of Catholic exorcists in the Graubünden. In the cellar of a former tavern at Ilanz, the spirits of two innkeepers, man and wife, often appeared to visitors and said: "So many thumbs also make a measure." This was their punishment for having cheated customers by sticking their thumbs in the pitchers while drawing wine. The present owners, who were Protestants, sent for the Catholic priest from a nearby village to drive the spirits from their cellar. The priest agreed, but only if the householders would ask their own Protestant pastor to join him in the task. As the two brothers of the cloth stood before the house, the priest asked, "Will you go in and bring them out?" The pastor went in but shortly returned to report that the spirits refused to come. Then the priest went down into the cellar and brought the spirits out, and he and the pastor led them through the town. After the priest banished them to a cave along the Rhine, they never bothered mortals again. This event happened "a long time ago," said the informant in 1943.[86] The historian, heeding the folklorist's warning that all is not ancient which seems so,[87] does not have to believe these practices extremely old in order to appreciate their point: in the absence of a centralized state, post-Reformation religion could not be thoroughly confessionalized. Through the process of confessionalization, we may conclude, the state "became the true beneficiary of the union with the Reformation."[88]

V

The long survival of the Holy Roman Empire's late-medieval characteristics—a traditional monarchy, small states, close union of religion and governance, and communalism—mocks every notion of a new departure, turning point, or *Sonderweg* among the German-speaking peoples before 1800.[89] Thereafter did begin a new story, a *Sonderweg* not away from "the West" but toward "the West," a passage of

---

[86] *Ibid.*, 2: pp. 399–400.

[87] Hermann Bausinger, "Traditionale Welten. Kontinuität und Wandel in der Volkskultur," *Historische Zeitschrift* 241 (1985): pp. 265–87.

[88] Karlheinz Blaschke, "The Reformation and the Rise of the Territorial State." trans. Thomas A. Brady, Jr., in *Luther and the Modern State in Germany*, ed. James D. Tracy, Sixteenth Century Essays & Studies 7 (Kirksville, Mo.: Sixteenth Century Journal Publishers, 1986), p. 75.

[89] I would add this fourth characteristic to Heinz Schilling's three (see note 19), despite his strictures in "Die deutsche Gemeindereformation" (n. 59).

German-speaking peoples from the Germanys to Germany. Nothing impelled them in this direction more than their experience of French imperial rule under Napoleon—so much so, that Thomas Nipperdey opens his account of nineteenth-century Germany with the words, "In the beginning was Napoleon."[90] The shocking appearance of a truly western ruler among the Germans is also suggested in a scene by the Alsatian writer René Schickele. As one of Napoleon's regiments— German speakers from Alsace—marches into Rheinweiler, a small town in Baden, the soldiers are heard to sing:

> Gott Vater hat einen Sohn, Und der heißt Napoleon.[91] (God the Father has a son, And his name's Napoleon.)

---

[90] Thomas Nipperdey, *Deutsche Geschichte 1800–1860. Bürgerwelt und starker Staat* (Munich: C. H. Beck, 1983), p. 11.

[91] René Schickele, *Maria Capponi* (Munich: Kurt Wolff, 1925), p. 70.

CHAPTER SIXTEEN

THE RISE OF MERCHANT EMPIRES, 1400–1700:
A EUROPEAN COUNTERPOINT

Glory of empire! Most unfruitful lust
After vanity that men call fame!
It kindles still, the hypocritic gust,
By rumor, which as honor men acclaim.
What thy vast avengeance and thy sentence just
On the vain heart that greatly loves thy name
What death, what peril, tempest, cruel woe,
Dost thou decree that he must undergo!

—Luis Vaz de Camoëns

Pride in their port, defiance in their eye,
I see the lords of human kind pass by.

—Oliver Goldsmith

Where is the flag of England?
Go East, North, South or West;
Wherever there's wealth to plunder
Or land to be possessed;
Wherever there's feeble people
To frighten, coerce or scare;
You'll find the butcher's apron,
The English flag is there.

—Derek Warfield of "The Wolfe Tones"

On July 8, 1497, as Vasco da Gama's men were embarking at Lisbon's
Belem docks, an old man, a soothsayer out of Greek drama, warned
the departing adventurers that the pursuit of glory, wealth, and power
in the East would doom their own souls. The Christian West would
lose its soul in the East—or at least that is how Luis Vaz de Camoëns
told it, many years later.[1] Da Gama's voyage and that of Columbus,
five years earlier, set Europeans on the path to global unification
through the rise of merchant empires. The transformation of Europe
from a lesser civilization perched on the western point of Eurasia
into a cluster of empires brawling for domination of world trade is

---

[1] Luis Vaz de Camoëns, *The Lusiads*, IV, p. 95, in Leonard Bacon's translation.

widely held to mark a turning point in world history. From the
events of the 1490s thus come the currently popular divisions of the
world into "developed" and "underdeveloped," "First World" and
"Third World," "North" and "South," and "white" and "colored."
Although commonly employed today to criticize Europe, these pairs
derive from a European vision of the post-1490s world. The Scot-
tish philosopher Adam Smith proclaimed it in the birth year of the
American Republic: "The discovery of America, and that of the passage to the East Indies by the Cape of Good Hope, are the two
greatest events recorded in the history of mankind."[2] Today, as this
vision shoulders aside a rival that claims "affiliation with a tradition
of Western Civilization that ran back through modern and medieval Europe to the ancient Greeks and Hebrews,"[3] the rise of merchant
empires is coming to mark the inception of modern history.

As they knitted the globe together, the European merchant empires
affected different parts of the world in different ways. In parts of the
Americas, ecological exchange made the initial contacts catastrophic;
in other parts of the Americas and some of Africa and Oceania,
peoples were drawn into the global trading system at a pace that
allowed for adaptation and even some control; and in much of Asia
the Europeans caused few important economic and political changes
until the eighteenth century.[4] Then, however, "institutional changes
in the international economic order speeded the process in banking,
finance, transportation, and communication," and their source, industrial technology, "made it virtually impossible for any non-Western
society to resist Westernization, at least in the field of trade and exchange."[5] The rise of merchant empires, therefore, formed the first
stage of European penetration of and continuous interaction with
the wider world, which led to radical transformations only after 1750.

More controversial is the merchant empires' part in the making
of modern Europe.[6] According to its usual plot, the story of modern

---

[2] Quoted by André Gunder Frank, *World Accumulation, 1492–1789* (London, 1978),
p. 25.
[3] William H. McNeill, "Mythistory," in his *Mythistory and Other Essays* (Chicago
and London, 1986), p. 10.
[4] Alfred W. Crosby, *Ecological Imperialism: The Biological Expansion of Europe, 900–1900*
(Cambridge, 1986); Eric R. Wolf, *Europe and the People without History* (Berkeley and
Los Angeles, 1982), pp. 131–231; Paul E. Lovejoy, *Transformations in Slavery: A History
of Slavery in Africa* (Cambridge, 1983), pp. 103–34; Michael N. Pearson, *Before
Colonialism: Some Theories on Asian-European Relations, 1500–1750* (New Delhi, 1988).
[5] Philip D. Curtin, *Cross-Cultural Trade in World History* (Cambridge, 1984), p. 251.
[6] The leading works are Immanuel Wallerstein, *The Modern World-System*, vol. 1:

Europe as "development" begins in Portugal around 1450 and migrates northward to find its proper home in England and the Netherlands around 1600, where it settles down to wait for the great transformation around 1750. The story of Europe can also be plotted, however, from the experiences of the peoples who did not go over the sea, as Bernal Diaz del Castillo once wrote, "to serve God and His Majesty, to give light to those who were in darkness, and to grow rich, as all men desire to do."[7] This chapter's goal is to replot the story from their perspective.

I. *Merchant Empires and European History*

Silks and cottons, coffee and tea, tobacco and opium, tomatoes and potatoes, rice and maize, porcelain and lacquerware—the impact of the merchant empires on European material culture proved profound and permanent. No less striking were the mental changes, beginning with wonder at strange plants, beasts, and men and culminating in the fruitful cultural relativism that sprouted from European encounters with Americans, Africans, and Asians.[8] The merchant empires' contribution to European economic development is more controversial, though the dominant opinion now seems to be that, whatever the vital role played by American silver in greasing the wheels of European trade in Asia, the share of imperial profits in the capitalization of the Industrial Revolution was not very great.[9] Much of empire's

Capitalist Agriculture and the Origins of the European World-Economy in the Sixteenth Century (New York, 1975); Eric L. Jones, *The European Miracle* (Cambridge, 1981); Eric R. Wolf, *Europe and the People without History* (Berkeley and Los Angeles, 1982); Peter Kriedte, *Peasants, Landlords, and Merchant Capitalists: Europe and the World Economy, 1500–1800*, trans. V. R. Berghahn (Cambridge, 1983), pp. 162–84; R. J. Holton, *The Transition from Feudalism to Capitalism* (New York, 1985); *The Brenner Debate: Agrarian Class Structure and Economic Development in Pre-Industrial Europe*, edited by T. H. Aston and C. H. E. Philpin (Cambridge, 1985).

[7] Quoted by J. H. Parry, *The Age of Reconnaissance: Discovery, Exploration, and Settlement, 1450–1650* (Berkeley and Los Angeles, 1963), p. 19.

[8] Anthony Pagden, *The Fall of Natural Man: The American Indian and the Origins of Comparative Ethnology* (Cambridge, 1982), p. 209; Donald F. Lach, *Asia in the Making of Europe*, vol. 2: *A Century of Wonder*, 3 parts (Chicago and London, 1970–1977), 3: p. 565.

[9] Wolfgang Reinhard, *Geschichte der europäischen Expansion*, vol. 1, *Die alte Welt bis 1818* (Stuttgart, 1983), pp. 157–70; Ward Barrett, "World Bullion Flows, 1450–1800," *The Rise of Merchant Empires*, edited by James D. Tracy (Cambridge, 1990), pp. 224–54. Reinhard's judgment (p. 232) is that "Die Gewinne aus dem Überseehandel waren zu gering, um als entscheidende Ursache für das beschleunigte wirtschaftliche Wachstum und die Industrialisierung Großbritanniens nach 1750 in Frage zu kommen." Kriedte,

profits flowed into the upkeep and expansion of the merchant empires themselves, which gradually merged into a single vast system of accumulation, out of which the industrial Revolution fashioned a global domination. The relationships between these two processes—the formation of the world economy and the coming of industrial capitalism—form the topic of the hottest debates between proponents respectively of "endogenous" and "exogenous" origins of European capitalism.[10] The debate contrasts with a hardening consensus about the European political order—a competitive system of small, centralized states—that seems to have promoted the rise of merchant empires. More and more, the roots of Europe's distinctiveness are being sought in political formation rather than in social structure; indeed, the proposition that Europe's social evolution may be seen as the paradigm of global social history is now under attack.[11] The shift of perspective toward state-building, however, merely poses the old question in a different form: Why did Europe diverge from world patterns of empire?

Empire, runs one useful definition,

> is a political system encompassing wide, relatively highly centralized territories, in which the center, as embodied both in the person of the emperor and in the central political institutions, constituted an autonomous entity. Further, ... empires ... have often embraced some idea, a potentially universal political and cultural orientation that went beyond that of any of their component parts.[12]

Neither in the age of merchant empires nor earlier did Europe produce any empires of this kind. Indeed, there is growing agreement that the failure of empire in Europe made possible the European pursuit of empire abroad, and that the most important agent of this change was the European "nation state." E. L. Jones attributes Europe's hegemony to its polycentric, competitive state system, and Immanuel

---

Peasants, Landlords and Merchant Capitalist, p. 160, and Holton, *Transition*, p. 207, agree; and the issue is reviewed by Patrick O'Brien, "European Economic Development: The Contribution of the Periphery," *Economic History Review* 35 (1982): pp. 1–18.

[10] There is a recent survey by William W. Hagen, "Capitalism and the Countryside in Early Modern Europe: Interpretations, Models, Debates," *Agricultural History* 62 (1988): pp. 13–47.

[11] See Wolf, *Europe and the People without History*, pp. 79–88, whose concept of "tributary society" is the most important contribution to this shift.

[12] Shmuel N. Eisenstadt, "Empires," *International Encyclopedia of Social Sciences* 5 (1968): p. 41. Michael Doyle, *Empires* (Ithaca, 1986), p. 45, overemphasizes the concept of sovereignty.

Wallerstein identifies the absence of true empire in Europe as the absolute precondition of the European seaborne world economy.[13] Paul Kennedy, finally, concludes that the dynamic expansion of late medieval Europe continued into the modern era because "the manifold rivalries of the European states, already acute, were spilling over into transoceanic spheres."[14]

The full realization of the potential for expansion came in one form, the nation-state, and in one region, northwestern Europe. As V. G. Kiernan writes, "among the various components making up the unique amalgam of modern north-western Europe, none was more important than its political component, the loosely named 'nation-state,'" which was a "political organization of society of a kind distinct from any other in history."[15] It arose not in Europe as a whole or even at its heart but on its far northwestern corner. There, in the Low Countries but above all in England, occurred the events that prompt all of the debates about what is variously called "the transition to capitalism," "the European advantage," or "the rise of the West."

II. *England, Europe, the West: a Synecdoche*

A synecdoche is a figure of speech in which a part stands for the whole.[16] The part, the essential locus of European modernity, was its northwestern corner, which became "leading part" or "leader" in the race for development, into which it drew much of the rest. Kiernan puts the notion as well as it can be put:

> In the seventeenth century there began that diffusion of ideas and technology from a corner of north-western Europe which is still continuing. . . . Within another century or two the southern part of this [Atlantic] region had dropped out, as Spain and Portugal sank into hopeless decadence, and the northern area—corresponding fairly closely

---

[13] Jones, *European Miracle*, pp. 85, 89–90, 93–5, 104–24; Wallerstein, *Modern World-System* 1: pp. 15–18.

[14] Paul Kennedy, *The Rise and Fall of the Great Powers: Economic Change and Military Conflict from 1500 to 2000* (New York, 1987), p. 29.

[15] V. G. Kiernan, "State and Nation in Western Europe," *Past and Present*, no. 31 (July 1965): pp. 20–38, here at p. 20. And see Holton, *Transition from Feudalism to Capitalism*, p. 208.

[16] Arthur Quinn, *Figures of Speech: 60 Ways to Turn a Phrase* (Salt Lake City, 1982), pp. 56–58.

with the one dominated or most strongly affected by Protestantism in its more active forms—went far ahead. This is how it has come about that in nine contexts out of ten today, when the world talks of something as "European," it means something that originated in this one small area, or growing-point of Europe.[17]

A strict review of the ingredients of development, indeed, reveals that only one country, England, produced all the requisites: a strong state without competing structures, an important seaborne empire, an agriculture transformed by capitalist investment, and its own Industrial Revolution.

England may be regarded as the only complete case of "development" in European history. In every account, England sets the pace and fixes the norms, flanked by the Netherlands and France, and trailed by Spain and Portugal. Germany and Italy, once in the van, after 1500 or so gallop to the rear, where they ride herd on the clouds of barbarian auxiliaries—Scandinavia, Eastern Europe, and the Muslim world. This hierarchy is reproduced from a wide variety of perspectives, from the consistently Marxist arguments of Maurice Dobb and Robert Brenner to the neo-classical exchange model of Douglass C. North and Robert Paul Thomas.[18]

In recent years, the discussion has begun to shift from economic development to state formation, which tends to relieve the blinding anglocentrism of the transition debate and makes different accounts defensible.[19] From within the broadly Marxist discourse, for example, Perry Anderson follows the trajectories of a romanized and a non-romanized Europe into a dynamic West and an imitative East.[20] Greater emphasis on government also tends to magnify the importance of French and German (usually Prussian) history,[21] and thus

---

[17] Kiernan, "State and Nation," p. 20.

[18] Maurice Dobb, *Studies in the Development of Capitalism*, rev. ed. (New York, 1963); Robert Brenner "Agrarian Class Structure and Economic Development in Pre-Industrial Europe," and "The Agrarian Roots of European Capitalism," in *Brenner Debate*, pp. 54–62, 213–327; Douglass C. North and Robert Paul Thomas, *The Rise of the Western World: A New Economic History* (Cambridge, 1973), p. 103, who classify England and the Netherlands as "winners," France as an "also ran," and Spain, Italy, and Germany as "clear losers."

[19] See Theda Skocpol, "Bringing the State Back In: Strategies of Analysis in Current Research," in *Bringing the State Back In*, edited by Peter B. Evans, Dietrich Rueschemeyer, and Theda Skocpol (Cambridge, 1985), pp. 3–43, here at pp. 4–8.

[20] Perry Anderson, *Lineages of the Absolutist State* (London, 1974).

[21] Gianfranco Poggi, *The Development of the Modern State; A Sociological Introduction* (Stanford, 1978), p. 17.

to turn attention away from what Marx called the first or "really revolutionary" path to capitalism, in which producers become capitalists, toward the second, less revolutionary path, in which merchants assume control of production.[22] It may well be that in Europe the first, "really revolutionary," way could and did occur only once; and that the second, less revolutionary, way has been the paramount one. If so, it suggests that the two ways were not alternatives at all, and that the unique English invention of capitalism transformed other societies by replicating its outcome but not its formative experience. In this view, what has happened to the world is not a social evolution toward "modernity" but the spread of capitalism as a kind of global "maladie anglaise."

One reason for the transition problem's intractability is its focus on the passage from feudal governments before the fourteenth-century crisis to absolute monarchies in the sixteenth.[23] The debate lacks the perspective of medieval Christendom's heartlands, based on a line running roughly from Cologne to Rome, where the failure of medieval imperial tendencies at the center enabled smaller, more efficient empires to form later at the western, especially the northwestern, periphery. The heartlands did produce rulers who aimed to unite Christendom into an empire of a classic sort, but they failed.[24] One reason for their failure was that, down to the end of the medieval era, much of the ideological and religious ground on which empire had to be built—and not a little of its material basis—served an institution which made rival imperial claims. I refer, of course, to the Latin church in general and to the Roman papacy in particular.

But, if empire in the heartlands fell victim to particularism the very success of this particularism held significance for the rise of Western Europe's merchant empires because among the small powers of Italy and Germany were to be found the pioneers of an especially European kind of dominion. At Venice and Genoa, at

---

[22] There is a good discussion of Marx's concept of two paths to capitalism by Kohachiro Takahashi, "A Contribution to the Discussion," in *The Transition from Feudalism to Capitalism*, edited by Rodney H. Hilton (London, 1976), pp. 68–97, here at pp. 88–97.

[23] Paul Sweezey, "A Critique," and Takahashi, "Contribution To The Discussion," in *ibid.*, pp. 46–52, 83–7.

[24] The will, if not the means to dominate Europe in this way, certainly existed. See, e.g., Hermann Wiesflecker, *Kaiser Maximilian I. Das Reich, Österreich und Europa an der Wende zur Neuzeit*, vol. 5: *Der Kaiser und seine Umwelt. Hof, Staat, Wirtschaft, Gesellschaft, und Kultur* (Munich, 1986), pp. 445–7, 641–2.

Lübeck and Hamburg, warrior-merchants pioneered seaborne raiding-and-trading empires; and, though they had all plunged into deep decline before 1500, their operations provoked emulation on a grander, oceanic scale by Portugal and Spain and the Netherlands and England respectively. The warrior-merchant, who is surely one of Europe's most distinctive social types, first appeared not in the western tier but in the Italian and German heartlands.

III. *The Church as Empire*

At the fall of the Roman power in the West, it has long been recognized, some imperial functions passed to the Latin Christian church. Some, but not all, for the church's authority was essentially spiritual or ideological, not military, and its claims were embodied in law, not in armies.[25] From the eleventh century onward, the church provided central leadership, models of bureaucratic government, a vocabulary of authority, association, and power, a common language and institutions for the spread of high culture, and an ecumenical ideology. Its center, the papal monarchy, grew as an essentially European creation to fill essentially European needs, and in its mature, twelfth-century form the papal monarchy may have been the most peculiarly European institution Europe ever knew. The language, symbols, and law that linked the papacy to the Roman imperium contained more shadow than substance, except in the sense that the papal monarchy filled a role that was in some respects similar to the one the Roman monarchy had filled. Some who recognized this fact could nevertheless hardly separate its functional aspect—Europe's need—from the historical one: the Roman heritage. Thomas Hobbes, for example, wrote that "the Papacy is no other than the ghost of the deceased Roman empire, sitting crowned upon the grave thereof."[26] This is the historical aspect, but Hobbes also recognized the functional aspect—the need that had given room to ecclesiastical authority—when he warned that "it is not the Roman clergy only, that pretends the Kingdom of God to be of this world, and thereby to have a power therein,

---

[25] See, for a general statement, John A. Hall, *Powers and Liberties: The Causes and Consequences of the Rise of the West* (Berkeley, 1985), pp. 120–1. See also Robert G. Wesson, *The Imperial Order* (Berkeley and Los Angeles, 1967), pp. 416–24.

[26] Thomas Hobbes, *Leviathan or the Matter, Forme, and Power of a Commonwealth, Ecclesiastical and Civil*, ch. 47 (edited by Michael Oakeshott [Oxford, 1960], p. 457).

distinct from that of the civil stat è."[27] He might have meant Calvin's Geneva,[28] he certainly meant the English Puritans, and he abhorred the idea that such forces might offer something that "the civil state" could not supply.

The papal monarchy flourished and must therefore be associated with European needs in the era from 1050 to about 1300, when the popes claimed the supreme lordship of Christendom and made their claim credible through victories over the Holy Roman emperors. Although armed by 1200 with a full theory of an imperial papacy, the thirteenth-century popes were unable to translate the theory into practice. The crucial test came under Pope Boniface VIII, whose great bull "Unam Sanctam" (1302) delivered "a fine [Augustinian] summary of the political consequences of that hierarchy of being where peace and justice in the world are derived from the sacred, from sanctification and legitimation through the sacraments and the jurisdiction of the Church."[29] His defeat by the French king, however, proved a turning point in the doctrine's application, and thereafter "the facade of Christian control over Europe was maintained . . . in large part because the secular powers of society had come to learn how the papal machine could in fact be operated to their best advantage."[30] Despite its imperial failure, the papacy played "a very notable role in making a secular empire impossible" because "the church refused to serve as a second fiddle in an empire equivalent to those of China and Byzantium, and thus did not create a Caesaropapist doctrine in which a single emperor was elevated to semi-divine status."[31]

Full recognition of the church's imperial role in the governance of Christendom has been hindered by the tired convention of treating religion as ideology or, more commonly, "mere ideology." This habit mars some of the best contributions to the transition debate, whose authors generally treat European Christianity as though it were significant only for changes in the attitudes of individuals, such as merchants.[32] All that must change, however, once we admit the

---

[27] *Ibid.*, p. 459.

[28] Harro Höpfl, *The Christian Polity of John Calvin* (Cambridge, 1982), pp. 188–206.

[29] Heiko A. Oberman, "The Shape of Late Medieval Thought," in his *The Dawn of the Reformation: Essays in Late Medieval and Early Reformation Thought* (Edinburgh, 1986), p. 32.

[30] Hall, *Powers and Liberties*, p. 134.

[31] *Ibid.*, pp. 134–5.

[32] See, e.g., Frank, *World Accumulation*, pp. 269–70, who is still mired in the debate about Weber and Tawney. The deficit is not made good by Wallerstein, though

lesson, drawn from the study of ancient religions, that religion is initially ritual and social and only secondarily mythic and individual,
and that religion forms a part of every social order's definition.[33]

Christendom resembled its sister civilization, Islam, far more than
it did the disintegrated religious cultures of modern Europe and
North America. Whatever else they attempted, Christendom's leaders
aimed to perform for many peoples the essential task of a religious system: to reveal the connections between the invisible and the
visible worlds and to make the former's power available for strengthening the latter's order. Most medieval Christian thinkers could have
heartily endorsed the view expressed by the Muslim philosopher Ibn
Khaldūn: "Only by God's help in establishing His religion do individual desires come together in agreement to press their claims, and
hearts become united."[34]

Christendom had its peculiarities, of course, and one of them arose
from its ordering of the relationship between religion and government. Their institutional separation was not in itself distinctive, for
in Islam, contrary to what is often said, by 1100 "the bifurcation of
the Islamic structure of domination into caliphate and rulership had
become fully established."[35] This arrangement permitted Islamic states
to function with legitimacy in the absence of any successor (caliph)

---

there are promising signs in Wolf's *Europe and the People without History*. There are
several ways to attack the veil of mystery, which this convention draws across Europe
before 1450 or so, among them Perry Anderson's revitalization of the view that the
peculiarities of medieval European civilization arose from a "synthesis" of Roman
and Germanic institutions. See Anderson, *Passages from Antiquity to Feudalism* (London,
1974), esp. pp. 128–42.

[33] Eugene D. Genovese, *Roll, Jordan, Roll: The World the Slaves Made* (New York,
1972), p. 161, muses that "few tasks present greater difficulty than that of com-
pelling the well educated to take religious matters seriously." The tide has, how-
ever, turned in studies of premodern Europe, as witness, e.g., Robert W. Scribner,
"Cosmic Order and Daily Life: Sacred and Secular in Pre-industrial German
Society," and "Ritual and Popular Belief in Catholic Germany at the Time of the
Reformation," in his *Popular Culture and Popular Movements in Reformation Germany*
(London and Ronceverte, 1987), pp. 1–16, 17–48.

[34] Ibn Khaldūn (= ʿAbd-ar-Rahmân Abû Zayd ibn Muhammad ibn Muhammad
ibn Khaldūn), *The Muqaddimah: An Introduction to History*, trans. Franz Rosenthal,
abridged edition by N. J. Dawood (Princeton, 1957), p. 125. See Thomas A. Brady,
Jr., "Godly Republics: The Domestication of Religion in the German Urban Reformation," in *The German People and the Reformation*, edited by R. Po-Chia Hsia (Ithaca,
1988), pp. 14–32, here at p. 15.

[35] Said Amir Arjomand, *The Shadow of God and the Hidden Imam: Religion, Political
Order, and Societal Change in Shiʾite Iran from the Beginning to 1890*, Publications of the
Center for Middle Eastern Studies, vol. 17 (Chicago and London, 1984), p. 94.

to the Prophet; and the postclassical "gunpowder empires"—Ottoman Turkey, Safavid Persia, and Mughal India—all practiced the de facto separation of religious from military authority.[36] Some Christian civilizations, notably the Byzantine, evolved a very similar pattern: a highly centralized monarchy and a clerical hierarchy, each recognizing the divine origin of the other's authority.

The rise of the papal monarchy blocked a similar solution in the Christian West, where the church evolved its own system of authority as well as its own imperial claims and sought to deny divine legitimacy to all other rulers. Tendencies of this sort appeared already in the late Roman era, when St. Augustine provided the normative doctrine of a world divided into two realms—being a Roman, he called them "cities"—but the full arrangement did not emerge until the eleventh and twelfth centuries. Then began the stupendous transformation of a fragmented, agrarian Europe into Latin Christendom, a civilization that came to rival and resemble its elder Islamic sibling. Between 1050 and 1250, under the Roman bishops' leadership, the church struggled "against domination of the clergy by emperors, kings, and lords and for the establishment of the Church of Rome as an independent, corporate, political and legal entity, under the papacy." The church thus won the liberty to "work for the redemption of the laity and the reformation of the world, through law,"[37] and, beneath the umbrella of its titanic clash with the emperors, there sprouted the legal autonomy of kings and princes, the self-confidence of thousands of more or less self-governing cities, and the ambitions of the universities, with their new sciences of theology and law.

The Roman papacy emerged from this history as chief claimant to hegemony over the peoples who made up "Christendom (*christianitas*)," a term that came into common use just in this era.[38] Its church alone mediated among these peoples and engaged in both the fundamentally religious task of "the redemption of the laity" and the fundamentally political one of "the reformation of the world." The

[36] Marshall Hodgson, *The Venture of Islam: Conscience and History in a World Civilization*, vol. 3: *The Gunpowder Empires and Modern Times* (Chicago and London, 1974), pp. 16–133, from whom the quoted phrase is taken.
[37] Harold J. Berman, *Law and Revolution: The Formation of the Western Legal Tradition* (Cambridge, Mass., 1983), pp. 520.
[38] Bernard Guénée, *States and Rulers in Later Medieval Europe*, trans. Juliet Vale (Oxford, 1985), p. 2.

church had become one of those "superstructures" that "necessarily enter into the constitutive structure of the mode of production."[39]

By A.D. 1200, therefore, the Roman papacy had grown into an incompletely articulated imperial power. Its lords' claims, most boldly stated in Pope Gregory VII's "Dictatus papae" (1075), held that the Roman church alone was founded by God, that the pope alone is called "universal," that he alone may make new laws and wear the imperial insignia, that he may depose emperors, and that he may revise the judgments of all other rulers and absolve subjects from their oaths of fealty. In principle, at least, these claims represented "a massive shift in power and authority both within the church and in the relations between the church and the secular polities."[40]

How could an imperial papacy make good such claims? Not through feudal lordship, for despite papal assumption of feudal lordship over a few realms, such as Sicily, England, and the lands of the Teutonic Order, feudal contract offered no very promising basis for imperium. Nor through military might, for, despite the popes' role in provoking the Crusades, they did not control the crusading forces. Some power accrued from papal assumption of the right to appoint to benefices, called "reservations,"[41] though the benefice system left most ecclesiastical property in local hands.[42] Then, too, the Roman popes contested possession of the symbols and vocabulary of Roman imperial authority with, first, the Holy Roman emperors, and, later on, the kings and princes.[43]

The most effective instrument of the sacerdotal imperium was neither military force nor Roman regalia but the idea of universal jurisdiction and universal law: God had set a law over the world, and the Roman bishop was the supreme judge. The definition of ecclesiastical jurisdiction and canon law "was a matter not merely of convenience but of principle, and of deep principle, for which

---

[39] Anderson, *Lineages of the Absolutist State*, p. 403. The point is made, though in different language, by Hall, *Powers and Liberties*, pp. 20–21.

[40] Berman, *Law and Revolution*, p. 100. A useful, if one-sided, special study is Walther Ullmann, *The Growth of Papal Government in the Middle Ages: A Study in the Ideological Relation of Clerical to Lay Power* (London, 1955).

[41] Geoffrey Barraclough, *The Papal Provisions: Aspects of Church History, Constitutional, Legal, and Administrative in the Late Middle Ages* (Oxford, 1935).

[42] Jörn Sieglerschmidt, *Territorialstaat und Kirchenregiment. Studien zur Rechtsdogmatik des Kirchenpatronatsrechts im 15. und 16. Jahrhundert*, Forschungen zur kirchlichen Rechtsgeschichte und zum Kirchenrecht, vol. 15 (Cologne and Vienna, 1987), pp. 7–28.

[43] Wesson, *Imperial Order*, pp. 423–5; Roy Strong, *Art and Power: Renaissance Festivals, 1450–1650* (Berkeley and Los Angeles, 1984), pp. 65–81.

men were ready to fight, bleed, and die."[44] The principle's popularity, in turn, depended on a broad sense of Christian community, of the (Latin) Christians as a *populus christianus*, which drew both from the communitarianism of Germanic folk culture and from the powerful, even predominant, socioreligious metaphor of the family.[45] Encompassing this whole community of peoples—Swedes and Sicilians, Celts and Croats, Portuguese and Poles—was the church, "a single state structure, governed by a single system of law, the canon law." The one church's universality firmly sanctioned the plurality of polities against all other claims to absolute or universal authority. Not only did the popes of the twelfth and thirteenth century defeat the German emperors, their rivals for the imperium, but the theory of imperial sacerdotium extended the principles of reason and redeemability to all other bodies of law, whether customary or statutory, royal, regional, or local. Above them all stood the church's canon law, which

> was, to be sure human law; yet it was supposed to be also a reflection of natural law and divine law. The secular order, however, was less perfect, more primitive, more earthbound. Its law was, therefore, more tied to irrational factors, to power, to superstition, to decadence. Yet it was capable of being regenerated; it was redeemable; it had positive significance. The church could help to make it conform more fully to natural law and ultimately to divine law. The canon law could serve as a model for the secular legal orders.[46]

Under the church's sponsorship, therefore, emerged Latin Christendom's ecumenical idea, universal law, which held that the universe itself was subject to law, that the duality of temporal and spiritual authorities placed limitations upon the power of each, that the supremacy of law was rooted in the plurality of secular authority within kingdoms and within Christendom, and that mutual obligation existed between superiors and inferiors, between central and local authorities, and between official and popular agencies of government.[47]

---

[44] Berman *Law and Revolution*, p. 531.

[45] *Ibid.*, p. 528; John Bossy, *Christianity in the West, 1400–1700* (Oxford, 1985), ch. 2.

[46] Berman, *Law and Revolution*, p. 531. See note 86 below.

[47] *Ibid.*, pp. 536–7. The papalist doctrine, which "designated the Pope as the *homo spiritualis*, the spiritual man, who cannot be judged by anyone and who judges everything in both realms of Church and State," was but one interpretation of the common view "that without the *vera iustitia* of the Church, the State has to disintegrate, can only become a latrocinium, a robber-state-as St. Augustine put it." Oberman "The Shape of Late Medieval Thought," p. 32. Against this view, the canon lawyers developed the position that the pope also stands under the law. See Francis W. Oakley, *The Western Church in the Later Middle Ages* (Ithaca, 1979), pp. 159–74.

The idea of universal law helped to sustain an ecumenical sense of the church during the fourteenth and fifteenth centuries, when the papal monarchy reeled from one disaster to another: the transfer of the papacy to Avignon in 1309; quarrels with the Spiritual Franciscans and with the Holy Roman emperor; the dissident movement of the Lollards in England and the Hussites' armed revolt in Bohemia; and the Great Western Schism of 1378–1415. These shocks eased the appropriation of legitimacy by the kings and princes and drove the Roman papacy to become locally more secular and universally more spiritual. Locally, the fifteenth-century popes began to form the Patrimony of Peter into a territorial state, the Papal State, the organization, symbols, and political culture of which exerted the profoundest influence on the other monarchies of the early modern era.[48] Ernst Kantorowicz formulated splendidly the effects of this influence: "Under the *pontificalis maiestas* of the pope, . . . the hierarchical apparatus of the Roman Church tended to become the perfect prototype of an absolute and rational monarchy on a mystical basis, while at the same time the State increasingly showed a tendency to become a quasi-Church or a mystical corporation on a rational basis."[49] In its union of temporal and spiritual government, the Renaissance papacy produced "a cultural typology which was to serve as a model of excellence for the whole of Europe of the ancien regime."[50]

The church's official reaction to the Reformation reaffirmed this union, and the Council of Trent proclaimed that "the Church is unquestionably a visible, jurisdictional institution, the structure and traditions of which are derived directly from the inspiration of the Holy Ghost."[51] Catholic theologians of the sixteenth century nevertheless adjusted theory to practice. Robert Bellarmine (1542–1621), for example, struck "a middle road" between the extreme theocratic doctrine of direct papal sovereignty and the denial of all papal authority, holding "that there should be power of indirect interven-

---

[48] Paolo Prodi, *The Papal Prince, One Body and Two Souls: The Papal Monarchy in Early Modern Europe*, trans. Susan Haskins (New York, 1987), p. 6, sees in the early modern Papal State a prototype of the way "in which some tendencies of the management of power made themselves known in a dialectical relationship . . . with the evolving states on the one hand, and with the papacy's primatial call . . . on the other."

[49] Ernst Kantorowicz, *The King's Two Bodies: A Study in Medieval Political Theology*, 3rd ed. (Princeton, 1973), p. 194.

[50] A. Quondam, quoted by Prodi, *Papal Prince*, p. 47.

[51] Quentin Skinner, *Foundations of Modern Political Thought*, 2 vols. (Cambridge, 1978), 2: p. 144.

tion exceptionally where spiritual welfare is concerned and because the problem of salvation affects all mankind."[52] In Spain some advanced theologians, such as Francisco de Vitoria (ca. 1485–1546), affirmed the papal supremacy within the church but denied that the pope, or anyone else, could have supreme, direct, and absolute governance over the whole world, for no power on this earth could dispense from the natural law or the law of nations.[53] The lawfulness of the universe, once an ecclesiastical instrument against the Holy Roman emperor's superior might, had taken on a life of its own.

The papacy's local retreat into the Papal State, plus the Catholic retrenchment on the issue of direct papal sovereignty, encouraged the growth of a new universalism, more religious and spiritual and less political than the theory of direct papal monarchy. Partly this arose from the fact that the Roman church became, just at the moment of its greatest losses in Europe, a global institution. The change may be illustrated by a contrast between Pope Alexander VI's (r. 1492–1503) imperial demarcation of the globe between Portugal and Spain in 1493 and Pope Paul III's (r. 1534–1549) pastoral "Sublimis Deus" of 1537, which forbade Christians to enslave the newly discovered peoples beyond the sea. As the church voyaged out with the merchant adventurers, traders, and conquerors, its agents expanded the Christian universalism far beyond the old boundaries.[55]

To this more universal universality is linked the growth of a more spiritualized form of papal supremacy, the doctrine of papal infallibility. The teaching that the pope cannot err in matters of doctrine is more a repudiation than a confirmation of Christendom's ecumenical ideology of universal law. It originated not with canon lawyers but among the mendicant orders of the thirteenth and early fourteenth centuries, especially the Franciscans, whose late thirteenth-century theologians evolved an increasingly radical doctrine of papal

[52] Prodi, *Papal Prince*, p. 26.

[53] See Venancio D. Carro, "The Spanish Theological-Juridical Renaissance and the Ideology of Bartolomé de Las Casas," in *Bartolomé de Las Casas in History: Toward an Understanding of the Man and His Work*, edited by Juan Fried and Benjamin Keen (DeKalb, Ill., 1971), pp. 236–77, here at pp. 250–63. For the intellectual context, see Skinner, *Foundations of Modern Political Thought*, 2: p. 151.

[54] Guenée, *States and Rulers*, p. 10, believes that the demarcation "was already arbitration within the jurisdiction of the law of nations rather than a sovereign decision of the Pope." On Paul III's bull, see Lewis Hanke, *All Mankind Is One: A Study of the Disputation Between Bartolomé de Las Casas and Juan Ginés de Sepúlveda in 1550 on the Intellectual and Religious Capacity of the American Indians* (DeKalb, Ill., 1974), pp. 17–22.

[55] See, e.g., Jonathan D. Spence, *The Memory Palace of Matteo Ricci* (New York, 1984).

infallibility. Itself a sign of radical skepticism about the church's
ability to govern the world through law, infallibility came to be taught
by some of the papacy's fiercest enemies, such as William of Ockham
(d. ca. 1349), who clung to the idea that, even if popes could err,
the true church could not. After a long life on the margins of orthodoxy, "only in the sixteenth century did the doctrine of the pope's
personal infallibility begin to find considerable acceptance in Catholic theology."[56]

The intensification of papal monarchy over the Papal State, the theoretical backpedaling to the Bellarminian doctrine of indirect power,
the development of the notion of a global religious mission, and a
growing orthodox acceptance of papal infallibility—these were all
signs that the sixteenth-century papacy was no longer a European
imperial monarchy. The pope's two new roles, local monarch over
the Papal State and leader of a global religious community, framed
the papacy's postmedieval history until 1870. On July 18, 1870, the
First Vatican Council proclaimed the dogma of papal infallibility; two months later, on September 20, Italian troops invaded the
Vatican and ended the Papal State. The church had failed to become
a true empire; it had briefly become a state; it remained a global
religious organization.

One of the imperial papacy's most enduring political legacies to
Europe was the idea of Rome as a paradigm of imperial rule. The
Roman heritage, long contested between popes and emperors, acquired
new vigor through the literary and artistic culture of the Renaissance.
This can be illustrated by the clash of claims. At the court of Pope
Julius II (r. 1503–1513), an orator promised that, though Julius Caesar
merely thought he ruled the world, Pope Julius II in fact did.[57] A
few years later, as if in reply, the imperial grand chancellor, Mercurino
Arborio di Gattinara (d. 1530), trumpeted grandiosely that the work
begun by Charles the Great would be completed by Charles the
Greatest, giving the world "one pastor and one flock."[58] Such bom-

[56] Brian Tierney, *Origins of Papal Infallibility, 1150–1350: A Study on the Concepts of Infallibility, Sovereignty, and Tradition in the Middle Ages*, Studies in the History of Christian Thought, vol. 6 (Leiden, 1972), pp. 57, 92–109, 171–237, 271, with the closing quote at p. 271.

[57] John W. O'Malley, "Giles of Viterbo: A Reformer's Thought on Renaissance Rome," *Renaissance Quarterly* 20 (1967): pp. 1–11, here at p. 10 (reprinted in John W. O'Malley, *Rome and the Renaissance: Studies in Culture and Religion* [London, 1981]).

[58] John M. Headley, "The Habsburg World Empire and the Revival of Ghibellinism," *Medieval and Renaissance Studies* 7 (1978): pp. 93–127, here at pp. 97–102.

bast may have charmed the humanist literati who flocked to the Hapsburg courts from lands, such as Germany, Italy, and the Netherlands, which lacked large, strong states, but they soon learned to venerate the particular monarchies as worthy successors to Rome.[59] Roman imperial language and symbols became tools in the kits of the Renaissance Italians, Burckhardt's "first-born among the sons of modern Europe,"[60] who poured forth an army of artists and architects, rivers of symbols, and a creeping wave of taste to feed the tastes of the powerful in all the European capitals.

The coming of the large states meant the doom of many smaller units, and a look backward from around 1600 teaches us how vital were the great universalist structures of medieval Europe to the peculiarly European success of very small political units.[61] This was true of the Italian communes, in which the bishops personified local autonomy, while the papacy sponsored anti-imperial urban leagues.[62] And it was sometimes true of the Holy Roman Empire's lands, where small semisovereignties flourished under what an early sixteenth-century Austrian official called "both wings of the [imperial] eagle."[63]

The old universalisms nevertheless proved ever more difficult to sustain, as fighters moved in to serve the papacy as they had served the Holy Roman Empire. Some did so in the belief that an imperial papacy hindered, even shackled, the church's efforts to preach the redemption of the world.[64] Others did so on behalf of the most powerful and ultimately most successful gravediggers of the papal imperium—the kings and princes, whose confidence and independence had earlier waxed under its protection of the church.[65] By the fifteenth century, the structures that had helped them to become more than tribal paramount chiefs or feudal tenants-in-chief, stood

---

[59] Skinner, *Foundations of Modern Political Thought*, 1: ch. 9; Thomas A. Brady, Jr., *Turning Swiss: Cities and Empire, 1450–1550* (Cambridge, 1985), pp. 22–8.

[60] Jacob Burckhardt, *The Civilization of the Renaissance in Italy*, trans. S. G. C. Middlemore, revised by Irene Gordon (New York, 1961), p. 121.

[61] Wallerstein offers this insight in *Modern World-System*, 1: pp. 172–3.

[62] J. K. Hyde, *Society and Politics in Medieval Italy: The Evolution of the Civil Life, 1000–1350* (New York, 1973), pp. 58–9; Daniel Waley, *The Italian City-Republics* (New York and Toronto, 1969), p. 127.

[63] Quoted by Brady, *Turning Swiss*, p. 78.

[64] For orientation, see Oakley, *The Western Church*, pp. 178–259; and *idem*, *Omnipotence, Covenant, and Order: An Excursion in the History of Ideas from Abelard to Leibniz* (Ithaca, 1984), pp. 55–65, 77–84, for William of Ockham's role.

[65] The inability to grasp the influence of the church on the political evolution of Europe is the greatest weakness of Reinhard Bendix's *Kings or People: Power and the Mandate to Rule* (Berkeley and Los Angeles, 1978).

in their way, and the assault on the papacy's material foundations began well before there erupted, sparked by quite different forces, the Protestant Reformation. Well before that time, Emperor Frederick III (r. 1440–1493) summed up Austrian practice in a sentence: "What the priests own, belongs to us."[66]

Legitimate or not, the European state, or nation-state, is the imperial papacy's true successor. It grew up in the house of Christendom, a space the Latin church had helped to create, it grew strong by feeding on the church's temporalities, and it eventually appropriated the spiritual claim to be the true foundation of human community. It became "one body and two souls,"[67] both empire and nation. Not, however, without a struggle, for the same forces that unsettled the feudal order—urbanization, trade, plague, and depression—opened space for a very different kind of voice, the demand for corporate-communal rule.

IV. *The Communal Way—Alternative to the State*

A state, to use the term in its sixteenth-century meaning, "is a political body subject to a government and to common laws." Although medieval Europeans hardly used the word (*status, état, estado, stato, Staat*), the patterns of governance that produced the European type of state—smaller and better integrated than an empire, larger and more powerful than a city-state—reach far back into the twelfth and thirteenth centuries.[68] Public opinion in Christendom nonetheless long held that "the peace of the world could only be safeguarded by the existence of a single universal power."[69] Down at least through Dante Alighieri (d. 1321), the vision of a neo-Roman universal monarchy became a major weapon against those who, like Giles of Rome (ca. 1246–1316), were beginning to argue that all political authority and even the ownership of property (*dominium*) depended on loyal

---

[66] "Pfaffengut ist Kammergut," quoted by Wiesflecker, *Kaiser Maximilian I.* vol. 1: *Jugend, burgundisches Erbe und Römisches Königtum bis zur Alleinherrschaft, 1459–1493* (Munich, 1971), p. 79; and in a slightly different form, "Pfaffenhab ist unser Kammergut," in *ibid.*, vol. 5: p. 156.

[67] Prodi, *Papal Prince*, p. 185.

[68] Joseph R. Strayer, *On the Medieval Origins of the Modern State* (Princeton, 1970), p. 12.

[69] Guénée, *States and Rulers*, p. 7.

membership in the church.[70] Lawyer-popes, indeed, proved more flexible than imperial propagandists, and the theory of papal monarchy allowed them to argue, as Pope Innocent III (r. 1198–1216) did in 1202, that kings and princes were not units of the Roman imperium and thus did not have to recognize a temporal superior, that is, the emperor. One party of the church's lawyers, it has been said, "held the national state over the baptismal font."[71]

With the *regnum*, the realm of well-defined boundaries associated with a strong core region, such as the king of France's Ile-de-France, the political future truly lay. By the fourteenth century, old-fashioned vassalage no longer supplied a sufficient basis for monarchy, not least because the economic crisis was steadily undermining the governmental functions of landlordship, on which feudal governance depended. Kings and princes came to deal with powerful subjects not as individuals but as members of corporate assemblies, called "estates." The dualistic state (*Ständesstaat*), a nearly universal phenomenon in Latin Christendom by the fourteenth century, formed a major transition stage between the feudal monarchy of the past and the centralized monarchy of the future.[72] Such corporate institutions formed and flourished during the 250 years after about 1250, beginning as "tools of government" through which kings and princes sought consent from the "politically active, propertied classes," and ending sometimes as their rivals, sometimes as their creatures.[73]

The passage from these dualistic governments of kings-and-parliaments to centralized monarchy unfolded since 1450 in Europe's western tier, often in ways that now seem inevitable.[74] That centralization of power proved more fundamental than its monarchical representations is proven by the case of England, where the ultimately successful assault on royal absolutism between 1640 and 1688

---

[70] John B. Morrall, *Political Thought in Medieval Times* (London, 1958; reprinted, New York, 1962), pp. 86–7.

[71] "Cum rex superiorem in temporalibus minime recognoscat," quoted by Guénée, *States and Rulers*, p. 7.

[72] Poggi, *Development of the Modern State*, pp. 36–59, summarizes the data and the theories; and see Guénée, *States and Rulers*, pp. 171–87.

[73] Strayer, *Medieval Origins of the Modern State*, pp. 66–67.

[74] See now, however, the very important volume edited by Helmut G. Koenigsberger, *Republiken und Republikanismus im Europa der Frühen Neuzeit*, Schriften des Historischen Kollegs, Kolloquien, vol. 11 (Munich, 1988), which shows that premodern republicanism remained an oppositional current that never developed a theoretical position, and that all tendencies to republicanism on a national level—England, Sweden—failed to come to fruition.

hardly challenged the centralized state's supremacy—any more than the French Revolution would in France. The true anomaly among the empire building peoples is not England but the Netherlands, which, because of its failure to centralize, is sometimes regarded as a case of "failed development."[75] The Netherlands, however, belonged by heritage and experience to the old Central European heartlands, where particularism had prevailed, and, though the experience of empire strained the older corporate structures, it did not smash them to make way for a thoroughly centralized state.

The Netherlands form the transition from the western states, whose experience shapes most accounts of European history in the early modern era, to the lands that had been the heartlands of medieval Christendom but became the semiperiphery of modern Europe. The experience of these lands, especially Germany and Italy, makes it unlikely that wholly endogenous causes produced the large, central-ized nation-states of the West. Indeed, history written from the per-spective of the Central European heartlands of Christendom reveals what is sometimes called "Old Europe," the continuity of whose life from about 1000 to about 1800 depended on its corporately organ-ized society, a vast, bewildering welter of assemblies, foundations, guilds, societies, and other corporate institutions of every conceiv-able type.[76] European history since 1800 can then be seen as the conformity, forced and induced, of this old society to the new type of the centralized, imperial European nation-state. One of the great values of the heartlands' premodern history is to show us a political experience that was relatively undisturbed by the experience of em-pire. Although this history has remained largely hidden from the centralist-developmentalist perspective, its recovery can throw a new and powerful light both on what Christendom was and on what Europe became.

Between 1250 and 1500, much of Europe witnessed innovations in governance that, in the absence of merchant empires, could some-times allow an exit from feudal governance quite different from

---

[75] Frederik Krantz and Paul M. Hohenberg, eds., *Failed Transitions to Modern Industrial Society: Renaissance Italy and Seventeenth-Century Holland. First International Colloquium, April 18–20, 1974* (Montreal, 1975); Strayer, *Medieval Origins*, p. 91.

[76] See Dietrich Gerhard, *Old Europe: A Study of Continuity, 1000–1800* (New York, 1981). For the present state of discussion on corporate society, see Winfried Schulze, ed., *Ständische Gesellschaft und soziale Mobilität*, Schriften des Historischen Kollegs, Kolloquien, vol. 12 (Munich, 1988).

absolute monarchy. First came a general devolution of political power: corporate bodies of powerful subjects came to play an important role in the government of kingdoms, duchies, and other principalities; guilds came to play an important role in the governments of some cities; and in a few places even villages gained a significant measure of self-administration. Second, the sense of place, of country, began to form and become the object of people's loyalties, as they began to identify themselves with their homelands. Gradually, as the sense of political community became more concrete, it attached to language as well, and political and ethnic communities (*populus* and *natio*) began to take shape.[77] The growing strength of such identifications made ever more remote the possibility of resubmerging them in an imperial loyalty of civilizational scale. Third, this era seethed with corporate ideology, ideas of community, of togetherness, of the whole superseding the parts, and of the common good that transcends ever particular good.[78] Although these three developments are often called "feudal," they represented a massive shift of governance away from government by contract and vassalage and toward participation in government by the body of subjects, or the *melior pars* thereof. Indeed, the community of the *populus* or *natio*, though not so comprehensive as the church, was far more so than the old assemblies of vassals. We find everywhere and on all levels of political life and thought this broadening, by means of which political life burst the lower bounds of the feudal age's concept of a society divided into clergy, nobility, and "workers," that is, the urban rich.[79] In a few places, this devolution brought even peasant householders into the political assemblies, while in civic governments the lesser merchants, shopkeepers, and artisan masters sometimes pushed their way into the town halls. At Florence in the 1370s, the political success of such folk even inspired the wool workers, called the *Ciompi*, to imitate them; and at Basel in 1521 the guildsmen briefly pushed the greater merchants out of government altogether.[80] The extreme examples of

[77] Guénée, *States and Rulers*, pp. 49–55.

[78] Antony Black, *Council and Commune: The Conciliar Movement and the Fifteenth-Century Heritage* (London, 1979); idem, *Guilds and Civil Society in European Political Thought from the Twelfth Century to the Present* (Ithaca, 1984).

[79] Georges Duby, *The Three Orders: Feudal Society Imagined*, trans. Arthur Goldhammer (Chicago and London, 1980), p. 5.

[80] See Hans Füglister, *Handwerksregiment. Untersuchungen und Materialien zur sozialen und politischen Struktur der Stadt Basel in der ersten Hälfte des 16. Jahrhunderts*, Basler Beiträge zur Geschichtswissenschaft, vol. 143 (Basel, 1981). On the political movements

devolution, however, came in certain naturally favored corners of the Central European countryside, especially the central Alpine lands. Here armed farmers and stockmen ruled themselves and answered with pike and sword all who challenged their right to do so. "The Swiss," as Machiavelli noted, "are best armed and most free."[81]

The popularization of corporate institutions and ideas aroused contempt and sometimes fear in the traditional elites. It was not enough to shout at the newcomers, "Canaille! Canaille! Canaille! May you die of starvation," or call them "these craftsmen of shit!"— as fourteenth-century Florentine aristocrats did.[82] Whole new terms had to be invented for groups whose voice had now and then to be heard, but who, by the lights of their betters, had no right to voice at all. This new actor on the political states, the Common Man (*popolo minuto, menu peuple, gemeiner Mann*), threatened to play an unpredictable role: he was stupid, he was cunning; he was docile, he was dangerous; he was subservient, he was sullen; he was hardworking, he was lazy; he was the wisest beast in the farmyard, he was a dangerous rebel. He and his comrades acted, as Emperor Maximilian sneered at the Swiss in 1499, like "wicked, crude, stupid peasants, in whom there is neither virtue, noble blood, nor proper moderation, but only immoderate display, disloyalty, and hatred for the German nation."[83]

Two features of the spread of corporate thinking through Europe merit special attention. First, it bore intimate connections to what was happening in the church, for not only did it draw vitality from the corporate-familial images that animated late medieval religious consciousness, it also expanded in a moral room created by the eleventh-century investiture controversy's "radical reappraisal of the relationship between church and state."[84] Second, corporate ideas came to serve the vast communal movement, which arose in the

of south German journeymen, and on the fall of real wages that undermined them, see Knut Schulz, *Handwerksgesellen und Lohnarbeiter. Untersuchungen zur oberrheinischen und oberdeutschen Stadtgeschichte des 14. bis 17. Jahrhunderts* (Sigmaringen, 1985); Jean-Pierre Kintz, *La société strasbourgeoise du milieu du XVIe siècle à la fin de la Guerre de Trente Ans 1560–1650. Essai d'histoire démographique, économique et sociale* (Paris, 1984).

[81] Machiavelli, *The Prince*, ch. 12.

[82] G. A. Brucker, *Florentine Politics and Society, 1343–1378* (Princeton, 1962), pp. 52–53.

[83] Quoted by Guy P. Marchal, "Die Antwort der Bauern. Elemente und Schichtungen des eidgenössischen Geschichtsbewußtseins am Ausgang des Mittelalters," in *Geschichtsschreibung und Geschichtsbewußtsein im späten Mittelalter*, edited by Hans Patze, Vorträge und Forschungen, vol. 31 (Sigmaringen, 1987), pp. 757–90, here at p. 757.

[84] Black, *Guilds and Civil Society*, p. 62. The corporate character of medieval religion is a principal theme of Bossy, *Christianity in the West*.

European cities during the twelfth and thirteenth centuries, and the outcome of which, most pronounced in Central Europe, brought elements of self-government into the hands of the Common Man.

The political Golden Age of the Common Man coincided with the depressed, stagnant, troubled, and disrupted fourteenth and fifteenth centuries. How were economic depression and political emancipation related? Economic dislocation, followed by famine and plague and a hundred years of economic stagnation, undermined both the economic viability of the manorial estates and the political vitality of the seigneuries—the two foundation stones of feudal government. On the land, some of the lords' administrative functions devolved upon the villages, while in the towns, the rise of real wages—commodity prices fell faster than wages—lent new political force to the craftsmen and laborers. The advance of market forces, which the depression accelerated rather than stemmed, lent new value and hence new power to human labor and new voice to those who labored, the commons, and this at a time when no new form of the state had definitively replaced feudal monarchy.[85]

The great devolution took many forms in many places. An immense wave of rural revolts began in England in 1381 and culminated in the great German Peasants' Revolt of 1525. In the cities, too, political agitation came in waves: guild revolts laced with anti-Jewish riots in the Rhenish towns in the mid-fourteenth century; terrible pogroms in the Castilian towns in the 1380s and a communal revolt in the early 1520s; and a tremendous wave of riots, revolts, and coups in the Italian cities during the first third of the sixteenth century. In Bohemia, revolt developed on a much greater scale: slashing, brutal campaigns in which Hussite armies, armed with religious enthusiasm,

---

[85] This paragraph recapitulates an argument I make in "Der Gemeine Mann und seine Feinde: Betrachtungen zur oberdeutschen Geschichte im 15. und 16. Jahrhundert," in *Stände und Gesellschaft im Alten Reich. Beiträge des zweiten deutsch-amerikanischen Kolloquiums zur frühneuzeitlichen Reichsgeschichte*, edited by Georg Schmidt, Veröffentlichungen des Instituts für Europäische Geschichte Mainz, 85 (Wiesbaden, 1988), pp. 50–6. It agrees closely with Peter Blickle, *Die Gemeindereformation. Die Menschen des 16. Jahrhunderts auf dem Weg zum Heil* (Munich, 1985), pp. 165–204. Closer study may uncover politically significant communalism in other parts of Europe. See the suggestive comment by Marc Bloch, *French Rural History: An Essay on Its Basic Characteristics*, translated by Janet Sondheimer (Berkeley and Los Angeles, 1966), p. 167. Although Emmanuel Le Roy Ladurie notes in passing "the universal strength of peasant communalism" in France, he calls it merely "colourful." Emmanuel Le Roy Ladurie, *The French Peasantry, 1450 1660*, trans. Alan Sheridan (Berkeley and Los Angeles, 1987), pp. 384, 391.

patriotism, wagon-forts, and cannon, held off one imperial army after another.[86]

All of this appeared as disorder, as chaos, as the unfortunate consequences of government's inadequate finance and military force—but only if seen from throne and castle. Seen from below, the same movements posed a corporate defense of local and regional rights, of the subjects' purses, and of the cause of law and justice.[87] Much of later fourteenth- and fifteenth-century Europe faced two possible political paths: "one, emancipation of the small producer, the peasant and the craftsman, from the higher classes in church and state; the other, reorganization of the higher classes, moral rearmament, pruning of excrescences, concentration of power."[88] By the first half of the sixteenth century, this choice was clearly resolved, at least in Europe's western tier, in favor of concentration, the road to the "national state."

The new state differed from the old monarchies in several ways: first, it controlled a well-defined, continuous territory; second, it was relatively centralized; third, it was differentiated from other organizations; and fourth, it reinforced its claims through a tendency to monopolize the concentrated means of physical coercion within its territory.[89] Such states possessed standing armies, bureaucracies staffed by lawyers, regular taxation, mercantilist trade policies, diplomatic services, and an ideology of sovereignty drawn more or less from Roman law.[90] Thus armed, states tackled the twin traditional tasks

---

[86] Peter Blickle, "Peasant Revolts in the Late Medieval German Empire," *Social History* 4 (1979): pp. 223–39; Peter Bierbrauer, "Bäuerliche Revolten im Alten Reich. Ein Forschungsbericht," in *Aufruhr und Empörung? Studien zum bäuerlichen Widerstand im Alten Reich*, edited by Peter Blickle (Munich, 1980), pp. 1–68; R. H. Hilton, *Bond Men Made Free: Medieval Peasant Movements and the English Rising of 1381* (London, 1979); Lauro Martines, *Power and Imagination: City-States in Renaissance Italy* (New York, 1979), pp. 295–6. See, in general, Guénée, *States and Rulers*, pp. 192–7; Michael Mollat and Philippe Wolff, *The Popular Revolutions of the Late Middle Ages*, trans. A. L. Lytton-Sells (London, 1973).

[87] Peter Blickle, "Communalism, Parliamentarism, Republicanism," trans. Thomas A. Brady, Jr., *Parliaments, Estates, and Representation* 6 (1986): pp. 1–13.

[88] Kiernan, "State and Nation," p. 28.

[89] Charles Tilly, "Reflections on the History of European State-Making," in *The Formation of National States in Western Europe*, edited by Charles Tilly (Princeton, 1975), p. 27.

[90] Anderson, *Lineages of the Absolutist State*, pp. 24–38. In the Holy Roman Empire, by contrast, the idea of sovereignty took no root before the eighteenth century. Helmut Quaritsch, *Souveränität. Entstehung und Entwicklung des Begriffs in Frankreich und Deutschland vom 13. Jahrhundert bis 1806*, Schriften zur Verfassungsgeschichte, vol. 38 (Berlin, 1986).

of government—the administration of justice and defense of the realm—in new and more effective ways. Royal law, codified in innovative lawbooks and administered by Latin-speaking lawyers and judges, became the knife that cut away at the vast riot of corporate immunities, privileges, and liberties.

Nowhere in Europe did the problem of reconstructing authority pose itself more acutely than in the German-speaking world, where in 1525 political devolution culminated in the greatest mass rebellion of premodern European history.[91] The rebels opposed not law but alien law—the book-based laws of the empire and the territorial states, against which so many bitter jokes circulated—in favor of their own "old law" and the "godly law."[92] They wanted government, but of their own choosing: where effective territorial governments existed, the rebels of 1525 proposed a new role in them for the commons; in hopelessly fragmented regions, they proposed new states based on popular representation; and everywhere they demanded an end to political privilege based on property in land and labor.[93] Sometimes they got their wishes. Rural householders came to sit in the parliaments (*Landschaften*) of many small Swiss and south German lands, and where there was little or no landed nobility, as in Graubunden and Valais, they pushed their demands toward truly republican government.[94] The uplands of the German-speaking world's southern tier formed the freest political zone in Europe, and the liberties of its armed, self-governing commoners exercised a powerful demonstration effect far beyond the Swiss Confederacy's borders. Deep in the heart of south Germany, it was said that the common folk wanted "to be free, like the Swiss" and "be their own lords."[95]

In very few places had the commons any real chance of becoming "free, like the Swiss," for the prospect of an empowerment of the primary producers sufficed to rally the elites to the early modern state. The landed nobles clearly had little choice, for the traditional combination of government with landlordship had failed, leaving

---

[91] Peter Blickle, *The Revolution of 1525: The German Peasants' War from a New Perspective*, trans. Thomas A. Brady, Jr., and H. C. Erik Midelfort (Baltimore, 1981).

[92] Gerald Strauss, *Law, Resistance, and the State: The Opposition to Roman Law in Reformation Germany* (Princeton, 1986), esp. pp. 3–30.

[93] Blickle, *Revolution of 1525*, pp. 125–45.

[94] Peter Blickle, *Landschaften im alten Reich. Die staatliche Funktion des gemeinen Mannes in Oberdeutschland* (Munich, 1973); *idem*, "Communalism, Parliamentarism, Republicanism," pp. 1–13.

[95] Brady, *Turning Swiss*, pp. 34–40.

rural society open to freeholding, wage labor, and representative government. Hence the aristocracies, and not only in the German-speaking world, supported "a *displacement* of politico-legal coercion upwards
towards a centralized, militarized summit."[96] In lands where the urban
element was weak, such as the Duchy of Upper Austria, the alliance
between landed nobility and the Hapsburg state operated in just this
way. Taking advantage of rural overpopulation, the state guaranteed
succession rights to the inheriting farmers, who helped to guard law
and order among their less fortunate kinsmen and kinswomen.[97]

Urban elites, too, longed for law and order, even at foreign hands.
In northern Italy between 1494 and 1530, for example, the ruling
classes of the city-states "could not command enough support or loyalty from the subject communities to have any firm faith in survival."[98] It is no wonder, then, that the Genoese elite in particular found
the Spanish hegemony as tolerable as it was lucrative.[99] Even in the
great ramshackle structure that was the Holy Roman Empire, "the
machinery of the imperial constitution played a crucial role in regulating and shaping the course of urban conflicts."[100]

Rural pacification lay at the core of the state's situation. The surest
way to rural peace lay in the fixity and security of peasant property
rights and tenures, a step with which not all landlords agreed. Indeed,
in England the landed class split over centralization, and in France
for a long time the process aroused powerful noble resistance.[101] In
the long run, however, enhanced peasant property rights helped to
pacify the countryside and forced landlords to rely on the state for
continued extraction of the agricultural surplus.[102] In some countries,
therefore, the state became the lord of all peasants and burghers,

---

[96] Anderson, *Lineages of the Absolutist State*, pp. 19–20 (emphasis in the original).

[97] Hermann Rebel, *Peasant Classes: The Bureaucratization of Property and Family Relations
under Early Habsburg Absolutism, 1511–1626* (Princeton, 1983).

[98] Martines, *Power and Imagination*, p. 288.

[99] Wallerstein, *Modern World-System*, I: pp. 171–3.

[100] Christopher R. Friedrichs, "Urban Conflicts and the Imperial Constitution in
Seventeenth-Century Germany," *The Journal of Modern History* 58, Supplement
(December, 1986), pp. S98–S123, here at p. S123.

[101] Brenner, "Agrarian Class Structure and Economic Development in Pre-Industrial
Europe," in *Brenner Debate*, pp. 54–62. On peasant property rights and the growth
of the French state, see William H. Beik, *Absolutism and Society in Seventeenth-Century
France: State and Provincial Aristocracy in Languedoc* (Cambridge, 1985), esp. ch. 1; Hilton
Root, *Peasants and King in Burgundy: Agrarian Foundations of French Absolutism* (Berkeley
and Los Angeles, 1987).

[102] See Brenner, "The Agrarian Roots of European Capitalism," in *Brenner Debate*,
pp. 286–91.

both now "subjects," and at least in some respects the guarantor of their property rights. The new pacification and security came at a very high price, for all the old rights, the entire "old law," became vulnerable to invasion by the king's or prince's law. Theirs was a written law preached by learned lawyers, "the priests of this law and the political theologians of the new state," whose gospel held that "princes and magistrates are called 'the living law.'"[103]

Two things about this process strike the eye. First, though it is sometimes argued that the early modern state's protection of property rights promoted economic development,[104] this is true only of certain types of rights, such as contracts, for wherever the state pacified the countryside by securing peasant property rights—the classic case is France—it did so at the expense of economic development. Economic development ultimately required a massive expropriation of the peasantry, which happened in the fullest sense only in England. "Ironically," concludes Robert Brenner, "the most complete freedom and property rights for the rural population meant poverty and a self-perpetuating cycle of backwardness. In England, it was precisely the absence of rights that facilitated the onset of real economic development."[105]

A second point about rural pacification is that more secure rights for peasants limited the extraction of the surplus and diminished the state's revenues. Rural pacification thus affected kings' and princes' ability to pursue what since about 1500 had become their leading enterprise: the business of war.

V. *The State as Military Enterprise*

One view of European history holds that the emergence of strong states encouraged and, indeed, proved vital to, something called "development."[106] This, if true, was the furthest thing from their

---

[103] Strauss, *Law, Resistance, and the State*, p. 164.

[104] This is the principal argument of North and Thomas, *Rise of the Western World*, though occasionally (see, e.g., 29–30) they acknowledge that the market had to be helped by force. For critiques, see Brenner, "Agrarian Class Structure," p. 16 n. 12; Charles Tilly, "War Making and State Making as Organized Crime," in *Bringing the State Back In*, pp. 169–91.

[105] Brenner, "Agrarian Class Structure," p. 52.

[106] Guénée, *States and Rulers*, pp. 20–21, cites the French version, but there are others.

builders' minds. State-building aimed to enhance the rulers' power to make war. "The new monarchy," Kiernan writes, "bore an essentially warlike character that it was never to lose. War for it was not an optional policy, but an organic need, . . . [and] the whole state apparatus that rulers were putting together piecemeal was largely a by-product of war."[107] Political consolidation began with conquest and ended with "an exchange of resources, including plunder, to merchants in return for goods and credit."[108] War and trade were complementary ways of gaining control of what belonged to others.

The European state's growth as a military enterprise shaped the rise of merchant empires, which were made possible by the absolute or relative superiority of Western weaponry and Western military organisation over all others.[109] The formation of the imperial arsenal began at home with the evolution of a new system of warfare that replaced an older pattern in which war might described as a kind of "violent housekeeping."[110] It emerged in full flower during the 1490s—the decade of Columbus and Da Gama—when the Italian Wars became the laboratory for a new style of land warfare, the essentials of which did not change for three hundred years.

Europe's "military revolution" began with innovations in management, organization, and weaponry.[111] The management of war as an enterprise bloomed in fourteenth and fifteenth-century Italy, whence it spread across Europe.[112] By 1451 the rulers of its homeland could establish a structure of collective security, which enabled them to gain control over the enormously expensive system of mercenary warfare.

---

[107] Kiernan, "State and Nation," p. 31.

[108] Wolf, *Europe and the People without History*, p. 105. As Charles Tilly so pungently puts it, "war making and state making—quintessential protection rackets with the advantage of legitimacy—qualify as our largest examples of organized crime." Tilly, "War Making and State Making," p. 169.

[109] Geoffrey Parker, in *The Political Economy of Merchant Empires*, ch. 4.

[110] John R. Hale, *War and Society in Renaissance Europe, 1450–1620* (Baltimore, 1985), pp. 13, 15. See also Kennedy, *Great Powers*, pp. 36–7, 41–6. Like most accounts, Kennedy's focuses too much on Charles V vs. Francis I and too little on the previous generation, when the French invasion of Italy in 1494 provoked the transformation of a Franco-Burgundian struggle into a European one. See Wiesflecker, *Kaiser Maximilian I*, 5: pp. 410–47.

[111] See the masterful synthesis by Geoffrey Parker, *The Military Revolution: Military Innovation and the Rise of the West, 1500–1800* (Cambridge, 1988); also William H. McNeill, *The Pursuit of Power: Technology, Armed Force, and Society Since A.D. 1000* (Chicago and London, 1982), pp. 79–81.

[112] Michael Mallet, *Mercenaries and their Masters: Warfare in Renaissance Italy* (Totowa, N.J., 1974), pp. 76–145.

The chief organizational innovation, the renaissance of infantry, began in 1302 at Courtrai, where the Flemish guild militias defeated a French feudal army. After the Burgundian Wars of 1474–1477, when the Swiss and Upper Rhenish forces smashed the Burgundian army in three stunning victories, the revival took on "world-historical influence, as the other peoples, recognizing the superiority of the Swiss way of war, began to imitate it."[113]

Guns, the new weaponry, had been known in Europe since around 1330, but 150 years passed before artillery and muskets became indispensable to field armies.[114] The Swiss used them sparingly, but during the Italian Wars Gonzalo Hernandez de Cordoba (1453–1515), Castile's "Great Captain," began to pack his infantry formations with gunners. By this time, too, every European warlord had invested heavily in cannon, especially after Charles VIII's French guns battered one fortress after another in his progress to Naples in 1494. Thereafter, as Spanish, French, and Italian gunners demonstrated the obsolescence of all older fortifications, a new system, the wickedly expensive *trace italienne*, began to spread across Italy and then into the rest of Europe.[115] Cannon won their place on the battlefield, too, and at Marignano in 1515, under the walls of Milan, a French army taught the Swiss what even the best infantry could expect, if they gave battle without them.

The Italian Wars were the laboratory of early modern warfare,[116] which, along with painting, architecture, classical scholarship, and music, belonged to the Renaissance culture that spread across Europe during the sixteenth century. Warfare's scale grew enormously: between 1530 and 1710 the total numbers of armed forces paid by the European states and the total numbers involved in European battles increased about tenfold.[117] The states passed these costs on to their subjects, who "paid higher taxes, and, thanks to higher

---

[113] Hans Delbrück, *Geschichte der Kriegskunst im Rahmen der politischen Geschichte*, vol. 4, *Neuzeit* (Berlin, 1920; reprinted, Berlin, 1962), p. 1. See Parker, *Military Revolution*, pp. 16–17.

[114] Carlo M. Cipolla, *Guns, Sails,* and Empires: Technological Innovation and the Early Phases of European Expansion, 1400–1700* (New York, 1965), pp. 21–31.

[115] Parker, *Military Revolution*, pp. 9–16.

[116] Mallet, *Mercenaries and their Masters*, pp. 231–8. On the wider background, see Philippe Contamine, *War in the Middle Ages*, trans. Michael Jones (Oxford, 1984), pp. 119–72.

[117] Geoffrey Parker, "The 'Military Revolution, 1560–1660'—A Myth?" in his *Spain and the Netherlands, 1559–1569* (London and Short Hills, N.J., 1979), pp. 86–103, here at pp. 95–96. See now Parker, *Military Revolution*, pp. 45–6.

imposts on commodities, they paid more for what they wore, ate
and drank. The increased size of armies was passed on still more
personally through the voracious appetite of the recruiting process."[118]
Still more went into fortifications, the bottomless hole into which the
peoples' substance disappeared.[119]

   Early military enterprising suffered from primitive bureaucracies and
poor field commanders, but most of all from lack of money. One
aggravating condition of the latter was corporate liberties, the growth
of which over the previous 150 years had made a narrow passage
for the royal fist into subjects' purses. Taxation without consent
generally passed for a mark of tyranny, as Philippe de Commynes
(ca. 1447–1511) wrote: "Is there any king or lord in this world who
has the power, outside of his own domain, to levy a single *denier* on
his subjects without the approval and consent of those who are to
pay it, unless he does it by tyranny or violence?"[120] As the states
grew stronger and sought more powerfully and effectively after their
subjects' wealth, corporate institutions provided just about the only
instruments of resistance. In no other large state was this truer than
in the Holy Roman Empire, where under Emperor Maximilian I
(r. 1493–1519) the imperial diet contributed so little to his Italian
Wars that in compensation he squeezed Austria dry: between 1508
and 1517, the modestly endowed Austrian lands produced perhaps
twenty times as much revenue annually (about 1,000,000 florins per
year) as did the entire remainder of the empire.[121] A similar disparity, arising from similar causes, existed between the Hapsburgs' two
European milch cows, Castile and the Netherlands.[122] The common
folk of Castile, where corporate powers of resistance were weak,
shouldered an ever greater burden of regressive, indirect taxes, de-

---

[118] Hale, *War and Society*, p. 47. See Parker, *Military Revolution*, pp. 61–4.
   [119] Parker, *Military Revolution*, p. 39, on the relative costs of offense and defense.
   [120] *The Memoirs of Philippe de Commynes*, edited by Samuel Kinser, trans. Isabelle
Cazeaux, 2 vols. (Columbia, S.C., 1969–1973), 1: p. 358 (Book V, ch. 19).
   [121] Wiesflecker, *Kaiser Maximilian I.*, 5: pp. 572–4.
   [122] This is based on John H. Elliott, *Imperial Spain, 1469–1716* (New York, 1964),
pp. 191–9; and M. R. Rodriguez-Salgado, *The Changing Face of Empire: Charles V,
Philip II, and Habsburg Authority, 1551–1559*, Cambridge Studies in Early Modern
History (Cambridge, 1988), pp. 50–72. The latter points out (p. 60) that the Aragonese
were thoroughly protected from taxation by their corporate liberties. Paul Kennedy's
account of Habsburg resources in *Great Powers*, pp. 43–44, suffers from too modern
a view of "incomes." The banking houses were not a "major source of income"
but a means for anticipating income from taxes at the cost of incomes from the
domain and regalian rights.

spite the rivers of American bullion that flowed through Spain into foreign hands. In the Hapsburg Netherlands, by contrast, the regent and the estates cooperated in funding the public debt in such a way that for "the first time in European history . . . the future revenues of whole provinces could be mobilized for present needs through the mechanism of credit."[123] After the Dutch revolt, this innovation worked against the Hapsburgs rather than for them.

Few European populations would tolerate the levels of taxation needed to pay for Europe's sixteenth-century wars, and few royal warlords could finance their enterprises of their own. The rulers turned, therefore, to Europe's merchant-bankers for the freedom to make war on credit.[124] The Germans led the way. Emperor Maximilian I raised two German infantry regiments, which were drilled and armed in the Swiss manner. To pay them he had to borrow often from the Fuggers and the other Augsburg firms, who financed his wars.[125] This alliance between banking and war-making fostered the rise of the German military enterprisers, who helped the German lansquenets replace the Swiss as kings of Europe's battlefields and promoted, a generation later, a parallel transformation of German cavalry (*Reiter*). The emperor's lack of regular taxes or a standing army made the Holy Roman Empire a fertile pasture for both the south German bankers and the military enterprisers. To them was owing much of the debt Maximilian left behind: 6,000,000 florins, or eighteen times his annual income, half of it to the Augsburg bankers.[126]

The German military enterprisers arose to meet the need to coordinate command with credit during the first half of the sixteenth century; they organized armies under contract, extended credit to equip and pay them, led them on campaign, and commanded them in battle.[127] In their ranks ranged some old-fashioned, hell-raising

---

[123] James D. Tracy, *A Financial Revolution in the Habsburg Netherlands: Renten and Renteniers in the County of Holland, 1515–1565* (Berkeley and Los Angeles, 1985), p. 221. See Geoffrey Parker, "Spain, Her Enemies, and the Revolt of the Netherlands," in *Spain and the Netherlands*, pp. 17–42, here at pp. 21–2.

[124] McNeill, *Pursuit of Power*, pp. 102–16.

[125] Wiesflecker, *Kaiser Maximilian I.*, 5: pp. 545–54.

[126] Brady, *Turning Swiss*, pp. 80–90. See Wiesflecker, *Kaiser Maximilian I.*, 5: pp. 566–70; Peter Schmid, "Reichssteuern, Reichsfinanzen und Reichsgewalt in der ersten Hälfte des 16. Jahrhunderts," in *Säkulare Aspekte der Reformationszeit*, edited by Heinz Angermeier, Schriften des Historischen Kollegs, Kolloquien, vol. 5 (Munich and Vienna, 1983), pp. 153–98.

[127] I draw details from Fritz Redlich, *The German Military Enterpriser and His Work Force: A Study in European Economic and Social History*, 2 vols. (Wiesbaden, 1964).

nobles, such as Count William IV of Fürstenberg (1491–1541), but also men who combined military with entrepreneurial talents, such as Georg von Frundsberg (1473–1528), the south German warlord whose 10,000 lansquenets helped to sack Rome in 1527. No Welser or Fugger ever prepared his son more carefully to enter the family business than he did his son, Caspar. Such men raised and financed German mercenaries for wars from Russia to America and from North Africa to Scotland. The Germans spread through Europe a practice that the more centralized western monarchies put to more efficient use than any German ruler could, giving rise to "the seemingly symbiotic relationship . . . between the state, military power, and the private economy's efficiency in the age of absolutism. Behind every successful dynasty stood an array of opulent banking families."[128]

The merchant empires gave new scope and opportunities to military enterprising and found new uses for its practices and skills. The Iberian conquests employed specialists from among all the peoples who made a business of war, and no conquistador would have felt strange in Frundsberg's army. It was chiefly Germans and Italians who developed "the absolute or relative superiority of Western weaponry and Western military organization,"[129] while Portuguese, Spaniards, Frenchmen, Dutchmen, and Englishmen took this superiority over the sea into the wider world.

The state's growth as a military enterprise accelerated its appropriation of church property in the wake of the Reformation. In the Holy Roman Empire, the century of religious wars (1546–1648) wedded the "confessions," religious alliances of small states, to military enterprising, while the confessional systems protected each state's appropriation of its church's wealth, personnel, and means of social discipline.[130] Elsewhere, the advance of the Reformation quickened the state's appropriation of the identification of church and people, which had so powerfully supported both local and universal corporate feeling during the preceding era.[131] Reforming kings marshaled local patri-

---

[128] Jan de Vries, quoted by Tilly, "War Making and State Making," p. 179.
[129] Geoffrey Parker, in *The Political Economy of Merchant Empires*, ch. 4.
[130] Hale, *War and Society*, pp. 35–9.
[131] In England, at least the process began well before the Reformation, as Walter Ullmann shows in "'This Realm of England is an Empire,'" *Journal of Ecclesiastical History* 30 (1979): pp. 176–91. The growth of rulers' practical authority over the church has been studied with special intensity in Germany. See Heinz Schilling, "The Reformation and the Rise of the Early Modern State," and Karlheinz Blaschke, "The Reformation and the Rise of the Territorial State," both in *Luther and the*

otism (the sense of *natio*) for their own ends by merging it with a wider, sacral sense of community, which they wrested from the papacy.[132] As the identification of people and church ripened in kingdoms, such as England, and city-states, such those of Switzerland, the identity between "the church" and the subjects of a single ruler or regime became a mental habit.[133]

The Reformation and the imitative side of the Counter Reformation thus eased the church's passage from Christendom to the large but particular communities created by the states. This process, legitimated by the doctrine of sovereignty, occurred most completely in the states that competed for merchant empires, for competition and rule over non-Europeans provoked the growth of a sense of community in something called the "nation." In Germany and Italy, by contrast, states rarely if ever created communities of this sort before the nineteenth century. There never was a Prussian nation, and the German, Austrian, and Italian nations of today arose much later than the western imperial nations.[134]

The sovereign national state thus succeeded the papal imperium as the form of government; and the nation, the state's moral creature, succeeded the church as the ultimate community of fortune. Nations are postecclesiastical Europe's solution to the problem of mobilizing populations for imperial and other purposes.[135] The first nations were the first imperial peoples—England, Spain, Portugal, the Netherlands, and France—and other peoples invented nations

---

Modern State in Germany, edited by James D. Tracy, Sixteenth Century Essays and Studies, vol. 7 (Kirksville, Mo., 1986), pp. 21–30, 61–76. For Spain, see Elliott, *Imperial Spain*, pp. 204–41.

[132] The best study is Ullmann's "'This Realm of England is an Empire,'" esp. pp. 199–203. There is a good insight into how it worked in Gillian E. Brennan "Papists and Patriotism in Elizabethan England," *Recusant History* 19/1 (May, 1988): pp. 1–15.

[133] On the German-speaking free cities, see Gottfried W. Locher, *Die zwinglische Reformation im Rahmen der europäischen Kirchengeschichte* (Göttingen, 1979), pp. 167–71; Brady, "Godly Republics," pp. 14–32. This identity, as Bernd Hamm cogently argues, found its legitimacy in Huldrych Zwingli's rejection of Luther's doctrine of "two kingdoms" in favor of a one "kingdom" or "city" and a convergence of civil and Christian freedom. See Bernd Hamm, *Zwinglis Reformation der Freiheit* (Neukirchen-Vluyn, 1988), pp. 100–17.

[134] The formation of confessional networks supplied the German-speaking world with some of the sense of community that elsewhere the sense of nationality provided. See Wolfgang Reinhard, "Zwang zur Konfessionalisierung? Prolegomena zu einer Theorie des konfessionellen Zeitalters," *Zeitschrift für Historische Forschung* 10 (1983): pp. 257–77.

[135] See Kiernan, "State and Nation," to whose view my own is indebted.

either to imitate the imperial states or to get free of them. Examples of the former are the Germans and Italians, of the latter the Poles and the Irish. Each of Europe's old imperial nations, however, arose from a state that undertook imperial enterprise beyond the seas, and their sense of themselves fed from their feelings of linguistic, cultural, and racial superiority over European rivals and European and non-European inferiors.[136]

Such were some of the military and ideological links among military enterprising, state-building, and overseas empire. To them we may add another, social, link: the quintessentially European figure of the warrior-merchant.

VI. *The Merchant as Warrior*

As a historical problem, the rise of merchant empires intersects the debate about the transition from feudalism to capitalism in Europe. The debate's least tractable sector concerns the relationship of the merchants to the feudal order, on the one hand, and the capitalist bourgeoisie, on the other. Few discussions of the merchants' role in preindustrial Europe are free from thoughts about their connections to modern business classes. The notion that Europe witnessed the replacement of land-based feudal warriors by city-born business elites is very deeply rooted in European historiography, and a durable apologetic contrasts the merchant as bearer of peaceful trade with the noble as bearer of war.[137] It is an old idea, celebrated long ago by the English clergyman Edward Young (1683–1765) in these words:[138]

---

[136] Although the literature on early modern Europe emphasizes the strength of Spanish racialism, in modern times the leaders in racial thought have been Northern Europeans. See Hugh A. MacDougall, *Racial Myth in English History: Trojans, Teutons, and Anglo-Saxons* (Hanover, N. H., and London, 1982); Roger Chickering, *We Men Who Feel Most German: A Cultural Study of the Pan-German League, 1886–1914* (Boston, 1984), ch. 4.

[137] John Merrington suggests why this is so: ". . . to read the progressive role of the urban bourgeoisie backwards into history is to pose the market as the only dynamic force, the principle behind all movement, all change." John Merrington, "Town and Country in the Transition to Capitalism," in *Transition from Feudalism to Capitalism*, edited by R. H. Hilton, pp. 170–95, here at p. 173.

[138] Edward Young, "To a Solemn Musick," in *The Stuffed Owl: An Anthology, of Bad Verse*, edited by D. B. Wyndham Lewis and Charles Lee (London, 1962), p. 72.

Merchants o'er proudest heroes reign;
Those trade in blessing, these in pain,
At slaughter swell, and shout while nations groan
With purple monarchs merchants vie;
If great to spend, what to supply?
Priests pray for blessings; merchants pour them down.

Kings, merchants are in league and love,
Earth's odours play soft airs above,
That o'er the teeming field prolific range.
Planets are merchants; take, return,
Lustre and heat; by traffic burn:
The whole creation is one vast Exchange.

How utterly this notion of the world as "one vast Exchange" contrasts
with our image of the early medieval merchant, who huddles—
harmless and ghostlike, though pregnant with mighty revolutions—
at the foot of castles in which barbarian kings hold sway. This
image—it is Henri Pirenne's—haunts us still, even in our knowledge
of how neatly the merchant, his trade, and his cities nestled in the
violent bosom of feudal Europe. Once grown rich, the merchant
strove upward into the warrior classes because, as a fifteenth-century
Strasbourgeois insisted, "he whom God has granted wealth, also
wants honor."[139]

War and trade, K. N. Chaudhuri writes, "are the two indivisible
symbols of man's basic desire to look beyond his inner self and of the
urge to master the constraints of immediate natural environment."[140]
The great contemporary Asian empires—Ottoman Turkey, Mughal
India, and Ming China—are said to have separated government from
trade and warriors from merchants.[141] This was certainly not true in
Europe, where from an early time merchants governed and made
war. States ruled by merchants or by merchants and landowners

---

[139] Quoted by Thomas A. Brady, Jr., *Ruling Class, Regime, and Reformation at Strasbourg, 1520–1555*, Studies in Medieval and Reformation Thought, vol. 22 (Leiden,
1978), p. 49.
[140] K. N. Chaudhuri, "The Organising Principles of Premodern, Long-Distance
Trade, Merchants, and Objects of Trade," in *The Political Economy of Merchant Empires*,
ch. 11.
[141] See the grand overview by Michael N. Pearson in his chapter in *The Political
Economy of Merchant Empires: State Power and World Trade 1350–1750*, edited by James
D. Tracy (New York, 1991), where he writes that in Mughal India "mercantile
activity and tributary relationships thus function side by side," though "it is . . . quite
incorrect to see [the merchants] as other than passive vis-à-vis the elite." But the
chapter by K. N. Chaudhuri, also in this volume, expresses doubt on this point.

arose in Italy very shortly after A.D. 1000. Pisa, Genoa, and Venice led the pack, but all up and down Central Europe, from Tuscany to Flanders, from Brabant to Livonia, merchants not only supplied warriors—as they did all over Europe—they sat in governments that made war and, sometimes, buckled on armor and went into battle themselves. Such places make a long list: not only Florence, Milan, Venice, and Genoa, but also Augsburg, Nuremberg, Strasbourg, and Zurich; not only Lübeck, Hamburg, Bremen, and Danzig, but also Bruges, Ghent, Leiden, and Cologne. Some of them—Florence, Nuremberg, Siena, Bern, and Ulm come to mind—built consider-able territorial states; Genoa and Venice acquired Europe's first merchant empires; and the German Hansa dominated the northern trade and stimulated the commercial rise of the Dutch.[142] In very many respects, such as the organization of slave labor, management of colonies, imperial administration, commercial institutions, mari-time technology and navigation, and naval gunnery, the Italian city-states were the direct forerunners of the Portuguese and Spanish empires, to the shaping of which the Italians contributed so heavily, and in the profits of which they so largely shared.[143]

By 1500 only rags and tags remained of the Italian seaborne em-pires. The Genoese position in the East quickly crumbled before the Ottoman advance, whereupon the Genoese merchants—"a Genoese and therefore a merchant," the saying went—turned to feed at the Iberian trough.[144] The Venetian seaborne empire held out longer, but well before 1500 Venice began to build a compensatory empire on *terra ferma*. Supremacy in the European long-distance trade and banking had by this time passed to the south Germans.[145] The remark-

[142] G. V. Scammell, *The World Ecompassed: The First European Maritime Empires, c. 800–1650* (Berkeley and Los Angeles, 1981), gives this dimension its full due; Philippe Dollinger, *The German Hansa*, trans. D. S. Ault and S. H. Steinberg (Stanford, 1970), pp. 62–84, 281–329.

[143] As Chaudhuri says in his chapter in *Political Economy of Merchant Empires* "With the rise of the trading republics in Italy, the professional skills of their merchants gradually became an integral part of western social self-awareness and acceptance."

[144] Carla Rahn Phillips, "The Growth and Composition of Trade from Southern Europe, 1350–1750," in *Rise of Merchant Empires*, pp. 34–101; Herman Van der Wee, "Structural Changes in European Long-Distance Trade, and Particularly in the Re-export Trade from South to North, 1350–1750," in *ibid.*, p. 33.

[145] Jean-François Bergier, "From the Fifteenth Century in Italy to the Sixteenth Century in Germany: A New Banking Concept?" in *The Dawn of Modern Banking*, edited by the Center for Medieval and Renaissance Studies, University of California, Los Angeles (New Haven and London, 1979), pp. 105–30.

able continuity between big Italian and big south German trade and banking is hardly surprising in a purely institutional and technical sense because the Italians were the Germans' teachers, but it also had an ideological side.

Christianity is sometimes said to have been hostile to merchants and commerce, and it is true that "the Scholastic Doctors of the Middle Ages looked with favor upon husbandry but regarded trade with distrust because it was an occupation which, although not wicked in itself, nevertheless endangered the salvation of the soul."[146] The explosive expansion of trade, however, brought radical changes, and by the fifteenth century Italian writers, such as Bernardino of Siena (1380–1444) and Antonino of Florence (1389–1459), were wrestling realistically with economic issues and practices. Some humanists went further than that. In his *De avaritia* of 1428–1429, the Florentine humanist Poggio Bracciolini (1380–1459) rejected the ideal of evangelical poverty. He argued that wealth is a sign of divine favor, and that "everything we undertake is for the sake of money, and we are all led by desire for gain."[147]

Such arguments built self-confidence in men and families whose power came from trade rather than birth, status, or vocation. At Augsburg in the first half of the next century, the humanist politician Conrad Peutinger (1465–1547) set out to defend his Welser in-laws and the other big firms against the powerful German antimonopoly movement. He argued that the very pursuit of profit promoted the common good and should therefore be free of all restrictive legislation.[148] Although still a far step from viewing the world as "one

---

[146] Raymond de Roover, "The Scholastic Attitude toward Trade and Entrepreneurship," in *Business, Banking, and Economic Thought in Late Medieval and Early Modern Europe: Selected Studies of Raymond de Roover*, edited by Julius Kirshner (Chicago and London, 1974), pp. 336–45, here at p. 336, and see pp. 339–45 for what follows.

[147] Poggio Bracciolini, "On Avarice," translated by Benjamin G. Kohl and Elizabeth B. Welles, in *The Earthly Republic: Italian Humanists on Government and Society*, edited by Benjamin G. Kohl and Ronald G. Witt (Philadelphia, 1978), pp. 231–89. See Hans Baron, "Franciscan Poverty and Civic Wealth as Factors in the Rise of Humanistic Thought," *Speculum* 13 (1938): pp. 1–37, and more generally, Eugenio Garin, *Italian Humanism: Philosophy and Civic Life in the Renaissance*, trans. Peter Munz (New York, 1965).

[148] Erich Höffner, *Wirtschaftsethik und Monopole im 15. und 16. Jahrhundert* (Jena, 1941; reprinted, Stuttgart, 1969); and, on the context, see Brady, *Turning Swiss*, pp. 120–30. My point is hardly weakened by Raymond de Roover's doubt about the novelty of Peutinger's argument. Raymond de Roover, "Monopoly Theory Before Adam Smith," in his *Business, Banking, and Economic Thought*, pp. 285–7.

vast Exchange," Peutinger's argument lies on the same path toward the idea of a world governed by the market.

Like their Italian counterparts, the south German merchant-bankers had to grapple with the disparity between their political power and their economic interests. Genoa and Venice proved too weak to hold what their merchant-warriors had seized; the military power of Augsburg and Nuremberg hardly reached a half-day's ride from their walls. The really big firms, such as Augsburg's Fuggers, grew much too large for the protection such city-statelets could supply and cultivated a way of life too grand for their merchant colleagues. Sometimes they conducted separate foreign policies against their own governments or against their natural allies. The war between Charles V and the German Protestants in 1546–1547 and its aftermath supply some telling examples. At Augsburg the Fuggers stayed loyal to the emperor, but their government supported the Protestant league; at Nuremberg the big families, all Lutherans, kept the entire city loyal, despite the entreaties of their fellow Protestants; and at Strasbourg, the threat of outlawry if Charles won the war drove the Protestant merchants to face exile rather than resistance and ruin.[149] The lesson is clear: the great south German firms, having outgrown their hometowns, gravitated toward the monarchy for protection and favor.

This mismatch between commercial enterprise and political base presents a south German variation on an Italian theme and a forestate of a Dutch one, for the government of the United Provinces of the Netherlands proved itself unable to supply the political and military weight the Dutch merchants required in order to keep up with the English.[150] The north Italian, south German, and Dutch cases lead to a single conclusion: the expansion of long-distance trade required, sooner or later, a strong, highly centralized and militarized state, and the minimum size—in area, population, and wealth—of that state grew larger with each passing century. City-states simply could not command sufficient force in the changed world of the sixteenth and seventeenth centuries.

---

[149] Olaf Mörke, "Die Fugger im 16. Jahrhundert. Städtisches Elite oder Sonderstruktur?" *Archiv für Reformationsgeschichte* 74 (1983): pp. 141–61; Brady, *Turning Swiss*, pp. 202–21.

[150] See Peter Wolfgang Klein, "Dutch Capitalism and the European World-Economy," in *Dutch Capitalism and World Capitalism*, edited by Maurice Aymard (Cambridge, 1982), pp. 75–91, who believes that this weakness was deliberate.

The association of the big merchants with the centralized monarchies, it is sometimes argued, promoted economic development because the state provided security to private property, especially to contracts.[151] This is no doubt true so long as we recognize that, though it may have helped to assure private property rights of the domestic elites, the union of warfare and trade was bound by no law in dealings with other peoples. Indeed, the securing of some private property rights in the core countries of Europe went hand in hand with massive invasion of nearly every other form of property right in the world: communal and corporate rights in European lands; and ancient forms of land tenure in Ireland and Scotland, the Canary Islands, Mexico, and British North America.[152]

The rise of merchant empires thus continued a European union of trade and warfare, the continuous history of which had begun with the Italian maritime empires. The business of war on land flowed into the war of business at sea and across the seas, and it is often very difficult to separate them, for "in every instance European ventures on the oceans were sustained by a combination of public, quasi-public, and relentlessly private enterprise."[153] The entire English operation in the Atlantic prior to 1630, writes Kenneth R. Andrews, was a "predatory drive of armed traders and marauders to win by fair means or foul a share of the Atlantic wealth of the Iberian nations."[154] A Drake, a Fenner, or a Hawkins, to name but three of the great English families who lived from maritime plunder, can hardly be distinguished from some of the leading German military enterprisers.[155] And they were all fellows to the Portuguese Da Gamas, who traded spices in India in one generation and crusaded in Ethiopia in the next.[156] Such men continued a long European tradition of the union of warfare and trade. What was new in the sixteenth

---

[151] See note 104 above.

[152] Such invasions lay behind a fundamental change in the notion of property. See Winfried Schulze, "Vom Gemeinnutz zum Eigennutz. Über Normenwandel in der ständischen Gesellschaft der frühen Neuzeit," *Historische Zeitschrift* 243 (1986): pp. 591–626; Renate Blicke, "Nahrung und Eigentum als Kategorien in der ständischen Gesellschaft," in Schulze, ed., *Ständische Gesellschaft und soziale Mobilität*, pp. 73–93.

[153] McNeill, *Pursuit of Power*, p. 103.

[154] Kenneth R. Andrews, *Trade, Plunder, and Settlement: Maritime Enterprise and the Genesis of the British Empire, 1480–1630* (Cambridge, 1984), p. 356.

[155] David B. Quinn and A. N. Ryan, *England's Sea Empire, 1550–1642* (London, 1983), p. 69.

[156] Bailey W. Diffie and George D. Winius, *Foundations of the Portuguese Empire, 1415–1580* (Minneapolis, 1977), pp. 354–8.

century was the immense power of the relatively small imperial states they served, as they served themselves.

The Portuguese, first Europeans to go over the sea, partly grabbed and partly built an Asian trading network based on the cooperation of private traders with the Crown, on convincing naval superiority, and on the successful seizure of strategic ports. The role of the Crown, which managed trade through royal officials and the sale of licenses (*cartazes*), loomed greater than it would in the later Asian systems of the Dutch and the English, but it remained within the limits of the European type of seaborne empire.[157]

When, as in England, the state could not pay the costs of empire, or, as in the Netherlands, it would not, the imperial division of labor evolved a new form: the chartered company, in which the merchants themselves both conducted trade and policed the trading system. The vigorous young English seaborne empire was managed ashore by "men who had participated in the promotion of the drive for trans-oceanic trade and plunder; afloat its conduct was largely in the hands of men whose maritime experience had been accumulated in the same movement."[158] They and their Dutch counterparts had to shift from prevailing European methods of making war, which would not do in Asia, where Europeans could not transform the terms of trade through brute force. The more efficient kind of political management of trade, which they required, was supplied by the chartered companies.

The Dutch East India Company (VOC) and English East India Company (EIC) were just as closely linked to government and war as the Portuguese *Estado da India* had been.[159] Their Asian trade, according to Chaudhuri, "could not be strictly separated from the conduct of national foreign policy, and reasons of state dictated that the merchants should look to the government for a large measure of political support."[160] Although their centralization of the distribu-

---

[157] Niels Steensgaard, *The Asian Trade Revolution of the Seventeenth Century: The East India Companies and the Decline of the Caravan Trade* (Chicago and London, 1974), pp. 85, 95–113; Diffie and Winius, *Foundations*, pp. 301–37; K. N. Chaudhuri, *Trade and Civilisation in the Indian Ocean: An Economic History from the Rise of Islam to 1750* (Cambridge, 1985), pp. 63–79. For a critique of Steensgaard's thesis, see Sanjay Subrahmanyam and Luís Filipe F. R. Thomaz, in *The Political Economy of Merchant Empires*, ch. 8.
[158] Quinn and Ryan, *England's Sea Empire*, p. 69.
[159] See Chaudhuri, *Trade and Civilisation*, pp. 80–97.
[160] K. N. Chaudhuri, *The Trading World of Asia and the English East India Company, 1660–1760* (Cambridge, 1975), p. 455.

tion of Asian commodities in merchants' hands proved more efficient than the Portuguese system, the East India companies essentially extended and adapted the historic European union of warfare and trade. They functioned in many respects like states, but the kind of states Europe might have had, had merchants ever gained a completely free hand to manage the state as a profit-making enterprise. The companies built, maintained, and used fleets, organized and maintained armies, and conducted diplomacy, and their budgeting, accounting, and communications were far more efficient than those of any European state. Free of the cares of noncommercial, nonmilitary affairs, which so weighed down the merchants who ruled European city-states, for a long time the chartered companies had no subjects to manage. They drew from the wealth produced by hundreds of peoples, without the expenses, troubles, and dangers of managing the primary extraction of surplus.

Protected by guarantees of law at home and attracted by freedom from laws abroad, the company merchants resembled Spanish conquistadors or German military enterprisers more than they did the Fuggers of Augsburg or the Strozzi of Florence. They lived in two worlds: a home world in which the growing security of property protected their accumulations from the type of behavior they exhibited abroad; and a wider world that afforded release from restraints on freedom at home.

VII. *Conclusion*

The rise of European merchant empires capitalized on certain features of Christendom: the separation between ecumenical integration and military force, the success of small governments, the close integration of trade and government, and the operations of the warrior-merchants. These characteristics arose since 1000 in Christendom's heartlands, roughly the lands of Italy and the Holy Roman Empire; their consequences developed most freely between 1450 and 1650 in Europe's western tier, where the combined enterprises of governmental centralization, war-making, and overseas adventure and conquest began to transform the old kingdoms into the early modern states. From this time onward, Italy and Germany began to become "backward," while Portugal, Spain, France, England, and the Netherlands marched or trudged on the path to imperial-national statehood. In the nonimperial heartlands, the fundamental lines of medieval European development continued: the centrality of religious institutions and culture, the fragmentation of government, and the preservation of traditional property rights against capitalist invasion.

"Development," therefore, as defined by the experience of north-western Europe, and more especially by that of England, meant the transformation of European civilization through the acquisition of sea-borne empires into new patterns, which were not simply extensions of earlier European ones. The acquisition of power over non-Europeans abroad encouraged the European elites to integrate their realms into civilizations—called "nations"—a process that began with language and ended with biology.[161] The belated efforts, moreover, of the "back-ward" peoples to catch up, compete with, and surpass the Western European imperial nation-states on the stage of world history, pre-pared the ground for some of our own century's greatest tragedies.

The great going-out over the sea did not change everything, but it changed everything it touched. It did not create the warriors' quest for new lands or the merchants' for new markets, but it did open to European warrior-merchants realms where laws were less strict, less enforceable, or simply absent, and where popular resistance to invasion of rights was less effective than at home.[162] The merchant empires afforded new freedoms in new lands, where men could ob-tain greater wealth, prestige, and power than they could have won at home. If they did so at the expense of Africans, Amerindians, and other peoples, who cared, especially after death stilled Las Casas's bold tongue? Who abhorred the buying and selling of human beings, so long as it was not done at London, Paris, Seville, or Amster-dam—cities whose merchants bought and sold more Africans in three and-a-half centuries than the Islamic world did in more than a millennium?[163] Slavery, that ultimate human lordship over the socially dead,[164] completed the gradient of contempt which—to take the English example—"civilised and prosperous Englishmen" felt "for the

---

[161] "Nations," writes Ernest Gellner, "can be defined only in terms of the age of nationalism," which is, "essentially, the general imposition of a high culture on soci-ety [and the] generalized diffusion of a school-mediated, academy-supervised idiom, codified for the requirements of reasonably precise bureaucratic and technological requirements." Gellner, *Nations and Nationalism* (Ithaca and London, 1983), pp. 55, 57.

[162] Tilly, "War Making and State Making," p. 183, notes that "popular resistance to war making and state making made a difference."

[163] Lovejoy, *Transformations in Slavery*, pp. 24–42, 44–47.

[164] Orlando Patterson, *Slavery and Social Death: A Comparative Study* (Cambridge, Mass., 1982).

vagabonds of their own country, for the customs of the most backward parts of England, and for the dirty, cowkeeping Celts on its
fringes."[165] This gradient, boundless in its expansibility, began at
home and spread its shadow from nearby hearts of darkness to those
far over the sea.

The merchant empire-builders' freedom of action arose from European superiority in the organization and execution of war by land
and by sea, and of commerce. This "eccentric departure from the
human norm of command behavior," to use McNeill's language,[166]
may be associated with "the rise of capitalism," providing that certain qualifications are respected. First, the rise of merchant empires
does not signal a victory of a mercantile bourgeoisie over a warrior
nobility. The European nation-state was militarized and expansionist,
it policed agriculture, it allied with merchants bent on overseas profits
and plunder, and it articulated itself through the growth of civil and
military bureaucracy.[167] It generally acquired these characteristics,
moreover, before it became genuinely national, and perhaps the possession of overseas empire made the passage to nationhood possible or at least easier. This possibility is strongly supported by the
one case in which a centralized, militarized state created a nation in
the absence of foreign empire. In the Prussian creation of modern
Germany, foreign empire seemed very useful, even necessary, to the
stability of the state and social order. Whether German "social imperialism" owed more to a realistic appraisal of social strains in the
new Germany or to the German bourgeoisie's envy of the British
Empire, the point remains that empire seemed necessary to nation-
building.[168]

A second qualification to the association of merchant empires with
capitalism concerns the imperial contribution to European development. Apart from the grease that American bullion supplied to the
Europeans' Asian trade, the importance of the non-European world's
contribution to the capitalization of industrialism in Europe is still

---

[165] Angus Calder, *Revolutionary Empire: The Rise of the English-Speaking Empires from
the Fifteenth Century to the 1780s* (New York, 1981), p. 25.

[166] McNeill, *Pursuit of Power*, p. 116.

[167] Wolf, *Europe and the People without History*, p. 110.

[168] My thinking on this point owes a good deal to Geoff Eley, "The British Model
and the German Road: Rethinking the Course of German History Before 1914,"
in David Blackbourne and Geoff Eley, *The Peculiarities of German History: Bourgeois
Society and Politics in Nineteenth-Century Germany* (Oxford, 1984), pp. 39–155.

quite controversial. It may well be, however, that this contribution
came not just as capital accumulated through exchange but as the
vaulting confidence of Europe's rulers and elites in knowing history's
blessing upon their rule.

Once firm limits are fixed to the merchant's role, two neglected
aspects of the transition to capitalism emerge from obscurity. The
first aspect, the continuity of imperial enterprise from home to the
colonies, helps to ease the sometimes acrimonious conflict between
proponents respectively of endogenous and exogenous theories of
capitalist development.[169] Much can be clarified by glancing under-
neath the Europe organized by states to see the correspondences
between colonizations at home and abroad. The pursuit of profit,
which led some merchants to seek fortunes in the colonies or in the
Asia trade, led others to find the areas within Europe that were less
resistant to the controlling power of merchant capital than were the
guild-bound cities.[170] The export of commodity production into the
European countryside meant that the growth of the merchants' hegemony over production, which perhaps ended in Bengal, Java, and
Martinique, began just outside Bristol, Haarlem, and Rouen. Warfare
underwent a similar change, driven by the restless search for new
sources of money, guns, and men. Propelled by these forces of war
and trade, market relations penetrated the European "hinterlands"
in every possible geographical and social sense of the term: the urban
commons, the countryside, the backward sectors of core countries,
relatively backward countries (Wallerstein's semiperiphery), and the
seaborne empires. In this sense, European societies were also colonized and plundered, less catastrophically than the Americas but
more so than most of Asia. The rise of the enterprising classes from
military and mercantile backgrounds suggests that Marx's second,
"non-revolutionary" way to capitalism was Europe's journey, to which
the first, "really revolutionary," English way gave a massive impulse.
The rapid economic development yielded by the English path proved

---

[169] The best overview is provided by Pearson, *Before Colonialism*. For the basic
schema, see Wallerstein, *Modern World-System*, 1: pp. 349–50.

[170] On rural industry and proto-industrialization, see Kriedte, *Peasants, Landlords,
and Merchant Capitalists*, pp. 74–8; Myron P. Gutmann, *Toward the Modern Economy:
Early Industry in Europe, 1500–1800*, New Perspectives on European History (New York,
1988), pp. 5–6, 8–11, 94–5.

extremely destructive, both of traditional property rights at home and of institutions and cultures throughout the world.

The second aspect of the transition that this account brings to the fore, concerns the role of the Latin church in the origins and growth of the state system. Arguments about the origins of the European difference, whether conceived as "capitalism," "modernity," or "development," commonly cultivate a stubborn ignorance of the role of the Latin church in the governance of feudal Europe. Partly this stems from a retrograde mentality that deals with religious systems as "mere" ideology, but partly it reflects bewilderment at the spectacle of a civilization governed as was no other in world history. Once recognized, this fact in itself disqualifies European "feudalism" to serve as a stage in any universal scheme of social evolution.

To a very great degree, it was the popes' sacerdotal imperium that the European states came to ape, with this difference: the communities they created, the nations, were exclusive rather than universal. Above the national claims, of course, the ruling elites long claimed to represent more universal values embodied in something they called "civilization." That quickly fell by the wayside, however, when the imperial struggles came home, and World War I found each belligerent defining itself as a "civilization." Such definitions merely completed the logic of the European state system. If empire consists in centralized rule over disparate peoples, combined with an encompassing, integrative ideology and a circulation of wealth to the center and force to the periphery, then the major states of early modern Europe were all empires before they were national states, and the modern European nations are mostly their creations.

Imperial operations of the European type first attained full scope in the merchant empires constructed by Western Europeans during the early modern era. In their forefront was the warrior-merchant, whose presence reminds us how much the merchant empires owed to their predecessors, the seaborne raiding-and-trading empires built by small urban powers in the heartlands of medieval Europe.

Three things, therefore, seem to have determined that Central Europe and Western Europe would move since about 1450 on different paths: the temporary but decisive success of the imperial papacy in sheltering politico-military particularism in the heartlands; the greater scope afforded warrior-merchants by the kingdoms of the west; and the attainment of empire in lands that lay far beyond the

restraints which old European institutions and habits—corporate governance, communal ideals, collective holding of property, governance
split between civil and ecclesiastical authority—placed on the management of trade and property to utmost advantage.

The early commercial empires of Central European city-states
therefore, grew into nothing; the later commercial empires of Western
European kingdoms grew into imperial nations. The latter came to
compare themselves to the classical empires, though they never lost
a faint, ghostly sense of forming a civilization—the "West" as opposed
to all the "Easts."

All of the "Easts" participate in the history of the "West." The
seaborne empires served, for example, to dampen for a time the
scale and consequences of warfare in metropolitan Europe. For about
350 years before 1914, Europe exported some of its competitive
struggles into the wider, colonial world, though, when this relief valve
failed, the old pattern of perennial intra-European strife, which had
first appeared in the Italian Wars, reestablished itself in Europe in
new and terrible forms. The stakes, of course, were infinitely higher
now—domination not just of Europe but of the world—and the
costs had grown astronomically through the industrialization of war.
The warring powers, however, remained what they had become in
the era of merchant empires: morally autarchic entities, the military-
commercial competition among which was unrestrained by any
principles of law. Despite a vague allegiance to "civilization," their
elites respected no ecumenical ideology but the doctrine of the market, no common ritual but the business of exchange, and no common
morality but the pursuit of profit.

This is one way of looking at the European consequences of the
rise of merchant empires. There are others. One of them, starting
from the neo-classical theory of international trade, tends to park
most other historical forces—church, states, empires; religion, patriotism, racial consciousness; government, war, plunder—under the
ledger heading of "transaction costs."[171] From this perspective, the
merchant empires represent "a step from autarky, localized trade, to
larger trade and specialization, which at least for some economies . . .

---

[171] This is explained very lucidly by Douglass C. North, in *The Political Economy
of Merchant Empires*, ch. 1. The remaining quotes in this paragraph are from the
same source. See the critical remarks on North's views by Tilly, "War Making and
State Making," p. 177.

were steps along the route to a persistent evolution of more efficient forms of economic organization." Two changes, in this view, made greater efficiency possible: "economies of scale associated with the volume of exchange" and "improved methods of enforcing contracts."

Despite its very different language and assumptions, the trade-based account of the rise of merchant empires does not differ so radically from the one I have sketched above. Each emphasizes a valuable perspective on the process: European trade expanded its scope through military enterprising on a global scale; the security of contracts grew out of the state's tendency to favor merchant property over other forms of property right. And these two changes—expansion abroad, security of property at home—reveal the two faces of Europe's empire-builders: plunderers, slavers, and extortioners abroad; prudent, law-abiding businessmen at home. It is nonetheless worth considering whether the term "transaction costs" expresses adequately these two roles.

The end returns us to the beginning, where the old Portuguese soothsayer stood at the Belem docks on that fateful July day in 1497. He charged Da Gama with turning his back on Christendom for the sake of profit, glory, and empire. Ahead, the oceanic revolution opened to Europe's warrior-merchants worlds in which they could pursue these goals with a freedom Europe often denied and an efficiency it rarely tolerated. Their escape into the "Easts" from custom, law, and obligation gave them a taste of power they would crave forever more. At Sao Tomé and Mombasa, at Goa and Macao, at Jakarta and Malacca, at Cuzco and Tenochtitlan, and at Calcutta and Hanoi, Europeans finally learned to walk the earth as "the lords of human kind."

INDEX OF PERSONS

INDEX OF PLACES

Danube Valley, 121
Danzig, 276, 287–88, 300, 466
Darmstadt, 97
Denmark, 94, 293
Dillingen, 388
Ditmarsh, 365
Donauwörth, 396
Dortmund, 306
Dresden, 382
Düsseldorf, 119, 315; empire, 470

East Elbia, 302–4
East Prussia, 304
Eastern Europe, 436
Ebersmünster (Lower Alsace), 302
Eckbolsheim (Lower Alsace), 235
Eichstätt, prince-bishopric, 118
Elbe River, 303. See also East Elbia
Electorate of Saxony. See Saxony,
  electorate
Emden, 378-79
England, 201, 203, 205, 293, 317–18,
  321, 335, 379, 381, 408, 417, 431,
  433, 435–36, 438, 442, 444, 449–50,
  453, 456–57, 463, 470–73
empire, 470, 473
Ensisheim (Upper Alsace), 344
Erfurt, city, 287, 307–8, 342;
  university, 235
Erzgebirge, 295–96
Esslingen, 84
Ethiopia, 469
Ettlingen, 237

Flanders, county, 276, 291, 466
Florence, 17, 37, 40, 276, 451–52,
  466–67, 471
France, 16, 30, 40, 84, 89, 92, 94,
  116–17, 126, 149, 317, 320–21,
  335, 377, 379–81, 399–400, 408,
  417, 436, 449–50, 456–57, 463, 471
Franche-Comté, county, 87
Franconia, 114, 121, 174, 281, 283,
  349, 393, 420, 426
Frankfurt am Main, 89, 98, 110, 121,
  158, 182, 194, 287–89, 305, 307
Frankfurt an der Oder, university, 380
Freiburg im Breisgau, city, 305, 307;
  university, 99, 105, 131, 190, 237
Frisia, 379

Gastein valley (Salzburg), 295
Geispolsheim (Lower Alsace), 95, 97

Geneva, 354, 373, 380, 439
Genoa, 40, 218, 437, 456, 466, 468
German Democratic Republic, 1, 336,
  364
Germany. See Holy Roman Empire
Giessen, university, 382
Goa, 477
Gorizia/Görz, county, 313
Goslar, 122, 150, 153, 157, 160, 296,
  306
Göß Abbey (Styria), 283
Graubünden, 302, 385, 418, 427–28
Graz, city, 313, 388, 391; university,
  313
Greifswald, university, 316, 375
Grünberg (Hesse), 92–93

Haarlem, 474
Habsburg Netherlands.
  See Netherlands
Hagenau, colloquy (1539), 118
Hamburg, 193, 288–89, 293, 300, 305,
  309, 438, 466
Hanoi, 483
Hanover, 281
Hegau, 339
Heidelberg, city , 380, 382, 400;
  university, 105, 131
Heilbronn, 84, 421
Henneberg-Schleusingen, county, 109
Herborn, 380
Hesse, landgraviate, 109, 281
Hesse-Cassel, landgraviate, 382
Hesse-Darmstadt, landgraviate, 382
Hildesheim, prince-bishopric, 387
Hohentwiel, Castle, 83
Homberg (Hesse), 93
Horburg, county, 85
Hradcany Castle (Prague), 392
Hulst, 379
Hungary, 295, 322, 325, 328, 337,
  346
Hüningen, 302

Ilanz (Graubünden), 426–28
India, 441, 465
Inner Austria. See Austria, Inner
Innsbruck, city, 327–28, 333, 344–46,
  391; university, 315
Italy, 17, 30, 40, 99, 171, 175, 218,
  321, 323, 325, 327, 334, 341, 344,
  347, 399, 417, 436–37, 447, 450,
  456, 458–59, 463, 466, 471

INDEX OF SUBJECTS

Verlag. *See* putting out
villages, 280, 282–83, 286

Weisskunig, 326
women; guilds and crafts, 290–92; legal
rights, 234; urban reformation, 227–51

XIII. *See* Strasbourg, privy councils
XV. *See* Strasbourg, privy councils

Zwinglianism, 61–63, 66–67, 78, 101,
104, 177, 194, 198
Zwinglians, 58, 61, 65, 75, 180, 192

STUDIES IN MEDIEVAL
AND REFORMATION THOUGHT

EDITED BY HEIKO A. OBERMAN

1. DOUGLASS, E. J. D. *Justification in Late Medieval Preaching*. 2nd ed. 1989
2. WILLIS, E. D. *Calvin's Catholic Christology*. 1966 *out of print*
3. POST, R. R. *The Modern Devotion*. 1968 *out of print*
4. STEINMETZ, D. C. *Misericordia Dei*. The Theology of Johannes von Staupitz. 1968 *out of print*
5. O'MALLEY, J. W. *Giles of Viterbo on Church and Reform*. 1968 *out of print*
6. OZMENT, S. E. *Homo Spiritualis*. The Anthropology of Tauler, Gerson and Luther. 1969
7. PASCOE, L. B. *Jean Gerson: Principles of Church Reform*. 1973 *out of print*
8. HENDRIX, S. H. *Ecclesia in Via*. Medieval Psalms Exegesis and the *Dictata super Psalterium* (1513-1515) of Martin Luther. 1974
9. TREXLER, R. C. *The Spiritual Power*. Republican Florence under Interdict. 1974
10. TRINKAUS, Ch. with OBERMAN, H. A. (eds.). *The Pursuit of Holiness*. 1974 *out of print*
11. SIDER, R. J. *Andreas Bodenstein von Karlstadt*. 1974
12. HAGEN, K. *A Theology of Testament in the Young Luther*. 1974
13. MOORE, Jr., W. L. *Annotatiunculae D. Iohanne Eckio Praelectore*. 1976
14. OBERMAN, H. A. with BRADY, Jr., Th. A. (eds.). *Itinerarium Italicum*. Dedicated to Paul Oskar Kristeller. 1975
15. KEMPFF, D. *A Bibliography of Calviniana*. 1959-1974. 1975 *out of print*
16. WINDHORST, C. *Täuferisches Taufverständnis*. 1976
17. KITTELSON, J. M. *Wolfgang Capito*. 1975
18. DONNELLY, J. P. *Calvinism and Scholasticism in Vermigli's Doctrine of Man and Grace*. 1976
19. LAMPING, A. J. *Ulrichus Velenus (Oldřich Velenský) and his Treatise against the Papacy*. 1976
20. BAYLOR, M. G. *Action and Person*. Conscience in Late Scholasticism and the Young Luther. 1977
21. COURTENAY, W. J. *Adam Wodeham*. 1978
22. BRADY, Jr., Th. A. *Ruling Class, Regime and Reformation at Strasbourg, 1520-1555*. 1978
23. KLAASSEN, W. *Michael Gaismair*. 1978
24. BERNSTEIN, A. E. *Pierre d'Ailly and the Blanchard Affair*. 1978
25. BUCER, Martin. *Correspondance*. Tome I (Jusqu'en 1524). Publié par J. Rott. 1979
26. POSTHUMUS MEYJES, G. H. M. *Jean Gerson et l'Assemblée de Vincennes (1329)*. 1978
27. VIVES, Juan Luis. *In Pseudodialecticos*. Ed. by Ch. Fantazzi. 1979
28. BORNERT, R. *La Réforme Protestante du Culte à Strasbourg au XVIᵉ siècle (1523-1598)*. 1981
29. SEBASTIAN CASTELLIO. *De Arte Dubitandi*. Ed. by E. Feist Hirsch. 1981
30. BUCER, Martin. *Opera Latina*. Vol I. Publié par C. Augustijn, P. Fraenkel, M. Lienhard. 1982
31. BÜSSER, F. *Wurzeln der Reformation in Zürich*. 1985 *out of print*
32. FARGE, J. K. *Orthodoxy and Reform in Early Reformation France*. 1985
33, 34. BUCER, Martin. *Etudes sur les relations de Bucer avec les Pays-Bas*. I. Etudes; II. Documents. Par J. V. Pollet. 1985
35. HELLER, H. *The Conquest of Poverty*. The Calvinist Revolt in Sixteenth Century France. 1986

36. MEERHOFF, K. *Rhétorique et poétique au XVIe siècle en France.* 1986
37. GERRITS, G. H. *Inter timorem et spem.* Gerard Zerbolt of Zutphen. 1986
38. ANGELO POLIZIANO. *Lamia.* Ed. by A. Wesseling. 1986
39. BRAW, C. *Bücher im Staube.* Die Theologie Johann Arndts in ihrem Verhältnis zur Mystik. 1986
40. BUCER, Martin. *Opera Latina.* Vol. II. Enarratio in Evangelion Iohannis (1528, 1530, 1536). Publié par I. Backus. 1988
41. BUCER, Martin. *Opera Latina.* Vol. III. Martin Bucer and Matthew Parker: Florilegium Patristicum. Edition critique. Publié par P. Fraenkel. 1988
42. BUCER, Martin. *Opera Latina.* Vol. IV. Consilium Theologicum Privatim Conscriptum. Publié par P. Fraenkel. 1988
43. BUCER, Martin. *Correspondance.* Tome II (1524-1526). Publié par J. Rott. 1989
44. RASMUSSEN, T. *Inimici Ecclesiae.* Das ekklesiologische Feindbild in Luthers "Dictata super Psalterium" (1513-1515) im Horizont der theologischen Tradition. 1989
45. POLLET, J. *Julius Pflug et la crise religieuse dans l'Allemagne du XVIe siècle.* Essai de synthèse biographique et théologique. 1990
46. BUBENHEIMER, U. *Thomas Müntzer.* Herkunft und Bildung. 1989
47. BAUMAN, C. *The Spiritual Legacy of Hans Denck.* Interpretation and Translation of Key Texts. 1991
48. OBERMAN, H. A. and JAMES, F. A., III (eds.). in cooperation with SAAK, E. L. *Via Augustini.* Augustine in the Later Middle Ages, Renaissance and Reformation: Essays in Honor of Damasus Trapp. 1991 *out of print*
49. SEIDEL MENCHI, S. *Erasmus als Ketzer.* Reformation und Inquisition im Italien des 16. Jahrhunderts. 1993
50. SCHILLING, H. *Religion, Political Culture, and the Emergence of Early Modern Society.* Essays in German and Dutch History. 1992
51. DYKEMA, P. A. and OBERMAN, H. A. (eds.). *Anticlericalism in Late Medieval and Early Modern Europe.* 2nd ed. 1994
52, 53. KRIEGER, Chr. and LIENHARD, M. (eds.). *Martin Bucer and Sixteenth Century Europe.* Actes du colloque de Strasbourg (28-31 août 1991). 1993
54. SCREECH, M. A. *Clément Marot: A Renaissance Poet discovers the World.* Lutheranism, Fabrism and Calvinism in the Royal Courts of France and of Navarre and in the Ducal Court of Ferrara. 1994
55. GOW, A. C. *The Red Jews: Antisemitism in an Apocalyptic Age, 1200-1600.* 1995
56. BUCER, Martin. *Correspondance.* Tome III (1527-1529). Publié par Chr. Krieger et J. Rott. 1989
57. SPIJKER, W. VAN 'T. *The Ecclesiastical Offices in the Thought of Martin Bucer.* Translated by J. Vriend (text) and L.D. Bierma (notes). 1996
58. GRAHAM, M.F. *The Uses of Reform.* 'Godly Discipline' and Popular Behavior in Scotland and Beyond, 1560-1610. 1996
59. AUGUSTIJN, C. *Erasmus. Der Humanist als Theologe und Kirchenreformer.* 1996
60. McCOOG S J, T. M. *The Society of Jesus in Ireland, Scotland, and England 1541-1588.* 'Our Way of Proceeding?' 1996
61. FISCHER, N. und KOBELT-GROCH, M. (Hrsg.). *Außenseiter zwischen Mittelalter und Neuzeit.* Festschrift für Hans-Jürgen Goertz zum 60. Geburtstag. 1997
62. NIEDEN, M. *Organum Deitatis.* Die Christologie des Thomas de Vio Cajetan. 1997
63. BAST, R.J. *Honor Your Fathers.* Catechisms and the Emergence of a Patriarchal Ideology in Germany, 1400-1600. 1997
64. ROBBINS, K.C. *City on the Ocean Sea: La Rochelle, 1530-1650.* Urban Society, Religion, and Politics on the French Atlantic Frontier. 1997
65. BLICKLE, P. *From the Communal Reformation to the Revolution of the Common Man.* 1998
66. FELMBERG, B. A. R. *Die Ablaßtheorie Kardinal Cajetans (1469-1534).* 1998

67. CUNEO, P. F. *Art and Politics in Early Modern Germany.* Jörg Breu the Elder and the Fashioning of Political Identity, ca. 1475-1536. 1998
68. BRADY, Jr., Th. A. *Communities, Politics, and Reformation in Early Modern Europe.* 1998
69. McKEE, E. A. *The Writings of Katharina Schütz Zell.* 1. The Life and Thought of a Sixteenth-Century Reformer. 2. A Critical Edition. 1998
70. BOSTICK, C. V. *The Antichrist and the Lollards.* Apocalyticism in Late Medieval and Reformation England. 1998
71. BOYLE, M. O'ROURKE. *Senses of Touch.* Human Dignity and Deformity from Michelangelo to Calvin. 1998

Prospectus available on request

BRILL — P.O.B. 9000 — 2300 PA LEIDEN — THE NETHERLANDS